# grilling

charcoal • gas • smokers

## Grilling

Contributing Editor: Kristin Bienert
Contributing Designer: Craig Hanken, Studio P2
Copy Chief: Terri Fredrickson
Publishing Operations Manager: Karen Schirm
Senior Editor, Asset and Information Manager: Phillip Morgan
Edit and Design Production Coordinator: Mary Lee Gavin
Editorial Assistant: Cheryl Eckert
Book Production Managers: Pam Kvitne, Marjorie J. Schenkelberg,
 Rick von Holdt, Mark Weaver

## Meredith® Books

Executive Director, Editorial: Gregory H. Kayko
Executive Director, Design: Matt Strelecki
Managing Editor: Amy Tincher-Durik
Executive Editor/Group Manager: Jennifer Darling

Publisher and Editor in Chief: James D. Blume
Editorial Director: Linda Raglan Cunningham
Executive Director, New Business Development: Todd M. Davis
Executive Director, Sales: Ken Zagor
Director, Operations: George A. Susral
Director, Production: Douglas M. Johnston
Director, Marketing: Amy Nichols
Business Director: Jim Leonard

Vice President and General Manager: Douglas J. Guendel

## Meredith Publishing Group

President: Jack Griffin
Executive Vice President: Bob Mate

## Meredith Corporation

Chairman and Chief Executive Officer: William T. Kerr
President and Chief Operating Officer: Stephen M. Lacy

In Memoriam: E.T. Meredith III (1933-2003)

All of us at Meredith® Books are dedicated to providing you with
the information and ideas you need to enhance your home and
garden. We welcome your comments and suggestions. Write to us
at: Meredith Books, Garden Editorial Department, 1716 Locust St.,
Des Moines, IA 50309-3023.

Previously published as *Better Homes and Gardens®
The New Grilling Book.*

This version printed by Meredith Books for Borders Group.

Test Kitchen

Pictured on the front
cover: Steak-Lover's
Platter, page 119.

Pictured on the back cover:
Top left: Three-Way
Chicken Wings, page 59;
Top right: Burgers
Borracho, page 109;
Bottom left: Kansas City
Pork Spareribs, page 206;
Bottom right: Asparagus
with Parmesan Curls,
page 62.

# CONTENTS

**FIRE & FOOD**

So when did food and fire first hook up?
The truth is, getting a handle on the origins
of cooking outdoors over flame is like
grasping at smoke. Almost every self-
respecting culture claims to have dreamed
up this cooking method. In North America,
we can't even agree on what to call it.
Although barbecuing and grilling are used
synonymously in many areas, regional
purists still swear that barbecuing is
cooking with an indirect wood fire at a
relatively low temperature, while grilling
means cooking quickly over direct, hot
heat. (This Grilling Basics chapter helps
clear up the confusion.)

**THE RECIPES THROUGHOUT THIS BOOK INCLUDE THE FOLLOWING FEATURES:**

- Preparation and grilling times.
- Recipe introductions that include information about taste or hints on unique ingredients, preparation, and serving suggestions.
- Special equipment suggestions.
- Preparation steps for easy reference.
- Separate directions for gas and charcoal grills.
- Nutrition analyses.

# Grilling Basics

# GRILLING BASICS

Grilling is so popular that the mouthwatering aromas of grilled foods can be detected even on cold wintry days. And why not? Grilling is generally easy and oh-so tasty. To ensure succulent steaks, fork-tender fish, and perfect poultry, a little know-how and a few simple grilling techniques can go a long way. In this section, you'll find everything you need to know—from your initial purchase of a grill to understanding the difference between direct and indirect grilling. But first, a lesson in grilling semantics.

# WHAT'S IN A NAME?

Though cooking over a fire is one of the oldest, simplest, and quickest food-preparation methods, a difference of opinion remains as to what the process should be called—grilling, barbecuing, pit roasting, or smoking. Why the different labels? All of the terms involve the food's relationship to the fire, but there are some differences.

GRILLING is cooking food over direct heat. This means firing up briquettes in a charcoal grill or lighting a gas grill, then putting the food on the grill rack. The lid is left off of a charcoal grill, but the cover is closed with a gas grill. The heat intensity of direct grilling is similar to broiling, so tender meats—burgers, steaks, chops, and poultry—are best for this method.

BARBECUING originally referred more to the event of gathering around the grill to cook outdoors than the actual cooking procedure. But the term has come to mean cooking food for a long time over low heat. Barbecuing generally encompasses roasting bigger cuts of meats and vegetables that need long cooking times. It's traditionally done with the grill cover down over indirect heat. The indirect heat cooks the food slowly without burning or drying out. Ribs, pork tenderloins, beef roasts, whole birds, whole fish, corn on the cob, and casserole-type dishes are good candidates for this method of grilling.

Some barbecue devotees, especially competitive cookers, consider barbecuing to be the old-fashioned pit dug in the ground to cook a whole pig or lamb for 10 to 24 hours. That process typically is overseen by a seasoned pitmaster and involves great camaraderie and extensive socializing. Although this type of gathering is still called a barbecue, the cooking method is increasingly referred to as pit roasting.

SMOKING involves indirectly cooking food and adding wood chips to the grill to give a characteristic flavor. It can be done in a smoker, which is an outdoor cooker designed specifically for this method, or in a covered grill with a pan of water placed beneath the meat. Smoking is done much more slowly than grilling, so less tender cuts of meat—ham, brisket, pork shoulder, and game birds—benefit.

# REGIONAL VARIATIONS

Distinctions and preferences for grilling or barbecuing styles are uniquely regional. One issue concerns the favored type of meat, with pork preferred east of the Mississippi River and beef preferred to the west.

**Barbecue,** when it comes to pork, takes on two primary forms, either ribs or whole pieces of meat that have been barbecued, then sliced, chopped, or "pulled" off the bone (shredded). Southern chopped barbecue pork is usually served on a hamburger bun. Often the sandwich is topped with a generous portion of vinegar-sauced coleslaw. Texans, who are partial to beef, are famous for their barbecued beef brisket, which is heavily smoked and served with bread and condiments such as pickles or jalapeños.

**Sauce** is another issue, with Easterners favoring a vinegar-based sauce and Westerners preferring the sweet-and-sour taste that catsup and sugar add. In parts of the South, a wet sauce often will be used in addition to a dry rub of seasonings—such as cumin, black pepper, red pepper, and white pepper. The rubbed meat is cooked slowly while being continually basted with a sauce of tomato, vinegar, and sugar.

Variations on the sauce issue exist throughout the country. For example, folks in some areas of South Carolina and Georgia baste their barbecue with a yellow mustard sauce.

In Kansas City, the self-proclaimed barbecue capital, you might find backyard cooks marinating foods in vinegar-based mixtures, applying spicy rubs to the surfaces of meat, and finally topping the finished pork, beef, ribs, chicken, and lamb with tomato-based sauces sweetened with molasses.

**Pulling meat versus chopping or slicing** is yet another regional bone of contention. Pulled pork is slow-cooked, shredded by hand, then smothered with a sauce. The center of the pulled-pork region is Memphis, Tennessee, where a tomato-based sauce spiked with black pepper and molasses is served. In Alabama pork is pulled or chopped, but in eastern North Carolina, only chopped or sliced pork makes the menu.

# MASTERING DIRECT
# & INDIRECT HEAT

Foods are cooked on the grill with either direct or indirect heat. Once you master these techniques, you can grill almost any kind of meat, poultry, or fish, plus an amazing array of vegetables, appetizers, and baked items.

## DIRECT HEAT

Food cooks in minutes when placed directly over high heat because the intense temperature browns the outside, concentrating the flavors in a caramelized crust while cooking the inside by heat conduction. The high heat produces foods with a smoky flavor.

Direct grilling is best suited to foods that are tender, small or thin, and cook quickly—in less than 20 minutes—such as steaks, burgers, kabobs, hot dogs, boneless poultry, fish, and most vegetables.

Direct grilling can be done with the cover up or down. When the grill cover is closed, the grill begins to mimic an oven, and reflected heat, as well as the heat from the coals, cooks the foods. The closed cover lowers the temperature inside the grill by decreasing the oxygen supply to the coals, allowing larger foods, such as roasts and bone-in poultry, to cook more slowly. It also imparts a smoky flavor.

To set up a charcoal grill for direct grilling, light the coals as recommended by the manufacturer. Evenly arrange the coals directly under the section of the grill rack where the food will be placed.

To set up a gas grill, preheat it with the lid closed, then adjust the gas flow settings to the desired heat level.

Electric grills also make use of direct heat, though they generally can't reach as high a temperature as gas or charcoal grills. The good news is that indoor electric grills allow you to enjoy grilled boneless chicken, vegetables, seafood, and hamburgers year-round, no matter how much snow is on the ground.

## INDIRECT HEAT

Cooking by indirect heat means placing the food adjacent to, rather than directly over, the coals. The grill cover must be down. The setup is similar to a horizontal smoker, though cooking takes place in the same chamber as the fire, the temperature is generally higher, and wood chips are not required. Indirect grilling is the best of both worlds—great charcoal flavor and tenderness that results from slower cooking. In terms of timing and temperature control it's more forgiving and easier than

**For longer-cooking foods that are grilled indirectly, you can add water or other liquid to the drip pan.**

direct grilling because food cooks evenly without having to be turned.

Indirect grilling enables you to roast large or fatty cuts of meat without burning them to a crisp. It is definitely the choice for cooking whole birds, ribs, brisket, large roasts, whole fish, and whole vegetables such as squash, onions, potatoes, or corn on the cob.

However, for indirect grilling, resist lifting the cover to peek inside. Uncovering the grill allows heat to escape and can add as much as 15 minutes to the grilling time every time the lid is lifted. Let the foods grill the minimum time specified in the recipe before checking for doneness. When cooking indirectly, it's best to use a thermometer to test the doneness of meat and poultry (see page 13).

To set up a charcoal grill for indirect cooking, light the coals as recommended by the manufacturer. Arrange glowing coals around the grill perimeter using long-handle tongs. When the coals are covered with gray ash, set a drip pan in the center of the grill, surrounded by coals, directly under where the food

will be placed. If your grill is large, push the coals to one side of the grill and place the drip pan on the other side.

Indirect grilling on a gas grill takes even less preparation. Light the grill according to the manufacturer's instructions. Turn the setting to high, and let the grill preheat for 10 to 15 minutes. Then reduce the heat on one burner to medium or medium-high, and turn the other burner off to set up two heat zones. Place the drip pan directly on the lava rocks, ceramic briquettes, or flavorizer bars on the burner that's turned off. Adjust the gas flow to the burner that's on to maintain the desired temperature inside the firebox. Place the food on the grill rack directly over the drip pan.

The drip pan collects the fat drippings from the foods to minimize flare-ups. It also can be used to hold water or other liquid, such as juices, beer, or wine, to create steam and help add flavor during prolonged cooking. Some gas grills have built-in drip pans. If yours doesn't, use a disposable foil roasting pan or make your own using heavy-duty foil.

One key component to successful grilling is determining the point when the charcoal or gas grill have obtained the ideal temperature for cooking the food. If the heat is too high, food can become charred and dry on the outside before the inside is properly cooked. If the heat is too low, it will defeat the quick-cooking benefit of grilling.

Judging the temperature of the grill without a thermometer is a guess, but it can be an educated guess. Many grill chefs determine coal temperature by how long they can hold their hands above the coals at the cooking level. This method becomes more accurate when you know how the coals should look.

A grill thermometer offers an accurate temperature measurement, but can only be used when the grill is covered. Some grills come equipped with built-in thermometers. Separate grill thermometers are widely available. Follow the manufacturer's instructions for how to use your grill thermometer.

For our recipes, a **hot fire** allows a 2-second hand count and has a temperature reading of 400° to 450°. The coals should be burning down and appear barely covered with gray ash.

A **medium fire** equates to a hand count of 4 seconds and a temperature reading of 350° to 375°. At this point, the coals should glow through a layer of gray ash.

A **low fire** is considered a 5-second hand count and a temperature reading of 300° to 350°. At this point, the coals are covered with a thick layer of gray ash.

A **very low fire** has a temperature reading of less than 300° and is reserved for smoking and barbecuing.

Controlling the grill temperature is paramount. Whatever kind of grill you have, one of the simplest temperature-control methods is to regulate the airflow through the cooking chamber. Do this by adjusting the vents in the grill bottom or sides, closing them to restrict airflow and dampen the heat or opening them to promote heat. Leave the top vents in the grill cover open at all times during cooking or the fire will be smothered.

On a gas grill, you can change the temperature with the turn of a dial.

Managing the temperature in a charcoal grill is more challenging because it depends on the type and readiness of the briquettes or lump hardwood you use and the spacing of the coals. Briquettes reach cooking temperature when they are covered in gray ash, usually 30 to 40 minutes after lighting. Lump hardwood charcoal ignites faster, gets hotter, and burns more quickly.

To lower the temperature of a charcoal fire, arrange the hot coals in thinner layers and let them burn down about 5 to 10 minutes longer. To build a hotter charcoal fire, use more coals and don't let them burn down as much. If you want more heat from the coals while they're burning, gently tap them with long-handle tongs to shake off the excess ash, then move them closer together.

When grilling for a long period, use tongs to replenish the coals adding about 10 coals every 20 to 30 minutes. Never use lighter fluid on or near burning coals. If you cannot or choose not to change the temperature of the grill, change the distance between the food and the fire. To reduce the heat reaching the food, raise the grill rack.

Set up the grill outside on an even, stable surface and away from any material or items that may catch fire. Make sure the grilling rack is clean and the firebox is clear of excess ash that can block the vents. Open the grill cover and vents.

About 30 minutes before you put food on the grill, add the briquettes to the grill. When building a charcoal or wood fire, start with enough coals to cover an area about 3 inches larger on all sides than the size of the food you plan to cook. It's always best to err on the side of too many coals versus too few. After lighting the coals, leave them in a pile or in a chimney starter until they're glowing red (about 20 minutes) then spread them over the bottom grate in a single layer. Leave an area of the grill free of coals to provide a space to move food in case of flare-ups or when foods are cooking too quickly.

Let the coals burn until they're covered with a thin layer of gray ash, about 5 to 10 minutes more, before putting the food on the grill.

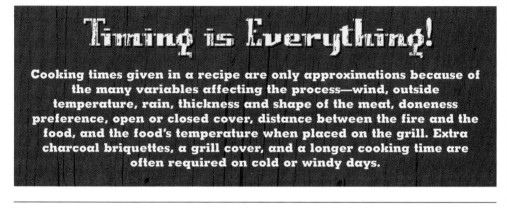

# Timing is Everything!

**Cooking times given in a recipe are only approximations because of the many variables affecting the process—wind, outside temperature, rain, thickness and shape of the meat, doneness preference, open or closed cover, distance between the fire and the food, and the food's temperature when placed on the grill. Extra charcoal briquettes, a grill cover, and a longer cooking time are often required on cold or windy days.**

# IS IT DONE YET?

**Many thermometers display the correct temperature range for various meats right on the dial.**

The safest way to judge the doneness of roasts, whole birds, and other large pieces of meat is with a thermometer. It is best to buy a meat thermometer that's made of stainless steel, with an easy-to-read dial and a shatterproof, clear lens.

**Liquid-filled thermometers** work well for roasts, whole poultry, and other thick pieces of food. These are readily available and can be left in the food while it cooks.

**Instant-read thermometers** check the internal temperature of food at the end of cooking, giving a reading in less than 20 seconds. They must be inserted at least two inches into the food. If the food has not yet reached the desired temperature, remove the thermometer and continue cooking.

**Digital thermometers** give readings in 10 seconds and can be used for thin foods, but cannot be used while food is being cooked.

When using a thermometer, insert it into the thickest part of the food, making sure it isn't touching any bones, fat, or gristle. Take the meat off the grill when it has reached the minimum internal temperature. Remember, food continues to cook for several minutes after being removed from the grill and can become overcooked if not removed promptly. Roasts and whole birds should stand 15 minutes before carving. The internal temperature will raise about five degrees with standing.

# BEYOND TRADITIONAL GRILLING

## Rotisserie Grilling

If your grill comes with a large spit or rotisserie, you will find it works best for cooking whole birds under five pounds or large pieces of meat. Smaller birds should be strung side to side on the spit, while larger birds can be strung head to tail along the spit axis. Truss birds before placing them on the spit. If they are heavy, determine the approximate center of gravity so they will balance well when turning. For best results with boneless spareribs, ask your butcher to cut them in half crosswise, forming two long strips, and thread them on the spit accordion-style.

**Rotisseries, such as the one shown here, is useful for larger cuts of meat.**

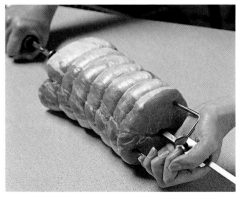

This type of grilling is similar to barbecuing, and should not be rushed. As in barbecuing, you should baste the spitted food as it cooks to add moistness and flavor.

## Adding Smoke Flavor

Aromatic woods—alder, apple, cherry, hickory, maple, mesquite, oak, or pecan—can be added to a charcoal or gas grill to give foods a more distinctive flavor. Be aware that this is a case of less is more. Too much smoke overpowers the food and can leave a bitter taste.

Wood chips, chunks, or pellets of your favorite wood can impart a mild smoke flavor to meats, poultry, and fish. The wood should be soaked in water according to the manufacturer's directions, drained well, and added to a charcoal fire just before putting food on the grill. Because wood chunks and chips can ignite, do not put food directly over them.

With outside gas or electric grills, place the wood in a metal smoker box or wrap it in heavy-duty foil that has holes poked in the top for steam to escape. A disposable drip pan also can be used to hold the wood. Place the box, foil package, or pan directly over the

**A variety of wood chips and other smoke enhancers are available for grills.**

lava rocks in a gas grill before preheating on high. Some gas grills come with a special attachment for adding wood.

For long-term cooking, keep extra wood soaking to periodically add to the fire. Presoaked wood chips should be replenished when you refuel your grill, adding another cup or a couple of chunks each time.

## Smoke Cooking

Increasingly, outdoor cooking is being done in smokers. Smoking enthusiasts agree there is nothing better than the dark golden skin of a smoked turkey or the deep crunchy crust of smoked salmon steaks. But strong opinions prevail regarding the best equipment, best fuel, and best technique. Some experts even have their equipment customized to meet their own specifications.

Before venturing into any big purchases, get acquainted with the smoking process on a simple scale by using your charcoal or gas grill (see *Adding Smoke Flavor,* page 14). If you become hooked on smoke cooking, then explore the special equipment available.

The most common types of smokers are vertical water smokers (right). These cylindrical cookers are divided into several stackable sections. The heat source is at the base of the smoker with a water pan positioned above it. The next level (or levels) includes either one or two racks that hold the food to be smoked.

Wood chunks can be used alone or along with charcoal as the primary fuel. Bear in mind that the temperature of a charcoal fire peaks, then starts to drop, so you will need to regularly add briquettes to maintain the proper temperature over a long cooking period. If your smoker is gas or electric, add wood chips to the hot lava rock base or place them near the heating element (or as directed in the owner's manual) where they will ignite and burn slowly.

Many dedicated chefs or grill masters prefer the horizontal dry smokers. These smokers generally consist of two separate sections,

which may be drum or box shape. The smaller drum or box is an offset fire chamber; it is attached to one end of the larger cooking chamber. Dry smokers allow the option of cooking over an all-wood fire, using either logs or wood chunks. However, charcoal or a combination of charcoal and wood chips also can fuel this type of smoker.

**This vertical-type smoker is relatively inexpensive.**

The firebox on this type of grill has a grid rack; some racks are adjustable so they can be moved closer or farther away from the fire. The cooking chamber is heated indirectly via an opening between the two sections, which, aided by the draw of a vented smokestack, allows the heat and smoke from the firebox to pass through into the cooking chamber. You can reduce or increase the airflow via the damper on the firebox and the smokestack to adjust the smoker temperature. If the smoker doesn't have a temperature gauge built in, invest in a good thermometer to monitor the temperature (see *Is it Done Yet?*, page 13). Checking for the doneness temperature is critical for smoked meats because most meats, especially poultry and beef, will still look pink inside even when done.

# MAKING YOUR CHOICE

## SELECT A GRILL THAT MEETS YOUR EXPECTATIONS AND MATCHES YOUR LIFESTYLE

# TYPE

If you grill on a limited basis or live in an apartment and are restricted to a tiny balcony, you might try a small hibachi. Most backyard grillers prefer a large charcoal or gas kettle or rectangular unit with a lid to enable them to roast, barbecue, and smoke.

# FIREPOWER

Both gas and charcoal grills deliver adequate heat output for the recipes in this book. Electric units and indoor grills offer viable options for people who live in apartment complexes or other places where open flames are not permitted.

# SIZE

Purchase a grill with as large a cooking area as you can afford, because a larger unit offers maximum flexibility. You'll be able to grill a full meal without cooking in shifts, and you'll have extra room to move foods around to different temperature zones.

# CONVENIENCE

If you prefer ease and no-fuss grilling, a gas or electric grill or smoker might be best for you.

These grills heat more quickly than charcoal models and you have no ashes to discard.

# DURABILITY

As with all cooking equipment purchases, consider durability. Look for heavy-gauge metal construction, preferably with a rust-resistant coating. Both stainless steel and cast aluminum resists rust and corrosion. Look for sturdy legs and wheels and tight-fitting parts. Purchase from a reputable company to help assure replacement parts and warranty service will be available.

## CHARCOAL GRILLS

Charcoal grills are the least expensive and deliver more intense heat than other grills. They tend to be a little messier, take more time to start, and, when it comes to heat, are harder to control. But many grill enthusiasts insist on using a charcoal grill. Here are a few of the variations on the theme.

**The hibachi** is very small and portable. The heavy metal fireboxes with vents allow them to achieve high heat. The grill racks are easily raised and lowered to control the heat.

**The kettle grill** is probably the most popular grill. It resembles two large metal bowls; the top one, with a vent and handle, serves as the cover. This allows you to cook over charcoal while using the grill as an oven.

**Steel drum grills** are popular on the professional barbecue circuit. Made from

55-gallon steel drums, these grills are hefty and best for barbecuing whole hogs and large cuts of meat.

**Brick or stone grills** were popular in the 1950s. A new generation of high-tech outdoor cooking centers is emerging in today's market place; some units are modular and can be installed in brick or stone walls or islands, and others must be custom-built by masonry artisans.

## GAS GRILLS

Gas grills have evolved into the most popular type of grill in backyards across the country. Although gas grills outsell charcoal grills and are used twice as often, this type of grill costs more than charcoal grills. The main advantage, however, is convenience and ease. Gas grills light easily and the heat is more easily controlled. Generally, gas grills also have covers, which are usually attached, so they can easily be used for smoking or indirect cooking.

A gas grill is basically a metal firebox with tube-shape gas burners at the bottom, topped by a grate that holds lava stones, ceramic briquettes, or inverted V-shape metal bars to deflect the heat. Be aware that lava rocks generally need replacing sooner than ceramic briquettes because they absorb grease. Metal bars have the added benefit of directing grease away from burners and minimizing flare-ups. Generally, parallel bar burners or long S-shape burners will heat the best and allow more temperature control.

Look for a gas grill that has at least two individual burners to allow you to grill different foods simultaneously and to grill indirectly. In addition, some grills will offer side burners, which are handy for simmering marinades and sauces. Other possible features might include towel bars, glass windows, utensil hooks, and condiment racks—all nonessential.

## OTHER GRILLS

Infrared gas grills are relatively new to the market. Developers say they will preheat in minutes with high-intensity infrared ceramic burners that cook up to 50 percent faster than regular grills. They claim to perform well even in below-freezing temperatures.

**Electric tabletop grills** run the gamut from moderately priced models to professional high-end units. They also may be found on ranges that have special grates and exhaust fans. Electric grills can only be used for direct grilling of foods up to 1 inch thick such as burgers; skinless, boneless chicken breasts; turkey tenderloin steaks; hot dogs; bratwurst; and steaks and chops up to 1 inch thick. (See charts for suggested timings, page 26.)

**Skillet grills** are frying pans with parallel ridges on the bottom that allow lower-fat frying. The ridges raise the meat so it has less contact with the fat, which flows into the lower ridges of the pan. These skillets approximate a grilled flavor as the ridges create searing and simulate grill marks.

## SMOKERS

Smokers can be electric, gas, or charcoal fueled. Many experienced cooks believe that electric versions are the most reliable. Electric and gas smokers generally are more expensive than charcoal, but they are exceptionally convenient and provide steady, consistent heat with little attention required during cooking.

**Vertical smokers** The typical vertical water smoker—with a dome-shape lid, a fire box in the bottom, a water tray in the middle, and a cooking rack at the top—is usually the least expensive and most compact smoker type. Both gas and electric models sometime have a bed of lava rock under the burner or coil.

**Gas water smokers** share many of the attributes of electric, especially the ease in maintaining more consistent temperatures and the overall convenience. However, they may be somewhat more costly and you must remember to check the gas cylinder periodically to be certain you won't run out during an extended cooking period.

**Charcoal water smokers** have the advantage of being the least expensive and most portable, but they do require attention during use, especially during cold and windy weather. There also is a bit more cleanup, since you're contending with ashes.

When purchasing a vertical smoker, look for one that is sturdy, has a built-in temperature gauge, and doors that slide open to easily add more water, wood, or charcoal.

**Horizontal smokers.** The horizontal dry or pit smokers range dramatically in size, starting with small barrels and progressing to huge models designed to turn out hundreds of pounds of deliciously smoked meat. Generally much larger and heavier than traditional grills, they aren't very portable. The hefty price tags—they can run from hundreds to many thousands of dollars—also mean they're a bigger investment than traditional grills. But these smokers will last for years and typically appeal to committed competi-tion barbecuers. Look for convenience features, such as doors that open or trays that pull out to empty ashes and vents and dampers that allow the regulation of heat and smoke. It's also an asset to have an adjustable-height cooking grid in the firebox as it gives maximum control.

The versatile all-in-one gas smoker-roaster grills require the same amount of space as a traditional gas grill, but they are more expensive. They provide effortless smoking and are both convenient and space-efficient—considering that one piece of equipment is capable of dry smoking, water smoking, and regular direct-heat grilling. Relying on natural or propane gas as a heat source also makes these grills convenient to use.

The type of fuel you use for grilling has little affect on the flavor of the food because the food doesn't stay on the grill long enough to absorb much of the fuel's flavor. In barbecuing, however, the food stays on the grill much longer and the smoke cooks the food. That's when the fuel has a real impact on flavor.

**Gas** is the winner when it comes to selecting a convenient, clean-burning fuel. In both propane and natural forms, it ignites with the turn of a knob, heats quickly, and cleans up easily. The standard 20-pound propane tank gives 12 to 18 hours of nonstop grilling. For safety and convenience, simply trade the empty tank for a full one at your local supermarket, home center, or convenience store.

If your home uses propane for heat, you can have your grill attached directly to the propane supply line to avoid the use of tanks. Some grills run on natural gas, which also can be hooked up directly by the utility company.

**Lump charcoal,** also called natural hardwood charcoal, is the fuel choice of chefs and professional barbecuers. Lump charcoal, is formed by burning whole logs or large pieces of aged low-resin hardwoods in a kiln at 900° until they become carbonized. It doesn't contain any industrial additives or petroleum, and it retains some of its original wood flavor. It is porous and lights more easily than briquettes, burns cleaner and hotter, and leaves fewer residues. The main drawbacks are that it occasionally sparks, can be hard to find, and costs more.

**Hardwood charcoal briquettes,** also called natural briquettes, are made from pulverized lump charcoal held together with natural binders, such as lime and starch. They don't have the petroleum, nitrates, and fillers found in other composite briquettes that can emit off-flavors to foods.

**Composition briquettes,** the most common charcoal briquettes, are made from burned wood and scraps, coal dust, camphor, and paraffin or petroleum binders. They're more uniform in shape, size, and consistency than lump charcoal. Find a quality brand, as some brands contain excessive amounts of fillers that can give foods an unpleasant taste and leave heavy ashes.

**Wood** is preferred by professional barbecuers. It is considered the best at delivering prolonged hot heat and releasing flavorful smoke. Green wood burns hotter, longer, and smokier than aged wood. Unless you have a large cooker and don't mind tending to it, logs are not the average barbecuer's choice for fuel. However, some companies now sell wood chunks that are easy to light in a chimney starter. Place the wood chunks on wads of newspapers in the starter and light the paper. After about 10 minutes, dump the blazing coals into the grill and spread them out over the bottom to burn until they glow. Some wood chunks are enclosed in paper sacks that can be put directly in the grill for lighting. Wood chunks burn hotter than charcoal, so less is needed; they're best used for direct grilling with the grill lid left off. Use only dried natural hardwood, not soft woods such as pine that can cause flare-ups and leave a sooty, tarry-resin flavor. Never use lumber or plywood that contain toxic chemicals. Use untreated wood for grilling.

## Good Grilling Advice

**Are you a grilling fanatic and want to know more? Visit these internet sites for more information on grilling, contests, and recipes.**

- **www.weberbbq.com (the Weber-Stephen Products Co.)**
- **www.bbqind.org (the Barbecue Industry Association)**
- **www.barbecuen.com (a free electronic newsletter)**
- **www.barbecuenews.com (National Barbecue News)**

# SPARKING THE FIRE

### LIGHTING A CHARCOAL GRILL

Starting a charcoal fire is a simple matter of mounding briquettes (approximately 30 briquettes per pound of meat to be cooked) on the charcoal grate and igniting them, leaving the lid off. It will take about 20 to 30 minutes for the coals to turn ashy gray, which means they are ready. The ignition process can be tricky, but there are plenty of aids to make the job easier.

**Instant-lighting briquettes,** which ash over in about 20 minutes, are saturated with a petroleum product that lights easily with a match.

**Fire-starter gels** are an alcohol-base, ecologically friendly way to start a fire for grilling. Put small dollops of the gel on the charcoal and light with a match for a low, quiet flame. After about 15 seconds of burning, there will be no trace of the gel and no odor.

**Paraffin fire starters** offer another environmentally safe, smokeless, and nontoxic method for starting a charcoal fire. Place a couple of pieces under a mound of charcoal and ignite with a match. They light easily, even if wet, and will burn hot for about 12 minutes.

**Chimney starters,** wide cylindrical steel pipes with vent holes at the bottom and a grate in the middle, help coals reach cooking stage faster than if they're started on a grill grate. Fill a chimney starter with charcoal and wood chunks, stuff newspapers under the starter grate, set the starter on the grill grate, and light the papers with a match. When the coals are ready, dump them from the chimney starter into the grill.

**Electric starters,** loop-shape heating elements, are placed under a mound of coals or wood chunks and plugged in and removed once the coals are lit. Follow the manufacturer's directions and place on a fireproof surface after removing from grill.

**Liquid lighter fluids,** once a popular option, are outlawed in many areas because of their emission of possible pollutants.

## LIGHTING A GAS GRILL

Follow the directions in your owner's manual for lighting a gas grill. This usually involves turning on the gas, then the burner and pressing an ignition button several times while the lid is open. Close the lid; preheat with all burners on high about 15 minutes or until the grill reaches at least 500°.

## Cleaning Your Grill

As with any appliance, some simple maintenance will add years to the life of your grill and keep it looking good, too.

■ Wipe the inside and outside surfaces of the grill with a soft cloth and warm, soapy water. Rinse with clear water and wipe dry.

■ Prevent grease build-up by wiping the inside of the lid with paper towels while it's still warm.

■ *For a gas grill:* After every use, turn your grill burners on HIGH for 10 to 15 minutes (with the lid closed); turn burners off. Then loosen residue from the grill rack with a brass bristle brush. This not only helps prevent sticking, but also avoids flare-ups the next time you grill.

■ *For a charcoal grill:* After every use, soak the grill rack in hot sudsy water to loosen cooked-on food. A rack that is too large for the sink can be wrapped in wet paper towels or newspaper and allowed to stand for about an hour. Unwrap the rack and wipe it clean with paper towels. If necessary, use a stiff scrub brush to remove stubborn burned on food. Your manufacturer may also recommend that certain abrasive cleaners not be used on the grill rack. Look for cleaners made specifically for grills.

■ Check your owner's manual for cleaning tips and specific manufacturer's cleaning instructions.

**Gas grills, similar to the one pictured at right, are the most popular type of grills purchased today.**

# SAFETY FIRST

Fire can be a friend if you're constantly on guard to its power to burn. Be aware of the potential for danger and treat the fire and the grill with respect.

## DON'T GET BURNED

■ Never leave infants, children, and pets unattended near a hot barbecue grill.

■ Never use gasoline or kerosene to start charcoal. Use fire-starter gels as directed and never apply starters to existing hot or even warm coals.

■ Do not use lighter fluid or an electric or a chimney starter with instant lighting briquettes.

■ Never wear loose clothing when cooking over a hot grill.

## DON'T BURN DOWN THE HOUSE

■ Never leave a grill unattended or try to move it while it's in use or hot.

■ Never use your grill in a garage or enclosed area.

■ Never use a barbecue grill unless all parts of the unit are firmly in place and the grill is level and stable.

■ A grill should not be used within five feet of any combustible materials.

## LET IT COOL

■ Make sure coals and ashes are dead before putting a grill away or covering it.

■ Never dump hot or warm coals or wood out of a grill. Never dump recently used coals or wood into a trash can.

■ Unplug electric starters and allow them to cool on a fireproof surface before storing.

## GIVE GAS GRILLS A CHECKUP

When your gas grill has been idle for a period of time or if you have just attached a new gas cylinder, make sure the unit is in good working order.

■ Read the owner's manual to review safety precautions specific to your grill.

■ Test for gas leaks. Use a spray bottle filled with soapy water to spritz joints and fittings; look for tiny bubbles, which indicate a leak. Do *not* light the grill if you detect a leak.

■ Check hoses for cracking, brittleness, and leaks. Make sure there are no sharp bends in the hose or tubing and that they are far away from heat or hot surfaces. Install a heat shield for protection, if necessary.

■ Clean your gas grill's venturi tubes (the tubes leading to the burners) regularly according to the manufacturer's instructions. Keep the grill clean, making sure that the tubes are not blocked. Spiders often may be the culprit of a block.

■ Be aware that if your grill was made prior to 1995, it may not have several safety features found on most newer models, such as a shut-off mechanism in the event of a hose rupture or leak.

■ Realize that the gas cylinder typically holds about 20 pounds of propane, which can leak or lead to an explosion if it isn't handled properly. Follow safe transport and storage procedures, as noted on the tank.

# ARE GRILLED FOODS SAFE?

You may have heard of possible health risks associated with cooking over high heat. Grilling, broiling, and smoking have all been implicated. These cooking methods can produce small amounts of harmful substances when fat from meat drips over hot coals, resulting in flare-ups. Although the risk is very low, you may want to take some precautions.

To play it safe, minimize flare-ups by choosing lean cuts of meat and trimming visible fat before grilling. During a flare-up, rescue food from scorching by moving it to a cooler area, and extinguishing the grill fire by temporarily covering the grill. Use minimal oil on foods and grill racks, and grill fatty foods or skin-on poultry indirectly. It is best to apply sugary sauces with a light hand toward the end of grilling to prevent burning. Most important, always clean the grill of charred food debris before grilling again.

If you are still concerned about possible risks, grill foods over indirect heat (see page 10). The grilling charts at the ends of the recipe chapters give timings for grilling foods with both direct and indirect heat.

# GRILLING GADGETS

**GRILLING ENTHUSIASTS HAVE MYRIAD ACCESSORIES TO CONSIDER. SOME ARE NECESSARY, OTHERS ARE EXTRAVAGANT GADGETS. CONSIDER THE OPTIONS.**

■ Heavy flame-retardant oven mitts or hot pads protect against burned hands.
■ Long-handle utensils help in moving food around on a grill rack. Tongs work for most foods, whereas a big-blade spatula is handy for foods that crumble, such as burgers and large pieces of fish.

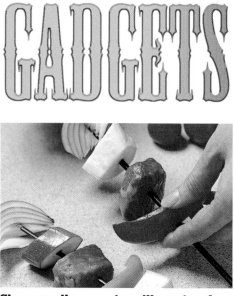

**Skewers allow you to grill meat and vegetables together. Be sure to leave space between pieces.**

**A grilling basket for kabobs eliminates the need for threading skewers.**

**Pans such as this one are perfect for making pizza on the grill.**

■ A barbecue brush is vital for oiling the rack before grilling and for brushing sauces over food.

■ Grill grate pickup devices can save the day whenever you need to remove your grill rack to replenish the coals or rescue food from occasional flare-ups.

■ A spray bottle filled with water helps tame charcoal flare-ups.

■ A cleaning brush is critical. A clean grill rack helps prevent food from sticking. Brush the grill rack vigorously during preheating, before placing food on it, and again at the end of grilling after the rack has cooled.

■ A waterproof vinyl grill cover helps protect the grill from the elements, extending its life.

■ A second gas tank can be a welcome meal-saver. You'll avoid a disheartening half-done meal on a cold grill.

■ A grilling night-light, designed to mount on the grill, is great for late-night cookouts.

■ An instant-read or digital thermometer can mean the difference between just right and overdone (see *Is It Done Yet?* on page 13 for more information on thermometers).

■ Skewers—metal or wood—are needed for grilling kabobs. (For wood or bamboo skewers, soak them in water for at least 30 minutes before using so they don't burn.)

■ Disposable foil drip pans are ideal for indirect grilling and for holding wood chips.

■ A hinged grilling basket is a useful device for holding fish, shrimp, or vegetables that need to be turned.

■ Nonstick enamel-coated grilling trays, woks, and pizza pans, with small holes that allow heat and smoke to penetrate foods, come in all shapes and sizes, with and without handles.

■ Grilling packets or heavy-duty foil are invaluable for baking food on the grill. Ready-made pouches, presealed on three sides, are large enough to hold four to six main-dish servings or a side dish. You also can make your own from heavy-duty foil.

# GRILLING GLOSSARY

- **BASTE:** To brush a seasoned liquid over a food surface to add moisture and flavor.

- **BROCHETTE:** French term for kabob, food cooked on a skewer.

- **CERAMIC BRIQUETTES:** Radiant materials compacted in a brick shape; used in gas grills. Ceramic briquettes don't burn completely like charcoal. Lava rocks and metal plates are similar alternatives.

- **CHARCOAL BRIQUETTES:** Ground charcoal, coal dust, and starch compacted in a brick shape and used as fuel in charcoal grills.

- **CHARCOAL GRATE:** The rack that holds charcoal in the firebox.

- **CHARCOAL GRILL:** A grill that uses charcoal briquettes as its principal fuel.

- **CHIMNEY STARTER:** A metal cylinder-shape container used to start a charcoal fire.

- **DIRECT GRILLING:** Method of quickly cooking food by placing it on a grill rack directly over the heat source. Food is most often cooked uncovered on a charcoal grill, but covered on a gas grill.

- **DRIP PAN:** A metal or disposable foil pan placed under food to catch drippings when grilling. A drip pan can also be made from heavy foil.

- **DRY SMOKING:** A method of cooking food by placing it on a grill rack indirectly over the heat source with the lid down and vents adjusted to allow the fire to burn and create smoke.

- **ELECTRIC GRILL:** A small tabletop grill that uses electricity for fuel. Also, many high-end rangetops include a grate or grill insert and a built-in exhaust fan for smokeless indoor grilling.

- **FIREBOX:** The bottom of the grill that holds the fire or heat.

- **FLARE-UPS:** Flames caused by fat dripping onto hot coals or lava rocks.

- **GAS GRILL:** A grill that uses gas from a propane tank or natural gas line for fuel.

- **GLAZE:** To form a glossy, flavorful coating on food as it cooks, usually by basting it.

■ **GRID:** The latticework of metal rods that holds food on a grill; sometimes referred to as grill grate.

■ **GRILL BASKET:** A hinged wire basket that is used to hold fish or vegetables for grilling.

■ **GRILL WOK:** A wok that is made specifically for grilling. With its sloped sides and numerous small holes, it makes small pieces of vegetables, meat, or seafoods easy to stir-fry on the grill.

■ **HIBACHI:** A small, portable, uncovered grill, often made of cast iron.

■ **INDIRECT GRILLING:** Method of cooking food slowly, off to one side of the heat source, usually over a drip pan in a covered grill.

■ **KABOBS:** Pieces of meat, poultry, seafood, and/or vegetables threaded on a skewer and grilled.

■ **KETTLE GRILL:** A round charcoal grill with a heavy cover. It usually stands on three legs and can be used for either direct or indirect grilling.

■ **LAVA ROCK:** This natural rock results from volcanic lava and is used as an alternative to ceramic briquettes in gas or electric grills. It can be used many times, but eventually needs to be replaced.

■ **LUMP CHARCOAL:** Carbon residue of wood that has been charred; usually in the form of lumps. Used for heat source in charcoal grills.

■ **MARINATE:** To soak food in a flavorful liquid mixture before it is cooked. Marinades add flavor to foods and tenderize certain cuts of meat. Beef cuts that benefit from marinating include boneless skirt steak, flank steak, round top round steak, round eye round steak, round tip steak, and chuck blade steak.

■ **MEDIUM DONENESS:** For this doneness, the center of the meat should have a slightly pink to red color. The meat will be slightly firm and springy when pressed. If using a thermometer, a medium doneness temperature is 160°.

■ **MEDIUM-RARE DONENESS:** For this doneness, the center of the meat should have a bright red color and be slightly springy when pressed. If using a thermometer, a medium-rare temperature is 145°. This temperature is not recommended for veal, pork, or ground meats.

■ **MEDIUM-WELL DONENESS:** For this doneness, the center of the meat should have very little pink color and be firm and springy when pressed. If using a thermometer, a medium-well temperature is 170°.

■ **ROTISSERIE:** The spit or long metal skewer that suspends and rotates food over the grill's heat source.

■ **RUB:** A blend of seasonings that is rubbed onto a food surface before grilling.

■ **SKEWER:** A long, narrow metal or wooden stick that can be inserted through pieces of meat or vegetables for grilling.

■ **SMOKER BOX:** Small, perforated steel or cast-iron container placed on a gas grill's lava rocks or ceramic briquettes, or the grill rack to hold wood chips and provide smoke.

■ **VENTS:** Holes in a grill cover or firebox that open and close. When open, air circulates through, increasing the heat of a fire.

■ **WATER/WET SMOKING:** Method of cooking food by placing a pan of water or other liquid in the grill to add moisture when smoking foods.

■ **WOOD CHIPS AND CHUNKS:** Natural hardwood materials added to a fire to impart smoky flavor to food as it cooks.

# Electric Grills

The following timings should be used as general guidelines. Refer to your owner's manual for preheating directions, suggested cuts, and recommended grilling times.

| Cut or Type | Thickness, Weight, or Size | Doneness | Grilling Time |
|---|---|---|---|
| **BEEF** | | | |
| Boneless Sirloin steak | 1 in. | Rare<br>Medium rare<br>Medium | 14 to 18 min.<br>17 to 19 min.<br>18 to 22 min. |
| Flank steak | ¾ to 1 in. | Medium | 12 to 14 min. |
| Ground meat patties | ¾ in.<br>(4 per lb.) | No pink remains | 14 to 18 min. |
| Steak (porterhouse, rib, rib eye, sirloin, T-bone, tenderloin, top loin) | 1 in. | Rare<br>Medium | 8 to 12 min.<br>12 to 15 min. |
| Top round steak | 1 in. | Rare<br>Medium | 14 to 16 min.<br>18 to 20 min. |
| Hotdogs | 6 per lb. | Heated through | 3 to 5 min. |
| **LAMB** | | | |
| Chop | 1 in. | Medium rare<br>Medium | 10 to 14 min.<br>14 to 16 min. |
| **PORK\*** | | | |
| Chop | ¾ to 1 in. | Medium to well-done | 8 to 12 min. |
| **POULTRY** | | | |
| Chicken breast half, skinned and boned | 4 to 5 oz. each | Tender, no longer pink | 12 to 15 min. . |
| Turkey breast tenderloin steak | 4 to 6 oz. each | Tender, no longer pink | 12 to 15 min. |
| **VEAL** | | | |
| Chop | 1 in. | Medium to well-done | 19 to 23 min. |
| **FISH AND SEAFOOD** | | | |
| Fillets, steaks, cubes (for kabobs) | ½- to 1-in. thick | Flakes | 4 to 6 min. per ½-in. thickness |
| Lobster tail, butterflied (rock lobster) | 6 oz. | Opaque | 6 to 10 min. |
| Sea scallops | 12 to 15 per lb. | Opaque | 5 to 8 min. |
| Shrimp | Medium (20 per lb.) | Opaque | 6 to 8 min. |
| | Jumbo (12 to 15 per lb.) | Opaque | 10 to 12 min. |

*Note: Pork should be cooked until juices run clear.

## Condiments

# Tomato-Molasses-Mustard Sauce

**Prep:** 20 minutes

*Consider this a melting pot sauce. It has plenty of regional echoes to satisfy purists from whatever part of the country who may converge at your picnic table.*

- ¼ cup finely chopped onion
- 6 cloves garlic, minced
- ½ teaspoon paprika
- ½ teaspoon crushed red pepper
- 1 tablespoon cooking oil
- 1 15-ounce can tomato puree
- 3 tablespoons cider vinegar
- 3 tablespoons molasses
- 2 tablespoons brown sugar
- 2 tablespoons stone-ground mustard
- ½ teaspoon salt
- ½ teaspoon dried oregano, crushed
- ½ teaspoon liquid smoke (optional)

**1** In a medium saucepan cook onion, garlic, paprika, and crushed red pepper in hot oil until onion is tender.

**2** Stir in the tomato puree, vinegar, molasses, brown sugar, mustard, salt, oregano, and, if desired, liquid smoke. Bring to boiling; reduce heat. Simmer, uncovered, about 10 minutes or until sauce is thickened, stirring frequently.

**3** To use, brush chicken, pork, or beef with some of the sauce during the last 10 minutes of grilling. If desired, reheat and pass remaining sauce. Makes about 2 cups.

Ⓥ Nutrition Facts per tablespoon: 19 calories, 1 g total fat (0 g saturated fat), 0 mg cholesterol, 100 mg sodium, 4 g carbohydrate, 0 g fiber, 0 g protein. Daily Values: 2% vit. A, 8% vit. C, 1% iron.

# KANSAS CITY BARBECUE SAUCE

**Prep:** 40 minutes

*Kansas City is a notoriously competitive barbecue town—so much so that the sauces are secrets taken to the grave. How'd we get this one? Work, work, work.*

- ½ cup finely chopped onion
- 2 cloves garlic, minced
- 1 tablespoon olive oil or cooking oil
- ¾ cup apple juice
- ½ of a 6-ounce can tomato paste (⅓ cup)
- ¼ cup cider vinegar
- 2 tablespoons brown sugar
- 2 tablespoons molasses
- 1 tablespoon paprika
- 1 tablespoon prepared horseradish
- 1 tablespoon Worcestershire sauce
- 1 teaspoon salt
- ½ teaspoon pepper

**1** In a medium saucepan cook onion and garlic in hot oil until onion is tender. Stir in apple juice, tomato paste, vinegar, brown sugar, molasses, paprika, horseradish, Worcestershire sauce, salt, and pepper. Bring to boiling; reduce heat. Simmer, uncovered, about 30 minutes or until desired consistency, stirring occasionally.

**2** To use, brush chicken, pork, or beef with some of the sauce during the last 10 minutes of grilling. If desired, reheat and pass additional sauce. Makes about 1⅓ cups.

Ⓥ Nutrition Facts per tablespoon: 26 calories, 1 g total fat (0 g saturated fat), 0 mg cholesterol, 150 mg sodium, 5 g carbohydrate, 0 g fiber, 0 g protein. Daily Values: 2% vit. A, 6% vit. C, 2% iron.

# Tangy Barbecue Sauce

**Prep:** 20 minutes

*Who wants some tang? Balsamic vinegar tarts up this sauce while corn syrup offers a sweet counterpoint.*

    1 cup catsup
    ⅓ cup balsamic vinegar or cider
        vinegar
    ⅓ cup light-colored corn syrup
    ¼ cup finely chopped onion or thinly
        sliced green onions
    ¼ teaspoon salt
      Several dashes bottled hot
        pepper sauce

**1** In a small saucepan combine the catsup, vinegar, corn syrup, onion, salt, and hot pepper sauce. Bring to boiling; reduce heat. Simmer, uncovered, for 10 to 15 minutes or until desired consistency, stirring sauce occasionally.

**2** Brush burgers, chicken, or pork with some of the sauce during the last 10 minutes of grilling. If desired, reheat and pass remaining sauce. Makes about 1½ cups.

Nutrition Facts per tablespoon: 29 calories, 0 g total fat (0 g saturated fat), 0 mg cholesterol, 161 mg sodium, 7 g carbohydrate, 0 g fiber, 0 g protein. Daily Values: 1% vit. A, 3% vit. C, 2% iron.

# HONEY-BEER-BARBECUE SAUCE

**Prep:** 25 minutes

*Here's a medley of flavors for the boldest of backyard barbecue chefs.*

    ⅓ cup chopped onion
    1 clove garlic, minced
    1 tablespoon cooking oil
    ¾ cup bottled chili sauce
    ½ cup beer
    ¼ cup honey
    2 tablespoons Worcestershire sauce
    1 tablespoon prepared mustard

**1** In a medium saucepan cook onion and garlic in hot oil until onion is tender. Stir in chili sauce, beer, honey, Worcestershire sauce, and mustard. Bring to boiling; reduce heat. Simmer, uncovered, about 20 minutes or until desired consistency, stirring occasionally.

**2** Brush beef, chicken, or pork with sauce during the last 10 minutes of grilling. If desired, reheat and pass remaining sauce. Makes about 1½ cups.

Nutrition Facts per tablespoon: 28 calories, 1 g total fat (0 g saturated fat), 0 mg cholesterol, 121 mg sodium, 5 g carbohydrate, 0 g fiber, 0 g protein. Daily Values: 1% vit. A, 5% vit. C, 1% iron.

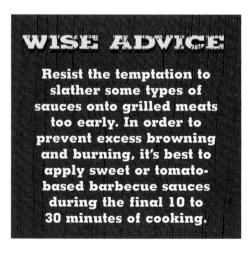

**WISE ADVICE**

**Resist the temptation to slather some types of sauces onto grilled meats too early. In order to prevent excess browning and burning, it's best to apply sweet or tomato-based barbecue sauces during the final 10 to 30 minutes of cooking.**

# Plum-Good Sauce

**Prep:** 15 minutes

*When Asian ingredients such as plums, ginger, soy, and citrus hit the grill, they offer up a tantalizing fusion of flavors. Wait to put the sauce on until the last 10 minutes of cooking or the considerable amount of sugar in the orange juice concentrate, catsup, and plums might burn.*

½ cup chopped onion
1 tablespoon margarine or butter
1 16-ounce can whole, unpitted
   purple plums
1 6-ounce can frozen orange juice
   concentrate, thawed (¾ cup)
¼ cup catsup
2 tablespoons soy sauce
1 tablespoon prepared mustard
2 teaspoons grated fresh ginger or
   1 teaspoon ground ginger
1 teaspoon Worcestershire sauce

**1** In a medium saucepan cook onion in hot margarine until tender. Drain plums, reserving syrup. Remove and discard pits from plums. In a blender container or food processor bowl combine plums and reserved syrup. Cover and blend or process until nearly smooth.

**2** Stir pureed plums, orange juice concentrate, catsup, soy sauce, mustard, ginger, and Worcestershire sauce into onion mixture. Bring to boiling; reduce heat. Simmer, uncovered, for 10 to 15 minutes or until reduced to about 2 cups, stirring often.

**3** To use, brush chicken or pork ribs with some of the sauce during the last 10 minutes of grilling. If desired, reheat and pass additional sauce. Makes about 2 cups.

Nutrition Facts per tablespoon: 30 calories, 0 g total fat (0 g saturated fat), 1 mg cholesterol, 104 mg sodium, 7 g carbohydrate, 0 g fiber, 0 g protein. Daily Values: 1% vit. A, 14% vit. C, 1% iron.

# PEANUT SATAY SAUCE

**Prep:** 10 minutes

*To really bring out the rich aroma of the sesame oil, keep this sauce bubbly warm in a saucepan right on the grill.*

¼ cup creamy peanut butter
2 tablespoons rice vinegar or white
   vinegar
2 tablespoons soy sauce
2 cloves garlic, minced
½ teaspoon toasted sesame oil
⅛ teaspoon crushed red pepper
2 tablespoons thinly sliced
   green onion

**1** In a small bowl stir together peanut butter, vinegar, soy sauce, garlic, sesame oil, and red pepper. Stir in green onion.

**2** To use, brush chicken, beef, pork, or lamb with some of the sauce during the last 5 minutes of grilling. If desired, reheat and pass additional sauce. Makes about ½ cup.

Nutrition Facts per tablespoon: 53 calories, 4 g total fat (1 g saturated fat), 0 mg cholesterol, 296 mg sodium, 3 g carbohydrate, 1 g fiber, 2 g protein. Daily Values: 1% iron.

**Smokin' Hot Tip**

**What's the easiest way to clean up a gas grill? After each use, turn the grill settings to high for 10 to 15 minutes (with the lid closed). Then simply brush off the grill rack using a brass bristle brush. This prevents charred bits of food from sticking and flare-ups next time around.**

Mango and Pepper BBQ Sauce (left)
Honey-Peach Sauce (right)

# Mango and Pepper BBQ Sauce

**Prep:** 20 minutes

*What starts out as a chunky fresh-fruit-and-vegetable salsa you could serve alongside your grilled food winds up being pureed into a terrific barbecue sauce for the top of it.*

> 2 cups chopped red sweet pepper
> ½ cup chopped onion
> 2 tablespoons cooking oil
> 2 medium mangoes, seeded, peeled, and chopped (2 cups)
> ¼ cup packed brown sugar
> 2 tablespoons rice vinegar
> ½ teaspoon crushed red pepper
> ¼ teaspoon salt
> 2 tablespoons finely chopped green onion

1 In a large skillet cook the sweet pepper and onion in hot oil just until tender. Stir in the mangoes, brown sugar, vinegar, crushed red pepper, and salt. Bring to boiling; reduce heat. Simmer, uncovered, about 10 minutes or until mangoes are tender. Cool mixture slightly. Transfer mixture to a blender container or food processor bowl. Cover and blend or process until nearly smooth. Stir in the green onion.

2 To use, brush chicken, shrimp, fish, or pork with some of the sauce during the last 10 minutes of grilling. If desired, reheat and pass additional sauce. Makes about 2½ cups.

Nutrition Facts per tablespoon: 19 calories, 1 g total fat (0 g saturated fat), 0 mg cholesterol, 14 mg sodium, 3 g carbohydrate, 0 g fiber, 0 g protein. Daily Values: 8% vit. A, 20% vit. C.

# HONEY-PEACH SAUCE

**Prep:** 20 minutes

*Nothing says summer like a perfect peach. Here's a sauce to highlight the season's bounty.*

> 4 medium peaches
> 2 tablespoons lemon juice
> 2 tablespoons honey
> ½ teaspoon cracked pepper
> 1 to 2 teaspoons snipped fresh thyme

1 Peel and cut up 3 of the peaches. Place in a blender container. Add lemon juice, honey, and pepper. Cover and blend until smooth. Transfer to a medium saucepan. Bring to boiling; reduce heat. Simmer, uncovered, about 15 minutes or until slightly thickened, stirring occasionally. Remove from heat. Peel and finely chop the remaining peach; stir into the sauce. Stir in thyme.

2 To use, brush pork, beef, or poultry with some of the sauce during the last 15 minutes of grilling. If desired, reheat and pass additional sauce. Makes about 1¾ cups.

Nutrition Facts per tablespoon: 15 calories, 0 g total fat (0 g saturated fat), 0 mg cholesterol, 0 mg sodium, 4 g carbohydrate, 0 g fiber, 0 g protein. Daily Values: 1% vit. A, 3% vit. C.

## Did You Know?

**Removing the large seed of a mango takes a little cutting expertise. It's best to place the fruit on its blossom end and align a sharp knife slightly off-center on the stem end of the fruit. Slice down through the peel and flesh, next to the pit. Repeat on the other side of the seed. Cut off the remaining flesh around the seed. Remove the peel, and cut the mango into pieces as directed in your recipe.**

# Soy-Citrus Marinade

**Prep:** 10 minutes  **Marinate:** 1 hour

*Citrus, salty soy, garlic, and brown sugar zing up this Asian-accented marinade.*

¼ cup soy sauce
1 tablespoon finely shredded orange
   peel
¼ cup orange juice
1 tablespoon finely shredded lemon
   peel
3 tablespoons lemon juice
1 tablespoon brown sugar
3 cloves garlic, minced
2 teaspoons toasted sesame oil

1 In a small bowl combine soy sauce, orange peel, orange juice, lemon peel, lemon juice, brown sugar, garlic, and sesame oil. Stir until the sugar is dissolved.

2 To use, pour marinade over seafood, fish, or chicken in a plastic bag set in a shallow dish; seal bag. Marinate in the refrigerator for 1 to 2 hours, turning bag occasionally. Drain, discarding marinade. Grill seafood, fish, or chicken according to the charts on pages 292 and 326. Makes about ¾ cup marinade (enough for about 2 pounds seafood, fish, or chicken).

ⓥNutrition Facts per tablespoon: 21 calories, 1 g total fat (0 g saturated fat), 0 mg cholesterol, 344 mg sodium, 3 g carbohydrate, 0 g fiber, 0 g protein. Daily Values: 14% vit. C, 1% iron.

# GINGER-RUM MARINADE

**Prep:** 10 minutes  **Marinate:** 4 hours

*For those instances where a Caribbean vacation isn't practical, this pineapple and ginger concoction—made merrier with rum—will take you there.*

½ cup unsweetened pineapple juice
⅓ cup rum
¼ cup soy sauce
1 tablespoon brown sugar
1 tablespoon grated fresh ginger
2 cloves garlic, minced
¼ teaspoon ground red pepper

1 In a small bowl combine pineapple juice, rum, soy sauce, brown sugar, ginger, garlic, and red pepper. To use, pour marinade over beef, pork, or chicken in a plastic bag set in a shallow dish; seal bag. Marinate in the refrigerator for 4 to 8 hours, turning bag occasionally. Drain, reserving marinade.

2 Grill beef, pork, or chicken according to the charts on pages 174, 224, and 292, brushing occasionally with the marinade up to the last 5 minutes of grilling. Discard any remaining marinade. Makes about 1¼ cups marinade (enough for 2½ to 3 pounds beef, pork, or chicken).

ⓥNutrition Facts per tablespoon: 17 calories, 0 g total fat (0 g saturated fat), 0 mg cholesterol, 206 mg sodium, 2 g carbohydrate, 0 g fiber, 0 g protein. Daily Values: 1% vit. C.

## Sizzlin' Solutions

Besides adding flavor, acid-containing marinades are a great way to tenderize meat. Acids such as citrus juice, vinegar, or wine are often used. Be extra careful when marinating fish and shellfish! The acid can "cook" the fish, making it tough and inedible. Also avoid using a metal container for marinating with an acid; it can pit the container.

# Lemon-Rosemary Marinade

**Prep:** 10 minutes **Marinate:** 1 hour

*If it clucks or comes out of the water, this refreshing lemon-essence marinade made with fresh, pungent rosemary is what you need to bring a summery lightness to your entrée.*

1 teaspoon finely shredded lemon
    peel
⅓ cup lemon juice
¼ cup olive oil or cooking oil
¼ cup white wine Worcestershire
    sauce
1 tablespoon sugar
1 tablespoon snipped fresh
    rosemary or 1 teaspoon dried
    rosemary, crushed
¼ teaspoon salt
⅛ teaspoon pepper

**1** In a small bowl combine the lemon peel, lemon juice, oil, Worcestershire sauce, sugar, rosemary, salt, and pepper. To use, pour marinade over fish, seafood, or chicken in a plastic bag set in a shallow dish; seal bag. Marinate in the refrigerator for 1 to 2 hours, turning the bag occasionally. Drain, reserving the marinade.

**2** Grill fish, seafood, or chicken according to the charts on pages 292 and 326, brushing occasionally with the marinade up to the last 5 minutes of grilling. Discard any remaining marinade. Makes about ¾ cup marinade (enough for about 2 pounds fish, seafood, or chicken).

Nutrition Facts per tablespoon: 49 calories, 5 g total fat (1 g saturated fat), 0 mg cholesterol, 87 mg sodium, 3 g carbohydrate, 0 g fiber, 0 g protein. Daily Values: 6% vit. C.

## FAJITA MARINADE

**Prep:** 10 minutes **Marinate:** 4 hours

*A good long soak in this lime-salsa-hot-sauce marinade will make a semi-tough cut of beef—such as flank steak—tender and terrific.*

½ cup Italian salad dressing
½ cup salsa
1 teaspoon finely shredded lime
    peel
2 tablespoons lime juice
1 tablespoon snipped fresh cilantro
¼ teaspoon bottled hot pepper sauce

**1** In a small bowl stir together salad dressing, salsa, lime peel, lime juice, cilantro, and hot pepper sauce. To use, pour marinade over beef or chicken in a plastic bag set in a shallow dish; seal bag. Marinate in the refrigerator about 4 hours for chicken or overnight for beef, turning bag occasionally. Drain, reserving marinade.

**2** Grill beef or chicken and vegetables for fajitas according to the charts on pages 174 and 292, brushing occasionally with the marinade up to the last 5 minutes of grilling. Slice beef or chicken for fajita filling. Bring any remaining marinade to boiling. Boil gently, uncovered, for 1 minute. Serve with fajitas. Makes about 1 cup marinade (enough for 2 to 2½ pounds beef or chicken).

Nutrition Facts per tablespoon: 37 calories, 4 g total fat (1 g saturated fat), 0 mg cholesterol, 86 mg sodium, 2 g carbohydrate, 0 g fiber, 0 g protein. Daily Values: 1% vit. A, 5% vit. C.

*Smokin' Hot Tip*

**The secret to getting the most juice from citrus fruit is to first roll the fruit on a hard surface, pressing firmly but gently with the palm of your hand. This is how much juice and peel you can expect to get: A medium orange yields about ¼ to ⅓ cup juice and 1 to 2 tablespoons finely shredded peel. A medium lemon or lime will yield about 2 to 3 tablespoons juice and ½ to 1 tablespoon finely shredded peel.**

# Best Beef Marinade

**Prep:** 10 minutes
**Marinate:** 30 minutes to 3 hours

*Here's a luxurious bath for good beef featuring the distinctive taste of shallots and lots of fresh thyme. Its flavors are particularly good paired with potatoes of any kind—sliced and grilled, baked, or mashed.*

¼ cup chopped shallots
3 tablespoons soy sauce
2 tablespoons olive oil
2 tablespoons balsamic vinegar or
     cider vinegar
4 teaspoons snipped fresh thyme
1 clove garlic, minced
½ teaspoon cracked black pepper

**1** In a small bowl combine shallots, soy sauce, olive oil, vinegar, thyme, garlic, and cracked pepper.

**2** To use, pour marinade over beef in a plastic bag set in a shallow dish; seal bag. Marinate in the refrigerator about 30 minutes for tender cuts (like tenderloin or sirloin) or for 3 to 24 hours for tougher cuts (like flank steak), turning bag occasionally. Drain, reserving marinade.

**3** Grill beef according to the chart on page 174, brushing occasionally with the marinade up to the last 5 minutes of grilling. Bring any remaining marinade to boiling. Boil gently, uncovered, for 1 minute. Serve with beef. Makes about ½ cup marinade (enough for about 1 to 1½ pounds beef).

Nutrition Facts per tablespoon: 42 calories, 3 g total fat (0 g saturated fat), 0 mg cholesterol, 387 mg sodium, 3 g carbohydrate, 0 g fiber, 1 g protein. Daily Values: 6% vit. A, 2% vit. C, 2% iron.

# SWEET AND SPICY RUB

**Prep:** 10 minutes

*Turn your backyard into a mecca for meat lovers with this Middle Eastern rub. If your cloves and cardamom haven't been called into service lately, pitch 'em and buy fresh.*

2 tablespoons margarine or butter
1 teaspoon ground cinnamon
½ teaspoon salt
½ teaspoon ground cumin
½ teaspoon ground turmeric
½ teaspoon ground red pepper
½ teaspoon ground black pepper
¼ teaspoon ground cardamom
⅛ teaspoon ground cloves
⅛ teaspoon ground nutmeg
1 tablespoon sugar

**1** In a small saucepan melt margarine or butter. Stir in cinnamon, salt, cumin, turmeric, red pepper, black pepper, cardamom, cloves, and nutmeg. Remove from heat. Stir in sugar; cool.

**2** To use, sprinkle evenly over meat or poultry; rub in with your fingers. Grill meat or poultry according to the charts on pages 174, 224, and 292. Makes about ¼ cup rub (enough for about 4 pounds meat or poultry).

Nutrition Facts per tablespoon: 70 calories, 6 g total fat (1 g saturated fat), 0 mg cholesterol, 335 mg sodium, 5 g carbohydrate, 0 g fiber, 0 g protein. Daily Values: 8% vit. A, 1% vit. C, 1% calcium, 5% iron.

# Jamaican Jerk Rub

**Prep:** 10 minutes

*Like all-American barbecue, Jamaican jerk can be wet or dry, sauced or rubbed, and both styles have their zealots. But life's just too short to do it one way all the time.*

  2 teaspoons sugar
1½ teaspoons onion powder
1½ teaspoons dried thyme, crushed
  1 teaspoon ground allspice
  1 teaspoon ground black pepper
 ½ to 1 teaspoon ground red pepper
 ½ teaspoon salt
 ¼ teaspoon ground nutmeg
 ⅛ teaspoon ground cloves

**1** In a small bowl stir together sugar, onion powder, thyme, allspice, black pepper, red pepper, salt, nutmeg, and cloves. To use, sprinkle mixture evenly over meat; rub in with your fingers.

**2** Grill meat according to the charts on pages 174 and 224. Makes about 8 teaspoons rub (enough for about 4 pounds meat).

Nutrition Facts per teaspoon: 8 calories, 0 g total fat (0 g saturated fat), 0 mg cholesterol, 134 mg sodium, 2 g carbohydrate, 0 g fiber, 0 g protein. Daily Values: 1% vit. C, 1% iron.

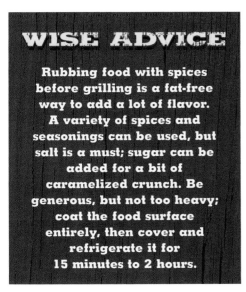

## WISE ADVICE

**Rubbing food with spices before grilling is a fat-free way to add a lot of flavor. A variety of spices and seasonings can be used, but salt is a must; sugar can be added for a bit of caramelized crunch. Be generous, but not too heavy; coat the food surface entirely, then cover and refrigerate it for 15 minutes to 2 hours.**

# HERBED PECAN RUB

**Prep:** 15 minutes

*Pecans gives this thyme-accented rub its depth of flavor and richness.*

 ½ cup broken pecans
 ½ cup fresh oregano leaves
 ½ cup fresh thyme leaves
  3 cloves garlic, cut up
 ½ teaspoon pepper
 ½ teaspoon finely shredded lemon
    peel
 ¼ teaspoon salt
 ¼ cup cooking oil

**1** In a blender container or food processor bowl combine pecans, oregano, thyme, garlic, pepper, lemon peel, and salt. Cover and blend or process with several on-off turns until well combined, stopping several times and scraping the sides.

**2** With the machine running, gradually add oil until the mixture forms a paste. To use, sprinkle mixture evenly over fish or chicken; rub in with your fingers. Grill fish or chicken, using indirect heat, according to the charts on pages 292 and 326. Makes about ½ cup rub (enough for about 3 pounds fish or chicken).

Nutrition Facts per 2 teaspoons: 72 calories, 8 g total fat (1 g saturated fat), 0 mg cholesterol, 45 mg sodium, 1 g carbohydrate, 0 g fiber, 0 g protein. Daily Values: 1% vit. C, 1% calcium, 1% iron.

Watermelon and Jicama Salsa (left)
Green Tangy Avocado Salsa (right)

# Green Tangy Avocado Salsa

**Prep:** 30 minutes   **Chill:** 1 hour

*Not that anyone's likely to tire of good old guacamole anytime soon, but this tomatillo salsa shows off the avocado's versatility. Leave the salsa on the chunky side so the ingredients retain their individual textures.*

6 fresh tomatillos, husked and
  halved
1 cup water
1 ripe avocado, seeded and peeled
½ cup coarsely chopped green
  onions
½ cup loosely packed fresh cilantro
  leaves
⅓ cup dairy sour cream
1 fresh jalapeño pepper, seeded and
  coarsely chopped
½ teaspoon salt

1 In a medium saucepan combine tomatillos and water. Bring to boiling; reduce heat. Simmer, uncovered, for 5 to 7 minutes or until soft, stirring occasionally. Remove tomatillos with a slotted spoon; cool slightly. Reserve 2 tablespoons of the cooking liquid.

2 In a food processor bowl or blender container combine tomatillos, the reserved 2 tablespoons cooking liquid, the avocado, green onions, cilantro, sour cream, jalapeño pepper, and salt. Cover and process or blend until combined but still slightly chunky. Transfer to a covered container; chill for 1 to 24 hours.

3 Serve with grilled meat, poultry, or seafood or as a dip with fresh vegetables and/or tortilla chips. Makes about 2 cups.

Nutrition Facts per tablespoon: 17 calories, 1 g total fat (0 g saturated fat), 1 mg cholesterol, 35 mg sodium, 1 g carbohydrate, 0 g fiber, 0 g protein. Daily Values: 1% vit. A, 3% vit. C.

# WATERMELON AND JICAMA SALSA

**Prep:** 25 minutes

*This salsa stands out in a crowd: sweet and juicy watermelon combined with crisp jicama. The addition of jalapeño adds heat to sweet.*

3 cups chopped seeded watermelon
1½ cups thinly sliced, peeled jicama
1 fresh jalapeño pepper, seeded and
  finely chopped
2 tablespoons chopped green onion
1 tablespoon snipped fresh cilantro
  or mint
1 tablespoon seasoned rice vinegar
⅛ to ¼ teaspoon ground red pepper
  (optional)

1 In a medium bowl stir together the watermelon, jicama, jalapeño pepper, green onion, cilantro or mint, vinegar, and red pepper (if desired).

2 If desired, cover and chill for up to 2 hours, or serve immediately. Serve with grilled chicken, fish, or pork. Makes about 5 cups.

Nutrition Facts per tablespoon: 7 calories, 0 g total fat (0 g saturated fat), 1 mg cholesterol, 0 mg sodium, 1 g carbohydrate, 0 g fiber, 1 g protein. Daily Values: 5% vit. C.

## Flaming Facts

**Jicama, a large, crunchy root vegetable, often is called the Mexican potato. Unlike the starchy potato, jicama has a sweet flavor and is good both raw and cooked. When cooked, it keeps its crisp water chestnut-like crunch. Available year-round, look for it in Mexican markets and larger supermarkets. Cut jicama will last up to 1 week if wrapped in plastic wrap and stored in the refrigerator.**

# Smoky Sicilian Salsa

**Prep:** 15 minutes   **Grill:** 40 minutes

*Any recipe that starts out with a whole bulb of garlic is mighty promising. As garlic cooks, it mellows and sweetens and, when done on the grill, gains a great smoky flavor.*

   1   garlic bulb
   2   tablespoons olive oil
  10   plum tomatoes
   2   onion slices (about ¾ inch thick)
   1 to 2   fresh jalapeño peppers
   ½   cup fresh basil leaves, cut into thin
         strips
   ⅛   teaspoon salt

1 Fold an 18×9-inch piece of heavy foil in half to make a 9-inch square. Place garlic in center of foil. Drizzle with 1 tablespoon of the olive oil. Bring up opposite edges of foil and seal with a double fold. Fold remaining edges together to completely enclose garlic, leaving space for steam to build.

2 *For a charcoal grill,* arrange medium coals in the bottom of an uncovered grill, leaving a small area on one side free of coals. Place garlic on grill rack not directly over coals. Cover and grill for 30 minutes, turning once halfway through.

3 Place the tomatoes, onion slices, and jalapeño peppers on the grill rack directly over coals. (Or, use a grill basket, grill tray, or heavy foil for vegetables; place on grill rack.) Grill, uncovered, about 10 minutes more or just until the tomato skins brown and onion is crisp-tender, turning once halfway through grilling. [*For a gas grill,* preheat grill. Reduce heat to medium. Adjust for indirect cooking (see page 10). Grill as above.]

4 Remove vegetables from grill; cool until easy to handle. For salsa, if desired, remove and discard the tomato skin and seeds. Coarsely chop tomatoes and onion; place in a medium bowl. Seed and finely chop the jalapeño pepper; stir into tomato mixture. Squeeze garlic pulp from each clove; stir into tomato mixture. Stir in the remaining oil, the basil leaves, and salt. Serve with grilled meat, poultry, or fish. Makes about 2½ cups.

Nutrition Facts per tablespoon: 11 calories, 1 g total fat (0 g saturated fat), 0 mg cholesterol, 8 mg sodium, 1 g carbohydrate, 0 g fiber, 0 g protein. Daily Values: 1% vit. A, 6% vit. C, 1% iron.

## "HOT" PEAR RELISH

**Prep:** 1½ hours

*Some like it hot, and if that means you, go for the gusto with three jalapeños. Don't worry about overwhelming the relish—there's plenty of sweetness, vinegary tartness, and spice here, too.*

   1½   cups finely chopped pears (2 to
          3 medium)
   1½   cups finely chopped onions
          (3 medium)
   1½   cups finely chopped green sweet
          peppers (2 medium)
   2   cups cider vinegar
   1   cup sugar
   1 to 3   fresh jalapeño peppers,
          seeded and finely chopped
   1   tablespoon prepared mustard or
          Dijon-style mustard
   ¾   teaspoon ground turmeric

1 In a large saucepan combine pears, onions, and sweet peppers. Stir in vinegar, sugar, jalapeño peppers, mustard, and turmeric. Bring to boiling; reduce heat. Boil gently, uncovered, about 1 hour or until most of the liquid has evaporated and mixture is thick, stirring occasionally. Cool.

2 Serve with grilled burgers, Polish sausages, or pork. Store in the refrigerator for up to 4 weeks. Makes about 3 cups.

Nutrition Facts per tablespoon: 23 calories, 0 g total fat (0 g saturated fat), 0 mg cholesterol, 4 mg sodium, 7 g carbohydrate, 0 g fiber, 0 g protein. Daily Values: 5% vit. C.

# Cantaloupe Relish

**Prep:** 20 minutes **Chill:** 1 hour

*This relish can be ready in as little as an hour after stirring it together, but allowing the ingredients to mingle for as long as 24 hours lets the cantaloupe and jicama absorb a whole palette of flavors.*

1 cup chopped Asian pear or
chopped, peeled jicama
1 cup chopped cantaloupe
1 cup chopped, peeled papaya or
mango
3 tablespoons lemon juice
¼ cup finely chopped green onions
1 teaspoon snipped fresh lemon
thyme or thyme
1 teaspoon olive oil

In a medium bowl combine pear or jicama, cantaloupe, papaya or mango, lemon juice, green onions, thyme, and olive oil. Cover and chill for 1 to 24 hours. Serve with grilled chicken or pork. Makes about 3 cups.

Nutrition Facts per tablespoon: 6 calories,
0 g total fat (0 g saturated fat), 0 mg cholesterol,
1 mg sodium, 1 g carbohydrate, 0 g fiber,
0 g protein. Daily Values: 2% vit. A, 7% vit. C.

## RED SWEET PEPPER RELISH

**Prep:** 10 minutes

*Keep a jar of roasted red sweet peppers on hand and you'll be surprised at all you can do with them. Here they become a tasty relish for your favorite grilled meat.*

½ cup purchased roasted red sweet
pepper strips
1 tablespoon finely chopped pitted
ripe olives
2 teaspoons snipped fresh thyme or
½ teaspoon dried thyme,
crushed
2 teaspoons olive oil
¼ teaspoon black pepper

In a food processor bowl combine red sweet pepper, olives, thyme, olive oil, and black pepper. Cover; process with several on-off turns until coarsely chopped. Transfer to a bowl. Serve immediately or cover and chill until ready to serve. Serve relish with grilled burgers, steaks, or chicken. Makes about ⅔ cup.

Nutrition Facts per tablespoon: 10 calories,
1 g total fat (0 g saturated fat), 0 mg cholesterol,
4 mg sodium, 1 g carbohydrate, 0 g fiber,
0 g protein. Daily Values: 3% vit. A, 31% vit. C.

# Red Onion Relish

**Prep:** 15 minutes

1 large red onion, thinly sliced and
separated into rings
1 teaspoon olive oil or cooking oil
¼ cup dry red wine
½ teaspoon dried sage, crushed
¼ teaspoon salt

In a medium skillet cook onion in hot oil over medium heat for 5 to 7 minutes or until crisp-tender. Carefully add wine, sage, and salt. Cook for 1 to 2 minutes or until most of the liquid is evaporated. Serve onion mixture with grilled steaks or burgers. Serves 4.

Nutrition Facts per serving: 34 calories,
1 g total fat (0 g saturated fat), 0 mg cholesterol,
144 mg sodium, 3 g carbohydrate, 1 g fiber,
0 g protein. Daily Values: 2% vit. C, 1% iron.

*Sizzlin' Solutions*

**Sweet or savory, most relishes will go with any type of meat. But, as a starting point, we suggest serving plain grilled wieners or bratwurst with a tangy relish. Poultry teams nicely with a sweet relish, and steaks sizzle when combined with a hot relish.**

## DRIED-FRUIT CHUTNEY

**Prep:** 50 minutes

*Dried apricots, pineapple, and raisins provide a sweet and rich concentration of flavors that make this versatile chutney an all-around, all-year winner. It keeps in the fridge up to three weeks, but it'll be gone long before that.*

¾ cup coarsely chopped dried
    apricots
¾ cup coarsely chopped dried
    pineapple
¾ cup raisins
1 cup boiling water
½ cup chopped onion
½ cup cider vinegar
¼ cup packed brown sugar
¼ teaspoon ground ginger
⅛ teaspoon ground allspice
⅛ teaspoon ground cardamom
⅛ teaspoon ground cinnamon
⅛ teaspoon ground red pepper
    Dash salt
    Dash ground cloves

**1** In a medium bowl combine apricots, pineapple, and raisins. Pour boiling water over mixture. Let stand about 30 minutes or until fruit is softened. Drain, reserving ⅓ cup of the liquid.

**2** In a medium saucepan combine the softened fruit, the ⅓ cup reserved liquid, the onion, vinegar, brown sugar, ginger, allspice, cardamom, cinnamon, red pepper, salt, and cloves. Bring to boiling, stirring frequently; reduce heat. Simmer, uncovered, for 8 to 10 minutes or until liquid has evaporated and mixture is thick, stirring frequently; cool.

**3** Serve with grilled pork, lamb, or chicken. Store in the refrigerator for up to 3 weeks. Makes about 2½ cups.

ⓥNutrition Facts per tablespoon: 25 calories, 0 g total fat (0 g saturated fat), 0 mg cholesterol, 9 mg sodium, 7 g carbohydrate, 1 g fiber, 0 g protein. Daily Values: 2% vit. A, 2% vit. C, 2% iron.

# Plantain and Pepper Chutney

**Prep:** 35 minutes

*Plantains—cousin to the banana—have a mild, slightly sweet, squashlike flavor. Here it's punched up with the help of a hot Scotch bonnet pepper. For meeker tongues, substitute the jalapeño.*

1 ripe plantain, peeled and cut in
    half lengthwise
½ medium green sweet pepper
½ medium red sweet pepper
1 small onion, cut into 1-inch slices
1 fresh Scotch bonnet or jalapeño
    pepper
1 tablespoon olive oil
2 tablespoons apricot preserves or
    orange marmalade
1 tablespoon lime juice
¼ teaspoon salt
¼ teaspoon ground allspice

**1** Brush plantain, sweet peppers, onion, and Scotch bonnet or jalapeño pepper with oil.

**2** *For a charcoal grill,* grill plantain, sweet peppers, onion, and Scotch bonnet or jalapeño pepper on the rack of an uncovered grill directly over medium coals for 8 to 10 minutes or until tender, turning occasionally. Watch plantain and vegetables closely so they do not char. (*For a gas grill,* preheat grill. Reduce heat to medium. Place vegetables and Scotch bonnet or jalapeño pepper on grill rack over heat. Cover; grill as above.)

**3** Transfer to a cutting board; cool until easy to handle. Finely chop plantain, sweet peppers, and onion; place in a bowl. Seed and finely chop the Scotch bonnet or jalapeño pepper; stir into plantain mixture. Stir in preserves or marmalade, lime juice, salt, and allspice; toss to coat. If desired, cover and chill up to 2 hours.

**4** Serve at room temperature with grilled chicken or pork. Makes about 2 cups.

ⓥNutrition Facts per tablespoon: 16 calories, 1 g total fat (0 g saturated fat), 0 mg cholesterol, 17 mg sodium, 3 g carbohydrate, 0 g fiber, 0 g protein. Daily Values: 2% vit. A, 10% vit. C.

## FRESH MANGO CHUTNEY

**Prep:** 25 minutes

¼ cup packed brown sugar
¼ cup finely chopped onion
¼ cup golden raisins
¼ cup cider vinegar
½ teaspoon ground nutmeg
½ teaspoon ground cinnamon
¼ teaspoon salt
⅛ teaspoon ground cloves
2 cups chopped, peeled mangoes or peaches
2 tablespoons water
2 tablespoons lemon or lime juice

**1** In a medium saucepan combine brown sugar, onion, raisins, vinegar, nutmeg, cinnamon, salt, and cloves. Bring to boiling; reduce heat. Cook, uncovered, for 5 minutes, stirring occasionally.

**2** Stir in mangoes or peaches and water. Return to boiling; reduce heat. Simmer, uncovered, about 5 minutes more or until slightly thickened, stirring frequently. Remove from heat. Stir in lemon or lime juice; cool.

**3** Serve with grilled burgers, steaks, pork, poultry, fish, or shrimp. Store in the refrigerator up to 1 week. Makes about 2 cups.

Nutrition Facts per tablespoon: 18 calories, 0 g total fat (0 g saturated fat), 0 mg cholesterol, 18 mg sodium, 5 g carbohydrate, 0 g fiber, 0 g protein. Daily Values: 5% vit. A, 6% vit. C.

## Plum Chutney

**Prep:** 40 minutes

*Here's an Asian-style chutney special enough to turn a midweek barbecue into a minor event. Try it on grilled duck.*

2½ cups chopped, pitted red or purple plums (about 1 pound)
⅓ cup packed brown sugar
⅓ cup sliced green onions
¼ cup raspberry vinegar
1 tablespoon soy sauce
1 fresh jalapeño pepper, seeded and finely chopped
1 teaspoon grated fresh ginger
1 clove garlic, minced

**1** In a medium saucepan combine plums, brown sugar, green onions, vinegar, soy sauce, jalapeño pepper, ginger, and garlic. Bring to boiling; reduce heat. Simmer, uncovered, about 25 minutes or until slightly thickened, stirring occasionally; cool. (Mixture will thicken more as it cools.)

**2** Serve with grilled duck, chicken, or pork. Store in the refrigerator for up to 1 week. Makes about 1¾ cups.

Nutrition Facts per tablespoon: 25 calories, 0 g total fat (0 g saturated fat), 0 mg cholesterol, 38 mg sodium, 6 g carbohydrate, 1 g fiber, 1 g protein. Daily Values: 1% vit. A, 6% vit. C, 1% iron.

## Did You Know?

**Chutneys, generally made from fruit, sugar, spices, and vinegar, can be chunky or smooth and hot or mildly hot. They are best known for being a partner to Indian curry dishes. But with the many combinations of fruit and spices that are possible, chutneys also can be used as a spread for bread, just like jam, or served with cheeses and crackers.**

## CITRUS-GARLIC BUTTER

**Prep:** 10 minutes  **Chill:** 2 hours

*Sometimes a flourish at the end is all you need to give flair to the most basic grilled food. Look no further than this butter to top off unadorned grilled meat, poultry, fish, or vegetables.*

½ cup butter, softened
2 tablespoons snipped fresh parsley
1 tablespoon finely shredded
   lemon peel
1 tablespoon finely shredded
   orange peel
2 cloves garlic, minced

1 In a small bowl stir together butter, parsley, lemon peel, orange peel, and garlic. If necessary, chill about 10 minutes or until easy to handle.

2 With your hands, shape the butter mixture into a 4-inch-long log. Wrap in plastic wrap; chill at least 2 hours or until firm.

3 To use, unwrap the butter and cut crosswise into 8 slices. Place one slice of butter on top of each serving of grilled chicken, beef, veal, fish, or vegetables. Makes ½ cup.

Nutrition Facts per tablespoon: 103 calories, 11 g total fat (7 g saturated fat), 31 mg cholesterol, 117 mg sodium, 1 g carbohydrate, 0 g fiber, 0 g protein. Daily Values: 11% vit. A, 5% vit. C.

## Tomato Aioli

**Prep:** 10 minutes

*With the addition of dried tomatoes, aioli—a garlicky Provençal mayonnaise popularly served with meat, fish, and vegetables—makes a perfect finishing touch for grilled lamb chops.*

½ cup mayonnaise
2 tablespoons oil-packed dried
   tomatoes, drained and finely
   chopped
1 tablespoon snipped fresh basil
2 cloves garlic, minced
1 teaspoon snipped fresh thyme

1 In a small bowl combine mayonnaise, tomatoes, basil, garlic, and thyme. Serve with grilled lamb, pork, or chicken. Makes about ⅔ cup.

Nutrition Facts per tablespoon: 75 calories, 8 g total fat (1 g saturated fat), 6 mg cholesterol, 60 mg sodium, 1 g carbohydrate, 0 g fiber, 0 g protein. Daily Values: 1% vit. A, 2% vit. C.

## TANGY COCONUT SAUCE

**Prep:** 10 minutes

*When you want a super-easy sauce for grilled shrimp or fish, try this 5-ingredient wonder. Wasabi paste, if you haven't tried it, is the Japanese counterpart to our horseradish. It has a sharp, assertive, and hot flavor. Use the lower range first to determine your level of preference.*

⅓ cup purchased unsweetened
   coconut milk
1 teaspoon cornstarch
2 to 4 teaspoons wasabi paste
2 teaspoons grated fresh ginger
1 teaspoon lime juice

1 In a small saucepan stir together the coconut milk and cornstarch. Cook and stir over low heat for 3 to 5 minutes. Set mixture aside to cool.

2 Meanwhile, in a small mixing bowl combine the wasabi paste, ginger, and the lime juice. Stir in thickened coconut milk mixture. Cover and cool mixture in refrigerator. Serve with grilled shrimp or fish. Makes 4 servings.

Nutrition Facts per serving: 40 calories, 4 g total fat (3 g saturated fat), 0 mg cholesterol, 25 mg sodium, 2 g carbohydrate, 0 g fiber, 0 g protein. Daily Values: 1% iron.

# APPETIZERS, SIDES, DESSERTS

3

# Appetizers, Sides, Desserts

# Herbed Roasted Garlic Spread

**Prep:** 20 minutes **Grill:** 35 minutes

*Long, slow roasting transforms garlic from sharp to mellow and changes its texture from firm to lusciously, spreadably soft. Roasted garlic isn't just for spreading on bread. You can mash the tender cloves into potatoes, a vinaigrette, or a shrimp and pasta toss.*

  4 **garlic bulbs**
  ¼ **cup olive oil**
  1 **teaspoon salt**
  1 **teaspoon dried basil, crushed**
  1 **teaspoon dried oregano, crushed**
  ½ **teaspoon pepper**
  8 **slices sourdough bread, toasted and halved**

**1** With a sharp knife, cut off the top ½ inch from each garlic bulb to expose the ends of the individual cloves. Leaving garlic bulbs whole, remove any loose, papery outer layers.

**2** Fold four 18×9-inch pieces of heavy foil in half to make 9-inch squares. Place each garlic bulb, cut side up, in center of a foil square. Drizzle the bulbs with olive oil and sprinkle with salt, basil, oregano, and pepper. Bring up opposite edges of foil and seal with a double fold. Fold remaining edges together completely to enclose garlic, leaving space for steam to build.

**3** *For a charcoal grill,* arrange medium-hot coals around a drip pan. Test for medium heat above the pan. Place foil packets with garlic on grill rack over drip pan. Cover and grill foil packets for 35 to 40 minutes or until garlic bulbs feel soft when packets are squeezed, turning packets occasionally. [*For a gas grill,* preheat grill. Reduce heat to medium. Adjust for indirect cooking (see page 10). Grill as above.]

**4** To serve, unwrap garlic and transfer to serving plates. Squeeze garlic pulp from each clove; spread onto toasted bread. Makes 4 appetizer servings.

Nutrition Facts per serving: 151 calories, 8 g total fat (1 g saturated fat), 0 mg cholesterol, 421 mg sodium, 18 g carbohydrate, 0 g fiber, 3 g protein. Daily Values: 8% vit. C, 4% calcium, 6% iron.

## GRILLED ENDIVE WITH PROSCIUTTO

**Prep:** 10 minutes **Grill:** 25 minutes

*Here's an uptown version of a Southern classic: ham hocks and greens. In this version, plump endive spears are brushed with mustard and cloaked in a thin veil of prosciutto, an Italian ham that is fully cured but not smoked. It's a black-tie appetizer even if you're a T-shirt cook.*

  1 **tablespoon olive oil**
  1 **tablespoon Dijon-style mustard**
  ¼ **teaspoon pepper**
  3 **heads Belgian endive, trimmed and halved lengthwise**
  6 **thin slices prosciutto (2 ounces)**

**1** For dressing, in a small bowl combine the oil, mustard, and pepper. Brush dressing over endive halves. Wrap each endive half in a thin slice of prosciutto and secure with wooden toothpicks.

**2** *For a charcoal grill,* arrange medium-hot coals around a drip pan. Test for medium heat above the pan. Place endive on grill rack over drip pan. Cover; grill about 25 minutes or until endive is tender and prosciutto is golden brown, turning once halfway through grilling. [*For a gas grill,* preheat grill. Reduce heat to medium. Adjust for indirect cooking (see page 10). Grill as above.] Makes 6 appetizer servings.

Nutrition Facts per serving: 57 calories, 5 g total fat (0 g saturated fat), 0 mg cholesterol, 232 mg sodium, 1 g carbohydrate, 0 g fiber, 3 g protein. Daily Values: 4% vit. C, 1% iron.

# South-of-the-Border Potato Skins

**Prep:** 15 minutes  **Grill:** 25 minutes

*An old favorite with a slightly new twist.*

> 6 4- to 6-ounce baking potatoes (such
> as russet or long white)
> 1 tablespoon cooking oil
> 1 clove garlic, minced
> ⅛ to ¼ teaspoon ground red pepper
> 1 cup shredded taco cheese
> (4 ounces)
> 1 6-ounce container frozen avocado
> dip, thawed
> ¾ cup thick and chunky salsa
> ¾ cup dairy sour cream

**1** Scrub potatoes; cut each potato in half lengthwise. In a small bowl combine the oil, garlic, and red pepper. Brush cut surfaces of potato halves with some of the oil mixture.

**2** *For a charcoal grill,* grill potatoes, cut sides down, on the rack of an uncovered grill directly over medium coals for 20 to 25 minutes or until tender, turning once halfway through grilling. (*For a gas grill,* preheat grill. Reduce heat to medium. Place potatoes, cut sides down, on grill rack over heat. Cover and grill as above.)

**3** Carefully scoop out the insides of each potato half, leaving a ½-inch shell. Brush the insides of the potato shells with the remaining oil mixture. Sprinkle potatoes with cheese. Return potatoes to grill, cut sides up. Grill for 5 to 7 minutes more or until cheese is melted. Transfer to a serving platter.

**4** To serve, top each potato shell with avocado dip, salsa, and sour cream. Makes 12 appetizer servings.

Nutrition Facts per serving: 148 calories,
10 g total fat (4 g saturated fat), 15 mg cholesterol,
255 mg sodium, 13 g carbohydrate, 0 g fiber,
4 g protein. Daily Values: 6% vit. A, 17% vit. C,
6% calcium, 4% iron.

# ASPARAGUS WITH SORREL DRESSING

**Prep:** 10 minutes  **Grill:** 15 minutes

*You can, of course, go down the safe road and make the dressing with spinach. But it's worth every effort to seek out sorrel. With its refreshing lemony flavor, sorrel is most complementary to the asparagus.*

> ¼ cup plain low-fat yogurt
> ¼ cup mayonnaise or salad dressing
> ¼ cup finely snipped sorrel or
> spinach
> 1 green onion, thinly sliced
> 1 teaspoon lemon-pepper seasoning
> (optional)
> 1 pound asparagus spears
> 2 tablespoons water

**1** For dressing, in a small bowl combine yogurt, mayonnaise, sorrel or spinach, green onion, and, if desired, lemon-pepper seasoning. Cover and refrigerate until ready to serve.

**2** Fold a 36×18-inch piece of heavy foil in half to make an 18×18-inch square. Snap off and discard the woody bases from asparagus. Place asparagus in center of foil. Fold up edges of foil slightly; drizzle asparagus with water. Bring up 2 opposite edges of foil; seal with a double fold. Fold remaining ends to completely enclose the asparagus, leaving space for steam to build.

**3** *For a charcoal grill,* grill asparagus packet on the rack of an uncovered grill directly over medium-hot coals about 15 minutes or until crisp-tender, turning once. (*For a gas grill,* preheat grill. Reduce heat to medium-hot. Place asparagus on grill rack over heat. Cover and grill as above.) Serve with dressing. Makes 6 appetizer servings or 4 side-dish servings.

Nutrition Facts per serving: 86 calories,
7 g total fat (1 g saturated fat), 6 mg cholesterol,
63 mg sodium, 3 g carbohydrate, 1 g fiber,
2 g protein.. Daily Values: 7% vit. A, 25% vit. C,
3% calcium, 3% iron.

South-of-the-Border Potato Skins

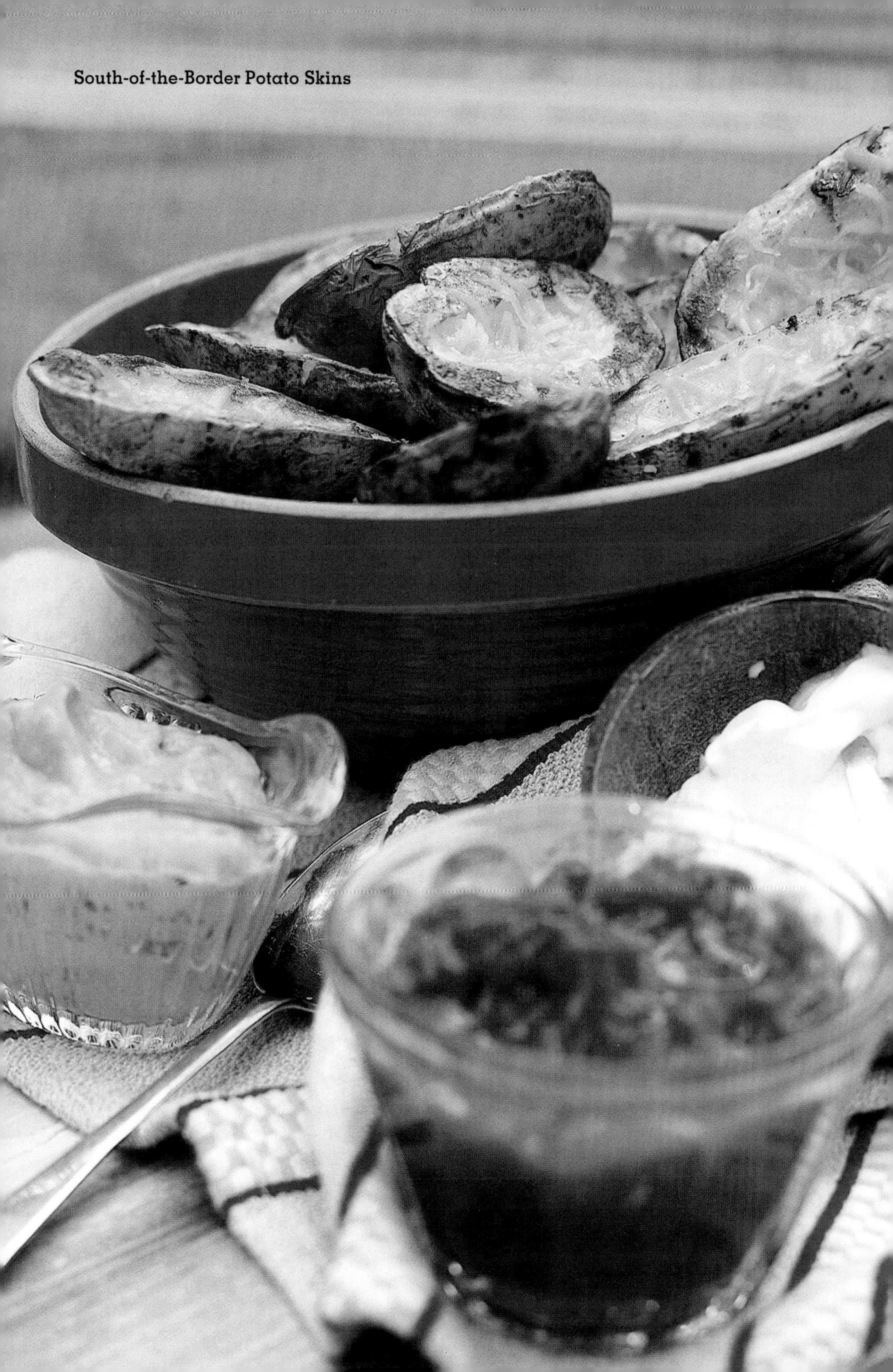

## Smokin' Hot Tip

**Easy to spot at the supermarket, portobello mushrooms are ideal for grilling and roasting because of their large size. Left whole, they make a great meatless sandwich because of the meaty texture. Portobellos range from 3 to 8 inches in diameter and have caps that are tan or light brown with dark gills. Their flavor, though similar to the simple white button mushroom, is more distinctive. Generally, the darker the gills on the underside of the cap, the more intense the flavor.**

## Grilled Portobellos with Avocado Salsa

**Prep:** 20 minutes   **Grill:** 8 minutes

*Portobellos arrived in markets as suddenly as, well, mushrooms after a spring rain. They quickly became popular because of their rich mushroom flavor and firm, meaty texture. They're especially tasty in this new-style salsa.*

  4  6- to 8-ounce fresh portobello
       mushrooms
  3  tablespoons balsamic vinegar
  2  tablespoons red wine vinegar
  2  tablespoons olive oil
  ¼  teaspoon crushed red pepper
  1  medium avocado, seeded, peeled,
       and chopped
  1  medium tomato, chopped
  ¼  cup sliced green onions
  ¼  cup crumbled, crisp-cooked bacon
       (about 4 slices)
  2  tablespoons snipped fresh cilantro

1  Cut off mushroom stems even with caps; discard stems. Lightly rinse mushroom caps. Gently pat dry with paper towels. In a bowl combine vinegars, olive oil, and red pepper. Reserve ¼ cup vinegar mixture for salsa.

2  *For a charcoal grill,* grill mushroom caps on the rack of an uncovered grill directly over medium coals for 8 to 10 minutes or until tender, turning and brushing once with the remaining vinegar mixture halfway through grilling. (*For a gas grill,* preheat grill. Reduce heat to medium. Place mushroom caps on grill rack over heat. Cover and grill as above.)

3  For salsa, in a medium bowl combine the reserved vinegar mixture, the avocado, tomato, green onions, bacon, and cilantro.

4  Slice the mushrooms about ½ inch thick. Spoon the salsa over the mushroom slices. Makes 8 appetizer servings.

Nutrition Facts per serving: 117 calories, 8 g total fat (2 g saturated fat), 2 mg cholesterol, 44 mg sodium, 10 g carbohydrate, 2 g fiber, 3 g protein. Daily Values: 4% vit. A, 18% vit. C, 13% iron.

## BABA GHANOUSH

**Prep:** 25 minutes   **Grill:** 30 minutes
**Chill:** 4 hours

*Baba ghanoush is good, but grilling the eggplant bumps it up a notch. One of the secrets is those delicious brown blisters that come from cooking over an outdoor fire, adding a roasted flavor to a traditional favorite.*

  1  medium eggplant (about 1 pound)
  2  tablespoons tahini (sesame seed
       paste)
  2  tablespoons loosely packed fresh
       mint leaves
  1  tablespoon lemon juice
  2  cloves garlic, halved
  ¼  teaspoon salt
       Crackers or assorted vegetable
       dippers

1 Pierce eggplant in several places with tines of a fork. *For a charcoal grill*, grill eggplant on the rack of an uncovered grill directly over medium coals for 30 to 35 minutes or until tender and skin is charred, turning frequently. (*For a gas grill*, preheat grill. Reduce heat to medium. Place eggplant on grill rack over heat. Cover and grill as above.)

2 Remove eggplant from grill; let cool until easy to handle. Peel, discarding skin, and cut up. In a blender container or food processor bowl combine the grilled eggplant, the tahini, mint, lemon juice, garlic, and salt. Cover and blend or process until smooth.

3 Cover and chill dip for 4 to 24 hours. Serve dip with crackers or vegetable dippers. Makes about 1 cup.

Nutrition Facts per 2 tablespoons dip: 36 calories, 2 g total fat (0 g saturated fat), 0 mg cholesterol, 69 mg sodium, 4 g carbohydrate, 2 g fiber, 1 g protein. Daily Values: 4% vit. C, 3% iron.

# Sweet Pepper Dip

**Prep:** 35 minutes    **Grill:** 10 minutes
**Chill:** 1 hour

*Grilling adds a smokiness to the sweetness of red peppers. A trick to peeling the charred skin off the peppers is letting them steam in foil awhile. Resist the temptation to rinse the peppers or peel them under water; it will wash away the prized flavor.*

- 2 **large red sweet peppers, quartered lengthwise**
- 4 **teaspoons olive oil**
- 1 **8-ounce carton dairy sour cream**
- 1 **3-ounce package cream cheese, softened**
- ½ **teaspoon salt**
- 2 **tablespoons finely chopped green onion**
- 2 **tablespoons snipped fresh basil or 1 teaspoon dried basil, crushed**
  **Assorted vegetable dippers, crackers, and/or chips**

1 Brush pepper pieces with olive oil. *For a charcoal grill*, grill peppers, cut sides up, on the rack of an uncovered grill directly over medium-hot coals about 10 minutes or until pepper skins are blistered and dark. (*For a gas grill*, preheat grill. Reduce heat to medium-hot. Place peppers, cut sides up, on grill rack over heat. Cover and grill as above.)

2 Wrap pepper pieces tightly in foil and let stand for 10 to 15 minutes or until cool enough to handle. Unwrap peppers. Using a paring knife, pull the skin off gently.

3 In a blender container or food processor bowl combine grilled peppers, sour cream, cream cheese, and salt. Cover and blend or process until smooth. Transfer to a medium bowl. Stir in green onion and basil. Cover and chill for 1 to 24 hours. Serve dip with vegetable dippers, crackers, and/or chips. Makes about 2¼ cups.

Nutrition Facts per 1 tablespoon dip: 27 calories, 3 g total fat (1 g saturated fat), 5 mg cholesterol, 40 mg sodium, 1 g carbohydrate, 0 g fiber, 0 g protein. Daily Values: 5% vit. A, 11% vit. C.

## GRILLED PITA TRIANGLES

**Prep:** 5 minutes    **Grill:** 2 minutes

*These pita triangles are simple and low-fat companions for dips. Serve them with any dip that calls for crackers.*

1 To make pita triangles, cut 4 large pita bread rounds in half crosswise. *For a charcoal grill*, grill the halves on the rack of an uncovered grill directly over medium coals about 2 minutes or until lightly browned, turning once halfway through grilling. (*For a gas grill*, preheat grill. Reduce heat to medium. Place the pita bread halves on grill rack over heat. Cover and grill as above.) Cut each half into 4 triangles. Makes 32 triangles.

Nutrition Facts per 2 triangles: 10 calories, 0 g total fat (0 g saturated fat), 0 mg cholesterol, 161 mg sodium, 17 g carbohydrate, 0 g fiber, 3 g protein.

Polenta with Ratatouille

# Polenta with Ratatouille

**Prep:** 35 minutes    **Chill:** 30 minutes
**Grill:** 26 minutes
**Special Equipment:** Grill tray

*While ratatouille on its own is a great side dish,
it easily moves to the center of the plate when
served with grilled polenta and smoked
mozzarella cheese.*

3⅓ cups water
  1 cup cornmeal
  ½ teaspoon salt
  ½ cup semi-soft goat cheese with
      garlic and herb
  2 small Japanese eggplants, halved
      lengthwise (8 ounces total)
  1 small red sweet pepper, quartered
      lengthwise
  1 small zucchini, halved lengthwise
  1 small yellow summer squash,
      halved lengthwise
  1 small onion, cut into ½-inch slices
  2 plum tomatoes, halved lengthwise
  1 to 2 tablespoons olive oil
  ¾ cup shredded smoked mozzarella
      cheese (3 ounces)

**1** For polenta, in a 2-quart microwave-safe
casserole combine water, cornmeal, and
salt. Cook, covered, on 100% power (high)
for 15 to 17 minutes or until thick, stirring
every 4 minutes. Stir in goat cheese.

**2** Immediately spread hot polenta into a
greased 2-quart square baking dish; cool
slightly. Cover; chill about 30 minutes or
until firm. Cut polenta into 6 rectangles; cut
each rectangle in half diagonally. Brush the
vegetables with olive oil.

**3** *For a charcoal grill,* grill vegetables on the
rack of an uncovered grill directly over
medium coals until tender, turning once
halfway through grilling. (Allow about
15 minutes for onion, 10 to 12 minutes for

eggplants and sweet pepper, and 5 to
6 minutes for zucchini, yellow squash, and
tomatoes.) Remove vegetables from grill.
(*For a gas grill,* preheat grill. Reduce heat to
medium. Place vegetables on grill rack
directly over heat. Cover and grill as above.)

**4** Transfer polenta to a lightly greased grill
tray; add to grill. Grill for 10 to 12 minutes
or until polenta is heated through, turning
once halfway through grilling. Remove
polenta from heat.

**5** For ratatouille, coarsely chop grilled
vegetables; place in a medium bowl. If
desired, season to taste with salt and pepper.
Spoon 2 to 3 tablespoons ratatouille onto
each grilled polenta triangle; sprinkle with
mozzarella cheese. Return polenta to grill.
Cover and grill for 1 to 2 minutes more or
until cheese is melted. Serve immediately.
Makes 12 appetizer servings.

Nutrition Facts per serving: 115 calories,
6 g total fat (3 g saturated fat), 12 mg cholesterol,
124 mg sodium, 12 g carbohydrate, 2 g fiber,
4 g protein. Daily Values: 7% vit. A, 16% vit. C,
4% calcium, 4% iron.

## Did You Know?

**You're missing out if you've
never had polenta. This
Italian mush is simply made
by boiling a mixture of
cornmeal or farina and water.
It's often made tastier by the
addition of Parmesan cheese.
The Italians eat it in a variety
of ways: as a thick porridge,
or molded (as it's done here),
sliced, fried, or broiled. Here
we've added goat cheese and
grilled it. It's a definite treat!**

## Provolone and Roasted Sweet Pepper Pizza

**Prep:** 40 minutes  **Rise:** 1 hour
**Grill:** 2 minutes

*This is great for an afternoon party where you want to keep food coming rather than choreograph everything to be done at once. A secret to making pizza on the grill is to keep the crust fairly small. Remember, you have to turn it!*

1 envelope active dry yeast
1 cup warm water (105° to 115°)
2 tablespoons cornmeal
1 teaspoon olive oil
½ teaspoon salt
  Dash sugar
2¾ to 3 cups all-purpose flour
2 cups shredded provolone cheese
  (8 ounces)
2 7-ounce jars roasted red sweet
  peppers, drained (see tip box,
  below)
¼ cup snipped fresh oregano
⅛ teaspoon coarsely ground black
  pepper

1 In a large bowl dissolve yeast in warm water. Stir in cornmeal, oil, salt, and sugar. Using a wooden spoon, stir in as much of the flour as you can.

2 Turn dough out onto a lightly floured surface. Knead in enough of the remaining flour to make a moderately stiff dough that is smooth and elastic (about 3 minutes total). Shape into a ball. Place in a lightly greased bowl, turning once to grease surface. Cover; let rise in a warm place until double in size (about 1 hour). Punch dough down. Turn out onto a lightly floured surface. Divide dough into fourths. Cover; let rest for 10 minutes. Roll each portion into a 10-inch circle.

3 For topping, in a medium bowl combine the shredded cheese, sweet peppers, oregano, and black pepper. Set aside.

4 *For a charcoal grill,* carefully slide a dough circle onto the rack of an uncovered grill directly over medium-hot coals. Grill for 1 to 2 minutes or until dough is puffed in some places and starting to become firm. When the dough is just starting to char on the underside, turn the crust. Sprinkle with about 1 cup of the topping. Grill for 1 to 2 minutes more or until cheese is melted and crust is crisp. Remove pizza from grill. (*For a gas grill,* preheat grill. Reduce heat to medium-hot. Place a dough circle on grill rack over heat. Cover and grill as above.)

5 Repeat with the remaining dough and topping. Cut each pizza into 4 wedges. Makes 16 appetizer servings.

Nutrition Facts per serving: 135 calories, 4 g total fat (3 g saturated fat), 10 mg cholesterol, 192 mg sodium, 17 g carbohydrate, 0 g fiber, 6 g protein. Daily Values: 14% vit. C.

## WISE ADVICE

You can buy roasted red sweet peppers, but if you have the time or you grow sweet peppers, it's easy to roast 'em yourself. To roast sweet peppers, cut them into quarters. Remove stems, membranes, and seeds. Brush skins lightly with oil. Place them on a grill rack directly over medium-slow coals with the skin sides down; grill, uncovered, for 15 minutes or until crisp-tender and charred. Wrap grilled peppers tightly in foil and let them stand for 10 minutes or until cool enough to handle. Using a paring knife, gently pull the skins off. Use as directed in recipes, or cut into strips and toss with salads, layer on sandwiches, or stir into vegetable dishes.

# Smoked Mozzarella and Dried Tomato Pizza

**Prep:** 10 minutes   **Grill:** 5 minutes

*Few appetizers are this chic, this fast, and this good. The rich taste of dried tomatoes goes well with smoked mozzarella and olives. For a sophisticated flourish, snip several leaves of basil from your garden over the hot pizzas.*

　　2　cups shredded smoked mozzarella cheese (8 ounces)
　⅓　cup oil-packed dried tomatoes, drained
　　1　clove garlic, minced
　¼　teaspoon dried oregano, crushed
　　　Dash crushed red pepper
　　4　large pita bread rounds
　⅓　cup fresh basil leaves cut into thin strips

**1** In a medium bowl stir together the mozzarella cheese, tomatoes, garlic, oregano, and crushed red pepper. Top pita rounds with cheese mixture, dividing equally.

**2** *For a charcoal grill,* arrange medium-hot coals around edge of grill. Test for medium heat above center of grill. Place pitas on grill rack over center of grill. Cover; grill for 5 to 7 minutes or until cheese is melted and bottoms of pitas are crisp. [*For a gas grill,* preheat grill. Reduce heat to medium. Adjust for indirect cooking (see page 10). Grill as above.] Remove pizzas from grill.

**3** To serve, sprinkle with basil strips. Cut each pizza into 4 wedges. Makes 8 appetizer servings.

Nutrition Facts per serving: 173 calories, 7 g total fat (4 g saturated fat), 22 mg cholesterol, 279 mg sodium, 19 g carbohydrate, 0 g fiber, 9 g protein. Daily Values: 7% vit. A, 7% vit. C, 14% calcium, 5% iron.

# BRUSCHETTA WITH SWEET ONION TOPPING

**Prep:** 20 minutes   **Grill:** 2 minutes

*Brew-SKET-a is all the rage. All it is, really, is toast made from a long, rustic loaf of bread, then topped with something delicious. Often the topping is a finely diced tomato salad, but this sweet onion version is an inspired alternative worth adding to your bruschetta repertoire.*

　　1　large onion, halved lengthwise and thinly sliced
　　1　tablespoon olive oil or cooking oil
　⅓　cup coarsely chopped walnuts
　　1　teaspoon sugar
　　1　tablespoon herb mustard or Dijon-style mustard
　　1　16-ounce loaf French bread baguette, cut into ¼-inch slices
　½　cup freshly grated Parmesan or Romano cheese

**1** For topping, in a large skillet cook onion in hot oil until tender. Add walnuts and sugar. Cook and stir about 5 minutes more or until onion is golden and walnuts are lightly toasted. Stir in mustard.

**2** Spoon some of the topping onto each bread slice. Sprinkle with cheese. If desired, cover bread slices and let stand at room temperature for up to 1 hour.

**3** *For a charcoal grill,* grill bread slices on the rack of an uncovered grill directly over medium-hot coals about 2 minutes or just until heated through and bottoms are toasted. (*For a gas grill,* preheat grill. Reduce heat to medium-hot. Place bread slices on grill rack over heat. Cover and grill as above.) Serve immediately. Makes 8 appetizer servings.

Nutrition Facts per serving: 246 calories, 9 g total fat (1 g saturated fat), 5 mg cholesterol, 500 mg sodium, 33 g carbohydrate, 1 g fiber, 9 g protein. Daily Values: 1% vit. A, 2% vit. C, 12% calcium, 10% iron.

## Flaming Facts

**Luscious, creamy goat cheese has won plenty of converts for several reasons. There are varieties for just about every occasion, need, or taste—fresh, soft-ripened, aged, cheddar-like chèvres, or even blue. You'll find it is delicious in lasagna, on pizza, in blintzes, and on grilled burgers. Another benefit of this trendy cheese is that it often agrees with those who are lactose intolerant. Many people who cannot tolerate regular cow's milk products find they can eat small amounts of goat cheese with no problems.**

## Goat Cheese Flatbread

**Prep:** 20 minutes   **Grill:** 18 minutes
**Special Equipment:** Baking sheet

*What cooks meat, roasts vegetables, and bakes bread? It's your very own grill!*

1 16-ounce loaf frozen bread dough, thawed
   Cornmeal
   Olive oil
½ cup chopped roasted red sweet peppers
½ cup crumbled soft goat cheese (chèvre)
¼ cup chopped, pitted Greek black olives
¼ cup fresh basil leaves cut into thin strips

**1** Place thawed bread dough on a lightly floured surface; roll into a 14×10-inch rectangle. Sprinkle cornmeal evenly on a baking sheet; place dough on baking sheet. Cover; let rest for 10 minutes. Using your finger, make ½-inch-deep indentations every 2 inches. Brush some olive oil evenly over dough. Sprinkle with roasted red peppers, goat cheese, and olives.

**2** *For a charcoal grill,* arrange hot coals around edge of grill. Test for medium-hot heat above center of grill. Place baking sheet with dough on grill rack over center of grill. Cover and grill for 18 to 22 minutes or until edges of flatbread are golden brown. [*For a gas grill,* preheat grill. Reduce heat to medium-hot. Adjust for indirect cooking (see page 10). Grill as above.]

**3** Remove flatbread from grill; sprinkle with basil. To serve, cut into 12 pieces. Makes 6 appetizer servings.

Nutrition Facts per serving: 242 calories, 5 g total fat (2 g saturated fat), 4 mg cholesterol, 97 mg sodium, 35 g carbohydrate, 1 g fiber, 7 g protein. Daily Values: 6% vit. A, 56% vit. C, 6% calcium, 3% iron.

**Swiss and Caramelized Onion Flatbread:** Prepare dough as directed above, except omit red pepper, goat cheese, olives, and basil. In a medium skillet cook 3 cups thinly sliced onions in 2 tablespoons olive oil, covered, over medium-low heat for 13 to 15 minutes or until tender. Add 4 teaspoons brown sugar. Cook and stir over medium-high heat for 4 to 5 minutes or until golden. Sprinkle onions over dough; sprinkle with 2 cups shredded smoked Swiss cheese (8 ounces) and 2 tablespoons pine nuts, toasted. Grill as above.

Nutrition Facts per serving: 439 calories, 19 g total fat (8 g saturated fat), 35 mg cholesterol, 101 mg sodium, 43 g carbohydrate, 1 g fiber, 18 g protein. Daily Values: 9% vit. A, 5% vit. C, 36% calcium, 5% iron.

## MEXICAN PITAS WITH TROPICAL SALSA

**Prep:** 25 minutes   **Grill:** 8 minutes

½ cup finely chopped fresh mango
½ cup finely chopped fresh pineapple
¼ cup finely chopped red onion

2 tablespoons snipped fresh cilantro
1 tablespoon lime juice
1 small fresh red serrano pepper,
    seeded and finely chopped
4 large pita bread rounds, halved
    crosswise
1½ cups shredded asadero,
    manchego, or Monterey Jack
    cheese (6 ounces)
4 teaspoons olive oil

**1** For salsa, in a bowl combine mango, pineapple, red onion, cilantro, lime juice, and serrano pepper. Cover and chill.

**2** Fill pita bread halves with shredded cheese. Gently press each pita half to flatten and seal slightly. Brush the outsides of the pita halves with olive oil.

**3** *For a charcoal grill,* grill pita halves on the rack of an uncovered grill directly over medium-hot coals for 8 to 10 minutes or until cheese is melted and bread is slightly crisp, turning once halfway through grilling. (*For a gas grill,* preheat grill. Reduce heat to medium-hot. Place pita halves on grill rack over heat. Cover and grill as above.)

**4** To serve, place pita halves on a serving platter on individual plates. Pass salsa, to be scooped up with torn pieces of pita. Makes 8 appetizer servings.

Nutrition Facts per serving: 170 calories,
7 g total fat (3 g saturated fat), 19 mg cholesterol,
372 mg sodium, 21 g carbohydrate, 1 g fiber,
8 g protein. Daily Values: 7% vit. A, 14% vit. C,
9% calcium, 5% iron.

# Polynesian Rumaki

**Prep:** 25 minutes   **Marinate:** 1 hour
**Grill:** 12 minutes

*Chicken livers take on Polynesian flavors from a soy-ginger marinade for a classic hors d'oeuvre. Curry adds an unexpected flavor note.*

1 pound chicken livers
3 tablespoons grated fresh ginger
3 tablespoons dry sherry
2 tablespoons soy sauce

1 tablespoon sugar
1 tablespoon cooking oil
1 teaspoon curry powder
1 clove garlic, minced
12 slices bacon, halved crosswise
12 whole water chestnuts, halved
    horizontally
12 fresh or canned pineapple chunks,
    halved

**1** Cut chicken livers in half (quarter any large livers). Place chicken livers in a plastic bag set in a deep bowl. For marinade, in a small bowl combine ginger, sherry, soy sauce, sugar, oil, curry powder, and garlic. Pour over chicken livers; seal bag. Marinate in the refrigerator for 1 to 2 hours, turning the bag occasionally.

**2** Meanwhile, in a large skillet cook bacon over medium heat about 2 minutes or just until the edges begin to curl. Do not let bacon brown. Drain; cool slightly. Drain chicken livers, discarding marinade.

**3** On a wooden toothpick, secure one end of a bacon slice. Add one water chestnut piece and one pineapple chunk. Add one liver piece; then wrap with the other end of bacon slice. Repeat with the remaining bacon, water chestnuts, pineapple, and livers.

**4** If desired, place skewers in a greased grill basket. *For a charcoal grill,* grill skewers on the rack of an uncovered grill directly over medium coals for 12 to 14 minutes or until livers are no longer pink, turning once halfway through grilling. (*For a gas grill,* preheat grill. Reduce heat to medium. Place skewers on grill rack over heat. Cover and grill as above.) Makes 24 appetizers.

ⓥNutrition Facts per appetizer: 45 calories,
2 g total fat (1 g saturated fat), 77 mg cholesterol,
85 mg sodium, 2 g carbohydrate, 0 g fiber,
4 g protein. Daily Values: 57% vit. A, 6% vit. C,
7% iron.

Three-Way Chicken Wings

## THREE-WAY CHICKEN WINGS

**Prep:** 10 minutes per sauce
**Grill:** 20 minutes

*There are no three ways about it: This flock of wings will fly off the serving platter. These irresistible morsels, perfect for a summer lawn party, are sticky, so you might want to have finger bowls available.*

1 recipe Easy Barbecue Sauce, Spicy Mustard Sauce, and/or Sweet-and-Sour Sauce
24 chicken wings (about 4 pounds)

**1** Prepare desired sauce(s). Set aside. Rinse chicken wings; pat dry with paper towels. Tuck under wing tips.

**2** *For a charcoal grill*, arrange medium-hot coals around a drip pan. Test for medium heat above the pan. Place chicken wings on grill rack over drip pan. Cover; grill for 20 to 25 minutes or until chicken is no longer pink, turning once and brushing occasionally with some of desired sauce(s) during the last 5 minutes of grilling. [*For a gas grill*, preheat grill. Reduce heat to medium. Adjust for indirect cooking (see page 10). Grill chicken as above.]

**3** To serve, reheat the remaining sauce(s). Transfer to a serving bowl or bowls and use as a dipping sauce for the grilled wings. Makes 24 wings.

**Easy Barbecue Sauce:** In a small saucepan stir together 1 cup bottled chili sauce, ½ cup currant jelly, 2 tablespoons snipped fresh chives, and 2 teaspoons prepared mustard. Cook and stir until jelly is melted. Makes about 1½ cups.

Nutrition Facts per wing: 71 calories, 2 g total fat (0 g saturated fat), 18 mg cholesterol, 160 mg sodium, 7 g carbohydrate, 0 g fiber, 7 g protein. Daily Values: 1% vit. A, 2% vit. C, 2% iron.

**Spicy Mustard Sauce:** In a small saucepan stir together 1⅓ cups chicken broth, ½ cup hot-style mustard, 4 teaspoons cornstarch, 2 teaspoons soy sauce, and, if desired, a few dashes bottled hot pepper sauce. Cook and stir until thickened and bubbly. Cook and stir for 2 minutes more. Makes about 1¾ cups.

Nutrition Facts per wing: 51 calories, 2 g total fat (1 g saturated fat), 18 mg cholesterol, 155 mg sodium, 1 g carbohydrate, 0 g fiber, 7 g protein. Daily Values: 2% iron.

**Sweet-and-Sour Sauce:** In a small saucepan stir together ⅔ cup unsweetened pineapple juice, ⅔ cup red wine vinegar, ½ cup packed brown sugar, 2 tablespoons cornstarch, 2 tablespoons soy sauce, and ¼ teaspoon ground ginger. Cook and stir until thickened and bubbly. Cook and stir for 2 minutes more. Makes about 1⅔ cups.

Nutrition Facts per wing: 64 calories, 2 g total fat (0 g saturated fat), 18 mg cholesterol, 106 mg sodium, 6 g carbohydrate, 0 g fiber, 7 g protein. Daily Values: 1% vit. C, 2% iron.

## DON'T GET BURNED!

**A lot of grillers hover protectively over their grills and flip and turn foods again and again. Restrain yourself! It's best to turn only once when you are direct grilling. This will help seal in those precious juices. When indirect grilling, it isn't necessary to turn the meat at all. Read your recipe in its entirety to determine if it is necessary to turn the food during grilling. Use long-handled tongs when turning foods on the grill rather than a fork. Tongs keep your hands from getting burned, and they are more gentle with the food. Forks pierce the food, and allow the tasty juices to escape!**

# Smoked Fish Pâté

**Prep:** 10 minutes    **Grill:** 8 minutes

*To smoke on a gas grill, use a small metal container, which is available where grill accessories are sold. Place the drained chips in the container and follow the manufacturer's directions.*

1 pound fresh or frozen skinless catfish fillet (about ¾ to 1 inch thick)
1 cup hardwood chips, soaked in water about 1 hour
1 3-ounce package cream cheese, cut up
¼ cup milk
2 tablespoons snipped fresh parsley
2 teaspoons finely shredded lemon peel
2 tablespoons lemon juice
2 cloves garlic, minced
¼ teaspoon salt
¼ teaspoon ground red pepper
Baguette-style French bread slices, toasted, or crackers

**1** Thaw fish, if frozen. *For a charcoal grill,* arrange medium-hot coals around a drip pan. Test for medium heat above the pan. Drain wood chips and sprinkle over coals. Prick a few holes in a piece of heavy foil large enough to hold fish and place on rack above drip pan. Place the fish on foil. Cover and grill 8 to 12 minutes (about 4 to 6 minutes per ½-inch thickness of fish) or until fish begins to flake easily with a fork. [*For a gas grill,* preheat grill. Reduce heat to medium. Adjust for indirect cooking (see page 10). Grill as above.] Cool completely; break fish into pieces, removing any bones.

**2** Place fish in a food processor bowl. Cover; process until nearly smooth. Add cream cheese, milk, parsley, lemon peel, lemon juice, garlic, salt, and red pepper. Cover; process until mixture is smooth.

**3** Spoon mixture into a serving bowl and chill at least 2 hours or for up to 2 days. Serve pâté with toasted baguette slices. Makes about 2 cups (eight ¼-cup servings).

Nutrition Facts per 1 tablespoon pâté and 2 baguette slices: 113 calories, 3 g total fat (1 g saturated fat), 12 mg cholesterol, 219 mg sodium, 15 g carbohydrate, 0 g fiber, 5 g protein. Daily Values: 1% vit. A, 1% vit. C, 1% iron.

## SKILLET-GRILLED MUSSELS

**Prep:** 20 minutes    **Soak:** 45 minutes
**Grill:** 6 minutes

*The mussels cook beautifully in a skillet, and the sauce that develops is perfect for dipping crusty pieces of bread. While this makes a lovely appetizer, add a crisp Chardonnay and a simple tossed salad and you have dinner.*

24 mussels in shells
⅓ cup butter, cut into small pieces
2 tablespoons olive oil
1 tablespoon lemon juice
⅛ teaspoon bottled hot pepper sauce
French bread or sourdough bread (optional)

**1** Scrub mussels under cold running water. Using your fingers, pull out the beards that are visible between the shells. In an 8-quart pot or Dutch oven combine 4 quarts cold water and ⅓ cup salt; add mussels. Soak for 15 minutes; drain and rinse. Discard water. Repeat soaking, draining, and rinsing twice.

**2** Evenly distribute the butter pieces in a large cast-iron skillet or 9×9×2-inch baking pan. Drizzle with olive oil, lemon juice, and hot pepper sauce. Place mussels on top of butter mixture.

**3** *For a charcoal grill,* place medium coals in bottom of grill. Place mussels in skillet on grill rack directly over coals. Cover and grill for 6 to 10 minutes or until the mussels have opened. Discard any mussels that do not open. (*For a gas grill,* preheat grill. Reduce heat to medium. Place mussels in skillet on grill rack over heat. Cover and grill as above.)

**4** If desired, serve mussels with French bread or sourdough, dipping bread into pan juices. Makes 6 to 8 appetizer servings.

Nutrition Facts per serving: 227 calories, 17 g total fat (7 g saturated fat), 59 mg cholesterol, 312 mg sodium, 4 g carbohydrate, 0 g fiber, 14 g protein. Daily Values: 14% vit. A, 14% vit. C, 1% calcium, 25% iron.

# Bacon Wrapped Shrimp

**Prep:** 25 minutes   **Marinate:** 30 minutes
**Grill:** 8 minutes

*As everyone knows, overcooked shrimp are dry and, well, overcooked. That's why it's a good idea to give the bacon a head start in this recipe. And you need time to offer your guests a lovely bottle of California Chardonnay.*

  **18 to 24 fresh jumbo shrimp in shells (about 1½ pounds total), peeled and deveined**
    **1 tablespoon sugar**
    **1 tablespoon olive oil**
    **1 tablespoon white vinegar**
  **1½ teaspoons paprika**
    **½ teaspoon salt**
    **½ teaspoon curry powder**
    **½ teaspoon ground cumin**
    **½ teaspoon black pepper**
    **¼ teaspoon ground red pepper**
    **9 to 12 slices bacon, halved crosswise**

**1** Rinse shrimp; pat dry with paper towels. Place shrimp in a large bowl. For marinade, in a small bowl stir together sugar, olive oil, vinegar, paprika, salt, curry powder, cumin, black pepper, and red pepper. Pour over shrimp; toss to coat. Cover and marinate at room temperature for 30 minutes.

**2** Meanwhile, in a large skillet cook bacon over medium heat about 2 minutes or just until the edges begin to curl. Do not let bacon brown. Drain; cool slightly.

**3** Drain shrimp, reserving marinade. For each appetizer, wrap one bacon piece around a shrimp and secure with a wooden toothpick. Repeat with the remaining bacon and shrimp.

**4** If desired, place wrapped shrimp in a greased grill basket. *For a charcoal grill,* grill shrimp on the rack of an uncovered grill directly over medium coals for 8 to 10 minutes or until shrimp are opaque, turning and brushing once with marinade halfway through grilling. (*For a gas grill,* preheat grill. Reduce heat to medium. Place skewers on grill rack over heat. Cover and grill as above.) Makes 18 to 24 appetizers.

Nutrition Facts per appetizer: 48 calories, 3 g total fat (1 g saturated fat), 41 mg cholesterol, 154 mg sodium, 1 g carbohydrate, 0 g fiber, 5 g protein. Daily Values: 2% vit. A, 2% vit. C, 5% iron.

**Poblano Pepper-Wrapped Shrimp:** Prepare Bacon-Wrapped Shrimp as directed, except roast 2 fresh poblano peppers as follows: Cut peppers in half lengthwise; remove stems, seeds, and membranes. *For a charcoal grill,* grill peppers, cut sides up, on the rack of an uncovered grill directly over medium-hot coals about 10 minutes or until pepper skins are blistered and dark. (*For a gas grill,* preheat grill. Reduce heat to medium-hot. Place peppers, cut sides up, on grill rack over heat. Cover and grill as above.) Wrap peppers in foil; let stand for 15 to 20 minutes or until cool enough to handle. Using a paring knife, pull the skin off gently. Cut poblano peppers into 4×¼-inch strips. Wrap a pepper strip around each shrimp before adding bacon.

Nutrition Facts per appetizer: 52 calories, 3 g total fat (1 g saturated fat), 41 mg cholesterol, 154 mg sodium, 2 g carbohydrate, 0 g fiber, 5 g protein. Daily Values: 2% vit. A, 46% vit. C, 5% iron.

## ASPARAGUS WITH PARMESAN CURLS

**Prep:** 15 minutes **Marinate:** 30 minutes
**Grill:** 3 minutes
**Special Equipment:** Grill tray or basket

*You don't need new equipment or split-second timing for this garnish. A potato peeler is all it takes to create the pile of Parmesan shavings. Simply scatter them over grilled asparagus like flower petals to create a stunning dish.*

1½ pounds asparagus spears,
    trimmed
2 tablespoons olive oil
2 tablespoons lemon juice
½ teaspoon salt
¼ teaspoon pepper
1 2-ounce block of Parmesan cheese

1 In a large skillet cook the asparagus in a small amount of boiling water 3 minutes. Drain well. Meanwhile, for marinade, in a 2-quart rectangular baking dish stir together olive oil, lemon juice, salt, and pepper. Add drained asparagus, turning to coat. Cover and marinate at room temperature for 30 minutes. Drain asparagus, discarding marinade. Place asparagus on a grill tray or in a grill basket.

2 *For a charcoal grill,* grill asparagus on the rack of an uncovered grill directly over medium coals for 3 to 5 minutes or until asparagus is tender and beginning to brown, turning once halfway through grilling. (*For a gas grill,* preheat grill. Reduce heat to medium. Place asparagus on grill rack over heat. Cover and grill as above.)

3 To serve, arrange asparagus on a serving platter. Working over asparagus, use a cheese plane or vegetable peeler to cut thin, wide strips from the side of Parmesan cheese. Makes 6 side-dish servings.

Nutrition Facts per serving: 95 calories,
7 g total fat (1 g saturated fat), 7 mg cholesterol,
287 mg sodium, 4 g carbohydrate, 1 g fiber,
6 g protein. Daily Values: 6% vit. A, 35% vit. C,
8% calcium, 3% iron.

# Corn with Ancho-Avocado Butter

**Prep:** 25 minutes **Chill:** 1 hour
**Grill:** 10 minutes

*Butter, salt, and pepper, step aside. Ancho chilies, lime, and avocado update an ear of corn. Ancho chilies, a deep reddish brown, are dried poblanos with a mild, smoky flavor.*

2 tablespoons water
2 tablespoons lime juice
½ to 1 small dried ancho pepper
3 tablespoons butter or margarine,
    softened
⅛ teaspoon salt
½ of a small avocado, seeded,
    peeled, and chopped
6 fresh ears of corn, with husks

1 In a small saucepan combine water, lime juice, and ancho pepper. Cook, covered, over low heat about 10 minutes or until pepper turns soft. Drain; cool. Remove stem and seeds from pepper; finely chop pepper. In a small bowl combine ancho pepper, softened butter or margarine, and salt. Slightly mash the avocado; stir into butter mixture. If desired, press into a small mold or cup lined with plastic wrap. Cover and chill for 1 hour.

2 Remove husks and silks from ears of corn. If desired, leave a few leaves of the husks intact. In a large covered saucepan cook corn in boiling water for 5 minutes; drain.

3 *For a charcoal grill,* grill corn on the rack of an uncovered grill directly over medium coals about 10 minutes or until corn kernels are tender, turning occasionally. (*For a gas grill,* preheat grill. Reduce heat to medium. Place corn on grill rack over heat. Cover and grill as above.)

4 If using a mold, remove butter mixture from mold; discard plastic wrap. Serve corn with butter mixture. Makes 6 side-dish servings.

Nutrition Facts per serving: 246 calories,
10 g total fat (2 g saturated fat), 8 mg cholesterol,
125 mg sodium, 40 g carbohydrate, 6 g fiber,
5 g protein. Daily Values: 10% vit. A, 32% vit. C,
7% iron.

Asparagus with Parmesan Curls

## ANTIPASTO KABOBS

**Prep:** 25 minutes    **Grill:** 8 minutes

*Don't be puzzled by the cipollini—they're little onion wannabes. They look like onions, taste like onions, but are really the bulbs of the grape hyacinth. You'll find cipollini in upscale supermarkets or Italian markets.*

⅓ cup balsamic vinegar
1 6-ounce jar marinated artichoke
      hearts
1 medium red sweet pepper, cut into
      1-inch pieces
1 medium yellow sweet pepper, cut
      into 1-inch pieces
8 small whole or 4 medium cipollini,
      halved, or 8 pearl onions
8 large crimini or button mushroom
      caps
2 ounces provolone cheese, cut into
      thin, short strips
¼ cup snipped fresh basil

**1** In a small saucepan bring vinegar to boiling; reduce heat. Simmer, uncovered, about 5 minutes or until vinegar is reduced to 3 tablespoons. Set aside to cool.

**2** Drain artichoke hearts, reserving 2 tablespoons liquid; set aside. On 4 long metal skewers, alternately thread sweet peppers, cipollini, and mushrooms, leaving ¼ inch between pieces. In a small bowl combine reduced vinegar and reserved artichoke liquid. Brush half of the vinegar mixture over vegetables.

**3** *For a charcoal grill*, grill skewers on the rack of an uncovered grill directly over medium coals for 8 to 10 minutes or until vegetables are tender, turning once and brushing frequently with remaining vinegar mixture. (*For a gas grill*, preheat grill. Reduce heat to medium. Place skewers on grill rack over heat. Cover and grill as above.)

**4** Remove vegetables from skewers; transfer to a large bowl. Add drained artichokes, cheese, and basil. Season to taste with salt and pepper, if desired. Toss gently to combine. Makes 6 side-dish servings.

Nutrition Facts per serving: 106 calories, 4 g total fat (2 g saturated fat), 7 mg cholesterol, 220 mg sodium, 14 g carbohydrate, 1 g fiber, 4 g protein. Daily Values: 18% vit. A, 94% vit. C, 7% calcium, 9% iron.

## Did You Know?

**Although relatively expensive by comparison to other vinegar types, balsamic vinegar is worth having on your shelf of staples. This aromatic dark, mellow Italian vinegar has a wonderful sweet-sour flavor. Balsamic vinegar is made by aging high-quality red wine vinegar in oak barrels for as long as 15 to 20 years. The longer it is aged, the more expensive it will be. Besides salad dressings, try it in place of cider or white vinegar in your favorite recipes; it adds exciting flavor when stirred into sauces or tossed into vegetable dishes. Balsamic vinegar can usually be found with the other vinegars in your supermarket, or look for it in Italian food markets.**

# Cast-Iron Skillet Cowboy Beans

**Prep:** 15 minutes   **Grill:** 30 minutes

*Cowboy cooking is back. And it's good! Whether you make this over a campfire on a fishing trip or on the latest state-of-the-art grill in your backyard, the bubbling satisfaction of a skillet full of beans can't be beat.*

> 2 15-ounce cans pinto beans, rinsed
>    and drained
> ½ cup chopped onion
> ½ cup catsup
> ½ cup hot strong coffee
> 6 slices bacon, crisp-cooked,
>    drained, and crumbled
> 2 tablespoons Worcestershire sauce
> 1 tablespoon brown sugar

**1** In a 9-inch cast-iron skillet combine pinto beans, onion, catsup, coffee, bacon, Worcestershire sauce, and brown sugar.

**2** *For a charcoal grill*, grill beans in skillet on the rack of an uncovered grill directly over medium coals about 15 minutes or until bubbly. Grill for 15 to 20 minutes more or until beans are desired consistency, stirring occasionally. (*For a gas grill*, preheat grill. Reduce heat to medium. Place beans in skillet on grill rack over heat. Cover and grill as above.) Makes 6 side-dish servings.

Nutrition Facts per serving: 184 calories, 4 g total fat (1 g saturated fat), 5 mg cholesterol, 1,003 mg sodium, 30 g carbohydrate, 8 g fiber, 9 g protein. Daily Values: 2% vit. A, 26% vit. C, 5% calcium, 19% iron.

# CURRIED RICE PILAF

**Prep:** 30 minutes   **Grill:** 5 minutes

*If you make the rice ahead and refrigerate it, you'll lop off about 20 minutes of final prep time.*

> 2 cups cooked long grain rice
> ½ cup chopped onion
> ½ cup mixed dried fruit bits
> ¼ cup chopped celery
> 1 tablespoon margarine or butter
> 1½ teaspoons instant chicken or beef
>    bouillon granules
> ½ to 1 teaspoon curry powder
> 1 clove garlic, minced
> ⅛ teaspoon pepper
> ¼ cup slivered almonds, toasted
>    (optional)

**1** In a large bowl combine cooked rice, onion, fruit bits, celery, margarine or butter, bouillon, curry powder, garlic, and pepper.

**2** Tear off a 36×18-inch piece of heavy foil. Fold in half to make an 18-inch square. Place pilaf in center of the foil. Bring up two opposite edges of foil and seal with a double fold. Fold remaining edges together to completely enclose rice mixture, leaving space for steam to build.

**3** *For a charcoal grill*, grill packet on the rack of an uncovered grill directly over medium coals for 15 to 20 minutes or until onion and celery is crisp-tender, turning packet once halfway through grilling. (*For a gas grill*, preheat grill. Reduce heat to medium. Place packet on grill rack over heat. Cover and grill as above.) Open packet and stir before serving and, if desired, add almonds. Makes 4 side-dish servings.

Nutrition Facts per serving: 182 calories, 3 g total fat (1 g saturated fat), 0 mg cholesterol, 376 mg sodium, 36 g carbohydrate, 0 g fiber, 3 g protein. Daily Values: 7% vit. A, 3% vit. C, 1% calcium, 8% iron.

# Grilled Corn Relish

**Prep:** 15 minutes  **Grill:** 25 minutes

*Lime, chili powder, and corn are a spectacular combination, especially if the corn's been grilled. This colorful relish is a great side for grilled chicken. Or, wrap the relish, grilled chicken strips, and shredded Jack cheese in warm flour tortillas and you'll have the makings for dynamite burritos.*

> 3 tablespoons lime juice
> 1 tablespoon cooking oil
> 2 cloves garlic, minced
> 2 fresh ears of corn, husked and cleaned
> 1 teaspoon chili powder
> 1 small avocado, seeded, peeled, and cut up
> ½ cup chopped red sweet pepper
> ¼ cup snipped fresh cilantro
> ¼ teaspoon salt

1 In a medium bowl combine lime juice, oil, and garlic. Brush corn lightly with some of the lime juice mixture. Sprinkle corn with chili powder.

2 *For a charcoal grill*, grill corn on the rack of an uncovered grill directly over medium coals for 25 to 30 minutes or until corn kernels are tender, turning occasionally. (*For a gas grill*, preheat grill. Reduce heat to medium. Place corn on grill rack over heat. Cover and grill as above.)

3 Meanwhile, add avocado, sweet pepper, cilantro, and salt to the remaining lime juice mixture; toss to combine. Cut corn kernels from cobs; stir into avocado mixture. Serve immediately at room temperature or cover and chill up to 2 hours. Makes 4 side-dish servings.

Nutrition Facts per serving: 159 calories, 12 g total fat (2 g saturated fat), 0 mg cholesterol, 152 mg sodium, 15 g carbohydrate, 3 g fiber, 3 g protein. Daily Values: 15% vit. A, 51% vit. C, 1% calcium, 6% iron.

# BEET AND FENNEL SALAD

**Prep:** 20 minutes  **Grill:** 25 minutes

> 4 medium beets without tops (about 1 pound)
> 1 fennel bulb, cored and thinly sliced
> 2 tablespoons butter or margarine
> 2 tablespoons red wine vinegar
> 2 teaspoons snipped fresh basil
> ¼ teaspoon salt
> 1 or 2 oranges, peeled and sectioned
> ⅓ cup chopped, toasted walnuts or pecans

1 Trim and peel beets. Halve beets lengthwise and cut into slices about ¼ inch thick. Tear off a 36×18-inch piece of heavy foil; fold in half to make an 18-inch square. Place sliced beets and fennel in center of foil. Add butter or margarine and 1 tablespoon water. Bring up opposite edges of foil and seal with a double fold. Fold remaining edges together to completely enclose vegetables, leaving space for steam to build.

2 *For a charcoal grill*, place foil packet on the rack of an uncovered grill directly over medium coals for about 25 minutes or until beets and fennel are just tender, turning packet over once. (*For a gas grill*, preheat grill. Reduce heat to medium. Place foil packet on grill rack over heat. Cover and grill as above.) Open packet and allow vegetables to cool while preparing dressing.

3 For dressing, in a small bowl stir together vinegar, basil, and salt.

4 In a large bowl combine the beets and fennel along with any juices, the orange sections, and nuts. Drizzle with vinegar mixture, tossing lightly to coat. Makes 4 side-dish servings.

Nutrition Facts per serving: 153 calories, 12 g total fat (4 g saturated fat), 15 mg cholesterol, 243 mg sodium, 11 g carbohydrate, 10 g fiber, 3 g protein. Daily Values: 5% vit. A, 25% vit. C, 3% calcium, 5% iron.

# Warm Asparagus, Fennel, and Spinach Salad

**Prep:** 15 minutes  **Grill:** 12 minutes

*Subtle, engaging, and thoroughly delicious, this trio of springtime favorites is a sophisticated study of texture, taste, and color.*

1 medium fennel bulb (about
    1 pound)
2 tablespoons water
2 tablespoons olive oil
¼ teaspoon finely shredded lemon
    peel
4 teaspoons lemon juice
⅛ teaspoon salt
⅛ teaspoon pepper
8 ounces asparagus spears, trimmed
4 cups fresh spinach
¼ cup shredded Parmesan cheese
    (1 ounce)
1 tablespoon fresh basil leaves cut
    into thin strips

1 Trim off stem end of fennel; quarter fennel but do not remove core. Place fennel in a small microwave-safe dish or pie plate. Add the water. Cover with vented plastic wrap. Microwave on 100% power (high) about 4 minutes or until nearly tender; drain.

2 Meanwhile, for dressing, in a small bowl combine oil, lemon peel, lemon juice, salt, and pepper; whisk until smooth. Brush fennel and asparagus with 1 tablespoon of the dressing; set remaining dressing aside.

3 *For a charcoal grill,* grill fennel on the rack of an uncovered grill directly over medium coals for 5 minutes, turning occasionally. Add asparagus to grill. Grill for 7 to 8 minutes more or until vegetables are tender, turning occasionally. (*For a gas grill,* preheat grill. Reduce heat to medium. Place fennel, then asparagus on grill rack over heat. Cover and grill as above.)

4 Transfer fennel to a cutting board; cool slightly and cut into ¼- to ½-inch slices, discarding core. To serve, divide fennel and asparagus among 4 dinner plates. Arrange spinach on top. Drizzle with remaining dressing. Top with Parmesan cheese and basil. Makes 4 side-dish servings.

Nutrition Facts per serving: 111 calories, 9 g total fat (1 g saturated fat), 5 mg cholesterol, 231 mg sodium, 5 g carbohydrate, 7 g fiber, 4 g protein. Daily Values: 4% vit. A, 23% vit. C, 7% calcium, 3% iron.

## EGGPLANT SALAD

**Prep:** 10 minutes  **Grill:** 8 minutes

3 tablespoons snipped fresh herbs
    (basil, oregano, and/or parsley)
3 tablespoons balsamic vinegar
2 tablespoons olive oil
2 cloves garlic, minced
    Salt and black pepper
3 Japanese eggplants, sliced
    lengthwise ¼ inch thick (about
    12 ounces)*
2 medium red sweet peppers,
    seeded and cut into 1-inch strips
2 medium sweet onions (such as
    Vidalia or Walla Walla), sliced
    ½ inch thick

1 In a small bowl combine the herbs, vinegar, oil, garlic, and salt and pepper to taste.

2 *For a charcoal grill,* grill vegetables on the rack of an uncovered grill directly over medium heat for 8 to 12 minutes or until vegetables are crisp-tender, turning once and brushing occasionally with some of the oil mixture. (*For a gas grill,* preheat grill. Reduce heat to medium. Place vegetables on grill rack over heat. Cover and grill as above.) Transfer vegetables to serving dish; toss with remaining oil mixture. Makes 4 to 6 servings

*Note: If desired, substitute 1 small regular eggplant for the Japanese variety. Slice and grill as above. Before serving, cut slices into quarters.

Nutrition Facts per serving: 116 calories, 7 g total fat (1 g saturated fat), 0 mg cholesterol, 39 mg sodium, 13 g carbohydrate, 3 g fiber, 1 g protein. Daily Values: 27% vit. A, 112% vit. C, 1% calcium, 6% iron.

# Potato Salad with Garlic Dressing

**Prep:** 15 minutes   **Grill:** 30 minutes
**Chill:** 4 hours

*Potato salad never had it so good. Tiny little new potatoes and creamy yellow Yukon golds grill up toasty on the outside and smooth on the inside.*

  1½ pounds tiny new potatoes, halved
   3 large yellow potatoes (about
        1 pound total), such as Yukon
        gold or Finnish yellow,
        quartered
   2 tablespoons olive oil
   1 clove garlic, minced
   ½ cup thinly sliced green onions
   ⅓ cup mayonnaise or salad dressing
   ⅓ cup dairy sour cream
   2 cloves garlic, minced
   ½ teaspoon salt
   ⅛ teaspoon pepper

**1** On 4 long metal skewers, thread potatoes, leaving a ¼-inch space between pieces. In a small bowl combine the olive oil and the clove garlic; brush over potatoes.

**2** *For a charcoal grill,* grill kabobs on the rack of an uncovered grill directly over medium coals about 30 minutes or until tender, turning occasionally. (*For a gas grill,* preheat grill. Reduce heat to medium. Place kabobs on grill rack over heat. Cover and grill as above.)

**3** Remove potatoes from grill. Cool slightly. Cut potatoes into 1-inch pieces; place in a large bowl; set aside. For dressing, in a small bowl combine green onions, mayonnaise or salad dressing, sour cream, the 2 cloves garlic, the salt, and pepper. Add to potatoes; toss gently to coat. Serve immediately or, if desired, cover and chill 4 to 24 hours. Before serving, stir in a little milk, if necessary, to thin dressing. Makes 8 side-dish servings.

Nutrition Facts per serving: 266 calories,
13 g total fat (3 g saturated fat), 10 mg cholesterol,
202 mg sodium, 35 g carbohydrate, 1 g fiber,
4 g protein. Daily Values: 4% vit. A, 37% vit. C,
2% calcium, 12% iron.

# WHEAT BERRY AND VEGETABLE SALAD

**Prep:** 1 hour   **Grill:** 10 minutes

*Wheat berries are whole, unprocessed kernels of wheat. They require patient simmering, but pack a nutritional wallop. The lemon-laced dressing and grilled vegetables combine with the chewy nutty wheat berries to create a satisfying main-course salad.*

   3 cups water
   1 cup wheat berries
   ¼ cup lemon juice
   ½ teaspoon sugar
   ½ teaspoon salt
   ½ teaspoon black pepper
   1 tablespoon Dijon-style mustard
   ¼ cup olive oil
   ¼ cup fresh basil leaves cut into thin
        strips
   2 tablespoons snipped fresh chives
   2 medium zucchini and/or yellow
        summer squash, cut lengthwise
        into ½-inch slices
   2 red and/or green sweet peppers,
        quartered lengthwise
   1 large red onion, cut into ½-inch
        slices

**1** In a medium saucepan bring water to boiling. Stir wheat berries into boiling water; reduce heat. Simmer, covered, for 45 to 60 minutes or until wheat berries are tender but chewy and most of the water is absorbed. Drain off any excess liquid. Transfer berries to a large bowl; cool slightly.

**2** Meanwhile, for dressing, in a small bowl combine lemon juice, sugar, salt, and black pepper. Using a wire whisk, stir briskly until sugar and salt dissolve. Stir in mustard. Whisking continuously, slowly pour in oil. Stir in half of the basil and the chives. Pour ¼ cup of the dressing over wheat berries; toss to coat. Cover; chill until needed.

**3** Brush zucchini, sweet peppers, and onion with the remaining dressing. *For a charcoal grill,* grill vegetables on the rack of an uncovered grill directly over medium coals about 10 minutes or until crisp-tender, turning once halfway through grilling. (*For a gas grill*, preheat grill. Reduce heat to medium. Place vegetables on grill rack over heat. Cover and grill as above.)

**4** Remove vegetables from grill; cool slightly. Cut into 1-inch pieces. Add vegetables and the remaining basil to wheat berry mixture; toss gently to combine. Serve immediately or cover and chill. If chilled, let salad stand at room temperature about 30 minutes before serving. Makes 8 to 10 side-dish servings.

Nutrition Facts per serving: 151 calories,
7 g total fat (1 g saturated fat), 0 mg cholesterol,
186 mg sodium, 20 g carbohydrate, 2 g fiber,
3 g protein. Daily Values: 22% vit. A, 72% vit. C,
1% calcium, 9% iron.

## Italian Bread Salad with Grilled Vegetables

**Prep:** 35 minutes   **Grill:** 12 minutes

*The traditional panzanella—an Italian salad of bread, tomatoes, and vinaigrette—is taken to a new level with grilled vegetables and a robust balsamic dressing.*

  5  1-inch slices Italian bread
  4  plum tomatoes, halved lengthwise
  1  medium red or yellow sweet
       pepper, quartered lengthwise
  ¼  cup olive oil
  4  cups torn romaine lettuce
  2  tablespoons balsamic vinegar
  2  teaspoons snipped fresh oregano
       or ½ teaspoon dried oregano,
       crushed
  1  clove garlic, minced
  ¼  teaspoon salt
  ⅛  teaspoon black pepper
  2  tablespoons finely shredded
       Parmesan cheese

**1** Lightly brush cut surfaces of bread, tomatoes, and sweet pepper with 2 tablespoons of the olive oil.

**2** For a charcoal grill, grill tomatoes and sweet pepper, cut sides up, on the rack of an uncovered grill directly over medium-hot coals until pepper skins are blistered and dark. (Allow about 10 minutes for sweet pepper and about 5 minutes for tomatoes.) Remove vegetables from grill. Wrap pepper in foil and let stand for 20 minutes. Meanwhile, add bread to grill. Grill about 2 minutes or until bread is lightly toasted, turning once halfway through grilling. Remove bread from grill. (*For a gas grill*, preheat grill. Reduce heat to medium-hot. Place tomatoes and pepper, cut sides up, then bread on grill rack over heat. Cover and grill as above.)

**3** Remove and discard skins from pepper and tomatoes. Coarsely chop vegetables, and cut bread into 1-inch cubes; place in a large bowl. Add the romaine lettuce.

**4** For dressing, in a screw-top jar combine remaining oil, the vinegar, oregano, garlic, salt, and black pepper. Cover and shake well. Drizzle over lettuce mixture; toss gently to coat. To serve, sprinkle with Parmesan cheese. Makes 6 side-dish servings.

Nutrition Facts per serving: 179 calories,
11 g total fat (1 g saturated fat), 2 mg cholesterol,
269 mg sodium, 17 g carbohydrate, 1 g fiber,
4 g protein. Daily Values: 21% vit. A, 63% vit. C,
4% calcium, 10% iron.

**Smokin' Hot Tip**

Choosing olive oil is easy. If you want no flavor from the oil, buy light olive oil (lighter in color and flavor). For a more pronounced flavor, choose extra virgin or virgin olive oil. Rule of thumb: The darker the color, the more pronounced the flavor. Regardless of the type chosen, olive oil is high in monounsaturated fats (better-for-you fats) and low in the not-so-good saturated fats.

Sante Fe Rice and Corn Salad

## SANTA FE RICE AND CORN SALAD

**Prep:** 30 minutes  **Soak:** 2 hours
**Grill:** 25 minutes

*This black bean and rice salad will take center
stage on your picnic plate. The vinaigrette nicely
complements all of the ingredients.*

    3 fresh ears of corn, with husks
    2½ cups water
    1¼ cups long grain rice
    ½ teaspoon salt
    1 medium red sweet pepper,
        quartered lengthwise
    1 fresh poblano pepper, halved
        lengthwise and seeded
    ½ cup canned black beans, rinsed
        and drained
    ⅓ cup snipped fresh cilantro
    1 recipe Dijon Vinaigrette

1 Peel back the corn husks, if present, but do
not remove. Remove the corn silks. Gently
rinse corn. Pull the husks back up around
corn. Using 100-percent-cotton string, tie the
husks shut. Cover corn with water. Soak for
2 to 4 hours. Drain well. (Or, remove husks
and silks. Place each ear of corn on a piece of
heavy foil; dot each ear with 1 tablespoon
butter. Wrap securely in foil.)

2 In a medium saucepan bring the 2½ cups
water to boiling. Stir in rice and salt.
Return to boiling; reduce heat. Simmer,
covered, about 15 minutes or until rice is
tender and the liquid is absorbed. Place in a
colander and rinse with cold water. Drain and
set aside.

3 *For a charcoal grill,* grill corn on the rack
of an uncovered grill directly over
medium-hot coals for 15 minutes. Add sweet
pepper and poblano pepper, cut sides up, to
grill. Grill about 10 minutes more or until
corn kernels are tender and pepper skins are
blistered and dark, turning corn frequently.
(*For a gas grill,* preheat grill. Reduce heat to
medium-hot. Place corn, then sweet pepper
and poblano pepper, cut sides up, on grill rack
over heat. Cover and grill as above.)

4 Wrap peppers in foil and let stand for
20 minutes. Cool corn slightly. Remove
and discard husks. Cut corn kernels from
cobs. Remove and discard skins from
peppers; chop the peppers.

5 In a large bowl combine rice, corn, peppers,
beans, and cilantro. Add Dijon Vinaigrette;
toss gently to coat. Serve at room temperature
or chilled. Makes 6 side-dish servings.

**Dijon Vinaigrette:** In a small screw-top jar
combine 3 tablespoons salad oil, 3 tablespoons
red wine vinegar, 1½ teaspoons Dijon-style
mustard, ½ teaspoon bottled hot pepper sauce
(optional), and ⅛ teaspoon salt. Cover and
shake well.

Nutrition Facts per serving: 260 calories,
8 g total fat (1 g saturated fat), 0 mg cholesterol,
310 mg sodium, 45 g carbohydrate, 3 g fiber,
5 g protein. Daily Values: 10% vit. A, 51% vit. C,
2% calcium, 14% iron.

## Flaming Facts

**If you've just started
experimenting with chile
peppers, and haven't tried
poblanos, check them out.
These dark green chiles
range from mild to slightly
hot. Riper poblanos are
reddish brown in color and
taste sweeter and richer than
green poblanos. They are
most well known for their use
in chile rellenos because of
their great flavor and fairly
large size—perfect for
stuffing. They generally
measure about 2½ to 3 inches
wide and from 4 to 5 inches
long. Look for these versatile
chiles in Mexican markets or
larger supermarkets. They're
most available in the summer
and early fall.**

# Eggplant with Gorgonzola

**Prep:** 10 minutes  **Grill:** 20 minutes

*This is packet cooking at its best—easy, pretty, and delicious. Toss a colorful medley of vegetables with pesto, wrap in a foil packets, and grill. At the last minute, when dinner is ready, transfer the vegetables to a bowl, sprinkle them with Gorgonzola, and serve.*

1 small eggplant (about 12 ounces)
1 medium yellow summer squash, halved lengthwise and sliced 1 inch thick
1 small red onion, cut into thin wedges
2 tablespoons pesto
¼ cup crumbled Gorgonzola or other blue cheese, feta cheese, or goat cheese (chèvre) (1 ounce)

1 If desired, peel eggplant. Cut into 1-inch cubes. In a large bowl combine the eggplant, squash, onion, and pesto; toss gently to coat. Fold a 36×18-inch piece of heavy foil in half to make an 18-inch square. Place vegetables in center of foil. Bring up opposite edges of foil and seal with a double fold. Fold remaining edges together to completely enclose vegetables, leaving space for steam to build.

2 *For a charcoal grill,* grill vegetables on the rack of an uncovered grill directly over medium coals for 20 to 25 minutes or until crisp-tender, turning occasionally. (*For a gas grill,* preheat grill. Reduce heat to medium. Place vegetables on grill rack over heat. Cover and grill as above.)

3 To serve, transfer vegetables to a serving bowl and sprinkle with cheese. Makes 4 side-dish servings.

Nutrition Facts per serving: 116 calories, 8 g total fat (2 g saturated fat), 7 mg cholesterol, 179 mg sodium, 9 g carbohydrate, 3 g fiber, 4 g protein. Daily Values: 3% vit. A, 5% vit. C, 4% calcium, 2% iron.

# LEEKS WITH MUSTARD VINAIGRETTE

**Prep:** 15 minutes  **Grill:** 15 minutes

*In France, where leeks often grow like weeds, they are known as a poor man's asparagus. That seems unfair in terms of flavor. Because of their refined onion flavor, we like to think of them as a rich man's onion and find that they're perfect with grilled or lightly smoked chicken.*

4 teaspoons red wine vinegar
4 teaspoons Dijon-style mustard
1 tablespoon snipped fresh tarragon
2 tablespoons olive oil
6 medium leeks (about 2 pounds total)
2 tablespoons water
2 cloves garlic, thinly sliced
⅛ teaspoon salt
⅛ teaspoon pepper
¼ cup crumbled blue cheese (1 ounce)

1 For dressing, in a small bowl combine the red wine vinegar, mustard, and half of the tarragon. Whisk in 1 tablespoon of the olive oil. Set aside.

2 Remove any tough outer leaves from leeks. Trim roots from bases. Trim all but 2 inches of the green leafy portions from leeks. Cut into quarters lengthwise. Wash leeks well. Fold a 36×18-inch piece of heavy foil in half to make an 18-inch square. Place leeks in center of foil. Drizzle with the remaining olive oil and the water. Sprinkle with garlic, salt, and pepper. Bring up opposite edges of foil and seal with a double fold. Fold remaining edges together to completely enclose leeks, leaving space for steam to build.

3 *For a charcoal grill,* grill leeks on the rack of an uncovered grill directly over medium coals about 15 minutes or until leeks are tender. (*For a gas grill,* preheat grill. Reduce heat to medium. Place leeks on grill rack over heat. Cover and grill as above.)

4 Transfer leeks to a serving platter. Drizzle with dressing. Sprinkle with blue cheese and

the remaining tarragon. Serve warm or at room temperature. Makes 4 side-dish servings.

Nutrition Facts per serving: 156 calories, 10 g total fat (3 g saturated fat), 6 mg cholesterol, 330 mg sodium, 16 g carbohydrate, 6 g fiber, 4 g protein. Daily Values: 2% vit. A, 13% vit. C, 8% calcium, 14% iron.

# Orzo-and-Spinach-Stuffed Portobellos

**Prep:** 20 minutes   **Grill:** 15 minutes

*The best portobellos to buy for this dish have caps that are thick and almost bowl-shaped. If you can, avoid portobellos that have opened up and resemble big saucers. They taste fine, but stuffing tends to roll off of them.*

  4 **cups water**
  1 **tablespoon instant chicken bouillon granules**
  ½ **cup orzo (rosamarina)**
  1 **10-ounce package frozen chopped spinach, thawed and well drained**
  1 **cup shredded Italian cheese blend or smoked mozzarella cheese (4 ounces)**
  2 **tablespoons chopped walnuts, toasted**
  ⅛ **teaspoon pepper**
  6 **3½-inch fresh portobello mushroom caps**
  1 **tablespoon olive oil**
  1 **clove garlic, minced**
  1 **small yellow or red sweet pepper, quartered lengthwise**

**1** In a medium saucepan bring water and bouillon granules to boiling; stir in orzo. Boil gently for 5 to 8 minutes or until orzo is tender but still firm; drain. In a medium bowl combine orzo, spinach, cheese, walnuts, and pepper; set aside.

**2** Rinse mushroom caps. Gently pat dry with paper towels. Combine oil and garlic; brush over mushrooms and sweet pepper. Sprinkle lightly with salt and pepper.

**3** *For a charcoal grill,* grill sweet pepper on the rack of an uncovered grill directly over medium coals for 7 minutes. Turn sweet pepper. Add mushrooms, gill sides down, to grill. Grill for 3 to 4 minutes more or until pepper is tender. Remove vegetables from grill. Chop pepper and stir into orzo mixture. Place mushrooms, gill sides up, on a piece of heavy foil. Fill with orzo mixture. Return to grill. Grill for 5 to 8 minutes or until heated through and cheese is melted. (*For a gas grill,* preheat grill. Reduce heat to medium. Place mushrooms, gill sides down, and sweet peppers on grill rack over heat. Cover and grill as above.) Serve immediately. Makes 6 side-dish servings.

Nutrition Facts per serving: 178 calories, 9 g total fat (3 g saturated fat), 14 mg cholesterol, 297 mg sodium, 17 g carbohydrate, 2 g fiber, 9 g protein. Daily Values: 26% vit. A, 27% vit. C, 13% calcium, 13% iron.

**Sizzlin' Solutions**

**Toasting nuts for recipes is easy, especially when you use your microwave. Place ½ to 1 cup nuts in a 2-cup glass measure. Cook, uncovered, on 100 percent power (high) until light brown, stirring after 2 minutes, then every 30 seconds. Cook from 2 to 4 minutes, watching carefully. Nuts will continue to toast as they stand.**

## GARLICKY MUSHROOMS

**Prep:** 15 minutes   **Grill:** 6 minutes

*Ingredients, like people, are sometimes just meant for each other. That's certainly the case with garlic, butter, and mushrooms. Portobellos, with their rich, meaty flavor, put butter and garlic to especially good use. One taste and you may move this side dish to the center of the plate.*

 1 pound fresh portobello mushrooms
 ¼ cup butter, melted
 3 cloves garlic, minced
 ¼ teaspoon salt
 ⅛ teaspoon pepper
 1 tablespoon snipped fresh chives

1 Cut off the mushroom stems even with the caps; discard stems. Rinse mushroom caps. Gently pat dry with paper towels.

2 In a small bowl stir together butter, garlic, salt, and pepper; brush over mushrooms.

3 *For a charcoal grill*, grill mushrooms on the rack of an uncovered grill directly over medium coals for 6 to 8 minutes or until mushrooms are just tender, turning once halfway through grilling. (*For a gas grill*, preheat grill. Reduce heat to medium. Place mushrooms on grill rack over heat. Cover and grill as above.)

4 To serve, sprinkle mushrooms with chives. Makes 4 side-dish servings.

Nutrition Facts per serving: 133 calories, 12 g total fat (7 g saturated fat), 31 mg cholesterol, 252 mg sodium, 6 g carbohydrate, 2 g fiber, 3 g protein. Daily Values: 10% vit. A, 9% vit. C, 1% calcium, 13% iron.

# Onion Blossoms

**Prep:** 15 minutes   **Grill:** 35 minutes

*Sweet onions, such as Vidalia and Walla Walla, are mellow enough to eat raw, but they move into the fast lane when "baked" on the grill with butter, mustard, and little hot sauce. They're especially good with grilled steak or burgers.*

 4 medium sweet onions (4 to
    5 ounces each)
 1 tablespoon margarine or butter,
    melted
 1 teaspoon Dijon-style mustard
 ⅛ teaspoon bottled hot pepper sauce
 1 tablespoon brown sugar
    Pepper

1 Peel onions; cut almost through each onion, forming 8 wedges. Fold four 24×18-inch pieces of heavy foil in half crosswise; trim into 12-inch squares. Place each onion in center of foil square. In a small bowl stir together the margarine or butter, mustard, and hot pepper sauce. Drizzle mixture over onions. Sprinkle with brown sugar. Bring up opposite edges of foil and seal with a double fold. Fold remaining edges together to completely enclose onions, leaving space for steam to build.

2 *For a charcoal grill*, arrange medium-hot coals around a drip pan. Test for medium heat above the pan. Place onion packets on grill rack over drip pan. Cover and grill about 25 minutes or until onions are nearly tender. Make a 2-inch opening in the top of each packet. Cover and grill about 10 minutes more or until the onions are lightly browned. [*For a gas grill*, preheat grill. Reduce heat to medium. Adjust for indirect cooking (see page 10). Grill as above.] Remove onion blossoms from foil packets; sprinkle with pepper. Makes 4 side-dish servings.

Nutrition Facts per serving: 83 calories, 3 g total fat (1 g saturated fat), 0 mg cholesterol, 70 mg sodium, 13 g carbohydrate, 2 g fiber, 1 g protein. Daily Values: 3% vit. A, 8% vit. C, 2% calcium, 2% iron.

## SWEET PEPPER STIR-FRY

**Prep:** 15 minutes   **Grill:** 8 minutes
**Special Equipment:** Grill wok

   Nonstick cooking spray
3 medium red, yellow, and/or green
   sweet peppers, cut into thin
   strips
2 green onions, cut into 2-inch pieces
1 fresh jalapeño pepper, seeded and
   cut into thin strips
1 teaspoon toasted sesame oil
1 teaspoon grated fresh ginger
1 clove garlic, minced
⅛ teaspoon salt
¼ cup coarsely chopped honey-
   roasted peanuts

**1** Lightly coat an unheated grill wok with
nonstick cooking spray.

**2** *For a charcoal grill,* preheat the grill wok
on the rack of an uncovered grill directly
over medium coals for 15 seconds. Add the
sweet peppers, green onions, and jalapeño
pepper to grill wok. Stir-fry for 8 to
10 minutes or until vegetables are crisp-
tender. *(For a gas grill,* preheat grill. Reduce
heat to medium. Preheat the grill wok on grill
rack over heat for 15 seconds. Add the sweet
peppers, green onions, and jalapeño pepper to
grill wok. Stir-fry as above.)

**3** Transfer to a serving bowl. In a small bowl
stir together the sesame oil, ginger, garlic,
and salt. Drizzle over the vegetables and toss
to combine. To serve, sprinkle with peanuts.
Makes 4 to 6 side-dish servings.

Nutrition Facts per serving: 76 calories,
5 g total fat (1 g saturated fat), 0 mg cholesterol,
91 mg sodium, 8 g carbohydrate, 2 g fiber,
2 g protein. Daily values: 18% vit. A, 184% vit. C,
3% iron.

# Oriental Green Beans

**Prep:** 10 minutes   **Grill:** 8 minutes
**Special Equipment:** Grill wok

2 tablespoons soy sauce
1 tablespoon water
⅛ teaspoon ground ginger
⅛ teaspoon pepper
   Nonstick cooking spray
2 cups bias-sliced green beans
½ cup sliced water chestnuts
2 tablespoons sliced or slivered
   almonds, toasted

**1** In a small bowl stir together soy sauce,
water, ginger, and pepper; set aside.

**2** Lightly coat an unheated grill wok with
nonstick cooking spray.

**3** *For a charcoal grill,* preheat grill wok on
the rack of an uncovered grill directly over
medium coals for 15 seconds. Add green
beans to grill wok. Stir-fry 8 to 10 minutes or
until crisp-tender. *(For a gas grill,* preheat
grill. Reduce heat to medium. Preheat grill
wok on grill rack over heat 15 seconds. Add
green beans to grill wok. Stir-fry as above.)

**4** Transfer to a serving bowl; add water
chestnuts. Drizzle soy sauce mixture over
the beans; toss to coat. To serve, sprinkle with
almonds. Makes 4 side-dish servings.

Nutrition Facts per serving: 70 calories,
2 g total fat (0 g saturated fat), 0 mg cholesterol,
519 mg sodium, 11 g carbohydrate, 2 g fiber,
3 g protein. Daily values: 4% vit. A, 12% vit. C,
3% calcium, 8% iron.

*Grilling Know-How*

**Grill woks are similar to grill
trays, except they have higher
sides, allowing you to turn
foods with greater abandon.
They are typically made of
nonstick enamel-coated metal
with small holes in the bottom
and sides to allow heat and
smoke to penetrate the food,
while preventing it from
falling into the fire. To use a
grill wok, oil it lightly and
place it directly on the grill
rack. Have a couple of long-
handled spatulas or spoons
ready for stirring.**

Peppers Stuffed with Goat Cheese

## PEPPERS STUFFED WITH GOAT CHEESE

**Prep:** 15 minutes  **Grill:** 10 minutes

*For a tantalizing twist on stuffed peppers, mix equal parts crumbled goat cheese and shredded Monterey Jack. Add fresh herbs and melt to perfection in sweet pepper halves. Serve with a good steak and a hearty red wine, such as a French Rhône wine or Australian Shiraz.*

    1 ounce soft goat cheese (chèvre)
    ¼ cup shredded Monterey Jack
        cheese (1 ounce)
    1 tablespoon snipped fresh chives
    1 tablespoon snipped fresh basil or
        1 teaspoon dried basil, crushed
    2 medium red, yellow, and/or green
        sweet peppers, quartered
        lengthwise

**1** For cheese mixture, in a small bowl combine goat cheese, Monterey Jack cheese, chives, and basil. Set aside.

**2** *For a charcoal grill,* grill sweet peppers on the rack of an uncovered grill directly over medium-hot coals about 8 minutes or until peppers are crisp-tender and beginning to brown, turning once halfway through grilling. (*For a gas grill,* preheat grill. Reduce heat to medium-hot. Place peppers on grill rack over heat. Cover and grill as above.) Remove peppers from grill.

**3** Spoon cheese mixture into sweet pepper pieces; return to grill. Grill for 2 to 3 minutes more or until cheese is melted. Serve stuffed peppers immediately. Makes 4 side-dish servings.

Nutrition Facts per serving: 60 calories, 4 g total fat (2 g saturated fat), 13 mg cholesterol, 80 mg sodium, 3 g carbohydrate, 0 g fiber, 3 g protein. Daily Values: 30% vit. A, 104% vit. C, 4% calcium.

## Jasmine Mint Tea Rice with Peas

**Prep:** 20 minutes  **Grill:** 25 minutes

*You've probably cooked with wine, and perhaps beer, but maybe not tea. This exceptional combination of sweet peas, mint tea, and the subtly aromatic jasmine rice is the perfect way to bring springtime to any meal.*

    1 bag mint-flavored tea
    1¼ cups boiling water
    1 cup jasmine rice
    1 tablespoon margarine or butter
    ½ teaspoon salt
    ½ cup fresh shelled or thawed frozen
        peas
    2 teaspoons snipped fresh mint

**1** Place tea bag in a small glass bowl. Pour boiling water over tea. Cover; let stand for 5 minutes. Remove tea bag and discard. Meanwhile, fold a 36×18-inch piece of heavy foil in half to make an 18-inch square. Bring up all sides of foil to form a pouch.

**2** Place uncooked rice in the center of the pouch. Place margarine on top of rice; sprinkle with salt. Carefully pour brewed tea over rice. Bring edges of foil together and seal tightly to form a pouch, leaving space for steam to build.

**3** *For a charcoal grill,* grill rice on the rack of an uncovered grill directly over medium-hot coals about 25 minutes or until liquid is absorbed and rice is tender. (*For a gas grill,* preheat grill. Reduce heat to medium-hot. Place rice on grill rack over heat. Cover and grill as above.)

**4** Remove rice from grill. Carefully open packet. Add peas. Seal packet and let stand for 10 minutes. Just before serving, toss with a fork. Sprinkle with fresh mint. Makes 4 side-dish servings.

Nutrition Facts per serving: 184 calories, 0 g total fat, 0 mg cholesterol, 270 mg sodium, 40 g carbohydrate, 1 g fiber, 4 g protein. Daily Values: 1% vit. A, 4% vit. C, 1% calcium, 16% iron.

## BUTTERMILK MASHED GRILLED POTATOES

**Prep:** 10 minutes    **Grill:** 50 minutes

*Maybe it's just their buttery color, but we do think that Yukon gold or Finnish yellow potatoes taste creamier than other varieties. And when you cook them on the grill, they acquire a roasted flavor that will make these mashed potatoes a summertime staple.*

> 6 medium yellow potatoes (about 2 pounds total), such as Yukon gold or Finnish yellow
> 1 teaspoon cooking oil
> ¾ cup buttermilk or milk
> 3 tablespoons margarine or butter
> ¼ teaspoon salt
> ¼ teaspoon ground white or black pepper

1 Scrub potatoes thoroughly with a brush; pat dry. Prick potatoes with a fork. Rub potatoes with oil.

2 *For a charcoal grill,* arrange medium-hot coals around edge of grill. Test for medium heat above center of grill. Place potatoes on grill rack over center of grill. Cover and grill for 50 to 60 minutes or until potatoes are tender. [*For a gas grill,* preheat grill. Reduce heat to medium. Adjust for indirect cooking (see page 10). Grill as above.]

3 A few minutes before potatoes are done, in a small saucepan combine buttermilk or milk, margarine or butter, salt, and pepper. Heat over low heat until warm, stirring frequently (do not boil).

4 When potatoes are done, cool slightly. If desired, peel potatoes. Transfer potatoes to a large mixing bowl; mash with a potato masher or beat with an electric mixer on low speed. Gradually add warmed buttermilk mixture, mashing or beating until smooth. Makes 6 side-dish servings.

Nutrition Facts per serving: 216 calories, 7 g total fat (1 g saturated fat), 1 mg cholesterol, 199 mg sodium, 35 g carbohydrate, 1 g fiber, 5 g protein. Daily Values: 7% vit. A, 32% vit. C, 5% calcium, 16% iron.

## Two-Potato Packet

**Prep:** 15 minutes    **Grill:** 30 minutes

*Sweet potatoes weren't designed just for marshmallows and Thanksgiving. You'll find sweet potatoes are great on the grill year round.*

> 2 medium sweet potatoes, peeled and thinly sliced (12 ounces)
> 4 small red potatoes, thinly sliced (8 ounces)
> 4 onion slices, separated into rings
> 2 tablespoons margarine or butter, cut into small pieces
> 4 small sprigs of fresh rosemary, basil, or oregano
> ⅛ teaspoon salt
> ⅛ teaspoon pepper
> ½ cup shredded smoked provolone or Gouda cheese (2 ounces)

1 Fold four 24×18-inch pieces of heavy foil in half to make 18×12-inch rectangles. Divide sweet potatoes and red potatoes among foil rectangles, alternating and overlapping the slices. Top with onion, margarine, herb, salt, and pepper. Bring up opposite edges of foil and seal with a double fold. Fold remaining edges together to completely enclose vegetables, leaving space for steam to build.

2 *For a charcoal grill,* arrange medium-hot coals around edge of grill. Test for medium heat above center of grill. Place vegetables on grill rack over center of grill. Cover and grill about 30 minutes or until potatoes are tender. [*For a gas grill,* preheat grill. Reduce heat to medium. Adjust for indirect cooking (see page 10). Grill as above.]

3 Remove packets from grill. Open packets; sprinkle vegetables with cheese. Let stand for 1 to 2 minutes or until cheese is melted. Makes 4 side-dish servings.

Nutrition Facts per serving: 234 calories, 10 g total fat (4 g saturated fat), 10 mg cholesterol, 260 mg sodium, 32 g carbohydrate, 3 g fiber, 6 g protein. Daily Values: 153% vit. A, 42% vit. C, 11% calcium, 7% iron.

## SPICY POTATO SLICES

**Prep:** 10 minutes **Grill:** 20 minutes

*Sometimes you have to give spuds a kick. And this spice mixture is just the ticket for creamy yellow potatoes such as Yukon gold or Finnish yellow. If you want to go above and beyond, offer a little sour cream and fresh chives on the side.*

  1 teaspoon dried thyme, crushed
  ½ teaspoon garlic salt
  ½ teaspoon paprika
  ⅛ teaspoon pepper
  3 large yellow potatoes (such as Yukon gold or Finnish yellow) or 2 russet potatoes (about 1 pound total), cut into ¼-inch slices
  1 sweet onion (such as Vidalia or Walla Walla), sliced
  2 tablespoons olive oil
  ¼ cup light dairy sour cream (optional)
  1 tablespoon snipped fresh chives (optional)

**1** For seasoning mixture, combine thyme, garlic salt, paprika, and pepper; set aside. Fold a 36×18-inch piece of heavy foil in half to make an 18-inch square. Place the potato slices and onion slices in center of foil. Drizzle with oil. Sprinkle with seasoning mixture. Bring up opposite edges of foil and seal with a double fold. Fold remaining edges together to completely enclose vegetables, leaving space for steam to build.

**2** *For a charcoal grill*, grill potatoes on the rack of an uncovered grill directly over medium coals for 20 to 25 minutes or until potatoes are tender. (*For a gas grill*, preheat grill. Reduce heat to medium. Place potatoes on grill rack over heat. Cover; grill as above.)

**3** If desired, serve potatoes with sour cream and chives. Makes 4 side-dish servings.

Nutrition Facts per serving: 186 calories, 7 g total fat (1 g saturated fat), 0 mg cholesterol, 266 mg sodium, 29 g carbohydrate, 1 g fiber, 3 g protein. Daily Values: 1% vit. A, 29% vit. C, 1% calcium, 11% iron.

# Sweet Potatoes and Apples

**Prep:** 20 minutes **Grill:** 20 minutes

*How sweet it is! Sweet potatoes are a treat you thought only came around at Thanksgiving time. Well, you can start thanking this recipe for bringing them to summertime fare for the grill!*

  2 medium sweet potatoes, peeled and cut into 1-inch cubes
  2 medium cooking apples, cored and cut into eighths
  ¼ cup maple-flavored syrup
  1 teaspoon finely shredded lemon peel
  ¼ teaspoon ground cinnamon
  ⅛ teaspoon salt
  ⅛ teaspoon pepper

**1** In a covered medium saucepan cook sweet potatoes in a small amount of boiling water for 10 minutes. Drain.

**2** Fold a 36×18-inch piece of heavy foil in half to make an 18-inch square. Place the sweet potatoes and apple pieces in center of foil. In a small bowl stir together the syrup, lemon peel, cinnamon, salt, and pepper. Drizzle over apples and potatoes. Bring up opposite edges of foil and seal with a double fold. Fold remaining edges together to completely enclose potatoes and apples, leaving space for steam to build.

**3** *For a charcoal grill*, grill foil packet on the grill rack of an uncovered grill directly over medium coals for 20 to 25 minutes or until apples are tender. (*For a gas grill*, preheat grill. Reduce heat to medium. Place foil packets on grill rack over heat. Cover; grill as above.) Makes 4 servings.

Nutrition Facts per serving: 144 calories, 0 g total fat (0 g saturated fat), 0 mg cholesterol, 73 mg sodium, 36 g carbohydrate, 3 g fiber, 1 g protein. Daily Values: 129% vit. A, 30% vit. C, 2% calcium, 2% iron.

## SMOKED PORTOBELLO AND WALNUT PASTA

**Prep:** 20 minutes    **Soak:** 1 hour
**Grill:** 30 minutes

*The art of grilling lies in knowing when to relax. For instance, when the wood chips start smoking, resist the natural urge to lift the lid of your grill. Relax instead, for you want to trap all that delicious wood smoke to flavor the vegetables.*

  4 to 6 hickory wood chunks or 4 cups
       hickory wood chips
  3 tablespoons olive oil
  2 tablespoons white wine vinegar
  1 tablespoon snipped fresh tarragon
  1 tablespoon snipped fresh thyme
  2 cloves garlic, minced
  ½ teaspoon black pepper
  ¼ teaspoon salt
  8 ounces fresh portobello
       mushrooms
  2 medium zucchini, halved
       lengthwise
  2 medium red sweet peppers, halved
       lengthwise, or 4 plum tomatoes,
       halved lengthwise and seeded
  ¾ cup walnut pieces
  2 cups packaged dried bow tie pasta
       (about 6 ounces)
  ½ cup finely shredded Parmesan
       cheese or 1 cup crumbled feta
       cheese
  ¼ cup fresh basil cut into thin strips

1 At least 1 hour before grilling, soak wood chunks in enough water to cover. For dressing, in a small bowl combine olive oil, vinegar, tarragon, thyme, garlic, black pepper, and salt; set aside. Cut off mushroom stems even with caps; discard stems. Lightly rinse mushroom caps and gently pat dry with paper towels.

2 Drain wood chunks. *For a charcoal grill,* arrange medium-hot coals around a drip pan. Test for medium heat above the pan. Sprinkle wood chunks over coals. Place mushrooms, zucchini, and sweet peppers on grill rack over drip pan; brush with some of the dressing. Place walnuts on a piece of heavy foil; add to grill. Cover and grill for 15 minutes. Remove walnuts from grill. Turn vegetables; brush with remaining dressing. Cover and grill about 15 minutes more or until peppers are crisp-tender and mushrooms are tender. [*For a gas grill,* preheat grill. Reduce heat to medium. Adjust for indirect cooking (see page 10). Grill as above.]

3 Meanwhile, cook pasta according to package directions; drain. Return pasta to hot pan. Cut vegetables into bite-size pieces. Add grilled vegetables, walnuts, cheese, and basil to cooked pasta; toss to combine. Serve immediately. Makes 6 side-dish servings.

Nutrition Facts per serving: 316 calories,
20 g total fat (2 g saturated fat), 31 mg cholesterol,
205 mg sodium, 27 g carbohydrate, 3 g fiber,
11 g protein. Daily Values: 20% vit. A, 76% vit. C,
9% calcium, 17% iron.

## Did You Know?

Fresh herbs turn ordinary dishes into extraordinary ones. Herbs have their own distinct flavors, but you can have one step in for another. Try these substitutions:
- **Sage: Use savory, marjoram, or rosemary**
- **Basil: Substitute oregano or thyme**
- **Thyme: Basil, marjoram, oregano, or savory**
- **Mint: Substitute basil, marjoram, or rosemary**
- **Rosemary: Try thyme, tarragon, or savory**
- **Cilantro: Substitute parsley**

Smoked Portobello and Walnut Pasta

# Fire-Roasted Acorn Squash

**Prep:** 10 minutes **Grill:** 45 minutes

*Falling leaves and chilly evenings set the stage for hard winter squash. But rather than the usual brown sugar-and-butter treatment, try basting rings of squash with tarragon butter, then grilling them. They're delicious with grilled pork and a dry white wine.*

    1 tablespoon olive oil
    ½ teaspoon salt
    ¼ teaspoon pepper
    2 small acorn squash, cut crosswise
        into 1-inch rings and seeded
    2 tablespoons margarine or butter,
        melted
    2 teaspoons snipped fresh tarragon
        or ½ teaspoon dried tarragon,
        crushed

1 In a small bowl combine oil, salt, and pepper; brush over squash rings. In another small bowl stir together melted margarine or butter and tarragon; set aside.

2 *For a charcoal grill,* arrange medium-hot coals around a drip pan. Test for medium heat above the pan. Place squash rings on grill rack over drip pan. Cover and grill about 45 minutes or until squash is tender, turning squash occasionally and brushing with margarine mixture after 30 minutes of grilling. [*For a gas grill,* preheat grill. Reduce heat to medium. Adjust for indirect cooking (see page 10). Grill as above.] Makes 4 side-dish servings.

Nutrition Facts per serving: 156 calories, 9 g total fat (2 g saturated fat), 0 mg cholesterol, 332 mg sodium, 20 g carbohydrate, 4 g fiber, 2 g protein. Daily Values: 138% vit. A, 48% vit. C, 6% calcium, 8% iron.

# TOMATOES WITH PESTO

**Prep:** 15 minutes **Grill:** 15 minutes

*Celebrate the arrival of tomatoes with this easy side dish. Visit a farmer's market for the best selection of red, yellow, and orange tomatoes. At the height of summer you can get them for a song, but they'll win you a chorus of praise.*

    3 to 5 small to medium red, orange,
        and/or yellow tomatoes, cored
        and halved crosswise
    2 tablespoons pesto
    6 thin onion slices
    ½ cup shredded Monterey Jack
        cheese (2 ounces)
    ⅓ cup smoky-flavored whole
        almonds, chopped
    2 tablespoons snipped fresh parsley

1 Using a spoon, hollow out the top ¼ inch of tomato halves. Top with pesto, then onion slices. Place tomatoes in a foil pie plate.

2 *For a charcoal grill,* arrange medium-hot coals around edge of grill. Test for medium heat above center of grill. Place tomatoes on grill rack over center of grill. Cover and grill for 10 to 15 minutes or until tomatoes are heated through. [*For a gas grill,* preheat grill. Reduce heat to medium. Adjust for indirect cooking (see page 10). Grill as above.]

3 Meanwhile, in a small bowl stir together cheese, almonds, and parsley. Sprinkle over tomatoes. Cover and grill about 5 minutes more or until cheese is melted. Sprinkle lightly with salt and pepper. Serve immediately. Makes 6 side-dish servings.

Nutrition Facts per serving: 132 calories, 10 g total fat (2 g saturated fat), 9 mg cholesterol, 119 mg sodium, 6 g carbohydrate, 2 g fiber, 5 g protein. Daily Values: 7% vit. A, 24% vit. C, 8% calcium, 5% iron.

# Zucchini with Tomatoes

**Prep:** 10 minutes  **Grill:** 17 minutes
**Stand:** 5 minutes  **Chill:** 2 hours

*When everyone else is wondering what to do
with their abundant supply of zucchini in the
garden, you'll be standing around watching it
grow so that you can pick it for this side dish.*

  2 **medium zucchini**
  4 **large roma tomatoes**
    **Olive oil**
  2 **large red and/or green sweet**
    **peppers, quartered and seeded**
½ **cup balsamic vinegar**
  2 **tablespoons orange juice**
  1 **tablespoon honey**
  1 **tablespoon snipped fresh basil**
    **Dash dried oregano, crushed**

**1** Bias-cut zucchini into ½-inch-thick slices.
Cut tomatoes into ½-inch-thick slices.
Brush both sides of zucchini and tomato
slices with olive oil.

**2** *For a charcoal grill,* grill vegetables on the
grill rack of an uncovered grill directly
over medium coals for 2 to 3 minutes or until
lightly golden and tender, turning once. Place
in a bowl. Grill sweet peppers about
15 minutes or until skins have blistered and
browned. (*For a gas grill,* preheat grill.
Reduce heat to medium. Place zucchini and
tomatoes, then peppers on grill rack over
heat. Cover and grill as above.)

**3** Wrap sweet peppers in foil and set aside
for 5 to 10 minutes. Using a small knife,
peel skins off sweet peppers. Add peppers to
zucchini and tomatoes in bowl. (If desired,
cover and refrigerate for 2 to 24 hours.)

**4** In a small bowl combine vinegar, orange
juice, and honey. Stir in basil and oregano.
Drizzle over vegetables. Serves 6 to 8.

Nutrition Facts per serving: 71 calories,
2 g total fat (0 g saturated fat), 0 mg cholesterol,
10 mg sodium, 14 g carbohydrate, 2 g fiber,
1 g protein. Daily Values: 22% vit. A, 100% vit. C,
8%iron.

# JAMAICAN GLAZED PLANTAINS

**Prep:** 10 minutes  **Grill:** 15 minutes

*The plantain, a larger variety of the banana, is
frequently used in Latin American cooking.
Because it is usually best when cooked, it is often
called a "cooking banana." The mild squashlike
flavor is enjoyed in Latin American countries to
the same degree that we enjoy potatoes.*

    **Cooking oil**
  3 **tablespoons orange marmalade**
  2 **tablespoons brown sugar**
  2 **tablespoons frozen pineapple-**
    **banana juice concentrate or**
    **pineapple-orange juice**
    **concentrate, thawed**
  1 **teaspoon ground allspice**
½ **to 1 teaspoon bottled habañero**
    **sauce or 1 to 2 teaspoons bottled**
    **Caribbean-style hot sauce**
  3 **large, ripe plantains**

**1** Lightly oil a purchased foil pan (about an
8-inch square) with cooking oil; set aside.

**2** In a small bowl stir together marmalade,
brown sugar, juice concentrate, allspice,
and hot sauce. Cut peel from plantains; halve
lengthwise and place in a single layer in the
oiled pan. Drizzle with marmalade mixture.

**3** *For a charcoal grill,* grill plantains in foil
pan on the grill rack of an uncovered grill
directly over medium-hot coals for
15 minutes or until just tender and glaze is
slightly thickened, turning once. (*For a gas
grill,* preheat grill. Reduce heat to medium-
hot. Place plantains on grill rack over heat.
Cover and grill as above.)

**4** To serve, spoon glaze over plantains.
Makes 6 servings.

Nutrition Facts per serving: 161 calories,
1 g total fat (0 g saturated fat), 0 mg cholesterol,
8 mg sodium, 14 g carbohydrate, 2 g fiber,
1 g protein. Daily Values: 10% vit. A, 33% vit. C.

# Smoky Gazpacho

**Prep:** 40 minutes  **Soak:** 1 hour
**Grill:** 40 minutes  **Chill:** 2 hours

*You can adjust a chile pepper's kick through its seeds. For milder soup, remove all the seeds from the pepper; for a hotter soup, leave in a few.*

2 cups hickory wood chips
5 medium red sweet peppers, quartered lengthwise
4 large tomatoes, halved lengthwise and seeded
1 medium onion, cut into ½-inch slices
3 or 4 fresh jalapeño peppers, halved lengthwise and seeded
2 tablespoons olive oil
2 cloves garlic, minced
1 14½-ounce can chicken broth
¾ cup chopped seeded cucumber
1 tablespoon snipped fresh cilantro
1 tablespoon lime juice
¼ teaspoon salt
¼ teaspoon black pepper
Lime slices (optional)

1 At least 1 hour before grilling, soak wood chips in enough water to cover. Brush sweet peppers, tomatoes, onion, and jalapeño peppers with olive oil.

2 Drain wood chips. *For a charcoal grill,* place medium-low coals in bottom of grill. Sprinkle wood chips over coals. Place vegetables on grill rack directly over coals. Cover and grill until vegetables are tender, turning once halfway through grilling. (Allow about 40 minutes for onion, 30 minutes for sweet peppers, and 20 minutes for tomatoes and jalapeño peppers.) (*For a gas grill,* preheat grill. Reduce heat to medium-low. Place vegetables on grill rack over heat. Grill as above.) Remove vegetables from grill.

3 Wrap sweet and jalapeño peppers in foil and let stand for 20 minutes. Remove and discard pepper skins. Place about half of the sweet peppers and jalapeño peppers, onion, tomatoes, and garlic in a blender container or food processor bowl. Cover and blend or process until smooth. Transfer to a large storage container. Repeat with the remaining vegetables and garlic. Add to storage container. Stir in chicken broth, cucumber, cilantro, lime juice, salt, and black pepper. Cover and chill gazpacho for 2 to 24 hours.

4 To serve, ladle into chilled bowls or mugs. If desired, garnish with lime slices. Makes 8 side-dish servings.

Nutrition Facts per serving: 78 calories, 4 g total fat (1 g saturated fat), 0 mg cholesterol, 240 mg sodium, 9 g carbohydrate, 2 g fiber, 3 g protein. Daily Values: 40% vit. A, 181% vit. C, 1% calcium, 5% iron.

## HERB-GRILLED TOMATOES

**Prep:** 15 minutes  **Grill:** 10 minutes

4 small tomatoes
3 tablespoons dairy sour cream or plain yogurt
1 tablespoon snipped fresh basil or 1 teaspoon dried basil, crushed
1 tablespoon fine dry bread crumbs
1 tablespoon finely shredded Parmesan cheese

1 Remove cores from tomatoes; cut tomatoes in half crosswise. Spread cut sides of tomatoes with sour cream or yogurt. Sprinkle each tomato with basil, bread crumbs, and Parmesan cheese; arrange in a foil pie pan.

2 *For a charcoal grill,* arrange medium-hot coals around a drip pan. Test for medium heat above the pan. Place foil pan of tomatoes on grill over drip pan. Cover and grill for 10 to 15 minutes or until tomatoes are heated through. [*For a gas grill,* preheat grill. Reduce heat to medium. Adjust for indirect cooking (see page 10). Grill as above.] Makes 4 side-dish servings.

Nutrition Facts per serving: 56 calories, 3 g total fat (1 g saturated fat), 6 mg cholesterol, 46 mg sodium, 6 g carbohydrate, 1 g fiber, 2 g protein. Daily Values: 8% vitamin A, 29% vitamin C, 2% calcium, 3% iron.

Smoky Gazpacho

# Pasta with Grilled Tomato Sauce

**Prep:** 20 minutes   **Grill:** 10 minutes

*The smaller plum tomato tends to be meatier than its big beefsteak cousin. That's why plum tomatoes are favored for making sauces.*

  2 cups packaged dried cavatelli
     (about 6 ounces)
  2 tablespoons olive oil
  1 tablespoon balsamic vinegar
  2 cloves garlic, minced
  ¼ teaspoon salt
  ¼ teaspoon crushed red pepper
  ¼ teaspoon freshly ground black
     pepper
  1 large red onion, cut into ½-inch
     slices
  6 plum tomatoes, halved lengthwise
  1 tablespoon fresh basil leaves cut
     into thin strips

1 Cook pasta according to package directions. Drain and keep warm. Meanwhile, in a small bowl combine oil, vinegar, garlic, salt, red pepper, and black pepper. Brush oil mixture over onion slices and tomato halves.

2 *For a charcoal grill,* grill onion and tomatoes on the rack of an uncovered grill directly over medium coals until onion is crisp-tender and tomatoes are heated through, turning and brushing once with oil mixture halfway through grilling. (Allow about 10 minutes for onion and about 5 minutes for tomatoes.) (*For a gas grill,* preheat grill. Reduce heat to medium. Place onion and tomatoes on grill rack over heat. Cover and grill as above.)

3 Chop the vegetables; place in a medium bowl. Add basil and any remaining oil mixture; toss gently to combine. Serve over cooked pasta. Makes 6 side-dish servings.

Nutrition Facts per serving: 174 calories, 5 g total fat (1 g saturated fat), 0 mg cholesterol, 97 mg sodium, 28 g carbohydrate, 2 g fiber, 5 g protein. Daily Values: 4% vit. A, 21% vit. C, 1% calcium, 10% iron.

# COUSCOUS WITH GRILLED VEGETABLES

**Prep:** 20 minutes   **Grill:** 10 minutes

*Couscous is a tiny, precooked pasta, making it practically instant. Besides being a friend to busy cooks, it is the perfect foil for grilled vegetables.*

  ¼ cup snipped fresh oregano
  ¼ cup snipped fresh parsley
  ¼ cup lemon juice
  3 tablespoons olive oil
  1 tablespoon water
  2 cloves garlic, minced
  2 red and/or green sweet peppers,
     quartered lengthwise
  1 medium red onion, cut into ½-inch
     slices
  2 small zucchini and/or yellow
     summer squash, halved
     lengthwise
  1 10-ounce package couscous
  ½ cup pistachio nuts or dry roasted
     peanuts (optional)

1 For dressing, in a small bowl combine oregano, parsley, lemon juice, oil, water, and garlic. Brush sweet peppers, onion, and zucchini and/or summer squash lightly with some of the dressing.

2 *For a charcoal grill,* grill vegetables on the rack of an uncovered grill directly over medium coals for 10 to 12 minutes or until vegetables are tender, turning occasionally. (*For a gas grill,* preheat grill. Reduce heat to medium. Place vegetables on grill rack over heat. Cover and grill as above.) Remove vegetables from grill; cool slightly.

3 Meanwhile, prepare couscous according to package directions. Coarsely chop vegetables; toss with couscous. Stir in remaining dressing. To serve, if desired, stir in nuts and season with salt and black pepper; toss gently. Makes 6 to 8 side-dish servings.

Nutrition Facts per serving: 259 calories, 7 g total fat (1 g saturated fat), 0 mg cholesterol, 32 mg sodium, 42 g carbohydrate, 8 g fiber, 7 g protein. Daily Values: 12% vit. A, 67% vit. C, 2% calcium, 6% iron.

# Vegetables with Dill Butter

**Prep:** 20 minutes **Grill:** 30 minutes

2 tablespoons butter or margarine
4 teaspoons snipped fresh dillweed
   or 1 teaspoon dried dillweed
¼ teaspoon salt
¼ teaspoon pepper
4 medium carrots, sliced (2 cups)
2 cups cubed potatoes
1 small yellow summer squash or
   zucchini, halved lengthwise and
   cut into ½-inch-thick slices
   (1 cup)
Nonstick cooking spray
4 slices bacon, crisp-cooked,
   drained, and crumbled, or ¼ cup
   diced cooked ham

**1** In a small saucepan melt butter or margarine. Remove from heat. Stir in dillweed, salt, and pepper. Set aside.

**2** Fold a 36×18-inch piece of heavy foil in half to make an 18-inch square. Lightly coat center of foil with nonstick cooking spray. Place vegetables in center of foil. Drizzle butter mixture over vegetables. Top with crumbled bacon or ham. Bring up opposite edges of foil and seal with a double fold. Fold remaining edges together to completely enclose vegetables, leaving space for steam to build.

**3** *For a charcoal grill,* grill vegetables on the rack of an uncovered grill directly over medium coals about 30 minutes or until vegetables are crisp-tender. (*For a gas grill,* preheat grill. Reduce heat to medium. Place vegetables on grill rack over heat. Cover and grill as above.) Serve immediately. Makes 4 to 5 side-dish servings.

Nutrition Facts per serving: 200 calories,
9 g total fat (5 g saturated fat), 21 mg cholesterol,
342 mg sodium, 26 g carbohydrate, 3 g fiber,
5 g protein. Daily Values: 165% vitamin A,
27% vitamin C, 3% calcium, 10% iron.

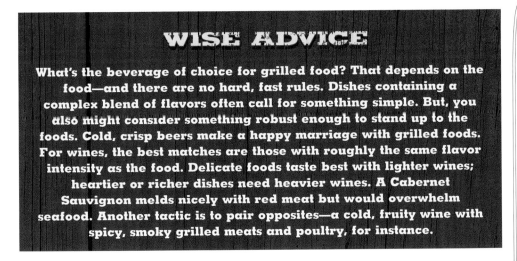

## WISE ADVICE

What's the beverage of choice for grilled food? That depends on the food—and there are no hard, fast rules. Dishes containing a complex blend of flavors often call for something simple. But, you also might consider something robust enough to stand up to the foods. Cold, crisp beers make a happy marriage with grilled foods. For wines, the best matches are those with roughly the same flavor intensity as the food. Delicate foods taste best with lighter wines; heartier or richer dishes need heavier wines. A Cabernet Sauvignon melds nicely with red meat but would overwhelm seafood. Another tactic is to pair opposites—a cold, fruity wine with spicy, smoky grilled meats and poultry, for instance.

## WINTER VEGETABLE PACKET

**Prep:** 20 minutes   **Grill:** 30 minutes

*Besides great flavor, another thing that makes "packet cooking" so appealing is that there is no pan to clean up. Another plus is the packet doesn't demand attention; it can sit off to one side while you grill your steaks to perfection.*

¼ cup margarine or butter, melted
2 teaspoons snipped fresh basil,
    thyme, or rosemary or
    ½ teaspoon dried basil, thyme,
    or rosemary, crushed
1 pound tiny new potatoes, cut into
    ¼-inch slices
4 medium carrots, cut into ½-inch
    pieces
1 medium green sweet pepper, cut
    into ½-inch strips
1 medium onion, thinly sliced

**1** In a small bowl stir together melted margarine or butter and desired herb; set aside. In a large bowl toss together the potatoes, carrots, sweet pepper, and onion.

**2** Fold a 36×18-inch piece of heavy foil in half to make an 18-inch square. Place the vegetables in center of foil. Drizzle herb mixture over vegetables. Sprinkle with salt and pepper. Bring up opposite edges of foil and seal with a double fold. Fold remaining edges together to completely enclose vegetables, leaving space for steam to build.

**3** *For a charcoal grill,* grill vegetables on the rack of an uncovered grill directly over medium coals for 30 to 35 minutes or until potatoes and carrots are tender. (*For a gas grill,* preheat grill. Reduce heat to medium. Place vegetables on grill rack over heat. Cover and grill as above.) Serve immediately. Makes 6 to 8 side-dish servings.

Nutrition Facts per serving: 176 calories,
8 g total fat (1 g saturated fat), 0 mg cholesterol,
171 mg sodium, 25 g carbohydrate, 3 g fiber,
3 g protein. Daily Values: 124% vit. A, 36% vit. C,
2% calcium, 1% iron.

**Summer Vegetable Packet:** Prepare Winter Vegetable Packet as directed, except substitute 8 ounces asparagus spears, trimmed and cut into 1-inch pieces; 1 medium red sweet pepper, cut into ½-inch strips; 1 small zucchini, cut into ½-inch slices; and 1 small yellow summer squash, cut into ½-inch slices for the potatoes, carrots, sweet pepper, and onion. Grill for 15 to 20 minutes. Makes 4 to 6 side-dish servings.

Nutrition Facts per serving: 124 calories,
12 g total fat (2 g saturated fat), 0 mg cholesterol,
203 mg sodium, 5 g carbohydrate, 2 g fiber,
2 g protein. Daily Values: 31% vit. A, 70% vit. C,
2% calcium, 3% iron.

## Vegetable Kabobs

**Prep:** 20 minutes   **Grill:** 10 minutes

*With the delicate flavor of baby vegetables, less is usually more. Here they are brushed with a rosemary-scented oil-and-vinegar dressing.*

8 tiny new potatoes, quartered
2 tablespoons water
8 baby sunburst squash
4 miniature red sweet peppers
    and/or 1 red sweet pepper, cut
    into 1-inch pieces
8 tiny red onions, halved, or 2 small
    red onions, each cut into
    8 wedges
8 baby zucchini or 1 small zucchini,
    halved lengthwise and sliced
¼ cup bottled oil-and-vinegar salad
    dressing
2 teaspoons snipped fresh rosemary
    or ½ teaspoon dried rosemary,
    crushed

**1** In a 2-quart microwave-safe casserole combine potatoes and water. Microwave, covered, on 100% power (high) for 5 minutes. Gently stir in sunburst squash, sweet peppers, and onions. Cook, covered, on high for 4 to 6 minutes or until nearly tender. Drain; cool slightly.

On eight 10-inch skewers, alternately thread the potatoes, sunburst squash, sweet peppers, onions, and zucchini. In a small bowl combine salad dressing and rosemary; brush over vegetables.

For a charcoal grill, grill kabobs on the rack of an uncovered grill directly over medium coals for 10 to 12 minutes or until vegetables are tender and browned, turning and brushing occasionally with dressing mixture. (For a gas grill, preheat grill. Reduce heat to medium. Place kabobs on grill rack over heat. Cover and grill as above.)

If desired, garnish with additional fresh rosemary. Makes 4 side-dish servings.

Nutrition Facts per serving: 161 calories, 8 g total fat (1 g saturated fat), 0 mg cholesterol, 217 mg sodium, 22 g carbohydrate, 2 g fiber, 3 g protein. Daily Values: 15% vit. A, 75% vit. C, 2% calcium, 7% iron.

## COUNTRY VEGETABLE MIX

**Prep:** 25 minutes    **Grill:** 20 minutes

*Tired of fussy flavor combinations? Weary of mile-high presentations? This recipe brings simple country flavors to your table with an assortment of farm-stand vegetables.*

    1½ cups sliced fennel
     1 cup sliced carrots
     8 ounces green beans, trimmed
     1 medium onion, cut into thin
        wedges
     ½ teaspoon salt
     ¼ teaspoon cracked black pepper
     2 tablespoons butter or olive oil
     2 tablespoons snipped fresh basil

Fold a 36×18-inch piece of heavy foil in half to make an 18-inch square. Place the vegetables in center of foil. Sprinkle with salt and pepper. Dot with butter or drizzle with olive oil. Bring up opposite edges of foil and seal with a double fold. Fold remaining edges together to completely enclose vegetables, leaving space for steam to build.

For a charcoal grill, grill vegetables on the rack of an uncovered grill directly over medium coals about 20 minutes or until vegetables are crisp-tender. (For a gas grill, preheat grill. Reduce heat to medium. Place vegetables on grill rack over heat. Cover and grill as above.) Open foil packet. Stir basil into vegetables. Makes 5 side-dish servings.

Nutrition Facts per serving: 81 calories, 5 g total fat (3 g saturated fat), 12 mg cholesterol, 292 mg sodium, 9 g carbohydrate, 9 g fiber, 2 g protein. Daily Values: 71% vit. A, 14% vit. C, 4% calcium, 5% iron.

### Did You Know?

**Fresh vegetables taste so great when grilled. A few tricks make it easy. If you use bamboo skewers, be sure to soak the skewers for 30 minutes first. Don't crowd the pieces; leave a small space (about ¼ inch) between pieces to ensure even grilling. Avoid pairing large hunks of meat with quick-cooking vegetables because they require different cooking times. Instead, make several skewers of meat and several skewers of vegetables so each can be removed from the grill when done. Cut the vegetables into uniform sizes and shapes so they will cook evenly. For those who like gadgets, look for grill baskets for kabobs—no skewers needed! Don't forget that leftover grilled vegetables are tasty added to everyday recipes. Stir them into pasta sauce, add to soups, stir into rice pilaf, or roll up in a tortilla.**

# Summer Squash Combo

**Prep:** 20 minutes  **Grill:** 5 minutes

*Walnut oil is prized by French cooks for its rich, full flavor. With a couple herbs and a drizzle of walnut oil, you will even have zucchini speaking perfect French in minutes.*

- 2 tablespoons walnut oil or olive oil
- 1 tablespoon olive oil
- 2 teaspoons snipped fresh rosemary or ½ teaspoon dried rosemary, crushed
- 1 clove garlic, minced
- ½ to 1 teaspoon crushed red pepper
- ½ teaspoon salt
- 2 medium red onions, cut crosswise into ¾-inch slices
- 2 medium zucchini, quartered lengthwise
- 2 medium yellow summer squash, quartered lengthwise

1 In a small bowl stir together walnut oil, the 1 tablespoon olive oil, the rosemary, garlic, red pepper, and salt. Brush the onions, zucchini, and yellow squash with some of the oil mixture.

2 *For a charcoal grill,* grill vegetables on the rack of an uncovered grill directly over medium to medium-hot coals for 5 to 6 minutes or until crisp-tender and lightly browned, turning and brushing once with the remaining oil mixture. (*For a gas grill,* preheat grill. Reduce heat to medium to medium-hot. Place vegetables on grill rack over heat. Cover and grill as above.) Serve immediately. Makes 4 to 6 side-dish servings.

Nutrition Facts per serving: 126 calories, 10 g total fat (1 g saturated fat), 0 mg cholesterol, 272 mg sodium, 8 g carbohydrate, 2 g fiber, 1 g protein. Daily Values: 4% vit. A, 12% vit. C, 2% calcium, 3% iron.

# PIQUANT BROCCOLI AND OLIVES

**Prep:** 15 minutes  **Marinate:** 10 minutes
**Grill:** 6 minutes

*You probably don't think of broccoli when you consider vegetables for the grill. But grilling gives it a great smoky flavor worth trying.*

- 3½ cups broccoli florets
- ½ cup pitted ripe olives
- ½ of a 2-ounce can anchovy fillets, drained and finely chopped (optional)
- 2 tablespoons snipped fresh oregano or Italian flat parsley
- 2 tablespoons red wine vinegar
- 2 tablespoons olive oil
- 5 cloves garlic, minced
- ½ teaspoon crushed red pepper
  Dash salt

1 In a large saucepan bring a small amount of water to boiling; add broccoli florets. Simmer, covered, for 2 minutes. Drain well. In a medium bowl combine broccoli and olives. For marinade, in a small bowl whisk together anchovies (if using), oregano, vinegar, oil, garlic, red pepper, and salt. Pour the marinade over the broccoli and olives. Marinate at room temperature for 10 minutes, stirring occasionally. Drain broccoli and olives; discard marinade.

2 On long metal skewers alternately thread broccoli florets and olives. *For a charcoal grill,* grill kabobs on the rack of an uncovered grill directly over medium coals for 6 to 8 minutes or until broccoli is lightly browned and tender, turning occasionally. (*For a gas grill,* preheat grill. Reduce heat to medium. Place kabobs on grill rack over heat. Cover and grill as above.) Makes 4 side-dish servings.

Nutrition Facts per serving: 91 calories, 8 g total fat (1 g saturated fat), 0 mg cholesterol, 125 mg sodium, 6 g carbohydrate, 3 g fiber, 3 g protein. Daily Values: 13% vit. A, 121% vit. C, 4% calcium, 6% iron.

Piquant Broccoli and Olives

# Corn Crunch Muffins

**Prep:** 15 minutes    **Grill:** 15 minutes

*A good way to bake during the summer months without heating up your kitchen is to keep a lid on it—on your grill, that is. The only trick for making muffins on your grill is to use foil baking cups rather than paper ones.*

  1 cup all-purpose flour
  ¾ cup cornmeal
  2 tablespoons thinly sliced green
     onion
  2 teaspoons baking powder
  1 8½-ounce can cream-style corn
  2 slightly beaten egg whites
  3 tablespoons cooking oil
  2 tablespoons fat-free milk
  24 2½-inch foil bake cups
  ⅓ cup bran cereal flakes, slightly
     crushed

**1** In a medium bowl combine flour, cornmeal, green onion, and baking powder. Make a well in the center. In a small bowl combine corn, egg whites, oil, and milk; add all at once to flour mixture. Stir just until moistened.

**2** For each muffin, layer 2 foil bake cups together. Spoon batter into cups, filling each two-thirds full. Sprinkle with cereal.

**3** *For a charcoal grill,* arrange medium-hot coals on both sides of grill. Test for medium heat above center of grill. Place muffins on grill rack over center of grill. Cover and grill for 15 to 20 minutes or until a wooden toothpick inserted in centers comes out clean. [*For a gas grill,* preheat grill. Reduce heat to medium. Adjust for indirect cooking (see page 10). Grill as above.] Makes 12 muffins.

Nutrition Facts per muffin: 120 calories, 4 g total fat (1 g saturated fat), 0 mg cholesterol, 139 mg sodium, 19 g carbohydrate, 1 g fiber, 3 g protein. Daily Values: 2% vit. A, 3% vit. C, 5% calcium, 12% iron.

# HERBED SOURDOUGH BREAD

**Prep:** 15 minutes    **Grill:** 15 minutes

*Choose a good quality sourdough bread from a bakery for these buttery slices. The best sourdough breads are dense, chewy, and possess a characteristic tangy flavor.*

  ¼ cup margarine or butter, softened
  2 tablespoons snipped fresh chives
     or thinly sliced green onion
  2 tablespoons snipped fresh parsley
  1 tablespoon snipped fresh tarragon
     or ½ teaspoon dried tarragon,
     crushed
  1 1-pound loaf unsliced sourdough
     bread

**1** In a small bowl stir together the margarine or butter, chives, parsley, and tarragon.

**2** Cut bread into twelve 1-inch slices, cutting to but not through bottom crust. Spread cut surfaces with margarine or butter mixture. Fold a 48×18-inch piece of heavy foil in half to make a 24×18-inch rectangle. Place bread in center of foil. Bring up opposite edges of foil and seal with a double fold. Fold remaining edges of foil together to completely enclose bread, leaving space for steam to build.

**3** *For a charcoal grill,* grill bread on the rack of an uncovered grill directly over medium to medium-hot coals about 15 minutes or until heated through. (*For a gas grill,* preheat grill. Reduce heat to medium to medium-hot. Place bread on grill rack over heat. Cover and grill as above.) Makes 12 servings.

Nutrition Facts per serving: 141 calories, 4 g total fat (1 g saturated fat), 0 mg cholesterol, 268 mg sodium, 22 g carbohydrate, 0 g fiber, 4 g protein. Daily Values: 5% vit. A, 1% vit. C, 7% iron.

# Savory Stuffed Breadsticks

**Prep:** 25 minutes    **Grill:** 8 minutes

*Be careful; after you taste this, you may never again be satisfied with plain breadsticks. With soft bread, crisp bacon, melted cheddar and Parmesan, green onions, and fresh thyme, you may never get to the main course either. But these breadsticks are worth the risk.*

4 slices bacon, cut up
½ cup chopped onion
¼ cup finely shredded Parmesan cheese
¼ cup shredded sharp cheddar cheese (1 ounce)
2 tablespoons sliced green onion
1 tablespoon snipped fresh thyme
6 soft breadsticks or dinner rolls

**1** In a medium skillet cook bacon until crisp. Remove bacon; drain on paper towels. Drain off fat, reserving 1 tablespoon drippings in skillet. Add onion to drippings. Cook over medium heat until tender, stirring occasionally. Cool slightly. Stir in bacon, cheeses, green onion, and thyme.

**2** Cut each breadstick in half lengthwise, cutting to but not through opposite side. Spread cut surfaces with bacon mixture.

**3** Fold six 24×18-inch pieces of heavy foil in half to make 18×12-inch rectangles. Place each breadstick in center of foil. Bring up opposite edges of foil and seal with a double fold. Fold remaining edges together to completely enclose breadsticks, leaving space for steam to build. If desired, chill for up to 8 hours.

**4** *For a charcoal grill,* grill breadstick packets on the rack of an uncovered grill directly over medium coals for 8 to 10 minutes or until cheddar cheese is beginning to melt, turning occasionally. (*For a gas grill,* preheat grill. Reduce heat to medium. Place breadstick packets on grill rack over heat. Cover; grill as above.) Makes 6 breadsticks.

Nutrition Facts per breadstick: 81 calories, 5 g total fat (2 g saturated fat), 12 mg cholesterol, 165 mg sodium, 4 g carbohydrate, 0 g fiber, 5 g protein. Daily Values: 2% vit. A, 3% vit. C, 6% calcium, 2% iron.

## CARAWAY-CHEESE PUMPERNICKEL BREAD

**Prep:** 10 minutes    **Grill:** 15 minutes

1 cup shredded Swiss cheese
¼ cup margarine or butter, softened
¼ cup mayonnaise or salad dressing
1 to 2 teaspoons caraway seed
1 16-ounce round or oval loaf unsliced pumpernickel bread

**1** In a small bowl combine shredded cheese, margarine or butter, mayonnaise or salad dressing, and caraway seed; set aside.

**2** Cut bread into 1-inch-thick slices, cutting to but not through bottom crust. Cut crosswise down the center of bread, cutting to but not through bottom crust (do not cut crosswise through end slices). Spread cut surfaces with cheese mixture.

**3** Tear off a 48×18-inch piece of heavy foil. Fold in half to make a 24×18-inch rectangle. Place bread in center of foil. Bring up opposite edges of foil and seal with a double fold. Fold remaining edges together to completely enclose bread, leaving space for steam to build.

**4** *For a charcoal grill,* grill bread packet on the rack of an uncovered grill directly over medium coals about 15 minutes or until heated through, turning once. (*For a gas grill,* preheat grill. Reduce heat to medium. Place bread packet on grill rack over heat. Cover and grill as above.) Makes 12 servings.

Nutrition Facts per serving: 198 calories, 11 g total fat (3 g saturated fat), 11 mg cholesterol, 349 mg sodium, 19 g carbohydrate, 0 g fiber, 6 g protein. Daily Values: 7% vitamin A, 10% calcium, 7% iron.

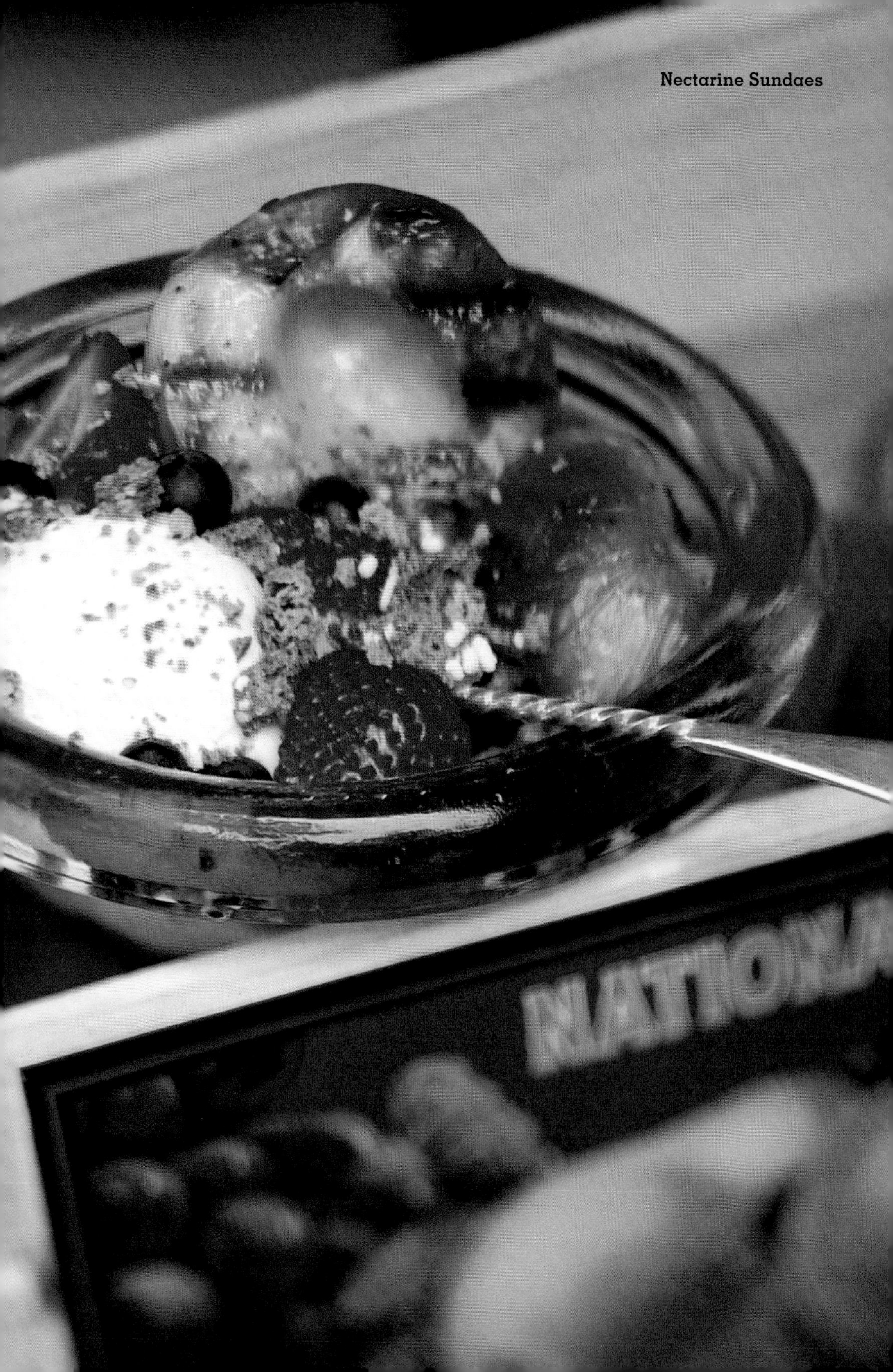


Nectarine Sundaes

# Nectarine Sundaes

**Prep:** 10 minutes    **Grill:** 10 minutes

*A nectarine transforms into the most amazing delicacy when grilled and brushed with honey. Choose nectarines that are fully ripe, but still firm.*

> 2 **medium nectarines, halved lengthwise and pitted**
> 1 **tablespoon margarine or butter, melted**
> 2 **tablespoons honey or flavored honey**
> 1/8 **teaspoon ground nutmeg**
> 1/2 **pint (1 cup) vanilla ice cream**
> 1 **cup blueberries**
> 1 **cup sliced strawberries**
> 1/4 **cup crushed amaretti cookies, crushed gingersnaps, or granola**

1 Brush cut sides of nectarines with margarine or butter.

2 *For a charcoal grill,* grill nectarines on the rack of an uncovered grill directly over medium coals for 10 to 12 minutes or until tender, turning and brushing once with honey halfway through grilling. (*For a gas grill,* preheat grill. Reduce heat to medium. Place nectarines on grill rack over heat. Cover and grill as above.)

3 To serve, sprinkle cut sides of nectarines with nutmeg. Place in dessert dishes, cut sides up. Top each nectarine half with some of the ice cream, blueberries, and strawberries. Sprinkle with crushed cookies. Makes 4 servings.

Nutrition Facts per serving: 212 calories, 7 g total fat (3 g saturated fat), 15 mg cholesterol, 93 mg sodium, 36 g carbohydrate, 2 g fiber, 2 g protein. Daily Values: 12% vit. A, 49% vit. C, 4% calcium, 4% iron.

# HONEY-GLAZED BANANAS

**Prep:** 5 minutes    **Grill:** 4 minutes

*Grill bananas, then serve them as a side dish? You bet. These honey-glazed wonders go especially well with spicy dishes. The trick to grilling bananas is to use ripe, yet still firm ones. Choose bananas that have just started to develop small black "sugar spots."*

> 2 **tablespoons margarine or butter, melted**
> 1 **tablespoon honey**
> 1 **teaspoon white vinegar**
> 1/8 **teaspoon ground red pepper**
> 2 **large ripe, yet firm, bananas or plantains**
> **Vanilla ice cream or pound cake (optional)**

1 In a small bowl combine margarine, honey, vinegar, and red pepper. Peel bananas or plantains; cut in half lengthwise. Brush generously with some of the honey mixture.

2 *For a charcoal grill,* grill bananas or plantains on the rack of an uncovered grill directly over medium coals until browned and heated through, turning once and brushing frequently with the remaining honey mixture. (Allow about 4 minutes for bananas and about 8 minutes for plantains.) (*For a gas grill,* preheat grill. Reduce heat to medium. Place bananas or plantains on grill rack over heat. Cover and grill as above.) If desired, serve over ice cream or pound cake. Makes 4 servings.

Nutrition Facts per serving: 133 calories, 6 g total fat (1 g saturated fat), 0 mg cholesterol, 68 mg sodium, 21 g carbohydrate, 1 g fiber, 1 g protein. Daily Values: 7% vit. A, 10% vit. C, 1% iron.

# Nectarine Raspberry Crisp

**Prep:** 15 minutes  **Grill:** 20 minutes

*"The check's in the mail." "I'll just be a minute." "Dessert is on the grill." In this string of dubious promises, the latter will come deliciously true. What makes this even better is you can prepare the crisp ahead, then let it "bake" while enjoying dinner.*

⅓ cup granulated sugar
5 tablespoons all-purpose flour
1 tablespoon lemon juice
1¼ teaspoons apple pie spice or ground nutmeg
6 medium nectarines (about 2 pounds), pitted and cut into 1-inch chunks
1 cup raspberries
¼ cup packed brown sugar
¼ cup rolled oats
¼ cup cold butter (no substitutes)
⅓ cup pecans, coarsely chopped
  Vanilla ice cream (optional)

1 In a large bowl combine granulated sugar, 2 tablespoons of the flour, the lemon juice, and ¼ teaspoon of the apple pie spice. Gently stir in nectarines and raspberries. Transfer to an 8½×½-inch round disposable foil baking pan. For the topping, combine the remaining flour, remaining apple pie spice, the brown sugar, and rolled oats. Using a pastry blender, cut in butter until mixture resembles coarse crumbs. Stir in nuts. Sprinkle topping evenly over fruit mixture.

2 *For a charcoal grill*, arrange medium coals in a doughnut shape in bottom of grill, leaving a 9-inch circle in the center without coals. Test for medium-low heat above the center. Place fruit crisp in pan on grill rack over center of grill. Cover and grill for 20 to 25 minutes or until fruit mixture is bubbly in center. [*For a gas grill*, preheat grill. Reduce heat to medium-low. Adjust for indirect cooking (see page 10). Grill as above.]

3 Serve warm. If desired, serve with ice cream. Makes 6 servings.

Nutrition Facts per serving: 291 calories, 13 g total fat (5 g saturated fat), 20 mg cholesterol, 80 mg sodium, 45 g carbohydrate, 4 g fiber, 3 g protein. Daily Values: 17% vit. A, 23% vit. C, 2% calcium, 8% iron.

## PEACHES WITH QUICK CHERRY SAUCE

**Prep:** 15 minutes  **Grill:** 6 minutes

*Don't tell anyone you're making this or they'll insist on skipping dinner. The beauty of this dessert is that you probably have most of the ingredients on hand, so you won't have to reveal your sweet intentions until the last minute.*

3 medium peaches or nectarines, pitted and quartered
3 tablespoons orange juice
1½ cups fresh or thawed frozen unsweetened pitted dark sweet cherries
½ cup cherry jam
3 cups vanilla ice cream
2 tablespoons coconut or almonds, toasted

1 Brush peaches with 1 tablespoon of the orange juice. Thread peaches onto 2 long metal skewers. For sauce, in a small saucepan combine the remaining orange juice, cherries, and cherry jam. Bring to boiling over medium heat, stirring frequently; reduce heat. Simmer, uncovered, for 3 minutes. Set aside.

2 *For a charcoal grill*, grill skewers on the rack of an uncovered grill directly over medium coals for 6 to 8 minutes or until heated through, turning once halfway through grilling. If desired, add sauce in saucepan to grill beside peaches to keep warm. (*For a gas grill*, preheat grill. Reduce heat to medium. Place skewers, then sauce in saucepan (if desired) on grill rack over heat. Cover and grill as above.)

3 To serve, spoon peaches and sauce over scoops of vanilla ice cream. Sprinkle with coconut. Makes 6 servings.

Nutrition Facts per serving: 273 calories,
8 g total fat (5 g saturated fat), 29 mg cholesterol,
56 mg sodium, 50 g carbohydrate, 2 g fiber,
3 g protein. Daily Values: 13% vit. A, 19% vit. C,
8% calcium, 3% iron.

# Caramel Apple Ice Cream Sauce

**Prep:** 20 minutes **Grill:** 15 minutes

*Old-fashioned flavors, old-fashioned pleasures:*
*What can possibly be better than sweet*
*cinnamon-scented apples over a scoop of vanilla*
*ice cream? Seconds, of course.*

  ⅓ cup packed brown sugar
  2 tablespoons margarine or butter,
     softened
  2 tablespoons light-colored corn
     syrup
  1 teaspoon ground cinnamon
  3 cups sliced, peeled cooking apples
     (3 medium), such as Rome
     Beauty or Granny Smith
  1 pint (2 cups) vanilla ice cream

**1** In a small bowl stir together the brown
sugar, margarine, corn syrup, and
cinnamon; set aside.

**2** Fold a 36×18-inch piece of heavy foil in
half to make an 18-inch square. Place
apples in center of foil. Dot with cinnamon
mixture. Bring up opposite edges of foil and
seal with a double fold. Fold remaining edges
together to completely enclose apples,
leaving space for steam to build.

**3** *For a charcoal grill,* grill apples on the rack
of an uncovered grill directly over medium
coals for 15 to 20 minutes or until apples are
tender. (*For a gas grill,* preheat grill. Reduce
heat to medium. Place apples on grill rack
over heat. Cover and grill as above.)

**4** To serve, spoon hot apple mixture over
scoops of ice cream. Serve immediately.
Makes 4 servings.

Nutrition Facts per serving: 397 calories,
18 g total fat (9 g saturated fat), 45 mg cholesterol,
124 mg sodium, 60 g carbohydrate, 1 g fiber,
3 g protein. Daily Values: 21% vit. A, 1% vit. C,
10% calcium, 8% iron.

# BANANA SUNDAES

**Prep/Grill:** 15 minutes

*Create the sundae of your dreams—grilled*
*banana, caramel topping, coconut, and almonds*
*make it a reality.*

  3 large firm bananas
  1 tablespoon margarine or butter,
     melted
  2 teaspoons orange juice
  ½ cup caramel ice-cream topping
  ¼ teaspoon ground cinnamon
  1 pint vanilla ice cream
  ¼ cup toasted coconut
  ¼ cup sliced almonds, toasted

**1** Cut bananas in half lengthwise; then cut
each piece in half crosswise. (You should
have 12 pieces.) Stir together margarine or
butter and 1 teaspoon of the orange juice.
Brush mixture over all sides of banana pieces.

**2** *For a charcoal grill,* grill bananas on the
rack of an uncovered grill directly over
medium-hot coals for 4 minutes or until
heated through, turning over halfway through
grilling. (*For a gas grill,* preheat grill. Reduce
heat to medium-hot. Place bananas on grill
rack over heat. Cover and grill as above.)

**3** Meanwhile, for the sauce, in a heavy,
medium skillet or saucepan combine the
caramel topping and the remaining orange
juice. Heat the caramel mixture on the grill
rack alongside bananas directly over the coals
or heat (or on a stovetop) until the mixture
boils, stirring frequently. Stir in the
cinnamon. Add the bananas to the sauce; stir
gently to coat.

**4** To serve, spoon sauce and bananas over
scoops of ice cream. Sprinkle with the
coconut and almonds. Serve immediately.
Makes 4 servings.

Nutrition Facts per serving: 556 calories,
24 g total fat (7 g saturated fat), 29 mg cholesterol,
243 mg sodium, 84 g carbohydrate, 5 g fiber,
6 g protein. Daily Values: 12% vit. A, 20% vit. C,
11% calcium, 7% iron.

# Pineapple with Sugared Wontons

**Prep:** 15 minutes **Grill:** 10 minutes

*Grilled wonton wrappers are a snappy partner to this island dessert of rum-glazed pineapple and toasted coconut.*

6 ¾-inch slices cored fresh
    pineapple, quartered
¼ cup packed brown sugar
2 tablespoons rice vinegar or
    seasoned rice vinegar
2 tablespoons rum
4 teaspoons lime juice
6 wonton wrappers, halved
    diagonally
1 tablespoon butter, melted (no
    substitutes)
3 tablespoons shredded coconut
1 tablespoon granulated sugar

**1** Place pineapple in a single layer in a shallow dish. In a small bowl stir together the brown sugar, vinegar, rum, and lime juice until sugar dissolves. Pour brown sugar mixture over the pineapple; set aside. Place a sheet of waxed paper on a cookie sheet. Lay wonton wrappers on waxed paper. Brush both sides with melted butter. Place coconut in a disposable foil pie pan or on a double thickness of heavy foil.

**2** Drain pineapple, reserving brown sugar mixture. *For a charcoal grill,* grill pineapple on the rack of an uncovered grill directly over medium coals for 6 to 8 minutes or until heated through, turning once and brushing occasionally with some of the brown sugar mixture. Transfer pineapple to dessert bowls. Add wonton wrappers to grill. Grill for 2 to 4 minutes or until browned, turning once halfway through grilling. Transfer grilled wontons to cookie sheet; immediately sprinkle with granulated sugar. Add coconut in pie pan to grill. Grill about 2 minutes or until coconut is lightly toasted, using tongs to shake pan back and forth. Remove coconut from grill. (*For a gas grill,* preheat grill. Reduce heat to medium. Place pineapple, then wonton wrappers and coconut in pie pan on grill rack over heat. Cover and grill as above.)

**3** To serve, drizzle remaining brown sugar mixture over pineapple and sprinkle with coconut. Serve with sugared wontons. Makes 4 servings.

Nutrition Facts per serving: 204 calories, 5 g total fat (3 g saturated fat), 9 mg cholesterol, 103 mg sodium, 38 g carbohydrate, 2 g fiber, 2 g protein. Daily Values: 2% vit. A, 32% vit. C, 2% calcium, 8% iron.

## WISE ADVICE

There are several easy ways to cut a fresh pineapple. The easiest is to slice the pineapple in half lengthwise, then into quarters. With a curved grapefruit knife, remove and discard the hard core; then slice and separate the flesh from the skin. Cut the remaining flesh crosswise into strips or chunks. Another simple method is to hollow the whole fruit by cutting off both the pineapple's crown and a slice from the bottom. Insert a knife close to the skin, and make your cut far enough inside the skin, or shell, of the pineapple to remove the eyes (similar to those found in a potato). Slice the skinned fruit lengthwise into quarters; then remove and discard the core.

Pineapple with Sugared Wontons

## STUFFED AUTUMN APPLES AND PEARS

**Prep:** 20 minutes    **Grill:** 25 minutes

*The aroma of this dessert will bring back memories of sitting on Grandpa's lap while he reads you the story of the Three Bears—for the umpteenth time! Like those sweet memories, you'll never tire of these rich, soothing flavors.*

2 medium cooking apples, such as Rome Beauty, Granny Smith, or Golden Delicious
2 medium ripe, yet firm, pears, such as Bosc, Anjou, or Bartlett
2 tablespoons brown sugar
2 tablespoons margarine or butter, melted
¼ cup coarsely chopped walnuts
¼ cup raisins
4 gingersnaps, finely crushed
1 teaspoon finely shredded orange peel

**1** Peel the apples and pears. Cut the apples and pears in half lengthwise. Core the apples and pears, hollowing out the centers of each half.

**2** In a large bowl combine the fruit halves, 1 tablespoon of the brown sugar, and 1 tablespoon of the margarine; toss gently to coat. Set aside. For filling, in a small bowl combine the remaining brown sugar, remaining margarine, walnuts, raisins, gingersnaps, and orange peel. Set aside.

**3** *For a charcoal grill,* arrange medium-hot coals around a drip pan. Test for medium heat above the pan. Place fruit, cut sides down, on grill rack over drip pan. Cover and grill for 20 minutes. Turn fruit; spoon the filling into hollowed-out centers. Cover and

grill about 5 minutes more or until fruit is tender. [*For a gas grill,* preheat grill. Reduce heat to medium. Adjust for indirect cooking (see page 10). Grill as above.] Serve warm. Makes 4 servings.

Nutrition Facts per serving: 258 calories, 11 g total fat (2 g saturated fat), 0 mg cholesterol, 102 mg sodium, 41 g carbohydrate, 4 g fiber, 2 g protein. Daily Values: 5% vit. A, 12% vit. C, 2% calcium, 7% iron.

# Gingered Fruit Compote

**Prep:** 20 minutes    **Grill:** 8 minutes

*Compote generally refers to fruit gently stewed until it's meltingly tender, yet still retaining it's shape. Here the process is abbreviated and the fruit is bathed in a lime-ginger sauce, then served over pound cake toast.*

3 tablespoons margarine or butter, melted
1 tablespoon brown sugar
¼ teaspoon ground nutmeg
¾ teaspoon finely shredded lime peel
¼ cup lime juice
¾ teaspoon grated fresh ginger
1 medium papaya, peeled, seeded, and cut into 1-inch slices
1 medium ripe plantain or 1 large very firm banana, halved lengthwise
1 small fresh pineapple, peeled, cored, and cut into 1-inch slices
6 1-inch slices frozen loaf pound cake, thawed

**1** In a small bowl combine 1 tablespoon of the margarine, the brown sugar, and nutmeg; set aside. In another small bowl combine the remaining margarine, the lime peel, lime juice, and ginger. Brush some of the lime mixture over the papaya, plantain or banana, and pineapple.

**2** *For a charcoal grill,* grill fruit on the rack of an uncovered grill directly over medium coals for 6 to 8 minutes or until heated through, turning once halfway through grilling. Remove fruit from grill; keep warm. Add cake slices to grill. Grill for 2 to 3 minutes or until lightly toasted, turning and brushing once with brown sugar mixture. (*For a gas grill,* preheat grill. Reduce heat to medium. Place fruit, then cake on grill rack over heat. Cover and grill as above.)

**3** Cut fruit into bite-size pieces; place in a medium bowl. Add the remaining lime mixture; toss gently to coat. To serve, spoon fruit mixture over grilled pound cake. Makes 6 servings.

Nutrition Facts per serving: 420 calories,
23 g total fat (11 g saturated fat),
112 mg cholesterol, 267 mg sodium,
51 g carbohydrate, 2 g fiber, 5 g protein.
Daily Values: 30% vit. A, 48% vit. C, 4% calcium,
10% iron.

## FRUIT KABOBS WITH LIME-YOGURT SAUCE

**Prep:** 15 minutes    **Grill:** 6 minutes

*After dinner, let fruit bask in the limelight with this lovely, light dessert. For the best results, choose fruit that is on the firm side of fully ripe.*

   6 6- to 8-inch bamboo skewers
   1 8-ounce carton vanilla low-fat
      yogurt
   1 teaspoon finely shredded lime
      peel
   1 tablespoon lime juice
   ¼ teaspoon ground cinnamon
   1 small fresh pineapple, peeled and
      cored
   2 large ripe, yet firm, nectarines or
      peeled peaches, pitted
   2 medium ripe, yet firm, bananas
   1 tablespoon margarine or butter,
      melted
   2 teaspoons lime juice

**1** Soak the skewers in warm water for several minutes; drain. Meanwhile, for the sauce, in a small bowl combine the yogurt, lime peel, the 1 tablespoon lime juice, and the cinnamon. Cover and chill until serving time.

**2** For the kabobs, cut pineapple into 1-inch slices; quarter slices. Cut nectarines into wedges. Cut bananas into chunks. Alternately thread pieces of fruit on the skewers. In a small bowl combine margarine and the 2 teaspoons lime juice; brush over kabobs.

**3** *For a charcoal grill,* grill kabobs on the rack of an uncovered grill directly over medium coals for 6 to 8 minutes or until heated through, turning once or twice. (*For a gas grill,* preheat grill. Reduce heat to medium. Place kabobs on grill rack over heat. Cover and grill as above.)

**4** Serve kabobs with the sauce. Serves 6.

Nutrition Facts per serving: 161 calories,
3 g total fat (1 g saturated fat), 2 mg cholesterol,
43 mg sodium, 33 g carbohydrate, 2 g fiber,
3 g protein. Daily Values: 6% vit. A, 39% vit. C,
5% calcium, 3% iron.

## Grilling Know-How

**Apples are delicious on the grill—either skewered and cooked directly over the fire or baked in a foil packet. You will find they need no more than 10 to 15 minutes of heat or just until their outsides are golden. For the best results, choose a good cooking apple, such as Rome Beauty, York Imperial, Newton Pippin, or Granny Smith.**

# Peanut Butter S'mores

**Prep:** 15 minutes  **Grill:** 7 minutes

*Though you may not own up to it, this variation on the s'mores theme could become one of those private pleasures. No one will ever have to know your secret obsession.*

¾ cup peanut butter
4 9- to 10-inch flour tortillas (burrito-
   size)
1 cup tiny marshmallows
½ cup miniature semisweet
   chocolate pieces
1 medium ripe, yet firm, banana,
   thinly sliced

**1** For s'mores, spread about 3 tablespoons peanut butter over half of each tortilla. Top each with some of the marshmallows, chocolate pieces, and banana slices. Fold tortillas in half, pressing gently to flatten and seal slightly.

**2** *For a charcoal grill,* grill s'mores on the rack of an uncovered grill directly over medium coals for 7 to 9 minutes or until tortillas are golden and chocolate is melted, turning once halfway through grilling. (*For a gas grill,* preheat grill. Reduce heat to medium. Place s'mores on grill rack over heat. Cover and grill as above.)

**3** To serve, cut each s'more into 4 wedges. Makes 8 servings.

Nutrition Facts per serving: 290 calories,
17 g total fat (3 g saturated fat), 0 mg cholesterol,
207 mg sodium, 31 g carbohydrate, 2 g fiber,
8 g protein. Daily Values: 2% vit. C, 3% calcium,
10% iron.

# CHOCOLATE-RASPBERRY BURRITOS

**Prep:** 15 minutes  **Grill:** 8 minutes

*Chocolate goes with all kinds of foods, but it's sublime with raspberries. Wrap the two in tortillas and grill, and you have a dessert to swoon for. (For the ultimate, try them with a scoop of vanilla ice cream.)*

4 7- to 8-inch flour tortillas
1 cup semisweet chocolate pieces
1 cup raspberries
2 tablespoons butter, melted (no
   substitutes)
2 teaspoons sugar
½ teaspoon ground cinnamon

**1** Stack the tortillas and wrap in a piece of foil. *For a charcoal grill,* grill tortillas on the rack of an uncovered grill directly over medium-low coals about 5 minutes or until tortillas are warm and pliable, turning packet once. Remove tortillas from grill. (*For a gas grill,* preheat grill. Reduce heat to medium-low. Place tortillas on grill rack over heat. Cover and grill as above.)

**2** For burritos, sprinkle ¼ cup of the chocolate pieces and ¼ cup of the raspberries in the center of each tortilla; fold in sides and roll up. Brush with half of the melted butter. Add burritos to grill. Grill about 3 minutes or until the tortillas begin to show grill marks and the chocolate is melted, turning once halfway through grilling. Transfer to a serving platter. Brush burritos with the remaining melted butter. In a small bowl combine the sugar and cinnamon; sprinkle over burritos. Serve immediately. Makes 4 servings.

Nutrition Facts per serving: 361 calories,
20 g total fat (4 g saturated fat), 15 mg cholesterol,
179 mg sodium, 49 g carbohydrate, 2 g fiber,
4 g protein. Daily Values: 6% vit. A, 12% vit. C,
4% calcium, 15% iron.

# Banana-Chocolate Tiramisu

**Prep:** 20 minutes    **Chill:** 1 hour
**Grill:** 6 minutes

*Tiramisu, an Italian dessert, literally means*
*"pick me up" in Italian. It was meant to go with*
*coffee for a mid-afternoon lift. This version will*
*lift you to dessert heaven!*

  1 8-ounce carton mascarpone cheese
    or one 8-ounce container cream
    cheese, softened
  ½ cup sifted powdered sugar
  ⅓ cup unsweetened cocoa powder
  1 teaspoon vanilla
  3 tablespoons reduced-fat milk
  1 cup whipping cream, whipped
  4 medium ripe, yet firm, bananas,
    peeled
  2 tablespoons margarine or butter,
    melted
  1 cup crushed amaretti cookies
    Chocolate curls (optional)

1 For chocolate cream, in a medium mixing
  bowl beat mascarpone cheese, powdered
sugar, cocoa powder, and vanilla with an
electric mixer on low speed until combined.
Gradually add milk, beating until smooth. By
hand, fold in whipped cream. Cover; chill for
1 to 8 hours.

2 Brush peeled bananas with melted margarine
  or butter. *For a charcoal grill,* grill bananas
on the rack of an uncovered grill directly over
medium coals for 6 to 8 minutes or until lightly
browned, turning once halfway through grilling.
(*For a gas grill,* preheat grill. Reduce heat to
medium. Place bananas on grill rack over heat.
Cover; grill as above.)

3 To serve, slice bananas. Layer banana
  slices, amaretti crumbs, and chocolate
cream in 4 to 6 dessert dishes. If desired,
sprinkle with chocolate curls. Serves 4 to 6.

Nutrition Facts per serving: 766 calories,
57 g total fat (30 g saturated fat), 154 mg cholesterol,
136 mg sodium, 61 g carbohydrate, 2 g fiber,
17 g protein. Daily Values: 34% vit. A, 17% vit. C,
11% calcium, 8% iron.

# CHOCOLATE-SAUCED DESSERT KABOBS

**Prep:** 15 minutes    **Grill:** 5 minutes

  ¾ cup semisweet chocolate pieces
  ¼ cup margarine or butter
  ⅔ cup sugar
  1 5-ounce can (⅔ cup) evaporated
    milk
  2 medium ripe nectarines or
    peaches
  2 ripe medium bananas, peeled
  ½ of a 10¾-ounce fresh or frozen
    pound cake
  6 whole strawberries

1 For sauce, in a heavy small saucepan melt
  chocolate pieces and margarine or butter
over low heat. Add sugar. Gradually stir in
milk. Bring to boiling; reduce heat. Boil
gently over low heat for 8 minutes, stirring
frequently. Remove from heat. Set aside.

2 Peel peaches, if using. Remove pits from
  nectarines or peaches; cut fruit into wedges.
Cut bananas into 1-inch pieces. Cut cake into
1-inch cubes. Remove stems from strawberries.
On 6 long skewers, alternately thread peaches
or nectarines, bananas, and cake cubes. Add
one strawberry to each skewer.

3 *For a charcoal grill,* grill kabobs on the
  rack of an uncovered grill directly over
medium coals about 5 minutes or until cake is
toasted, turning once halfway through
grilling. (*For a gas grill,* preheat grill. Reduce
heat to medium. Place kabobs on grill rack
over heat. Cover; grill as above.) To serve,
remove fruit and cake from kabobs; place on
6 dessert plates. Drizzle with chocolate sauce.
(Store any remaining sauce in the refrigerator
for another use.) Makes 6 servings.

Nutrition Facts per serving: 445 calories,
21 g total fat (5 g saturated fat), 7 mg cholesterol,
216 mg sodium, 66 g carbohydrate, 1 g fiber,
5 g protein. Daily Values: 19% vit. A, 22% vit. C.

# Hazelnut Pears

**Prep:** 30 minutes   **Grill:** 12 minutes

*The caramel-like sauce, spiced with nutmeg and cardamom, grills right along with the pears in a foil packet. Ice cream is optional but a perfect mate for this luscious dessert.*

⅓ cup packed brown sugar
2 tablespoons butter, softened
2 tablespoons light corn syrup
¼ teaspoon ground nutmeg
¼ teaspoon ground cardamom
3 cups cored sliced pears (3 medium)
⅓ cup chopped toasted hazelnuts
   Vanilla ice cream (optional)

**1** In a small bowl combine brown sugar, softened butter, corn syrup, nutmeg, and cardamom. Set aside. Fold a 36×18-inch piece of heavy foil in half to make an 18-inch square. Place pear slices in the center of the foil. Spoon brown sugar mixture over pears. Sprinkle with nuts. Bring up opposite edges of foil and seal with a double fold. Fold ends to completely enclose pears, leaving space for steam to build.

**2** *For a charcoal grill,* grill pear packet directly over medium coals for 12 to 15 minutes or until pears are tender. (*For a gas grill,* preheat grill. Reduce heat to medium. Grill packet on grill rack over heat. Cover and grill as above.) Serve warm pear mixture over ice cream, if desired. Makes 4 to 6 servings.

Nutrition Facts per serving: 289 calories,
14 g total fat (4 g saturated fat), 15 mg cholesterol,
163 mg sodium, 43 g carbohydrate, 5 g fiber,
2 g protein. Daily Values: 5% vit. A, 8% vit. C,
4% calcium, 9% iron.

# PEANUT AND BANANA PIZZA

**Prep:** 15 minutes   **Grill:** 11 minutes
**Special Equipment:** Grill pizza pan

*No need to heat up the oven for this cookie pizza. Your kids will want this dessert every time you fire up the grill.*

1 18-ounce package refrigerated chocolate chip or peanut butter cookie dough
½ cup caramel ice-cream topping
1 cup semisweet or milk chocolate pieces and/or miniature candy-coated semisweet baking bits
½ cup chopped dry-roasted peanuts
1 large banana, thinly sliced
2 tablespoons chocolate ice-cream topping (optional)

**1** For crust, grease a 12-inch grill pizza pan. Press cookie dough into prepared pan.

**2** *For a charcoal grill,* grill crust directly over medium coals for 10 to 15 minutes or until edges of cookie crust are lightly golden and top is set but not dry. (*For a gas grill,* preheat grill. Reduce heat to medium. Grill cookie crust on grill rack over heat. Cover and grill as above.) Remove crust from grill (cookie crust may puff and fall at this point).

**3** Drizzle caramel topping over cookie crust. Sprinkle chocolate pieces and/or baking bits and peanuts over caramel. Return pan to grill for 1 to 2 minutes more or until chocolate pieces soften. Remove from grill and cool on a wire rack.

**4** To serve, top pizza with sliced banana and, if desired, drizzle with chocolate topping. Cut into wedges. Makes 12 servings.

Nutrition Facts per serving: 334 calories,
16 g total fat (3 g saturated fat), 11 mg cholesterol,
185 mg sodium, 48 g carbohydrate, 1 g fiber,
4 g protein. Daily Values: 10% iron.

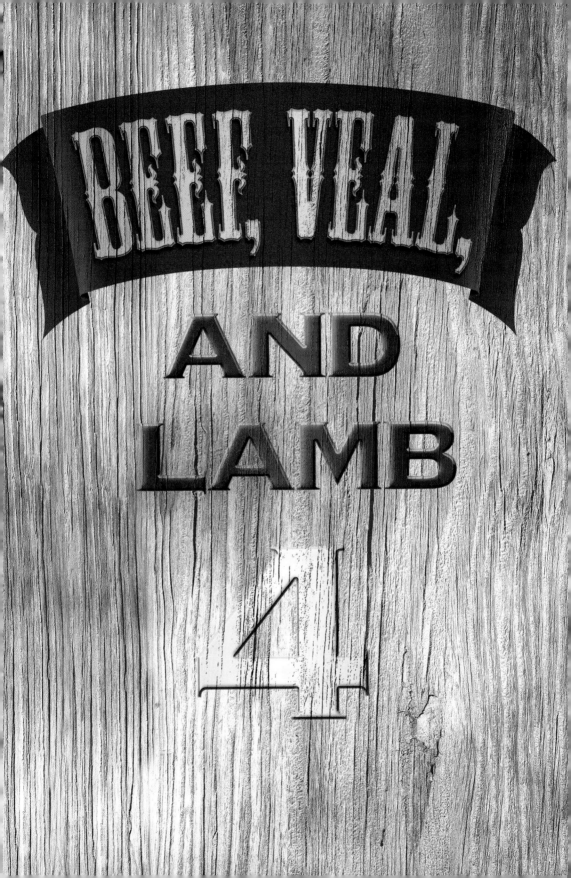

# Beef, Veal, and Lamb

# Sun-Dried Tomato Burgers

**Prep:** 15 minutes   **Grill:** 12 minutes

*The juicy burger's rich, tart taste comes from flavor-packed dried tomatoes, but it's the mayo, which gets its kick from a jalapeño pepper, that's truly memorable.*

  1 **pound lean ground beef**
  1 **tablespoon finely chopped oil-packed dried tomatoes**
  1 **teaspoon finely shredded lemon or lime peel**
  ½ **teaspoon salt**
  ¼ **teaspoon black pepper**
  4 **onion hamburger buns, split and toasted**
  ¼ **cup light mayonnaise dressing or salad dressing**
  2 **tablespoons snipped fresh basil**
  1 **fresh jalapeño pepper, seeded and finely chopped**
  1 **cup lightly packed arugula or spinach leaves**

**1** In a medium bowl combine ground beef, tomatoes, lemon peel, salt, and black pepper; mix well. Shape into four ½-inch-thick patties.

**2** *For a charcoal grill,* grill burgers on the rack of an uncovered grill directly over medium coals for 12 to 16 minutes or until meat is no longer pink, turning once halfway through grilling. (*For a gas grill,* preheat grill. Reduce heat to medium. Place burgers on grill rack over heat. Cover and grill as above.) Remove burgers from grill.

**3** Meanwhile, in a small bowl combine mayonnaise dressing, basil, and jalapeño pepper. Serve burgers on buns with mayonnaise mixture and arugula or spinach leaves. Makes 4 servings.

Nutrition Facts per serving: 450 calories, 20 g total fat (6 g saturated fat), 71 mg cholesterol, 784 mg sodium, 40 g carbohydrate, 2 g fiber, 26 g protein. Daily Values: 1% vit. A, 13% vit. C, 6% calcium, 25% iron.

# BASIL BURGERS

**Prep:** 15 minutes   **Grill:** 14 minutes

*These mixed-meat patties (beef and turkey) get an Italian accent from the cinnamon-pepper flavor of basil and the tang of Parmesan cheese.*

  1 **slightly beaten egg**
  ⅔ **cup chopped onion**
  ½ **cup grated Parmesan cheese**
  ¼ **cup snipped fresh basil or**
     1 **tablespoon dried basil, crushed**
  ¼ **cup catsup**
  2 **cloves garlic, minced**
  ¼ **teaspoon salt**
  ¼ **teaspoon pepper**
  1 **pound lean ground beef**
  1 **pound ground turkey**
  8 **hamburger buns, split and toasted**
  8 **lettuce leaves**
  8 **tomato slices**

**1** In a large bowl combine egg, onion, Parmesan cheese, basil, catsup, garlic, salt, and pepper. Add ground beef and turkey; mix well. Shape meat mixture into eight ¾-inch-thick patties.

**2** *For a charcoal grill,* grill burgers on the rack of an uncovered grill directly over medium coals for 14 to 18 minutes or until meat juices run clear, turning once halfway through grilling. (Burgers will appear pink when done because of the catsup in the mixture.) (*For a gas grill,* preheat grill. Reduce heat to medium. Place burgers on grill rack over heat. Cover and grill as above.) Remove burgers from grill.

**3** Serve burgers on buns with lettuce and tomato. Makes 8 servings.

Nutrition Facts per serving: 340 calories, 14 g total fat (5 g saturated fat), 88 mg cholesterol, 533 mg sodium, 26 g carbohydrate, 2 g fiber, 25 g protein. Daily Values: 5% vit. A, 11% vit. C, 11% calcium, 20% iron.

Burgers Borracho

# Burgers Borracho

**Prep:** 15 minutes  **Marinate:** 6 to 24 hours
**Grill:** 14 minutes

¼ cup finely chopped onion
2 tablespoons tomato paste
4 cloves garlic, minced
½ teaspoon salt
½ teaspoon dried rosemary, crushed
½ teaspoon pepper
¼ teaspoon ground allspice
1½ pounds lean ground beef
1½ cups beer
6 hamburger buns, split and toasted
1 recipe Mustard Sauce
Lettuce leaves and onion slices (optional)

**1** In a bowl combine onion, tomato paste, garlic, salt, rosemary, pepper, and allspice. Add ground beef; mix well. Shape mixture into six ¾-inch-thick patties. Place in a shallow dish. Reserve 1 tablespoon of beer for Mustard Sauce; pour remaining beer over burgers. Cover; marinate in the refrigerator for 6 to 24 hours, turning burgers once. Prepare Mustard Sauce. Cover and chill until needed.

**2** Drain burgers, discarding beer. *For a charcoal grill,* grill burgers on the rack of an uncovered grill directly over medium coals for 14 to 18 minutes or until meat is no longer pink, turning once halfway through grilling. (*For a gas grill,* preheat grill. Reduce heat to medium. Place burgers on grill rack over heat. Cover; grill as above.) Remove burgers from grill. Serve burgers on buns with sauce. If desired, add lettuce and onion slices. Makes 6 servings.

**Mustard Sauce:** In a small bowl combine 3 tablespoons stone-ground mustard, ¾ teaspoon Worcestershire sauce, and the reserved 1 tablespoon beer.

Nutrition Facts per serving: 324 calories, 13 g total fat (5 g saturated fat), 71 mg cholesterol, 547 mg sodium, 24 g carbohydrate, 1 g fiber, 24 g protein. Daily Values: 1% vit. A, 8% vit. C, 4% calcium, 23% iron.

# BBQ BURGERS

**Prep:** 15 minutes  **Grill:** 14 minutes

1 clove garlic, minced
¼ cup catsup
2 tablespoons steak sauce
1 tablespoon water
1 teaspoon sugar
1 teaspoon vinegar
Few dashes bottled hot pepper sauce (optional)
1 pound lean ground beef
¼ teaspoon salt
¼ teaspoon pepper
4 hamburger buns, split and toasted
American cheese slices, lettuce leaves, tomato slices, onion slices, pickle slices (optional)

**1** For sauce. in a small saucepan combine garlic, catsup, steak sauce, water, sugar, vinegar, and, if desired, hot pepper sauce. Bring to boiling; reduce heat. Simmer, uncovered, for 3 minutes. Remove from heat; set aside.

**2** In a medium bowl combine beef, salt, and pepper. Shape mixture into four ¾-inch-thick patties.

**3** *For a charcoal grill,* grill burgers on the rack of an uncovered grill directly over medium coals for 14 to 18 minutes or until meat is no longer pink, turning once halfway through grilling and brushing once or twice with sauce during the last 5 minutes. (*For a gas grill,* preheat grill. Reduce heat to medium. Adjust heat for direct grilling. Place burgers on grill rack over heat. Cover and grill as above.) Remove burgers from grill. Serve patties on buns. Spoon any remaining sauce over burgers. If desired, top burgers with cheese, lettuce, tomato, onion, and pickles. Makes 4 servings.

Nutrition Facts per serving: 332 calories, 13 g total fat (5 g saturated fat), 71 mg cholesterol, 713 mg sodium, 29 g carbohydrate, 1 g fiber, 24 g protein. Daily Values: 1% vit. A, 4% vit. C, 3% calcium, 21% iron.

# Burgers Italiano

**Prep:** 20 minutes  **Grill:** 13 minutes

*The grill goes to Little Italy. Two of America's favorite foods—hamburgers and pizza—come together in patties flavored with Italian staples.*

    1 slightly beaten egg
 1¼ cups meatless spaghetti sauce
    ⅓ cup fine dry bread crumbs
    ⅓ cup chopped onion
    3 tablespoons snipped fresh basil or
        oregano or 1 teaspoon dried
        basil or oregano, crushed
    2 cloves garlic, minced
    1 pound lean ground beef
    1 pound bulk Italian sausage
    2 medium green, yellow, and/or red
        sweet peppers, cut into rings
        and halved
    1 tablespoon olive oil or cooking oil
    4 ounces sliced mozzarella cheese
    8 kaiser rolls, split and toasted

**1** In a large bowl combine egg and ¼ cup of the spaghetti sauce. Stir in bread crumbs, onion, basil, and garlic. Add ground beef and sausage; mix well. Shape meat mixture into eight ½-inch-thick patties.

**2** Fold a 24×18-inch piece of heavy foil in half crosswise. Trim it into a 12-inch square. Place the sweet peppers in center of foil square. Drizzle with oil. Bring up opposite edges of foil; seal with a double fold. Fold remaining edges together to completely enclose peppers, leaving space for steam to build.

**3** *For a charcoal grill,* grill burgers and peppers on the rack of an uncovered grill directly over medium coals until meat is no longer pink and peppers are tender, turning once halfway through grilling. (Allow 12 to 16 minutes for burgers and 10 to 12 minutes for peppers.) (*For a gas grill,* preheat grill. Reduce heat to medium. Place burgers and peppers on grill rack over heat. Cover and grill as above.) Remove burgers and peppers from grill.

**4** Top burgers with peppers and cheese; return to grill. Cover and grill about 15 seconds more or until cheese is melted. Remove burgers from grill.

**5** Meanwhile, in a small saucepan cook and stir remaining 1 cup spaghetti sauce until heated through. Serve burgers on rolls; top with some of the spaghetti sauce. Pass the warm sauce. Makes 8 servings.

Nutrition Facts per serving: 540 calories, 27 g total fat (10 g saturated fat), 106 mg cholesterol, 995 mg sodium, 41 g carbohydrate, 0 g fiber, 31 g protein. Daily Values: 24% vit. A, 66% vit. C, 19% calcium, 27% iron.

## PEPPER-BACON BURGERS

**Prep:** 15 minutes  **Grill:** 14 minutes

*A word to the wise: When handling hot peppers, wear plastic gloves to keep the heat in the meat and off your hands.*

    1 small onion, thinly sliced and
        separated into rings
    1 fresh Anaheim or mild green chile
        pepper, seeded and cut into rings
    2 tablespoons margarine or butter
    1 slightly beaten egg
    ¼ cup fine dry bread crumbs
    6 slices crisp-cooked bacon,
        crumbled
    4 to 6 fresh serrano peppers or 2 to
        3 fresh jalapeño peppers, seeded
        and finely chopped
    2 tablespoons milk
    1 pound lean ground beef
    4 kaiser rolls or hamburger buns,
        split and toasted
    4 lettuce leaves

**1** In a small saucepan cook onion and Anaheim pepper in hot margarine about 10 minutes or until onion is tender. Meanwhile, in a medium bowl combine egg, bread crumbs, bacon, serrano peppers, and milk. Add ground beef; mix well. Shape meat mixture into four ¾-inch-thick patties.

**2** *For a charcoal grill,* grill burgers on the rack of an uncovered grill directly over medium coals for 14 to 18 minutes or until meat is no longer pink, turning once halfway through grilling. (*For a gas grill,* preheat grill. Reduce heat to medium. Place burgers on grill rack over heat. Cover and grill as above.) Remove burgers from grill. Add split rolls, cut sides down, to grill. Grill for 1 to 2 minutes or until lightly toasted.

**3** Serve burgers on rolls with onion mixture and lettuce leaves. Makes 4 servings.

Nutrition Facts per serving: 550 calories, 29 g total fat (9 g saturated fat), 132 g cholesterol, 733 mg sodium, 38 g carbohydrate, 1 g fiber, 32 g protein. Daily Values: 11% vit. A, 34% vit. C, 8% calcium, 29% iron.

## Mexican-Style Burgers

**Prep:** 15 minutes    **Grill:** 14 minutes

*Tortillas step in for buns in this south-of-the-border version of the all-American burger. Serve toasted corn chips and guacamole on the side.*

1   slightly beaten egg
1   4-ounce can diced green chile peppers, drained
⅓   cup finely crushed tortilla chips
2   tablespoons chopped onion
2   tablespoons taco sauce
1   clove garlic, minced
¼   teaspoon salt
1½   pounds lean ground beef
6   10-inch flour tortillas
1   cup shredded Monterey Jack, Monterey Jack with jalapeño peppers, or cheddar cheese (4 ounces)
1   medium tomato, chopped
¾   cup shredded lettuce
   Taco sauce (optional)

**1** In a large bowl combine egg, chile peppers, tortilla chips, onion, taco sauce, garlic, and

salt. Add ground beef; mix well. Shape the meat mixture into six ¾-inch-thick patties. Stack the tortillas and wrap in a piece of foil.

**2** *For a charcoal grill,* grill burgers and tortillas on the rack of an uncovered grill directly over medium coals until meat is no longer pink and tortillas are warm and pliable, turning once halfway through grilling. (Allow 14 to 18 minutes for burgers and about 5 minutes for tortillas.) (*For a gas grill,* preheat grill. Reduce heat to medium. Place burgers and tortillas on grill rack over heat. Cover and grill as above.)

**3** To serve, place burgers on warmed tortillas. Top with cheese, tomato, and lettuce. Wrap tortillas around burgers. Pass additional taco sauce, if desired. Serves 6.

Nutrition Facts per serving: 430 calories, 25 g total fat (10 g saturated fat), 122 mg cholesterol, 684 mg sodium, 21 g carbohydrate, 1 g fiber, 28 g protein. Daily Values: 11% vit. A, 30% vit. C, 16% calcium, 21% iron.

## Sizzlin' Solutions

**Making burgers is simple— right? Yes, if you follow a few tips:**

• **Be sure your ground meat is fresh. It should be bright pink without any unpleasant odors or dark spots.**

• **Grill burgers over medium heat to keep them flavorful and juicy.**

• **Resist pressing down on the burgers with a spatula while they grill! This squeezes out the juices, making them dry and tough.**

• **Never cook burgers to the point of dryness—the meat should show no signs of pinkness and the juices should run clear.**

Spanish Meat Loaves

## SPANISH MEAT LOAVES

**Prep:** 15 minutes    **Grill:** 18 minutes

*Serve these diminutive, green-olive-stuffed loaves with Barcelona-style Spanish rice or thinly sliced potatoes and onions cooked in a foil pack alongside them on the grill.*

　1 slightly beaten egg
　¾ cup quick-cooking rolled oats
　½ cup pimiento-stuffed green olives, sliced
　¼ cup snipped fresh parsley
　¼ cup tomato paste
　¼ teaspoon pepper
　1 pound lean ground beef
　¼ cup jalapeño pepper jelly or apple jelly, melted
　1 medium tomato, chopped
　⅓ cup chunky salsa
　¼ cup chopped, seeded cucumber
　2 tablespoons sliced pimiento-stuffed green olives (optional)

**1** In a medium bowl combine the egg, rolled oats, the ½ cup olives, the parsley, tomato paste, and pepper. Add ground beef; mix well. Shape into four 4×2½×1-inch meat loaves.

**2** *For a charcoal grill,* grill meat loaves on the rack of an uncovered grill directly over medium coals for 16 to 18 minutes or until meat is no longer pink, turning once halfway through grilling. Brush with melted jelly; grill for 2 minutes more. (*For a gas grill,* preheat grill. Reduce heat to medium. Place meat loaves on grill rack over heat. Cover and grill as above.)

**3** Meanwhile, for relish, in a small bowl combine the tomato, salsa, cucumber, and, if desired, the 2 tablespoons olives. Serve the meat loaves with relish. Makes 4 servings.

Nutrition Facts per serving: 362 calories, 16 g total fat (5 g saturated fat), 125 mg cholesterol, 479 mg sodium, 31 g carbohydrate, 2 g fiber, 26 g protein. Daily Values: 15% vit. A, 47% vit. C, 4% calcium, 30% iron.

# Stuffed Meat Loaf

**Prep:** 25 minutes    **Grill:** 50 minutes
**Stand:** 15 minutes

　2 cups sliced fresh mushrooms
　1 medium onion, thinly sliced
　1 tablespoon margarine or butter
　2 tablespoons snipped fresh parsley
　1 slightly beaten egg
　½ cup rolled oats
　⅓ cup milk
　¾ teaspoon salt
　¼ teaspoon pepper
　1½ pounds lean ground beef
　2 tablespoons catsup
　1 teaspoon prepared mustard

**1** In a small saucepan cook mushrooms and onion in hot margarine over medium heat about 5 minutes or until vegetables are tender. Stir in parsley. Cool slightly.

**2** In a medium bowl combine egg, rolled oats, milk, salt, and pepper. Add ground beef; mix well. Place on waxed paper and flatten to a 12×8-inch rectangle. Spoon mushroom mixture evenly over meat. Starting from a short side, roll up; pinch seam and ends together to seal. For sauce, in a small bowl stir together catsup and mustard.

**3** Fold a 24×18-inch piece of heavy foil in half crosswise. Trim into a 12-inch square. Cut several slits in the foil. Place meat on foil.

**4** *For a charcoal grill,* arrange medium coals around a drip pan. Test for medium-low heat above pan. Place foil with meat loaf on grill rack over drip pan. Cover; grill for 50 to 60 minutes or until meat is no longer pink, brushing with sauce during the last 5 minutes of grilling. [*For a gas grill,* preheat grill. Reduce heat to medium-low. Adjust for indirect cooking (see page 10). Grill as above.]

**5** Remove meat loaf from grill. Cover with foil; let stand for 15 minutes before slicing. Makes 6 servings.

Nutrition Facts per serving: 296 calories, 17 g total fat (6 g saturated fat), 107 mg cholesterol, 445 mg sodium, 9 g carbohydrate, 1 g fiber, 25 g protein. Daily Values: 6% vit. A, 7% vit. C, 3% calcium, 19% iron.

## MUSHROOM-HORSERADISH-STUFFED STEAKS

**Prep:** 20 minutes   **Grill:** 10 minutes

1½ cups sliced fresh mushrooms
½ cup chopped onion
2 cloves garlic, minced
1 tablespoon margarine or butter
2 tablespoons prepared horseradish
¼ teaspoon salt
⅛ teaspoon pepper
4 8-ounce boneless beef top loin
    steaks, cut 1 inch thick
2 tablespoons margarine or butter
1 tablespoon Worcestershire sauce

**1** For stuffing, in a medium saucepan cook mushrooms, onion, and garlic in the 1 tablespoon margarine or butter until tender. Remove from heat; stir in horseradish, salt, and pepper.

**2** To prepare meat, trim fat from steaks. Cut a pocket in each steak by cutting from one side almost to, but not through, the other side. Spoon stuffing into pockets. If necessary, fasten pockets with wooden toothpicks.

**3** For sauce, in a small saucepan melt remaining 2 tablespoons margarine over low heat. Remove from heat; stir in Worcestershire sauce. Set aside.

**4** *For a charcoal grill*, grill steaks on the rack of an uncovered grill directly over medium coals until desired doneness, turning once halfway through grilling. (Allow 8 to 12 minutes for medium-rare and 12 to 15 minutes for medium doneness.) (*For a gas grill*, preheat grill. Reduce heat to medium. Place steaks on grill rack over heat. Cover and grill as above.) To serve, spoon sauce over steaks. Makes 4 servings.

Nutrition Facts per serving: 378 calories, 19 g total fat (5 g saturated fat), 130 mg cholesterol, 451 mg sodium, 5 g carbohydrate, 1 g fiber, 45 g protein. Daily Values: 10% vit. A, 11% vit. C, 3% calcium, 38% iron.

## Garlic Steaks with Nectarine-Onion Relish

**Prep:** 20 minutes   **Marinate:** 20 minutes
**Grill:** 8 minutes

*The sweet-spicy relish makes these aromatic steaks the star of any backyard barbecue. Refreshing mint and nectarines combine for a perfect flavor match.*

4 boneless beef top loin steaks, cut
    1 inch thick
6 cloves garlic, thinly sliced
  Salt
  Pepper
2 medium onions, coarsely chopped
1 teaspoon olive oil
2 tablespoons cider vinegar
1 tablespoon honey
1 medium nectarine, chopped
2 teaspoons snipped fresh mint

**1** Trim fat from steaks. With the point of a paring knife, make small slits in steaks. Insert half of the garlic into slits. Wrap steaks in plastic wrap; marinate at room temperature for 20 minutes. (For more intense flavor, marinate in the refrigerator for up to 8 hours.) Sprinkle with salt and pepper.

**2** Meanwhile, for relish, in a large nonstick skillet cook the remaining garlic and the onions in hot oil over medium heat about 10 minutes or until onions are a deep golden color, stirring occasionally. Stir in vinegar and honey. Stir in nectarine and mint; heat through. Set aside.

**3** *For a charcoal grill*, grill steaks on the rack of an uncovered grill directly over medium coals until desired doneness, turning once halfway through grilling. (Allow 8 to 12 minutes for medium rare and 12 to 15 minutes for medium.) (*For a gas grill*, preheat grill. Reduce heat to medium. Place steaks on grill rack over heat. Cover and grill as above.)

4 Serve the steaks with relish. If desired, garnish with additional fresh mint. Makes 4 servings.

🕙Nutrition Facts per serving: 272 calories, 9 g total fat (3 g saturated fat), 97 mg cholesterol, 108 mg sodium, 13 g carbohydrate, 1 g fiber, 34 g protein. Daily Values: 2% vit. A, 9% vit. C, 2% calcium, 27% iron.

## BEEF STEAKS WITH TOMATO-GARLIC BUTTER

**Prep:** 12 minutes   **Grill:** 8 minutes

*Beef steaks take kindly to the enhancement of butter, especially this tangy, garlic-infused blend. (Double the butter recipe if you want to spread it on warm bread.)*

½ cup butter, softened
1 tablespoon snipped oil-packed dried tomatoes
1 tablespoon chopped kalamata olives
1 tablespoon finely chopped green onion
1 clove garlic, minced
4 boneless beef top loin steaks, cut 1 inch thick

1 For butter, in a small bowl stir together the butter, dried tomatoes, kalamata olives, green onion, and garlic. Set aside. Trim fat from steaks. *For a charcoal grill,* grill steaks on the rack of an uncovered grill directly over medium coals until desired doneness, turning once halfway through grilling. (Allow 8 to 12 minutes for medium-rare and 12 to 15 minutes for medium doneness.) (*For a gas grill,* preheat grill. Reduce heat to medium. Place steaks on grill rack over heat. Cover and grill as above.)

2 If desired, sprinkle steaks with salt and pepper. To serve, spread 1 tablespoon of the butter mixture over each steak. Cover and chill the remaining butter mixture for another time (also can be used as a spread for bread). Makes 4 servings.

Nutrition Facts per serving: 383 calories, 22 g total fat (11 g saturated fat), 161 mg cholesterol, 227 mg sodium, 0 g carbohydrate, 0 g fiber, 45 g protein. Daily Values: 10% vit. A, 1% vit. C, 1% calcium, 32% iron.

## Did You Know?

**Did you know that every time you grill a steak, you are repeating the ritual that gave the meat its name? The Saxons and Jutes, who invaded England in the fifth century, brought along their skills as cattlemen. They were master grillers, cooking their beef on pointed sticks over campfires and calling it "steik," which means meat on a stick.**

## Sizzlin' Solutions

**Gorgonzola is a rich and creamy blue cheese made from cow's milk. The strong-flavored cheese has an ivory interior that is streaked with the characteristic blue-green veins. If the cheese is aged for more than 6 months, the flavor and aroma can become quite strong—in fact, down right unpleasant. This flavorful cheese teams nicely with sliced pears, apples, peaches, and hearty red wines. Adventuresome cooks will find it especially tasty melted over grilled steaks or baked potatoes or crumbled into salads.**

# Beef and Gorgonzola Salad

**Prep:** 15 minutes   **Grill:** 14 minutes

*Real men eat salad. (And besides, any plate of greens topped off with sirloin, grilled onions, and tangy blue cheese is really too hearty to nibble.)*

    3 tablespoons balsamic vinegar
    2 tablespoons olive oil
    1 clove garlic, minced
    ½ teaspoon salt
    ½ teaspoon pepper
    1 boneless beef sirloin steak, cut
        1 inch thick
    1 tablespoon snipped fresh thyme
    2 teaspoons snipped fresh rosemary
    4 ¼-inch slices red onion
    6 cups lightly packed mesclun or
        torn mixed salad greens
    8 yellow and/or red pear tomatoes,
        halved
    2 tablespoons crumbled Gorgonzola
        or other blue cheese

**1** For vinaigrette, in a screw-top jar combine vinegar, oil, garlic, salt, and pepper; cover and shake well. Trim fat from steak. Remove 1 tablespoon vinaigrette from jar and brush evenly onto both sides of steak. Press thyme and rosemary onto both sides of steak. Brush both sides of onion slices with some of the remaining vinaigrette, reserving the rest.

**2** *For a charcoal grill,* grill steak and onion slices on the rack of an uncovered grill directly over medium coals until steak is desired doneness and onion is tender, turning once halfway through grilling. (For steak, allow 14 to 18 minutes for medium-rare and 18 to 22 minutes for medium doneness. For onion, allow about 10 minutes.) (*For a gas grill,* preheat grill. Reduce heat to medium. Place steak and onion slices on grill rack over heat. Cover and grill as above.)

**3** Divide mesclun among 4 dinner plates. To serve, thinly slice the steak across the grain. Separate onion slices into rings. Arrange warm steak and onion on mesclun. Drizzle with the reserved vinaigrette. Top with tomatoes and blue cheese. Makes 4 servings.

Nutrition Facts per serving: 266 calories, 16 g total fat (5 g saturated fat), 59 mg cholesterol, 373 mg sodium, 9 g carbohydrate, 2 g fiber, 22 g protein. Daily Values: 7% vit. A, 28% vit. C, 4% calcium, 22% iron.

## BEEF STEAK IN THAI MARINADE

**Prep:** 10 minutes   **Grill:** 14 minutes
**Marinate:** 4 hours   **Stand:** 5 minutes

    1 2½-pound boneless beef sirloin
        steak, cut 1 inch thick
    ½ cup unsweetened coconut milk
    ½ stalk lemongrass, trimmed and
        coarsely chopped, or ⅛ teaspoon
        finely shredded lemon peel
    3 tablespoons lime juice
    2 tablespoons fish sauce or soy
        sauce
    2 to 4 tablespoons red curry paste
    2 teaspoons sugar

1 Trim fat from steak. Place steak in a plastic bag set in a shallow dish.

2 For marinade, in a blender container or food processor bowl combine coconut milk, lemongrass, lime juice, fish sauce, red curry paste, and sugar. Cover and blend or process until smooth. Pour marinade over steak; seal bag. Marinate in the refrigerator for 4 to 24 hours, turning bag occasionally.

3 Drain steak, reserving marinade. *For a charcoal grill*, grill steak on the rack of an uncovered grill directly over medium coals until desired doneness, turning once and brushing with reserved marinade halfway through grilling. (Allow 14 to 18 minutes for medium-rare or 18 to 22 minutes for medium doneness.) (*For a gas grill*, preheat grill. Reduce heat to medium-hot. Place steak on grill rack over heat. Cover; grill as above.) Discard any remaining marinade. Remove steak from grill; let stand for 5 minutes. Thinly slice meat across the grain. Makes 10 servings.

Nutrition Facts per serving: 233 calories, 12 g total fat (6 g saturated fat), 77 mg cholesterol, 210 mg sodium, 3 g carbohydrate, 0 g fiber, 26 g protein. Daily Values: 3% vit. A, 2% vit. C, 1% calcium, 20% iron.

## Southwest Steak

**Prep:** 20 minutes  **Marinate:** 6 to 24 hours
**Grill:** 14 minutes

- 1 1-pound boneless beef sirloin steak, cut 1¼ to 1½ inches thick
- 1 medium onion, chopped
- ⅓ cup lime juice
- ¼ cup snipped fresh cilantro
- 3 fresh jalapeño peppers, seeded and finely chopped
- 3 tablespoons water
- 2 tablespoons cooking oil
- 1 teaspoon ground cumin
- 1 teaspoon bottled minced garlic
- ½ teaspoon ground red pepper
- ¼ teaspoon salt

1 Trim fat from steak. Place steak in a plastic bag set in a shallow dish. For marinade, combine onion, lime juice, 2 tablespoons of the cilantro, the jalapeño peppers, water, oil, cumin, garlic, red pepper, and salt. Pour marinade over steak; seal bag. Marinate in refrigerator 6 to 24 hours, turning bag occasionally.

2 Drain steak, reserving marinade. *For a charcoal grill*, grill steak on the rack of an uncovered grill directly over medium coals to desired doneness, turning once and brushing occasionally with marinade up to the last 5 minutes of grilling. (Allow 14 to 18 minutes for medium-rare and 18 to 22 minutes for medium doneness.) (*For a gas grill*, preheat grill. Reduce heat to medium. Place steak on grill rack over heat. Cover and grill as above.) Discard any remaining marinade. Sprinkle steak with the remaining 2 tablespoons cilantro. Makes 4 servings.

Nutrition Facts per serving: 256 calories, 15 g total fat (5 g saturated fat), 76 mg cholesterol, 148 mg sodium, 3 g carbohydrate, 0 g fiber, 26 g protein. Daily Values: 1% vit. A, 27% vit. C, 1% calcium, 22% iron.

## Flaming Facts

**Several cuts of beef have interesting names, but few cooks know why. Sirloin, so it's told, likely comes from the French word surlonge (over the loin). Filet mignon is French for small and boneless; the name first appeared in a book by O. Henry in 1906. It is cut from the small end of the beef tenderloin. London Broil is actually the name of a recipe, not a cut—but some markets sell an appropriate cut to use (flank, top round, or chuck shoulder) by that name anyway. It is named after England's capital city.**

## STEAK-LOVER'S PLATTER

**Prep:** 40 minutes  **Marinate:** 4 to 6 hours
**Grill:** 14 minutes

*A meat-and-potatoes meal gets real flavorful
with a beer-and-vinegar marinade and a
generous amount of marjoram.*

      2 pounds boneless beef top sirloin
            steak, cut 1 inch thick
   ½ cup cider vinegar
      5 tablespoons snipped fresh
            marjoram or 3 teaspoons dried
            marjoram, crushed
   ¼ cup dark beer or nonalcoholic beer
   ¼ cup olive oil or cooking oil
      1 clove garlic, minced
      1 recipe Onion Sauce
      3 medium baking potatoes, each cut
            lengthwise into 8 wedges (about
            1 pound total)
      3 medium yellow, orange, red,
            and/or green sweet peppers, cut
            into 1-inch rings
      2 medium zucchini, quartered
            lengthwise

**1** Trim fat from steak. Place steak in a plastic
bag set in a shallow dish. For marinade, in
a small bowl combine vinegar, 2 tablespoons
of the fresh marjoram or 2 teaspoons of the
dried marjoram, the beer, 2 tablespoons of the
oil, the garlic, ½ teaspoon salt, and
½ teaspoon pepper. Pour over steak; seal bag.
Marinate in the refrigerator for 4 to 6 hours,
turning bag occasionally.

**2** Prepare Onion Sauce. Keep warm. In a
covered medium saucepan cook potato
wedges in boiling water for 4 minutes; drain.
In a large bowl stir together potatoes, sweet
peppers, and zucchini. In a small bowl stir
together the remaining oil, 1 tablespoon of
the fresh marjoram or 1 teaspoon of the dried
marjoram, ¼ teaspoon salt, and ¼ teaspoon
pepper. Sprinkle over vegetables and toss
gently to coat.

**3** Drain steak, discarding marinade. *For a
charcoal grill*, grill steak on the rack of an
uncovered grill directly over medium coals
until desired doneness, turning once halfway
through grilling. (Allow 14 to 18 minutes for
medium-rare and 18 to 22 minutes for
medium doneness.) While the steak is
grilling, add potatoes, sweet peppers, and
zucchini to grill.* Grill vegetables until
tender, turning once halfway through grilling.
(Allow 10 to 12 minutes for potatoes and
peppers and 5 to 6 minutes for zucchini.) (*For
a gas grill*, preheat grill. Reduce heat to
medium. Place steak, then potatoes, sweet
peppers, and zucchini on grill rack over heat.
Cover and grill as above.)

**4** To serve, cut steak across the grain into
¼-inch slices. Transfer steak slices to a
serving platter and arrange potatoes,
zucchini, and peppers around steak. If using,
sprinkle with the remaining fresh marjoram.
Drizzle with half of the sauce; pass the
remaining sauce. Makes 6 servings.

**Onion Sauce:** In a small saucepan cook
1 cup chopped onion and 1 clove garlic,
minced, in 1 tablespoon hot margarine or
butter over medium heat until onion is tender.
In a small bowl combine ½ cup dark beer or
nonalcoholic beer, ½ cup beef broth,
1 tablespoon cornstarch, and 1 tablespoon
Worcestershire sauce; add to onion mixture.
Cook and stir until thickened and bubbly.
Cook and stir for 2 minutes more. Makes
about 1⅓ cups.

Nutrition Facts per serving: 510 calories,
23 g total fat (6 g saturated fat), 101 mg cholesterol,
445 mg sodium, 34 g carbohydrate, 2 g fiber,
39 g protein. Daily Values: 38% vit. A, 165% vit. C,
4% calcium, 41% iron.

*\*Note:* If all of the food won't fit on your grill
at one time, cook it in two batches, cooking
vegetables first. If the vegetables get too cool
while the remaining food is cooking, reheat
them on the grill while you slice the meat.

# Basil-Stuffed Beef

**Prep:** 20 minutes  **Grill:** 1 hour
**Stand:** 10 minutes

*Cooking this garlic-and-basil-stuffed roast over indirect heat makes it taste like filet mignon.*

1 3- to 3½-pound boneless beef top
    sirloin roast, cut 1¾ inches thick
¼ teaspoon salt
¼ teaspoon pepper
2 cups loosely packed fresh basil
    leaves, snipped
8 to 10 cloves garlic, minced
2 teaspoons olive oil

1 Trim fat from meat. Make five or six 5-inch-long slits along the top of the meat, cutting almost through it. Sprinkle with salt and pepper.

2 For filling, in a small bowl combine basil and garlic. Stuff the filling into the slits in the meat. Tie the meat with 100-percent-cotton string to hold the slits closed. Drizzle with olive oil. Insert a meat thermometer in center of meat.

3 For a charcoal grill, arrange medium coals around a drip pan. Test for medium-low heat above the pan. Place meat on grill rack over drip pan. Cover and grill for 1 to 1½ hours or until meat thermometer registers 155°. [*For a gas grill,* preheat grill. Reduce heat to medium-low. Adjust for indirect cooking (see page 10). Grill as above, except place meat on a rack in a roasting pan.]

4 Remove meat from grill. Cover with foil; let stand for 10 minutes before carving. (The meat's temperature will rise 5° during standing.) Makes 10 to 12 servings.

Nutrition Facts per serving: 255 calories,
13 g total fat (5 g saturated fat), 91 mg cholesterol,
121 mg sodium, 1 g carbohydrate, 0 g fiber,
31 g protein. Daily Values: 1% vit. C, 2% calcium,
23% iron.

# BEEF AND AVOCADO TACOS

**Prep:** 20 minutes  **Grill:** 10 minutes

*Threading the ingredients on skewers keeps things organized on the grill, allowing you to kick back like a caballero at the end of a long day's ride.*

2 tablespoons lemon juice
1 avocado, seeded, peeled, and cut
    into ½-inch cubes
1 pound boneless beef sirloin or eye
    round steak, cut 1 inch thick
1 medium onion, cut into wedges
2 fresh cubanelle, Anaheim, or
    poblano peppers, cut into 1-inch
    squares
1 tablespoon olive oil
½ cup picante sauce
2 cups shredded lettuce
4 7- to 8-inch flour tortillas, warmed

1 Drizzle lemon juice over avocado; toss gently to coat. Set aside.

2 Trim fat from steak. Cut steak into 2×1-inch thin strips. On four 12-inch skewers, thread steak accordion-style. On four 12-inch skewers, alternately thread onion and peppers. Brush vegetables with oil.

3 For a charcoal grill, grill kabobs on the rack of an uncovered grill directly over medium coals for 10 to 12 minutes or until meat is slightly pink in center, turning once and brushing occasionally with picante sauce. (*For a gas grill,* preheat grill. Reduce heat to medium. Place kabobs on grill rack over heat. Cover and grill as above.)

4 To serve, divide the avocado, steak, onion, peppers, and lettuce among the warm tortillas. Fold tortillas over filling. If desired, serve tacos with additional picante sauce. Makes 4 servings.

Nutrition Facts per serving: 425 calories,
24 g total fat (6 g saturated fat), 76 mg cholesterol,
403 mg sodium, 24 g carbohydrate, 3 g fiber,
30 g protein. Daily Values: 7% vit. A, 105% vit. C,
5% calcium, 32% iron.

# Italian Steak Sandwiches

**Prep:** 20 minutes   **Grill:** 16 minutes

*Flavors of Italian cuisine dominate in this sandwich. The intensely flavorful, garlicky olive oil sauce elevates the steak sandwich from ordinary to outstanding.*

> 1 1-pound boneless beef sirloin steak, cut 1 inch thick
> 1 cup loosely packed fresh Italian flat-leaf parsley
> 3 tablespoons olive oil
> 4 teaspoons lemon juice
> 1 tablespoon capers, drained
> 2 cloves garlic, minced
> Dash salt
> Dash bottled hot pepper sauce
> 4 1-inch slices sourdough bread
> 1 medium onion, thinly sliced and separated into rings
> 1 cup mesclun

**1** Trim fat from steak. For sauce, in a blender container or food processor bowl combine parsley, olive oil, lemon juice, capers, garlic, salt, and hot pepper sauce. Cover and blend or process until nearly smooth, stopping and scraping sides as necessary. Set aside.

**2** *For a charcoal grill,* grill steak on the rack of an uncovered grill directly over medium coals until desired doneness, turning once halfway through grilling. (Allow 14 to 18 minutes for medium-rare and 18 to 22 minutes for medium doneness.) Remove steak from grill. Add bread slices, cut sides down, to grill. Grill for 2 to 4 minutes or until bread is lightly browned, turning once halfway through grilling. (*For a gas grill,* preheat grill. Reduce heat to medium. Place steaks, then bread on grill rack over heat. Cover and grill as above.)

**3** Thinly slice steak. To serve, arrange onion rings and mesclun on bread slices; top with steak slices. Drizzle with sauce. Makes 4 servings.

Nutrition Facts per serving: 211 calories, 13 g total fat (2 g saturated fat), 13 mg cholesterol, 244 mg sodium, 17 g carbohydrate, 1 g fiber, 7 g protein. Daily Values: 8% vit. A, 41% vit. C, 4% calcium, 14% iron.

## Flaming Facts

Here's a list of the 10 most tender steaks (listed from most tender to least tender), according to the National Cattlemen's Beef Association:
1. Tenderloin
2. Chuck Top Blade
3. Top Loin
4. Porterhouse/T-Bone
5. Rib Eye
6. Rib
7. Chuck Eye
8. Top Sirloin
9. Round Tip
10. Chopped

To help make less tender steaks more tender, consider marinating them before grilling. (See page 34 for tips on marinades.)

Jalapeño Beef Kabobs

## JALAPEÑO BEEF KABOBS

**Prep:** 15 minutes   **Grill:** 12 minutes

*Firecracker-hot but as sweet-as-pie, jalapeño pepper jelly adds zing to these kabobs. Look for it with other jams and jellies at the supermarket.*

1 10-ounce jar jalapeño pepper jelly
2 tablespoons lime juice
1 clove garlic, minced
4 small purple or white boiling onions
4 baby pattypan squash, halved crosswise
1 pound boneless beef sirloin steak, cut 1 inch thick
4 fresh tomatillos, husked and cut into quarters
½ of a medium red or green sweet pepper, cut into 1-inch squares
Hot cooked polenta (optional)

**1** For glaze, in a small saucepan combine the jalapeño jelly, lime juice, and garlic. Cook and stir over medium heat until jelly is melted. Remove from heat.

**2** In a small covered saucepan cook onions in a small amount of boiling water for 3 minutes. Add squash; cook for 1 minute more; drain. Trim fat from steak. Cut steak into 1-inch cubes. On eight 6- to 8-inch metal skewers, alternately thread onions, squash, steak, tomatillos, and sweet pepper.

**3** *For a charcoal grill,* grill kabobs on the rack of an uncovered grill directly over medium coals for 12 to 14 minutes or until meat is slightly pink in center, turning once and brushing occasionally with glaze during the last 5 minutes of grilling. (*For a gas grill,* preheat grill. Reduce heat to medium. Place kabobs on grill rack over heat. Cover; grill as above.)

**4** Serve kabobs with hot polenta, if desired, and any remaining glaze. Serves 4.

Nutrition Facts per serving: 444 calories, 11 g total fat (4 g saturated fat), 76 mg cholesterol, 71 mg sodium, 61 g carbohydrate, 2 g fiber, 27 g protein. Daily Values: 9% vit. A, 54% vit. C, 4% calcium, 27% iron.

# Beef and Fruit Salad

**Prep:** 20 minutes   **Marinate:** 30 minutes
**Grill:** 14 minutes

12 ounces boneless beef sirloin steak, cut 1 inch thick
⅓ cup reduced-sodium teriyaki sauce
¼ cup lemon juice
¼ cup water
2 teaspoons toasted sesame oil
⅛ teaspoon bottled hot pepper sauce
3 cups shredded napa cabbage
1 cup torn or shredded spinach
2 cups fresh fruit (such as sliced plums, nectarines, or kiwi fruit; halved seedless grapes or strawberries; and/or raspberries)

**1** Trim fat from steak. Place steak in a plastic bag set in a shallow dish. For marinade, combine teriyaki sauce, lemon juice, water, oil, and hot pepper sauce; reserve ⅓ cup for dressing. Pour remaining marinade over steak; seal bag. Marinate at room temperature up to 30 minutes, turning bag occasionally. (Or, marinate in refrigerator up to 8 hours.)

**2** Drain steak, reserving marinade. *For a charcoal grill,* grill steak on the rack of an uncovered grill directly over medium coals until desired doneness, turning once halfway through grilling and brushing occasionally with reserved marinade up to the last 5 minutes of grilling. (Allow 14 to 18 minutes for medium-rare or 18 to 22 minutes for medium doneness.) (*For a gas grill,* preheat grill. Reduce heat to medium. Place steak on grill rack over heat. Cover and grill as above.) Discard any remaining marinade.

**3** To serve, divide cabbage and spinach among 4 serving plates. Thinly slice steak across the grain. Arrange steak and fruit on greens. Drizzle with reserved dressing. Makes 4 servings.

Nutrition Facts per serving: 248 calories, 10 g total fat (3 g saturated fat), 57 mg cholesterol, 307 mg sodium, 19 g carbohydrate, 2 g fiber, 22 g protein. Daily Values: 19% vit. A, 86% vit. C, 6% calcium, 19% iron.

## LETTUCE-WRAPPED VIETNAMESE BEEF

**Prep:** 15 minutes **Marinate:** 2 to 24 hours
**Grill:** 8 minutes

*Vietnamese cuisine is increasingly popular, and this fresh, flavorful dish makes it easy to see why. The marinade is key here, giving strips of sirloin an enticing lightness. To eat, wrap the lettuce leaves around the beef slices and eat out-of-hand.*

   1 pound beef top sirloin steak, cut
      1 inch thick
  ¼ cup chopped green onions
   2 stalks lemongrass, chopped
   2 tablespoons sugar
   2 tablespoons lime juice
   2 tablespoons fish sauce
   3 cloves garlic, minced
   1 recipe Rice Vinegar Sauce
   8 large lettuce leaves
     Assorted toppings (such as
      shredded carrot, fresh cilantro
      leaves, shredded fresh mint
      leaves, and/or chopped peanuts)

**1** Trim fat from steak. Place steak in a plastic bag set in a shallow dish. For marinade, in a small bowl combine the green onions, lemongrass, sugar, lime juice, fish sauce, and garlic. Pour over steak; seal bag. Marinate in the refrigerator for 2 to 24 hours, turning bag occasionally. Drain steak, discarding marinade.

**2** *For a charcoal grill,* grill steak on the rack of an uncovered grill directly over medium coals until desired doneness, turning once halfway through grilling. (Allow 8 to 12 minutes for medium-rare and 12 to 15 minutes for medium doneness.) (*For a gas grill,* preheat grill. Reduce heat to medium. Place steaks on grill rack over heat. Cover and grill as above.)

**3** Meanwhile, prepare Rice Vinegar Sauce. To serve, overlap 2 lettuce leaves on individual serving plates. Thinly slice steak. Arrange steak slices on lettuce leaves. Add the desired toppings; drizzle with Rice Vinegar Sauce. Roll lettuce leaves around meat. Makes 4 servings.

**Rice Vinegar Sauce:** In a small bowl combine ¼ cup sugar; ¼ cup rice vinegar; 2 tablespoons lime juice; 2 tablespoons fish sauce; 2 cloves garlic, minced; and dash ground red pepper. Makes about ½ cup.

Nutrition Facts per serving: 348 calories, 13 g total fat (5 g saturated fat), 76 mg cholesterol, 671 mg sodium, 30 g carbohydrate, 1 g fiber, 29 g protein. Daily Values: 43% vit. A, 19% vit. C, 3% calcium, 28% iron.

# Beef Brochettes Tamarind

**Prep:** 30 minutes **Marinate:** 2 to 24 hours
**Grill:** 12 minutes

  1½ pounds boneless beef sirloin steak
   ¼ cup honey
   ¼ cup water
   1 to 2 tablespoons grated fresh
      ginger
   1 tablespoon tamarind concentrate
      (no water added)
  ¾ teaspoon salt
   2 cups assorted fresh vegetables
      (such as whole mushrooms,
      ½-inch slices of zucchini or
      yellow summer squash, and/or
      1-inch pieces of sweet pepper)

### Did You Know?

Tamarind is a sour pulp that is often used as a flavoring in Indian and Middle Eastern cuisines. Known as an Indian date, the tamarind is the fruit of a tall shade tree found in Asia, northern Africa, and India. The large, 5-inch-long pods envelop small seeds and a sweet-sour pulp. When dried, the pulp becomes very sour. You'll find it listed as an ingredient in the ever-popular Worcestershire sauce.

**1** Trim fat from steak. Cut into 1½-inch cubes. Place steak cubes in a plastic bag set in a shallow dish. For marinade, in a small bowl stir together the honey, water, ginger, tamarind, and salt. Pour over steak; seal bag. Marinate in the refrigerator for 2 to 24 hours, turning bag occasionally.

**2** Drain steak, reserving marinade. On six 10- to 12-inch metal skewers, alternately thread steak cubes and vegetables, leaving a ¼-inch space between pieces.

**3** *For a charcoal grill,* grill kabobs on the rack of an uncovered grill directly over medium coals for 12 to 15 minutes or until desired doneness, turning once and brushing occasionally with marinade during the first half of grilling. (*For a gas grill,* preheat grill. Reduce heat to medium. Place kabobs on grill rack over heat. Cover; grill as above.) To serve, remove meat and vegetables from skewers. Makes 6 servings.

ⓥNutrition Facts per serving: 257 calories, 10 g total fat (4 g saturated fat), 76 mg cholesterol, 424 mg sodium, 14 g carbohydrate, 1 g fiber, 26 g protein. Daily Values: 1% vit. C, 1% calcium, 22% iron.

## TROPICAL FIESTA STEAK

**Prep:** 20 minutes  **Grill:** 14 minutes
**Marinate:** 12 hours

⅓ cup frozen orange juice
   concentrate, thawed
3 tablespoons cooking oil
3 tablespoons honey
1 tablespoon sliced green onion
2 teaspoons spicy brown or Dijon-
   style mustard
1 teaspoon snipped fresh mint or
   ¼ teaspoon dried mint, crushed
   Few drops bottled hot pepper
   sauce
1 1½-pound boneless beef sirloin
   steak, cut 1 to 1¼ inches thick
½ cup chopped red sweet pepper
½ cup chopped red apple
½ cup chopped pear
½ cup chopped peeled peach
¼ cup chopped celery

2 tablespoons sliced green onion
2 teaspoons lemon juice
1 recipe Pineapple-Mustard Sauce
   (optional)
   Salt and pepper

**1** For marinade, in a small mixing bowl stir together the orange juice concentrate, oil, honey, the 1 tablespoon green onion, the mustard, mint, and hot pepper sauce. Remove ¼ cup of the mixture to make the relish; cover and refrigerate until needed.

**2** Trim fat from steak. Place the steak in a large plastic bag set in a shallow dish. Pour remaining marinade over steak; seal bag. Marinate in the refrigerator for 12 to 24 hours, turning bag occasionally.

**3** For fruit relish, in a bowl combine the reserved marinade, sweet pepper, apple, pear, peach, celery, the 2 tablespoons green onion, and lemon juice. Cover; refrigerate until serving time or up to 24 hours. If desired, prepare Pineapple-Mustard Sauce; refrigerate until serving time or up to 24 hours.

**4** Drain steak, reserving marinade. *For a charcoal grill,* grill steak on the rack of an uncovered grill directly over medium coals until desired doneness, turning once halfway through grilling and brushing occasionally with marinade up to the last 5 minutes of grilling. (Allow 14 to 20 minutes for medium-rare or 18 to 22 minutes for medium doneness.) (*For a gas grill,* preheat grill. Reduce heat to medium. Place steak on grill rack over heat. Cover and grill as above.) Season to taste with salt and pepper.

**5** To serve, thinly slice steak across the grain. Serve with the fruit relish. If desired, pass the Pineapple-Mustard Sauce. Serves 6.

Pineapple-Mustard Sauce: In a bowl stir together one 8-ounce carton pineapple yogurt, 2 tablespoons milk, and 1 teaspoon spicy brown mustard or Dijon-style mustard.

Nutrition Facts per serving: 344 calories, 17 total fat (5 g saturated fat), 76 mg cholesterol, 107 mg sodium, 21 g carbohydrate, 1 g fiber, 27 g protein. Daily Values: 33% vit. C, 10% calcium, 13% iron.

# Chili-Rubbed Steaks

**Prep:** 10 minutes **Marinate:** 1 to 2 hours
**Grill:** 8 minutes

*Down in the Rio Grande Valley they called it
comino and put it on everything but their corn
flakes. No question—cumin in the rub makes
these steaks great.*

2 12-ounce beef rib eye steaks, cut
    1 inch thick
1 tablespoon chili powder
1 tablespoon olive oil
1½ teaspoons dried oregano, crushed
½ teaspoon salt
½ teaspoon ground cumin

1 Trim fat from steaks. Place steaks in a
single layer in a shallow dish. For rub, in a
small bowl combine the chili powder, oil,
oregano, salt, and cumin. Spoon mixture
evenly over steaks; rub in with your fingers.
Cover and marinate in the refrigerator for 1 to
2 hours.

2 *For a charcoal grill,* grill steaks on the rack
of an uncovered grill directly over medium
coals until desired doneness, turning once
halfway through grilling. (Allow 8 to
12 minutes for medium-rare and 12 to
15 minutes for medium doneness.) (*For a gas
grill,* preheat grill. Reduce heat to medium.
Place steaks on grill rack over heat. Cover
and grill as above.)

3 To serve, cut steaks into serving-size
pieces. Makes 4 servings.

Nutrition Facts per serving: 323 calories,
16 g total fat (5 g saturated fat), 92 mg cholesterol,
376 mg sodium, 1 g carbohydrate, 1 g fiber,
42 g protein. Daily Values: 7% vit. A, 2% vit. C,
1% calcium, 24% iron.

# ROASTED GARLIC STEAK

**Prep:** 15 minutes **Grill:** 30 minutes

*To some minds, not liking garlic is as bad as not
liking sunshine. A word to the timid: Roasting
makes "the stinking rose" soft, sweet, and polite
as pie. You may want to throw on an extra bulb to
smear on bread.*

1 or 2 garlic bulbs
3 to 4 teaspoons snipped fresh basil
    or 1 teaspoon dried basil,
    crushed
1 tablespoon snipped fresh
    rosemary or 1 teaspoon dried
    rosemary, crushed
2 tablespoons olive oil or cooking oil
1½ pounds boneless beef rib eye
    steaks or sirloin steak, cut 1 inch
    thick
1 to 2 teaspoons cracked pepper
½ teaspoon salt

1 With a sharp knife, cut off the top ½ inch
from each garlic bulb to expose the ends of
the individual cloves. Leaving garlic bulbs
whole, remove any loose, papery outer layers.

2 Fold a 20×18-inch piece of heavy foil in
half crosswise. Trim into a 10-inch square.
Place garlic bulbs, cut sides up, in center of
foil square. Sprinkle the bulbs with basil and
rosemary and drizzle with oil. Bring up
opposite edges of foil and seal with a double
fold. Fold remaining edges together to
completely enclose garlic, leaving space for
steam to build.

3 *For a charcoal grill,* grill garlic on the rack
of an uncovered grill directly over medium
coals about 30 minutes or until garlic bulbs
feel soft when packet is squeezed, turning
garlic occasionally.

4 Meanwhile, trim fat from steaks. Sprinkle
pepper and salt evenly over steaks; rub in
with your fingers. While the garlic is grilling,
add steaks to grill. Grill until desired
doneness, turning once halfway through
grilling. (For rib eye steaks, allow 8 to
12 minutes for medium-rare and 12 to
15 minutes for medium doneness. For sirloin

steak, allow 14 to 18 minutes for medium-rare and 18 to 22 minutes for medium doneness.) (*For a gas grill,* preheat grill. Reduce heat to medium. Place garlic, then steaks on grill rack over heat. Cover and grill as above.) Remove garlic and steaks from grill.

**5** To serve, cut steaks into serving-size pieces. Remove garlic from foil, reserving the oil mixture. Squeeze garlic pulp from each clove onto steaks. Mash pulp slightly with a fork; spread over steaks. Drizzle with the reserved oil mixture. Makes 6 servings.

Nutrition Facts per serving: 251 calories, 15 g total fat (5 g saturated fat), 76 mg cholesterol, 235 mg sodium, 2 g carbohydrate, 0 g fiber, 26 g protein. Daily Values: 3% vit. C, 2% calcium, 20% iron.

# Steak with Sweet-Pepper Mustard

**Prep:** 30 minutes    **Grill:** 18 minutes

*Here are steaks with a Gallic touch—a Dijon mustard sauce enlivened by grilled sweet peppers and a rub featuring a French favorite, thyme.*

  2 medium red sweet peppers, quartered lengthwise
    Olive oil
  2 tablespoons snipped fresh thyme or 2 teaspoons dried thyme, crushed
  1 tablespoon Dijon-style mustard
  3 cloves garlic, minced
  2 beef T-bone steaks, cut 1 inch thick
  ¼ teaspoon salt
  ¼ teaspoon pepper

**1** Brush sweet peppers with olive oil. *For a charcoal grill,* grill peppers, cut sides up, on the rack of an uncovered grill directly over medium-hot coals about 10 minutes or until pepper skins are blistered and dark. (*For a gas grill,* preheat grill. Reduce heat to medium-hot. Place peppers, cut sides up, on grill rack over heat. Cover and grill as above.)

**2** Wrap peppers in foil and let stand for 20 minutes. Remove and discard pepper skins. Cut 2 pepper pieces lengthwise into thin strips; set aside. In a blender container or food processor bowl combine the remaining pepper pieces, 1 tablespoon of the fresh thyme or 1 teaspoon of the dried thyme, the Dijon mustard, and 1 clove of the garlic. Cover and blend or process until smooth.

**3** Meanwhile, trim fat from steaks. For rub, in a small bowl combine the remaining thyme, the remaining garlic, salt, and pepper. Sprinkle mixture evenly over steaks; rub in with your fingers. Add steaks to grill. Grill until desired doneness, turning once halfway through grilling. (Allow 8 to 12 minutes for medium-rare and 12 to 15 minutes for medium doneness.)

**4** Garnish the steaks with the grilled pepper strips. Serve with the mustard mixture. Makes 2 to 4 servings.

Nutrition Facts per serving: 467 calories, 25 g total fat (8 g saturated fat), 111 mg cholesterol, 560 mg sodium, 7 g carbohydrate, 1 g fiber, 50 g protein. Daily Values: 54% vit. A, 211% vit. C, 2% calcium, 32% iron.

## Grilling Know-How

Many professional cooks say they can judge a steak's doneness just by touch. Rare meat should feel like the area between your thumb and index finger when that hand is hanging relaxed—soft and spongy. For medium-rare, the same area feels springy but not hard when you form a loose fist. And for medium, the meat will feel similar to that same area when the fist is tightly clinched—firm, with minimal give. If this sounds a little beyond your tactile talents, then you might want to stick with your thermometer. Remember that medium-rare doneness is 145°; medium doneness is 160°.

## STEAK WITH BLUE CHEESE BUTTER

**Prep:** 10 minutes  **Grill:** 8 minutes

*The decadent combination of a good thick steak, Maytag blue cheese, butter, garlic, and fresh-from-the-garden basil is so rich, you'll think you've won the lottery.*

- ½ cup butter or margarine, softened
- ½ cup crumbled blue cheese (2 ounces)
- 1 tablespoon snipped fresh parsley
- 1 tablespoon snipped fresh basil or 1 teaspoon dried basil, crushed
- 1 clove garlic, minced
- 2 beef or T-bone porterhouse steaks, cut 1 to 1¼ inches thick

**1** For butter mixture, in a small bowl stir together butter, blue cheese, parsley, basil, and garlic. Set aside.

**2** Trim fat from steaks. *For a charcoal grill,* place medium coals in bottom of grill. Place steaks on grill rack directly over coals. Cover and grill until steaks are desired doneness, turning once halfway through grilling. (Allow 8 to 14 minutes for medium-rare and 12 to 18 minutes for medium doneness.) (*For a gas grill,* preheat grill. Reduce heat to medium. Place steaks on grill rack over heat. Grill as above.)

**3** To serve, cut steaks into serving-size pieces and top each piece with a generous 1 tablespoon butter mixture. Cover and chill the remaining butter mixture for another time (also can be served tossed with hot cooked vegetables.) Makes 2 to 4 servings.

Nutrition Facts per serving: 458 calories, 28 g total fat (13 g saturated fat), 161 mg cholesterol, 270 mg sodium, 0 g carbohydrate, 0 g fiber, 49 g protein. Daily Values: 8% vit. A, 3% calcium, 34% iron.

## Beer-Marinated Peppered Steaks

**Prep:** 10 minutes  **Marinate:** 4 to 24 hours
**Grill:** 8 minutes

*A simple marinade of beer and chili sauce gives T-bones a lip-smacking flavor. Spice lovers will enjoy the final sprinkling of cracked pepper.*

- 1 cup chopped onion
- ½ of a 12-ounce can (¾ cup) or bottle beer
- ¾ cup chili sauce
- ¼ cup snipped fresh parsley
- 3 tablespoons Dijon-style mustard
- 1 tablespoon Worcestershire sauce
- 2 teaspoons brown sugar
- ½ teaspoon paprika
- ½ teaspoon ground black pepper
- 3 beef T-bone or 6 top loin steaks, cut 1 inch thick
- 1 to 1½ teaspoons cracked black pepper

**1** For marinade, combine onion, beer, chili sauce, parsley, mustard, Worcestershire sauce, brown sugar, paprika, and the ground black pepper.

**2** Trim fat from steaks. Place steaks in a plastic bag set in a shallow dish. Pour marinade over steaks; seal bag. Marinate in the refrigerator for at least 4 to 24 hours, turning bag occasionally.

**3** Drain steaks, discarding marinade. Sprinkle both sides of steaks with the cracked black pepper.

**4** *For a charcoal grill,* grill steaks on the rack of an uncovered grill directly over medium coals until of desired doneness, turning once halfway through grilling. (Allow 8 to 12 minutes for rare and 12 to 15 minutes for medium doneness.) (*For a gas grill,* preheat grill. Reduce heat to medium. Place steaks on grill rack over heat. Cover and grill as above.) Makes 6 servings.

Nutrition Facts per serving: 224 calories, 10 g total fat (4 g saturated fat), 62 mg cholesterol, 212 mg sodium, 3 g carbohydrate, 0 g fiber, 27 g protein. Daily Values: 18% iron.

Steak with Blue Cheese Butter

## STUFFED STEAK PINWHEELS

**Prep:** 20 minutes   **Grill:** 12 minutes

*Popeye would serve these pinwheels with pride. Overstuffed with spinach and bacon, they are nice to look at and good to eat. (Just don't forget to take out the toothpicks.)*

  8 slices bacon
  1 1- to 1½-pound beef flank steak or
      top round steak
  ¾ teaspoon lemon-pepper seasoning
  ¼ teaspoon salt
  1 10-ounce package frozen chopped
      spinach, thawed and well
      drained
  2 tablespoons fine dry bread crumbs
  ½ teaspoon dried thyme, crushed
      Dash salt

**1** In a large skillet cook bacon over medium heat just until brown but not crisp. Remove from skillet; drain on paper towels. Set aside.

**2** Trim fat from steak. Score both sides of steak by making shallow diagonal cuts at 1-inch intervals in a diamond pattern. Place steak between two pieces of plastic wrap. Working from center to the edges, use flat side of a meat mallet to pound steak into a 12×8-inch rectangle. Remove plastic wrap. Sprinkle with ½ teaspoon of the lemon-pepper seasoning and the ¼ teaspoon salt. Arrange bacon lengthwise on steak.

**3** For filling, in a medium bowl combine spinach, bread crumbs, thyme, the remaining ¼ teaspoon lemon-pepper seasoning, and the dash salt. Spread over bacon. Starting from a short side, roll up. Secure with wooden toothpicks at 1-inch intervals, starting ½ inch from one end. Slice between toothpicks into eight 1-inch pinwheels. Thread 2 pinwheels onto each of 4 metal skewers.

**4** *For a charcoal grill,* grill pinwheels on the rack of an uncovered grill directly over medium coals until desired doneness, turning once halfway through grilling. (Allow 12 to 14 minutes for medium doneness.) (*For a gas grill,* preheat grill. Reduce heat to medium. Place pinwheels on grill rack over heat. Cover and grill as above.) To serve, remove from skewers. Makes 4 servings.

Nutrition Facts per serving: 265 calories, 15 g total fat (6 g saturated fat), 64 mg cholesterol, 702 mg sodium, 5 g carbohydrate, 2 g fiber, 27 g protein. Daily Values: 36% vit. A, 16% vit. C, 7% calcium, 21% iron.

*Grilling Know-How*

**Flank steak is a great steak for grilling. But, unless you tenderize it by marinating or tenderizing, you're in for some real tug of war when you bite into it (see page 34 on marinating). Once marinated, flank steak is perfect for both broiling and grilling. To serve, use a sharp knife to cut it across the grain into very thin slices.**

## Pepper-Marinated Flank Steak

**Prep:** 10 minutes   **Marinate:** 6 to 24 hours
**Grill:** 12 minutes

*This'll get their attention: A trio of peppers (including assertive red pepper flakes), red wine, lime juice, and soy sauce make this flank steak a bold one.*

  1 1- to 1½-pound beef flank steak
  ½ cup dry red wine
  ⅓ cup finely chopped onion
  2 tablespoons lime juice
  1 tablespoon cooking oil
  1 tablespoon reduced-sodium soy
      sauce

3 cloves garlic, minced
1 teaspoon crushed red pepper
½ teaspoon coarsely ground black
   pepper
½ teaspoon dried whole green
   peppercorns, crushed
1 tablespoon snipped fresh parsley

**1** Trim fat from steak. Score both sides of
steak in a diamond pattern by making
shallow diagonal cuts at 1-inch intervals.
Place in a plastic bag set in a shallow dish.

**2** For marinade, in a small bowl stir together
wine, onion, lime juice, oil, soy sauce,
garlic, red pepper, black pepper, and green
peppercorns. Pour over steak; seal bag.
Marinate in the refrigerator for 6 to 24 hours,
turning bag occasionally.

**3** Drain steak, reserving marinade. *For a
charcoal grill*, grill steak on the rack of an
uncovered grill directly over medium coals
until desired doneness, turning and brushing
once with marinade halfway through grilling.
(Allow 12 to 14 minutes for medium
doneness.) (*For a gas grill*, preheat grill.
Reduce heat to medium. Place steak on grill
rack over heat. Cover and grill as above.)

**4** To serve, thinly slice steak diagonally
across the grain. Sprinkle with parsley.
Makes 4 to 6 servings.

Ⓥ Nutrition Facts per serving: 199 calories,
10 g total fat (4 g saturated fat), 53 mg cholesterol,
145 mg sodium, 2 g carbohydrate, 0 g fiber,
22 g protein. Daily Values: 2% vit. A, 5% vit. C,
1% calcium, 15% iron.

## LEMONY FLANK STEAK

**Prep:** 15 minutes   **Marinate:** 2 to 24 hours
**Grill:** 12 minutes

*Lemon provides a subtle tartness to the oregano-
enhanced marinade. Embellish the strips of beef
with ultra-thin lemon slices and sprigs of fresh
oregano.*

1 1½-pound beef flank steak or
   boneless beef top sirloin steak
1 teaspoon finely shredded lemon
   peel
½ cup lemon juice
2 tablespoons sugar
2 tablespoons soy sauce
2 teaspoons snipped fresh oregano
   or ½ teaspoon dried oregano,
   crushed
⅛ teaspoon pepper
   Lemon slices (optional)

**1** Trim fat from steak. Score both sides of
steak in a diamond pattern by making
shallow diagonal cuts at 1-inch intervals.
Place steak in a plastic bag set in a shallow
dish. For marinade, in a small bowl combine
the lemon peel, lemon juice, sugar, soy sauce,
oregano, and pepper. Pour over steak; seal
bag. Marinate in the refrigerator for 2 to
24 hours, turning bag occasionally.

**2** Drain steak, reserving marinade. *For a
charcoal grill*, grill steak on the rack of an
uncovered grill directly over medium coals
until desired doneness, turning and brushing
once with marinade halfway through grilling.
(Allow 12 to 14 minutes for medium
doneness.) (*For a gas grill*, preheat grill.
Reduce heat to medium. Place steak on grill
rack over heat. Cover and grill as above.)

**3** To serve, thinly slice steak diagonally
across the grain. If desired, garnish with
lemon slices and additional fresh oregano.
Makes 6 servings.

Ⓥ Nutrition Facts per serving: 134 calories,
6 g total fat (3 g saturated fat), 40 mg cholesterol,
179 mg sodium, 3 g carbohydrate, 0 g fiber,
17 g protein. Daily Values: 6% vit. C, 1% calcium,
11% iron.

# Beef Satay

**Prep:** 25 minutes **Marinate:** 30 minutes
**Grill:** 3 minutes

*Satay, an Indonesian specialty, simply refers to cubes of marinated meat grilled on skewers and dipped in a sweet and spicy peanut sauce. Satay is often eaten as an appetizer or snack, but a generous serving of it makes a great meal.*

1 1- to 1¼-pound beef flank steak
⅓ cup plus 2 tablespoons light
    teriyaki sauce
½ teaspoon bottled hot pepper sauce
4 green onions, cut into 1-inch pieces
1 medium green or red sweet
    pepper, cut into ¾-inch chunks
3 tablespoons reduced-fat or regular
    peanut butter
3 tablespoons water
    Pomegranate seed (optional)

**1** Trim fat from steak. Thinly slice steak diagonally across the grain. For marinade, in a medium bowl combine the ⅓ cup teriyaki sauce and ¼ teaspoon of the pepper sauce. Add steak; toss to coat. Cover and marinate in the refrigerator for 30 minutes, stirring once. If using bamboo skewers, soak in warm water for 20 minutes; drain.

**2** Drain steak, reserving marinade. On 10- to 12-inch bamboo or metal skewers, alternately thread steak slices, accordion style, with green onion and sweet pepper pieces. Brush with marinade; discard any remaining marinade. Set aside.

**3** For peanut sauce, in a small saucepan combine the peanut butter, water, the 2 tablespoons teriyaki sauce, and the remaining pepper sauce. Cook and stir over medium heat just until smooth and heated through. Keep warm.

**4** *For a charcoal grill,* grill kabobs on the rack of an uncovered grill directly over medium coals for 3 to 4 minutes or until steak is slightly pink in center, turning once halfway through grilling. (*For a gas grill,* preheat grill. Reduce heat to medium. Place skewers on grill rack over heat. Cover and grill as above.)

**5** To serve, remove steak and vegetables from skewers; serve with warm peanut sauce. If desired, garnish with pomegranate seed. Makes 5 servings.

Nutrition Facts per serving: 221 calories, 10 g total fat (3 g saturated fat), 43 mg cholesterol, 567 mg sodium, 11 g carbohydrate, 1 g fiber, 21 g protein. Daily Values: 4% vit. A, 54% vit. C, 13% iron.

## ASIAN SALAD WITH BEEF

**Prep:** 15 minutes **Marinate:** 30 minutes
**Grill:** 12 minutes

*Many Vietnamese restaurants are famous for pho, noodle soup served in monster-size bowls. This beefy fusilli salad is inspired by the other side of the menu, where cool salads made of enticing blends of noodles, meat, herbs, and vegetables are found.*

1 1¼- to 1½-pound beef flank steak
½ cup red wine vinegar
3 tablespoons sugar
3 tablespoons cooking oil
1 tablespoon toasted sesame oil
1 tablespoon fish sauce or soy sauce
4 cloves garlic, minced
2 teaspoons grated fresh ginger
½ teaspoon salt
½ teaspoon crushed red pepper
12 ounces packaged dried fusilli
2 medium carrots, thinly bias-sliced
1 medium red or yellow sweet pepper,
    cut into cubes or thin strips
⅓ cup snipped fresh mint or cilantro

**1** Trim fat from steak. Score both sides of steak in a diamond pattern by making shallow diagonal cuts at 1-inch intervals. Place in a plastic bag set in a shallow dish.

**2** For marinade, in a screw-top jar combine vinegar, sugar, cooking oil, sesame oil, fish sauce, garlic, ginger, salt, and crushed red pepper; cover and shake well. Pour ⅓ cup of the marinade over steak; seal bag. Marinate at room temperature for 30 minutes or in the refrigerator for up to 8 hours, turning bag occasionally. Cover and chill the remaining marinade until needed.

**3** In a large pot or Dutch oven cook pasta in lightly salted boiling water for 10 to 15 minutes or until tender but still firm, adding carrots to pasta the last 1 minute of cooking. Drain pasta and carrots in colander. Rinse with cold water; drain well. Transfer to a large bowl; drizzle with the reserved marinade. Add sweet pepper and mint; toss gently to coat.

**4** Meanwhile, drain steak, discarding marinade. *For a charcoal grill,* grill steak on the rack of an uncovered grill directly over medium coals until desired doneness, turning once halfway through grilling. (Allow 12 to 14 minutes for medium doneness.) (*For a gas grill,* preheat grill. Reduce heat to medium. Place steak on grill rack over heat. Cover and grill as above.)

**5** To serve, thinly slice steak diagonally across the grain. Add to the pasta mixture; toss gently to coat. Makes 6 servings.

Nutrition Facts per serving: 474 calories, 16 g total fat (4 g saturated fat), 45 mg cholesterol, 311 mg sodium, 56 g carbohydrate, 3 g fiber, 26 g protein. Daily Values: 68% vit. A, 41% vit. C, 2% calcium, 34% iron.

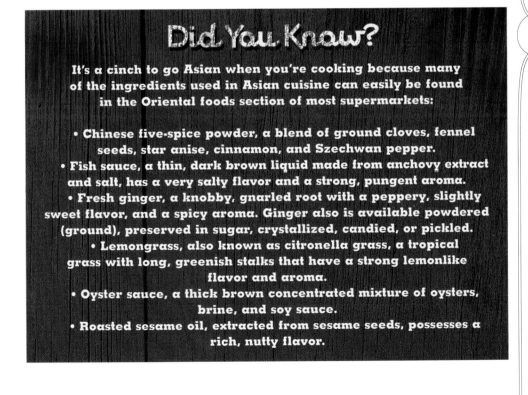

## Did You Know?

It's a cinch to go Asian when you're cooking because many of the ingredients used in Asian cuisine can easily be found in the Oriental foods section of most supermarkets:

- **Chinese five-spice powder**, a blend of ground cloves, fennel seeds, star anise, cinnamon, and Szechwan pepper.
- **Fish sauce**, a thin, dark brown liquid made from anchovy extract and salt, has a very salty flavor and a strong, pungent aroma.
- **Fresh ginger**, a knobby, gnarled root with a peppery, slightly sweet flavor, and a spicy aroma. Ginger also is available powdered (ground), preserved in sugar, crystallized, candied, or pickled.
- **Lemongrass**, also known as citronella grass, a tropical grass with long, greenish stalks that have a strong lemonlike flavor and aroma.
- **Oyster sauce**, a thick brown concentrated mixture of oysters, brine, and soy sauce.
- **Roasted sesame oil**, extracted from sesame seeds, possesses a rich, nutty flavor.

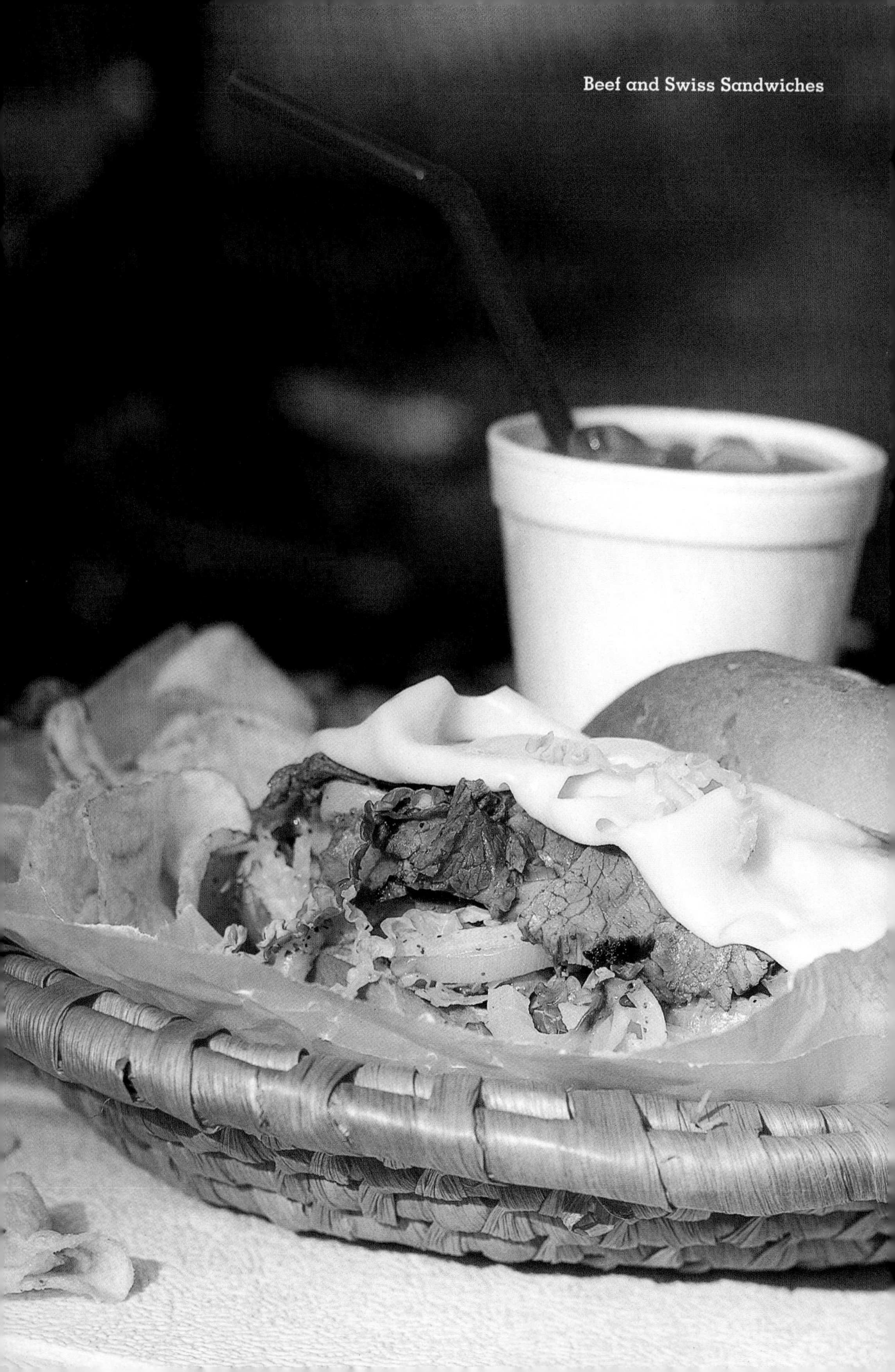

Beef and Swiss Sandwiches

# Beef and Swiss Sandwiches

**Prep:** 20 minutes   **Marinate:** 6 to 24 hours
**Grill:** 13 minutes

- 1   1- to 1¼-pound beef flank steak
- 1   medium sweet onion (such as Vidalia), thinly sliced
- ½   cup bottled clear Italian salad dressing or oil and vinegar salad dressing
- 2   tablespoons horseradish mustard
- 1½   cups packaged shredded cabbage with carrot (coleslaw mix)
- 6   kaiser or French-style rolls, split and toasted
- 4   ounces thinly sliced Swiss cheese

1 Trim fat from steak. Score both sides of steak in a diamond pattern by making shallow diagonal cuts at 1-inch intervals. Place steak and onion in a plastic bag set in a shallow dish. For marinade, in a bowl combine salad dressing and mustard. Pour over steak and onion; seal bag. Marinate steak in refrigerator 6 to 24 hours, turning bag occasionally.

2 Drain steak and onion, reserving marinade. Fold a 24×18-inch piece of heavy foil in half to make an 18×12-inch rectangle. Place onion in center of foil. Drizzle 2 tablespoons of marinade over onion. Bring up opposite edges of foil; seal with a double fold. Fold remaining edges together to completely enclose onion, leaving space for steam to build.

3 *For a charcoal grill,* grill steak and onion on the rack of an uncovered grill directly over medium coals for 12 to 14 minutes or until steak is slightly pink in center and onion is tender, turning steak and onion once and brushing steak once with marinade halfway through grilling. (*For a gas grill,* preheat grill. Reduce heat to medium. Place steak and onion on grill rack over heat. Cover; grill as above.) Remove steak and onion from grill. Add split rolls, cut sides down, to grill. Grill for 1 to 2 minutes or until lightly toasted.

4 To serve, thinly slice steak diagonally across the grain. Toss together onion and cabbage. Fill the rolls with steak slices and onion mixture. Top with cheese. Makes 6 servings.

Nutrition Facts per serving: 394 calories, 22 g total fat (7 g saturated fat), 53 mg cholesterol, 530 mg sodium, 25 g carbohydrate, 1 g fiber, 24 g protein. Daily Values: 18% vit. A, 16% vit. C, 19% calcium, 17% iron.

## SOY FLANK STEAK

**Prep:** 20 minutes   **Grill:** 12 minutes
**Marinate:** 2 hours

- 3   tablespoons rice vinegar
- 2   tablespoons thinly sliced green onion
- 2   tablespoons toasted sesame seed
- 2   tablespoons reduced-sodium soy sauce
- 2   tablespoons grated fresh ginger
- 2   teaspoons brown sugar
- ⅓   cup peanut oil
- 1   tablespoon toasted sesame oil
- 1   1¼-pound beef flank steak
- 6   cups shredded Chinese cabbage
- 1   cup coarsely shredded carrots
- 2   tablespoons snipped fresh cilantro

1 For dressing, in a bowl combine vinegar, onion, sesame seed, soy sauce, ginger, and brown sugar; stir until sugar dissolves. Slowly whisk in peanut oil and sesame oil.

2 Trim fat from steak. Place steak in a plastic bag set in a shallow dish. Pour half of dressing over steak; seal bag. Marinate in refrigerator 2 hours, turning bag occasionally.

3 Meanwhile, for slaw, combine cabbage, carrots, cilantro, and remaining dressing; toss to coat. Cover; chill until serving time.

4 Drain steak; discard marinade. *For a charcoal grill,* grill steak on the rack of an uncovered grill directly over medium coals until desired doneness, turning once halfway through grilling. (Allow 12 to 14 minutes for medium doneness.) (*For a gas grill,* preheat grill. Reduce heat to medium. Place steak on grill rack over heat. Cover; grill as above.) Thinly slice steak across grain; serve with slaw. Makes 6 servings.

Nutrition Facts per serving: 292 calories, 20 g total fat (5 g saturated fat), 44 mg cholesterol, 217 mg sodium, 9 g carbohydrate, 2 g fiber, 20 g protein. Daily Values: 61% vit. A, 37% vit. C, 6% calcium, 16% iron.

# Jerk London Broil

**Prep:** 15 minutes  **Marinate:** 30 minutes
**Grill:** 12 minutes

*The small Scotch bonnet pepper—one of the
hottest peppers on the planet and the star in
Jamaican cooking—packs a mouth-sizzling
punch. If you can't find these potent peppers or
want less heat, substitute a jalapeño pepper.*

1 1¼- to 1½-pound beef flank steak
4 green onions
¼ cup lime juice
2 tablespoons cooking oil
1 Scotch bonnet pepper, stem and
    seeds removed (optional)
2 teaspoons Jamaican jerk
    seasoning
1 1-inch piece fresh ginger, sliced
3 cloves garlic

**1** Trim fat from steak. Score both sides of
steak in a diamond pattern by making
shallow diagonal cuts at 1-inch intervals.
Place steak in a shallow glass dish. For
marinade, in a blender container combine
green onions, lime juice, oil, Scotch bonnet
pepper (if desired), jerk seasoning, ginger,
and garlic. Cover and blend until smooth.
Spread the marinade over steak. Cover and
marinate at room temperature for 30 minutes
or in the refrigerator for 6 to 24 hours.

**2** *For a charcoal grill,* grill steak on the rack
of an uncovered grill directly over medium
coals until desired doneness, turning once
halfway through grilling. (Allow 12 to 14
minutes for medium.) (*For a gas grill,*
preheat grill. Reduce heat to medium. Place
steak on grill rack over heat. Cover and grill
as above.)

**3** To serve, cut steak diagonally across
the grain into ⅛- to ¼-inch slices. Makes
6 servings.

Nutrition Facts per serving: 187 calories,
11 g total fat (3 g saturated fat), 44 mg cholesterol,
117 mg sodium, 2 g carbohydrate, 0 g fiber,
18 g protein. Daily Values: 4% vit. A, 8% vit. C,
1% calcium, 13% iron.

## BRISKET WITH SPICY BARBECUE SAUCE

**Prep:** 25 minutes  **Marinate:** 4 to 24 hours
**Grill:** 2 hours  **Stand:** 15 minutes

*Many a would-be barbecue master has hung up
his or her apron after failing the ultimate test:
brisket. The trick is to smoke the unforgiving cut
into submission, and slice it extra thin to serve.*

2 teaspoons seasoned salt
1 teaspoon paprika
1 teaspoon black pepper
1 2- to 3-pound fresh beef brisket
4 to 6 cups mesquite wood chips
¼ cup dry red wine
4 teaspoons Worcestershire sauce
1 tablespoon cooking oil
1 tablespoon red wine vinegar or
    cider vinegar
1 clove garlic, minced
½ teaspoon hot-style mustard
¼ teaspoon ground coriander
    Dash ground red pepper
1 recipe Spicy Barbecue Sauce

**1** For rub, in a small bowl combine seasoned
salt, paprika, and black pepper. Sprinkle
mixture evenly over meat (do not trim fat);
rub in with your fingers. Cover and marinate
in the refrigerator for 4 to 24 hours.

**2** At least 1 hour before grilling, soak wood
chips in enough water to cover. For basting
sauce, in a small bowl combine wine,
Worcestershire sauce, oil, vinegar, garlic,
mustard, coriander, and red pepper. Set aside.

**3** Drain wood chips. *For a charcoal grill,*
arrange medium-low coals around a drip
pan. Pour 1 inch of water into drip pan. Test
for low heat above the pan. Sprinkle one-
fourth of the wood chips over the coals. Place
meat, fat side up, on grill rack over drip pan.
Cover and grill for 2 to 2½ hours or until
meat is tender, brushing with basting sauce
every 30 minutes of grilling. Add more wood
chips every 30 minutes. [*For a gas grill,*
preheat grill. Reduce heat to low. Adjust for
indirect cooking (see page 10). Add wood

chips according to manufacturer's directions. Grill as above, except place meat, fat side up, on a rack in a roasting pan.]

**4** Remove meat from grill. Cover with foil; let stand for 15 minutes before slicing. Trim off layer of fat; thinly slice meat diagonally across grain. Serve meat with Spicy Barbecue Sauce. Makes 8 servings.

**Spicy Barbecue Sauce:** In a small saucepan stir together 1 cup catsup; 1 large tomato, peeled, seeded, and chopped; 1 small green sweet pepper, chopped; 2 tablespoons brown sugar; 2 tablespoons chopped onion; 1 to 2 tablespoons bottled steak sauce; 1 to 2 tablespoons Worcestershire sauce; ½ teaspoon garlic powder; ¼ teaspoon ground nutmeg; ¼ teaspoon ground cinnamon; ¼ teaspoon ground cloves; ¼ teaspoon ground red pepper; and ⅛ teaspoon ground ginger. Bring to boiling; reduce heat. Simmer, covered, about 5 minutes or until sweet pepper is crisp-tender. Serve warm or at room temperature. Makes about 2 cups.

Nutrition Facts per serving: 287 calories, 13 g total fat (4 g saturated fat), 78 mg cholesterol, 871 mg sodium, 16 g carbohydrate, 1 g fiber, 26 g protein. Daily Values: 7% vit. A, 41% vit. C, 2% calcium, 22% iron.

## Spicy Grilled Brisket

**Prep:** 25 minutes   **Soak:** 1 hour
**Grill:** 2½ hours   **Stand:** 10 minutes

*This tasty brisket makes enough for a crowd. The homemade sauce lends an additional zesty kick. Or, opt for a bottled sauce with some heat.*

 1½ **pounds mesquite wood chunks**
  1 **5- to 6-pound fresh beef brisket**
  3 **cloves garlic, cut into slivers**
  2 **tablespoons cooking oil**
  2 **tablespoons coarse or kosher salt**
  2 **tablespoons paprika**
  1 **tablespoon ground black pepper**
  1 **teaspoon ground red pepper**
  1 **teaspoon dried thyme, crushed**
    **Sweet and Hot Barbecue Sauce or bottled barbecue sauce**

**1** At least 1 hour before grilling, soak wood chunks in enough water to cover.

**2** Trim fat from brisket. Make several slits in surface of the brisket. Insert a sliver of garlic into each slit. Brush brisket with oil. In a small bowl stir together salt, paprika, black pepper, red pepper, and thyme. Rub pepper mixture over all sides of the meat.

**3** Drain wood chunks. *For a charcoal grill,* arrange medium-low coals around a drip pan. Test for medium-low heat above pan. Place about half of the drained wood chunks over the coals. Place brisket, fat side up, on grill rack over drip pan. Cover and grill for 2½ to 3 hours or until meat is tender. Add more wood chunks as necessary. [*For a gas grill,* preheat grill. Reduce heat to low. Adjust for indirect cooking (see page 10). Add wood chips according to manufacturer's directions. Grill as above, except place meat, fat side up, on a rack in a roasting pan.]

**4** Meanwhile, prepare Sweet and Hot Barbecue Sauce or warm bottled barbecue sauce in a small saucepan over low heat. To serve, let meat stand 10 minutes. Slice meat across the grain. Serve with barbecue sauce. Makes 15 servings.

**Sweet and Hot Barbecue Sauce:** In a large saucepan cook ½ cup chopped onion; 6 jalapeño chile peppers, seeded and chopped; and 2 cloves garlic, minced, in 1 tablespoon hot oil until onion is tender. Stir in 2 cups catsup, ¼ cup brown sugar, ¼ cup white wine vinegar, ¼ cup orange juice, 3 tablespoons Worcestershire sauce, and 1 teaspoon dry mustard. Bring mixture to boiling; reduce heat. Simmer, uncovered, for 10 to 15 minutes or until of desired consistency. Makes about 3 cups.

Nutrition Facts per serving: 243 calories, 11 g total fat (3 g saturated fat), 76 g cholesterol, 1,343 mg sodium, 11 g carbohydrate, 0 g fiber, 25 g protein. Daily Values: 9% vit. A, 2% vit. C, 1% calcium, 18% iron.

## RIB ROAST WITH DIJON SAUCE

**Prep:** 20 minutes **Marinate:** 6 to 24 hours
**Soak:** 1 hour **Grill:** 2 hours
**Stand:** 15 minutes

1 4-pound beef rib roast
¾ cup dry red wine
½ cup finely chopped onion
¼ cup lemon juice
1 tablespoon Worcestershire sauce
½ teaspoon dried rosemary, crushed
½ teaspoon dried marjoram, crushed
¼ teaspoon garlic salt
4 cups mesquite wood chips
1 8-ounce carton dairy sour cream
2 to 3 tablespoons Dijon-style mustard
1 green onion, thinly sliced
2 tablespoons ranch salad dressing
2 tablespoons milk

1 Trim fat from meat. Place in plastic bag set in shallow dish. Combine wine, onion, lemon juice, Worcestershire, rosemary, marjoram, garlic salt, and ¼ cup water. Pour over meat; seal bag. Marinate in refrigerator 6 to 24 hours, turning occasionally. At least 1 hour before grilling, soak wood chips in enough water to cover.

2 Drain meat, reserving marinade. Insert a meat thermometer into the center of meat without it touching bone.

3 Drain wood chips. *For a charcoal grill,* arrange medium coals around a drip pan. Pour 1 inch of water into drip pan. Test for medium-low heat above pan. Sprinkle one-fourth of the wood chips over the coals. Place meat, fat side up, on grill rack over drip pan. Cover and grill until thermometer registers 140° for medium-rare (2 to 2½ hours) or 155° for medium doneness (2½ to 3 hours), brushing occasionally with marinade during the first 1¾ hours of grilling. Add more wood chips every 30 minutes. [*For a gas grill,* preheat grill. Reduce heat to medium-low. Adjust for indirect cooking (see page 10). Add wood chips according to manufacturer's directions. Grill as above, except place meat, fat side up, in a roasting pan.] Remove meat

from grill. Cover; let stand for 15 minutes. (The meat's temperature will rise 5° during standing.)

4 For sauce, combine sour cream, mustard, onion, dressing, and milk. Slice meat; serve with sauce. Makes 8 servings.

Nutrition Facts per serving: 425 calories,
27 g total fat (12 g saturated fat), 126 mg cholesterol,
319 mg sodium, 3 g carbohydrate, 0 g fiber,
39 g protein. Daily Values: 7% vit. A, 7% vit. C,
4% calcium, 25% iron.

## Peppered Rib Roast

**Prep:** 10 minutes **Grill:** 2¼ hours
**Stand:** 15 minutes

4 teaspoons coarsely ground pepper
2 tablespoons finely chopped shallots
1 teaspoon coarse salt
1 teaspoon dried basil, crushed
1 teaspoon dried thyme, crushed
1 6-pound beef rib roast
1 tablespoon olive oil

1 Combine pepper, shallots, salt, basil, and thyme; set aside. Trim fat from meat. Brush meat with oil. Rub pepper mixture over surface of roast. Insert a meat thermometer into center of meat without touching bone.

2 *For a charcoal grill,* arrange medium coals around drip pan. Test for medium-low heat above pan. Place roast, bone side down, on grill rack over pan. Cover; grill until meat thermometer registers 140° for medium-rare (2¼ to 2¾ hours) or 155° for medium (2¾ to 3¼ hours). [*For a gas grill,* preheat grill. Reduce heat to medium. Adjust for indirect cooking (see page 10). Add wood chips according to manufacturer's directions. Grill as above, except place meat in roasting pan.]

3 Remove meat from grill. Cover with foil; let stand for 15 minutes before carving. (The meat's temperature will rise 5° during standing.) Makes 10 to 12 servings.

Nutrition Facts per serving: 310 calories,
18 g total fat (7 g saturated fat), 100 mg cholesterol,
305 mg sodium, 1 g carbohydrate, 0 g fiber,
34 g protein. Daily Values: 2% vit. A, 2% vit. C,
1% calcium, 23% iron.

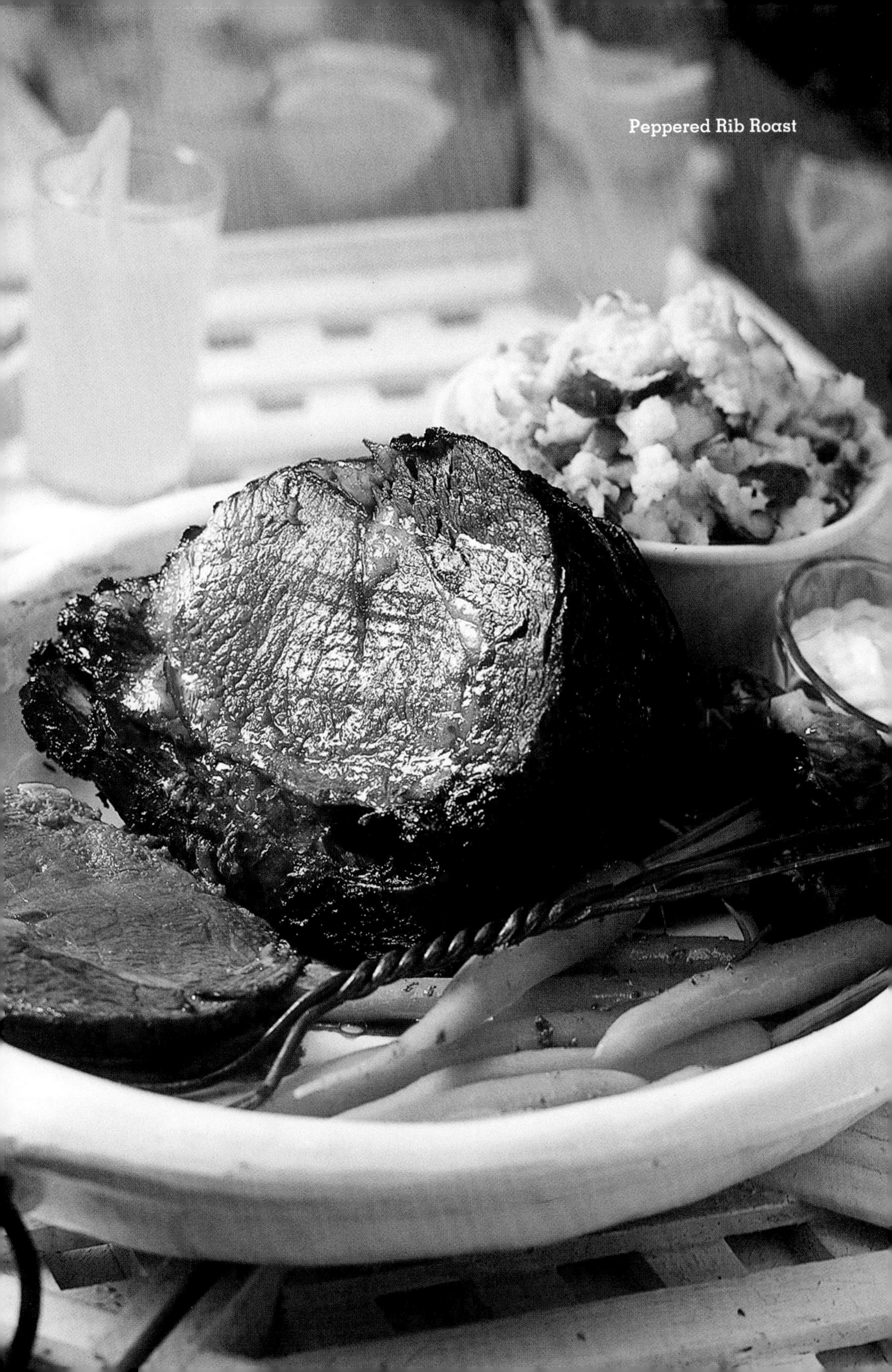

Peppered Rib Roast

## WINE-MARINATED BEEF ROAST

**Prep:** 15 minutes   **Marinate:** 6 to 24 hours
**Grill:** 1 hour   **Stand:** 15 minutes

*Don't toss out the marinade this time. It returns
as a finishing topper for this dill-scented roast
and mingles enticingly with a horseradish sauce.*

> 1 2- to 3-pound beef eye round roast
> 2 medium onions, sliced and
>    separated into rings
> ½ cup dry white wine
> ¼ cup olive oil or cooking oil
> 1 tablespoon dried dillweed
> 2 teaspoons coarsely ground pepper
> ½ teaspoon salt
> ⅔ cup mayonnaise or salad dressing
> ⅓ cup dairy sour cream
> 2 tablespoons prepared horseradish
> ⅛ teaspoon salt
> ⅛ teaspoon pepper

**1** Trim fat from meat. Place meat and onions
in a plastic bag set in a shallow dish. For
marinade, in a small bowl combine wine, oil,
2 teaspoons of the dillweed, the 2 teaspoons
coarse pepper, and the ½ teaspoon salt. Pour
over meat and onions; seal bag. Marinate in
the refrigerator 6 to 24 hours, turning bag
occasionally.

**2** Drain meat and onions, reserving
marinade. Chill onions and marinade while
grilling meat. Insert a meat thermometer into
the center of the meat.

**3** *For a charcoal grill,* arrange medium coals
around a drip pan. Test for medium-low
heat above the pan. Place meat on grill rack
over drip pan. Cover and grill until meat
thermometer registers 140° for medium-rare
(1 to 1½ hours) or 155° for medium doneness
(1½ to 2 hours). [*For a gas grill,* preheat grill.
Reduce heat to medium-low. Adjust for
indirect cooking (see page 10). Grill as above,
except place meat on a rack in a roasting
pan.] Remove meat from grill. Cover the
meat with foil; let stand for 15 minutes before
carving. (The meat's temperature will rise 5°
during standing.)

**4** Meanwhile, for sauce, in a small bowl
combine remaining dillweed, mayonnaise,
sour cream, horseradish, the ⅛ teaspoon salt,
and the ⅛ teaspoon pepper. Cover and chill
until ready to serve. In a large skillet bring the
onions and marinade to boiling; reduce heat.
Simmer, covered, about 12 minutes or until
onions are tender.

**5** To serve, thinly slice the meat. Serve meat
slices with the onion mixture and sauce.
Makes 8 servings.

Nutrition Facts per serving: 374 calories,
28 g total fat (6 g saturated fat), 74 mg cholesterol,
373 mg sodium, 4 g carbohydrate, 0 g fiber,
26 g protein. Daily Values: 3% vit. A, 3% vit. C,
2% calcium, 15% iron.

## Marinated Beef on Sourdough

**Prep:** 25 minutes   **Marinate:** 4 to 24 hours
**Grill:** 1¼ hours   **Stand:** 15 minutes

*A sturdy cabernet, assisted by plenty of garlic,
does wonderful things to a round roast.*

> 1 2-pound beef round tip roast or
>    sirloin tip roast
> 8 cloves garlic, sliced
> ⅔ cup Cabernet Sauvignon or other
>    dry red wine
> ½ cup finely chopped onion
> ¼ cup olive oil
> 2 tablespoons red wine vinegar
> ¼ teaspoon salt
> ¼ teaspoon pepper
> 1 clove garlic, minced
> 8 ½-inch-thick slices sourdough
>    bread, toasted

**1** Trim fat from meat. With the point of a
paring knife, make small slits in meat.
Insert garlic slices into slits. Place meat in a
plastic bag set in a shallow dish. For
marinade, in a small bowl combine the wine,
onion, 2 tablespoons of the olive oil, and the
vinegar. Pour over meat; seal bag. Marinate in
the refrigerator for 4 to 24 hours, turning the
bag occasionally.

**2** Drain meat, discarding marinade. Sprinkle meat with salt and pepper. Insert a meat thermometer into center of meat. In a small bowl combine the remaining olive oil and the minced garlic; brush over one side of each bread slice. Set aside.

**3** *For a charcoal grill,* arrange medium coals around a drip pan. Test for medium-low heat above the pan. Place meat on grill rack over drip pan. Cover and grill until meat thermometer registers 140° for medium-rare (1¼ to 1½ hours) or 155° for medium doneness (1½ to 1¾ hours). A few minutes before meat is done, add bread to grill. [*For a gas grill,* preheat grill. Reduce heat to medium-low. Adjust for indirect cooking (see page 10). Grill as above, except place meat on a rack in a roasting pan.]

**4** Remove meat from grill. Cover with foil; let stand for 15 minutes before slicing. (The meat's temperature will rise 5° during standing.) To serve, thinly slice meat. Arrange meat slices on toasted bread. Makes 8 servings.

Nutrition Facts per serving: 232 calories, 8 g total fat (2 g saturated fat), 54 mg cholesterol, 265 mg sodium, 14 g carbohydrate, 0 g fiber, 23 g protein. Daily Values: 1% vit. C, 2% calcium, 17% iron.

## RANCH-STYLE BEEF

**Prep:** 15 minutes    **Marinate:** 6 to 24 hours
**Grill:** 2 hours    **Stand:** 15 minutes

>    1 4-pound boneless rolled beef rib
>       roast from small end
>    4 teaspoons pepper
>    ½ teaspoon ground cardamom
>    ⅔ cup soy sauce
>    ⅓ cup vinegar
>    ½ teaspoon paprika
>    ¼ teaspoon garlic powder

**1** Trim fat from meat. Combine pepper and cardamom; rub over entire surface of meat.

**2** For marinade, in a bowl stir together soy sauce, vinegar, paprika, and garlic powder. Place meat in a large plastic bag set in a shallow dish. Pour marinade over meat; seal bag. Marinate in refrigerator for 6 to 24 hours, turning bag occasionally.

**3** Drain meat, reserving marinade. Chill marinade while grilling meat. Insert a meat thermometer into the center of the meat.

**4** *For a charcoal grill,* arrange medium coals around a drip pan. Test for medium-low heat above pan. Place roast on grill rack over drip pan. Cover; grill until meat thermometer registers 140° for medium-rare (2 to 2½ hours) or 155° for medium doneness (2½ to 3 hours). [*For a gas grill,* preheat grill. Reduce heat to medium-low. Adjust for indirect cooking (see page 10). Grill as above, except place meat on a rack in roasting pan.]

**5** Remove meat from grill; let stand for 15 minutes before carving. (The meat's temperature will rise 5° during standing.) Heat reserved marinade until bubbly; strain and serve with meat. Makes 10 servings.

Nutrition Facts per serving: 324 calories, 18 g total fat (8 g saturated fat), 107 mg cholesterol, 646 mg sodium, 2 g carbohydrate, 0 g fiber, 37 g protein. Daily Values: 26% iron.

## Flaming Facts

Getting graded isn't just for students. Beef gets graded, too—but by a system determined by the United States Department of Agriculture. The grade reflects how flavorful, juicy, and tender the meat will be. Inspectors look at the degree of marbling, or the way the fat is distributed throughout the meat. Marbling helps keep meat juicy and tender during cooking—the more the marbling, the higher the grade. Most meat sold at supermarkets is choice and select. Prime, the top grade, is usually reserved for fine restaurants and top butchers.

# Chipotle Tenderloin Steak and Potatoes

**Prep:** 15 minutes  **Grill:** 20 minutes

*These steaks have all the attributes of a classic Mexican dish—chile peppers, cilantro, garlic, and lime. Enjoy a margarita while dinner grills.*

> 4 **beef tenderloin or rib eye steaks, cut 1 to 1¼ inches thick**
> 2 to 4 **tablespoons finely chopped, drained chipotle peppers in adobo sauce**
> 2 **tablespoons snipped fresh cilantro**
> 1 **tablespoon lime juice**
> 4 **cloves garlic, minced**
> ½ **teaspoon salt**
> 3 **medium potatoes, each cut lengthwise into 8 wedges**
> 2 **teaspoons olive oil**
> 1 **teaspoon coarse or kosher salt**
> 1 **lime, cut into wedges**

**1** Trim fat from steaks. In a small bowl stir together chipotle peppers, cilantro, lime juice, garlic, and salt. Brush mixture onto both sides of steaks. Brush potato wedges with olive oil and sprinkle with salt.

**2** *For a charcoal grill,* place medium coals in bottom of grill. Place potatoes on grill rack directly over coals. Cover and grill for 20 to 25 minutes or until potatoes are tender and brown, turning once halfway through grilling. While the potatoes are grilling, add steaks to grill. Cover and grill until steaks are desired doneness, turning once halfway through grilling. (Allow 8 to 14 minutes for medium-rare and 12 to 18 minutes for medium doneness.) (*For a gas grill,* preheat grill. Reduce heat to medium. Place potatoes, then steaks on grill rack over heat. Grill as above.) To serve, pass lime wedges with steaks. Makes 4 servings.

Nutrition Facts per serving: 385 calories, 13 g total fat (4 g saturated fat), 96 mg cholesterol, 959 mg sodium, 30 g carbohydrate, 1 g fiber, 35 g protein. Daily Values: 9% vit. A, 32% vit. C, 3% calcium, 37% iron.

## Sizzlin' Solutions

**Add some smoke and heat with chipotles! Made by drying and smoking jalapeños, chipotles add a smoky, almost chocolate-like flavor to foods. Chipotles are available dried, canned in adobo sauce (a sauce made of ground chiles, herbs, and vinegar), and pickled. The smoky chile pepper is generally added to stews and sauces; the pickled variety is often eaten as an appetizer.**

# FILET MIGNON WITH PORTOBELLO SAUCE

**Prep:** 15 minutes  **Grill:** 8 minutes

*The meaty portobello is perfectly fit to dress up a fillet. A splash of Madeira sweetens the mushroom's loamy presence and adds elegance.*

> 4 **beef tenderloin steaks, cut 1 inch thick**
> 1 **teaspoon olive oil**
> ¼ **teaspoon pepper**
> 2 **fresh large portobello mushrooms, halved and sliced**
> 8 **green onions, cut into 1-inch pieces**
> 1 **tablespoon margarine or butter**
> ⅓ **cup beef broth**
> 2 **tablespoons Madeira or port wine**

**1** Trim fat from steaks. Rub both sides of steaks with oil and pepper.

**2** *For a charcoal grill,* grill steaks on the rack of an uncovered grill directly over medium coals until desired doneness, turning once halfway through grilling. (Allow 8 to 12 minutes for medium-rare and 12 to 15 minutes for medium doneness.) (*For a gas grill,* preheat grill. Reduce heat to medium. Place steaks on grill rack over heat. Cover and grill as above.)

❸ Meanwhile, for sauce, in a large skillet cook and stir mushrooms and green onions in hot margarine over medium heat about 5 minutes or until tender. Stir in beef broth and Madeira. Bring to boiling. Remove from heat. Thinly slice steaks diagonally and serve with sauce. Makes 4 servings.

Nutrition Facts per serving: 260 calories, 13 g total fat (4 g saturated fat), 80 mg cholesterol, 160 mg sodium, 4 g carbohydrate, 1 g fiber, 29 g protein. Daily Values: 8% vit. A, 11% vit. C, 1% calcium, 31% iron.

## Peppercorn Beef

**Prep:** 12 minutes **Marinate:** 15 minutes **Grill:** 12 minutes

*Pick up some white and pink peppercorns if your spice rack doesn't have them already. A three-pepper blend flavors these steaks more subtly than basic black.*

   4 beef tenderloin steaks or 1 to
      1½ pounds boneless beef sirloin
      steak, cut 1¼ inches thick
   ⅓ cup bottled oil and vinegar salad
      dressing
   ⅓ cup dry red wine
   ¼ cup snipped fresh garlic chives or
      ¼ cup snipped fresh chives plus
      2 cloves garlic, minced
   1 teaspoon cracked multicolor or
      black peppercorns

❶ Trim fat from steaks. Place steaks in a plastic bag set in a shallow dish. For marinade, in a small bowl combine the salad dressing, wine, garlic chives, and peppercorns. Pour over steaks; seal bag. Marinate at room temperature for 15 minutes or in the refrigerator for 8 to 12 hours, turning bag occasionally.

❷ Drain steaks, reserving marinade. *For a charcoal grill,* place medium coals in bottom of grill. Place steaks on grill rack directly over coals. Cover and grill until

steaks are desired doneness, turning and brushing once with marinade halfway through grilling. (Allow 12 to 14 minutes for medium-rare and 16 to 18 minutes for medium doneness.) (*For a gas grill,* preheat grill. Reduce heat to medium. Place steaks on grill rack over heat. Grill as above.)

❸ If using sirloin steak, cut steak into 4 serving-size pieces. Makes 4 servings.

Nutrition Facts per serving: 287 calories, 16 g total fat (5 g saturated fat), 96 mg cholesterol, 218 mg sodium, 1 g carbohydrate, 0 g fiber, 32 g protein. Daily Values: 2% vit. C, 28% iron.

## WISE ADVICE

Marinades and rubs offer a whole new world of flavors for grilled meats. Both add flavor but they serve two different purposes. A marinade is a seasoned liquid that can also tenderize—if it contains an acidic ingredient, such as lemon juice, yogurt, wine, or vinegar. A small amount of oil helps the ingredients adhere to the meat better. A rub is a blend of herbs and spices rubbed into the surface of meat. A rub does not tenderize. Some cooks prefer rubs that are made into a paste by adding a little oil, crushed garlic, or mustard.

Beef Kabobs and Noodles

# Beef Kabobs and Noodles

**Prep:** 25 minutes **Marinate:** 30 minutes
**Grill:** 12 minutes

⅓ cup sake or dry white wine
3 tablespoons hoisin sauce
2 tablespoons soy sauce
4 teaspoons sugar
1 teaspoon grated fresh ginger
⅛ teaspoon ground red pepper
1 pound beef tenderloin
6 ounces dried soba (buckwheat
    noodles) or spaghetti
4 ounces pea pods, halved (1¾ cups)
1 medium carrot, cut into thin strips
1 tablespoon toasted sesame oil
3 medium green onions, bias-sliced
    into ¼- to ½-inch pieces
1 tablespoon sesame seed, toasted

**1** For dressing, in a small saucepan combine the sake, 2 tablespoons of the hoisin sauce, the soy sauce, sugar, ginger, and ground red pepper. Bring to boiling; remove from heat. Cool slightly.

**2** Trim fat from meat. Cut meat into 1-inch cubes. Place meat in a plastic bag set in a shallow dish. Add 2 tablespoons of the dressing and the remaining hoisin sauce; seal bag. Marinate at room temperature for 30 minutes or in the refrigerator for up to 3 hours, turning bag occasionally. If using bamboo skewers, soak 4 skewers in warm water for 20 minutes; drain. Drain meat, discarding marinade. Thread meat onto 10- to 12-inch long bamboo or metal skewers.

**3** *For a charcoal grill,* grill kabobs on the rack of an uncovered grill directly over medium coals for 12 to 14 minutes or until meat is slightly pink in center, turning once halfway through grilling. (*For a gas grill,* preheat grill. Reduce heat to medium. Place kabobs on grill rack over heat. Cover; grill as above.)

**4** Meanwhile, in a large saucepan cook soba noodles in boiling water about 6 minutes or until tender but still firm, adding pea pods and carrot the last 2 minutes of cooking; drain. Return mixture to hot pan. Add remaining dressing and sesame oil; toss gently to coat.

**5** Transfer soba mixture to a small serving platter. Place kabobs on noodle mixture. Sprinkle with onions and sesame seed. Serves 4.

Nutrition Facts per serving: 418 calories, 9 g total fat (2 g saturated fat), 81 mg cholesterol, 1,160 mg sodium, 48 g carbohydrate, 2 g fiber, 33 g protein. Daily Values: 43% vit. A, 32% vit. C, 4% calcium, 24% iron.

## BEEF TENDERLOIN FILLETS WITH HORSERADISH CHILI

**Prep:** 30 minutes **Grill:** 18 minutes

1½ pounds beef tenderloin, cut into
    4 fillets about 1¼ inches thick
½ teaspoon dried sage, crushed
¼ to 1 teaspoon coarsely ground
    pepper
¼ teaspoon salt
2 teaspoons cooking oil
1 cup coarsely chopped tomatoes
2 tablespoons chili seasoning mix
2 cloves garlic, minced
½ cup drained canned red beans,
    rinsed and drained
¼ to ½ cup grated horseradish

**1** Trim fat from fillets. Rub both sides of fillets with sage, pepper, and salt. For chili, in a heavy skillet heat oil over medium-high heat. Add tomatoes, chili seasoning, and garlic to skillet; cook 1 to 2 minutes or until tomatoes just start to soften. Reduce heat to medium-low. Add beans and horseradish. Cook and stir for 2 minutes more. Cover loosely and keep warm.

**2** *For a charcoal grill,* grill fillets on the rack of an uncovered grill directly over medium coals until desired doneness, turning once halfway through grilling. (Allow 18 to 20 minutes for medium doneness.) (*For a gas grill,* preheat grill. Reduce heat to medium. Place steaks on grill rack over heat. Cover; grill as above.) To serve, place one fillet on each plate; spoon warm chili over fillets. Serves 4.

Nutrition Facts per serving: 347 calories, 14 g total fat (5 g saturated fat), 96 mg cholesterol, 759 mg sodium, 18 g carbohydrate, 1 g fiber, 37 g protein. Daily Values: 15% vit. A, 45% vit. C, 5% calcium, 39% iron.

# Crab-Stuffed Tenderloin

**Prep:** 20 minutes  **Grill:** 43 minutes
**Stand:** 15 minutes

*They said beef tenderloin couldn't be improved, but we went and did it. Then again, what wouldn't sweet and delicate crab, artichoke hearts, and garlic-herb cream cheese improve?*

  4 ounces cooked crabmeat
  ½ of a 14-ounce can artichoke hearts,
      drained and chopped
  ¼ of a 5-ounce container semisoft
      goat cheese with garlic and herb
  2 tablespoons thinly sliced green
      onion
  1 2-pound center-cut beef tenderloin
  1 tablespoon coarsely ground
      pepper

**1** For filling, in a small bowl combine crabmeat, artichoke hearts, cheese, and green onion.

**2** Trim fat from beef. Butterfly the meat by making a lengthwise cut down center of meat, cutting to within ½ inch of the other side. Spread open. Place knife in the "v" of the first cut. Cut away from the first cut and parallel to the cut surface to within ½ inch of the other side of the meat. Repeat on opposite side of "v." Spread these sections open. Gently pound meat to ¾-inch thickness. Spoon filling over meat. Starting from a short side, roll up meat. Tie with 100-percent-cotton string. Sprinkle pepper evenly over meat; rub in with your fingers.

**3** *For a charcoal grill,* arrange medium-hot coals around a drip pan. Test for medium heat above the pan. Place meat on grill rack directly over coals. Grill for 8 to 10 minutes or until meat is browned, turning frequently. Place meat over drip pan. Cover and grill until desired doneness. (Allow 35 to 50 minutes for medium-rare doneness.) [*For a gas grill,* preheat grill. Reduce heat to

medium. Adjust for indirect cooking (see page 10). Grill as above, except place meat on a rack in a roasting pan after browning.]

**4** Remove meat from grill. Cover with foil; let stand for 15 minutes before slicing. Makes 6 to 8 servings.

Nutrition Facts per serving: 260 calories, 12 g total fat (5 g saturated fat), 110 mg cholesterol, 135 mg sodium, 3 g carbohydrate, 1 g fiber, 34 g protein. Daily Values: 1% vit. A, 7% vit. C, 3% calcium, 29% iron.

## TEX-MEX SMOKED SHORT RIBS

**Prep:** 20 minutes  **Soak:** 1 hour
**Grill:** 1½ hours

*The meat of choice in the state of Texas is beef. The neighboring country of Mexico influences Texas cuisine in a big way. These beef ribs show off their Mexican influence with hot pepper-spiked picante and cumin.*

  4 pounds beef short ribs
  4 cups hickory or apple wood chips
  1 tablespoon cooking oil
  1½ teaspoons chili powder
  1 teaspoon dry mustard
  ½ teaspoon ground cumin
  ⅛ teaspoon garlic powder
  ½ cup hot picante sauce
  ¼ teaspoon bottled hot pepper sauce

**1** Trim fat from ribs. Cut ribs into serving-size pieces. Place ribs in a 4- to 6-quart pot or Dutch oven. Add enough water to cover ribs. Bring to boiling; reduce heat. Simmer, covered, about 1½ hours or until tender. Drain ribs.

**2** At least 1 hour before grilling, soak wood chips in enough water to cover.

**3** Meanwhile, for sauce, in a small saucepan combine oil, chili powder, dry mustard, cumin, and garlic powder. Cook and stir over medium heat until bubbly. Remove from heat. Stir in picante sauce and hot pepper sauce. Set aside.

**4** Drain wood chips. *For a charcoal grill,* arrange medium-low coals around a drip pan. Pour 1 inch of water into drip pan. Test for low heat above the pan. Sprinkle half of the wood chips over the coals. Place ribs, bone side down, on grill rack over drip pan. Brush ribs with some of the sauce. Cover and grill for 20 to 30 minutes or until browned, brushing occasionally with sauce. Add the remaining wood chips halfway through grilling. [*For a gas grill,* preheat grill. Reduce heat to low. Adjust for indirect cooking (see page 10). Add wood chips according to manufacturer's directions. Grill as above.] To serve, reheat the sauce and pass with ribs. Makes 6 servings.

Nutrition Facts per serving: 474 calories, 30 g total fat (12 g saturated fat), 139 mg cholesterol, 242 mg sodium, 2 g carbohydrate, 0 g fiber, 46 g protein. Daily Values: 3% vit. A, 10% vit. C, 2% calcium, 37% iron.

# K.C.-Style Beef Ribs

**Prep:** 25 minutes   **Marinate:** 4 to 24 hours
**Soak:** 1 hour   **Grill:** 1¼ hours

  ½ cup cider vinegar
  3 tablespoons sugar
  2 teaspoons dry mustard
  ⅛ teaspoon salt
  2 cups pineapple juice
  ½ cup Worcestershire sauce
  ⅓ cup chopped onion
  2 tablespoons cooking oil
2½ to 3 pounds boneless beef
     short ribs
  4 teaspoons paprika
1½ teaspoons sugar
  1 teaspoon garlic powder
  ½ teaspoon pepper
  ¼ teaspoon salt
  4 cups wood chips or 10 to 12 wood
     chunks (hickory or oak)

**1** For marinade, in a medium saucepan bring the vinegar to boiling. Remove from heat. Stir in the 3 tablespoons sugar, the dry mustard, and the ⅛ teaspoon salt. Stir until sugar is dissolved. Stir in the pineapple juice, Worcestershire sauce, onion, and oil. Cool marinade to room temperature.

**2** Trim fat from ribs. Cut ribs into serving-size pieces. Place ribs in a large plastic bag set in a shallow dish. Pour marinade over ribs; seal bag. Marinate in the refrigerator for 4 to 24 hours, turning bag occasionally.

**3** Meanwhile, for rub, in a small bowl stir together the paprika, the 1½ teaspoons sugar, the garlic powder, pepper, and the ¼ teaspoon salt; set aside.

**4** At least 1 hour before grilling, soak wood chips in enough water to cover.

**5** Drain ribs, discarding marinade. Pat dry with paper towels. Generously sprinkle both sides of ribs with the rub mixture; rub mixture into ribs.

**6** Drain wood chips. *For a charcoal grill,* arrange medium-hot coals around a drip pan. Test for medium heat above the pan. Sprinkle one-fourth of the wood chips over the coals. Place ribs on grill rack directly over drip pan. Cover and grill for 1¼ to 1½ hours or until tender. Add more wood chips every 15 minutes and add more coals as necessary. [*For a gas grill,* preheat grill. Reduce heat to medium. Adjust for indirect cooking (see page 10). Add wood chips according to manufacturer's directions. Grill as above, except place meat, fat side up, in a roasting pan.] Makes 6 to 8 servings.

Nutrition Facts per serving: 770 calories, 69 g total fat (30 g saturated fat), 144 mg cholesterol, 231 mg sodium, 7 g carbohydrate, 0 g fiber, 28 g protein. Daily Values: 8% vit. A, 17% vit. C, 2% calcium, 24% iron.

## BARBECUED BEEF RIBS

**Prep:** 20 minutes   **Grill:** 1½ hours

*You could be waiting until after the sun burns out if you do ribs from start to finish on the grill. A preliminary boil gives them a good start.*

  3 to 4 pounds beef short ribs
  1 8-ounce can tomato sauce
  ¼ cup water
  2 tablespoons brown sugar
  2 tablespoons vinegar or lemon juice
  1 tablespoon finely chopped onion
  1 tablespoon Worcestershire sauce
  1 teaspoon crushed red pepper

**1** Trim fat from ribs. Cut ribs into serving-size pieces. Place ribs in a 4- to 6-quart pot or Dutch oven. Add enough water to cover ribs. Bring to boiling; reduce heat. Simmer, covered, about 1½ hours or until tender. Drain ribs.

**2** Meanwhile, for sauce, in a small saucepan combine tomato sauce, water, brown sugar, vinegar, onion, Worcestershire sauce, and red pepper. Bring to boiling; reduce heat; Simmer, uncovered, for 10 minutes, stirring once or twice. Set aside.

**3** *For a charcoal grill,* arrange medium-hot coals around a drip pan. Test for medium heat above the pan. Place ribs, bone side down, on grill rack over drip pan. Brush with some of the sauce. Cover and grill about 15 minutes or until browned, brushing occasionally with sauce. [*For a gas grill,* preheat grill. Reduce heat to medium. Adjust for indirect cooking (see page 10). Grill as above.] To serve, reheat sauce and pass with ribs. Makes 5 or 6 servings.

Nutrition Facts per serving: 433 calories, 25 g total fat (10 g saturated fat), 126 mg cholesterol, 389 mg sodium, 9 g carbohydrate, 1 g fiber, 42 g protein. **Daily Values:** 7% vit. A, 13% vit. C, 2% calcium, 35% iron.

# Pesto Veal Burgers on Focaccia

**Prep:** 15 minutes   **Grill:** 14 minutes

*Remember life before focaccia bread was readily available? We didn't know what we were missing. It's the perfect vehicle for these pesto-laced burgers.*

  1 slightly beaten egg white
  ½ cup soft bread crumbs
  ½ teaspoon salt
  ⅛ teaspoon pepper
  1 pound ground veal
  ¼ cup light mayonnaise dressing or
     salad dressing
  1 tablespoon pesto
  8 3-inch squares of focaccia bread or
     8 slices sourdough bread,
     toasted
  4 lettuce leaves
  4 tomato slices

**1** In a medium bowl combine egg white, bread crumbs, salt, and pepper. Add ground veal; mix well. Shape mixture into four ¾-inch-thick patties.

**2** *For a charcoal grill,* grill burgers on the rack of an uncovered grill directly over medium coals for 14 to 18 minutes or until meat is no longer pink, turning once halfway through grilling. (*For a gas grill,* preheat grill. Reduce heat to medium. Place burgers on grill rack over heat. Cover; grill as above.)

**3** Meanwhile, for sauce, in a small bowl combine mayonnaise and pesto. Serve burgers on toasted focaccia bread with sauce, lettuce, and tomato. Makes 4 servings.

Nutrition Facts per serving: 309 calories, 13 g total fat (3 g saturated fat), 95 mg cholesterol, 623 mg sodium, 18 g carbohydrate, 1 g fiber, 29 g protein. **Daily Values:** 1% vit. A, 8% vit. C, 4% calcium, 8% iron.

## LEMON-MUSTARD VEAL CHOPS

**Prep:** 10 minutes   **Grill:** 19 minutes

*Make your own fresh-herb mustard to dress up these veal chops. To enhance the lemon flavor, use lemon thyme—or, for a change of pace, substitute fresh rosemary.*

> 4 veal rib or loin chops, cut 1 inch thick
> 1 tablespoon snipped fresh thyme or 1 teaspoon dried thyme, crushed
> 1 tablespoon country Dijon-style mustard
> 2 teaspoons lemon juice
> 1 teaspoon lemon-pepper seasoning
> 1 teaspoon garlic-pepper seasoning

**1** Trim fat from chops. For sauce, in a small bowl combine thyme, mustard, lemon juice, lemon-pepper seasoning, and garlic pepper.

**2** *For a charcoal grill,* grill chops on the rack of an uncovered grill directly over medium coals until desired doneness, turning once and brushing occasionally with sauce during the last 5 minutes of grilling. (Allow 19 to 23 minutes for medium doneness.) (*For a gas grill,* preheat grill. Reduce heat to medium. Place chops on grill rack over heat. Cover and grill as above.) Makes 4 servings.

Nutrition Facts per serving: 189 calories, 8 g total fat (2 g saturated fat), 116 mg cholesterol, 460 mg sodium, 1 g carbohydrate, 0 g fiber, 26 g protein. Daily Values: 2% vit. C, 1% calcium, 7% iron.

## Garlic Studded Veal Chops and Asparagus

**Prep:** 15 minutes   **Grill:** 12 minutes
**Marinate:** 30 minutes

> 1 pound asparagus spears
> 2 tablespoons dry sherry
> 2 tablespoons olive oil
> 1 clove garlic, minced

> 4 boneless veal top loin chops, cut ¾ inch thick
> 3 or 4 cloves garlic, cut into thin slivers
> 1 tablespoon snipped fresh thyme or 1 teaspoon dried thyme, crushed
> ⅛ teaspoon salt
> ⅛ teaspoon pepper

**1** Snap off and discard woody stems from asparagus spears. In a medium skillet bring a small amount of water to boiling; add asparagus. Simmer, covered, about 3 minutes or until crisp-tender; drain. Place asparagus in a plastic bag; add sherry, 1 tablespoon of the olive oil, and the minced garlic. Marinate at room temperature for 30 minutes.

**2** Meanwhile, trim fat from meat. With the tip of a sharp knife, make a few small slits in each veal chop; insert garlic slivers. Combine remaining tablespoon olive oil, the thyme, salt, and pepper; brush over meat.

**3** *For a charcoal grill,* grill chops on the rack of an uncovered grill directly over medium coals for 22 to 13 minutes or until juices run clear, turning meat once halfway through grilling. (*For a gas grill,* preheat grill. Reduce heat to medium. Place chops on grill rack over medium heat. Cover and grill as above.)

**4** Add asparagus spears to grill (lay spears perpendicular to wires on grill rack so they won't fall into coals). Grill for 3 to 4 minutes or until crisp-tender and lightly browned, turning occasionally. Serve with chops. Makes 4 servings.

Nutrition Facts per serving: 237 calories, 11 g total fat (3 g saturated fat), 92 mg cholesterol, 131 mg sodium, 5 g carbohydrate, 2 g fiber, 27 g protein. Daily Values: 6% vit. A, 37% vit. C, 2% calcium, 9% iron.

Veal Chops with Apples

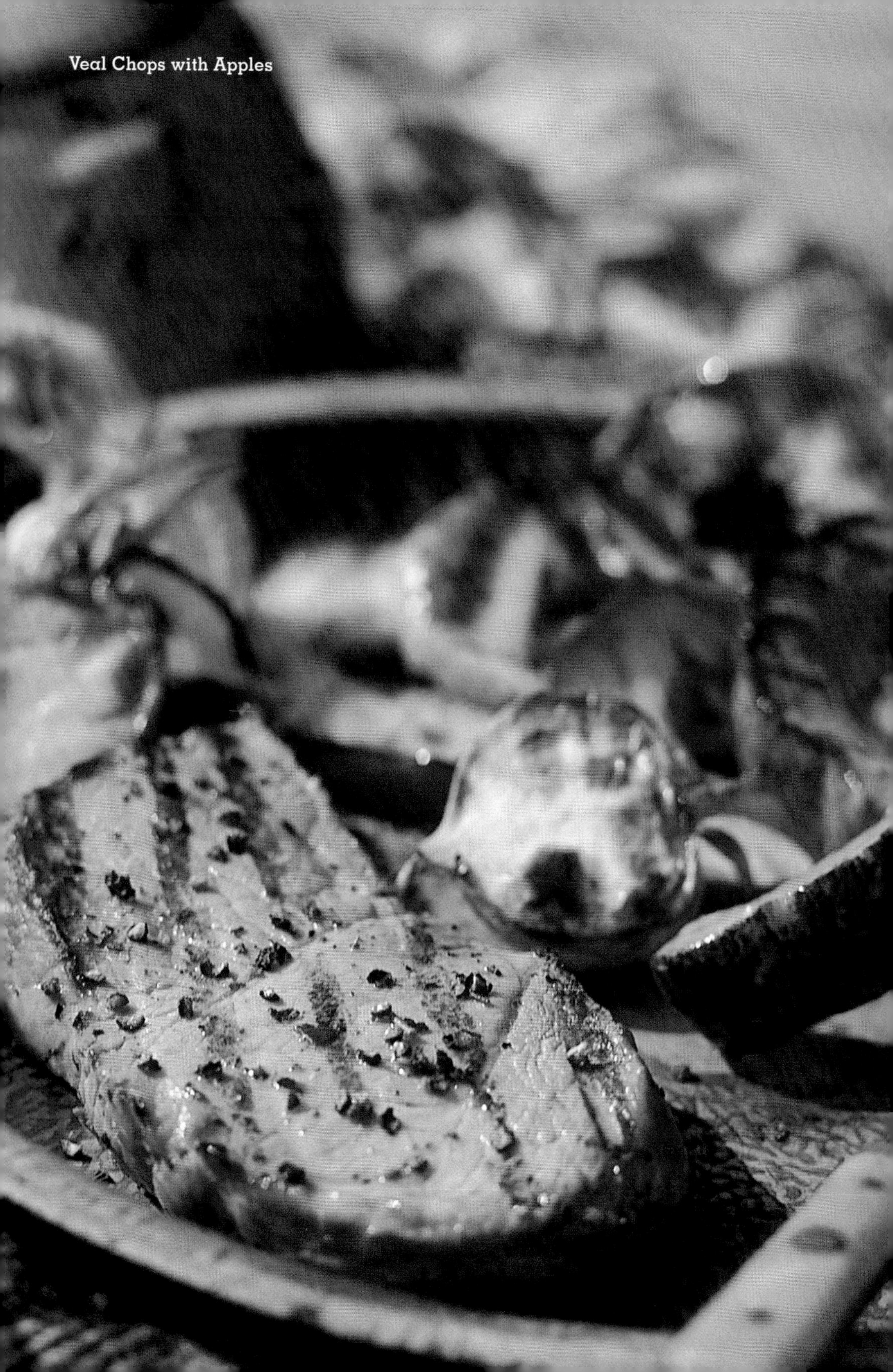

## VEAL CHOPS WITH APPLES

**Prep:** 10 minutes   **Marinate:** 6 to 24 hours
**Grill:** 15 minutes

*Americans are apple-eaters. We love them baked, stewed, and whirled into applesauce. Try them sliced into thick pieces and grilled alongside veal chops jazzed up with white wine and sage.*

4 boneless veal top loin chops, cut
   ¾ inch thick
½ cup dry white wine
2 tablespoons cooking oil
2 teaspoons dried sage, crushed
½ teaspoon salt
½ teaspoon pepper
2 medium tart cooking apples
   Assorted grilled vegetables
   (optional)

1 Trim fat from chops. Place chops in a plastic bag set in a shallow dish. For marinade, in a small bowl combine wine, oil, sage, salt, and pepper. Pour over chops; seal bag. Marinate in the refrigerator for 6 to 24 hours, turning bag occasionally.

2 Drain chops, reserving marinade. Just before grilling, core apples. Cut crosswise into 1-inch slices.

3 *For a charcoal grill,* grill chops and apple slices on the rack of an uncovered grill directly over medium coals for 15 to 17 minutes or until chops are slightly pink in center and apples are tender, turning and brushing once with marinade halfway through grilling. (*For a gas grill,* preheat grill. Reduce heat to medium. Place chops and apple slices on grill rack over heat. Cover and grill as above.)

4 Serve chops with apple slices and, if desired, grilled vegetables. Makes 4 servings.

Nutrition Facts per serving: 271 calories,
13 g total fat (3 g saturated fat), 95 mg cholesterol,
354 mg sodium, 9 g carbohydrate, 1 g fiber,
24 g protein. Daily Values: 5% vit. C, 2% calcium,
7% iron.

# Orange-Ginger Veal Chops

**Prep:** 15 minutes   **Marinate:** 2 hours
**Grill:** 19 minutes

*Grilled veal goes Chinese in this chop recipe. For the most authentic flavor, use rice vinegar and peanut oil.*

4 veal loin chops, cut 1 inch thick
½ cup frozen orange juice
   concentrate, thawed
½ cup rice vinegar or cider vinegar
3 tablespoons olive oil or peanut oil
2 tablespoons grated fresh ginger
2 tablespoons soy sauce
4 cloves garlic, minced
¼ teaspoon ground cinnamon
½ teaspoon toasted sesame oil

1 Trim fat from chops. Place chops in a plastic bag set in a shallow dish. For marinade, in a small bowl combine orange juice concentrate, vinegar, oil, ginger, soy sauce, garlic, and cinnamon. Pour over chops; seal bag. Marinate in the refrigerator for 2 hours, turning bag occasionally.

2 Drain chops, reserving marinade. *For a charcoal grill,* grill chops on the rack of an uncovered grill directly over medium coals for 11 to 13 minutes or until juices run clear, turning once and brushing occasionally with marinade up to the last 5 minutes of grilling. (*For a gas grill,* preheat grill. Reduce heat to medium. Place chops on grill rack over heat. Cover and grill as above.)

3 To serve, drizzle chops with sesame oil and sprinkle with freshly ground pepper. Makes 4 servings.

Nutrition Facts per serving: 345 calories,
17 g total fat (4 g saturated fat), 135 mg cholesterol,
511 mg sodium, 13 g carbohydrate, 0 g fiber,
35 g protein. Daily Values: 68% vit. C, 3% calcium,
10% iron.

## STUFFED VEAL CHOPS WITH GORGONZOLA

**Prep:** 15 minutes   **Grill:** 12 minutes

*Grill these unmistakably autumnal chops—with their stuffing of leeks, apples, and fresh sage—on a crisp fall day. Crumble blue cheese over each chop, and pair with a chilled Riesling.*

½ cup finely chopped tart apple
½ cup finely chopped leek
½ teaspoon snipped fresh sage
¼ teaspoon salt
¼ teaspoon pepper
4 boneless veal top loin chops, cut
　　¾ inch thick
1 tablespoon olive oil
½ cup crumbled blue cheese
　　(2 ounces)

1 For stuffing, in a small bowl combine the apple, leek, sage, salt, and pepper.

2 Trim fat from chops. Make a pocket in each chop by cutting horizontally from the fat side almost to the opposite side. Spoon about ¼ cup of the stuffing into each pocket. If necessary, secure with wooden toothpicks. Brush chops with olive oil; sprinkle lightly with additional salt and pepper.

3 *For a charcoal grill,* grill chops on the rack of an uncovered grill directly over medium coals for 11 to 13 minutes or until juices run clear, turning once halfway through grilling. (*For a gas grill,* preheat grill. Reduce heat to medium. Place chops on grill rack over heat. Cover and grill as above.)

4 If using, toothpicks, remove them. To serve, sprinkle crumbled blue cheese over chops. Makes 4 servings.

Nutrition Facts per serving: 260 calories,
14 g total fat (5 g saturated fat), 105 mg cholesterol,
422 mg sodium, 6 g carbohydrate, 2 g fiber,
27 g protein. Daily Values: 3% vit. A, 4% vit. C,
9% calcium, 9% iron.

## Veal Chops with Sweet Pepper Sauce

**Prep:** 20 minutes   **Grill:** 29 minutes

*Sometimes a basic paste—just garlic, oil, sage, salt, and pepper—is unbeatable. The real fun (and flavor) here is roasting the peppers on the grill for a sauce that goes over the chops and the pasta.*

6 veal loin chops, cut 1 inch thick
2 teaspoons dried sage, crushed
3 cloves garlic, minced
¾ teaspoon black pepper
½ teaspoon salt
2 teaspoons olive oil
2 medium red sweet peppers,
　　quartered lengthwise
1 14½-ounce can chunky pasta-style
　　tomatoes
1 teaspoon sugar
3 cups hot cooked pasta

1 Trim fat from chops. For rub, in a small bowl combine sage, 2 of the garlic cloves, ½ teaspoon of the black pepper, and ¼ teaspoon of the salt. Stir in olive oil. Spoon mixture evenly over the chops; rub in with your fingers.

2 *For a charcoal grill,* grill sweet peppers, cut sides up, on the rack of an uncovered grill directly over medium coals for 10 to 15 minutes or until pepper skins are blistered and dark. Wrap peppers in foil and let stand for 20 minutes. While peppers are standing, add chops to grill. Grill until desired doneness, turning once halfway through grilling. (Allow 19 to 23 minutes for medium doneness.) (*For a gas grill,* preheat grill. Reduce heat to medium. Place sweet peppers, cut sides up, then chops on grill rack over heat. Cover and grill as above.)

3 Using a paring knife, pull the pepper skins off gently. For sauce, place pepper pieces in a blender container or food processor bowl. Add the remaining garlic clove, remaining black pepper, remaining salt, the undrained

tomatoes, and sugar. Cover and blend or process until nearly smooth. Transfer to a small saucepan; heat through. To serve, spoon sauce over chops and pasta. Makes 6 servings.

⊕Nutrition Facts per serving: 289 calories, 9 g total fat (3 g saturated fat), 99 mg cholesterol, 544 mg sodium, 22 g carbohydrate, 2 g fiber, 28 g protein. Daily Values: 22% vit. A, 83% vit. C, 4% calcium, 12% iron.

## VEAL CHOPS WITH PESTO-STUFFED MUSHROOMS

**Prep:** 10 minutes **Marinate:** 15 minutes
**Grill:** 20 minutes

*A quick bath in white wine will do for these chops, although they'll thank you with more flavor if they can soak for a full 24 hours.*

   4 veal loin chops, cut ¾ inch thick
  ¼ cup dry white wine
   1 tablespoon snipped fresh sage or
      thyme
   1 tablespoon white wine
      Worcestershire sauce
   1 tablespoon olive oil
   3 large cloves garlic, minced
      Freshly ground pepper
   8 large fresh mushrooms (2 to
      2½ inches in diameter)
   2 to 3 tablespoons pesto

**1** Trim fat from chops. Place chops in a plastic bag set in a shallow dish. For marinade, in a small bowl combine wine, herb, Worcestershire sauce, oil, and garlic. Pour over chops; seal bag. Marinate at room temperature for 15 minutes or in the refrigerator for up to 24 hours, turning bag occasionally.

**2** Drain chops, reserving marinade. Sprinkle chops with ground pepper. *For a charcoal grill,* grill chops on the rack of an uncovered grill directly over medium coals until desired doneness, turning once halfway through grilling. (Allow 12 to 14 minutes for medium-rare and 15 to 17 minutes for medium doneness.) (*For a gas grill,* preheat grill. Reduce heat to medium. Place chops on grill rack over heat. Cover and grill as above.) Remove chops from grill.

**3** Meanwhile, cut off the mushroom stems even with the caps; discard stems. Rinse mushroom caps. Gently pat dry with paper towels. Brush mushroom caps with marinade. Add mushrooms, stemmed sides down, to grill. Grill for 4 minutes. Turn mushrooms; fill with pesto. Grill about 4 minutes more or until heated through. Serve mushrooms with chops. Makes 4 servings.

Nutrition Facts per serving: 285 calories, 16 g total fat (2 g saturated fat), 100 mg cholesterol, 157 mg sodium, 4 g carbohydrate, 1 g fiber, 28 g protein. Daily Values: 3% vit. C, 3% calcium, 9% iron.

## DON'T GET BURNED!

When the meat's on sale, and you have the freezer space to store it, there are a few guidelines to keep in mind for keeping it as good as the day you bought it: • If you plan to use the meat within 2 weeks after purchase, freeze it in the retail packing. For longer storage, rewrap or overwrap with moisture- and vapor-proof wrap, such as freezer paper, heavy-duty aluminum foil, or plastic wrap. • Freeze the meat quickly and maintain your freezer's temperature at 0° or below. • Thaw the frozen meat in the refrigerator on a plate or in a pan to catch any juices. Do not thaw meat at room temperature. • Meat can be thawed in a microwave oven. Follow the manufacturer's directions. After thawing, cook the meat right away.

## Apple-Sauced Veal Chops

**Prep:** 25 minutes **Grill:** 19 minutes

1 teaspoon ground cinnamon
½ teaspoon dried thyme, crushed
¼ teaspoon onion salt
¼ teaspoon dry mustard
4 veal loin chops, cut 1 inch thick
2 tablespoons margarine or butter
1 medium onion, cut into thin
    wedges
1 large cooking apple (such as Rome
    Beauty), cored and thinly sliced
1 tablespoon brown sugar
½ cup whipping cream

**1** For spice rub, in a small bowl stir together the cinnamon, thyme, onion salt, and dry mustard.

**2** Trim fat from chops. Sprinkle spice rub evenly over chops; rub in with fingers.

**3** *For a charcoal grill,* grill chops on the rack of an uncovered grill directly over medium coals for 19 to 23 minutes or until chops are slightly pink in center, turning once. (*For a gas grill,* preheat grill. Reduce heat to medium. Place chops on grill rack over heat. Cover and grill as above.)

**4** Meanwhile, for sauce, in a medium skillet heat margarine or butter over medium-low heat until melted. Add the onion. Cover and cook for 13 to 15 minutes or until onion is tender. Uncover; add apple slices and sugar. Cook and stir over medium-high heat about 5 minutes or until onions are golden and apples are tender. Stir in cream. Bring just to boiling; reduce heat. Boil gently for 2 to 3 minutes or until slightly thickened. Serve sauce over chops. Makes 4 servings.

Nutrition Facts per serving: 312 calories, 22 g total fat (10 g saturated fat), 110 mg cholesterol, 234 mg sodium, 12 g carbohydrate, 1 g fiber, 18 g protein. Daily Values: 18% vit. A, 6% vit. C, 4% calcium, 7% iron.

## Veal Kabobs with Romesco Sauce

**Prep:** 30 minutes    **Grill:** 12 minutes

1 pound boneless veal
1 medium yellow, green, or red
    sweet pepper, cut into 1½-inch
    pieces
1 medium zucchini, cut into
    ¾-inch slices
1 medium yellow summer squash,
    cut into ¾-inch slices
3 tablespoons olive oil
2 tablespoons snipped fresh oregano
    or 1½ teaspoons dried oregano,
    crushed
1 teaspoon bottled hot pepper sauce
1 cup finely chopped roasted red
    sweet peppers
1 cup bottled spicy pasta sauce
1 clove garlic, minced
2 cups hot cooked orzo (rosamarina)

**1** Trim fat from meat. Cut meat into 1¼-inch pieces. On four 10- to 12-inch metal skewers, alternately thread meat, sweet pepper, zucchini, and yellow squash, leaving a ¼-inch space between pieces. In a bowl combine olive oil, oregano, and hot pepper sauce. Set aside half of the oil mixture. Brush kabobs with the remaining oil mixture.

**2** *For a charcoal grill,* grill kabobs on the rack of an uncovered grill directly over medium coals for 12 to 14 minutes or until meat is slightly pink in center, turning once halfway through grilling. (*For a gas grill,* preheat grill. Reduce heat to medium. Place kabobs on grill rack over heat. Cover; grill as above.)

**3** For sauce, in a small saucepan combine the roasted red sweet peppers, pasta sauce, and garlic. Bring to boiling; remove from heat. Keep warm. Toss the reserved oil mixture with cooked orzo. To serve, arrange kabobs on a bed of orzo; top with sauce. Serves 4.

Nutrition Facts per serving: 346 calories, 17 g total fat (3 g saturated fat), 71 mg cholesterol, 377 mg sodium, 26 g carbohydrate, 4 g fiber, 21 g protein. Daily Values: 28% vit. A, 214% vit. C, 3% calcium, 17% iron.

Veal Kabobs with Romesco Sauce

# Sweet and Sour Veal Chops

**Prep:** 15 minutes   **Marinate:** 2 hours
**Grill:** 19 minutes

*Orange juice and vinegar, with the flavor additions of ginger and cinnamon, become the perfect marinade for these veal chops. Toasted sesame oil, either drizzled or brushed over the chops after grilling, adds even more flavor depth.*

  4 **veal loin chops, cut 1 inch thick
     (2 pounds)**
½ **cup frozen orange juice
     concentrate, thawed**
½ **cup rice vinegar or cider vinegar**
  3 **tablespoons olive oil or peanut oil**
  2 **tablespoons soy sauce**
  2 **tablespoons grated fresh ginger**
  4 **cloves garlic, minced**
¼ **teaspoon ground cinnamon**
½ **teaspoon toasted sesame oil
     Freshly ground black pepper**

**1** Trim fat from meat. Place chops in a plastic bag set in a shallow dish. For marinade, combine orange juice concentrate, rice vinegar, olive oil, soy sauce, ginger, garlic, and cinnamon. Pour over chops. Close bag. Marinate in the refrigerator for 2 hours, turning bag occasionally.

**2** Drain chops, reserving marinade. *For a charcoal grill,* place veal chops on the rack of an uncovered grill directly over medium coals for 19 to 23 minutes or until juices run clear, turning once and brushing occasionally with reserved marinade during the first 15 minutes of grilling. (*For a gas grill,* preheat grill. Reduce heat to medium. Place veal chops on grill rack over heat. Cover and grill as above.)

**3** Discard any remaining marinade. To serve, brush chops with sesame oil and sprinkle with freshly ground black pepper. Serves 4.

Nutrition Facts per serving: 345 calories,
17 g total fat (4 g saturated fat), 135 mg cholesterol,
511 mg sodium, 13 g carbohydrate, 0 g fiber,
35 g protein. Daily Values: 68% vit. C, 3% calcium,
10% iron.

# VEAL RIB CHOPS WITH SALSA

**Prep:** 20 minutes   **Grill:** 19 minutes

*Purchased chili sauce becomes the base for this easy salsa. A sprinkling of Cajun seasoning gives the chops a zip of flavor.*

½ **cup snipped dried tomatoes (not
     oil pack)**
½ **cup bottled chili sauce**
½ **teaspoon finely shredded orange
     peel**
¼ **cup orange juice**
  2 **tablespoons thinly sliced green
     onion**
  4 **veal rib or loin chops, cut 1 inch
     thick (2 pounds)**
  1 **to 2 teaspoons Cajun seasoning or
     jerk seasoning**

**1** For salsa, place dried tomatoes in a small bowl. Add hot water to cover; let stand for 10 minutes. Drain tomatoes, discarding liquid. In a small saucepan combine the tomatoes, chili sauce, orange peel, orange juice, and green onion. Bring just to boiling; remove from heat. Set salsa aside.

**2** Trim fat from meat. Rub the Cajun or jerk seasoning evenly onto both sides of the chops.

**3** *For a charcoal grill,* place veal chops on the rack of an uncovered grill directly over medium coals for 19 to 23 minutes or until juices run clear, turning once. (*For a gas grill,* preheat grill. Reduce heat to medium. Place veal chops on grill rack over heat. Cover and grill as above.) Serve salsa with chops. Makes 4 servings.

Nutrition Facts per serving: 250 calories,
8 g total fat (2 g saturated fat), 123 mg cholesterol,
693 mg sodium, 13 g carbohydrate, 0 g fiber,
30 g protein. Daily Values: 8% vit. C, 26% vit. C,
2% calcium, 9% iron.

# Bacon-Tarragon Veal Brochettes

**Prep:** 15 minutes   **Marinate:** 2 hours
**Grill:** 12 minutes

*Brochette (broh-SHEHT) is a French term for skewer. Veal, in this case, is threaded onto skewers. Fresh tarragon imparts a slight licoricelike flavor to the marinade.*

  2 pounds boneless veal
  3 tablespoons dry white wine
  2 tablespoons snipped fresh tarragon
  2 tablespoons olive oil
  2 tablespoons lemon juice
  ½ teaspoon salt
  ½ teaspoon pepper
  8 slices bacon
    Hot cooked rice pilaf (optional)

1 Trim fat from meat. Cut meat into 1-inch cubes. Place meat in a plastic bag set in a shallow dish. For marinade, combine wine, tarragon, olive oil, lemon juice, salt, and pepper. Pour over meat; seal bag. Marinate in the refrigerator for 2 hours, turning bag occasionally. Drain meat, reserving marinade.

2 In a large skillet cook bacon over medium heat just until brown but still limp. Drain on paper towels. On 10- to 12-inch metal skewers, alternately thread meat and bacon, weaving bacon between and around meat in an "S" fashion.

3 *For a charcoal grill,* grill kabobs on the rack of an uncovered grill directly over medium coals for 12 to 14 minutes or until meat is slightly pink in center, turning once and brushing occasionally with marinade up to the last 5 minutes of grilling. (*For a gas grill,* preheat grill. Reduce heat to medium. Place kabobs on grill rack over heat. Cover; grill as above.)

4 If desired, arrange kabobs on a bed pilaf; garnish with tarragon. Makes 4 to 6 servings.

Nutrition Facts per serving: 429 calories, 21 g total fat (6 g saturated fat), 195 mg cholesterol, 591 mg sodium, 1 g carbohydrate, 0 g fiber, 54 g protein. **Daily Values:** 13% vit. C, 1% calcium, 13% iron.

# FRUIT-AND-CHEESE-STUFFED VEAL ROLLS

**Prep:** 25 minutes   **Grill:** 20 minutes

  1 to 1¼ pounds veal leg round steak, cut ¼ to ½ inch thick
  ¼ teaspoon salt
  ¼ teaspoon pepper
  1 cup shredded Havarti or Swiss cheese (4 ounces)
  ½ cup finely chopped apple or pear
  2 tablespoons finely chopped pecans
  2 tablespoons snipped fresh parsley
  2 tablespoons margarine or butter, melted
  ¼ teaspoon ground nutmeg
  1 ounce Havarti or Swiss cheese, cut into strips

1 Trim fat from meat. Cut meat into 4 serving-size pieces. Place meat between 2 pieces of plastic wrap. Working from center to edges, use the flat side of a meat mallet to pound meat to ⅛-inch thickness. Remove plastic wrap. Sprinkle meat with salt and pepper.

2 For filling, in a bowl toss together the 1 cup shredded cheese, fruit, nuts, and parsley. Place about ⅓ cup of filling on each piece of meat. Fold in sides; roll up meat. Seal edges with small metal skewers. In a bowl combine melted margarine and nutmeg; brush meat rolls with some of the margarine mixture.

3 *For a charcoal grill,* arrange medium-hot coals around a drip pan. Test for medium heat above the pan. Place meat rolls on grill rack over drip pan. Cover and grill for 20 to 25 minutes or until meat is no longer pink. [*For a gas grill,* preheat grill. Reduce heat to medium. Adjust for indirect cooking (see page 10). Grill as above.]

4 Remove skewers from meat rolls. Place rolls on a serving platter. Brush rolls with remaining margarine mixture; top with cheese strips. Makes 4 servings.

Nutrition Facts per serving: 376 calories, 26 g total fat (3 g saturated fat), 136 mg cholesterol, 437 mg sodium, 3 g carbohydrate, 1 g fiber, 33 g protein. **Daily Values:** 14% vit. A, 5% vit. C, 17% calcium, 7% iron.

# Middle Eastern-Style Pizza

**Prep:** 15 minutes  **Grill:** 13 minutes
**Special Equipment:** Grill pizza pan

  12 ounces ground lamb
   1 8-ounce can tomato sauce
   1 clove garlic, minced
 ¼ teaspoon allspice
     Nonstick cooking spray
   1 10-ounce package refrigerated
     pizza dough
   2 plum tomatoes, thinly sliced
 ½ cup chopped green sweet pepper
 ½ cup crumbled feta cheese
     (2 ounces) (optional)
 ¼ cup minced fresh mint
   1 tablespoon pine nuts, toasted
     Plain low-fat yogurt (optional)

**1** For sauce, in a large skillet cook ground lamb over medium heat until meat is no longer pink. Drain well. Stir in tomato sauce, garlic, and allspice. Set aside.

**2** Lightly coat a 12-inch pizza pan with nonstick cooking spray. With your fingers, pat the pizza dough onto the prepared pan.

**3** *For a charcoal grill,* grill pizza crust in pan on the rack of an uncovered grill directly over medium coals for 5 minutes. (*For a gas grill,* preheat grill. Reduce heat to medium. Place pizza crust in pan on grill rack over heat. Cover and grill as above.) Carefully remove pizza crust from grill.

**4** Turn crust; spread with sauce. Top with tomatoes and sweet pepper. Return pizza to grill. Cover and grill for 8 to 10 minutes more or until pizza is heated through, checking occasionally to make sure the crust doesn't overbrown. Remove pizza from grill.

**5** Sprinkle with feta cheese (if desired), mint, and pine nuts. If desired, top with yogurt. Makes 4 servings.

Nutrition Facts per serving: 388 calories,
16 g total fat (5 g saturated fat), 57 mg cholesterol,
784 mg sodium, 40 g carbohydrate, 2 g fiber,
22 g protein. Daily Values: 9% vit. A, 35% vit. C,
2% calcium, 29% iron.

# LAMB BURGERS WITH FETA AND MINT

**Prep:** 15 minutes  **Grill:** 14 minutes

*For an extra flavor boost in these lamb burgers, try one of the feta cheeses flavored with dill—which goes especially well with mint—or cracked black pepper.*

   1 pound ground lamb or lean ground
     beef
   2 teaspoons freshly ground pepper
   4 kaiser rolls, split
   4 lettuce leaves
 ½ cup crumbled feta cheese
     (2 ounces)
   4 tomato slices
   1 tablespoon snipped fresh mint

**1** Shape ground lamb into four ¾-inch-thick patties. Press pepper evenly into patties.

**2** *For a charcoal grill,* grill burgers on the rack of an uncovered grill directly over medium coals for 14 to 18 minutes or until meat is no longer pink, turning once halfway through grilling. (*For a gas grill,* preheat grill. Reduce heat to medium. Place burgers on grill rack over heat. Cover; grill as above.)

**3** Serve burgers on rolls with lettuce, feta cheese, tomato, and mint. Makes 4 servings.

Nutrition Facts per serving: 435 calories,
21 g total fat (9 g saturated fat), 88 mg cholesterol,
535 mg sodium, 33 g carbohydrate, 1 g fiber,
28 g protein. Daily Values: 4% vit. A, 11% vit. C,
12% calcium, 27% iron.

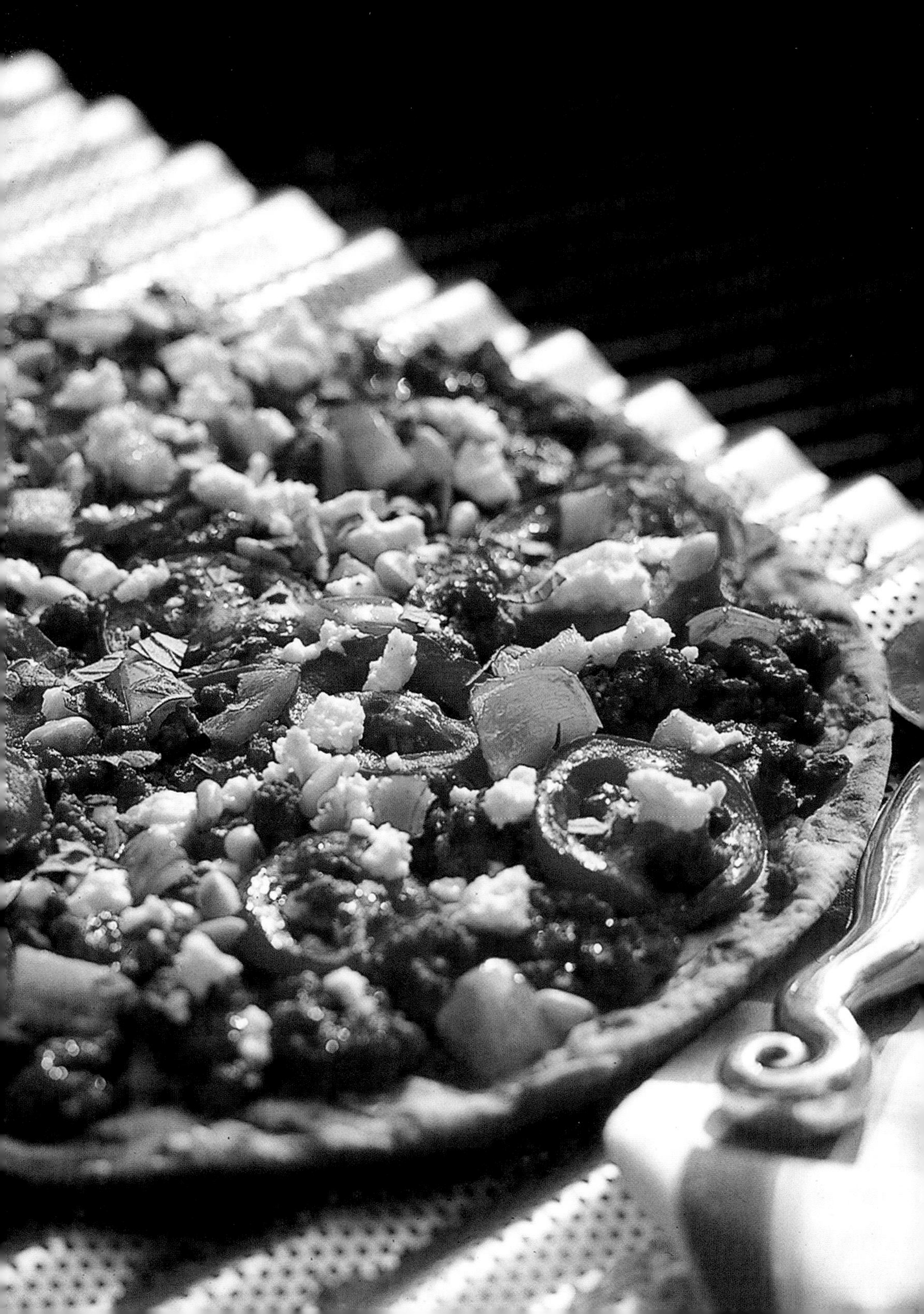
Middle Eastern-Style Pizza

# Spiced Lamb Patties

**Prep:** 20 minutes **Grill:** 10 minutes

*These flavorful lamb patties gain their notoriety because of the trio of spices they contain—ground cumin, cinnamon, and red pepper.*

> 3 tablespoons grated onion
> 2 tablespoons snipped fresh parsley
> 2 tablespoons snipped fresh cilantro
> ½ teaspoon ground cumin
> ½ teaspoon ground cinnamon
> ¼ teaspoon salt
> ¼ teaspoon ground red pepper
> 1 pound ground lamb or a mixture of ground lamb and ground beef
>   Thinly sliced cucumber (optional)
>   Lemon wedges (optional)

**1** In a medium bowl combine onion, parsley, cilantro, cumin, cinnamon, salt, and red pepper. Add ground meat; mix well. Shape about ¼ cup of the mixture into 8 oval patties about ¾ inch thick.

**2** *For a charcoal grill,* grill patties on the rack of an uncovered grill directly over medium coals for 14 to 18 minutes or until meat is no longer pink, turning once halfway through grilling. (*For a gas grill,* preheat grill. Reduce heat to medium. Place patties on grill rack over heat. Cover and grill as above.) Remove patties from grill.

**3** If desired, serve patties on a bed of cucumber slices and garnish with lemon wedges. Makes 4 servings.

Nutrition Facts per serving: 232 calories, 16 g total fat (6 g saturated fat), 76 mg cholesterol, 199 mg sodium, 2 g carbohydrate, 0 g fiber, 20 g protein. Daily Values: 1% vit. A, 5% vit. C, 2% calcium, 13% iron.

# CUCUMBER-LAMB BURGERS

**Prep:** 20 minutes **Grill:** 14 minutes

*Creamy buttermilk ranch dressing adds moistness to these delicious burgers. The savory flavor is repeated in the saladlike topper.*

> 1 beaten egg
> ⅓ cup finely chopped cucumber
> ¼ cup toasted wheat germ
> 2 tablespoons buttermilk ranch salad dressing or creamy cucumber salad dressing
> ½ teaspoon garlic salt
> ¼ teaspoon dried marjoram, crushed
>   Dash pepper
> 1 pound lean ground lamb
> 4 kaiser rolls, toasted
> 8 thin cucumber slices
> ¼ cup buttermilk ranch salad dressing or creamy cucumber salad dressing
>   Shredded lettuce

**1** In a bowl combine egg, chopped cucumber, wheat germ, the 2 tablespoons salad dressing, the garlic salt, marjoram, and pepper. Add ground lamb; mix well. Shape mixture into four ¾-inch-thick patties.

**2** *For a charcoal grill,* grill patties on the rack of an uncovered grill directly over medium coals for 14 to 18 minutes or until meat is no longer pink, turning once halfway through grilling. (*For a gas grill,* preheat grill. Reduce heat to medium. Place patties on grill rack over heat. Cover and grill as above.) Remove burgers from grill.

**3** Serve burgers on rolls with cucumber slices, remaining salad dressing, and shredded lettuce. Makes 4 servings.

Nutrition Facts per serving: 518 calories, 28 g total fat (8 g saturated fat), 135 mg cholesterol, 791 mg sodium, 35 g carbohydrate, 29 g protein. Daily Values: 4% vit. A, 2% vit. C, 7% calcium, 28% iron.

# Greek Meat Loaf

**Prep:** 20 minutes   **Grill:** 18 minutes

⅓ cup dairy sour cream
½ cup peeled, seeded, and finely
      chopped cucumber
2 tablespoons finely chopped red
      onion
1 clove garlic, minced
¼ teaspoon dried mint or basil,
      crushed
1 beaten egg
½ cup sliced pitted ripe olives
¼ cup fine dry bread crumbs
¼ cup crumbled feta cheese (1 ounce)
¼ cup milk
½ teaspoon dried mint or basil,
      crushed
8 ounces lean ground lamb
8 ounces lean ground beef
½ cup chopped tomato

1 For sauce, stir together sour cream, cucumber, onion, garlic, the ¼ teaspoon mint or basil, ⅛ teaspoon pepper, and dash salt. Cover and chill.

2 For meat loaf, in a large bowl combine the egg, olives, bread crumbs, feta cheese, milk, the ½ teaspoon mint or basil, ¼ teaspoon salt, and ¼ teaspoon pepper. Add ground lamb and beef; mix well. Shape into four 4×2½×¾-inch meat loaves.

3 For a charcoal grill, grill meat loaves on the rack of an uncovered grill directly over medium coals for 18 to 20 minutes or until meat is no longer pink, turning once halfway through grilling. (For a gas grill, preheat grill. Reduce heat to medium. Place meat loaves on grill rack over heat. Cover and grill as above.)

4 To serve, spoon some of the sauce over each serving and sprinkle with tomato. Makes 4 servings.

Nutrition Facts per serving: 367 calories, 25 g total fat (11 g saturated fat), 151 mg cholesterol, 557 mg sodium, 10 g carbohydrate, 1 g fiber, 26 g protein. Daily Values: 12% vit. A, 11% vit. C, 13% calcium, 17% iron.

# DIJON-CRUSTED LAMB RIB ROAST

**Prep:** 10 minutes   **Grill:** 50 minutes
**Stand:** 15 minutes

*Sour cream, Dijon mustard, garlic, and thyme grill up into a wonderful crust that has a twofold purpose—to provide flavor, of course, and to seal in the juices of the succulent lamb.*

1 2½-pound lamb rib roast (8 ribs)
3 tablespoons Dijon-style mustard
1 tablespoon olive oil
2 cloves garlic, minced
1 teaspoon snipped fresh thyme or
      ½ teaspoon dried thyme, crushed
¼ teaspoon salt
¼ teaspoon pepper
¼ cup dairy sour cream

1 Trim fat from meat. In a bowl stir together mustard, oil, garlic, thyme, salt, and pepper. Set aside 2 tablespoons of the mustard mixture; cover and chill. Brush meat with remaining mustard mixture. Insert a meat thermometer into meat without it touching bone.

2 For a charcoal grill, arrange medium-hot coals around a drip pan. Test for medium heat above pan. Place meat, bone side down, on grill rack over drip pan. Cover and grill until meat thermometer registers 140° for medium-rare (50 to 60 minutes) or 155° for medium doneness (1 to 1¼ hours). [For a gas grill, preheat grill. Reduce heat to medium. Adjust for indirect cooking (see page 10). Grill as above, except place meat, bone side down, in a roasting pan.]

3 Remove meat from grill. Cover with foil; let stand for 15 minutes before carving. (The meat's temperature will rise 5° during standing.) Meanwhile, for sauce, in a bowl stir together sour cream and reserved mustard mixture. To serve, cut meat into four 2-rib portions. Pass sauce with meat. Makes 4 servings.

Nutrition Facts per serving: 404 calories, 26 g total fat (9 g saturated fat), 129 mg cholesterol, 539 mg sodium, 2 g carbohydrate, 0 g fiber, 38 g protein. Daily Values: 3% vit. A, 1% vit. C, 4% calcium, 17% iron.

# Rack of Lamb with Creamy Pesto

**Prep:** 20 minutes  **Grill:** 50 minutes
**Stand:** 15 minutes

*Sometimes the simplest preparations make for a breathtaking dinnertime presentation, and few dishes engage the senses more fully than this rack of lamb. Be careful not to overcook the lamb. For the most mouthwatering results, the meat should be slightly pink.*

1  2½-pound lamb rib roast (8 ribs)
¼  cup pesto
2  tablespoons finely chopped
     hazelnuts or walnuts, toasted
½  cup plain yogurt or dairy sour
     cream
2  tablespoons pesto

1 Trim fat from meat. In a small bowl stir together the ¼ cup pesto and the nuts. Spread over meat. Insert a meat thermometer into the meat without it touching bone.

2 *For a charcoal grill,* arrange medium-hot coals around a drip pan. Test for medium heat above the pan. Place meat, bone side down, on grill rack over drip pan. Cover and grill until meat thermometer registers 140° for medium-rare (50 to 60 minutes) or 155° for medium doneness (1 to 1¼ hours). [*For a gas grill,* preheat grill. Reduce heat to medium. Adjust for indirect cooking (see page 10). Grill as above, except place meat, bone side down, in a roasting pan.]

3 Remove meat from grill. Cover with foil; let stand for 15 minutes before carving. (The meat's temperature will rise 5° during standing.) Meanwhile, for sauce, in a small bowl combine yogurt or sour cream and the 2 tablespoons pesto.

4 To serve, cut meat into four 2-rib portions. Pass the sauce with meat. Serves 4.

Nutrition Facts per serving: 530 calories, 37 g total fat (7 g saturated fat), 127 mg cholesterol, 308 mg sodium, 7 g carbohydrate, 0 g fiber, 42 g protein. Daily Values: 7% calcium, 17% iron.

# MONGOLIAN-STYLE LAMB CHOPS

**Prep:** 15 minutes  **Marinate:** 30 minutes
**Grill:** 10 minutes

*Tongue-tingling but far from fierce, the marinade for these chops has a hint of brown sugar that makes for a perfect balance of sweet and heat.*

4  to 6 lamb loin chops, cut 1 inch
     thick
2  tablespoons soy sauce
1  tablespoon brown sugar
6  cloves garlic, minced
1½  teaspoons grated fresh ginger
1  teaspoon toasted sesame oil
     Snipped fresh cilantro (optional)
     Lemon wedges (optional)

1 Trim fat from chops. Place chops in a plastic bag set in a shallow dish. For marinade, in a small bowl stir together the soy sauce, brown sugar, garlic, ginger, and sesame oil. Pour marinade over chops; seal bag. Marinate at room temperature for 30 minutes or in the refrigerator for 2 to 3 hours, turning bag occasionally. Drain chops, discarding marinade.

2 *For a charcoal grill,* grill chops on the rack of an uncovered grill directly over medium coals until desired doneness, turning once halfway through grilling. (Allow 10 to 14 minutes for medium-rare and 14 to 16 minutes for medium doneness.) (*For a gas grill,* preheat grill. Reduce heat to medium. Place chops on grill rack over heat. Cover and grill as above.)

3 If desired, garnish chops with cilantro and lemon wedges. Makes 4 to 6 servings.

Nutrition Facts per serving: 225 calories, 10 g total fat (4 g saturated fat), 83 mg cholesterol, 579 mg sodium, 5 g carbohydrate, 0 g fiber, 26 g protein. Daily Values: 3% vit. C, 2% calcium, 17% iron.

Mongolian-Style Lamb Chops

# Apple-Glazed Lamb Chops

**Prep:** 15 minutes   **Grill:** 10 minutes

*As fast as it is fancy, these chops get a quick glaze with an apple jelly mixture while on the grill. Apples and mint take on supporting roles.*

- 3 tablespoons apple jelly
- 1 green onion, thinly sliced
- 1 tablespoon soy sauce
- 2 teaspoons lemon juice
- ⅛ teaspoon curry powder
  Dash ground cinnamon
  Dash ground red pepper
- 2 small red and/or green apples, cut crosswise into ¼-inch slices
  Lemon juice
- 8 lamb loin chops, cut 1 inch thick
  Hot cooked couscous (optional)
- 1 tablespoon snipped fresh mint

**1** For glaze, in a saucepan cook and stir apple jelly, green onion, soy sauce, lemon juice, curry powder, cinnamon, and red pepper over medium heat until bubbly. Remove from heat. Remove seeds from apple slices. Brush apples with additional lemon juice. Set aside.

**2** Trim fat from chops. *For a charcoal grill,* grill chops on the rack of an uncovered grill directly over medium coals until desired doneness, turning once halfway through grilling. (Allow 10 to 14 minutes for medium-rare and 14 to 16 minutes for medium doneness.) While the chops are grilling, add apple slices to grill. Grill about 5 minutes or until tender, turning and brushing once with glaze halfway through grilling. (*For a gas grill,* preheat grill. Reduce heat to medium. Place chops, then apple slices on grill rack over heat. Cover; grill as above.)

**3** Serve chops with grilled apples and, if desired, hot couscous. Sprinkle with mint. Makes 4 servings.

Nutrition Facts per serving: 385 calories, 14 g total fat (5 g saturated fat), 133 mg cholesterol, 378 mg sodium, 20 g carbohydrate, 1 g fiber, 43 g protein. Daily Values: 1% vit. A, 11% vit. C, 3% calcium, 23% iron.

# TANDOORI-STYLE LAMB CHOPS

**Prep:** 20 minutes   **Grill:** 10 minutes

*The brick-and-clay tandoor ovens of India cook super-hot (usually more than 500°) and super-fast (half of a chicken cooks in less than five minutes). While your grill can't quite keep that pace, these chops emulate the spirit of this cooking technique.*

- 8 lamb loin chops, cut 1 inch thick
- 2 tablespoons cooking oil
- 6 cloves garlic, minced
- 1 tablespoon garam masala*
- 2 teaspoons grated fresh ginger
- ½ teaspoon salt
- 2 medium yellow summer squash and/or zucchini, halved lengthwise
- 4 pita bread rounds
- ½ cup plain low-fat yogurt
- 1 tablespoon snipped fresh mint
- ¼ cup chutney or hot chutney

**1** Trim fat from chops. For rub, in a small bowl combine oil, garlic, garam masala, ginger, and salt. Spoon evenly over chops and squash; rub in with your fingers.

**2** *For a charcoal grill,* grill chops and squash on the rack of an uncovered grill directly over medium coals until chops are desired doneness and squash is tender, turning once halfway through grilling. (For chops, allow 10 to 14 minutes for medium-rare and 14 to 16 minutes for medium doneness. For squash, allow 5 to 6 minutes.) While the chops and squash are grilling, add pita bread to grill. Grill about 2 minutes or until heated through. (*For a gas grill,* preheat grill. Reduce heat to medium. Place chops and squash, then pita bread on grill rack over heat. Cover and grill as above.)

**3** Meanwhile, in a small bowl combine yogurt and mint. Transfer squash to a cutting board; cool slightly and cut diagonally into ½-inch slices. Serve the chops with squash, pita bread, yogurt mixture, and chutney. Makes 4 servings.

Nutrition Facts per serving: 615 calories,
22 g total fat (6 g saturated fat), 135 mg cholesterol,
735 mg sodium, 51 g carbohydrate, 1 g fiber,
51 g protein. Daily Values: 3% vit. A, 11% vit. C,
14% calcium, 40% iron.

*Note:* For homemade garam masala, in a
small bowl combine 1 teaspoon ground
cumin, 1 teaspoon ground coriander,
½ teaspoon pepper, ½ teaspoon ground
cardamom, ¼ teaspoon ground cinnamon,
and ¼ teaspoon ground cloves.

## Jalapeño-and-Mint Lamb Chops

**Prep:** 15 minutes   **Grill:** 12 minutes

*The marriage of mint and lamb is a classic
flavor combination. A blast of jalapeño sets these
chops apart.*

   8 lamb loin chops, cut 1¼ inches
       thick
   ⅓ cup jalapeño pepper jelly
   4 teaspoons snipped fresh mint
   1 tablespoon lime juice
   1 small jalapeño pepper, finely
       chopped
   2 cloves garlic, minced

1 Trim fat from chops. If desired, sprinkle
with salt and pepper.

2 For glaze, in a small saucepan combine
jalapeño jelly, mint, lime juice, jalapeño
pepper, and garlic. Cook and stir over
medium-low heat until jelly is melted.
Remove from heat.

3 *For a charcoal grill,* place medium coals in
bottom of grill. Place chops on grill rack
directly over coals. Cover and grill until
chops are desired doneness, turning once and
brushing occasionally with glaze during the
first 5 minutes of grilling. (Allow 12 to 16
minutes for medium-rare and 16 to 18
minutes for medium doneness.) (*For a gas
grill,* preheat grill. Reduce heat to medium.
Place chops on grill rack over heat. Grill as
above.) Makes 4 servings.

Nutrition Facts per serving: 439 calories,
17 g total fat (6 g saturated fat), 160 mg cholesterol,
147 mg sodium, 19 g carbohydrate, 0 g fiber,
51 g protein. Daily Values: 15% vit. C, 3% calcium,
27% iron.

## Did You Know?

**Sheep, at one time, were bred to produce both wool and meat.
Unfortunately, the meat usually tasted strong and unpleasant. Today,
younger sheep are raised just for eating, making the meat leaner,
tastier, and more tender.
There are, however, flavor and size differences between imported
and domestic lamb because of varying feed options and breeding
techniques. Domestic lamb often has a milder flavor than imported
lamb because in the United States the animals are raised on grain
rather than grass. Cuts from domestic lamb tends to be meatier and
up to twice the size of the same cut from imported animals because
U.S. farmers endeavor to raise bigger, meatier animals.**

## Apricot-Stuffed Lamb Chops

**Prep:** 15 minutes  **Grill:** 10 minutes

*There's sweetness in the center of these chops, which are stuffed with apricots, raisins, onion, and orange peel. Be sure to soak those toothpicks so they don't turn into fuel on the grill.*

  ⅓ cup snipped dried apricots
  3 tablespoons raisins
  1 tablespoon finely chopped onion
  1 teaspoon finely shredded orange peel
  8 lamb rib chops, cut 1 inch thick
  2 teaspoons ground coriander
  ½ teaspoon salt
  ¼ teaspoon pepper

**1** For stuffing, in a small bowl combine the apricots, raisins, onion, and orange peel.

**2** Trim fat from chops. Make a pocket in each chop by cutting horizontally from the fat side almost to the bone. Spoon stuffing into pockets. If necessary, secure the openings with wooden toothpicks.

**3** For rub, in a small bowl combine the coriander, salt, and pepper. Sprinkle evenly over chops; rub in with your fingers.

**4** *For a charcoal grill,* grill chops on the rack of an uncovered grill directly over medium coals until desired doneness, turning once halfway through grilling. (Allow 10 to 14 minutes for medium-rare and 14 to 16 minutes for medium doneness.) (*For a gas grill,* preheat grill. Reduce heat to medium. Place chops on grill rack over heat. Cover and grill as above.) If using toothpicks, remove before serving. Makes 4 servings.

Nutrition Facts per serving: 358 calories, 14 g total fat (5 g saturated fat), 133 mg cholesterol, 388 mg sodium, 13 g carbohydrate, 1 g fiber, 43 g protein. Daily Values: 7% vit. A, 2% vit. C, 4% calcium, 25% iron.

# Pineapple Lamb Chops

**Prep:** 20 minutes  **Grill:** 10 minutes

  1 8¼-ounce can crushed pineapple
  ½ cup cooked rice
  1 tablespoon thinly sliced green onion
  ¼ teaspoon ground ginger
  ⅛ teaspoon salt
  8 lamb rib chops, cut 1 inch thick
  1 tablespoon honey
  2 teaspoons soy sauce
  1 teaspoon cornstarch

**1** For stuffing, drain pineapple, reserving syrup. In a bowl toss together ⅓ cup of the drained pineapple (set aside remaining pineapple), rice, onion, ginger, and salt.

**2** Trim fat from chops. Make a pocket in each chop by cutting horizontally from fat side almost to the bone. Spoon about 1 tablespoon stuffing into each pocket. If necessary, secure openings with wooden toothpicks.

**3** For glaze, combine 3 tablespoons of the reserved pineapple syrup, the honey, and soy sauce; set glaze aside. *For a charcoal grill,* grill chops on the rack of an uncovered grill directly over medium coals until desired doneness, turning once halfway through grilling and brushing with some of the glaze the last 2 minutes of grilling. (Allow 10 to 14 minutes for medium-rare and 14 to 16 minutes for medium doneness.) (*For a gas grill,* preheat grill. Reduce heat to medium. Place chops on grill rack over heat. Cover and grill as above.)

**4** In a small saucepan stir together remaining glaze, reserved crushed pineapple, remaining pineapple syrup, and cornstarch. Cook and stir over medium heat until thickened and bubbly. Cook and stir 1 minute more. Serve over lamb chops. Makes 4 servings.

Nutrition Facts per serving: 237 calories, 8 g total fat (3 g saturated fat), 69 mg cholesterol, 292 mg sodium, 19 g carbohydrate, 0 g fiber, 22 g protein. Daily Values: 7% vit. C, 2% calcium, 16% iron.

## INDONESIAN SATAY

**Prep:** 25 minutes    **Marinate:** 2 to 24 hours
**Grill:** 12 minutes

*This hearty dish satisfies all of the top picks of a
real meat lover. Savor the trio of lamb, beef, and
turkey all in one flavor-filled dish. Serve over
rice along with steamed green beans for a
memorable meal.*

  1 pound boneless leg of lamb, cut
      into 1½-inch cubes
  1 1-pound boneless beef sirloin
      steak, cut into 1½-inch cubes
  8 ounces skinless, boneless turkey
      breast, cut into 1½-inch cubes
  1 cup purchased unsweetened
      coconut milk
  ⅓ cup finely chopped onion
  2 cloves garlic, minced
  2 teaspoons dry mustard
  2 teaspoons ground coriander
  ½ teaspoon ground turmeric
  ¼ teaspoon salt
  ¼ teaspoon ground cumin
 10 green onions, trimmed and each
      cut into 4 pieces
  1 recipe Peanut Sauce
      Hot cooked rice (optional)

**1** Place the lamb, beef, and turkey cubes in a
plastic bag set in a shallow dish. Set aside.

**2** For marinade, in a bowl combine coconut
milk, onion, garlic, mustard, coriander,
turmeric, salt, and cumin. Pour over cubed
meat. Seal bag. Marinate in refrigerator for
2 to 24 hours, turning bag occasionally.

**3** Drain lamb, beef, and turkey cubes,
reserving marinade. On twenty 8-inch
metal skewers, alternately thread lamb, beef,
turkey, and green onion pieces leaving a
¼-inch space between pieces.

**4** *For a charcoal grill,* grill kabobs on the
rack of an uncovered grill directly over
medium coals for 12 to 16 minutes or until
lamb and beef are of desired doneness and
turkey is no longer pink, turning once and
brushing occasionally with marinade during
the first half of grilling. (*For a gas grill,*
preheat grill. Reduce heat to medium. Place
kabobs on grill rack over heat. Cover and grill
as above.)

**5** Serve kabobs with Peanut Sauce. If
desired, serve with hot cooked rice. Makes
10 servings.

**Peanut Sauce:** In a small saucepan place
¾ cup reduced-sodium chicken broth. Add
2 tablespoons sliced green onion and 1 clove
garlic, minced. Cook, covered, about
2 minutes or until onion is tender. Add
1 tablespoon reduced-sodium soy sauce,
½ teaspoon finely shredded lemon peel,
1 tablespoon lemon juice, 1 to 1½ teaspoons
chili powder, and ½ teaspoon brown sugar.
Bring to boiling; reduce heat. Simmer,
uncovered, for 5 minutes, stirring frequently.
Stir in ⅓ cup peanut butter and 1 tablespoon
grated fresh ginger or ¾ teaspoon ground
ginger; heat through without boiling. If
desired, thin sauce with a little unsweetened
coconut milk. Serve at room temperature.
Cover and chill sauce to store. Makes about
1½ cups.

Nutrition Facts per serving: 224 calories,
12 g total fat (7 g saturated fat), 62 mg cholesterol,
198 mg sodium, 4 g carbohydrate, 0 g fiber,
25 g protein. Daily Values: 2% vit. A, 5% vit. C,
1% calcium, 15% iron.

Greek-Inspired Lamb Pockets

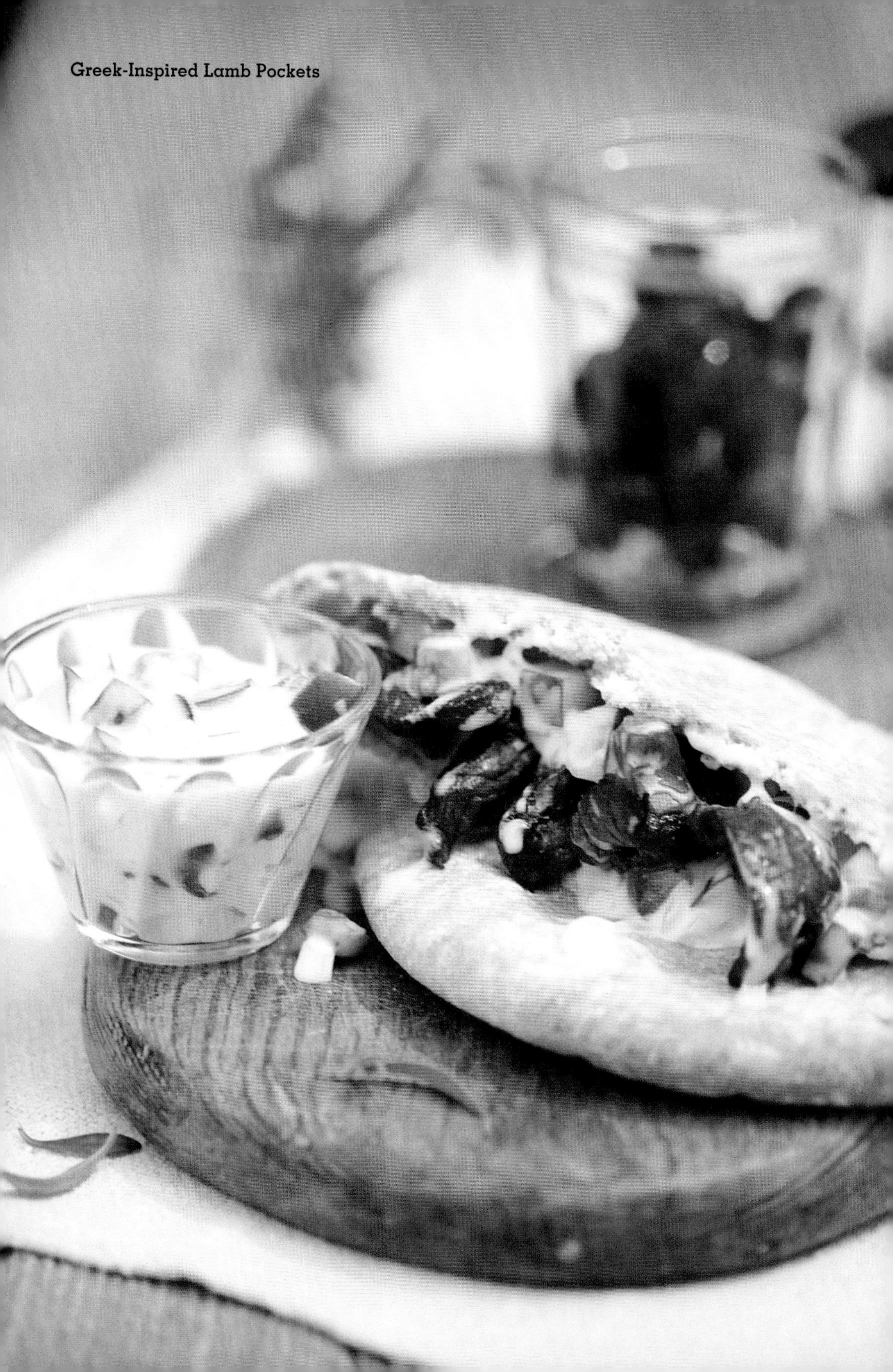

# Greek-Inspired Lamb Pockets

**Prep:** 20 minutes **Marinate:** 10 minutes
**Grill:** 10 minutes

- 1 pound boneless leg of lamb
- ¼ cup balsamic vinegar
- 1 tablespoon snipped fresh savory or 1 teaspoon dried savory, crushed
- ½ teaspoon pepper
- 1 8-ounce carton plain low-fat yogurt
- 1 small cucumber, seeded and chopped (¾ cup)
- 2 plum tomatoes, chopped
- 1 small onion, finely chopped
- 4 whole wheat pita bread rounds

**1** Trim fat from meat. Cut meat into 2×1-inch thin strips. Place meat in a plastic bag set in a shallow dish. For marinade, in a bowl combine vinegar, savory, and pepper. Pour over meat; seal bag. Marinate for 10 minutes at room temperature or in the refrigerator for up to 4 hours, turning bag occasionally. Meanwhile, for sauce, in a medium bowl combine yogurt, cucumber, tomatoes, and onion. Cover and chill until ready to serve. Stack pita bread and wrap in a piece of foil. Set aside.

**2** Drain meat, reserving marinade. On four 10- to 12-inch metal skewers, thread meat accordion-style. *For a charcoal grill,* grill kabobs on the rack of an uncovered grill directly over medium coals for 10 to 12 minutes or until meat is slightly pink in center, turning once and brushing occasionally with marinade up to the last 5 minutes of grilling. While the kabobs are grilling, add pita bread to grill. Grill about 5 minutes or until heated through. (*For a gas grill,* preheat grill. Reduce heat to medium. Place kabobs, then pita bread on grill rack over heat. Cover; grill as above.) Cut pita bread in half crosswise. Spoon sauce into pita halves; fill with lamb strips. Serves 4.

Ⓥ Nutrition Facts per serving: 361 calories, 8 g total fat (3 g saturated fat), 61 mg cholesterol, 430 mg sodium, 46 g carbohydrate, 1 g fiber, 28 g protein. Daily Values: 3% vit. A, 20% vit. C, 10% calcium, 15% iron.

# LEMON-ROSEMARY LAMB KABOBS

**Prep:** 15 minutes **Marinate:** 2 to 6 hours
**Grill:** 12 minutes

- 1 pound lean boneless leg of lamb
- ¼ cup olive oil
- 1 teaspoon finely shredded lemon peel
- 3 tablespoons lemon juice
- 1 tablespoon snipped fresh rosemary
- 2 cloves garlic, minced
- ½ teaspoon ground cumin
- ½ teaspoon freshly ground pepper
- ¼ teaspoon salt
- 2 small red onions, each cut lengthwise into 8 wedges

**1** Trim fat from meat. Cut meat into 1½-inch pieces. Place meat in a plastic bag set in a shallow dish. For marinade, in a small bowl combine olive oil, lemon peel, lemon juice, rosemary, garlic, cumin, pepper, and salt. Pour over meat; seal bag. Marinate in the refrigerator for 2 to 6 hours, turning bag occasionally.

**2** In a medium covered saucepan cook onions in a small amount of boiling water for 3 minutes; drain onions. Drain meat, reserving marinade. On 8 rosemary branches or metal skewers, alternately thread the meat and onion wedges, leaving about a ¼-inch space between pieces. Brush onion with some of the marinade.

**3** *For a charcoal grill,* place medium coals in bottom of grill. Place kabobs on grill rack directly over coals. Cover and grill for 12 to 16 minutes or until meat is slightly pink in center, turning and brushing once with marinade halfway through grilling. (*For a gas grill,* preheat grill. Reduce heat to medium. Place kabobs on grill rack over heat. Grill as above.) Makes 4 servings.

Nutrition Facts per serving: 264 calories, 19 g total fat (4 g saturated fat), 57 mg cholesterol, 46 mg sodium, 5 g carbohydrate, 1 g fiber, 19 g protein. Daily Values: 13% vit. C, 1% calcium, 12% iron.

# Grilled Greek Leg of Lamb

**Prep:** 20 minutes   **Marinate:** 20 minutes
**Grill:** 8 minutes

*Grilled leg of lamb in under an hour? Sure, if it's
sliced thin and flash-grilled after a quick soak
in a lemon-oregano marinade. The flavorful
topper—grilled tomatoes, cinnamon, feta cheese,
and Greek olives—creates a superb dish.*

1½ to 2 pounds boneless leg of lamb
   1 tablespoon finely shredded lemon
        peel
   ⅔ cup lemon juice
   6 tablespoons olive oil
   ⅓ cup snipped fresh oregano
   ½ teaspoon salt
   ⅛ teaspoon pepper
   ½ cup snipped fresh parsley
   ½ cup crumbled feta cheese
        (2 ounces)
   ¼ cup pitted, sliced kalamata olives
   ¼ teaspoon ground cinnamon
   ¼ teaspoon pepper
   2 pounds plum tomatoes

1 Trim fat from meat. Cut meat across the
grain into ½- to ¾-inch-thick slices. Place
meat in a large bowl. For marinade, in a small
bowl stir together the lemon peel, ⅓ cup of
the lemon juice, 4 tablespoons of the oil, the
oregano, salt, and the ⅛ teaspoon pepper.
Pour over meat. Cover and marinate at room
temperature for 20 minutes or in the
refrigerator for 8 to 24 hours, stirring
occasionally. In a small bowl combine the
remaining lemon juice, 1 tablespoon of the
oil, the parsley, feta cheese, olives, cinnamon,
and the ¼ teaspoon pepper; set aside.

2 Drain meat, discarding marinade. Brush
tomatoes with the remaining oil. *For a
charcoal grill,* grill meat and tomatoes on the
rack of an uncovered grill directly over
medium coals for 8 to 10 minutes or until
meat is slightly pink in center and tomatoes
are slightly charred, turning once halfway
through grilling. (*For a gas grill,* preheat

grill. Reduce heat to medium. Place meat and
tomatoes on grill rack over heat. Cover and
grill as above.)

3 Transfer tomatoes to a cutting board; cool
slightly and slice. Toss the tomatoes with
the feta cheese mixture; serve with meat.
Makes 6 servings.

Nutrition Facts per serving: 256 calories,
14 g total fat (4 g saturated fat), 66 mg cholesterol,
493 mg sodium, 11 g carbohydrate, 0 g fiber,
22 g protein. Daily Values: 15% vit. A, 80% vit. C,
6% calcium, 18% iron.

## ROSEMARY-AND-GARLIC-CRUSTED LAMB

**Prep:** 30 minutes   **Grill:** 1¾ hours
**Stand:** 15 minutes
**Special Equipment:** Rotisserie

*By grilling this leg of lamb on the spit of a
rotisserie, the heat circulates around the meat.*

1 3½- to 4-pound boneless leg of
        lamb, rolled and tied
2 tablespoons snipped fresh
        rosemary
2 to 3 teaspoons coarsely ground
        pepper
2 to 3 cloves garlic, minced

1 Trim fat from meat. For rub, in a small bowl
combine rosemary, pepper, and garlic.
Sprinkle mixture evenly over meat; rub in
with your fingers.

2 To mount on a spit rod, place one holding
fork on rod, tines toward point. Insert rod
through meat, pressing tines of holding fork
firmly into meat. Place the second holding
fork, tines toward the meat; press tines of
holding fork firmly into meat. Adjust forks
and tighten screws. Test the balance.

3 *For a charcoal grill,* arrange medium-hot
coals around a drip pan. Test for medium
heat above the pan. Attach spit; turn on the
motor and lower the grill hood. Let the meat
rotate over drip pan until an instant-read

thermometer registers 140° for medium-rare (1¾ to 2¼ hours) or 155° for medium doneness (2 to 2½ hours). [*For a gas grill*, preheat grill. Reduce the heat to medium. Adjust for indirect cooking (see page 10). Grill as above.]

**4** Remove meat from spit. Cover with foil; let stand for 15 minutes before carving. (The meat's temperature will rise 5° during standing.) To serve, remove strings and thinly slice meat. Makes 6 to 8 servings.

ⓥNutrition Facts per serving: 291 calories, 12 g total fat (4 g saturated fat), 134 mg cholesterol, 103 mg sodium, 1 g carbohydrate, 0 g fiber, 43 g protein. Daily Values: 2% vit. C, 1% calcium, 22% iron.

# Rosemary Lamb

**Prep:** 15 minutes    **Grill:** 1¾ hours
**Marinate:** 6 to 24 hours    **Stand:** 15 minutes

*If ever there were ever two flavors meant for each other, it has to be lamb and rosemary. Wine, lemon juice, and mustard round out the match.*

⅓ **cup dry red wine**
⅓ **cup lemon juice**
⅓ **cup cooking oil**
¼ **cup Dijon-style mustard**
3 **tablespoons snipped fresh**
   **rosemary or 2 teaspoons dried**
   **rosemary, crushed**
4 **cloves garlic, minced**
½ **teaspoon salt**
½ **teaspoon pepper**
1 **3- to 4-pound boneless leg of lamb,**
   **rolled and tied**

**1** For marinade, combine wine, lemon juice, oil, mustard, rosemary, garlic, salt, and pepper; mix well.

**2** Untie roast and trim fat. Place lamb in a plastic bag in a shallow dish. Pour marinade over lamb; seal bag. Marinate in the refrigerator for 6 to 24 hours, turning bag occasionally. Drain meat, reserving

marinade. Retie meat with butcher's string. Insert a meat thermometer into the center of meat.

**3** *For a charcoal grill*, arrange medium coals around a drip pan. Test for medium-low heat above pan. Place lamb on grill rack over drip pan. Cover and grill until meat thermometer registers 140° for medium-rare (1¾ to 2¼ hours) or 155° for medium doneness (2 to 2½ hours), brushing occasionally with marinade during the first 1½ hours of grilling. [*For a gas grill*, preheat grill. Reduce heat to medium-low. Adjust for indirect cooking (see page 10). Grill as above, except place meat on rack in a roasting pan.]

**4** Remove meat from grill. Cover with foil; let stand for 15 minutes (the meat's temperature will rise 5° during standing). To serve, remove strings and thinly slice meat. Makes 8 servings.

Nutrition Facts per serving: 285 calories, 17 g total fat (4 g saturated fat), 86 mg cholesterol, 384 mg sodium, 2 g carbohydrate, 0 g fiber, 28 g protein. Daily Values: 8% vit. C, 1% calcium, 14% iron.

**Grilling Know-How**

**Thermometers work best for those who don't consider their sense of touch good enough for checking doneness. Smaller cuts of meats, such as chops or steaks, may not be thick enough to give you an accurate reading, however. In these cases, check the recipe for further instructions for determining appropriate doneness.**

## MARINATED LEG OF LAMB

**Prep:** 15 minutes   **Marinate:** 6 to 24 hours
**Grill:** 1¾ hours   **Stand:** 15 minutes

*Lamb legs are rolled and tied for practical reasons. But it's OK to undo the butcher's handiwork in this case, to allow the marinade to have more contact with the surface of the meat making for more flavorful results. Before grilling, reroll and tie the meat.*

1 4-pound boneless leg of lamb,
   rolled and tied
1 tablespoon finely shredded
   lemon peel
⅓ cup lemon juice
¼ cup finely chopped onion
3 tablespoons Dijon-style mustard
2 tablespoons snipped fresh parsley
2 tablespoons cooking oil
1 tablespoon snipped fresh thyme or
   1 teaspoon dried thyme, crushed
1 tablespoon snipped fresh basil or
   1 teaspoon dried basil, crushed
1 tablespoon snipped fresh tarragon
   or 1 teaspoon dried tarragon,
   crushed

**1** Untie meat and trim fat. Place meat in a plastic bag set in a shallow dish. For marinade, in a small bowl combine lemon peel, lemon juice, onion, mustard, parsley, oil, thyme, basil, tarragon, and ½ teaspoon salt. Pour over meat; seal bag. Marinate in the refrigerator for 6 to 24 hours, turning bag occasionally. Drain meat, reserving marinade. Retie meat with butcher's string. Insert meat thermometer into center of meat.

**2** *For a charcoal grill,* arrange medium coals around a drip pan. Test for medium-low heat above the pan. Place meat on grill rack over drip pan. Cover and grill until meat thermometer registers 140° for medium-rare (1¾ to 2¼ hours) or 155° for medium doneness (2 to 2½ hours), brushing occasionally with marinade during the first 1½ hours of grilling. [*For a gas grill,* preheat grill. Reduce heat to medium-low. Adjust for indirect cooking (see page 10). Grill as

above, except place the meat on a rack in a roasting pan.]

**3** Remove meat from grill. Cover with foil; let stand for 15 minutes. (The meat's temperature will rise 5° during standing.) To serve, remove strings and thinly slice meat. Makes 10 to 12 servings.

Nutrition Facts per serving: 232 calories, 11 g total fat (3 g saturated fat), 92 mg cholesterol, 291 mg sodium, 2 g carbohydrate, 0 g fiber, 30 g protein. Daily Values: 9% vit. C, 1% calcium, 15% iron.

# Herbed Roast Lamb with Black Beans

**Prep:** 25 minutes   **Grill:** 1¾ hours
**Stand:** 15 minutes

1 4-pound boneless leg of lamb,
   rolled and tied
2 cloves garlic, peeled and sliced
1 medium lime, halved
1 recipe Herb Rub
1 cup chopped onion
2 15-ounce cans black beans, rinsed
   and drained
1 4½-ounce can diced green chile
   peppers
1 4-ounce jar chopped pimiento,
   drained
¼ cup snipped fresh cilantro
1 tablespoon red wine vinegar

**1** Untie meat and trim fat. Retie meat. With the point of a paring knife, make small slits in meat. Insert garlic into slits. Squeeze lime juice over lamb; rub surface with Herb Rub.

**2** *For a charcoal grill,* arrange medium coals around edges of grill. Test for medium-low heat where meat will cook. Place meat on rack in a roasting pan. Place roasting pan on grill rack, but not directly over coals. Cover and grill until meat thermometer registers 140° for medium-rare (1¾ to 2¼ hours) or 155° for medium doneness (2 to 2½ hours). [*For a gas grill,* preheat grill. Reduce heat to medium-low. Adjust for indirect cooking (see page 10). Grill as above.]

**3** Cover meat with foil; let stand 10 minutes. (The meat's temperature will rise about 5° during standing.)

**4** Drain fat from roasting pan; if necessary add cooking oil to fat to equal 1 tablespoon. In a saucepan combine the 1 tablespoon fat and onion; cook until tender. Stir in black beans, chile peppers, pimiento, cilantro, and red wine vinegar. Bring to boiling; reduce heat. Cook, uncovered, for 5 minutes. To serve, remove strings and thinly slice meat. Serve black bean mixture with lamb. Makes 10 to 12 servings.

**Herb Rub:** Combine 1 teaspoon dried oregano, crushed; 1 teaspoon ground coriander; ½ teaspoon dried thyme, crushed; ½ teaspoon ground cumin; ½ teaspoon chili powder; and ¼ teaspoon salt.

Nutrition Facts per serving: 266 calories, 7 g total fat (3 g saturated fat), 92 mg cholesterol, 371 mg sodium, 14 g carbohydrate, 4 g fiber, 35 g protein. Daily Values: 3% vit. A, 26% vit. C, 5% calcium, 24% iron.

## LAMB WITH HERB-DIJON SAUCE

**Prep:** 20 minutes **Marinate:** 1 to 24 hours
**Grill:** 1 hour **Stand:** 15 minutes

  1  5- to 6-pound leg of lamb, boned
      and butterflied
  1  8-ounce jar (¾ cup) Dijon-style
      mustard
 ⅓ cup dry white wine
 ¼ cup cooking oil
  2  cloves garlic, minced
  1  teaspoon dried rosemary, crushed
  1  teaspoon dried basil, crushed
 ½ teaspoon dried oregano, crushed
 ½ teaspoon dried thyme, crushed
 ¼ teaspoon pepper

**1** Trim fat from meat. For marinade, in a medium bowl combine mustard, wine, oil, garlic, rosemary, basil, oregano, thyme, and pepper. Place lamb in a shallow dish. Spread lamb with mustard mixture. Cover and marinate at room temperature for 1 hour or in the refrigerator for 4 to 24 hours.

**2** Drain meat, reserving marinade. Chill marinade while grilling meat. Thread two 12- to 14-inch metal skewers diagonally through the meat to keep it flat during cooking. Insert a meat thermometer into the center of meat.

**3** *For a charcoal grill,* arrange medium coals around a drip pan. Test for medium-low heat above pan. Place meat on grill rack over drip pan. Cover and grill until a meat thermometer registers 140° for medium-rare or 155° for medium (1 to 1½ hours), brushing occasionally with reserved marinade during the last 15 minutes of grilling. [For a gas grill, preheat grill. Reduce heat to medium-low. Adjust for indirect cooking (see page 10). Grill as above.]

**4** Remove meat from grill. Cover with foil; let stand for 15 minutes. (The meat's temperature will rise 5° during standing.) To serve, remove strings and thinly slice meat. Heat the remaining marinade until bubbly; serve with meat. Makes 12 servings.

Nutrition Facts per serving: 251 calories, 15 g total fat (4 g saturated fat), 85 mg cholesterol, 530 mg sodium, 6 g carbohydrate, 0 g fiber, 29 g protein. Daily Values: 12% iron.

Test for the desired temperature (see How Hot is It? page 11). Place the meat on the rack of a grill directly over the preheated coals (for direct grilling) or directly over a drip pan (for indirect grilling). Grill meat (uncovered for direct grilling or covered for indirect grilling) for the time given below or until done, turning the meat over halfway through the grilling time.

# Grilling Chart

| Cut | Thickness or weight | Coal Temperature | Doneness | Direct Grilling* Time | Indirect Grilling* Time |
|---|---|---|---|---|---|
| **BEEF** | | | | | |
| Boneless | 1 inch | Medium | Medium rare | 14 to 18 min. | 22 to 26 min. |
| | | | Medium | 18 to 22 min. | 26 to 30 min. |
| Sirloin steak | 1½ inches | Medium | Medium rare | 32 to 36 min. | 32 to 36 min. |
| | | | Medium | 36 to 40 min. | 36 to 40 min. |
| Flank steak | ¾ to 1 inch | Medium | Medium | 12 to 14 min. | 18 to 22 min. |
| Ground meat patties | ¾ inch (4 per pound) | Medium | No pink remains | 14 to 18 min. | 20 to 24 min. |
| Steak (blade, chuck, top round) | 1 inch | Medium | Medium rare | 14 to 16 min. | 45 to 55 min. |
| | | | Medium | 18 to 20 min. | 60 to 70 min. |
| | 1½ inches | Medium | Medium rare | 19 to 26 min. | 50 to 60 min. |
| | | | Medium | 27 to 32 min. | 1 to 1¼ hrs. |
| Steak (porterhouse, rib, rib eye, sirloin, T-bone, tenderloin, top loin) | 1 inch | Medium | Medium rare | 8 to 12 min. | 16 to 20 min. |
| | | | Medium | 12 to 15 min. | 20 to 24 min. |
| | 1¼ to 1½ inches | Medium | Medium rare | 14 to 18 min. | 20 to 22 min. |
| | | | Medium | 18 to 22 min. | 22 to 26 min. |
| **LAMB** | | | | | |
| Chop | 1 inch | Medium | Medium rare | 10 to 14 min. | 16 to 18 min. |
| | | Medium | Medium | 14 to 16 min. | 18 to 20 min. |
| Boneless rolled leg roast | 3 to 4 pounds | Medium-low | Medium rare | | 1¾ to 2¼ hrs. |
| | | Medium-low | Medium | | 2 to 2½ hrs. |
| **VEAL** | | | | | |
| Chop | 1 inch | Medium | Medium | 19 to 23 min. | 14 to 16 min. |
| | | Medium | Well-done | | 16 to 18 min. |
| Kabobs | 1-inch cubes | Medium | Medium | 12 to 14 min. | |

*Note: For differences in direct and indirect grilling methods, see page 10.*

# Pork

# Mesquite Mixed Grill

**Prep:** 10 minutes  **Soak:** 1 hour
**Grill:** 9 minutes

> 2 cups mesquite wood chips
> 4 boneless pork top loin chops, cut
>   ¾ inch thick
> 4 small leeks or 1 medium red sweet
>   pepper, cut into 1-inch strips
> ¼ teaspoon black pepper
> ⅛ teaspoon garlic salt
> 8 ounces cooked turkey Polish
>   sausage, cut into 4 equal
>   portions
> ⅓ cup whole-grain mustard
> 2 teaspoons white wine vinegar or
>   cider vinegar
> 1 teaspoon snipped fresh tarragon

**1** At least 1 hour before grilling, soak wood chips in enough water to cover.

**2** Trim fat from chops. If using leeks, rinse well; trim root ends. Cut 3 inches off each top; discard. Sprinkle pepper and garlic salt evenly over chops and leeks or sweet pepper.

**3** Drain wood chips. *For a charcoal grill,* arrange medium coals in bottom of grill. Sprinkle wood chips over coals. Place chops and leeks or sweet pepper on grill rack directly over coals. Cover and grill for 5 minutes. Turn chops; add sausage to grill. Cover and grill for 4 to 6 minutes more or until chops are slightly pink in center and juices run clear, turning sausage once halfway through grilling. (*For a gas grill,* preheat grill. Reduce heat to medium. Grill as above, adding wood chips according to manufacturer's directions.)

**4** Meanwhile, for dipping sauce, in a small bowl combine mustard, vinegar, and tarragon. Serve with chops, leeks or sweet pepper, and sausage. Makes 4 servings.

Nutrition Facts per serving: 282 calories, 12 g total fat (3 g saturated fat), 86 mg cholesterol, 880 mg sodium, 12 g carbohydrate, 4 g fiber, 27 g protein. Daily Values: 29% vit. C, 7% calcium, 19% iron.

# ASIAN-STYLE PORK CHOPS

**Prep:** 15 minutes  **Soak (optional):** 1 hour
**Marinate:** 6 to 24 hours  **Grill:** 35 minutes

> 4 cups hickory wood chips or
>   mesquite wood chips (optional)
> 4 pork loin or rib chops, cut
>   1¼ inches thick (about 3 pounds)
> 4 teaspoons finely shredded orange
>   peel
> ½ cup orange juice
> ¼ cup reduced-sodium soy sauce
> 2 tablespoons cooking oil
> 1 tablespoon brown sugar
> 1 tablespoon grated fresh ginger
> 1 teaspoon ground turmeric

**1** At least 1 hour before grilling, soak wood chips, if using, in enough water to cover. Trim fat from chops. Place chops in a plastic bag set in a shallow dish. For marinade, in a small bowl combine the orange peel, orange juice, soy sauce, oil, brown sugar, ginger, and turmeric. Pour marinade over chops; seal bag. Marinate in the refrigerator for 6 to 24 hours, turning bag occasionally. Drain chops, reserving marinade.

**2** Drain wood chips, if using. *For a charcoal grill,* arrange medium-hot coals around a drip pan. Test for medium heat above pan. Sprinkle half of the wood chips over the coals. Place chops on grill rack over drip pan. Cover and grill for 35 to 45 minutes or until chops are slightly pink in center and juices run clear, turning and brushing once with marinade halfway through grilling. Add remaining wood chips, if using, halfway through grilling. [*For a gas grill,* preheat grill. Reduce heat to medium. Adjust for indirect cooking (see page 10). Grill as above, adding wood chips according to manufacturer's directions.] Makes 4 servings.

Nutrition Facts per serving: 417 calories, 20 g total fat (6 g saturated fat), 168 mg cholesterol, 286 mg sodium, 2 g carbohydrate, 0 g fiber, 55 g protein. Daily Values: 8% vit. C, 11% iron.

# Glazed Pork Chops and Pineapple Relish

**Prep:** 30 minutes   **Grill:** 25 minutes

*Put this glaze from the Orient on an express to your table. A pineapple relish transports these pork chops far from the ordinary.*

¼ cup pineapple preserves
4 teaspoons soy sauce
1 teaspoon toasted sesame oil
1½ teaspoons grated fresh ginger
1 clove garlic, minced
4 boneless pork top loin chops, cut
   1¼ inches thick
1 tablespoon sesame seed, toasted
   (optional)
1 recipe Pineapple Relish

**1** For glaze, in a small saucepan combine preserves, soy sauce, oil, ginger, and garlic. Cook and stir over low heat just until preserves are melted; set aside. Trim fat from chops.

**2** *For a charcoal grill,* place medium coals in bottom of grill. Place chops on grill rack directly over coals. Cover and grill for 25 to 32 minutes or until chops are slightly pink in center and juices run clear, turning once and brushing occasionally with the glaze during the last 10 minutes of grilling. (*For a gas grill,* preheat grill. Reduce heat to medium. Grill as above.)

**3** If desired, sprinkle chops with sesame seed. Serve with Pineapple Relish. Makes 4 servings.

**Pineapple Relish:** In a small bowl stir together 1 cup chopped fresh pineapple; ½ cup chopped red sweet pepper; ¼ cup chopped green onions; 3 tablespoons snipped fresh cilantro; and ½ to 1 fresh jalapeño pepper, seeded and finely chopped. Cover and chill until ready to serve. Before serving, bring to room temperature. Makes 2 cups.

**Nutrition Facts per serving:** 364 calories, 16 g total fat (5 g saturated fat), 102 mg cholesterol, 425 mg sodium, 21 g carbohydrate, 1 g fiber, 33 g protein. **Daily Values:** 16% vit. A, 62% vit. C, 1% calcium, 12% iron.

## PECAN-STUFFED CHOPS

**Prep:** 10 minutes   **Marinate:** 6 to 24 hours
**Grill:** 40 minutes

4 pork loin chops, cut 1½ inches
   thick
1 teaspoon finely shredded orange
   peel
1 cup orange juice
2 tablespoons soy sauce
¼ cup finely chopped onion
¼ cup finely chopped celery
1 tablespoon margarine or butter
¾ cup corn bread stuffing mix
2 tablespoons chopped pecans

**1** Trim fat from chops. Make a pocket in each chop by cutting horizontally from the fat side almost to the bone. Place chops in a plastic bag set into a shallow dish. For marinade, combine orange peel, ¾ cup of the orange juice, and soy sauce. Pour over chops; seal bag. Marinate in the refrigerator for 6 to 24 hours, turning bag occasionally.

**2** Meanwhile, for stuffing, in a saucepan cook onion and celery in margarine or butter until tender. Stir in remaining ¼ cup orange juice; bring to boiling. Remove from heat. In a bowl combine stuffing mix and pecans; add onion mixture. Toss lightly to mix.

**3** Drain meat, reserving marinade. Spoon stuffing into pockets. If necessary, secure openings with wooden toothpicks.

**4** *For a charcoal grill,* arrange medium-hot coals around a drip pan. Test for medium heat above pan. Place chops on the grill rack over drip pan. Cover and grill for 40 to 45 minutes or until chops are slightly pink in the center and the juices run clear, turning once halfway through grilling and brushing occasionally with marinade. [*For a gas grill,* preheat grill. Adjust for indirect cooking (see page 10.) Grill as above.] If using, remove toothpicks before serving. Makes 4 servings.

**Nutrition Facts per serving:** 405 calories, 20 g total fat (6 g saturated fat), 102 mg cholesterol, 557 mg sodium, 19 g carbohydrate, 1 g fiber, 35 g protein. **Daily Values:** 4% vit. A, 35% vit. C, 1% calcium, 13% iron.

# Adobo Pork Chops

**Prep:** 15 minutes **Marinate:** 2 to 24 hours
**Grill:** 8 minutes

*For an extra hit of heat, add the ground red
pepper to the marinade mixture.*

> 6 boneless pork loin chops, cut
> ¾ inch thick
> 2 tablespoons brown sugar
> 2 tablespoons olive oil
> 2 tablespoons orange juice
> 1 tablespoon red wine vinegar or
> cider vinegar
> 2 teaspoons hot chili powder
> 1 teaspoon ground cumin
> 1 teaspoon dried oregano, crushed
> ½ teaspoon salt
> ¼ teaspoon ground red pepper
> (optional)
> ¼ teaspoon ground cinnamon
> 3 cloves garlic, minced
> 2 tablespoons snipped fresh cilantro

1 Trim fat from chops. Place chops in a
plastic bag set in a shallow dish. For
marinade, in a small bowl combine brown
sugar, oil, orange juice, vinegar, chili powder,
cumin, oregano, salt, red pepper (if desired),
cinnamon, garlic, and cilantro. Pour over
chops; seal bag. Marinate in the refrigerator
for 2 to 24 hours, turning bag occasionally.
Drain chops, discarding marinade.

2 *For a charcoal grill,* grill chops on the rack
of an uncovered grill directly over medium
coals for 8 to 11 minutes or until chops are
slightly pink in center and juices run clear,
turning once halfway through grilling. (*For a
gas grill,* preheat grill. Reduce heat to
medium. Place chops on grill rack over heat.
Cover and grill as above.) Makes 6 servings.

Nutrition Facts per serving: 180 calories,
11 g total fat (3 g saturated fat), 51 mg cholesterol,
166 mg sodium, 4 g carbohydrate, 0 g fiber,
16 g protein. Daily Values: 2% vit. A, 4% vit. C,
1% calcium, 7% iron.

# TERIYAKI PORK SALAD

**Prep:** 15 minutes **Marinate:** 20 minutes
**Grill:** 8 minutes

*Succulent pork chops soak up a homemade
teriyaki marinade for a great summertime salad.*

> 4 boneless pork top loin chops, cut
> ¾ inch thick
> ⅓ cup rice vinegar
> ⅓ cup orange juice
> 2 tablespoons reduced-sodium
> teriyaki sauce
> 1 tablespoon peanut oil or salad oil
> 1 teaspoon sesame seed, toasted
> 2 cloves garlic, minced
> 6 cups torn mixed salad greens
> ¾ cup sliced red radishes
> ¼ cup thinly sliced green onions

1 Trim fat from chops. Place chops in a
plastic bag set in a shallow dish. For
marinade/dressing mixture, whisk together
vinegar, orange juice, teriyaki sauce, oil,
sesame seed, and garlic. Reserve half of
mixture for dressing. Pour the remaining
mixture over the chops; seal bag. Marinate in
the refrigerator for at least 20 minutes or for
up to 8 hours, turning bag occasionally. Drain
chops, reserving marinade.

2 *For a charcoal grill,* grill chops on the rack
of an uncovered grill directly over medium
coals for 8 to 11 minutes or until chops are
slightly pink in center and juices run clear,
turning and brushing once with marinade
halfway through grilling. (*For a gas grill,*
preheat grill. Reduce heat to medium. Place
chops on grill rack over heat. Cover and grill
as above.)

3 Divide mixed greens, radishes, and green
onions among 4 dinner plates. Thinly slice
pork diagonally and arrange on top of greens.
Drizzle with reserved dressing mixture.
Makes 4 servings.

Nutrition Facts per serving: 199 calories,
11 g total fat (3 g saturated fat), 51 mg cholesterol,
172 mg sodium, 7 g carbohydrate, 1 g fiber,
18 g protein. Daily Values: 4% vit. A, 28% vit. C,
2% calcium, 8% iron.

# Pesto-Packed Pork Chops

**Prep:** 35 minutes    **Grill:** 35 minutes

*Rubbed with seasonings and fully packed with a pesto-feta filling, these chops will please the multitude. Use jalapeño or apple jelly for the glaze, depending on how much you like the heat.*

    2 tablespoons jalapeño jelly
    5 tablespoons pesto
    1 tablespoon balsamic vinegar
    3 tablespoons crumbled feta cheese
    1 tablespoon pine nuts, toasted
    2 cloves garlic, minced
    1 teaspoon freshly ground black
        pepper
    ½ teaspoon ground red pepper
    ½ teaspoon celery seed
    ½ teaspoon fennel seed, crushed
    ¼ teaspoon dried thyme, crushed
    ¼ teaspoon ground cumin
    4 bone-in or boneless pork loin
        chops, cut 1¼ inches thick
        Fresh basil leaves (optional)

**1** For glaze, in a small saucepan cook and stir jelly over low heat until melted. Stir in the 3 tablespoons of the pesto and the balsamic vinegar; heat through.

**2** Meanwhile, for filling, in a small bowl stir together the remaining 2 tablespoons of the pesto, the feta cheese, and the pine nuts; set aside. For rub, in a small bowl combine garlic, black pepper, red pepper, celery seed, fennel seed, thyme, and cumin. Set aside.

**3** Trim fat from chops. Make a pocket in each chop by cutting horizontally from the fat side almost to the bone or the opposite side. Spoon filling into pockets. If necessary, secure the openings with wooden toothpicks. Sprinkle rub evenly over chops; rub in with your fingers.

**4** *For a charcoal grill,* arrange medium-hot coals around a drip pan. Test for medium heat above the pan. Place chops on grill rack over drip pan. Cover and grill for 35 to 40 minutes or until chops are slightly pink in center and juices run clear, turning once and brushing occasionally with glaze during the last 10 minutes of grilling. [*For a gas grill,* preheat grill. Reduce heat to medium. Adjust for indirect cooking (see page 10). Grill as above.] If using, remove toothpicks before serving. If desired, garnish chops with basil. Makes 4 servings.

Nutrition Facts per serving: 393 calories, 25 g total fat (6 g saturated fat), 89 mg cholesterol, 312 mg sodium, 12 g carbohydrate, 0 g fiber, 29 g protein. Daily Values: 2% vit. A, 4% vit. C, 6% calcium, 13% iron.

## Did You Know?

**Believe it or not, the highly aromatic garlic bulb is a member of the lily family. It has become such a mainstay of everyday cooking that it's good to know how to keep it fresh. Stored in an open container in a cool, dark place, a fresh, unbroken garlic head will keep for up to 8 weeks. If broken, the cloves will last from 3 to 10 days. If you don't use garlic that often, it is also available as dehydrated garlic flakes, garlic powder, garlic salt, garlic extract, garlic juice, bottled minced or chopped garlic, and bottled chopped roasted garlic. Handy tip: 1 clove garlic equals ½ teaspoon bottled minced garlic or ⅛ teaspoon garlic powder.**

Curried Mustard Pork Chops

## CURRIED MUSTARD PORK CHOPS

**Prep:** 10 minutes   **Marinate:** 6 to 24 hours
**Grill:** 30 minutes

4 boneless pork loin chops, cut
   1 inch thick
½ cup spicy brown mustard
¼ cup dry white wine
1 tablespoon curry powder
1 tablespoon olive oil
1 green onion, sliced
1 clove garlic, minced
¼ to ½ teaspoon crushed red pepper

1 Trim fat from chops. Place chops in a plastic bag set in a shallow dish. For marinade, in a small bowl stir together brown mustard, wine, curry powder, oil, green onion, garlic, and red pepper. Pour over chops; seal bag. Marinate in the refrigerator for 6 to 24 hours, turning bag occasionally. Drain chops, reserving marinade.

2 *For a charcoal grill,* arrange medium-hot coals around a drip pan. Test for medium heat above pan. Place chops on grill rack over pan. Cover; grill for 30 to 35 minutes or until chops are slightly pink in center and juices run clear, turning and brushing once with marinade halfway through grilling. [*For a gas grill,* preheat grill. Reduce heat to medium. Adjust for indirect cooking (see page 10). Grill as above.] Makes 4 servings.

Nutrition Facts per serving: 225 calories,
13 g total fat (4 g saturated fat), 64 mg cholesterol,
353 mg sodium, 2 g carbohydrate, 1 g fiber,
22 g protein. Daily Values: 1% vit. A, 1% vit. C,
3% calcium, 10% iron.

## Pork Chops with Grilled Vegetables

**Prep:** 20 minutes   **Grill:** 35 minutes

4 pork loin chops, cut 1¼ inches thick
2 teaspoons olive oil
1 teaspoon lemon-pepper seasoning
   or garlic-pepper seasoning
⅓ cup plain low-fat yogurt
1¼ teaspoons snipped fresh thyme or
   rosemary
¼ teaspoon salt
¼ teaspoon black pepper
1 medium Vidalia or other sweet
   onion, cut into ½-inch slices
1 green or yellow sweet pepper,
   seeded and cut into quarters
4 plum tomatoes, halved lengthwise
1 tablespoon balsamic vinegar
1 tablespoon olive oil

1 Trim fat from chops. Brush chops on both sides using the 2 teaspoons oil; sprinkle with lemon-pepper or garlic-pepper seasoning. In a small bowl combine yogurt, ¾ teaspoon of the thyme or rosemary, ⅛ teaspoon of the salt, and ⅛ teaspoon of the black pepper. Cover and refrigerate.

2 *For a charcoal grill,* arrange medium-hot coals around a drip pan. Test for medium heat above pan. Place chops on grill rack over drip pan. Cover and grill for 35 to 40 minutes or until chops are slightly pink in the center and juices run clear, turning once halfway through grilling. Place onions on grill rack directly over coals the last 15 minutes of grilling or until crisp-tender, turning once. Place sweet peppers and tomatoes directly over coals the last 5 to 8 minutes or until peppers are crisp-tender and tomatoes begin to soften, turning once. [*For a gas grill,* preheat grill. Reduce heat to medium. Adjust for indirect cooking (see page 10). Grill as above.]

3 Meanwhile, in a large bowl combine vinegar, the 1 tablespoon olive oil, the remaining ½ teaspoon thyme, and the remaining ⅛ teaspoon of the salt and black pepper. Add vegetables; toss gently to coat. To serve, spoon vegetables over each chop. Serve with yogurt mixture. Makes 4 servings.

Nutrition Facts per serving: 225 calories,
13 g total fat (4 g saturated fat), 64 mg cholesterol,
353 mg sodium, 2 g carbohydrate, 1 g fiber,
22 g protein. Daily Values: 1% vit. A, 1% vit. C,
3% calcium, 10% iron.

## BARBECUED PORK CHOP SANDWICHES

**Prep:** 10 minutes   **Grill:** 25 minutes

*Two simple ingredients—curry and cumin— transform purchased chili sauce into a perfect sauce for grilled pork.*

- ⅓ cup bottled chili sauce
- ½ to 1 teaspoon curry powder
- ¼ teaspoon ground cumin
- 3 boneless pork loin chops, cut 1¼ to 1½ inches thick
  Salt and pepper (optional)
- 4 kaiser rolls, split and toasted
  Leaf lettuce (optional)

1 For sauce, in a small bowl stir together chili sauce, curry powder, and cumin. Set aside. Trim fat from chops. If desired, sprinkle lightly with salt and pepper.

2 *For a charcoal grill,* place medium coals in bottom of grill. Place chops on grill rack directly over coals. Cover and grill for 25 to 30 minutes or until chops are slightly pink in center and juices run clear, turning once and brushing occasionally with sauce during the last 10 minutes of grilling. (*For a gas grill,* preheat grill. Reduce heat to medium. Grill as above.) Remove chops from grill.

3 To serve, thinly slice pork. Top rolls with sliced pork and, if desired, leaf lettuce. Makes 4 servings.

Nutrition Facts per serving: 393 calories, 14 g total fat (4 g saturated fat), 77 mg cholesterol, 637 mg sodium, 35 g carbohydrate, 0 g fiber, 30 g protein. Daily Values: 3% vit. A, 5% vit. C, 5% calcium, 21% iron.

## Southwest Pork Chops with Corn Salsa

**Prep:** 20 minutes   **Grill:** 8 minutes

- ¼ cup white wine vinegar
- 3 tablespoons snipped fresh cilantro
- 1 teaspoon olive oil
- 1 cup fresh or frozen whole kernel corn
- 3 plum tomatoes, chopped
- ½ cup thinly sliced green onions
- 1 small fresh jalapeño pepper, seeded and minced
- 4 center-cut pork loin chops, cut ¾ inch thick

1 For sauce, in a small bowl combine 3 tablespoons of the vinegar, 1 tablespoon of the cilantro, and the oil. For salsa, thaw corn, if frozen. In a medium bowl combine the remaining vinegar, remaining cilantro, the corn, tomatoes, green onions, and jalapeño pepper. Set aside.

2 Trim fat from chops. *For a charcoal grill,* grill chops on the rack of an uncovered grill directly over medium coals for 8 to 11 minutes or until chops are slightly pink in center and juices run clear, turning once and brushing occasionally with sauce. (*For a gas grill,* preheat grill. Reduce heat to medium. Cover and grill as above.) Serve chops with salsa. Makes 4 servings.

Nutrition Facts per serving: 201 calories, 9 g total fat (3 g saturated fat), 51 mg cholesterol, 51 mg sodium, 14 g carbohydrate, 2 g fiber, 18 g protein. Daily Values: 7% vit. A, 35% vit. C, 8% iron.

## PLUM GOOD PORK CHOPS

**Prep:** 15 minutes    **Grill:** 25 minutes

*An inventive melding of plum preserves, curry, red pepper, and garlic takes these chops from ho hum to I-want-some. The magic is in the glaze.*

  3 tablespoons plum preserves
  1 green onion, thinly sliced
  1 tablespoon soy sauce
  2 teaspoons lemon juice
  ⅛ teaspoon curry powder
    Dash ground cinnamon
    Dash ground red pepper
  4 pork loin or rib chops, cut
      1¼ inches thick
  1 clove garlic, halved

1 For sauce, in a small saucepan combine plum preserves, green onion, soy sauce, lemon juice, curry powder, cinnamon, and red pepper. Cook and stir over medium heat until bubbly. Set aside. Trim fat from chops. Rub both sides of chops with cut sides of garlic.

2 *For a charcoal grill,* place medium coals in bottom of grill. Place chops on grill rack directly over coals. Cover and grill for 25 to 35 minutes or until chops are slightly pink in center and juices run clear, turning once and brushing occasionally with sauce during the last 10 minutes of grilling. (*For a gas grill,* preheat grill. Reduce heat to medium. Grill as above.) Makes 4 servings.

Nutrition Facts per serving: 224 calories, 11 g total fat (4 g saturated fat), 66 mg cholesterol, 283 mg sodium, 11 g carbohydrate, 0 g fiber, 20 g protein. Daily Values: 3% vit. C, 1% calcium, 6% iron.

# Flaming Facts

**Though beef is sold by official cuts, pork has evolved in the marketplace into six preferred forms. Chops can be boneless or bone-in, thick or thin. Ribs can be cut spare, back, or country-style to star in any barbecued dinner.**
**Pork cutlets are thin, boneless slices of meat.**
**Roasts are larger cuts of meat and, as the name implies, are great for roasting in the oven or over indirect heat on your grill. Strips are just right for stir-frying. Cubes are great for kabobs or stews. There's a cut for every need.**

# Sage-Marinated Chops with Sweet Potatoes

**Prep:** 25 minutes  **Marinate:** 8 to 24 hours
**Grill:** 25 minutes

- 4 pork rib or loin chops, cut 1¼ inches thick
- ⅔ cup cider vinegar
- ⅓ cup balsamic vinegar
- 2 tablespoons olive oil
- 2 teaspoons dried sage, crushed
- ½ teaspoon salt
- ¼ teaspoon pepper
- 2 sweet potatoes, quartered lengthwise (about 1 pound)
- 1 medium sweet onion (such as Vidalia), cut into ¾-inch slices

**1** Trim fat from chops. Place chops in a plastic bag set in a shallow dish. For marinade, in a small saucepan combine cider vinegar and balsamic vinegar. Bring to boiling; reduce heat. Boil gently, uncovered, about 8 minutes or until reduced to about ⅔ cup. Cool slightly. Stir in oil, sage, salt, and pepper. Reserve ¼ cup marinade; set aside.

**2** Pour remaining marinade over chops; seal bag. Marinate in the refrigerator for 8 to 24 hours, turning bag occasionally. Drain chops, discarding marinade. Brush potatoes and onion with the reserved marinade.

**3** *For a charcoal grill,* place medium coals in bottom of grill. Place chops, potatoes, and onion on grill rack directly over coals. Cover and grill for 25 to 30 minutes or until chops are slightly pink in center and vegetables are tender, turning chops once and vegetables occasionally. (*For a gas grill,* preheat grill. Reduce heat to medium. Place chops, potatoes, and onion on grill rack over heat. Grill as above.) Makes 4 servings.

Nutrition Facts per serving: 354 calories, 16 g total fat (4 g saturated fat), 77 mg cholesterol, 249 mg sodium, 28 g carbohydrate, 4 g fiber, 26 g protein. Daily Values: 193% vit. A, 41% vit. C, 3% calcium, 13% iron.

# MAPLE-MUSTARD PORK CHOPS

**Prep:** 30 minutes  **Grill:** 50 minutes

- ¼ cup pure maple syrup
- 2 tablespoons country Dijon-style mustard
- 1 to 2 teaspoons cider vinegar
- ¼ teaspoon pepper
- 1 medium acorn squash (1 pound)
- 1 teaspoon olive oil
  Salt (optional)
- 4 pork rib or loin chops, cut 1½ inches thick (2½ to 3 pounds)

**1** For glaze, in a small saucepan combine maple syrup, mustard, vinegar, and pepper. Cook over low heat until slightly thickened, stirring occasionally.

**2** Meanwhile, cut squash in half lengthwise; remove seeds. Lightly brush cut surfaces with olive oil. If desired, sprinkle with salt.

**3** *For a charcoal grill,* arrange medium-hot coals around a drip pan. Test for medium heat above the pan. Place squash, cut side down, on grill rack over drip pan. Cover and grill for 15 minutes. Add pork chops to grill rack over drip pan. Cover and grill for 25 minutes, turning after 18 minutes. Turn squash cut side up; brush chops and squash with glaze. Cover and grill for 10 to 15 minutes more or until squash is tender and chops are slightly pink in center and juices run clear. [*For a gas grill,* preheat grill. Reduce heat to medium. Adjust for indirect cooking (see page 10). Grill as above, except omit drip pan.]

**4** To serve, cut each squash half into 2 wedges. Spoon any remaining glaze over chops and squash. Makes 4 servings.

Nutrition Facts per serving: 599 calories, 20 g total fat (6 g saturated fat), 168 mg cholesterol, 347 mg sodium, 23 g carbohydrate, 2 g fiber, 56 g protein. Daily Values: 67% vit. A, 25% vit. C, 4% calcium, 14% iron.

Sage-Marinated Chops
with Sweet Potatoes

# Rosemary and Garlic Smoked Pork Roast

**Prep:** 20 minutes   **Soak:** 1 hour
**Grill:** 1 hour   **Stand:** 10 minutes

  4 cups apple or hickory wood chips
  1 2- to 3-pound boneless pork top
     loin roast (single loin)
  2 tablespoons snipped fresh
     rosemary
  1 tablespoon olive oil
  4 cloves garlic, minced
  ½ teaspoon pepper
  ¼ teaspoon salt
  4 sprigs fresh rosemary
  ½ of a lemon or lime

1 At least 1 hour before grilling, soak wood chips in enough water to cover.

2 Trim fat from meat. For rub, in a bowl combine the snipped rosemary, the oil, garlic, pepper, and salt. Sprinkle rub evenly over meat; rub in with your fingers. Insert a meat thermometer into the center of meat.

3 Drain wood chips. *For a charcoal grill,* arrange medium coals around a drip pan. Pour 1 inch of water into drip pan. Test for medium-low heat above the pan. Sprinkle half of the wood chips over the coals. Sprinkle rosemary sprigs over wood chips. Place meat on grill rack over drip pan. Cover and grill for 1 to 1¼ hours or until meat thermometer registers 155°. Add the remaining wood chips halfway through grilling. [*For a gas grill,* preheat grill. Reduce heat to medium-low. Adjust for indirect cooking (see page 10). Grill as above, except place meat on a rack in a roasting pan.]

4 Remove meat from grill. Squeeze the juice from the half lemon or lime over the meat. Cover meat with foil; let stand for 10 minutes before carving. (The meat's temperature will rise about 5° during standing.) Makes 8 to 10 servings.

Nutrition Facts per serving: 154 calories, 9 g total fat (3 g saturated fat), 51 mg cholesterol, 106 mg sodium, 1 g carbohydrate, 0 g fiber, 16 g protein. Daily Values: 4% vit. C, 4% iron.

# PEANUT-BUTTERED PORK LOIN

**Prep:** 10 minutes   **Grill:** 1½ hours
**Stand:** 15 minutes

*Try it—you'll like it! Peanut butter and orange juice create an excellent glaze for pork.*

  1 3- to 4-pound boneless pork top
     loin roast (double loin, tied)
  ⅓ cup orange juice
  ¼ cup creamy peanut butter
  ¼ cup dry roasted peanuts, finely
     chopped

1 Trim fat from meat. Insert a meat thermometer into the center of meat.

2 *For a charcoal grill,* arrange medium coals around a drip pan. Test for medium-low heat above the pan. Place meat on grill rack over drip pan. Cover and grill for 1 to 1½ hours or until meat thermometer registers 140°. [*For a gas grill,* preheat grill. Reduce heat to medium-low. Adjust for indirect cooking (see page 10). Grill as above, except place meat on a rack in a roasting pan.]

3 Meanwhile, for sauce, in a small bowl whisk together orange juice and peanut butter until smooth. Brush meat with some of the sauce. Cover and grill about 30 minutes more or until meat thermometer registers 155°, brushing occasionally with remaining sauce. Remove meat from grill. Cover with foil; let stand for 15 minutes before carving. (The meat's temperature will rise about 5° during standing.) Sprinkle with peanuts. Makes 10 to 14 servings.

Nutrition Facts per serving: 225 calories, 14 g total fat (4 g saturated fat), 61 mg cholesterol, 107 mg sodium, 3 g carbohydrate, 1 g fiber, 22 g protein. Daily Values: 7% vit. C, 6% iron.

# Rhubarb-Glazed Pork Roast

**Prep:** 45 minutes   **Grill:** 1¼ hours
**Stand:** 15 minutes

  12 ounces fresh or frozen rhubarb,
      sliced (about 2 cups)
   1 6-ounce can (⅔ cup) frozen apple
      juice concentrate
      Several drops of red food coloring
      (optional)
   2 tablespoons honey
   1 3-pound pork loin center rib roast
      (backbone loosened)

**1** For glaze, in a saucepan combine rhubarb, juice concentrate, and, if desired, red food coloring. Bring to boiling; reduce heat. Simmer, covered, for 15 to 20 minutes or until rhubarb is very tender. Strain, pressing liquid out of pulp. Discard pulp. Return liquid to pan. Bring to boiling; reduce heat. Simmer, uncovered, about 15 minutes or until reduced to about ½ cup. Remove from heat. Stir in honey. Reserve ¼ cup glaze; set aside.

**2** Meanwhile, trim fat from meat. Insert a meat thermometer into center of meat without it touching bone.

**3** *For a charcoal grill,* arrange medium coals around a drip pan. Test for medium-low heat above pan. Place meat, bone side down, on grill rack over pan. Cover; grill for 1¼ to 1¾ hours or until meat thermometer registers 155°, brushing occasionally with reserved glaze the last 15 minutes of grilling. [*For a gas grill,* preheat grill. Reduce heat to medium-low. Adjust for indirect cooking (see page 10). Grill as above, except place meat, bone side down, in a roasting pan.]

**4** Remove meat from grill. Cover; let stand 15 minutes before carving. (The temperature will rise 5° during standing.) In a saucepan cook remaining glaze over medium-low heat until heated through. Pass with meat. Serves 4 to 8.

Nutrition Facts per serving: 391 calories,
15 g total fat (5 g saturated fat), 102 mg cholesterol,
93 mg sodium, 30 g carbohydrate, 2 g fiber,
33 g protein. Daily Values: 1% vit. A, 13% vit. C,
7% calcium, 12% iron.

# PORK LOIN WITH JALAPEÑO GRAVY

**Prep:** 15 minutes   **Grill:** about 1 hour
**Stand:** 10 minutes

   1 2- to 2½-pound pork boneless top
      loin (single loin)
   1 teaspoon garlic powder
   1 teaspoon paprika
   ½ teaspoon salt
   ½ teaspoon black pepper
   2 jalapeño peppers, halved, seeded,
      and stemmed
      Cooking oil
   2 tablespoons all-purpose flour
  1⅔ cups half-and-half or milk

**1** Trim fat from meat. In a bowl combine garlic powder, paprika, salt, and black pepper. Sprinkle over meat; rub in. Insert a meat thermometer into the center of meat.

**2** *For a charcoal grill,* arrange medium-hot coals around a drip pan. Test for medium heat above pan. Place meat on a rack in a roasting pan over drip pan. Cover; grill for 1 to 1¼ hours or until meat thermometer registers 155°. [*For a gas grill,* preheat grill. Reduce heat to medium. Adjust for indirect cooking (see page 10). Grill as above, except place meat on a rack in a roasting pan.] Remove meat from grill. Reserve drippings in roasting pan. Cover meat; let stand 10 minutes. (The temperature will rise 5°.)

**3** Meanwhile, lightly brush jalapeño peppers with oil. Add peppers to grill, skin side down (lay peppers perpendicular to wires on grill rack so they won't fall into coals). Grill about 5 minutes or until soft and slightly charred. Cool slightly; finely chop.

**4** For gravy, pour 2 tablespoons of reserved drippings into a saucepan (add oil, if necessary, to make 2 tablespoons); add flour. Stir until smooth. Add half-and-half. Cook and stir until bubbly; add peppers. Cook and stir for 1 minute more. Serve with meat. Serves 4.

Nutrition Facts per serving: 431 calories,
28 g total fat (12 g saturated fat), 139 mg cholesterol,
386 mg sodium, 8 g carbohydrate, 0 g fiber,
36 g protein. Daily Values: 16% vit. A, 22% vit. C,
9% calcium, 11% iron.

# Gruyère and Pork Sandwiches

**Prep:** 15 minutes   **Grill:** 1 hour
**Stand:** 10 minutes

- 1 2-pound boneless pork top loin roast (single loin)
- 1 tablespoon paprika
- 1 teaspoon dried oregano, crushed
- ½ teaspoon salt
- ½ teaspoon garlic powder
  Coarse-grain brown mustard
- 1 10- to 12-inch Italian flat bread (focaccia), split horizontally and toasted
- 3 ounces thinly sliced cooked ham
- 4 slices Gruyère or Swiss cheese (about 4 ounces)
  Dill pickle slices

1 Trim fat from meat. For rub, in a small bowl combine paprika, oregano, salt, and garlic powder. Sprinkle rub evenly over meat; rub in with your fingers. Insert a meat thermometer into the center of meat.

2 *For a charcoal grill,* arrange medium coals around a drip pan. Test for medium-low heat above the pan. Place meat on grill rack over drip pan. Cover and grill for 1 to 1¼ hours or until thermometer registers 155°. [*For a gas grill,* preheat grill. Reduce heat to medium-low. Adjust for indirect cooking (see page 10). Grill as above, except place meat on a rack in a roasting pan.] Remove meat from grill. Cover with foil; let stand for 10 minutes before carving. (The meat's temperature will rise 5° during standing.)

3 To serve, thinly slice meat. Spread mustard on the bottom halves of bread. Layer with grilled pork, ham, cheese, and pickles. Spread mustard on top halves of bread; press firmly onto sandwiches. Cut into wedges. Serves 8.

Nutrition Facts per serving: 344 calories, 15 g total fat (6 g saturated fat), 72 mg cholesterol, 425 mg sodium, 25 g carbohydrate, 2 g fiber, 28 g protein. Daily Values: 10% vit. A, 5% vit. C, 16% calcium, 9% iron.

# PORK LOIN STUFFED WITH DRIED FRUIT AND GORGONZOLA

**Prep:** 30 minutes   **Grill:** 1¼ hours
**Stand:** 15 minutes

- ⅓ cup chopped onion
- 2 tablespoons butter or margarine
- 1½ cups snipped dried pears or dried apples
- 1 to 2 tablespoons balsamic vinegar
- ½ cup chopped toasted walnuts
- ¼ cup crumbled Gorgonzola cheese
- 1 3- to 4-pound boneless pork top loin roast (double loin, tied)
- 1 tablespoon snipped fresh rosemary
- 2 large cloves garlic, minced
- ½ teaspoon coarsely ground pepper

1 For stuffing, in a large skillet cook onion in hot butter over medium heat until tender. Stir in pears and vinegar. Remove from heat; stir in walnuts and cheese.

2 Untie roast; trim fat from meat. Spoon stuffing on flat side of one loin. Replace second loin and retie roast. Stir together rosemary, garlic, and pepper. Sprinkle evenly over meat; rub in with your fingers. Insert a meat thermometer into the center of meat.

3 *For a charcoal grill,* arrange medium-hot coals around a drip pan. Test for medium heat above pan. Place meat on grill rack over drip pan. Cover and grill for 1¼ to 2 hours or until thermometer registers 155°. [*For a gas grill,* preheat grill. Reduce heat to medium. Adjust for indirect grilling (see page 10). Grill as above, except place meat on a rack in a roasting pan.]

4 Remove meat from grill. Cover with foil; let stand 15 minutes before carving. (The meat's temperature will rise 5° during standing.) Makes 10 to 14 servings.

Nutrition Facts per serving: 306 calories, 16 g total fat (5 g saturated fat), 70 mg cholesterol, 112 mg sodium, 21 g carbohydrate, 2 g fiber, 21 g protein. Daily Values: 2% vit. A, 5% vit. C, 3% calcium, 10% iron.

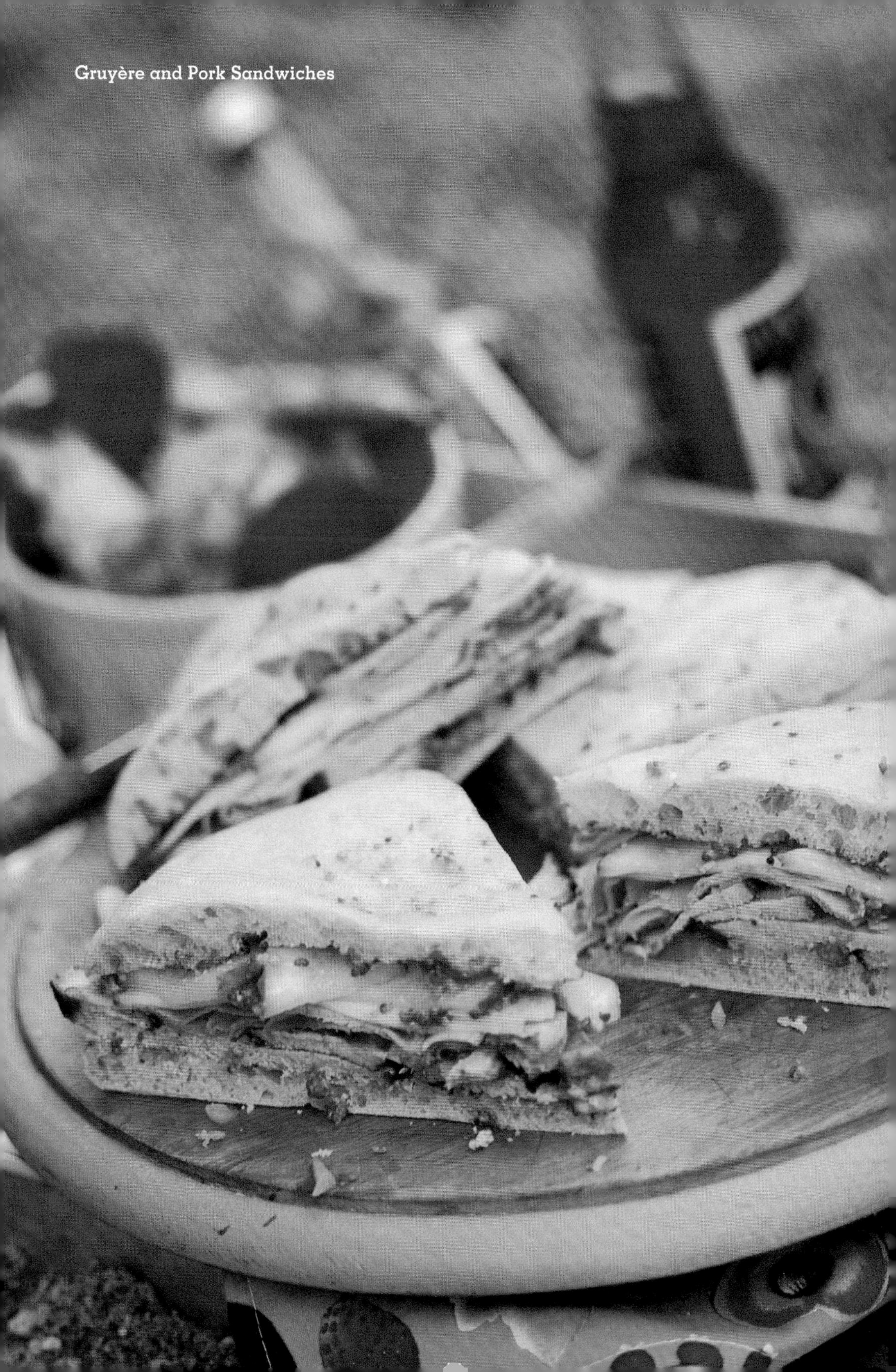
Gruyère and Pork Sandwiches

# Smoky Pork and Mushroom Kabobs

**Prep:** 15 minutes    **Marinate:** 10 minutes
**Grill:** 14 minutes

*Just a little hickory smoke flavoring added to this
maple-flavored sauce provides a smoky taste.*

1 pound lean boneless pork
8 ounces fresh mushroom caps
2 medium apples, such as Rome
    Beauty or Granny Smith, cored
    and quartered
1 medium onion, cut into wedges
¼ cup maple-flavored syrup
¼ cup tomato paste
2 tablespoons cider vinegar
¼ to ½ teaspoon hickory smoke
    flavoring
⅛ teaspoon pepper

**1** Trim fat from meat. Cut meat into 1½-inch
cubes. Place meat, mushrooms, apples, and
onion in a plastic bag set in a shallow dish. For
marinade, combine syrup, tomato paste, vinegar,
smoke flavoring, and pepper. Reserve ¼ cup
marinade for dipping sauce. Pour remaining
marinade over meat mixture in bag; seal bag.
Marinate in the refrigerator at least 10 minutes
or up to 4 hours, turning bag occasionally.

**2** Drain meat mixture, reserving marinade.
On 4 long metal skewers, alternately thread
meat, mushrooms, apples, and onion, leaving
a ¼-inch space between each piece.

**3** *For a charcoal grill,* grill kabobs on the
greased rack of an uncovered grill directly
over medium coals for 14 to 16 minutes or
until meat is slightly pink in center and juices
run clear, turning and brushing once with
marinade halfway through grilling. (*For a gas
grill,* preheat grill. Reduce heat to medium.
Place kabobs on grill rack over heat. Cover;
grill as above.) Serve kabobs with dipping
sauce. Makes 4 servings.

Nutrition Facts per serving: 261 calories,
8 g total fat (3 g saturated fat), 51 mg cholesterol,
54 mg sodium, 32 g carbohydrate, 3 g fiber,
18 g protein. Daily Values: 4% vit. A, 23% vit. C,
1% calcium, 16% iron.

# YOGURT-MINT PORK KABOBS

**Prep:** 25 minutes    **Marinate:** 1 hour
**Grill:** 12 minutes

1½ pounds lean boneless pork
1 16-ounce container plain fat-free
    yogurt
2 tablespoons lemon juice
2 to 4 cloves garlic, minced
2 teaspoons dried oregano, crushed
1 teaspoon dried mint, crushed
½ cup seeded, finely chopped tomato
½ cup seeded, finely chopped
    cucumber
4 cups fresh vegetables, cut into
    1-inch pieces (such as eggplant,
    zucchini, yellow summer
    squash, red onion, and/or
    mushrooms)
Nonstick cooking spray

**1** Trim fat from meat. Cut meat into 1-inch
cubes. For marinade, in a medium bowl
combine yogurt, lemon juice, garlic,
1 teaspoon of the oregano, and the mint.
Divide mixture in half. Stir meat cubes into
half of the yogurt mixture. Cover and
refrigerate meat and remaining yogurt
mixture for 1 to 4 hours.

**2** For sauce, up to 1 hour before serving, stir
tomato and cucumber into remaining yogurt
mixture. Cover; chill until serving time.

**3** Combine desired vegetables in a large
bowl. Lightly coat vegetables with
nonstick cooking spray, tossing to coat. Stir
in remaining 1 teaspoon oregano. Set aside.

**4** Drain pork, discarding yogurt mixture. On
twelve 6-inch metal skewers, alternately
thread meat and vegetables, leaving a ¼-inch
space between pieces.

**5** *For a charcoal grill,* grill kabobs on the rack
of an uncovered grill directly over medium
coals for 12 to 14 minutes or until meat is
slightly pink in center, turning once halfway
through grilling. (*For a gas grill,* preheat grill.
Reduce heat to medium. Place kabobs on grill
rack over heat. Cover; grill as above.) Serve
kabobs with yogurt mixture. Makes 6 servings.

Nutrition Facts per serving: 207 calories, 8 g total fat (3 g saturated fat), 53 mg cholesterol, 97 mg sodium, 13 g carbohydrate, 2 g fiber, 22 g protein. Daily Values: 3% vit. A, 44% vit. C, 14% calcium, 9% iron.

# Pine Nut and Corn Bread-Stuffed Pork Tenderloin

**Prep:** 35 minutes  **Grill:** 1 hour
**Stand:** 10 minutes

  2  12-ounce pork tenderloins
¾  cup shredded Monterey Jack
     cheese with jalapeño peppers
     (3 ounces)
¼  cup chopped onion
  1  tablespoon margarine or butter
  1  cup corn bread stuffing mix
  3  tablespoons chopped pine nuts or
     almonds, toasted
  2  tablespoons water
¼  teaspoon ground cumin
     Cooking oil
  1  cup fruit or tomato salsa (optional)

**1** Trim fat from meat. Split each tenderloin lengthwise, cutting to but not through the opposite side. Spread meat open. Place meat between 2 pieces of plastic wrap, overlapping one long side of each tenderloin about 2 inches. Working from the center to the edges, use the flat side of a meat mallet to pound meat into a 10-inch square. Remove plastic wrap. Sprinkle meat with cheese to within 1 inch of edges.

**2** For stuffing, in a small saucepan cook onion in hot margarine or butter until tender. Remove from heat. Stir in stuffing mix, pine nuts, water, and cumin. Spoon stuffing mixture over cheese layer to within 1 inch of edges of meat. Fold in sides; roll up. Press edge to seal. Tie with 100-percent-cotton string at 1-inch intervals. Brush all surfaces of meat with a little oil.

**3** *For a charcoal grill,* arrange medium-hot coals around a drip pan. Test for medium heat above the pan. Place meat on grill rack over drip pan. Cover; grill for 1 to 1¼ hours or until meat is slightly pink in center and

juices run clear, brushing occasionally with oil. [*For a gas grill,* preheat grill. Reduce heat to medium. Adjust for indirect cooking (see page 10). Grill as above, except place meat on a rack in a roasting pan.]

**4** Remove meat from grill. Cover with foil; let stand for 10 minutes. Remove string. Slice meat. If desired, serve with salsa. Makes 6 servings.

Nutrition Facts per serving: 311 calories, 15 g total fat (5 g saturated fat), 93 mg cholesterol, 317 mg sodium, 12 g carbohydrate, 0 g fiber, 31 g protein. Daily Values: 6% vit. A, 10% calcium, 16% iron.

## HONEY-MUSTARD PORK SANDWICHES

**Prep:** 10 minutes  **Grill:** 8 minutes

  1  1-pound pork tenderloin
     Pepper
  2  tablespoons Dijon-style mustard
  2  tablespoons honey
  4  kaiser rolls or hamburger
     buns, split and toasted
¼  cup mayonnaise
  4  tomato slices

**1** Trim fat from meat. Cut meat into ¾-inch slices. Sprinkle with pepper. For glaze, in a bowl combine mustard and honey; set aside.

**2** *For a charcoal grill,* grill meat on the rack of an uncovered grill directly over medium coals for 8 to 10 minutes or until meat is slightly pink in center and juices run clear, turning and brushing once with glaze halfway through grilling. (*For a gas grill,* preheat grill. Reduce heat to medium. Place meat on grill rack over heat. Cover and grill as above.) Remove meat from grill.

**3** To serve, spread cut sides of toasted rolls with mayonnaise. Top with meat and tomato slices. Makes 4 servings.

Nutrition Facts per serving: 459 calories, 18 g total fat (3 g saturated fat), 89 mg cholesterol, 639 mg sodium, 41 g carbohydrate, 0 g fiber, 32 g protein. Daily Values: 3% vit. A, 10% vit. C, 5% calcium, 23% iron.

# Peppered Pork and Pasta Salad

**Prep:** 35 minutes   **Grill:** 30 minutes

*Pork and pasta are peppered with colors. These flavors are just as bright to the tongue as this vinaigrette-tossed salad is to the eye.*

   1 recipe Italian Balsamic Vinaigrette
   2 12-ounce pork tenderloins
   2 red sweet peppers, halved
       lengthwise
   1 yellow sweet pepper, halved
       lengthwise
   1 green sweet pepper, halved
       lengthwise
   8 ounces packaged dried bow tie
       pasta
   ⅓ cup thinly sliced fresh basil

**1** Prepare Italian Balsamic Vinaigrette. Trim fat from meat. Lightly brush meat and insides of peppers with 2 tablespoons of the vinaigrette.

**2** *For a charcoal grill,* grill peppers, cut sides up, on the rack of an uncovered grill directly over medium coals for 10 to 12 minutes or until tender. Wrap peppers in foil; let stand for 20 minutes. While peppers are standing, add meat to grill. Grill about 20 minutes or until meat is slightly pink in center, turning occasionally to brown evenly. (*For a gas grill,* preheat grill. Reduce heat to medium. Place peppers, cut sides up, on grill rack over heat. Cover and grill as above.) Wrap and let stand. Meanwhile, add meat to grill; cover and grill as above. Using a paring knife, pull the skin off peppers gently. Cut peppers into 1-inch pieces; set aside.

**3** Meanwhile, cook pasta according to package directions; drain. Set aside.

**4** To serve, slice each tenderloin in half lengthwise; cut into ¼-inch slices. In a large bowl combine pasta, pork, peppers, and basil. Add the remaining vinaigrette; toss gently to coat. Serve immediately or cover and chill for up to 8 hours. Makes 6 servings.

**Italian Balsamic Vinaigrette:** In a screw-top jar combine 3 tablespoons balsamic vinegar; 3 tablespoons olive oil; 1 large clove garlic, minced; ½ teaspoon salt; and ¼ teaspoon pepper. Cover and shake well. Shake before serving. Makes about ⅓ cup.

Nutrition Facts per serving: 359 calories, 13 g total fat (3 g saturated fat), 113 mg cholesterol, 245 mg sodium, 30 g carbohydrate, 2 g fiber, 30 g protein. Daily Values: 20% vit. A, 138% vit. C, 2% calcium, 22% iron.

## PORK SATAY WITH TAHINI-COCONUT SAUCE

**Prep:** 40 minutes   **Marinate:** 2 to 3 hours
**Grill:** 10 minutes

*Sail with the South Sea winds. Here's a sweet and lively dish that will find a port on any shore. Tahini, coconut, curry—it just keeps getting better.*

   1½ pounds pork tenderloin
   ¼ cup coconut milk
   2 tablespoons lime juice
   1 tablespoon brown sugar
   1 tablespoon mild curry powder
   1½ teaspoons cooking oil
   1 tablespoon prepared red curry
       paste
   ⅛ teaspoon crushed red pepper
   ¾ cup coconut milk
   ¼ cup tahini (sesame seed paste)
   4 teaspoons orange juice
   2 teaspoons brown sugar
   1½ teaspoons fish sauce

**1** Trim fat from meat. Cut meat into ¾-inch cubes. For marinade, in a medium bowl stir together the ¼ cup coconut milk, the lime juice, the 1 tablespoon brown sugar, and the curry powder. Add the meat and stir to coat. Cover and marinate in the refrigerator for 2 to 3 hours, stirring occasionally.

**2** For dipping sauce, in a small saucepan heat oil over medium heat. Add the curry paste and crushed red pepper; reduce heat to low. Cook and stir about 1 minute or until fragrant. Stir in the ¾ cup coconut milk, the tahini, orange juice, the 2 teaspoons brown sugar, and the fish sauce. Bring just to simmering. Simmer gently, uncovered, about 5 minutes or until blended and thickened, stirring frequently. Cover and keep warm.

**3** Drain meat, discarding marinade. Thread the meat cubes onto long metal skewers, leaving ¼-inch space between each piece.

**4** *For a charcoal grill,* grill kabobs on the rack of an uncovered grill directly over medium coals for 10 to 12 minutes or until meat is slightly pink in center and juices run clear, turning occasionally to brown evenly. (*For a gas grill,* preheat grill. Reduce heat to medium. Place kabobs on grill rack over heat. Cover and grill as above.) Serve with dipping sauce. Makes 6 servings.

Nutrition Facts per serving: 283 calories, 15 g total fat (7 g saturated fat), 81 mg cholesterol, 223 mg sodium, 9 g carbohydrate, 1 g fiber, 28 g protein. Daily Values: 6% vit. C, 2% calcium, 16% iron.

## Did You Know?

**Try a little tahini for a change. Tahini is simply a paste, similar to natural peanut butter, that is made from sesame seeds rather than peanuts, of course. Nutritionally, tahini is high in fat, but it's also a good source of protein and calcium. It traditionally is used in Middle Eastern cuisine as a flavoring ingredient. Look for it with other ethnic foods in the supermarket.**

# Pork Tenderloin with Green Olive Tapenade

**Prep:** 20 minutes **Grill:** 1 hour
**Stand:** 10 minutes

1 cup pitted green olives, drained
1 tablespoon capers, drained
1 tablespoon Dijon-style mustard
1 tablespoon olive oil
1 tablespoon lemon juice
2 teaspoons anchovy paste
1 teaspoon snipped fresh thyme
1 small clove garlic, minced
2 12-ounce pork tenderloins

**1** For tapenade, in a food processor bowl combine olives, capers, mustard, oil, lemon juice, anchovy paste, thyme, and garlic. Cover; process until smooth, scraping sides as necessary. Cover and chill up to 24 hours.

**2** Trim fat from meat. Split each tenderloin lengthwise, cutting to but not through the opposite side. Spread meat open. Place meat between 2 pieces of plastic wrap overlapping one long side of each tenderloin about 2 inches. Working from the center to the edges, use the flat side of a meat mallet to pound meat into a 10×12-inch rectangle. Remove plastic wrap. Spread tapenade over meat to within 1 inch of edges. Fold in long sides just to cover edge of stuffing. Starting at one of the short sides, roll up. Tie with 100-percent-cotton string at 1-inch intervals.

**3** *For a charcoal grill,* arrange medium-hot coals around a drip pan. Test for medium heat above the pan. Place meat on grill rack over drip pan. Cover; grill for 1 to 1¼ hours or until meat is slightly pink in center and juices run clear. [*For a gas grill,* preheat grill. Reduce heat to medium. Adjust for indirect cooking (see page 10). Grill as above, except place meat on a rack in a roasting pan.)

**4** Remove meat from grill. Cover with foil; let stand for 10 minutes. Remove strings from meat and slice. Makes 6 servings.

Nutrition Facts per serving: 201 calories, 10 g total fat (2 g saturated fat), 83 mg cholesterol, 347 mg sodium, 1 g carbohydrate, 0 g fiber, 27 g protein. Daily Values: 2% vit. C, 2% calcium, 11% iron.

## SMOKY CHIPOTLE TENDERLOIN

**Prep:** 15 minutes  **Marinate:** 1 to 4 hours
**Grill:** 30 minutes  **Stand:** 10 minutes

*In Santa Fe, the masters of pepper love their carne adovada, and this fiery tenderloin takes its inspiration from the high desert country.*

   6 cloves garlic, minced
   1 teaspoon ground cumin
   1 teaspoon dried oregano, crushed
   ¼ teaspoon ground cinnamon
   1 tablespoon cooking oil
   1 8-ounce can tomato sauce
   ½ cup water
   ¼ cup cider vinegar
   2 teaspoons sugar
   ½ teaspoon salt
   2 12- to 16-ounce pork tenderloins
   3 to 5 canned chipotle peppers in
     adobo sauce

**1** For marinade, in a medium skillet cook garlic, cumin, oregano, and cinnamon in hot oil for 1 minute. Stir in tomato sauce, water, vinegar, sugar, and salt. Bring to boiling. Remove skillet from heat; cool mixture slightly.

**2** Meanwhile, trim fat from meat. Place meat in a plastic bag set in a shallow dish. Set aside. In a food processor bowl or blender container combine the tomato mixture and chipotle peppers. Cover and process or blend until smooth. Pour over meat in bag; seal bag. Marinate in the refrigerator 1 to 4 hours, turning bag occasionally. Drain, reserving marinade.

**3** *For a charcoal grill,* arrange medium-hot coals around a drip pan. Test for medium heat above the pan. Place meat on grill rack over drip pan. Cover and grill for 30 to 45 minutes or until meat is slightly pink in center and juices run clear, brushing occasionally with marinade during the first 20 minutes of grilling. [*For a gas grill,* preheat grill. Reduce heat to medium. Adjust for indirect cooking (see page 10). Grill as above, except place meat on a rack in a roasting pan.]

**4** Remove meat from grill. Cover with foil; let stand for 10 minutes. To serve, slice meat diagonally across the grain. Makes 6 to 8 servings.

Nutrition Facts per serving: 198 calories, 7 g total fat (2 g saturated fat), 81 mg cholesterol, 545 mg sodium, 8 g carbohydrate, 1 g fiber, 26 g protein. Daily Values: 13% vit. A, 11% vit. C, 2% calcium, 15% iron.

# Indonesian Pork and Noodles

**Prep:** 20 minutes  **Marinate:** 30 minutes
**Grill:** 12 minutes

   1 1-pound pork tenderloin
   ¼ cup Brazil nuts
   ¼ cup light soy sauce
   3 tablespoons lemon juice
   1 tablespoon olive oil
   1 tablespoon ground coriander
   1 tablespoon brown sugar
   ¾ teaspoon pepper
   1 clove garlic, minced
   8 ounces thin egg noodles
   1 tablespoon margarine or butter,
     softened
   2 tablespoons toasted sesame seed

**1** Trim fat from meat. Cut meat into 1-inch cubes. Place meat in a plastic bag set in a shallow dish. For marinade, in a food processor bowl combine nuts, soy sauce, lemon juice, oil, coriander, brown sugar, ½ teaspoon of the pepper, and garlic. Cover; process until combined. Pour marinade over meat; seal bag. Marinate in refrigerator for 30 to 60 minutes, turning bag occasionally.

**2** Drain meat, discarding marinade. Thread meat cubes onto 4 long metal skewers, leaving a ¼-inch space between pieces.

**3** *For a charcoal grill,* grill kabobs on the rack of an uncovered grill directly over medium coals for 12 to 14 minutes or until meat is slightly pink in center and juices run clear, turning once halfway through grilling. (*For a gas grill,* preheat grill. Reduce heat to medium. Place kabobs on grill rack over medium heat. Cover and grill as above.)

**4** Meanwhile, cook noodles according to package directions. Drain and return noodles to hot pan. Toss with margarine or butter, sesame seeds, and the remaining ¼ teaspoon of pepper. Serve noodles with kabobs. Makes 4 servings.

Nutrition Facts per serving: 490 calories, 20 g total fat (4 g saturated fat), 130 mg cholesterol, 458 mg sodium, 43 g carbohydrate, 3 g fiber, 36 g protein. Daily Values: 4% vit. A, 7% vit. C, 5% calcium, 33% iron.

## JAMAICAN PORK KABOBS

**Prep:** 15 minutes  **Grill:** 12 minutes

*Pickapeppa sauce can be found in most supermarkets with other sauces, such as Worcestershire sauce. Don't use red pepper sauce as a substitute—it will be too hot!*

> 2 ears of corn, husked and cleaned
> 1 12- to 14-ounce pork tenderloin
> 1 small red onion, cut into ½-inch wedges
> 16 baby pattypan squash, about 1 inch in diameter, or 4 fresh tomatillos, quartered
> ¼ cup mango chutney, finely chopped
> 3 tablespoons Pickapeppa sauce
> 1 tablespoon cooking oil
> 1 tablespoon water

**1** Cut corn crosswise into 1-inch pieces. In a medium saucepan cook corn pieces in small amount of boiling water for 3 minutes; drain and rinse with cold water. Meanwhile, trim fat from meat. Cut meat into 1-inch slices. On long metal skewers, alternately thread meat, corn, onion, and squash or tomatillos, leaving a ¼-inch space between each piece.

**2** For glaze, in a bowl combine chutney, Pickapeppa sauce, oil, and water. Set aside.

**3** *For a charcoal grill,* grill kabobs on the rack of an uncovered grill directly over medium coals for 12 to 14 minutes or until meat is slightly pink in center and vegetables are tender, turning once and brushing occasionally

with glaze during the last 5 minutes of grilling. (*For a gas grill,* preheat grill. Reduce heat to medium. Place kabobs on grill rack over heat. Cover; grill as above.) Makes 4 servings.

Nutrition Facts serving: 252 calories, 7 g total fat (2 g saturated fat), 60 mg cholesterol, 127 mg sodium, 27 g carbohydrate, 3 g fiber, 21 g protein. Daily Values: 3% vit. A, 13% vit. C, 2% calcium, 10% iron.

## Five-Spice Pork

**Prep:** 10 minutes  **Grill:** 25 minutes
**Stand:** 30 + 10 minutes

> 3 tablespoons ground cinnamon
> 2 teaspoons anise seed
> 1½ teaspoons whole black pepper
> 1 teaspoon fennel seed
> ½ teaspoon ground cloves
> 1 12-ounce pork tenderloin
> 3 cloves garlic, quartered
> Cooking oil

**1** For spice blend, in a blender container combine cinnamon, anise seed, pepper, fennel seed, and cloves. Cover; blend until powdery.

**2** Trim fat from pork. With the point of a paring knife, make small slits in meat. Insert garlic into slits. Brush pork with oil. Sprinkle about 1 tablespoon of spice mixture evenly over pork; rub in with your fingers. (Reserve remaining spice blend for another use.) Let meat stand 30 minutes before grilling.

**3** *For a charcoal grill,* arrange medium-hot coals around a drip pan. Test for medium heat above pan. Place pork on grill rack over pan. Cover; grill for 25 to 30 minutes or until meat is slightly pink in center and juices run clear. [*For a gas grill,* preheat grill. Reduce heat to medium. Adjust for indirect cooking (see page 10). Grill as above, except place meat on a rack in a roasting pan.] Remove pork from grill. Cover; let stand 10 minutes. Serves 4.

Nutrition Facts per serving: 133 calories, 6 g total fat (1 g saturated fat), 60 mg cholesterol, 44 mg sodium, 1 g carbohydrate, 0 g fiber, 19 g protein. Daily Values: 1% vit. C, 2% calcium, 10% iron.

## MOROCCAN PORK WITH WILTED GREENS

**Prep:** 40 minutes    **Grill:** 30 minutes
**Stand:** 10 minutes

*Cumin and coriander transform apricots and pork into a Moroccan masterpiece. Slice and serve over greens for an exotic treat.*

1 12-ounce pork tenderloin
⅓ cup snipped dried apricots
2 tablespoons snipped fresh cilantro
1 tablespoon raisins
2 teaspoons lemon juice
1 teaspoon ground cumin
1 teaspoon ground coriander
1 teaspoon paprika
⅛ teaspoon salt
1 to 1½ pounds mixed greens (such as Swiss chard, beet greens, mustard greens, and/or spinach)
2 tablespoons olive oil
2 cloves garlic, minced
    Lemon wedges

1 Trim fat from pork. Butterfly the meat by making a lengthwise cut down center of meat, cutting to within ½ inch of the other side. Spread open. Place knife in the "v" of the first cut. Cut away from the first cut and parallel to the cut surface to within ½ inch of the other side of the meat. Repeat on opposite side of "v." Spread these sections open. Sprinkle apricots, cilantro, and raisins over meat. Sprinkle with lemon juice. Starting from a long side, roll up. Tie with 100-percent-cotton string at 1-inch intervals.

2 For rub, in a small bowl combine cumin, coriander, paprika, and salt. Sprinkle rub evenly over meat; rub in with your fingers. Insert a meat thermometer into center of meat.

3 *For a charcoal grill,* arrange medium-hot coals around a drip pan. Test for medium heat above the pan. Place meat on grill rack over drip pan. Cover and grill for 30 to 45 minutes or until meat thermometer registers 155°. [*For a gas grill,* preheat grill. Reduce heat to medium. Adjust for indirect cooking (see page 10). Grill as above, except place meat on a rack in a roasting pan.] Remove meat from grill. Cover with foil; let stand for 10 minutes.

4 Meanwhile, wash and thoroughly dry the greens. Pat greens dry with paper towels. If desired, remove stems. Cut greens lengthwise into 2-inch strips; set aside. In a large heavy skillet heat oil over medium-high heat. Add garlic. Cook and stir garlic for 30 to 60 seconds or just until brown. Add the greens. Cook and stir for 2 to 3 minutes or just until greens are limp. To serve, slice meat diagonally across the grain; serve with greens. Squeeze the juice from lemon wedges over meat and greens. Makes 4 servings.

Nutrition Facts per serving: 234 calories, 11 g total fat (2 g saturated fat), 60 mg cholesterol, 317 mg sodium, 15 g carbohydrate, 3 g fiber, 22 g protein. Daily Values: 47% vit. A, 38% vit. C, 8% calcium, 34% iron.

## WISE ADVICE

**Nobody likes eating something akin to shoe leather. So to ensure juicy, tender results, pork shouldn't be overcooked. For small cuts of pork, such as cubed meat on kabobs or chops, use the time guidelines suggested in the recipe. It is recommended that you use a meat thermometer to judge the doneness of larger cuts of pork. For the correct final cooking temperatures for various cuts of pork, see grilling chart on page 224.**

Moroccan Pork with Wilted Greens

# Texas Rib Sandwich with Coleslaw

**Prep:** 10 minutes **Grill:** 1½ hours

*When you want a barbecue sandwich that's a barbecue sandwich, stick to the ribs—country-style boneless ribs, that is. Coleslaw is a must.*

> 2 pounds boneless pork country-style ribs
> ¾ cup bottled or homemade barbecue sauce
> 6 crusty dinner rolls or hamburger buns, split and toasted
> Bottled hot pepper sauce (optional)
> 1 cup prepared coleslaw

**1** Trim fat from ribs. *For a charcoal grill,* arrange medium-hot coals around a drip pan. Test for medium heat above the pan. Place ribs on grill rack over drip pan. (Or, place ribs in a rib rack; place on grill rack.) Cover and grill for 1½ to 2 hours or until ribs are tender, brushing occasionally with sauce during the last 10 minutes of grilling. [*For a gas grill,* preheat grill. Reduce heat to medium. Adjust for indirect cooking (see page 10). Grill as above, except place ribs on a rack in a roasting pan.] Remove ribs from grill and brush with the remaining sauce. Cut ribs into serving-size pieces.

**2** Top the toasted rolls with the ribs, hot pepper sauce (if desired), and coleslaw. Makes 6 servings.

Nutrition Facts per serving: 464 calories, 22 g total fat (7 g saturated fat), 89 mg cholesterol, 635 mg sodium, 37 g carbohydrate, 1 g fiber, 28 g protein. Daily Values: 4% vit. A, 15% vit. C, 6% calcium, 21% iron.

# SWEET AND TANGY COUNTRY-STYLE RIBS

**Prep:** 10 minutes **Grill:** 1½ hours

*Enjoy hot and tangy country-style ribs, just right for a picnic with coleslaw and garlic-buttered Texas toast.*

> ½ cup bottled chili sauce
> 2 tablespoons apple jelly
> 1 tablespoon vinegar
> 1 teaspoon prepared mustard
> 1 teaspoon Worcestershire sauce
> ¼ teaspoon chili powder
> 2 to 2½ pounds pork country-style ribs

**1** For sauce, in a small saucepan combine chili sauce and apple jelly. Cook and stir over medium heat until jelly is melted. Remove from heat. Stir in vinegar, mustard, Worcestershire sauce, and chili powder. Trim fat from ribs.

**2** *For a charcoal grill,* arrange medium-hot coals around a drip pan. Test for medium heat above the pan. Place ribs, bone side down, on grill rack over drip pan. (Or, place ribs in a rib rack; place on grill rack.) Cover and grill for 1½ to 2 hours or until ribs are tender, brushing occasionally with sauce during the last 15 minutes of grilling. [*For a gas grill,* preheat grill. Reduce heat to medium. Adjust for indirect cooking (see page 10). Grill as above, except place ribs in a roasting pan.]

**3** Reheat any remaining sauce and pass with ribs. Makes 4 servings.

Nutrition Facts per serving: 449 calories, 28 g total fat (10 g saturated fat), 129 mg cholesterol, 533 mg sodium, 15 g carbohydrate, 0 g fiber, 33 g protein. Daily Values: 5% vit. A, 11% vit. C, 2% calcium, 12% iron.

# Maple-Glazed Country Ribs

**Prep:** 15 minutes   **Grill:** 1½ hours

½ cup apple jelly
½ cup maple syrup or maple-flavored
   syrup
1 tablespoon cider vinegar
1 tablespoon coarse-grain brown
   mustard
1 clove garlic, minced
2½ to 3 pounds pork country-style ribs

**1** For sauce, in a small saucepan combine apple jelly, maple syrup, vinegar, mustard, and garlic. Bring to boiling; reduce heat. Simmer, uncovered, about 10 minutes or until desired consistency, stirring frequently. Remove from heat. Trim fat from ribs.

**2** *For a charcoal grill,* arrange medium-hot coals around a drip pan. Test for medium heat above pan. Place ribs, bone side down, on grill rack over pan. (Or, place ribs in a rib rack; place on grill rack.) Cover and grill for 1½ to 2 hours or until ribs are tender, brushing occasionally with sauce during the last 10 minutes of grilling. [*For a gas grill,* preheat grill. Reduce heat to medium. Adjust for indirect cooking (see page 10). Grill as above, except place ribs in a roasting pan.] Pass remaining sauce with ribs. Serves 4.

Nutrition Facts per serving: 572 calories, 21 g total fat (7 g saturated fat), 98 mg cholesterol, 155 mg sodium, 53 g carbohydrate, 0 g fiber, 41 g protein. Daily Values: 3% vit. C, 3% calcium, 15% iron.

# CRANBERRY-SAUCED COUNTRY-STYLE RIBS

**Prep:** 15 minutes   **Grill:** 1½ hours

1 8-ounce can jellied cranberry sauce
2 tablespoons steak sauce
2 teaspoons brown sugar
2 teaspoons prepared mustard
½ teaspoon finely shredded lemon
   peel
¼ teaspoon celery seed
2 to 2½ pounds pork country-style
   ribs

**1** For sauce, in a small saucepan combine cranberry sauce, steak sauce, brown sugar, mustard, lemon peel, and celery seed. Cook and stir until combined; remove from heat. Trim fat from ribs.

**2** *For a charcoal grill,* arrange medium-hot coals around a drip pan. Test for medium heat above the pan. Place ribs, bone side down, on grill rack over drip pan. (Or, place ribs in a rib rack; place on grill rack.) Cover and grill for 1½ to 2 hours or until ribs are tender, brushing occasionally with sauce during the last 15 minutes of grilling [*For a gas grill,* preheat grill. Reduce heat to medium. Adjust for indirect cooking (see page 10). Grill as above, except place ribs in a roasting pan.] Serve ribs with any remaining sauce. Makes 4 servings.

Nutrition Facts per serving: 374 calories, 17 g total fat (6 g saturated fat), 105 mg cholesterol, 269 mg sodium, 25 g carbohydrate, 2 g fiber, 29 g protein. Daily Values: 5% vit. C, 2% calcium, 10% iron.

## Did You Know?

**Kansas City-style barbecue emerged in the 1920s from a melting pot of sauces and traditions brought up the Mississippi and Missouri Rivers from open-pit grilling in the Deep South. The father of K.C. barbecue is Henry Perry, who, during the Depression, opened a streetcar barn and began barbecuing ribs in an outdoor pit. He served the ribs in newspapers to keep costs down.**

# Thai-Coconut Ribs

**Prep:** 15 minutes  **Marinate:** 8 to 24 hours
**Grill:** 1¼ hours

*These grilled ribs marinate in a spicy and gingery coconut-milk sauce that will send your taste buds to Thailand.*

4 pounds pork loin back ribs
1 cup coconut milk
3 tablespoons brown sugar
3 tablespoons soy sauce
1 tablespoon grated fresh ginger
1 teaspoon finely shredded
   lime peel
1 tablespoon lime juice
4 cloves garlic, minced
1 teaspoon crushed red pepper

1 Trim fat from ribs. Cut ribs into 6 serving-size pieces. Place ribs in a plastic bag set in a shallow dish. For marinade, in a small bowl combine coconut milk, brown sugar, soy sauce, ginger, lime peel, lime juice, garlic, and red pepper. Pour over ribs; seal bag. Marinate in the refrigerator for 8 to 24 hours, turning bag occasionally. Drain ribs, reserving marinade.

2 *For a charcoal grill,* arrange medium-hot coals around a drip pan. Test for medium heat above the pan. Place ribs, bone side down, on grill rack over drip pan. Cover and grill for 1¼ to 1½ hours or until ribs are tender, brushing frequently with marinade during the first hour of grilling. Discard marinade. [*For a gas grill,* preheat grill. Reduce heat to medium. Adjust for indirect cooking (see page 10). Grill as above, except place the ribs in a roasting pan.] Makes 6 servings.

Nutrition Facts per serving: 431 calories, 32 g total fat (16 g saturated fat), 99 mg cholesterol, 607 mg sodium, 9 g carbohydrate, 0 g fiber, 25 g protein. Daily Values: 2% vit. A, 8% vit. C, 4% calcium, 15% iron.

# WARREN'S BARBECUED RIBS

**Prep:** 15 minutes  **Grill:** 1¼ hours

*Who is Warren? We discovered that he was the husband of a past Test Kitchen director during the '60s. Originally published in a Better Homes and Gardens® barbecue cookbook 30 years ago, this recipe has stood the test of time!*

1 cup catsup
1 cup water
3 tablespoons vinegar
1 tablespoon sugar
1 tablespoon Worcestershire sauce
1 teaspoon celery seed
¼ teaspoon bottled hot pepper sauce
4 pounds pork loin back ribs or
   meaty spareribs
Salt
Black pepper

1 For sauce, in a medium saucepan combine catsup, water, vinegar, sugar, Worcestershire sauce, celery seed, and hot pepper sauce. Bring to boiling; reduce heat. Simmer, uncovered, for 30 minutes, stirring occasionally. Remove sauce from heat; set aside.

2 Trim fat from ribs. Season ribs lightly with salt and pepper. *For a charcoal grill,* arrange medium-hot coals around a drip pan. Test for medium heat above the pan. Place ribs, bone side down, on grill rack over drip pan. (Or, place ribs in a rib rack; place on grill rack.) Cover; grill for 1¼ to 1½ hours or until ribs are tender, brushing occasionally with sauce during the last 15 minutes of grilling. [*For a gas grill,* preheat grill. Reduce heat to medium. Adjust for indirect cooking (see page 10). Grill as above, except place the ribs in a roasting pan.] Brush ribs with sauce the last 15 minutes of grilling. Pass any remaining sauce. Makes 4 servings.

Nutrition Facts per serving: 571 calories, 37 g total fat (14 g saturated fat), 148 mg cholesterol, 996 mg sodium, 23 g carbohydrate, 1 g fiber, 37 g protein. Daily Values: 7% vit. A, 28% vit. C, 6% calcium, 21% iron.

Thai-Coconut Ribs

# Peanut-Sauced Pork Ribs

**Prep:** 10 minutes   **Grill:** 1¼ hours

*These ribs will remind you of a Southeast Asian favorite called satay. Peanut butter is the star ingredient in the traditional satay sauce.*

   3 tablespoons hot water
   ⅓ cup peanut butter
   ½ of a 6-ounce can (⅓ cup) frozen
       apple juice concentrate, thawed
   3 tablespoons cooking oil
   2 tablespoons teriyaki sauce
   1 tablespoon curry powder
   2 cloves garlic, minced
       Several dashes bottled hot
       pepper sauce
   4 pounds pork loin back ribs or
       meaty spareribs

**1** For sauce, in a small bowl gradually stir hot water into peanut butter (the mixture will stiffen at first). Stir in apple juice concentrate, oil, teriyaki sauce, curry powder, garlic, and hot pepper sauce until mixture is smooth. Trim fat from ribs.

**2** *For a charcoal grill,* arrange medium-hot coals around a drip pan. Test for medium heat above the pan. Place ribs, bone side down, on grill rack over drip pan. (Or, place ribs in a rib rack; place on grill rack.) Cover and grill for 1¼ to 1½ hours or until ribs are tender, brushing occasionally with sauce during the last 10 minutes of grilling. [*For a gas grill,* preheat grill. Reduce heat to medium. Adjust for indirect cooking (see page 10). Grill as above, except place ribs in a roasting pan.]

**3** In a small saucepan cook and stir any remaining sauce over medium-low heat until heated through. Pass sauce with ribs. Makes 6 servings.

Nutrition Facts per serving: 531 calories,
39 g total fat (11 g saturated fat), 117 mg cholesterol,
393 mg sodium, 11 g carbohydrate, 1 g fiber,
33 g protein. Daily Values: 1% vit. C, 2% calcium,
13% iron.

# GINGERY APRICOT-GLAZED PORK RIBS

**Prep:** 20 minutes   **Marinate:** 6 to 24 hours
**Grill:** 1¼ hours

*You're gonna love these baby back ribs. Maybe it's the apricot flavor or the ginger that you can't resist. Don't dwell on it—the combination of flavors is perfect.*

   4 pounds pork loin back ribs
   1 cup finely chopped onion
   ⅓ cup dry sherry
   ¼ cup finely grated fresh ginger
   ¼ cup rice vinegar
   ¼ cup soy sauce
   2 tablespoons minced garlic (about
       12 cloves)
   ½ teaspoon black pepper
   ⅔ cup apricot preserves
   3 tablespoons spicy brown mustard
   1 tablespoon toasted sesame oil
   ¼ teaspoon ground red pepper

**1** Trim fat from ribs. Place ribs in a large plastic bag set in a shallow dish. For marinade, in a medium bowl combine onion, sherry, ginger, vinegar, soy sauce, garlic, and black pepper. Pour over ribs; seal bag. Marinate in the refrigerator for 6 to 24 hours, turning bag occasionally. Drain, reserving ¼ cup of the marinade.

**2** For sauce, in a small saucepan combine apricot preserves, mustard, oil, and ground red pepper. Add the reserved marinade. Bring to boiling; reduce heat. Simmer, uncovered, about 3 minutes or until slightly thickened.

**3** *For a charcoal grill,* arrange medium-hot coals around a drip pan. Test for medium heat above the pan. Place ribs, bone side down, on grill rack over drip pan. (Or, place ribs in a rib rack; place on grill rack.) Cover and grill for 1¼ to 1½ hours or until ribs are tender, brushing occasionally with sauce during the last 15 minutes of grilling. [*For a gas grill*, preheat grill. Reduce heat to medium. Adjust for indirect cooking (see page 10). Grill as above, except place ribs in a roasting pan.] Makes 4 servings.

Nutrition Facts per serving: 740 calories, 42 g total fat (14 g saturated fat), 176 mg cholesterol, 637 mg sodium, 42 g carbohydrate, 1 g fiber, 45 g protein. Daily Values: 1% vit. A, 5% vit. C, 4% calcium, 19% iron.

# Asian-Style Gingered Ribs

**Prep:** 25 minutes   **Marinate:** 6 to 24 hours
**Soak:** 1 hour   **Grill:** 1¼ hours

*Don't be tempted to brush on the sauce early in the grilling process! With sugar in the rub and sauce, you might end up with burned ribs. Brush it on during just the last 15 minutes of grilling.*

　4 cups hickory or fruit wood chips
　¼ cup catsup
　¼ cup soy sauce
　2 tablespoons brown sugar
　2 tablespoons water
　2 tablespoons grated fresh ginger or
　　　1 teaspoon ground ginger
　2 tablespoons granulated sugar
　¼ teaspoon paprika
　¼ teaspoon ground turmeric
　¼ teaspoon celery seed
　¼ teaspoon dry mustard
　4 pounds pork loin back ribs or
　　　meaty spareribs

1 At least one hour before grilling, soak wood chips in enough water to cover.

2 For sauce, in a small mixing bowl combine catsup, soy sauce, brown sugar, water, and ginger. Cover and refrigerate up to 24 hours.

3 Trim fat from ribs. For rub, in a small bowl combine granulated sugar, paprika, turmeric, celery seed, and dry mustard. Sprinkle rub evenly over ribs; rub in with your fingers. Cover and refrigerate for 6 to 24 hours.

4 Drain wood chips. *For a charcoal grill*, arrange medium-hot coals around a drip pan. Test for medium heat above pan. Sprinkle one-fourth of the wood chips over the coals. Place ribs, bone side down, on grill rack over drip pan. (Or, place ribs in a rib rack; place on grill rack.) Cover and grill for 1¼ to 1½ hours or until ribs are tender, brushing occasionally with sauce during the last 15 minutes of grilling. Add more wood chips every 15 minutes. [*For a gas grill*, preheat grill. Reduce heat to medium. Adjust for indirect cooking (see page 10). Grill as above, except place ribs in a roasting pan; add wood chips according to manufacturer's directions.] Makes 6 to 8 servings.

Nutrition Facts per serving: 362 calories, 25 g total fat (10 g saturated fat), 98 mg cholesterol, 899 mg sodium, 10 g carbohydrate, 0 g fiber, 24 g protein. Daily Values: 1% vit. A, 3% vit. C, 3% calcium, 13% iron.

**Did You Know?**

A whopping 23% of consumers' refrigerators aren't kept cold enough. Keeping your refrigerator's temperature at no higher than 40° F is important in discouraging the growth of foodborne bacteria that can cause illness. It's a good idea to check the temperature of your refrigerator on a regular basis, especially in the summer when frequent opening of your refrigerator door during hot weather can increase the temperature inside the refrigerator.

## KANSAS CITY PORK SPARERIBS

**Prep:** 10 minutes **Soak:** 1 hour
**Grill:** 1¼ hours

*In this recipe from the classic barbecue city, Kansas City genius and wood smoke combine for unforgettable baby back ribs.*

4 cups hickory, oak, or apple wood
   chips
4 pounds meaty pork spareribs or
   loin back ribs
1 tablespoon brown sugar
1 tablespoon garlic pepper
1 tablespoon paprika
1½ teaspoons chili powder
1 teaspoon salt
½ teaspoon celery seed
¼ cup cider vinegar
1 recipe Kansas City Barbecue
   Sauce (recipe, page 29)

**1** At least 1 hour before grilling, soak wood chips in enough water to cover. Trim fat from ribs. For rub, in a small bowl combine brown sugar, garlic pepper, paprika, chili powder, salt, and celery seed. Brush ribs with vinegar. Sprinkle rub evenly over ribs; rub in with your fingers.

**2** Drain wood chips. *For a charcoal grill,* arrange medium-hot coals around a drip pan. Test for medium heat above the pan. Sprinkle one-fourth of the wood chips over the coals. Place ribs, bone side down, on grill rack over drip pan. (Or, place ribs in a rib rack; place on grill rack.) Cover and grill for 1¼ to 1½ hours or until ribs are tender. Add more wood chips every 15 minutes. [*For a gas grill,* preheat grill. Reduce heat to medium. Adjust for indirect cooking (see page 10). Grill as above, except place ribs in a roasting pan; add wood chips according to manufacturer's directions.]

**3** Serve ribs with Kansas City Barbecue Sauce. Makes 4 servings.

Nutrition Facts per serving: 688 calories,
42 g total fat (14 g saturated fat), 176 mg cholesterol,
1,470 mg sodium, 34 g carbohydrate, 2 g fiber,
46 g protein. Daily Values: 28% vit. A, 38% vit. C,
8% calcium, 34% iron.

## Did You Know?

**Not certain about which ribs to buy or how much?
Here's a quick review:**
**Spareribs** come from the belly or side of the hog, have the least amount of meat, and are less tender than other ribs. Count on a minimum of 1 pound per person.
**Back ribs** are cut from the blade and center section of the loin and are meatier, with "finger meat" between the bones, and are easier to handle than spareribs. Allow at least 1 pound per person.
**Country-style ribs,** cut from the rib end of the loin, are the meatiest of pork ribs. These ribs usually offer more meat than bone and can be eaten with knife and fork. Plan on about ½ pound per person to satisfy most appetites.

Kansas City Pork Spareribs

# Southwestern Ribs with a Rub

**Prep:** 35 minutes **Soak:** 1 hour
**Grill:** 1¼ hours

- **4 cups mesquite wood chips**
- **1 cup catsup**
- **½ cup light-colored corn syrup**
- **¼ cup white vinegar**
- **¼ cup packed brown sugar**
- **¼ cup finely chopped onion**
- **2 tablespoons prepared mustard**
- **1½ teaspoons Worcestershire sauce**
- **2 cloves garlic, minced**
- **½ teaspoon coarsely ground black pepper**
- **½ teaspoon bottled hot pepper sauce**
- **¼ teaspoon ground cumin or chili powder**
- **⅛ teaspoon ground red pepper**
- **1 recipe Rib Rub**
- **4 pounds pork loin back ribs**

**1** At least 1 hour before grilling, soak wood chips in enough water to cover. For sauce, in a 1½-quart saucepan combine catsup, corn syrup, vinegar, brown sugar, onion, mustard, Worcestershire sauce, garlic, black pepper, hot pepper sauce, cumin, and ground red pepper. Bring to boiling; reduce heat. Simmer, uncovered, for 25 to 30 minutes or until thickened, stirring occasionally.

**2** Prepare Rib Rub. Trim fat from ribs. Sprinkle rub over ribs; rub in with fingers.

**3** Drain wood chips. *For a charcoal grill,* arrange medium-hot coals around drip pan. Test for medium heat above the pan. Sprinkle half of the wood chips over the coals. Place ribs, bone side down, on grill rack over drip pan. (Or, place ribs in a rib rack; place on grill rack.) Cover and grill for 1¼ to 1½ hours or until ribs are tender, brushing occasionally with sauce during the last 10 minutes of grilling. (Add more wood chips every 15 minutes.) [*For a gas grill,* preheat grill. Reduce heat to medium. Adjust for indirect cooking (see page 10). Grill as above, except place ribs in a roasting pan; add wood chips according to manufacturer's directions.] Pass any remaining sauce. Makes 6 servings.

**Rib Rub:** In a blender container combine 2 teaspoons each dried rosemary, crushed; dried thyme, crushed; dried minced onion; dried minced garlic; 1 teaspoon coarse salt; and ¾ teaspoon black pepper. Cover and blend until coarsely ground.

Nutrition Facts per serving: 497 calories, 17 g total fat (6 g saturated fat), 84 mg cholesterol, 1,057 mg sodium, 44 g carbohydrate, 1 g fiber, 42 g protein. Daily Values: 5% vit. A, 20% vit. C, 5% calcium, 26% iron.

## CHUTNEY SPARERIBS

**Prep:** 15 minutes **Cook:** 1 hour
**Grill:** 10 minutes

- **3 to 4 pounds meaty pork spareribs or loin back ribs**
- **1 cup mango chutney**
- **¼ cup bottled chili sauce**
- **2 tablespoons vinegar**
- **1 tablespoon Worcestershire sauce**
- **1 tablespoon water**
- **1 teaspoon dry mustard**
- **½ teaspoon onion powder**
- **Several dashes bottled hot pepper sauce**

**1** Trim fat from ribs. Cut ribs into 6 serving-size pieces. Place ribs in a large Dutch oven. Add enough water to cover ribs. Bring to boiling; reduce heat. Simmer, covered, about 1 hour or until meat is tender. Drain ribs; sprinkle lightly with salt.

**2** Meanwhile, for sauce, in a medium saucepan combine chutney, chili sauce, vinegar, Worcestershire sauce, water, mustard, onion powder, and pepper sauce. Cook and stir over medium heat until heated through.

**3** *For a charcoal grill,* grill ribs, meaty side down, on the rack of an uncovered grill directly over medium coals for 10 to 15 minutes or until ribs are tender, turning once and brushing with sauce during the last 5 minutes of grilling. (*For a gas grill,* preheat grill. Reduce heat to medium. Place ribs on grill rack over heat. Cover and grill as above.) Pass any remaining sauce. Makes 6 servings.

Nutrition Facts per serving: 421 calories, 23 g total fat (9 g saturated fat), 70 mg cholesterol, 297 mg sodium, 29 g carbohydrate, 1 g fiber, 23 g protein. Daily Values: 4% vit. A, 13% vit. C, 4% calcium, 14% iron.

# Plum-Glazed Spareribs

**Prep:** 15 minutes    **Grill:** 1¼ hours

- 1 16-ounce can whole, unpitted purple plums
- 2 tablespoons orange juice concentrate
- 2 tablespoons bottled hoisin sauce
- 1 tablespoon soy sauce
- 1 teaspoon grated fresh ginger
- ¼ teaspoon pepper
- 2 tablespoons toasted sesame seeds
- 4 pounds meaty pork spareribs
  Salt
  Pepper

**1** For glaze, drain plums, reserving liquid. Pit plums. In a food processor bowl combine pitted plums and their reserved liquid, orange juice concentrate, hoisin sauce, soy sauce, ginger, and pepper. Cover and process until mixture is nearly smooth. Transfer to saucepan. Bring to boiling; reduce heat. Simmer, uncovered, about 15 minutes or until slightly thickened. Stir in sesame seeds.

**2** Trim fat from ribs. Cut ribs into 6 serving-size pieces. Sprinkle ribs with salt and pepper. *For a charcoal grill,* arrange medium-hot coals around a drip pan. Test for medium heat above the pan. Place ribs, bone side down, on grill rack over drip pan. Cover; grill for 1¼ to 1½ hours or until ribs are tender, brushing with glaze the last 10 minutes of grilling. [*For a gas grill,* preheat grill. Reduce heat to medium. Adjust for indirect cooking (see page 10). Grill as above, except place ribs in a roasting pan.] Pass any remaining glaze with ribs. Makes 6 servings.

Nutrition Facts per serving: 428 calories, 27 g total fat (10 g saturated fat), 103 mg cholesterol, 372 mg sodium, 18 g carbohydrate, 1 g fiber, 26 g protein. Daily Values: 2% vit. A, 15% vit. C, 4% calcium, 16% iron.

# SPICED AND SMOKED RIBS

**Prep:** 10 minutes    **Soak:** 1 hour
**Grill:** 1¼ hours

- 4 cups hickory wood chips
- 4 pounds meaty pork spareribs or loin back ribs
- 1 tablespoon brown sugar
- 1 teaspoon five-spice powder
- ½ teaspoon paprika
- ¼ teaspoon celery seed
- ¼ teaspoon salt
- ¼ teaspoon black pepper
- ½ cup catsup
- 2 tablespoons molasses
- 1 tablespoon lemon juice
- 1 tablespoon soy sauce
  Several dashes bottled hot pepper sauce

**1** At least 1 hour before grilling, soak wood chips in enough water to cover. Trim fat from ribs. Cut ribs into 4 to 6 serving-size pieces.

**2** For rub, in a small bowl stir together brown sugar, five-spice powder, paprika, celery seed, salt, and black pepper. Sprinkle rub evenly over ribs; rub in with your fingers.

**3** For glaze, combine catsup, molasses, lemon juice, soy sauce, and hot sauce.

**4** Drain wood chips. *For a charcoal grill,* arrange medium-hot coals around drip pan. Test for medium heat above pan. Sprinkle half of the wood chips over the coals. Place ribs, bone side down, on grill rack over drip pan. Cover; grill for 1¼ to 1½ hours or until ribs are tender, brushing occasionally with glaze the last 15 minutes of grilling. Add more wood chips every 20 minutes. [*For a gas grill,* preheat grill. Reduce heat to medium. Adjust for indirect cooking (see page 10). Grill as above, except place ribs in a roasting pan; add wood chips according to manufacturer's directions.] Makes 4 to 6 servings.

Nutrition Facts per serving: 561 calories, 37 g total fat (14 g saturated fat), 148 mg cholesterol, 913 mg sodium, 20 g carbohydrate, 1 g fiber, 36 g protein. Daily Values: 5% vit. A, 12% vit. C, 7% calcium, 23% iron.

# Jambalaya-Style Pork Chops

**Prep:** 15 minutes   **Grill:** 12 minutes

*Serving grilled pork chops with a New Orleans-style jambalaya sauce means you're gonna have some bayou-style fun.*

 4 smoked pork loin chops, cut
    ¾ inch thick
 ¼ teaspoon black pepper
 ½ of a medium onion, halved
 ½ of a medium green sweet pepper,
    halved
 1 cup water
 1 tablespoon cornstarch
 ½ teaspoon instant chicken bouillon
    granules
 1 14½-ounce can Cajun-style
    stewed tomatoes, undrained
 1 tablespoon snipped fresh parsley
 2 cups hot cooked brown rice

**1** Trim fat from chops. Sprinkle chops with black pepper; set aside. On a metal skewer, thread onion and sweet pepper, leaving a ¼-inch space between each piece.

**2** *For a charcoal grill,* grill vegetable kabobs on the rack of an uncovered grill directly over medium coals for 4 minutes. Turn kabobs; add chops to grill. Grill for 8 to 11 minutes more or until chops are heated through and vegetables are tender, turning once halfway through grilling. (*For a gas grill,* preheat grill. Reduce heat to medium. Place vegetable kabobs, then chops on grill rack over heat. Cover and grill as above.) Coarsely chop vegetables; set aside.

**3** For sauce, in a large saucepan combine water, cornstarch, and bouillon granules. Stir in undrained tomatoes (snip any large pieces). Cook and stir over medium heat until thickened and bubbly. Cook and stir for 2 minutes more. Stir in chopped vegetables; heat through. To serve, spoon sauce over chops; sprinkle with parsley. Serve with hot cooked brown rice. Makes 4 servings.

Nutrition Facts per serving: 210 calories, 6 g total fat (2 g saturated fat), 51 mg cholesterol, 1,202 mg sodium, 19 g carbohydrate, 0 g fiber, 20 g protein. Daily Values: 34% vit. C, 1% calcium, 11% iron.

# MAPLE-GLAZED SMOKED PORK CHOPS WITH APPLES

**Prep:** 15 minutes   **Grill:** 8 minutes

*Can it get any better than maple and apple on these ample chops? It's the perfect recipe for fall, when apples are at their best.*

 4 smoked pork loin chops, cut
    ¾ inch thick
 ¼ cup maple syrup
 3 tablespoons margarine or butter
 ¼ teaspoon ground cinnamon
 ⅛ teaspoon ground nutmeg
 2 medium cooking apples, cored and
    cut crosswise into ¾-inch rings

**1** Trim fat from chops. For glaze, in a small saucepan combine the maple syrup, margarine or butter, cinnamon, and nutmeg. Cook and stir until heated through. Brush chops and apple rings with some of the glaze.

**2** *For a charcoal grill,* grill chops and apple rings on the rack of an uncovered grill directly over medium coals for 8 to 11 minutes or until chops are heated through and apples are tender and golden, turning and brushing once with glaze halfway through grilling. (*For a gas grill,* preheat grill. Reduce heat to medium. Place chops and apple rings on grill rack over heat. Cover; grill as above.)

**3** To serve, arrange apple rings on top of chops. Spoon any remaining glaze over apple rings. Makes 4 servings.

Nutrition Facts per serving: 357 calories, 17 g total fat (5 g saturated fat), 81 mg cholesterol, 2,004 mg sodium, 21 g carbohydrate, 1 g fiber, 30 g protein. Daily Values: 8% vit. A, 5% vit. C, 5% iron.

# Peach-Glazed Ham Steaks

**Prep:** 5 minutes  Grill: 12 minutes

*Combining ham, peaches, and mustard has to be genius because it defies all logic. It produces a ham with attitude (but just the right attitude).*

2 tablespoons brown sugar
2 tablespoons spicy brown mustard
⅓ cup peach or apricot nectar
1 1-pound cooked ham center slice,
  cut ¾ to 1 inch thick
4 medium peaches, peeled and
  halved lengthwise
2 small green and/or red sweet
  peppers, each cut crosswise
  into 4 rings

**1** For glaze, in a small bowl combine brown sugar and mustard. Gradually whisk in peach nectar until smooth. To prevent ham from curling, make shallow cuts around the edge at 1-inch intervals. Brush 1 side of ham with glaze.

**2** *For a charcoal grill,* grill ham, glazed side down, on the rack of an uncovered grill directly over medium-hot coals for 6 minutes. Turn ham. Add peaches and sweet peppers to grill. Brush ham, peaches, and sweet peppers with glaze. Grill for 6 to 10 minutes more or until ham, peaches, and peppers are heated through, brushing occasionally with glaze. (*For a gas grill,* preheat grill. Reduce heat to medium-hot. Place ham, then peaches and sweet peppers on grill rack over heat. Cover and grill as above.) Makes 4 servings.

Ⓥ Nutrition Facts per serving: 284 calories, 7 g total fat (2 g saturated fat), 60 mg cholesterol, 1,468 mg sodium, 31 g carbohydrate, 3 g fiber, 26 g protein. Daily Values: 11% vit. A, 94% vit. C, 2% calcium, 15% iron.

## GRILLED HAM STEAKS WITH SPICY APRICOT GLAZE

**Prep:** 10 minutes   **Grill:** 8 minutes

*You can substitute peach or pineapple preserves for the apricot flavor if you like.*

3 tablespoons apricot jam or
  preserves
2 tablespoons coarse-grain mustard
1 teaspoon cider vinegar
⅛ teaspoon ground red pepper
1 pound cooked boneless smoked
  ham, cut into four ½-inch-thick
  slices

**1** For glaze, in a small bowl stir together apricot jam or preserves, mustard, vinegar, and red pepper.

**2** *For a charcoal grill,* grill ham on the rack of an uncovered grill directly over medium-hot coals for 8 to 10 minutes or until browned, turning once and brushing occasionally with glaze. (*For a gas grill,* preheat grill. Reduce heat to medium-hot. Place ham on grill rack over heat. Cover and grill as above.) Makes 4 servings.

Ⓥ Nutrition Facts per serving: 190 calories, 6 g total fat (2 g saturated fat), 51 mg cholesterol, 1,273 mg sodium, 12 g carbohydrate, 0 g fiber, 21 g protein. Daily Values: 34% vit. C, 1% calcium, 11% iron.

## DON'T GET BURNED!

**When checking for doneness of meat, it's best to use a meat thermometer. Smaller cuts of meat, such as chops or steaks, may not be thick enough to give you an accurate reading, however. In these cases, check the recipe for further instructions.**

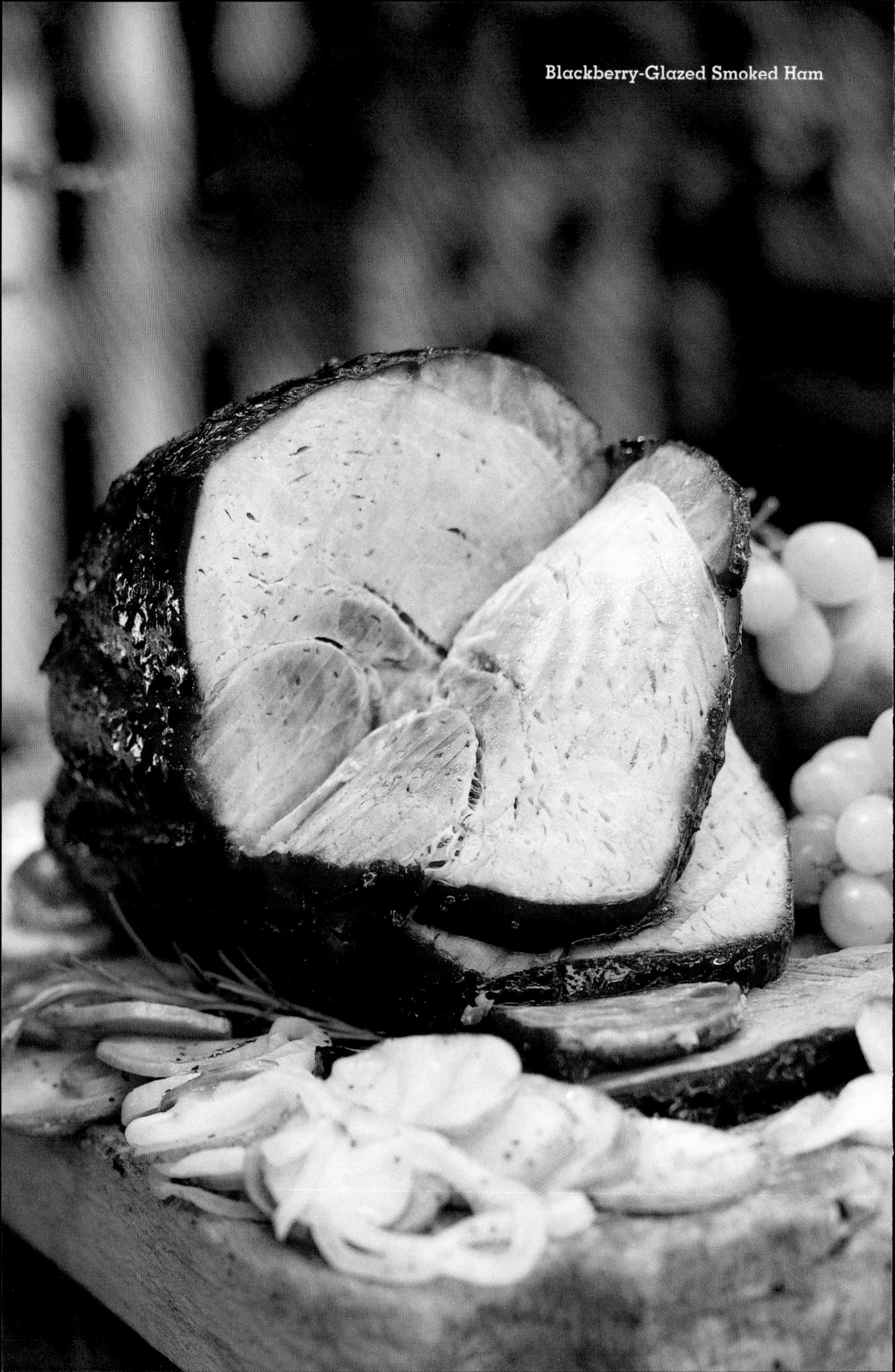

Blackberry-Glazed Smoked Ham

# Blackberry-Glazed Smoked Ham

**Prep:** 10 minutes   **Grill:** 2¼ hours
**Stand:** 15 minutes

*Blackberries speak of the great wild days of
summer. They also make a delicious glaze on this
smoked ham (no picking required with the ease
of blackberry jam). This makes enough for up to
28 people, so plan on it for a hungry crowd.*

   1 6- to 8-pound cooked ham shank
 1½ cups seedless blackberry jam or
         other seedless berry jam
   ¼ cup coarse-grain brown mustard
   2 tablespoons balsamic vinegar

1 Score ham by making shallow cuts in a
diamond pattern. Insert a meat thermometer
into thickest portion of ham without it
touching bone.

2 *For a charcoal grill,* arrange medium coals
around a drip pan. Test for medium-low
heat above the pan. Place ham on grill rack
over drip pan. Cover and grill for 2 to
2½ hours or until thermometer registers 130°.
[*For a gas grill,* preheat grill. Reduce heat to
medium-low. Adjust for indirect cooking (see
page 10). Grill as above, except place ham on
a rack in a roasting pan.]

3 Meanwhile, for sauce, in a medium
saucepan stir together the jam, mustard,
and vinegar. Bring just to boiling; reduce
heat. Simmer, uncovered, for 5 minutes.

4 Brush ham with some of the sauce. Cover
and grill for 15 to 20 minutes more or until
thermometer registers 135°, brushing once or
twice with sauce. Remove ham from grill.
Cover with foil; let stand for 15 minutes
before carving. (The meat's temperature will
rise 5° during standing.)

5 To serve, slice ham. Reheat and pass any
remaining sauce with ham. Makes 20 to
28 servings.

Nutrition Facts per serving: 210 calories,
6 g total fat (2 g saturated fat), 51 mg cholesterol,
1,202 mg sodium, 19 g carbohydrate, 0 g fiber,
20 g protein. Daily Values: 34% vit. C, 1% calcium,
11% iron.

## PIZZA BURGERS

**Prep:** 20 minutes   **Grill:** 14 minutes

   1 beaten egg
   ⅓ cup chopped canned mushrooms,
         drained
   ¼ cup seasoned fine dry bread
         crumbs
   2 tablespoons milk
   ½ teaspoon dried Italian seasoning,
         crushed
   ¼ teaspoon salt
   1 pound ground pork
   1 8-ounce can pizza sauce
   ¼ cup sliced pitted ripe olives
   4 ¾-inch-thick French bread slices,
         toasted
   ¼ cup shredded mozzarella cheese
         (1 ounce)

1 In a medium bowl combine egg,
mushrooms, bread crumbs, milk, Italian
seasoning, and salt. Add ground pork; mix
well. Shape meat mixture into four ¾-inch-
thick patties.

2 *For a charcoal grill,* grill meat on the grill
rack of an uncovered grill directly over
medium coals for 14 to 18 minutes or until
juices run clear, turning once halfway
through grilling. (*For a gas grill,* preheat
grill. Reduce heat to medium. Place meat on
grill rack over heat. Cover and grill as above.)
Remove burgers from grill.

3 In a small saucepan warm the pizza sauce
and olives. To serve, spoon some of the
sauce over toasted bread. Top with burgers.
Spoon remaining sauce over burgers and
sprinkle with cheese. Makes 4 servings.

Nutrition Facts per serving: 316 calories,
15 g total fat (5 g saturated fat), 112 mg cholesterol,
990 mg sodium, 25 g carbohydrate, 22 g protein.
Daily Values: 18% vit. A, 24% vit. C, 8% calcium,
13% iron.

# Apricot-Glazed Ham Burgers

**Prep:** 25 minutes   **Grill:** 15 minutes

*Put the ham back in your burgers. A tangy apricot sauce is the perfect accompaniment for these taste-packed grilled ham and pork patties.*

2 tablespoons brown sugar
4 teaspoons cornstarch
1¼ cups apricot nectar
2 tablespoons vinegar
1 beaten egg
½ cup corn bread stuffing mix
¼ cup sliced green onions
  Dash pepper
1 pound ground cooked ham
1 pound ground pork
8 hamburger buns, split and toasted
8 lettuce leaves

**1** For sauce, in a small saucepan stir together brown sugar and cornstarch. Stir in 1 cup of the apricot nectar and the vinegar. Cook and stir until thickened and bubbly. Cook and stir for 2 minutes more. Keep warm.

**2** In a medium bowl combine the remaining apricot nectar, the egg, stuffing mix, green onions, and pepper. Add ground ham and pork; mix well. Shape the meat mixture into eight ¾-inch-thick patties.

**3** *For a charcoal grill,* grill burgers on the rack of an uncovered grill directly over medium coals for 14 to 18 minutes or until juices run clear, turning once halfway through grilling. (*For a gas grill,* preheat grill. Reduce heat to medium. Place burgers on grill rack over heat. Cover and grill as above.) Remove burgers from grill.

**4** Serve burgers on toasted buns with lettuce leaves. Spoon sauce on burgers. Makes 8 servings.

Nutrition Facts per serving: 339 calories, 10 g total fat (4 g saturated fat), 83 mg cholesterol, 977 mg sodium, 37 g carbohydrate, 1 g fiber, 24 g protein. Daily Values: 8% vit. A, 45% vit. C, 4% calcium, 19% iron.

# CURRANT-GLAZED PORK BURGERS

**Prep:** 15 minutes   **Grill:** 14 minutes

¼ cup currant jelly
3 tablespoons catsup
1 tablespoon vinegar
⅛ teaspoon ground cinnamon
  Dash ground cloves
1 beaten egg
3 tablespoons fine dry bread crumbs
2 tablespoons chopped onion
2 tablespoons milk
¼ teaspoon salt
¼ teaspoon dried thyme, crushed
⅛ teaspoon pepper
1 pound lean ground pork
4 whole wheat hamburger buns, split and toasted
4 lettuce leaves

**1** For sauce, in a small saucepan combine currant jelly, catsup, vinegar, cinnamon, and cloves. Cook and stir just until boiling. Remove from heat and keep warm.

**2** In a medium bowl combine egg, bread crumbs, onion, milk, salt, thyme, and pepper. Add ground pork; mix well. Shape mixture into four ¾-inch-thick patties.

**3** *For a charcoal grill,* grill burgers on the rack of an uncovered grill directly over medium coals for 14 to 18 minutes or until juices run clear, turning once halfway through grilling. (*For a gas grill,* preheat grill. Reduce heat to medium. Place burgers on grill rack over heat. Cover and grill as above.) Remove burgers from grill.

**4** Serve burgers on toasted buns with lettuce leaves. Spoon sauce over burgers. Makes 4 servings.

Nutrition Facts per serving: 347 calories, 11 g total fat (4 g saturated fat), 107 mg cholesterol, 612 mg sodium, 43 g carbohydrate, 3 g fiber, 21 g protein. Daily Values: 5% vit. A, 6% vit. C, 6% calcium, 18% iron.

# Canadian Bacon Pizza

**Prep:** 20 minutes  **Grill:** 8 minutes

*Pizza on the grill is child's play—well, almost. When you use purchased Italian bread shells, all you have to do is toss on the ingredients, put it on the grill for 8 minutes, then cut into wedges.*

  1 6-ounce jar marinated artichoke
    hearts
  4 6-inch Italian bread shells (Boboli)
  ½ cup shredded fontina or
    mozzarella cheese (2 ounces)
  4 slices Canadian-style bacon, cut
    into strips (2 ounces)
  2 plum tomatoes, sliced
  ¼ cup crumbled feta cheese (1 ounce)
  1 green onion, thinly sliced
  2 teaspoons snipped fresh oregano
    or basil

**1** Drain artichoke hearts, reserving marinade. Halve the artichoke hearts lengthwise and set aside.

**2** Brush the bread shells with some of the marinade. Sprinkle with fontina cheese. Divide the artichoke hearts, Canadian bacon, tomatoes, feta cheese, green onion, and oregano among bread shells. Transfer the bread shells to a large piece of double-thickness foil.

**3** *For a charcoal grill,* arrange medium coals in bottom of grill. Place bread shells on grill rack directly over coals. Cover and grill about 8 minutes or until heated through and cheese is melted. (*For a gas grill,* preheat grill. Reduce heat to medium. Place bread shells on grill rack over heat. Grill as above.) Makes 4 servings.

Nutrition Facts per serving: 465 calories, 19 g total fat (6 g saturated fat), 44 mg cholesterol, 1,264 mg sodium, 56 g carbohydrate, 2 g fiber, 23 g protein. Daily Values: 13% vit. A, 34% vit. C, 24% calcium, 19% iron.

# HOMEMADE PORK SAUSAGE

**Prep:** 15 minutes  **Grill:** 14 minutes

*Why make your own sausage? Because it is lower in fat than store-bought and you can tailor the seasonings to your liking. Slip these grilled and skewered sausages onto a plate for a main course or nestle them in hotdog buns for a meal you can wrap your hands around.*

  3 tablespoons finely snipped
    fresh basil
  2 cloves garlic, minced
  1 teaspoon sugar
  1 teaspoon fennel seed
  1 teaspoon crushed red pepper
  ¾ teaspoon salt
  ½ teaspoon black pepper
  1½ pounds lean ground pork

**1** In a large bowl combine the basil, garlic, sugar, fennel seed, red pepper, salt, and black pepper. Add ground pork; mix well. Divide the meat mixture into 4 equal portions. Shape each portion around a flat-sided metal skewer into a 6-inch-long log.

**2** *For a charcoal grill,* grill meat on the rack of an uncovered grill directly over medium coals for 14 to 18 minutes or until meat is no longer pink, turning once halfway through grilling. (*For a gas grill,* preheat grill. Reduce heat to medium. Place meat on grill rack over heat. Cover and grill as above.)

**3** To serve, use the tines of a fork to remove the meat from skewers. Makes 4 servings.

Nutrition Facts per serving: 210 calories, 12 g total fat (5 g saturated fat), 79 mg cholesterol, 469 mg sodium, 2 g carbohydrate, 0 g fiber, 21 g protein. Daily Values: 3% vit. A, 1% vit. C, 1% calcium, 10% iron.

## Flaming Facts

**Aromatic fennel, with its pale green, celerylike stems, and bright green, downy plumes, has a delicate anise-like flavor. The broad, bulbous base can be eaten raw in salads or cooked along with meats, in soups, or in vegetable dishes. The feathery tops make a great garnish snipped over soups or vegetables. You'll find fennel from fall through spring at many supermarkets. It can be stored in the refrigerator in a plastic bag for up to five days.**

## Fennel and Pork Sausage with Grape Relish

**Prep:** 15 minutes    **Grill:** 14 minutes

*Why not make your own classic sausage? Two kinds of fennel make the sausage extraordinary, and the grape relish is out of this world.*

    1  slightly beaten egg
    1  tablespoon bourbon (optional)
    ½  cup quick-cooking rolled oats
    1  tablespoon fennel seed, crushed
    1  large clove garlic, minced
    1  teaspoon finely shredded
          lemon peel
    1  teaspoon paprika
    ½  teaspoon salt
    ½  teaspoon pepper
    1  pound lean ground pork
 1½  cups red seedless grapes, halved
    1  small fennel bulb, coarsely
          chopped (1 cup)
    2  tablespoons balsamic vinegar
    1  tablespoon margarine or butter
       Salt and pepper
    ¼  cup snipped fresh parsley

**1** In a medium bowl combine the egg and, if desired, bourbon. Stir in rolled oats, fennel seed, garlic, lemon peel, paprika, the ½ teaspoon salt, and the ½ teaspoon pepper. Add ground pork; mix well. Shape mixture into four ¾-inch-thick patties. Set aside.

**2** For relish, fold a 36×18-inch piece of heavy foil in half to make an 18-inch square. Place the grapes, chopped fennel, vinegar, and margarine or butter in the center of the foil. Sprinkle with salt and pepper. Bring up opposite edges of foil and seal with a double fold. Fold remaining edges together to completely enclose the grape mixture, leaving space for steam to build.

**3** *For a charcoal grill,* grill patties and relish on the rack of an uncovered grill directly over medium coals for 14 to 18 minutes or until patties are no longer pink, turning once halfway through grilling. (*For a gas grill,* preheat grill. Reduce heat to medium. Place patties and relish on grill rack over heat. Cover and grill as above.)

**4** To serve, spoon relish over sausage patties. Sprinkle with parsley. Makes 4 servings.

Nutrition Facts per serving: 284 calories, 14 g total fat (5 g saturated fat), 106 mg cholesterol, 409 mg sodium, 23 g carbohydrate, 7 g fiber, 18 g protein. Daily Values: 11% vit. A, 28% vit. C, 5% calcium, 17% iron.

## SAUSAGE AND FENNEL KABOBS

**Prep:** 20 minutes    **Grill:** 7 minutes

*Italian sausage and fennel unite for a wonderful taste combination made all the better by the cider-and-fennel glaze.*

    1  pound uncooked sweet or hot
          Italian sausage links
    3  small fennel bulbs with tops
 1⅓  cups apple cider or juice
    2  tablespoons brown sugar
    1  teaspoon snipped fresh oregano
    1  teaspoon fennel seed, crushed
    1  teaspoon olive oil
    ¼  teaspoon ground cumin

**1** Use the tines of a fork to prick several holes in each sausage link. Trim tops from fennel. If desired, reserve tops. Quarter fennel bulbs lengthwise. In a large saucepan combine the sausage, fennel bulbs, and 1 cup of the apple cider. Bring to boiling; reduce heat. Simmer, covered, about 10 minutes or until sausage is no longer pink and fennel is almost tender. Drain; cool slightly.

**2** For glaze, in a small bowl combine remaining apple cider, the brown sugar, oregano, fennel seed, oil, and cumin. Bias-slice each sausage link into 3 pieces. On four 10-inch metal skewers, alternately thread sausage and fennel, leaving ¼-inch space between each piece. Brush with some of the glaze.

**3** For a charcoal grill, grill kabobs on the rack of an uncovered grill directly over medium coals for 7 to 8 minutes or until sausage and fennel are browned and heated through, turning once and brushing occasionally with glaze. (For a gas grill, preheat grill. Reduce heat to medium. Place kabobs on grill rack over heat. Cover; grill as above.) To serve, if desired, arrange kabobs on a bed of the reserved fennel tops. Makes 4 servings.

Nutrition Facts per serving: 382 calories, 23 g total fat (8 g saturated fat), 65 mg cholesterol, 835 mg sodium, 28 g carbohydrate, 33 g fiber, 18 g protein. Daily Values: 28% vit. C, 8% calcium, 13% iron.

## Italian Sausage Pizza

**Prep:** 15 minutes    **Grill:** 28 minutes
**Special equipment:** grill tray or basket

*Grill this classic Italian sausage pizza, that's set apart by the smoky vigor of outdoor cooking. Suddenly you're a gourmet cook.*

    1 cup chopped plum tomatoes
    ½ cup snipped fresh basil
    1 clove garlic, minced
    ¼ teaspoon salt
    12 ounces uncooked sweet or hot
        Italian sausage links
    1 medium onion, cut into ½-inch
        slices

    1 red or yellow sweet pepper, cut
        into 1-inch strips
    4 7-inch packaged prebaked pizza
        crusts
    1 cup shredded mozzarella cheese
        (4 ounces)
    ¼ cup grated Parmesan cheese

**1** In a small bowl combine the tomatoes, basil, garlic, and salt; set aside.

**2** For a charcoal grill, arrange medium-hot coals around a drip pan. Test for medium heat above the pan. Place sausage on grill rack over drip pan. Cover and grill for 12 minutes. Turn sausage. Place onion and sweet pepper on a grill tray or in a grill basket; add to grill directly over coals. Cover and grill for 8 to 12 minutes more or until sausage juices run clear and vegetables are tender, turning once halfway through grilling. [For a gas grill, preheat grill. Reduce heat to medium. Adjust for indirect cooking (see page 10). Grill as above placing onion and sweet pepper directly over heat.] Remove sausage and vegetables from grill. Thinly slice sausage; set aside.

**3** Add pizza crusts to grill directly over coals. Cover and grill crust for 3 minutes. Turn crusts. Divide mozzarella cheese, tomato mixture, sausage, onion, and sweet pepper among the pizza crusts. Sprinkle with Parmesan cheese. Cover and grill about 5 minutes more or until heated through and cheese is melted. Makes 4 servings.

Nutrition Facts per serving: 597 calories, 26 g total fat (10 g saturated fat), 70 mg cholesterol, 1,470 mg sodium, 56 g carbohydrate, 1 g fiber, 32 g protein. Daily Values: 23% vit. A, 72% vit. C, 25% calcium, 9% iron.

## SAUSAGE AND SWEET PEPPER SANDWICHES

**Prep:** 20 minutes   **Grill:** 10 minutes

*Sure, you can easily squirt mustard on your sausage sandwich, but glazed over the meat (and peppers) and grilled gives it a chance to permeate every savory inch.*

4 uncooked sweet or hot Italian sausage links
¼ cup coarse-grain mustard
1 tablespoon water
2 green, yellow, and/or red sweet peppers, quartered lengthwise
¼ cup mayonnaise or salad dressing
4 6-inch French-style rolls, split and toasted

1 Use the tines of a fork to prick several holes in each sausage link. In a large saucepan combine sausage and enough water to cover. Bring to boiling; reduce heat. Simmer, covered, for 5 minutes; drain.

2 For glaze, in a small bowl combine 2 tablespoons of the mustard and the 1 tablespoon water; set aside.

3 For a charcoal grill, grill sausage and sweet peppers on the rack of an uncovered grill directly over medium coals for 10 to 12 minutes or until sausage is evenly browned and the juices run clear, turning and brushing sausage and peppers once with glaze halfway through grilling. (*For a gas grill,* preheat grill. Reduce heat to medium. Place sausage and sweet peppers on grill rack over heat. Cover and grill as above.) Remove sausage and peppers from grill.

4 In a small bowl combine remaining mustard and the mayonnaise. To serve, spread mustard mixture on cut sides of toasted rolls. Fill rolls with sausage and peppers; cut sandwiches in half. Makes 4 servings.

Nutrition Facts per serving: 548 calories, 36 g total fat (10 g saturated fat), 73 mg cholesterol, 1,390 mg sodium, 33 g carbohydrate, 0 g fiber, 23 g protein. Daily Values: 3% vit. A, 46% vit. C, 8% calcium, 22% iron.

# Jalapeño Sausages

**Prep:** 15 minutes   **Chill:** 6 to 24 hours
**Grill:** 20 minutes

*Southwestern-style sausages swaddled in warm tortillas make a blazingly satisfying meal.*

4 ounces fresh jalapeño peppers, seeded and finely chopped, or one 4-ounce can jalapeño peppers, drained and chopped
2 tablespoons snipped fresh cilantro
2 tablespoons beer or water
1 teaspoon cumin seed, crushed
1 clove garlic, minced
½ teaspoon salt
¼ teaspoon black pepper
⅛ teaspoon ground red pepper
1 pound lean ground pork
4 8-inch whole wheat flour or corn tortillas or frankfurter buns
Leaf lettuce (optional)

1 In a medium bowl combine jalapeño peppers, cilantro, beer, cumin seed, garlic, salt, black pepper, and red pepper. Add ground pork; mix well. Shape meat mixture into four 6-inch-long logs or ¾-inch-thick patties. Cover; chill for 6 to 24 hours or until mixture is firm. Stack tortillas; wrap in foil. Set aside.

2 For a charcoal grill, arrange medium-hot coals around a drip pan. Test for medium heat above the pan. Place meat on grill rack over drip pan. Cover; grill for 15 minutes, turning occasionally. Add tortillas to grill directly over coals. Cover; grill for 5 to 10 minutes more or until meat is no longer pink and tortillas are heated through, turning once halfway through grilling. [*For a gas grill,* preheat grill. Reduce heat to medium. Adjust for indirect cooking (see page 10). Grill as above.] To serve, place sausages in warm tortillas. If desired, top with lettuce. Serves 4.

Ⓝutrition Facts per serving: 240 calories, 11 g total fat (4 g saturated fat), 53 mg cholesterol, 432 mg sodium, 18 g carbohydrate, 1 g fiber, 17 g protein. Daily Values: 2% vit. A, 115% vit. C, 50% calcium, 16% iron.

Jalapeño Sausages

## GRILLED ITALIAN SAUSAGE WITH SWEET AND SOUR PEPPERS

**Prep:** 20 minutes    **Grill:** 10 minutes

    3 tablespoons slivered almonds
    ¼ cup raisins
    3 tablespoons red wine vinegar
    2 tablespoons sugar
    ¼ teaspoon salt
    ⅛ teaspoon black pepper
    1 tablespoon olive oil
    2 green sweet peppers, cut into
        1-inch-wide strips
    2 red sweet peppers, cut into 1-inch-
        wide strips
    1 medium red onion, thickly sliced
    6 uncooked sweet Italian sausage
        links

**1** In a small nonstick skillet cook and stir almonds for 1 to 2 minutes or until golden brown; stir in raisins. Remove skillet from heat. Let stand for 1 minute. Carefully stir in the vinegar, sugar, salt, and black pepper. Return to heat; cook and stir just until the sugar dissolves.

**2** Brush oil over sweet pepper strips and onion slices. Use the tines of a fork to prick several holes in each sausage link. *For a charcoal grill,* grill sausages and vegetables on the rack of an uncovered grill directly over medium coals for 10 to 15 minutes or until sausage is evenly browned and the juices run clear, turning once halfway through grilling. (*For a gas grill,* preheat grill. Reduce heat to medium. Place sausages and vegetables on grill rack over heat. Cover and grill as above.)

**3** In the large bowl toss the vegetables with the almond mixture; spoon onto a serving platter. Place the sausages on top of vegetables. Makes 6 servings.

Nutrition Facts per serving: 276 calories, 19 g total fat (6 g saturated fat), 59 mg cholesterol, 604 mg sodium, 15 g carbohydrate, 1 g fiber, 13 g protein. Daily Values: 19% vit. A, 102% vit. C, 2% calcium, 9% iron.

## Italian Pizza Sandwiches

**Prep:** 15 minutes    **Grill:** 20 minutes

    1 medium green sweet pepper, cut
        into thin strips
    1 medium onion, thinly sliced
    1 tablespoon margarine or butter
    4 uncooked sweet or hot Italian
        sausage links
    4 individual French-style rolls, split
        and toasted
    ½ cup pizza sauce, heated
    2 tablespoons grated Parmesan
        cheese

**1** Fold a 36×18-inch piece of heavy foil in half to make an 18-inch square. Place sweet pepper and onion in the center of the foil. Dot with margarine or butter. Bring up opposite edges of foil and seal with double fold. Fold remaining edges together to completely enclose the vegetables, leaving space for steam to build.

**2** Use the tines of a fork to prick several holes in each sausage link.

**3** *For a charcoal grill,* arrange medium-hot coals around a drip pan. Test for medium heat above the pan. Place sausages and foil packet on grill rack over drip pan. Cover and grill for 20 to 25 minutes or until sausage is evenly browned and juices run clear and vegetables are tender. [*For a gas grill,* preheat grill. Reduce heat to medium. Adjust heat for indirect cooking (see page 10). Grill as above.] Remove sausages and foil packet from grill.

**4** To serve, halve sausage links lengthwise, cutting to but not through the other side. Place sausage links in the toasted rolls. Top each with vegetable mixture and pizza sauce. Sprinkle with Parmesan cheese. Makes 4 servings.

Nutrition Facts per serving: 376 calories, 22 g total fat (7 g saturated fat), 51 mg cholesterol, 1,067 mg sodium, 26 g carbohydrate, 0 g fiber, 18 g protein. Daily Values: 11% vit. A, 37% vit. C, 14% iron.

## CHEESE-STUFFED BRATWURST

**Prep:** 10 minutes  **Grill:** 8 minutes

> 5 fully cooked bratwurst or fully cooked smoked Polish sausage
> 2 ounces Monterey Jack cheese with caraway
> ¼ cup thinly sliced green onions
> 5 6-inch French-style rolls or frankfurter buns, split and toasted
>  Catsup, mustard, and/or pickle relish (optional)

**1** Cut a lengthwise slit in each bratwurst or Polish sausage about ½ inch deep. Cut cheese into 5 strips that are 2½×½×¼ inches. Insert a cheese strip and some of the green onion into each bratwurst or Polish sausage.

**2** *For a charcoal grill,* arrange medium-hot coals around a drip pan. Test for medium heat above the pan. Place sausages, cheese side up, on the grill rack over the drip pan. Cover and grill for 8 to 10 minutes or until cheese is melted and bratwurst is heated through. [*For a gas grill,* preheat grill. Reduce heat to medium. Adjust heat for indirect cooking (see page 10). Grill as above.] Remove sausages from grill.

**3** Place sausages in rolls or buns. If desired, serve with catsup, mustard, and/or pickle relish. Makes 5 servings.

Nutrition Facts per serving: 581 calories, 34 g total fat (3 g saturated fat), 10 mg cholesterol, 1,442 mg sodium, 45 g carbohydrate, 23 g protein. Daily Values: 4% vit. A, 1% vit. C, 13% calcium, 16% iron.

# Deluxe Franks with BBQ Sauce

**Prep:** 20 minutes  **Grill:** 8 minutes

> 1 8-ounce can tomato sauce
> ¼ cup chopped onion
> 1 tablespoon coarse-grain brown mustard
> 1 teaspoon sugar
> 1 teaspoon lemon juice
> ¼ teaspoon garlic powder
> 8 frankfurters
> 8 2½×½×¼-inch strips American or cheddar cheese
> 8 slices bacon
> 8 frankfurter buns, split and toasted

**1** For sauce, in a medium saucepan combine tomato sauce, onion, mustard, sugar, lemon juice, and garlic powder. Bring to boiling; reduce heat. Simmer, covered, about 15 minutes or until onion is tender. Remove from heat; set aside.

**2** Cut a lengthwise slit in each frankfurter about ½ inch deep. Insert one strip of cheese into each slit.

**3** In a skillet cook bacon until nearly done but not crisp. Wrap one slice of bacon around each filled frankfurter.

**4** *For a charcoal grill,* grill frankfurters, cheese side up, on the rack of an uncovered grill directly over medium coals for 8 to 10 minutes or until bacon is cooked and frankfurters are heated through. (*For a gas grill,* preheat grill. Reduce heat to medium. Place frankfurters on grill rack over heat. Cover and grill as above.) Remove frankfurters from grill.

**5** To serve, dip frankfurters in sauce and place in buns. Serve with remaining sauce. Makes 8 servings.

Nutrition Facts per serving: 375 calories, 24 g total fat (10 g saturated fat), 46 mg cholesterol, 1,183 mg sodium, 26 g carbohydrate, 1 g fiber, 14 g protein. Daily Values: 5% vit. A, 30% vit. C, 7% calcium, 14% iron.

## CHICAGO-STYLE HOT DOGS

**Prep:** 10 minutes   **Grill:** 14 minutes

*They know how to do things right in the Windy City. Why not try these Chicago-style dogs, and maybe catch a Cubs game on the tube?*

⅓ cup catsup
¼ cup chopped pickled peppers
2 tablespoons pickle relish
2 tablespoons chopped onion
¼ teaspoon poppy seed
4 jumbo frankfurters (about 1 pound total)
4 frankfurter buns, split and toasted

**1** For sauce, in a small bowl combine the catsup, pickled peppers, relish, onion, and poppy seed.

**2** *For a charcoal grill,* grill frankfurters on the rack of an uncovered grill directly over medium coals for 14 to 16 minutes or until heated through, turning and brushing once with sauce halfway through grilling. (*For a gas grill,* preheat grill. Reduce heat to medium. Place frankfurters on grill rack over heat. Cover and grill as above.) Remove frankfurters from grill.

**3** Serve frankfurters in toasted buns; top with sauce. Makes 4 servings.

Nutrition Facts per serving: 528 calories, 35 g total fat (13 g saturated fat), 58 mg cholesterol, 2,052 mg sodium, 35 g carbohydrate, 0 g fiber, 17 g protein. Daily Values: 52% vit. A, 68% vit. C, 6% calcium, 19% iron.

# Hot Tots and Brats

**Prep:** 15 minutes   **Grill:** 47 minutes

4 uncooked bratwurst links (about 12 ounces total)
½ cup Italian salad dressing
3 tablespoons Dijon-style mustard
1 pound tiny new potatoes, quartered
1 medium onion, cut into wedges
Cracked black pepper
3 medium red, yellow, or green sweet peppers, quartered lengthwise

**1** Use the tines of a fork to prick several holes in each bratwurst. For sauce, in a small bowl stir together Italian salad dressing and Dijon mustard. Reserve ¼ cup of the sauce.

**2** Fold a 36×18-inch piece of heavy foil in half to make an 18-inch square. Place potatoes and onion in center of foil. Drizzle with remaining sauce. Sprinkle with black pepper. Bring up opposite edges of foil and seal with a double fold. Fold remaining edges together to completely enclose potato-and-onion mixture, leaving space for steam to build.

**3** *For a charcoal grill,* arrange medium-hot coals around a drip pan. Test for medium heat above the pan. Place foil packet on grill rack directly over coals. Cover and grill for 25 minutes. Turn packet over. Add bratwursts to grill over drip pan; brush with some of the reserved sauce. Cover and grill for 15 minutes. Turn bratwursts; brush with the rest of the reserved sauce.

**4** Add sweet peppers to grill directly over coals. Cover and grill peppers, foil packet, and bratwurst for 7 to 8 minutes or until peppers are crisp-tender, potatoes are tender, and bratwurst juices run clear, turning peppers once halfway through grilling. [*For a gas grill,* preheat grill. Reduce heat to medium. Adjust for indirect cooking (see page 10). Grill as above.] To serve, combine peppers with potatoes and onion. Serve over grilled bratwurst. Makes 4 servings.

Nutrition Facts per serving: 568 calories, 41 g total fat (2 g saturated fat), 51 mg cholesterol, 1,139 mg sodium, 35 g carbohydrate, 2 g fiber, 15 g protein. Daily Values: 41% vit. A, 181% vit. C, 2% calcium, 14% iron.

## BRATWURSTS IN BEER

**Prep:** 30 minutes   **Grill:** 17 minutes

- **6 uncooked bratwurst links (about 1¼ pounds total)**
- **3 12-ounce cans beer**
- **6 frankfurter buns, split and toasted**
  **Various mustards**
  **Catsup**
- **1 8-ounce can sauerkraut, heated and drained (optional)**

**1** Use the tines of a fork to prick several holes in each bratwurst. In a Dutch oven combine bratwursts and beer. Bring to boiling; reduce heat. Simmer, covered, about 20 minutes or until bratwursts are no longer pink; drain.

**2** *For a charcoal grill,* grill bratwursts on the rack of an uncovered grill directly over medium coals for 7 to 8 minutes or until bratwursts are browned, turning once halfway through grilling. (*For a gas grill,* preheat grill. Reduce heat to medium. Place bratwursts on grill rack over heat. Cover and grill as above.) Remove bratwursts from grill.

**3** Serve bratwursts in toasted buns with mustards, catsup, and, if desired, sauerkraut. Makes 6 servings.

Nutrition Facts per serving: 379 calories, 24 g total fat (8 g saturated fat), 51 mg cholesterol, 676 mg sodium, 23 g carbohydrate, 1 g fiber, 15 g protein. Daily Values: 1% vit. C, 5% calcium, 13% iron.

# Mustardy Brats with Sauerkraut

**Prep:** 15 minutes   **Grill:** 20 minutes

- **1 tablespoon margarine or butter**
- **½ cup chopped green sweet pepper**
- **1 small onion, chopped (⅓ cup)**
- **2 tablespoons brown sugar**
- **1 teaspoon prepared mustard**
- **½ teaspoon caraway seed**
- **1 cup drained sauerkraut**
- **6 uncooked bratwurst links (1¼ to 1½ pounds)**
- **6 hoagie buns, split and toasted**

**1** In a small skillet heat margarine or butter over medium heat until melted. Add green pepper and onion. Cook over medium heat about 5 minutes or until tender. Stir in brown sugar, mustard, and caraway seed. Add sauerkraut; toss to mix. Fold a 36×18-inch piece of heavy foil in half to make an 18-inch square. Place sauerkraut mixture in center of foil. Bring up opposite edges of foil and seal with a double fold. Fold remaining edges together to completely enclose sauerkraut mixture, leaving space for steam to build.

**2** Use the tines of a fork to prick several holes in each bratwurst. *For a charcoal grill,* arrange medium-hot coals around a drip pan. Test for medium heat above the pan. Place bratwurst and the foil packet on grill rack over drip pan. Cover and grill for 20 to 25 minutes or until bratwurst juices run clear, turning once halfway through grilling. [*For a gas grill,* preheat grill. Reduce heat to medium. Adjust for indirect cooking (see page 10). Grill as above.] Remove bratwurst and packet from grill.

**3** Serve bratwurst on toasted buns; top with sauerkraut mixture. Makes 6 servings.

Nutrition Facts per serving: 663 calories, 27 g total fat (10 g saturated fat), 46 mg cholesterol, 1,472 mg sodium, 83 g carbohydrate, 5 g fiber, 22 g protein. Daily Values: 2% vit. A, 48% vit. C, 6% calcium, 29% iron.

Test for the desired temperature (see How Hot is It? page 11). Place the meat on the rack of a grill directly over the preheated coals (for direct grilling) or directly over a drip pan (for indirect grilling). Grill meat (uncovered for direct grilling or covered for indirect grilling) for the time given below or until done, turning the meat over halfway through the grilling time.

# Grilling Chart

| Cut | Thickness or Weight | Coal Temperature | Grilling** Doneness | Direct Grilling** Time | Indirect Time |
|---|---|---|---|---|---|
| **PORK*** | | | | | |
| Boneless top loin roast | 2 to 4 lbs. (single loin) | Medium-low | 160° | | 1 to 1¼ hrs. |
| | 3 to 5 lbs. (double loin, tied) | Medium-low | 160° | | 1¼ to 2¼ hrs. |
| Chop | ¾ inch | Medium | Medium | 8 to 11 min. | 20 to 24 min. |
| | 1¼ to 1½ inches | Medium | Medium | 25 to 30 min. | 35 to 40 min. |
| Ham (fully cooked) Boneless half | 4 to 6 lbs. | Medium-low | 140° | | 1¼ to 2½ hrs. |
| Boneless portion | 3 to 4 lbs. | Medium-low | 140° | | 1½ to 2¼ hrs. |
| Smoked picnic | 5 to 6 lbs. | Medium-low | 140° | | 2 to 3 hrs. |
| Ham slice (fully cooked) | 1 inch | Medium-hot | Heated through | | 20 to 24 min. |
| Loin blade or sirloin roast | 3 to 4 lbs. | Medium-low | 170° | | 1¾ to 2½ hrs. |
| Loin center rib roast (backbone loosened) | 3 to 5 lbs. | Medium-low | 160° | | 1¼ to 2½ hrs. |
| Ribs, baby back | 2 to 4 lbs. | Medium | Medium | | 1¼ to 1½ hrs. |
| Ribs, country-style | 2 to 4 lbs. | Medium | Well-done | | 1½ to 2 hrs. |
| Ribs, loin back or spareribs | 2 to 4 lbs. | Medium | Well-done | | 1¼ to 1½ hrs. |
| Tenderloin | ¾ to 1 lb. | Medium | 160° | | 30 to 45 min. |

*Note: Pork should be cooked until juices run clear.
**Note: For differences in direct and indirect grilling methods, see page 10.

# Chicken and Turkey

# Southwestern Chicken Burgers

**Prep:** 15 minutes **Grill:** 15 minutes

*Get along, little chicken burgers. These burgers are like a taco in a bun, obtaining some of their flavor from nacho-flavored tortilla chips. Jack cheese, avocado slices, and salsa top the burgers.*

1 slightly beaten egg
¼ cup crushed nacho-flavor or plain tortilla chips
3 tablespoons finely chopped green sweet pepper
¾ teaspoon chili powder
¼ teaspoon salt
¼ teaspoon black pepper
1 pound uncooked ground chicken
1 avocado, seeded, peeled, and sliced
4 ounces sliced Monterey Jack cheese with jalapeño peppers
4 kaiser rolls or hamburger buns, split and toasted
   Lettuce leaves
   Salsa

1 In a bowl combine egg, tortilla chips, sweet pepper, chili powder, salt, and black pepper. Add chicken; mix well. Shape the chicken mixture into four ¾-inch-thick patties.

2 *For a charcoal grill,* grill burgers on the rack of an uncovered grill directly over medium coals for 14 to 18 minutes or until no longer pink, turning once halfway through grilling. (*For a gas grill,* preheat grill. Reduce heat to medium. Place burgers on grill rack over heat. Cover and grill as above.) Remove burgers from grill.

3 Top burgers with avocado and cheese. Grill for 1 to 2 minutes more or until cheese is melted. Remove burgers from grill.

4 Serve burgers on toasted rolls with lettuce and salsa. Makes 4 servings.

Nutrition Facts per serving: 424 calories,
23 g total fat (9 g saturated fat), 133 mg cholesterol,
674 mg sodium, 26 g carbohydrate, 2 g fiber,
29 g protein. Daily Values: 23% vit. A, 20% vit. C,
37% calcium, 20% iron.

# CANTONESE CHICKEN BURGERS

**Prep:** 15 minutes **Grill:** 16 minutes

1 slightly beaten egg
1 teaspoon toasted sesame oil
1 teaspoon soy sauce
⅓ cup fine dry bread crumbs
¼ cup chopped peanuts
1 green onion, thinly sliced
2 tablespoons shredded carrot
⅛ teaspoon garlic powder
1 pound uncooked ground chicken or turkey
4 hamburger buns with sesame seeds, split and toasted
8 fresh spinach leaves, shredded
¼ cup plum sauce

1 In a large bowl combine egg, sesame oil, and soy sauce. Stir in the bread crumbs, peanuts, green onion, carrot, and garlic powder. Add ground chicken or turkey, stirring to mix well. Shape chicken mixture into four ¾-inch-thick patties.

2 *For a charcoal grill,* grill burgers on the rack of an uncovered grill directly over medium coals 16 to 18 minutes or until no longer pink, turning once halfway through grilling. (*For a gas grill,* preheat grill. Reduce heat to medium. Place burgers on grill rack over heat. Cover and grill as above.) Remove burgers from grill.

3 Serve burgers on toasted buns with shredded spinach and plum sauce. Makes 4 servings.

Nutrition Facts per serving: 377 calories,
15 g total fat (3 g saturated fat), 108 mg cholesterol,
429 mg sodium, 35 g carbohydrate, 2 g fiber,
25 g protein. Daily Values: 17% vit. A, 4% vit. C,
5% calcium, 17% iron.

# Smoky Chicken Wraps

**Prep:** 20 minutes   **Soak:** 1 hour
**Marinate:** 15 minutes   **Grill:** 10 minutes

*Pine nuts, dried tomatoes, and mesquite-smoked chicken blend deliciously in tortillas spread with cream cheese. That's a wrap, folks.*

>  2 cups mesquite wood chips
>  3 medium skinless, boneless
>     chicken breast halves (about
>     12 ounces total)
>  1 tablespoon cooking oil
>  1 tablespoon Worcestershire sauce
>  1 teaspoon snipped fresh thyme
>  ¼ teaspoon pepper
>  ½ of an 8-ounce tub cream cheese
>  2 oil-packed dried tomatoes, drained
>     and finely chopped
>  2 tablespoons chopped pine nuts or
>     almonds (optional)
>     Salt and pepper
>  4 8- to 9-inch tomato tortillas
>     or plain flour tortillas
> 16 fresh basil leaves, cut into thin
>     strips

**1** At least 1 hour before grilling, soak wood chips in enough water to cover. Place chicken in a shallow dish. For marinade, in a small bowl combine oil, Worcestershire sauce, thyme, and pepper. Pour over chicken, turning chicken pieces to coat with marinade. Marinate at room temperature for 15 minutes.

**2** Meanwhile, in small bowl stir together cream cheese, dried tomatoes, and, if desired, pine nuts or almonds. If necessary, stir in enough water to make of spreading consistency. Season to taste with salt and pepper; set aside. Stack tortillas and wrap in a piece of heavy foil.

**3** Drain wood chips. *For a charcoal grill,* place medium-hot coals in bottom of grill. Sprinkle wood chips over coals. Place chicken and tortillas on grill rack directly over coals. Cover and grill until chicken is tender and no longer pink and tortillas are heated through, turning chicken once halfway through. (Allow 10 to 12 minutes for chicken

and about 5 minutes for tortillas.) (*For a gas grill,* preheat grill. Reduce heat to medium-hot. Add wood chips according to manufacturer's directions. Place chicken and tortillas on grill rack over heat. Cover and grill as above.)

**4** Transfer chicken to a cutting board; cool slightly and thinly slice. Spread the cream cheese mixture over tortillas; sprinkle with basil. Divide chicken among tortillas; roll up. Makes 4 servings.

Nutrition Facts per serving: 454 calories, 21 g total fat (6 g saturated fat), 77 mg cholesterol, 798 mg sodium, 42 g carbohydrate, 1 g fiber, 26 g protein. Daily Values: 5% vit. A, 17% vit. C, 7% calcium, 21% iron.

# VIETNAMESE-STYLE CHICKEN BREASTS

**Prep:** 15 minutes   **Grill:** 12 minutes

*Sweet-and-spicy peanut sauce tops chicken for a sandwich that will wake up your tastebuds.*

>  2 tablespoons sugar
>  2 tablespoons peanut butter
>  2 tablespoons soy sauce
>  2 tablespoons water
>  1 tablespoon cooking oil
>  1 clove garlic, minced
>  2 teaspoons toasted sesame oil
>  ½ teaspoon crushed red pepper
>  4 medium skinless, boneless
>     chicken breast halves
>     (about 1 pound total)
>  4 French-style rolls, split and
>     toasted
>  ½ cup packaged shredded broccoli
>     (broccoli slaw mix)
>  ¼ cup chopped peanuts (optional)

**1** For sauce, in a small saucepan* stir together sugar, peanut butter, soy sauce, water, cooking oil, and garlic. Set aside. Combine sesame oil and crushed red pepper; brush over chicken.

**2** *For a charcoal grill,* grill chicken on the rack and sauce in saucepan on the rack of an uncovered grill directly over medium coals for 12 to 15 minutes or until chicken is tender and no longer pink and sauce is heated through, turning chicken once halfway through and stirring sauce frequently. (*For a gas grill*, preheat grill. Reduce heat to medium. Place chicken and sauce in saucepan on grill rack over heat. Cover and grill as above.) Remove chicken and sauce from grill.

**3** Serve chicken on toasted rolls with sauce, shredded broccoli, and, if desired, peanuts. Makes 4 servings.

Nutrition Facts per serving: 409 calories, 15 g total fat (3 g saturated fat), 59 mg cholesterol, 959 mg sodium, 38 g carbohydrate, 1 g fiber, 29 g protein. Daily Values: 3% vit. A, 17% vit. C, 6% calcium, 18% iron.

*Note:* The heat from the grill will blacken the outside of the saucepan, so use an old one or a small cast-iron skillet.

# Mesquite-Grilled Chicken Sandwich

**Prep:** 15 minutes    **Grill:** 5 minutes

*A lime and mayonnaise mixture is the perfect partner to the flavor of these mesquite-kissed chicken sandwiches which are special enough to serve the most regal of guests.*

> 2 cups mesquite wood chips
> ¼ cup fat-free mayonnaise or salad dressing
> 1 teaspoon white wine Worcestershire sauce
> ½ teaspoon finely shredded lime peel or lemon peel
> 4 medium skinless, boneless chicken breast halves (about 1 pound total)
> 2 tablespoons white wine Worcestershire sauce
> ¼ to ½ teaspoon garlic pepper
> ⅛ teaspoon salt

> ½ cup shredded part-skim mozzarella cheese (2 ounces)
> 4 whole wheat hamburger buns, split and toasted
> 4 tomato slices
> ½ of a large avocado, seeded, peeled, and thinly sliced

**1** At least 1 hour before grilling, soak wood chips in enough water to cover.

**2** Meanwhile, combine mayonnaise, the 1 teaspoon Worcestershire sauce, and lime peel. Cover and refrigerate until serving time.

**3** Place each chicken piece between two pieces of plastic wrap. Use the flat side of a meat mallet to pound chicken to about ½ inch thick. Brush both sides of each chicken piece with the 2 tablespoons Worcestershire sauce; sprinkle with garlic pepper and salt.

**4** Drain wood chips. *For a charcoal grill,* place medium coals in the bottom of grill. Sprinkle wood chips over coals. Grill chicken on the rack of an uncovered grill directly over medium coals for 5 to 7 minutes or until tender and no longer pink, turning once halfway through grilling. Sprinkle each piece of chicken with cheese. Continue grilling just until cheese melts. (*For a gas grill,* preheat grill. Reduce heat to medium. Place chicken on grill rack over heat. Add wood chips according to manufacturer's directions. Cover and grill as above.) Remove the chicken from the grill.

**5** Serve chicken on toasted buns; top with mayonnaise mixture, tomatoes, and avocado. Makes 4 servings.

Nutrition Facts per serving: 320 calories, 10 g total fat (3 g saturated fat), 67 mg cholesterol, 680 mg sodium, 29 g carbohydrate, 3 g fiber, 30 g protein. Daily Values: 6% vit. A, 10% vit. C, 13% calcium, 14% iron.

## CHICKEN MOLE SANDWICH

**Prep:** 25 minutes   **Grill:** 12 minutes
**Chill:** 30 minutes

*It's the mole that makes this sandwich a zinger. Would you believe a sauce of chocolate and Mexican chile peppers could taste this good?*

¼ cup chopped onion
3 cloves garlic, minced
1 tablespoon cooking oil
½ cup water
3 dried chile peppers (New Mexico or pasilla), seeded and coarsely chopped
3 tablespoons chopped Mexican-style sweet chocolate or semisweet chocolate (1½ ounces)
4 medium skinless, boneless chicken breast halves (about 1 pound total)
Salt (optional)
1 small avocado, seeded, peeled, and mashed
2 tablespoons light mayonnaise dressing
¼ teaspoon ground red pepper (optional)
⅛ teaspoon salt
4 hard rolls (about 6 inches in diameter), split and toasted
Tomato slices
Baby romaine or other lettuce leaves

**1** For mole, in a large skillet cook onion and garlic in hot oil over medium-high heat until onion is tender. Add water and dried chile peppers. Reduce heat to medium; stir in chocolate. Cook and stir for 3 to 5 minutes or until thickened and bubbly. Cool slightly. Transfer mixture to a food processor bowl or blender container. Cover and process or blend until a smooth paste forms. Reserve 1 to 2 tablespoons of the mole.

**2** If desired, sprinkle chicken with salt. Using a sharp knife, cut a slit horizontally two-thirds of the way through each chicken piece.

Spread meat open; fill with remaining mole. Fold closed. Rub the outside of the chicken with the reserved mole.

**3** *For a charcoal grill,* grill chicken on the rack of an uncovered grill directly over medium coals for 12 to 15 minutes or until tender and no longer pink, turning once halfway through. (*For a gas grill,* preheat grill. Reduce heat to medium. Place chicken on grill rack over heat. Cover and grill as above.) Cover and chill for 30 minutes.

**4** In a small bowl stir together avocado, mayonnaise dressing, ground red pepper (if desired), and the ⅛ teaspoon salt. To serve, cut chicken into ¼- to ½-inch slices. Spread avocado mixture on split rolls; layer with tomato, chicken, and romaine. Serves 4.

Nutrition Facts per sandwich: 496 calories, 22 g total fat (5 g saturated fat), 59 mg cholesterol, 542 mg sodium, 45 g carbohydrate, 5 g fiber, 30 g protein. Daily Values: 34% vit. A, 15% vit. C, 8% calcium, 29% iron.

## Sizzlin' Solutions

**Boneless chicken breasts are ideal for grilled sandwiches. Try these simple ideas:**
• **Toss chopped grilled chicken with a spoonful of mayonnaise and pesto. Serve on a hard roll and top with a tomato slice.**
• **Sprinkle boneless chicken breasts with Cajun seasoning; grill. Serve on toasted buns and top with sliced avocado.**
• **Marinate boneless chicken breasts in a little olive oil and balsamic vinegar; grill. Serve on toasted buns; top with roasted red sweet peppers and mayonnaise.**

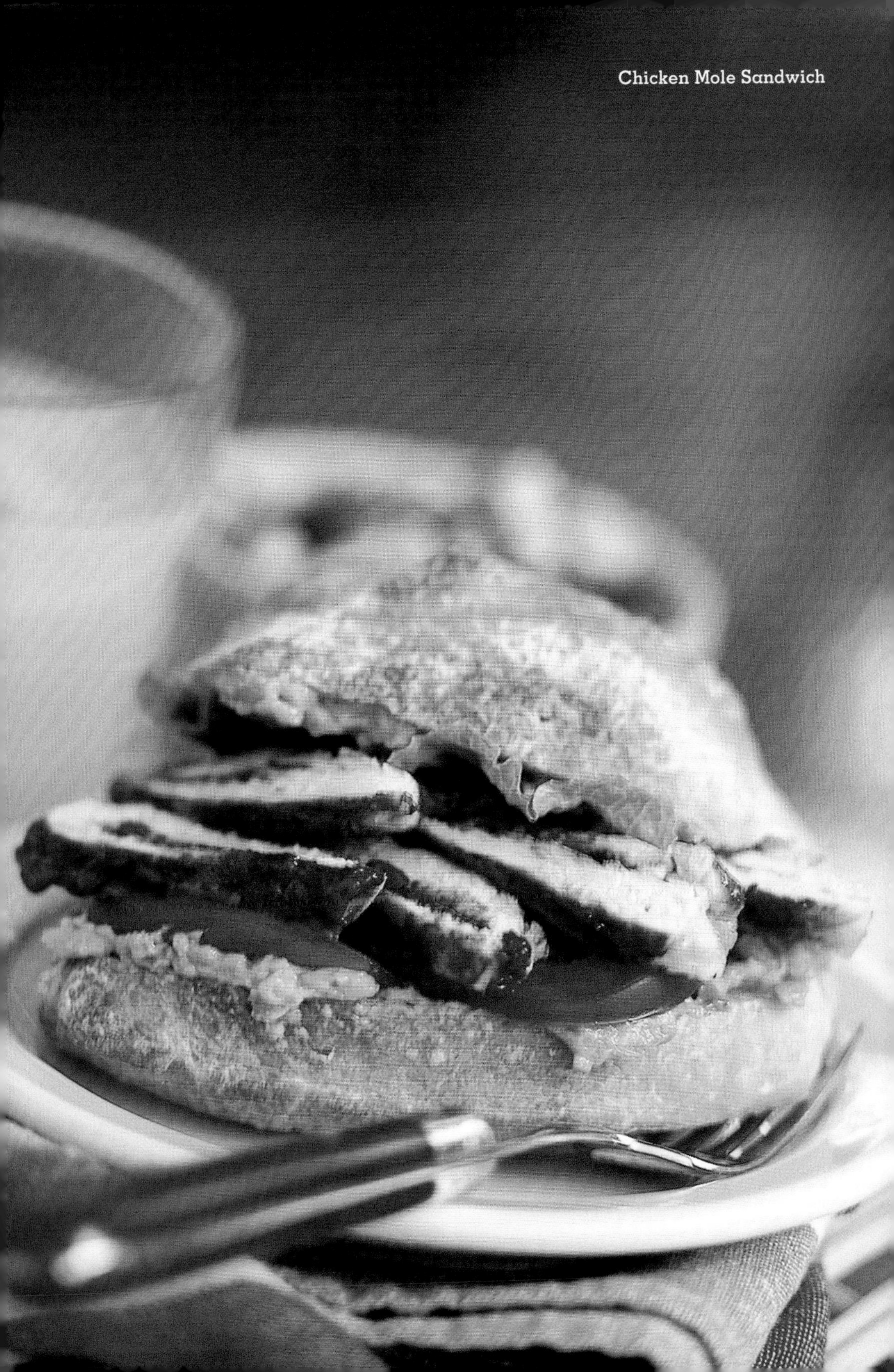

Chicken Mole Sandwich

# Apple and Chicken Salad

**Prep:** 20 minutes **Grill:** 12 minutes

*Tart apples and an apple jelly glaze on the grilled chicken make a delightful combination in this Waldorf-inspired salad.*

⅓ cup apple jelly
¼ cup horseradish mustard
4 medium skinless, boneless chicken breast halves (about 12 ounces total)
4 cups mesclun or torn mixed salad greens
2 tart medium apples, such as Granny Smith, Jonathan, or McIntosh, cored and sliced
⅓ cup coarsely chopped walnuts (toasted, if desired)
1 tablespoon cider vinegar
1 tablespoon salad oil

**1** For glaze, in a small saucepan cook and stir apple jelly over low heat until melted. Remove from heat; stir in mustard. Reserve all but 2 tablespoons of the glaze.

**2** *For a charcoal grill,* grill chicken on the rack of an uncovered grill directly over medium coals for 12 to 15 minutes or until tender and no longer pink, turning once and brushing occasionally with the 2 tablespoons glaze during the last 5 minutes of grilling. (*For a gas grill,* preheat grill. Reduce heat to medium. Place chicken on grill rack over heat. Cover and grill as above.) Transfer chicken to a cutting board; cool slightly. Slice chicken diagonally.

**3** Meanwhile, in a medium bowl toss mesclun with the apples and walnuts. For dressing, stir together reserved glaze, vinegar, and oil. Divide greens mixture among 4 dinner plates. Arrange chicken on greens; drizzle with the dressing. Makes 4 servings.

Nutrition Facts per serving: 307 calories, 13 g total fat (2 g saturated fat), 45 mg cholesterol, 186 mg sodium, 30 g carbohydrate, 2 g fiber, 19 g protein. Daily Values: 2% vit. A, 11% vit. C, 3% calcium, 10% iron.

# CHICKEN AND VEGETABLE SALAD

**Prep:** 20 minutes **Grill:** 17 minutes

1 cup sliced cauliflower or broccoli florets
1 cup baby carrots
1 medium red and/or yellow sweet pepper, cut into strips
1 small red onion, thinly sliced and separated into rings
½ cup bottled honey-mustard salad dressing
4 medium skinless, boneless chicken breast halves (about 1 pound total)
6 cups torn mixed salad greens
1½ cups cherry tomatoes, halved

**1** Fold a 48×18-inch piece of heavy foil in half to make a 24×18-inch rectangle. Place cauliflower, carrots, sweet pepper, and onion in center of foil. Pour ¼ cup of the dressing over vegetables; toss to coat. Bring up opposite edges of foil and seal with a double fold. Fold remaining edges together to completely enclose vegetables, leaving space for steam to build. Brush chicken with the remaining dressing.

**2** *For a charcoal grill,* grill vegetables on the rack of an uncovered grill directly over medium coals for 5 minutes. Add chicken to grill. Grill for 12 to 15 minutes more or until chicken is tender and no longer pink and vegetables are tender, turning once halfway through. (*For a gas grill,* preheat grill. Reduce heat to medium. Place vegetables, then chicken on grill rack over heat. Cover and grill as above.)

**3** To serve, divide greens and tomatoes among 4 dinner plates. Diagonally slice chicken; arrange on top of greens. Divide vegetables among plates. If desired, drizzle with additional dressing. Makes 4 servings.

Nutrition Facts per serving: 320 calories, 19 g total fat (3 g saturated fat), 64 mg cholesterol, 342 mg sodium, 15 g carbohydrate, 4 g fiber, 24 g protein. Daily Values: 102% vit. A, 109% vit. C, 5% calcium, 14% iron.

# Southwest Chicken Salad

**Prep:** 15 minutes   **Grill:** 12 minutes

- ½ cup bottled poppy seed salad dressing
- 1 small fresh jalapeño pepper, seeded and finely chopped
- ½ teaspoon finely shredded orange peel
- 4 medium skinless, boneless chicken breast halves (about 1 pound total)
- 2 oranges, peeled and sliced ½ inch thick
- 1 red sweet pepper, quartered lengthwise
- 8 cups torn mixed salad greens
- 1 small jicama, peeled and cut into thin, bite-size strips

**1** In a small bowl combine dressing, jalapeño pepper, and orange peel. Reserve all but 1 tablespoon of dressing mixture. Brush chicken, orange slices, and sweet pepper with the 1 tablespoon dressing mixture.

**2** *For a charcoal grill*, grill chicken, orange slices, and sweet pepper on the rack of an uncovered grill directly over medium coals for 12 to 15 minutes or until chicken and pepper are tender, chicken is no longer pink, and oranges are heated through, turning once halfway through grilling. (*For a gas grill*, preheat grill. Reduce heat to medium. Place chicken, orange slices, and sweet pepper on grill rack over heat. Cover; grill as above.) Transfer chicken, orange slices, and sweet pepper to a cutting board; cool slightly. Cut chicken and sweet pepper into bite-size strips; quarter the orange slices.

**3** Meanwhile, in a salad bowl toss together greens and jicama. Add chicken, oranges, and sweet pepper. Drizzle with reserved dressing mixture; toss to coat. Serves 4.

Nutrition Facts per serving: 339 calories, 18 g total fat (3 g saturated fat), 59 mg cholesterol, 194 mg sodium, 22 g carbohydrate, 3 g fiber, 24 g protein. Daily Values: 26% vit. A, 147% vit. C, 5% calcium, 11% iron.

# CHICKEN AND SALSA SALAD

**Prep:** 15 minutes   **Grill:** 12 minutes

- 4 small tomatoes, peeled, seeded, and finely chopped
- ½ of a 4-ounce can (3 tablespoons) diced green chile peppers, drained
- 2 tablespoons chopped green sweet pepper
- 2 tablespoons sliced green onion
- 2 tablespoons snipped fresh cilantro
- 2 tablespoons lemon juice
- 1 clove garlic, minced
- ⅛ teaspoon black pepper
- 4 medium skinless, boneless chicken breast halves (about 1 pound total)
  Cooking oil
  Salt
  Black pepper
- 1 10-ounce package (about 8 cups) torn mixed salad greens

**1** For salsa, combine tomatoes, chile peppers, sweet pepper, green onion, cilantro, lemon juice, garlic, and black pepper. Cover and chill, stirring occasionally. Bring to room temperature to serve.

**2** Brush chicken lightly with cooking oil; sprinkle with salt and black pepper. *For a charcoal grill*, grill chicken on the rack of an uncovered grill directly over medium coals for 12 to 15 minutes or until tender and no longer pink, turning once halfway through grilling. (*For a gas grill*, preheat grill. Reduce heat to medium. Place chicken on grill rack over heat. Cover and grill as above.)

**3** Line 4 salad plates with mixed greens. Top each with a chicken breast and salsa. Makes 4 servings.

Nutrition Facts per serving: 157 calories, 4 g total fat (1 g saturated fat), 59 mg cholesterol, 111 mg sodium, 8 g carbohydrate, 2 g fiber, 23 g protein. Daily Values: 11% vit. A, 70% vit. C, 4% calcium, 9% iron.

# Chicken Kabobs with Plum Vinaigrette

**Prep:** 35 minutes   **Grill:** 10 minutes

*Sometimes a kabob is just plum good. Plum sauce is used in the vinaigrette and fresh plums are threaded onto skewers.*

⅓ cup white wine vinegar
¼ cup plum sauce
3 tablespoons salad oil
¼ teaspoon ground coriander
¼ teaspoon coarsely ground black
  pepper
4 medium skinless, boneless
  chicken breast halves (about
  1 pound total)
Salt and black pepper (optional)
1 medium yellow, red, or green
  sweet pepper, cut into
  1-inch pieces
4 medium plums
6 cups torn red-tip leaf lettuce
1 cup fresh pea pods, tips and
  strings removed and halved

**1** For vinaigrette, in a small bowl combine vinegar, plum sauce, oil, coriander, and black pepper. Set aside 3 tablespoons to brush on kabobs; reserve the remaining mixture for the dressing.

**2** If desired, sprinkle chicken with salt and black pepper. Cut chicken into 2×1-inch strips. On 4 long metal skewers, alternately thread chicken strips, accordion style, with sweet pepper pieces, leaving a ¼-inch space between each piece. Pit plums; cut each plum into 8 wedges. Thread plums onto 4 more metal skewers.

**3** *For a charcoal grill,* grill chicken and plum kabobs on the rack of an uncovered grill directly over medium coals until chicken and pepper are tender, chicken is no longer pink, and plums are heated through, turning once and brushing occasionally with the 3 tablespoons vinaigrette during the last half of grilling. (Allow 10 to 12 minutes for chicken kabobs and 3 to 5 minutes for plum kabobs.) (*For a gas grill,* preheat grill. Reduce heat to medium. Place chicken and plum kabobs on grill rack over heat. Cover and grill as above.)

**4** Remove chicken, sweet pepper, and plums from skewers. Divide leaf lettuce among 4 dinner plates. Top with chicken, sweet pepper, plums, and pea pods. Serve with the remaining vinaigrette. Makes 4 servings.

Nutrition Facts per serving: 305 calories, 14 g total fat (2 g saturated fat), 59 mg cholesterol, 67 mg sodium, 22 g carbohydrate, 4 g fiber, 25 g protein. Daily Values: 20% vit. A, 149% vit. C, 7% calcium, 19% iron.

# JERK CHICKEN SALAD

**Prep:** 20 minutes  **Grill:** 12 minutes

⅓ cup olive oil
2 tablespoons lime juice
2 teaspoons snipped fresh thyme or
  ½ teaspoon dried thyme,
  crushed
1 teaspoon honey
4 skinless, boneless chicken breast
  halves (about 1 pound total)
1 plantain, 2 red bananas, or 1 large
  yellow banana, sliced
2 tablespoons Jamaican jerk
  seasoning
1 medium red or yellow sweet
  pepper, cut into strips
6 cups torn mixed salad greens
1 medium avocado, seeded, peeled,
  and cut into thin wedges
1 medium mango, peeled and cut
  into thin wedges

**1** For dressing, in a screw-top jar combine oil, lime juice, thyme, and honey; cover and shake well. Remove 1 tablespoon dressing. Set remaining dressing aside.

**2** Brush chicken and plantain or red bananas with the 1 tablespoon reserved dressing. Rub jerk seasoning onto chicken.

**3** *For a charcoal grill,* grill chicken on the rack of an uncovered grill directly over medium coals for 5 minutes. Turn chicken.

Add plantain or red bananas (if using yellow banana, do not grill) and sweet pepper strips to grill. Grill for 7 to 10 minutes more or until chicken is tender and no longer pink and plantain or red bananas and sweet pepper strips are tender. (*For a gas grill*, preheat grill. Reduce heat to medium. Place chicken, then plantains or red bananas and sweet pepper strips on grill rack over medium heat. Cover and grill as above.)

4 In a large bowl toss together salad greens and remaining dressing. Divide greens among 4 dinner plates. Top each with chicken, plantain or banana, sweet pepper strips, avocado, and mango. Makes 4 servings.

Nutrition Facts per serving: 492 calories, 29 g total fat (5 g saturated fat), 59 mg cholesterol, 364 mg sodium, 38 g carbohydrate, 7 g fiber, 26 g protein. Daily Values: 84% vit. A, 131% vit. C, 8% calcium, 25% iron.

# Chicken and Fruit Salad with Mango Vinaigrette

**Prep:** 30 minutes    **Grill:** 12 minutes

2 to 3 mangoes
½ teaspoon curry powder
⅛ teaspoon salt
¼ teaspoon coarsely ground pepper
3 medium skinless, boneless chicken breast halves (about 12 ounces)
6 cups torn mixed salad greens
½ of a medium cantaloupe, seeded, peeled, and cut into 1-inch chunks
1 cup halved or sliced strawberries
1 recipe Mango Vinaigrette
2 green onions, thinly bias-sliced

1 Peel and slice mangoes. Measure 1½ cups for use in the vinaigrette; set remaining slices aside for salad.

2 Stir together the curry, salt, and pepper. Sprinkle curry mixture over chicken; rub into chicken with your fingers. *For a charcoal grill,* grill chicken on the rack of an uncovered grill directly over medium coals about 12 to 15 minutes or until tender and no longer pink, turning once halfway through grilling. (*For a gas grill*, preheat grill. Reduce heat to medium. Place chicken on grill rack over medium heat. Cover and grill as above.) Cool chicken slightly; slice into ¼-inch strips.

3 Arrange salad greens on 4 dinner plates. Top with chicken, melon, strawberries, and reserved mango slices. Drizzle each salad with Mango Vinaigrette. Sprinkle green onion over all. Makes 4 servings.

**Mango Vinaigrette:** In a blender container combine the 1½ cups mango, ¼ cup orange juice, 3 tablespoons rice vinegar or white wine vinegar, 2 teaspoons honey, and 1 teaspoon Dijon-style mustard. Cover and blend until smooth. Cover; chill until serving time. Makes about 1¼ cups.

Nutrition Facts per serving: 239 calories, 3 g total fat (1 g saturated fat), 45 mg cholesterol, 155 mg sodium, 37 g carbohydrate, 5 g fiber, 19 g protein. Daily Values: 74% vit. A, 157% vit. C, 4% calcium, 11% iron.

## NORTHWEST CHICKEN SALAD

**Prep:** 15 minutes  **Marinate:** 15 minutes
**Grill:** 12 minutes

- 2 medium skinless, boneless chicken breast halves
- 1 recipe Raspberry Vinaigrette
- 10 thick asparagus spears, trimmed
- 4 cups shredded mixed salad greens
- 6 to 8 strawberries
- 1 pear, cored and sliced
- 2 tablespoons chopped sweet onion
  Pecan halves, toasted (optional)

**1** Place chicken in a plastic bag set in a shallow dish. Prepare Raspberry Vinaigrette; reserve half for dressing. Pour remaining vinaigrette over chicken; seal bag. Marinate at room temperature 15 minutes. Drain chicken; reserve marinade.

**2** *For a charcoal grill,* grill chicken and asparagus on the rack of an uncovered grill directly over medium coals for 12 to 15 minutes or until chicken and asparagus are tender and chicken is no longer pink, turning and brushing once with marinade halfway through grilling. (*For a gas grill,* preheat grill. Reduce heat to medium. Place chicken and asparagus on grill rack over heat. Cover; grill as above.)

**3** Divide greens between 2 dinner plates. Slice chicken into strips; arrange on greens. Top with asparagus, strawberries, pear, and onion. Drizzle with dressing. If desired, sprinkle with pecans. Makes 2 servings.

**Raspberry Vinaigrette:** In a screw-top jar combine ¼ cup pear nectar; 2 tablespoons salad oil; 2 tablespoons raspberry vinegar; 1 teaspoon Dijon-style mustard; 1 teaspoon toasted sesame oil; 1 teaspoon dried basil, crushed; and ⅛ teaspoon pepper. Cover and shake well. Makes about ½ cup.

Nutrition Facts per serving: 379 calories,
20 g total fat (3 g saturated fat), 59 mg cholesterol,
131 mg sodium, 28 g carbohydrate, 6 g fiber,
25 g protein. Daily Values: 9% vit. A, 85% vit. C,
5% calcium, 15% iron.

# Tropical Chicken Salad

**Prep:** 20 minutes  **Grill:** 12 minutes

- ½ cup low-calorie seedless blackberry spread
- ⅓ cup salad oil
- 3 tablespoons white wine vinegar
- 2 tablespoons pineapple juice
- 2 tablespoons dry white wine
- 4 medium skinless, boneless chicken breast halves
- 8 cups mixed salad greens
- 1 medium banana, sliced
- 1 orange, peeled and sliced
- 1 cup sliced strawberries
- 2 kiwi fruit, peeled and sliced
- 1 recipe Caramelized Walnuts

**1** For dressing, whisk together blackberry spread, oil, vinegar, pineapple juice, and wine. Cover and chill until ready to serve.

**2** *For a charcoal grill,* grill chicken on the rack of an uncovered grill directly over medium coals for 12 to 15 minutes or until chicken is tender and no longer pink, turning once halfway through grilling. (*For a gas grill,* preheat grill. Reduce heat to medium. Place chicken on grill rack over heat. Cover; grill as above.)

**3** To serve, slice chicken diagonally into strips. Divide salad greens among 4 dinner plates. Top with chicken strips, banana, orange slices, strawberries, and kiwi fruit. Drizzle with dressing; sprinkle with Caramelized Walnuts. Makes 4 servings.

**Caramelized Walnuts:** In a small skillet combine ½ cup broken walnuts and 2 tablespoons sugar. Cook over medium heat, shaking skillet occasionally, until sugar begins to melt. Do not stir. Reduce heat to low; cook until sugar is golden brown, stirring occasionally. Turn nuts out onto buttered foil to cool.

Nutrition Facts per serving: 588 calories,
31 g total fat (3 g saturated fat), 60 mg cholesterol,
88 mg sodium, 56 g carbohydrate, 6 g fiber,
27 g protein. Daily Values: 30% vit. A., 160% vit. C,
8% calcium, 19% iron.

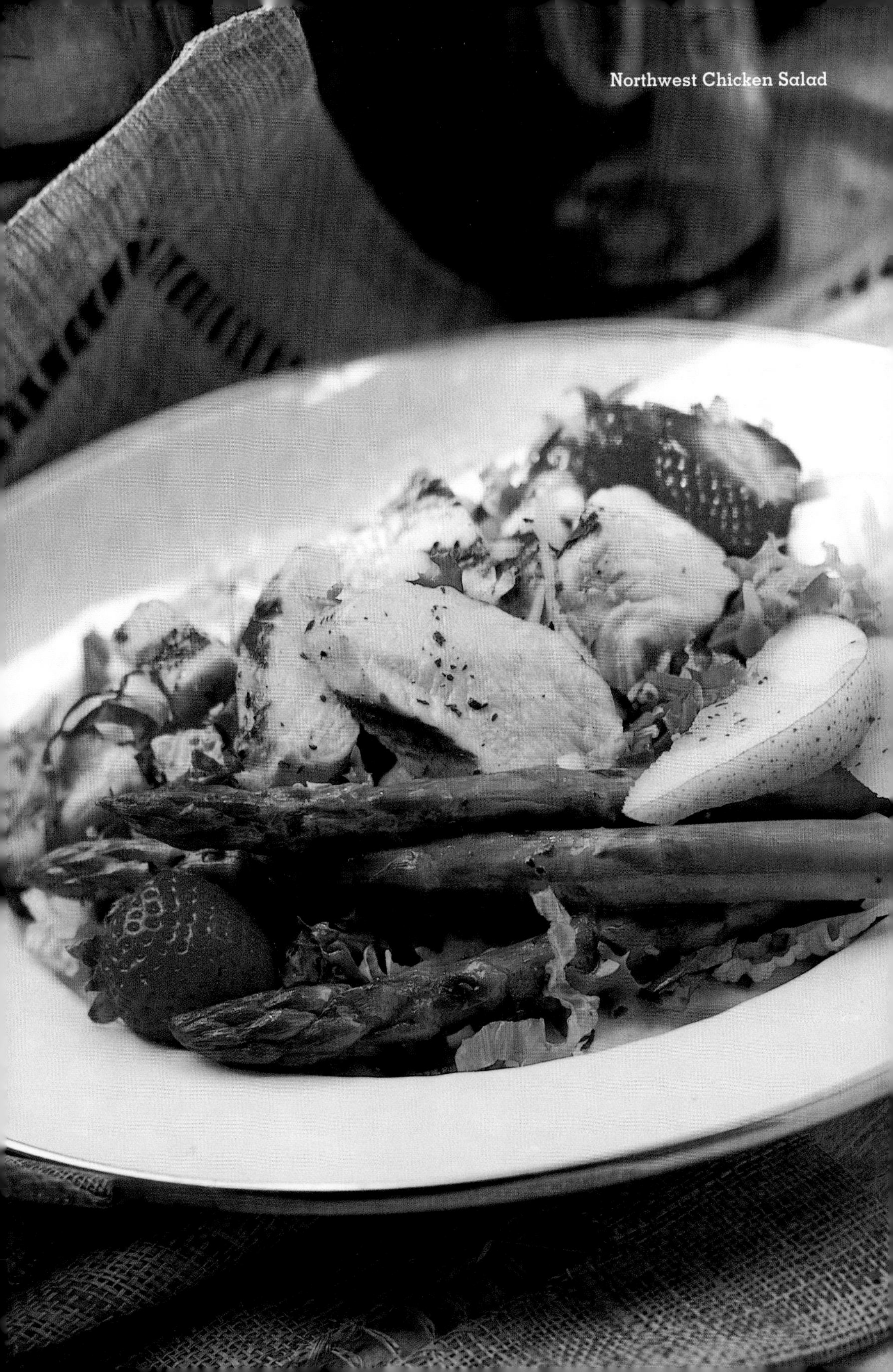
Northwest Chicken Salad

## SZECHWAN CHICKEN STRIPS

**Prep:** 15 minutes **Marinate:** 15 minutes
**Grill:** 10 minutes

    4 medium skinless, boneless
        chicken breast halves (about
        1 pound total)
  ⅓ cup rice vinegar
  ¼ cup hoisin sauce
    1 to 2 teaspoons Szechwan chili
        sauce or ½ teaspoon crushed red
        pepper
    1 clove garlic, minced
  12 cherry tomatoes
    2 cups packaged shredded
        broccoli (broccoli slaw mix)
    1 tablespoon chopped peanuts

**1** If using bamboo skewers, soak four 12-inch skewers in warm water for 20 minutes; drain. Cut chicken into bite-size strips. Place chicken in a plastic bag set in a shallow dish. For marinade, in a small bowl combine vinegar, hoisin sauce, Szechwan chili sauce, and garlic. Reserve half of the marinade for the dressing. Pour remaining marinade over chicken; seal bag. Marinate in the refrigerator at least 15 minutes or for up to 2 hours, turning the bag once.

**2** Drain chicken, reserving marinade. On bamboo or metal skewers, thread chicken, accordion style. *For a charcoal grill,* grill kabobs on the rack of an uncovered grill directly over medium coals for 10 to 12 minutes or until chicken is tender and no longer pink, turning once and brushing twice with marinade up to the last 5 minutes of grilling. Add tomatoes to ends of skewers the last 2 to 3 minutes of grilling. (*For a gas grill,* preheat grill. Reduce heat to medium. Place kabobs on grill rack over heat. Cover and grill as above.)

**3** Serve chicken over shredded broccoli. Drizzle with the dressing and sprinkle with peanuts. Makes 4 servings.

☺Nutrition facts per serving: 202 calories, 4 g total fat (1 g saturated fat), 59 mg cholesterol, 400 mg sodium, 15 g carbohydrate, 2 g fiber, 23 g protein. Daily Values: 8% vit. A, 51% vit. C, 2% calcium, 8% iron.

# Pakistani Chicken Kabobs

**Prep:** 30 minutes **Marinate:** 30 minutes
**Grill:** 12 minutes

    4 medium skinless, boneless
        chicken breast halves (about
        1 pound total)
  ⅓ cup plain yogurt
    2 teaspoons curry powder
    2 teaspoons brown sugar
    1 teaspoon grated fresh ginger
  ⅛ teaspoon salt
    2 limes
    4 cups peeled and cubed mango,
        papaya, and/or pineapple

**1** Cut chicken into 1-inch pieces. Place in a medium bowl. For marinade, in a small bowl combine yogurt, curry powder, brown sugar, ginger, and salt. Squeeze the juice from half of 1 lime; stir into yogurt mixture. Pour marinade over chicken; stir to coat. Cover and marinate in the refrigerator for at least 30 minutes or for up to 2 hours. Cut the remaining limes into wedges; set aside.

**2** Drain chicken, discarding marinade. Thread chicken onto 8 long metal skewers, leaving a ¼-inch space between each piece.

**3** *For a charcoal grill,* grill kabobs on the rack of an uncovered grill directly over medium coals for 12 to 14 minutes or until chicken is tender and no longer pink, turning once halfway through. (*For a gas grill,* preheat grill. Reduce heat to medium. Place kabobs on grill rack over heat. Cover and grill as above.) Remove kabobs from grill.

**4** To serve, place fruit on the ends of kabobs. Serve with lime wedges. Makes 4 servings.

☺Nutrition Facts per serving: 227 calories, 4 g total fat (1 g saturated fat), 61 mg cholesterol, 138 mg sodium, 25 g carbohydrate, 3 g fiber, 24 g protein. Daily Values: 32% vit. A, 95% vit. C, 5% calcium, 9% iron.

Szechwan Chicken Strips

## Italian Chicken and Sausage Kabobs

**Prep:** 20 minutes   **Marinate:** 2 to 8 hours
**Grill:** 12 minutes

>     4 medium skinless, boneless
>       chicken breast halves (about
>       1 pound total)
>     1 cup dry red wine
>     ½ cup olive oil
>     ¼ cup red wine vinegar
>     ¼ cup orange juice
>     2 tablespoons lemon juice
>     1 tablespoon snipped fresh sage
>     2 or 3 sprigs fresh parsley
>     3 large cloves garlic, minced
>    10 black peppercorns
>     2 bay leaves
>     1 pound uncooked Italian sausage
>       links
>    16 leaves fresh sage
>       Pita bread rounds (optional)

1 Cut chicken into 1-inch pieces. Place in a medium bowl. For marinade, in a small bowl combine wine, oil, vinegar, orange juice, lemon juice, the snipped sage, the parsley, garlic, peppercorns, and bay leaves. Pour over chicken; stir to coat. Cover and marinate in the refrigerator for 2 to 8 hours, stirring occasionally.

2 Drain chicken, reserving marinade. Cut sausage into 1-inch chunks. On 12- to 16-inch metal skewers, alternately thread sausage, chicken, and sage leaves, leaving a ¼-inch space between pieces.

3 *For a charcoal grill*, grill kabobs on the rack of an uncovered grill directly over medium coals for 12 to 14 minutes or until chicken and sausage are no longer pink, turning and brushing once with marinade halfway through. (*For a gas grill*, preheat grill. Reduce heat to medium. Place kabobs on grill rack over heat. Cover and grill as above.) Remove kabobs from grill.

4 If using, add pita bread to grill. Grill for 2 to 4 minutes or until lightly toasted, turning once halfway through. Serve kabobs with pita bread. Makes 8 servings.

Nutrition Facts per serving: 268 calories, 19 g total fat (5 g saturated fat), 62 mg cholesterol, 419 mg sodium, 2 g carbohydrate, 0 g fiber, 19 g protein. Daily Values: 6% vit. C, 1% calcium, 7% iron.

# Five-Spice Chicken Kabobs

**Prep:** 15 minutes   **Grill:** 12 minutes

>     ¼ cup frozen orange juice
>       concentrate, thawed
>     2 tablespoons honey
>     1 tablespoon soy sauce
>     ¼ teaspoon five-spice powder
>       Dash ground ginger
>     1 pound skinless, boneless chicken
>       breast halves or thighs
>     1 cup fresh pineapple chunks or one
>       8-ounce can pineapple chunks
>       (juice pack), drained
>     1 medium green sweet pepper, cut
>       into 1-inch pieces
>     1 medium red sweet pepper, cut into
>       1-inch pieces
>     2 cups hot cooked rice

1 For glaze, in a small bowl combine orange juice concentrate, honey, soy sauce, five-spice powder, and ginger. Set aside.

2 Cut chicken into 1-inch pieces. On six long skewers, alternately thread chicken, pineapple, green pepper, and red pepper, leaving a ¼-inch space between pieces.

3 *For a charcoal grill*, grill kabobs on the rack of an uncovered grill directly over medium coals for 12 to 14 minutes or until tender and no longer pink, turning and brushing once with glaze up to the last 5 minutes of grilling. (*For a gas grill*, preheat grill. Reduce heat to medium. Place kabobs on grill rack over heat. Cover and grill as above.) Serve with hot cooked rice. Makes 6 servings.

Nutrition Facts per serving: 218 calories, 2 g total fat (1 g saturated fat), 40 mg cholesterol, 210 mg sodium, 32 g carbohydrate, 1 g fiber, 17 g protein. Daily Values: 17% vit. A, 132% vit. C, 2% calcium, 10% iron.

## SPICY CHICKEN AND MELON KABOBS

**Prep:** 15 minutes **Grill:** 12 minutes

 1 tablespoon cooking oil
 2 cloves garlic, minced
 ½ teaspoon dried rosemary, crushed
 ¼ teaspoon ground cumin
 ⅛ teaspoon ground coriander
 ⅛ teaspoon ground black pepper
   Dash ground red pepper
 2 tablespoons balsamic vinegar or
   red wine vinegar
 12 ounces skinless, boneless chicken
   breast halves, cut into 1-inch
   pieces
 ½ medium cantaloupe, peeled and
   cut into 1½-inch pieces
 16 green onions, cut into 2-inch pieces
 2 tablespoons peach or apricot
   preserves

**1** Heat and stir oil, garlic, rosemary, cumin, coriander, black and red pepper, and ⅛ teaspoon salt in a small saucepan for 1 minute. Remove from heat; cool slightly. Stir in vinegar. Set aside.

**2** Alternately thread chicken, cantaloupe, and green onions on four 12- to 15-inch skewers. Brush with vinegar mixture. Stir preserves into remaining vinegar mixture.

**3** *For a charcoal grill,* grill kabobs on the rack of an uncovered grill directly over medium coals for 12 to 14 minutes or until tender and no longer pink, turning kabobs once and brushing with preserve-vinegar mixture halfway through grilling. (*For a gas grill,* preheat grill. Reduce heat to medium. Place kabobs on grill rack over heat. Cover and grill as above.) Makes 4 servings.

Nutrition Facts per serving: 185 calories, 6 g total fat (1 g saturated fat), 45 mg cholesterol, 116 mg sodium, 16 g carbohydrate, 1 g fiber, 17 g protein. Daily Values: 30% vit. A, 60% vit. C, 11% iron.

## Potato and Chicken Kabobs

**Prep:** 20 minutes **Grill:** 12 minutes

 12 whole tiny new potatoes, halved
   (1 pound)
 12 ounces skinless, boneless chicken
   breast halves
 1 lemon, cut into 4 wedges
 3 tablespoons olive oil
 1 tablespoon snipped fresh oregano
   or 1 teaspoon dried oregano,
   crushed
 1 large clove garlic, minced

**1** In a small saucepan bring a small amount of water to boiling; add potatoes. Simmer, covered, about 10 minutes or until almost tender. Drain well; halve potatoes lengthwise.

**2** Cut chicken into 1½-inch pieces. On 4 long metal skewers, alternately thread chicken and potatoes, leaving a ¼-inch space between pieces. Add a lemon wedge to the end of each skewer. In a small bowl combine olive oil, oregano and garlic; brush kabobs with oil mixture.

**3** *For a charcoal grill,* grill kabobs on the rack of an uncovered grill directly over medium coals for 12 to 14 minutes or until tender and no longer pink, turning kabobs once and brushing with remaining oil mixture halfway through grilling. (*For a gas grill,* preheat grill. Reduce heat to medium. Place kabobs on grill rack over heat. Cover and grill as above.)

**4** To serve, remove from skewers and squeeze lemon over chicken and potatoes. Makes 4 servings.

Nutrition Facts per serving: 293 calories, 13 g total fat (2 g saturated fat), 45 mg cholesterol, 49 mg sodium, 26 g carbohydrate, 1 g fiber, 19 g protein. Daily Values: 33% vit. C, 2% calcium, 16% iron.

## CHICKEN FAJITAS WITH GUACAMOLE

**Prep:** 25 minutes
**Chill (Guacamole):** Up to 4 hours
**Marinate:** 1 hour   **Grill:** 12 minutes

*There's nothing flat about these tortillas filled with chili-crazed chicken strips. Guacamole on the side, and you're in Southwest heaven.*

    1 recipe Guacamole
    3 medium skinless, boneless
        chicken breast halves (about
        12 ounces total)
    ¼ cup snipped fresh cilantro or
        parsley
    ¼ cup olive oil or cooking oil
    1 teaspoon finely shredded lemon
        peel
    2 tablespoons lemon juice
    1 teaspoon chili powder
    ½ teaspoon ground cumin
    ½ teaspoon pepper
    8 8-inch flour tortillas
    2 cups shredded lettuce
    1 cup shredded cheddar cheese
        (4 ounces)
    1 large tomato, chopped
    ½ cup sliced pitted ripe olives

**1** Prepare the Guacamole. Cover and chill for up to 4 hours. Place chicken in a shallow dish. For marinade, in a small bowl combine cilantro, oil, lemon peel, lemon juice, chili powder, cumin, and pepper. Pour over chicken; turn to coat. Cover and marinate in the refrigerator for 1 hour, turning chicken once. Stack tortillas and wrap in a piece of foil.

**2** Drain chicken, reserving marinade. *For a charcoal grill,* grill chicken and tortillas on the rack of an uncovered grill directly over medium coals until chicken is tender and no longer pink and tortillas are heated through, turning chicken and brushing once with marinade halfway through. (Allow 12 to 15 minutes for chicken and about 5 minutes for tortillas.) (*For a gas grill,* preheat grill. Reduce heat to medium. Place chicken and tortillas on grill rack over heat. Cover and grill as above.)

**3** To serve, cut chicken into bite-size strips. On each tortilla, arrange chicken strips, lettuce, cheese, tomato, and olives. Fold in sides; roll up tortillas. Serve with Guacamole. Makes 4 servings.

**Guacamole:** Seed and peel 1 ripe avocado. In a small bowl coarsely mash avocado. Stir in 1 medium tomato, seeded, chopped, and drained; 2 tablespoons finely chopped onion; 1 tablespoon lemon juice; and ¼ teaspoon salt. Makes about ¾ cup.

**Nutrition Facts per serving:** 576 calories, 32 g total fat (10 g saturated fat), 74 mg cholesterol, 745 mg sodium, 45 g carbohydrate, 5 g fiber, 30 g protein. **Daily Values:** 19% vit. A, 39% vit. C, 28% calcium, 31% iron.

# Fiery Chicken and Potato Fingers

**Prep:** 20 minutes   **Marinate:** 30 minutes
**Grill:** 24 minutes

*Hot and sweet describes the flavor of this dynamic duo. Grilled zucchini would make a fine side dish.*

    4 medium skinless, boneless
        chicken breast halves (about
        1 pound total)
    3 tablespoons olive oil
    3 tablespoons bottled hot pepper
        sauce
    2 tablespoons snipped fresh parsley
        (optional)

1 tablespoon honey or brown sugar
3 cloves garlic, minced
½ teaspoon salt
½ teaspoon ground red pepper
½ teaspoon cracked black pepper
2 large baking potatoes (about
1 pound total)

1 Cut each chicken breast half lengthwise into 3 strips. Place chicken in a plastic bag set in a shallow dish. For sauce, in a small bowl stir together oil, hot pepper sauce, parsley (if desired), honey, garlic, salt, red pepper, and black pepper. Pour 2 tablespoons of the sauce over chicken; seal bag. Marinate in the refrigerator for at least 30 minutes or for up to 24 hours, turning bag occasionally. Cover and chill the remaining sauce for basting.

2 Drain chicken, discarding marinade. Just before grilling, cut each potato lengthwise into 8 wedges. Lightly brush wedges with some of the remaining sauce.

3 *For a charcoal grill,* grill potatoes on the rack of an uncovered grill directly over medium coals for 15 minutes. Turn potatoes. Add chicken to grill. Grill for 9 to 12 minutes more or until chicken and potatoes are tender and chicken is no longer pink, turning chicken and brushing once with the remaining sauce halfway through. (*For a gas grill,* preheat grill. Reduce heat to medium. Place potatoes, then chicken on grill rack over heat. Cover and grill as above.) Makes 4 servings.

⊕**Nutrition facts per serving:** 335 calories, 12 g total fat (2 g saturated fat), 59 mg cholesterol, 340 mg sodium, 32 g carbohydrate, 1 g fiber, 25 g protein. **Daily Values:** 2% vit. A, 41% vit. C, 2% calcium, 15% iron.

## CHICKEN WITH HOTTER-THAN-HECK BARBECUE SAUCE

**Prep:** 25 minutes **Grill:** 12 minutes

*Not for the meeker tongue, this sauce contains chipotle peppers, which are smoked jalapeño peppers. For a milder sauce, reduce the amount of peppers to a couple of tablespoons.*

¼ cup chipotle peppers in adobo
sauce
Nonstick cooking spray
⅓ cup finely chopped onion
3 cloves garlic, minced
1 cup catsup
3 tablespoons white wine vinegar
3 tablespoons molasses or sorghum
1 tablespoon Worcestershire sauce
6 medium skinless, boneless
chicken breast halves

1 For the sauce, remove any stems from chipotle peppers. Place peppers and adobo sauce in a blender container. Cover and blend until smooth. Set aside.

2 Lightly coat an unheated medium saucepan with nonstick spray. Cook onion and garlic in saucepan until tender. Stir in chipotle pepper mixture, catsup, vinegar, molasses, and Worcestershire sauce. Bring to boiling; reduce heat. Simmer, uncovered, about 10 minutes or until mixture is slightly thickened.

3 *For a charcoal grill,* grill chicken on the rack of an uncovered grill directly over medium coals for 12 to 15 minutes or until chicken is tender and no longer pink, turning once halfway through grilling, and brushing with sauce the last 5 minutes of grilling. (*For a gas grill,* preheat grill. Reduce heat to medium. Place chicken on grill rack over heat. Cover and grill as above.)

4 Bring remaining sauce to boiling; pass with chicken. Makes 6 servings.

⊕**Nutrition Facts per serving:** 291 calories, 6 g total fat (1 g saturated fat), 59 mg cholesterol, 1,399 mg sodium, 36 g carbohydrate, 1 g fiber, 23 g protein. **Daily Values:** 101% vit. A, 26% vit. C, 17% iron.

## Middle-Eastern Chicken

**Prep:** 15 minutes **Grill:** 15 minutes

1 8-ounce carton plain fat-free
yogurt
1 small onion, finely chopped
1 tablespoon snipped fresh oregano
or savory or 1 teaspoon dried
oregano or savory, crushed
3 cloves garlic, minced
1 teaspoon sesame seed, toasted
½ teaspoon ground cumin
¼ teaspoon ground turmeric
(optional)
⅛ teaspoon salt
1 small cucumber, seeded and
chopped (about ⅔ cup)
4 medium skinless, boneless
chicken breast halves (about
1 pound total)
Hot cooked couscous (optional)

**1** In a medium bowl combine yogurt, onion, oregano, garlic, sesame seed, cumin, turmeric (if desired), and salt. Transfer half of the yogurt mixture to a small bowl and stir in cucumber; cover and refrigerate until ready to serve. Set remaining yogurt mixture aside.

**2** *For a charcoal grill,* arrange medium-hot coals around a drip pan. Test for medium heat above the pan. Place chicken on grill rack over drip pan. Spoon remaining yogurt mixture over chicken. Cover; grill for 15 to 18 minutes or until chicken is tender and no longer pink. [*For a gas grill,* preheat grill. Reduce heat to medium. Adjust for indirect cooking (see page 10). Grill as above.]

**3** Serve chicken with cucumber mixture and, if desired, couscous. Makes 4 servings.

Nutrition Facts per serving: 169 calories,
4 g total fat (1 g saturated fat), 60 mg cholesterol,
166 mg sodium, 7 g carbohydrate, 0 g fiber,
26 g protein. Daily Values: 1% vit. A, 4% vit. C,
11% calcium, 9% iron.

## BASIL-AND-GARLIC-STUFFED CHICKEN

**Prep:** 20 minutes **Grill:** 20 minutes

½ teaspoon finely shredded lemon
peel
2 tablespoons lemon juice
1 tablespoon margarine or butter,
melted
¼ cup grated Parmesan cheese
2 to 3 tablespoons snipped fresh
basil or 2 teaspoons dried basil,
crushed
1 tablespoon margarine or butter,
melted
2 cloves garlic, minced
4 medium skinless, boneless
chicken breast halves (about
1 pound total)

**1** For sauce, in a small bowl combine lemon peel, lemon juice, and the 1 tablespoon melted margarine.

**2** For stuffing, in a small bowl combine Parmesan cheese, basil, 1 tablespoon margarine or butter, and garlic. Set aside.

**3** Place each chicken piece between 2 pieces of plastic wrap. Use the flat side of a meat mallet to pound chicken into rectangles about ⅛-inch thick. Remove plastic wrap. Spread stuffing on chicken. Fold in sides of each chicken breast; roll up chicken. Secure with wooden toothpicks.

**4** *For a charcoal grill,* arrange medium-hot coals around a drip pan. Test for medium heat above the pan. Place chicken on grill rack over drip pan. Cover and grill for 20 to 25 minutes or until chicken is tender and no longer pink, brushing occasionally with sauce the last 10 minutes of grilling. [*For a gas grill,* preheat grill. Reduce heat to medium. Adjust for indirect cooking (see page 10). Grill as above.] Makes 4 servings.

Nutrition Facts per serving: 205 calories,
11 g total fat (3 g saturated fat), 64 mg cholesterol,
237 mg sodium, 2 g carbohydrate, 0 g fiber,
24 g protein. Daily values: 9% vit. A, 7% vit. C,
8% calcium, 5% iron.

# Chicken and Prosciutto Roll-ups

**Prep:** 25 minutes   **Grill:** 15 minutes

*Prosciutto, sweet peppers, and fontina let you "speak" Italian when you serve this dish.*

¼ cup dry white wine
2 teaspoons snipped fresh thyme or
   ½ teaspoon dried thyme, crushed
4 medium skinless, boneless
   chicken breast halves (about
   1 pound total)
4 thin slices prosciutto (about
   1 ounce total), trimmed of fat
2 ounces fontina cheese, thinly sliced
½ of a 7-ounce jar roasted red sweet
   peppers, drained and cut into
   thin strips (about ½ cup)
Fresh thyme (optional)

1 For sauce, in a small bowl combine wine and thyme. Set aside.

2 Place each chicken piece between 2 pieces of plastic wrap. Use the flat side of a meat mallet to pound chicken into rectangles about ⅛ inch thick. Remove plastic wrap.

3 Place a slice of prosciutto and one-fourth of the cheese on each chicken piece. Arrange one-fourth of the roasted peppers on cheese near bottom edge of chicken. Starting from bottom edge, roll up chicken; secure with wooden toothpicks. (At this point, chicken may be individually wrapped in plastic wrap and refrigerated for up to 4 hours.)

4 *For a charcoal grill,* grill chicken on the rack of an uncovered grill directly over medium coals for 15 to 17 minutes or until chicken is tender and no longer pink, turning to cook evenly and brushing twice with sauce up to the last 5 minutes of grilling. (*For a gas grill,* preheat grill. Reduce heat to medium. Place chicken on grill rack over heat. Cover and grill as above.) If desired, garnish with additional fresh thyme. Makes 4 servings.

Nutrition Facts per serving: 214 calories, 9 g total fat (4 g saturated fat), 76 mg cholesterol, 294 mg sodium, 2 g carbohydrate, 0 g fiber, 27 g protein. Daily Values: 14% vit. A, 85% vit. C, 7% calcium, 7% iron.

## CHICKEN CARIBBEAN

**Prep:** 15 minutes   **Grill:** 12 minutes

4 medium skinless, boneless
   chicken breast halves (about
   1 pound total)
½ teaspoon Jamaican jerk seasoning
½ cup purchased unsweetened
   coconut milk
1 teaspoon finely shredded orange
   peel (optional)
¼ cup orange juice
2 tablespoons snipped fresh basil
2 cups hot cooked rice

1 Rub both sides of chicken breasts with jerk seasoning.

2 *For a charcoal grill,* grill chicken on the rack of an uncovered grill directly over medium coals for 12 to 15 minutes or until chicken is tender and no longer pink, turning once halfway through grilling. (*For a gas grill,* preheat grill. Reduce heat to medium. Place chicken on grill rack over heat. Cover and grill as above.)

3 Meanwhile, for sauce, in a small saucepan combine coconut milk, orange juice, and 1 tablespoon of the basil. Bring to boiling; reduce heat. Simmer, uncovered, about 5 minutes or until reduced to ½ cup.

4 If desired, stir orange peel into cooked rice. Serve chicken and sauce over rice. Sprinkle with the remaining basil. Makes 4 servings.

Nutrition Facts per serving: 287 calories, 9 g total fat (6 g saturated fat), 59 mg cholesterol, 85 mg sodium, 25 g carbohydrate, 0 g fiber, 24 g protein. Daily Values: 2% vit. A, 13% vit. C, 2% calcium, 13% iron.

# Provençal Grilled Chicken and Herbed Penne

**Prep:** 20 minutes  **Grill:** 12 minutes

    8 ounces packaged dried plain
        penne pasta or tomato or garlic-
        and-herb-flavored penne pasta
    4 medium skinless, boneless
        chicken breast halves
    1 medium zucchini, halved
        lengthwise
    8 thick asparagus spears
        (8 to 10 ounces total), trimmed
    3 tablespoons olive oil
    1 tablespoon fines herbes or
        herbes de Provence, crushed
    ½ teaspoon salt
    1 tablespoon snipped fresh thyme
    ½ cup finely shredded Asiago cheese
        (optional)
        Pepper

**1** Cook pasta according to package directions; drain. Return pasta to hot pan. Meanwhile, brush chicken, zucchini, and asparagus with 1 tablespoon of the oil; sprinkle all sides with fines herbes and salt.

**2** *For a charcoal grill,* grill chicken, zucchini, and asparagus on the rack of an uncovered grill directly over medium coals for 12 to 15 minutes or until chicken and vegetables are tender and chicken is no longer pink, turning once halfway through grilling. (*For a gas grill,* preheat grill. Reduce heat to medium. Place chicken, zucchini, and asparagus on grill rack over heat. Cover and grill as above.)

**3** Transfer chicken and vegetables to a cutting board; cool slightly. Cut chicken and zucchini into 1-inch cubes; cut asparagus into 1-inch pieces. Add chicken, vegetables, the remaining oil, and thyme to pasta; toss to coat. Serve warm or chilled. Divide among 4 dinner plates; top with cheese (if desired) and season with pepper. Makes 4 servings.

Nutrition Facts per serving: 441 calories,
14 g total fat (2 g saturated fat), 59 mg cholesterol,
324 mg sodium, 46 g carbohydrate, 3 g fiber,
30 g protein. Daily Values: 3% vit. A, 14% vit. C,
3% calcium, 22% iron.

## ORANGE-DIJON CHICKEN

**Prep:** 20 minutes  **Grill:** 12 minutes
**Marinate:** 4 to 8 hours

    4 medium skinless, boneless
        chicken breast halves
    ½ cup olive oil
    3 cloves garlic, minced
    ½ teaspoon salt
    ⅛ teaspoon pepper
    1 recipe Orange-Dijon Glaze
        Coarsely ground pepper

**1** Place chicken in a plastic bag set in a shallow dish. For marinade, combine olive oil, garlic, salt, and the ⅛ teaspoon pepper in a small bowl. Pour over chicken; seal bag. Marinate in the refrigerator for 4 to 8 hours, turning bag occasionally.

**2** Drain chicken, discarding marinade. *For a charcoal grill,* grill chicken on the rack of an uncovered grill directly over medium coals for 12 to 15 minutes or until chicken is tender and no longer pink, turning once halfway through grilling. (*For a gas grill,* preheat grill. Reduce heat to medium. Place chicken, on grill rack over heat. Cover; grill as above.)

**3** Meanwhile, heat the Orange-Dijon Glaze in a saucepan until heated through. Transfer the chicken to 4 dinner plates and, if desired, cut into slices. Spoon Orange-Dijon Glaze on top; sprinkle with the coarsely ground pepper. Makes 4 servings.

**Orange-Dijon Glaze:** In a small bowl combine ¼ cup frozen orange juice concentrate, thawed; 2 to 4 tablespoons Dijon-style mustard; 2 tablespoons water; 1 tablespoon balsamic vinegar, if desired; 1 tablespoon olive oil; 1 teaspoon snipped fresh basil; 1 teaspoon snipped fresh mint; and ½ teaspoon snipped fresh rosemary. (If desired, prepare up to one day ahead. Store, covered, in the refrigerator.) Makes ¾ cup.

Nutrition Facts per serving: 249 calories,
14 g total fat (2 g saturated fat), 59 mg cholesterol,
310 mg sodium, 7 g carbohydrate, 0 g fiber,
23 g protein. Daily Values: 1% vit A, 46% vit. C,
2% calcium, 7% iron.

Provençal Grilled Chicken
and Herbed Penne

# Spicy Chicken and Star Fruit

**Prep:** 15 minutes **Grill:** 12 minutes

2 tablespoons balsamic vinegar or
     red wine vinegar
1 tablespoon olive oil
½ teaspoon dried rosemary, crushed
¼ teaspoon ground cumin
⅛ teaspoon ground coriander
⅛ teaspoon black pepper
     Dash ground red pepper
2 star fruit, sliced
8 green onions, cut into 2-inch
     pieces, and/or 4 small purple
     boiling onions, cut into wedges
4 medium skinless, boneless
     chicken breast halves (about
     1 pound total)
2 cups hot cooked rice
1 teaspoon finely shredded orange
     peel (optional)
2 tablespoons peach or apricot
     preserves, melted (optional)

**1** In a small bowl combine vinegar, oil,
rosemary, cumin, coriander, black pepper,
and red pepper. On eight 6-inch metal
skewers, alternately thread star fruit and
onions, leaving about a ¼-inch space between
each piece. Set aside.

**2** For a charcoal grill, grill chicken and
kabobs on the rack of an uncovered grill
directly over medium coals until chicken and
onions are tender, chicken is no longer pink,
and star fruit is heated through, turning and
brushing once with vinegar mixture halfway
through. (Allow 12 to 15 minutes for chicken
and about 5 minutes for kabobs.) (For a gas
grill, preheat grill. Reduce heat to medium.
Place chicken and kabobs on grill rack over
heat. Cover and grill as above.)

**3** To serve, if desired, toss the hot cooked
rice with the orange peel. Serve chicken,
star fruit, and onion over rice. If desired,
drizzle with preserves. Makes 4 servings.

Nutrition Facts per serving: 286 calories,
7 g total fat (1 g saturated fat), 59 mg cholesterol,
57 mg sodium, 30 g carbohydrate, 1 g fiber,
24 g protein. Daily Values: 8% vit. A, 32% vit. C,
2% calcium, 17% iron.

## CHICKEN WITH ROQUEFORT SAUCE

**Prep:** 12 minutes **Grill:** 12 minutes

*The pungent Roquefort cheese and sweet pears
combine for a memorable chicken dish.*

½ cup plain fat-free yogurt
¼ cup chopped red onion
2 tablespoons crumbled Roquefort or
     other blue cheese
1 tablespoon snipped fresh chives
⅛ teaspoon white pepper
2 ripe small pears, halved
     lengthwise, cored, and stemmed
     Lemon juice
4 medium skinless, boneless
     chicken breast halves (about
     1 pound total)
     Salt and black pepper

**1** For sauce, in a small bowl combine yogurt,
onion, Roquefort cheese, chives, and white
pepper. Cover and chill until ready to serve.
Brush the cut sides of pears with lemon juice.
Set aside.

**2** Sprinkle chicken with salt and black
pepper. For a charcoal grill, grill chicken
on the rack of an uncovered grill directly over
medium coals for 5 minutes. Turn chicken.
Add pears, cut sides down, to grill. Grill for
7 to 10 minutes more or until chicken is
tender and no longer pink and pears are
heated through. (For a gas grill, preheat grill.
Reduce heat to medium. Place chicken, then
pears on grill rack over heat. Cover and grill
as above.) Serve chicken and pears with
sauce. Makes 4 servings.

Nutrition Facts per serving: 199 calories,
5 g total fat (2 g saturated fat), 63 mg cholesterol,
168 mg sodium, 14 g carbohydrate, 2 g fiber,
25 g protein. Daily Values: 2% vit. A, 9% vit. C,
8% calcium, 6% iron.

# Raspberry Chicken with Plantains

**Prep:** 20 minutes   **Grill:** 12 minutes

*Using plantains instead of bananas fosters a Caribbean mood in this lighthearted chicken dish. Fresh raspberries make a terrific accent.*

1 cup raspberries or one 10-ounce package frozen unsweetened raspberries
2 tablespoons granulated sugar
1 teaspoon margarine or butter
2 ripe plantains or firm bananas, sliced
2 tablespoons brown sugar
2 tablespoons white wine vinegar
2 green onions, thinly sliced
1 small fresh jalapeño pepper, seeded and finely chopped
4 medium skinless, boneless chicken breast halves (about 1 pound total)
Salt and black pepper
Ti leaves (optional)

1 For sauce, in a small saucepan combine raspberries and granulated sugar. Cook and stir over low heat about 3 minutes or until berries are softened. Press berry mixture through a fine-mesh sieve; discard seeds.

2 For plantains, in a large nonstick skillet heat margarine or butter over medium heat. Add plantains, if using. Cook and stir about 2 minutes or until lightly browned and slightly softened. Add bananas (if using), brown sugar, and vinegar; heat through. Remove from heat; stir in green onions and jalapeño pepper.

3 Sprinkle chicken breasts with salt and black pepper. *For a charcoal grill,* grill chicken on the rack of an uncovered grill directly over medium coals for 12 to 15 minutes or until tender and no longer pink, turning once halfway through. (*For a gas grill,* preheat grill. Reduce heat to medium. Place chicken on grill rack over heat. Cover and grill as above.)

4 If desired, place a chicken piece on a ti leaf. Spoon sauce over chicken. Serve with plantain mixture. Makes 4 servings.

Nutrition Facts per serving: 300 calories, 5 g total fat (1 g saturated fat), 59 mg cholesterol, 103 mg sodium, 45 g carbohydrate, 4 g fiber, 23 g protein. Daily Values: 13% vit. A, 48% vit. C, 2% calcium, 11% iron.

## DON'T GET BURNED!

**Taking a few precautions when cooking chicken or turkey will ensure a dish that is wholesome and safe.**

- **Do not thaw poultry on the countertop or in the sink because bacteria reproduces faster at room temperature. Always thaw poultry in the refrigerator.**
- **Wash your hands, utensils, cutting boards, and work surfaces with hot soapy water after handling poultry to prevent spreading bacteria to other foods.**
- **Use separate dishes for raw and cooked poultry. When grilling, carry raw poultry to the grill on one plate, and bring the cooked poultry back to the kitchen on another clean plate.**

## WEST INDIES CHICKEN WITH FRUIT

**Prep:** 15 minutes **Grill:** 12 minutes

*A marmalade glaze on this chicken with a medley of fruit will have you sailing the tropical islands of your mind.*

- 1 small ruby red grapefruit
- 3 tablespoons orange marmalade
- 1 tablespoon snipped fresh thyme
- 2½ teaspoons ground coriander
- 2 teaspoons olive oil
- ½ teaspoon hot Hungarian paprika or
⅛ teaspoon ground red pepper
- ¼ teaspoon salt
- 2 ripe, yet firm, kiwi fruit
- 2 medium ripe, yet firm, nectarines
- 2 ripe, yet firm, star fruit
- 4 medium skinless, boneless chicken breast halves (about 1 pound total)

**1** Finely shred 2 teaspoons peel from grapefruit. For glaze, in a small bowl combine grapefruit peel, orange marmalade, thyme, coriander, olive oil, paprika, and salt; set aside.

**2** Peel and quarter grapefruit and kiwi fruit. Pit and quarter nectarines. Cut star fruit into ½-inch slices. Thread fruit onto 4 long metal skewers.

**3** For a charcoal grill, grill chicken and fruit kabobs on the rack of an uncovered grill directly over medium coals until chicken is tender and no longer pink and fruit is heated through, turning once and brushing frequently with glaze during the last half of grilling. (Allow 12 to 15 minutes for chicken and about 8 minutes for fruit.) (For a gas grill, preheat grill. Reduce heat to medium. Place chicken and fruit kabobs on grill rack over heat. Cover and grill as above.) Makes 4 servings.

Nutrition Facts per serving: 288 calories, 7 g total fat (1 g saturated fat), 59 mg cholesterol, 192 mg sodium, 36 g carbohydrate, 3 g fiber, 24 g protein. Daily Values: 12% vit. A, 142% vit. C, 5% calcium, 11% iron.

## Tarragon Chicken with Rice

**Prep:** 30 minutes **Grill:** 12 minutes
**Special Equipment:** Grill basket

*Tarragon's airy sweetness lifts this dish of rice, grilled vegetables, and chicken completely out of the ordinary.*

- 12 ounces asparagus spears, trimmed
- 4 medium carrots, halved lengthwise
- ¼ cup dry white wine
- 2 tablespoons olive oil or cooking oil
- 1 tablespoon snipped fresh tarragon or 1 teaspoon dried tarragon, crushed
- 1 clove garlic, minced
- ¼ teaspoon pepper
- 4 medium skinless, boneless chicken breast halves (about 1 pound total)
- 1⅓ cups chicken broth
- ⅔ cup basmati or regular rice
- 1 teaspoon snipped fresh tarragon or ¼ teaspoon dried tarragon, crushed
- 1 green onion, thinly sliced
Fresh tarragon (optional)

**1** In a large skillet cook asparagus and carrots in a small amount of boiling water for 3 minutes; drain. In a small bowl combine white wine, oil, the 1 tablespoon fresh or 1 teaspoon dried tarragon, the garlic, and pepper. Brush some of the mixture over chicken and vegetables.

**2** Meanwhile, in a medium saucepan bring chicken broth to boiling. Add rice and the ¼ teaspoon dried tarragon (if using). Return to boiling; reduce heat. Simmer, covered, about 20 minutes or until rice is tender (do not lift cover). Stir in the 1 teaspoon snipped fresh tarragon (if using). Cover; keep warm.

**3** Place asparagus and carrots in a grill basket. *For a charcoal grill*, grill chicken and vegetables on the rack of an uncovered grill directly over medium coals until chicken and vegetables are tender and chicken is no longer pink, turning and brushing once with the remaining wine mixture halfway through. (Allow 12 to 15 minutes for chicken and about 5 minutes for vegetables.) (*For a gas grill*, preheat grill. Reduce heat to medium. Place chicken and vegetables on grill rack over heat. Cover and grill as above.)

**4** Coarsely chop vegetables. Toss chopped vegetables and green onion with hot cooked rice. Serve chicken with rice mixture. If desired, garnish with additional fresh tarragon. Makes 4 servings.

ⓥNutrition Facts per serving: 364 calories, 11 g total fat (2 g saturated fat), 60 mg cholesterol, 363 mg sodium, 35 g carbohydrate, 4 g fiber, 28 g protein. Daily Values: 177% vit. A, 28% vit. C, 5% calcium, 21% iron.

## CITRUS-GRILLED CHICKEN

**Prep:** 20 minutes     **Marinate:** 30 minutes
**Grill:** 12 minutes

*Lightly toasted spices—coriander seed and anise seed—contribute to the aroma and flavor of this chicken. If you don't have a mortar and pestle, you can grind the spices in a pepper grinder.*

½ teaspoon coriander seed
¼ teaspoon anise seed
1½ pounds skinless, boneless chicken
　　breast halves
⅓ cup honey
¼ cup lemon juice
3 tablespoons orange juice
3 tablespoons lime juice
2 green onions, thinly sliced
1 teaspoon snipped fresh sage
1 teaspoon snipped fresh thyme
½ teaspoon snipped fresh rosemary
¼ teaspoon salt
⅛ teaspoon coarsely ground pepper

**1** In a small skillet cook and stir the coriander and anise seed over medium heat for 5 to 7 minutes or until seeds are fragrant and toasted, stirring constantly. Remove skillet from heat; let cool. Grind spices with a mortar and pestle. Set aside.

**2** Place chicken in a plastic bag set in a shallow dish. For marinade, in a large nonmetal bowl combine honey, lemon juice, orange juice, lime juice, green onions, sage, thyme, rosemary, salt, and pepper. Stir in ground spices. Pour marinade over chicken; seal bag. Marinate at room temperature for 30 minutes, turning bag occasionally. Drain chicken, reserving marinade.

**3** *For a charcoal grill*, grill chicken on the rack of an uncovered grill directly over medium coals 12 to 15 minutes or until chicken is tender and no longer pink, turning once and brushing occasionally with remaining marinade during the first 8 minutes of grilling. (*For a gas grill*, preheat grill. Reduce heat to medium. Place chicken on grill rack over heat. Cover and grill as above.) Makes 6 servings.

ⓥNutrition Facts per serving: 188 calories, 3 g total fat (1 g saturated fat), 59 mg cholesterol, 144 mg sodium, 18 g carbohydrate, 22 g protein. Daily Values: 1% vit. A, 19% vit. C, 1% calcium, 6% iron.

# Asian Chicken and Noodles

**Prep:** 25 minutes   **Grill:** 12 minutes

*East meets West in this great grilled chicken salad. Udon, thick Japanese wheat or corn flour noodles, are available at most Asian markets.*

    8 ounces packaged dried udon or
        Chinese curly noodles
    ¼ cup light soy sauce
    2 tablespoons toasted sesame oil
    2 tablespoons rice vinegar
    4 cloves garlic, minced
    1½ teaspoons grated fresh ginger
    ¼ teaspoon crushed red pepper
    4 medium skinless, boneless
        chicken breast halves
        (about 1 pound total)
    1 small eggplant, sliced
    4 cups packaged shredded cabbage
        with carrot (coleslaw mix)
    ¼ cup chopped cashews (optional)
    2 to 3 tablespoons snipped
        fresh cilantro

**1** Cook noodles according to package directions; drain. Transfer noodles to a large bowl. Meanwhile, in a small bowl combine soy sauce, oil, vinegar, garlic, ginger, and crushed red pepper. Reserve 2 tablespoons of the soy sauce mixture. Pour the remaining soy sauce mixture over noodles; toss gently to coat.

**2** *For a charcoal grill,* grill chicken and eggplant on the rack of an uncovered grill directly over medium coals until chicken and eggplant are tender and chicken is no longer pink, turning once and brushing occasionally with the reserved soy sauce mixture during the last half of grilling. (Allow 12 to 15 minutes for chicken and about 8 minutes for eggplant.) (*For a gas grill,* preheat grill. Reduce heat to medium. Place chicken and eggplant on grill rack over heat. Cover and grill as above.)

**3** Transfer chicken and eggplant to a cutting board; cool slightly. Cut into cubes. Add chicken, eggplant, and cabbage to noodle mixture; toss gently to combine. Sprinkle with cashews (if desired) and cilantro. Makes 4 servings.

Nutrition Facts per serving: 442 calories, 12 g total fat (2 g saturated fat), 108 mg cholesterol, 646 mg sodium, 51 g carbohydrate, 6 g fiber, 32 g protein. Daily Values: 81% vit. A, 60% vit. C, 6% calcium, 28% iron.

# JAMAICAN JERK CHICKEN

**Prep:** 25 minutes   **Grill:** 12 minutes
**Marinate:** 30 minutes

    ½ cup chopped onion
    2 tablespoons lime juice
    1 teaspoon salt
    1 teaspoon crushed red pepper
    ½ teaspoon ground allspice
    ¼ teaspoon black pepper
    ¼ teaspoon curry powder
    ⅛ teaspoon dried thyme, crushed
    ⅛ teaspoon ground red pepper
    ⅛ teaspoon ground ginger
    2 cloves garlic, quartered
    4 medium skinless, boneless
        chicken breast halves
    1 medium red, yellow, or green
        sweet pepper, cut into 1½-inch
        pieces
    1 small zucchini, sliced ½ inch thick
    1 tablespoon cooking oil
    ¼ teaspoon coarsely ground black
        pepper

**1** In a blender container combine onion, lime juice, salt, crushed red pepper, allspice, black pepper, curry powder, thyme, ground red pepper, ginger, and garlic. Cover and blend until smooth.

**2** Place chicken in a shallow nonmetal dish. Pour onion mixture over chicken; turn chicken to coat both sides. Cover and marinate in the refrigerator for 30 minutes.

**3** Meanwhile, thread sweet pepper and zucchini pieces onto 4 long metal skewers. Brush with oil and sprinkle with coarsely ground pepper.

4 Drain chicken, reserving onion mixture. *For a charcoal grill*, grill chicken and vegetable kabobs on the rack of an uncovered grill directly over medium coals until chicken is tender and no longer pink and vegetables are tender, turning and brushing once with onion mixture halfway through grilling. (Allow 12 to 15 minutes for chicken and about 10 minutes for vegetables.) (*For a gas grill*, preheat grill. Reduce heat to medium. Place chicken and vegetable kabobs on grill rack over heat. Cover and grill as above.) Makes 4 servings.

Nutrition Facts per serving: 174 calories, 7 g total fat (1 g saturated fat), 59 mg cholesterol, 594 mg sodium, 6 g carbohydrate, 1 g fiber, 22 g protein. Daily Values: 18% vit. A, 60% vit. C, 2% calcium, 8% iron.

## Curried Chicken and Potato Packets

**Prep:** 15 minutes  **Grill:** 25 minutes

*Offer your family these quick-and-easy packets, and they'll be packing it in as fast as they can eat. The potatoes offer heartiness; the sour cream and curry provide exuberant flavor.*

- 1 9-ounce package frozen cooked chicken breast strips
- 4 medium potatoes, cut into ¾-inch cubes
- 1½ cups packaged peeled baby carrots
- 1 small onion, thinly sliced
- ½ cup dairy sour cream or plain low-fat yogurt
- 1 teaspoon curry powder
- 1 teaspoon Dijon-style mustard
- ½ teaspoon salt
- ½ teaspoon paprika
- ⅛ teaspoon crushed red pepper

1 In a large bowl combine frozen chicken, potatoes, carrots, and onion; set aside. In a small bowl combine sour cream, curry powder, mustard, salt, paprika, and crushed red pepper. Pour over chicken mixture; toss gently to coat.

2 Fold four 24×18-inch pieces of heavy foil in half to make 18×12-inch rectangles. Divide chicken mixture among the foil rectangles. Bring up opposite edges of foil and seal with a double fold. Fold remaining edges together to completely enclose chicken mixture, leaving space for steam to build.

3 *For a charcoal grill*, grill chicken packets on the rack of an uncovered grill directly over medium coals about 25 minutes or until vegetables are tender. (*For a gas grill*, preheat grill. Reduce heat to medium. Place chicken packets on grill rack over heat. Cover and grill as above.) Makes 4 servings.

Nutrition Facts per serving: 371 calories, 11 g total fat (5 g saturated fat), 70 mg cholesterol, 414 mg sodium, 44 g carbohydrate, 3 g fiber, 24 g protein. Daily Values: 129% vit. A, 41% vit. C, 6% calcium, 21% iron.

## Flaming Facts

**Heard the health disadvantages of eating the skin on chicken or turkey? There's no need to remove it before grilling. Leaving it on actually adds flavor and keeps moistness in, yet the meat doesn't absorb much of the fat. On the other hand, removing the skin before eating does significantly lower the fat and calories. If you prefer to grill chicken without skin, brush the cold grill rack with oil or lightly coat with nonstick cooking spray (don't spray over hot coals) to prevent the chicken from sticking.**

Sticky-Sloppy Barbecue Chicken

## STICKY-SLOPPY BARBECUE CHICKEN

**Prep:** 45 minutes    **Marinate:** 2 to 4 hours
**Grill:** 50 minutes

*Country meets city in this finger-licking barbecue recipe. Sherry supplies the uptown flavor.*

  3 to 4 pounds meaty chicken pieces
    (breasts, thighs, and drumsticks)
1½ cups dry sherry
  1 cup finely chopped onion
  ¼ cup lemon juice
  6 cloves garlic, minced
  2 bay leaves
  1 15-ounce can tomato puree
  ¼ cup honey
  3 tablespoons molasses
  1 teaspoon salt
  ½ teaspoon dried thyme, crushed
  ¼ to ½ teaspoon ground red pepper
  ¼ teaspoon black pepper
  2 tablespoons white vinegar

**1** Place chicken in a plastic bag set in a shallow dish. For marinade, in a medium bowl stir together sherry, onion, lemon juice, garlic, and bay leaves. Pour over chicken; seal bag. Marinate in the refrigerator for 2 to 4 hours, turning bag occasionally. Drain chicken, reserving marinade. Cover and chill chicken until ready to grill.

**2** For sauce, in a large saucepan combine the reserved marinade, the tomato puree, honey, molasses, salt, thyme, red pepper, and black pepper. Bring to boiling; reduce heat. Simmer, uncovered, about 30 minutes or until reduced to 2 cups. Remove from heat; remove bay leaves. Stir in vinegar.

**3** *For a charcoal grill,* arrange medium-hot coals around a drip pan. Test for medium heat above the pan. Place chicken pieces, bone sides down, on grill rack over drip pan. Cover and grill for 50 to 60 minutes or until tender and no longer pink, brushing with some of the sauce during the last 15 minutes of grilling. [*For a gas grill,* preheat grill. Reduce heat to medium. Adjust for indirect cooking (see page 10). Grill as above.] To serve, reheat and pass the remaining sauce with chicken. Makes 6 servings.

Nutrition Facts per serving: 446 calories,
13 g total fat (4 g saturated fat), 104 mg cholesterol,
735 mg sodium, 33 g carbohydrate, 2 g fiber,
35 g protein. Daily Values: 14% vit. A, 52% vit. C,
5% calcium, 20% iron.

## WISE ADVICE

When grilling chicken, if you follow some simple tips, you'll end up with moist, flavorful chicken that is cooked to perfection.
• **Bone-in and skin-on chicken pieces grill best over indirect medium-low heat. This allows slow, even cooking and minimizes flare-ups.**
• **Leave the skin on. The skin holds a great deal of flavor and helps retain the moistness of the meat. It can be removed after grilling, if you like.**
• **If grilling skinless poultry, marinate it first, and take care not to overcook it. Turn it with tongs, not a fork, and baste it frequently while on the grill.**
• **Cook all whole poultry until the juices run clear, not pink, and the temperature registers 180° to 185°.**

# Curried Barbecued Chicken

**Prep:** 15 minutes   **Marinate:** 4 to 24 hours
**Grill:** 50 minutes

 2½ to 3 pounds meaty chicken pieces
      (breasts, thighs, and drumsticks)
   2 teaspoons finely shredded lime
      peel
 ⅓ cup lime juice
   1 tablespoon curry powder
   1 tablespoon cooking oil
   2 cloves garlic, minced
 ½ teaspoon salt
 ¼ teaspoon ground cumin
 ¼ teaspoon ground coriander
 ⅛ teaspoon ground red pepper

**1** Place chicken in a plastic bag set in a shallow dish. For marinade, stir together the lime peel, lime juice, curry powder, cooking oil, garlic, salt, cumin, coriander, and red pepper. Pour over chicken; seal bag. Marinate in the refrigerator 4 to 24 hours, turning the bag occasionally. Drain chicken, reserving the marinade.

**2** *For a charcoal grill,* arrange medium-hot coals around a drip pan. Test for medium heat above the pan. Place chicken pieces, bone sides down, on grill rack over pan. Cover and grill for 50 to 60 minutes or until chicken is tender and no longer pink, brushing with some of the marinade during the first 40 minutes of grilling. [*For a gas grill,* preheat grill. Reduce heat to medium. Adjust for indirect cooking (see page 10). Grill as above.] Makes 4 to 6 servings.

Nutrition Facts per serving: 366 calories,
20 g total fat (5 g saturated fat), 130 mg cholesterol,
382 mg sodium, 4 g carbohydrate, 1 g fiber,
42 g protein. Daily Values: 5%vit. A, 13% vit. C,
3% calcium, 16% iron.

## PLUM-GOOD CHICKEN

**Prep:** 15 minutes   **Grill:** 35 minutes

 ½ cup plum jam
   2 tablespoons lemon juice
   2 tablespoons water
   1 tablespoon soy sauce
 ½ teaspoon onion powder
 ¼ teaspoon ground ginger
   2 to 2½ pounds meaty chicken pieces
      (breasts, thighs, and drumsticks)

**1** For sauce, in a saucepan combine jam, lemon juice, water, soy sauce, onion powder, and ginger. Cook and stir until jam melts. Sprinkle chicken with salt and pepper.

**2** *For a charcoal grill,* grill chicken pieces, bone side up, on the rack of an uncovered grill directly over medium coals for 35 to 45 minutes or until chicken is tender and no longer pink, turning once halfway through grilling and brushing often with sauce during the last 15 minutes of grilling. (*For a gas grill,* preheat grill. Reduce heat to medium. Place chicken on grill rack over heat. Cover and grill as above.) Drizzle any remaining sauce on chicken before serving. Makes 4 to 6 servings.

Nutrition Facts per serving: 372 calories,
13 g total fat (4 g saturated fat), 104 mg cholesterol,
353 mg sodium, 29 g carbohydrate, 0 g fiber,
34 g protein. Daily Values: 3% vit. A, 5% vit. C,
2% calcium, 12% iron.

# Orange-Glazed Chicken

**Prep:** 15 minutes   **Grill:** 35 minutes

 ⅓ cup frozen orange juice
      concentrate, thawed
 ¼ cup honey
 ¼ cup soy sauce
   1 teaspoon five-spice powder
 ½ teaspoon garlic powder
   2 pounds meaty chicken pieces
      (breasts, thighs, and drumsticks)
   1 small orange

1 For glaze, in a small mixing bowl combine the orange juice concentrate, honey, soy sauce, five-spice powder, and garlic powder. Set aside.

2 If desired, remove skin from chicken. *For a charcoal grill*, grill chicken pieces, bone side up, on the rack of an uncovered grill directly over medium coals for 35 to 45 minutes or until chicken is tender and no longer pink, turning once halfway through grilling and brushing occasionally with sauce during the last 10 minutes of grilling. (*For a gas grill*, preheat grill. Reduce heat to medium. Place chicken on grill rack over heat. Cover and grill as above.)

3 To serve, cut the orange into thin slices. Garnish chicken with orange slices. Makes 4 servings.

Nutrition Facts per serving: 385 calories, 13 g total fat (3 g saturated fat), 104 mg cholesterol, 865 mg sodium, 32 g carbohydrate. Daily Values: 5% vit. A, 89% vit. C, 3% calcium, 14% iron.

## APPLE-GLAZED CHICKEN AND VEGETABLES

**Prep:** 20 minutes   **Grill:** 12 minutes

  1 **recipe Apple Glaze**
    **Nonstick cooking spray**
  2 **cloves garlic, minced**
  1 **medium leek, trimmed, cleaned thoroughly, and sliced, or 1/3 cup chopped onion**
  2 **medium apples, cored and coarsely chopped**
  2 **tablespoons apple cider or chicken broth**
  1 **10-ounce bag prewashed spinach, stems removed (about 10 cups)**
    **Salt**
    **Pepper**
  4 **small skinless, boneless chicken breast halves (about 12 ounces)**

1 Prepare Apple Glaze; set aside. Lightly coat an unheated large saucepan or Dutch oven with nonstick cooking spray. Add garlic, leek, and apples; cook over medium heat for 3 minutes. Add 1/4 cup of the Apple Glaze and the cider or broth; bring to boiling. Add spinach; toss just until wilted. Season with salt and pepper.

2 *For a charcoal grill*, grill chicken on the rack of an uncovered grill directly over medium coals for 12 to 15 minutes or until chicken is tender and no longer pink, turning once halfway through grilling and brushing often with glaze during the last 5 minutes of grilling. (*For a gas grill*, preheat grill. Reduce heat to medium. Place chicken on grill rack over heat. Cover and grill as above.)

3 To serve, slice each chicken breast crosswise into 6 to 8 pieces. Divide spinach mixture among 4 dinner plates and top with sliced chicken. Makes 4 servings.

**Apple Glaze:** In a small saucepan heat 1/2 cup apple jelly; 1 teaspoon finely shredded lemon peel; 1 tablespoon snipped fresh thyme or 1 teaspoon dried thyme, crushed; 1 teaspoon grated fresh ginger; and 2 tablespoons soy sauce just until jelly is melted.

Nutrition Facts per serving: 263 calories, 3 g total (1 g saturated fat), 45 mg cholesterol, 654 mg sodium, 42 g carbohydrate, 4 g fiber, 19 g protein. Daily values: 48% vit. A, 27% vit. C, 24% iron.

# Zesty Drumsticks

**Prep time:** 20 minutes **Grill:** 50 minutes

*Need a sauce fast? Here's the one. Currant jelly and chili sauce make an incredible match.*

¼ cup currant jelly
¼ cup bottled chili sauce
1 tablespoon vinegar
1 tablespoon Worcestershire sauce
⅛ teaspoon garlic powder
Several drops bottled hot pepper sauce
8 chicken drumsticks (about 1½ pounds total)

**1** For sauce, in a small saucepan combine currant jelly, chili sauce, vinegar, Worcestershire sauce, garlic powder, and hot pepper sauce. Cook over low heat about 5 minutes or until bubbly, stirring occasionally to melt jelly. Remove from heat. If desired, remove skin from chicken.

**2** *For a charcoal grill,* arrange medium-hot coals around a drip pan. Test for medium heat above the pan. Place chicken on grill rack over drip pan. Cover and grill for 50 to 60 minutes or until chicken is tender and no longer pink, brushing with sauce during the last 10 minutes of grilling. [*For a gas grill,* preheat grill. Reduce heat to medium. Adjust for indirect cooking (see page 10). Grill as above.]

**3** To serve, reheat and pass the remaining sauce with chicken. Makes 4 servings.

Nutrition Facts per serving: 295 calories, 12 g total fat (3 g saturated fat), 96 mg cholesterol, 335 mg sodium, 18 g carbohydrate, 29 g protein. Daily Values: 5% vit. A, 15% vit. C, 1% calcium, 13% iron.

# TEXAS-STYLE BARBEQUED CHICKEN LEGS

**Prep:** 20 minutes **Grill:** 40 minutes

*This is serious chicken, barbecue wranglers. There won't be one leg left, you can bet.*

1 medium onion, finely chopped
2 cloves garlic, minced
1 teaspoon chili powder
¼ teaspoon ground sage
1 tablespoon margarine or butter
½ cup catsup
2 tablespoons water
2 tablespoons vinegar
1 tablespoon sugar
1 tablespoon lemon juice
1 tablespoon Worcestershire sauce
½ teaspoon salt
½ teaspoon bottled hot pepper sauce
¼ teaspoon cracked black pepper
6 whole chicken legs (drumstick and thigh) (about 2½ pounds total)

**1** For sauce, in a small saucepan cook onion, garlic, chili powder, and sage in hot margarine or butter until onion is tender. Stir in catsup, water, vinegar, sugar, lemon juice, Worcestershire sauce, salt, hot pepper sauce, and black pepper. Bring to boiling; reduce heat. Simmer, uncovered, for 5 minutes, stirring occasionally. Remove from heat.

**2** *For a charcoal grill,* grill chicken on the rack of an uncovered grill directly over medium coals for 40 to 50 minutes or until tender and no longer pink, turning once and brushing with some of the sauce during the last 10 minutes of grilling. (*For a gas grill,* preheat grill. Reduce heat to medium. Place chicken, skin side down, on grill rack over heat. Cover and grill as above.)

**3** To serve, reheat and pass the remaining sauce with chicken. Makes 6 servings.

Nutrition Facts per serving: 276 calories, 15 g total fat (4 g saturated fat), 86 mg cholesterol, 596 mg sodium, 11 g carbohydrate, 1 g fiber, 25 g protein. Daily Values: 10% vit. A, 16% vit. C, 2% calcium, 11% iron.

# Polynesian Honey-Pineapple Chicken

**Prep:** 25 minutes **Marinate:** 6 to 24 hours
**Grill:** 40 minutes

½ cup pineapple juice
¼ cup honey
4 cloves garlic, minced
3 tablespoons Worcestershire sauce
1 tablespoon grated fresh ginger or
   1 teaspoon ground ginger
1 teaspoon salt
12 chicken drumsticks and/or thighs
   (about 3 pounds)

1 For marinade, in a large saucepan stir together pineapple juice, honey, garlic, Worcestershire sauce, ginger, and salt. Bring to boiling; reduce heat. Simmer, uncovered, about 15 minutes or until the marinade is reduced to ½ cup, stirring occasionally. Let mixture cool to room temperature.

2 Place chicken in a plastic bag set in a shallow dish. Pour marinade over chicken. Seal bag. Marinate in the refrigerator for 6 to 24 hours, turning bag occasionally. Drain chicken pieces, reserving marinade.

3 *For a charcoal grill,* arrange medium-hot coals around a drip pan. Test for medium heat above pan. Place chicken on grill rack over pan. Cover; grill for 50 to 60 minutes or until chicken is tender and no longer pink, brushing occasionally with the reserved marinade for the first 30 minutes. [*For a gas grill,* preheat grill. Reduce heat to medium. Adjust for indirect cooking (see page 10). Grill as above.] Makes 6 to 8 servings.

Nutrition Facts per serving: 424 calories,
22 g total fat (6 g saturated fat), 129 mg cholesterol,
553 mg sodium, 16 g carbohydrate, 37 g protein.
Daily Values: 27% vit. C, 16% iron.

# CHICKEN WITH PEACH SALSA

**Prep:** 20 minutes **Marinate:** 1 hour
**Grill:** 35 minutes

6 chicken breast halves with skin
   and bone (about 3 pounds total)
1 recipe Wine Marinade
2 medium peaches or nectarines
½ cup chopped red or green sweet
   pepper
1 ripe avocado, seeded, peeled, and
   finely chopped
2 green onions, finely chopped
½ teaspoon finely shredded lime peel
2 tablespoons lime juice
1 tablespoon snipped fresh cilantro

1 Place chicken in a plastic bag set in a shallow dish. Pour Wine Marinade over chicken; seal bag. Marinate in the refrigerator about 1 hour, turning bag occasionally.

2 Meanwhile, for salsa, peel, pit, and finely chop peaches or nectarines. In a medium bowl combine peaches or nectarines, sweet pepper, avocado, green onions, lime peel, lime juice, and cilantro. Cover and refrigerate.

3 Drain chicken, reserving marinade. *For a charcoal grill,* grill chicken on the rack of an uncovered grill directly over medium coals for 35 to 40 minutes or until tender and no longer pink, turning once halfway through grilling and brushing with marinade during the last 5 minutes of grilling. (*For a gas grill,* preheat grill. Reduce heat to medium. Place chicken on grill rack over heat. Cover and grill as above.) Serve with salsa. Serves 6.

Wine Marinade: In a bowl combine ½ cup dry white wine; 1½ teaspoons finely shredded orange peel; ⅓ cup orange juice; 2 tablespoons olive oil; 1½ teaspoons snipped fresh rosemary or ½ teaspoon dried rosemary, crushed; and 1 bay leaf.

Nutrition Facts per serving: 264 calories,
16 g total fat (3 g saturated fat), 57 mg cholesterol,
57 mg sodium, 11 g carbohydrate, 2 g fiber,
17 g protein. Daily Values: 12% vit. A, 50% vit. C,
2% calcium, 9% iron.

# Peanut-Ginger Chicken

**Prep:** 25 minutes   **Marinate:** 12 to 24 hours
**Chill (salsa):** 1 to 2 hours
**Grill:** 50 minutes

*A ginger-peanut-soy-sauce marinade takes you on a Far Eastern taste trip, and fruit salsa brings you home happy. Chicken never had it so good.*

12 chicken thighs (about 3 pounds total)
½ cup water
½ cup creamy peanut butter
¼ cup bottled chili sauce
¼ cup soy sauce
3 tablespoons cooking oil
3 tablespoons vinegar
1 tablespoon grated fresh ginger or ¾ teaspoon ground ginger
4 cloves garlic, minced
¼ to ½ teaspoon ground red pepper
1 cup chopped fresh fruit (such as peeled peaches, nectarines, pears, and/or plums)
1 cup chopped, seeded cucumber
2 tablespoons thinly sliced green onion
1 tablespoon sugar
1 recipe Napa Cabbage Slaw (optional)

1 If desired, remove skin from chicken. Place chicken in a plastic bag set in a shallow dish. For marinade, in a medium bowl gradually stir water into peanut butter. (The mixture will stiffen at first.) Stir in chili sauce, soy sauce, 2 tablespoons of the oil, 2 tablespoons of the vinegar, the ginger, garlic, and red pepper. Pour over chicken; seal bag. Marinate in the refrigerator for 12 to 24 hours, turning bag occasionally.

2 For salsa, in a medium bowl combine the remaining oil, the remaining vinegar, the fruit, cucumber, green onion, and sugar. Cover and chill for 1 to 2 hours. Drain chicken, discarding marinade.

3 *For a charcoal grill,* arrange medium-hot coals around a drip pan. Test for medium heat above the pan. Place chicken on grill rack over drip pan. Cover and grill for 50 to 60 minutes or until tender and no longer pink. [*For a gas grill*, preheat grill. Reduce heat to medium. Adjust for indirect cooking (see page 10). Grill as above.]

4 To serve, spoon salsa onto 6 dinner plates and place chicken on salsa. If desired, garnish with additional fruit and serve with Napa Cabbage Slaw. Makes 6 servings.

**Napa Cabbage Slaw:** In a large bowl combine 3 cups finely shredded napa cabbage, 1 cup finely shredded bok choy, and 2 to 3 tablespoons slivered sweet pepper. In a bowl stir together ¼ cup seasoned rice vinegar or white vinegar and 1 tablespoon toasted sesame oil. Pour vinegar mixture over cabbage mixture; toss to coat. Makes about 3 cups.

Nutrition Facts per serving: 455 calories, 30 g total fat (7 g saturated fat), 103 mg cholesterol, 715 mg sodium, 12 g carbohydrate, 2 g fiber, 34 g protein. Daily Values: 10% vit. A, 8% vit. C, 2% calcium, 14% iron.

## MUSTARD CHICKEN BARBECUE

**Prep:** 15 minutes   **Marinate:** 4 hours
**Grill:** 50 minutes

*Way down South they put mustard in their barbecue sauce. That's yellow mustard, generally. This sauce relies on Dijon for a different flavor experience.*

4 chicken drumsticks and 4 chicken thighs (about 3 pounds total); 4 whole chicken legs (drumstick and thigh); or 2 whole medium chicken breasts (about 2 pounds total), halved lengthwise
½ cup Dijon-style mustard
3 tablespoons vinegar
4 teaspoons Worcestershire sauce
1 teaspoon snipped fresh thyme or ⅛ teaspoon dried thyme, crushed
2 tablespoons mild-flavored molasses

1 If desired, remove skin from chicken. Place chicken in a plastic bag set in a shallow dish. For marinade, in a small bowl stir together mustard, vinegar, Worcestershire sauce, and thyme. Pour over chicken; seal bag. Marinate in the refrigerator for 4 to 24 hours, turning bag occasionally. Drain chicken, reserving marinade. Set aside ⅓ cup of the marinade for sauce.

2 *For a charcoal grill,* arrange medium-hot coals around a drip pan. Test for medium heat above the pan. Place chicken, bone side down, on grill rack over drip pan. Cover and grill for 50 to 60 minutes or until tender and no longer pink, brushing occasionally with marinade up to the last 5 minutes of grilling. [*For a gas grill,* preheat grill. Reduce heat to medium. Adjust for indirect cooking (see page 10). Grill as above.]

3 Meanwhile, for sauce, in a small saucepan combine the reserved ⅓ cup marinade and the molasses. Bring to boiling; reduce heat. Simmer, covered, for 5 minutes. To serve, pass sauce with chicken. Makes 4 servings.

Nutrition Facts per serving: 327 calories, 17 g total fat (4 g saturated fat), 103 mg cholesterol, 904 mg sodium, 10 g carbohydrate, 0 g fiber, 31 g protein. Daily Values: 4% vit. A, 14% vit. C, 3% calcium, 15% iron.

# Indian-Style Chicken

**Prep:** 10 minutes    **Grill:** 35 minutes

½ cup bottled barbecue sauce
¼ cup peanut butter
½ teaspoon finely shredded orange peel
1 to 2 tablespoons orange juice
1½ pounds chicken drumsticks, thighs, and/or breast halves

1 For sauce, stir together barbecue sauce, peanut butter, orange peel, and orange juice for desired consistency. Set aside.

2 *For a charcoal grill,* grill chicken on the rack of an uncovered grill directly over medium coals for 35 to 45 minutes or until tender and no longer pink, turning once halfway through grilling and brushing with sauce during the last few minutes of grilling. (*For a gas grill,* preheat grill. Reduce heat to medium. Place chicken on grill rack over heat. Cover and grill as above.)

3 Heat any remaining sauce until bubbly; serve with chicken. Makes 6 servings.

Nutrition Facts per serving: 292 calories, 16 g total fat (5 g saturated fat), 76 mg cholesterol, 367 mg sodium, 8 g carbohydrate, 1 g fiber, 29 g protein. Daily Values: 3% vit. A, 4% vit. C, 1% calcium, 7% iron.

## Good Grilling Advice

Grilling a great vegetable side dish to go along with your entree makes a lot of sense. Here are several ways to tackle the job:
• **Foil packets.** Packets made from folded heavy foil are convenient and clean-up is easy with this method, but you will sacrifice grilled flavor.
• **Direct grilling.** Use larger, sturdy produce, such as halved zucchini or squash. Lightly oil the rack before grilling.
• **Mesh grilling baskets.** No worry about food falling into the fire with these.
• **Grilling trays and woks.** These work with cut-up vegetables.
• **Foil pans.** These work for foods that aren't easily turned, such as tomatoes.

Sesame-Gingered Barbecued Chicken

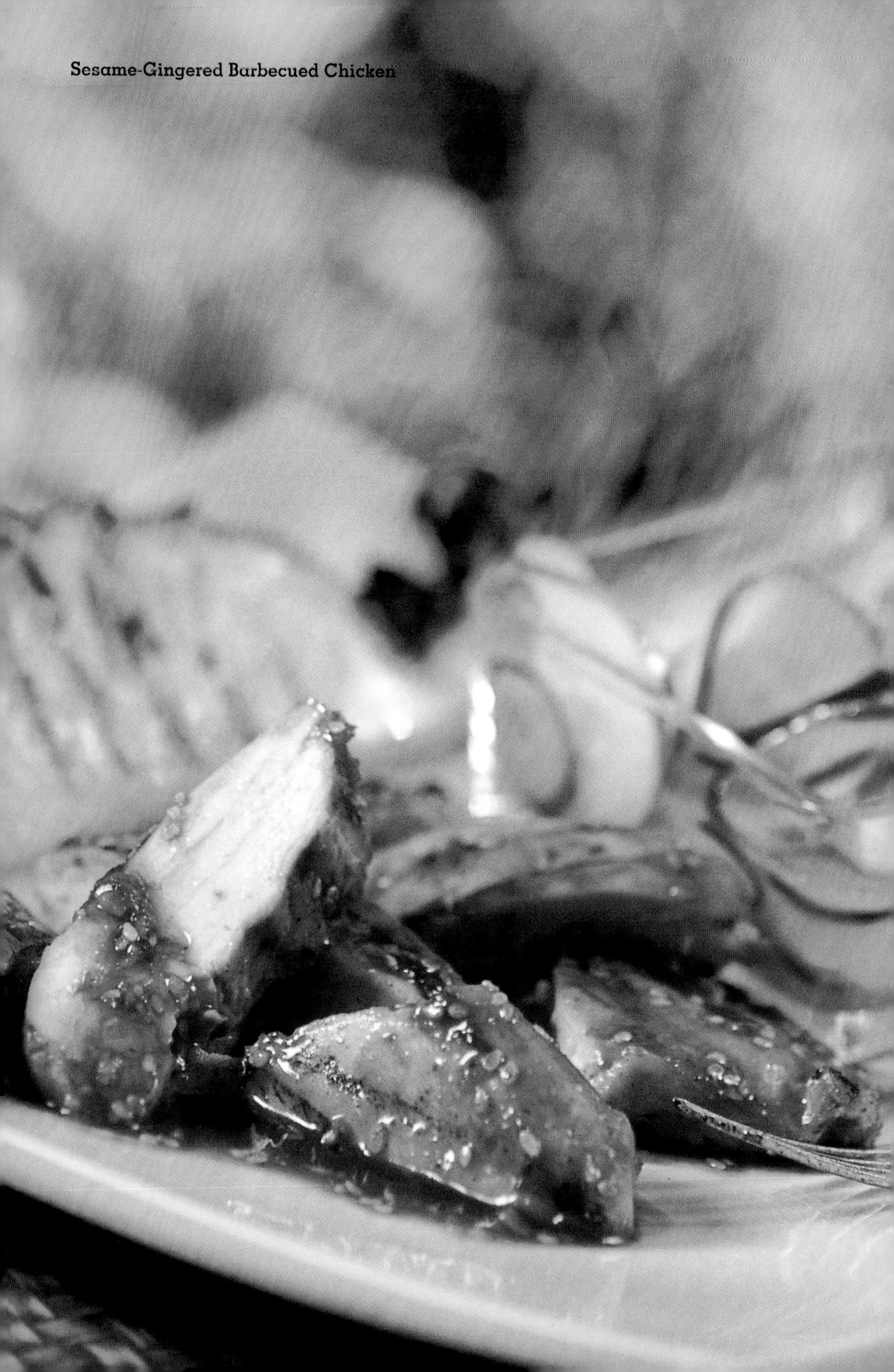

## Sesame-Gingered Barbecued Chicken

**Prep:** 15 minutes  **Grill:** 12 minutes

*What do the Orient and the Occident have in common? Well, a love of good barbecue, for one thing. This sweet-and-sour-hoisin-ginger-sesame sauce will please all palates.*

⅓ cup plum sauce or sweet-and-sour sauce
¼ cup water
3 tablespoons hoisin sauce
1½ teaspoons sesame seed (toasted, if desired)
1 teaspoon grated fresh ginger or ¼ teaspoon ground ginger
1 clove garlic, minced
¼ to ½ teaspoon Oriental chili sauce or several dashes bottled hot pepper sauce
6 medium skinless, boneless chicken breast halves and/or thighs (about 1½ pounds total)

**1** For sauce, in a small saucepan combine plum sauce, water, hoisin sauce, sesame seed, ginger, garlic, and Oriental chili sauce. Bring to boiling over medium heat, stirring frequently; reduce heat. Simmer, covered, for 3 minutes. Remove from heat.

**2** *For a charcoal grill,* grill chicken on the rack of an uncovered grill directly over medium coals for 12 to 15 minutes or until tender and no longer pink, turning once and brushing once or twice with some of the sauce during the last 5 minutes of grilling. (*For a gas grill,* preheat grill. Reduce heat to medium. Place chicken on grill rack over heat. Cover and grill as above.)

**3** Reheat and pass the remaining sauce with chicken. Makes 6 servings.

Nutrition Facts per serving: 166 calories, 4 g total fat (1 g saturated fat), 59 mg cholesterol, 216 mg sodium, 9 g carbohydrate, 0 g fiber, 22 g protein. Daily Values: 1% vit. A, 1% vit. C, 1% calcium, 5% iron.

## CHICKEN WITH MANGO CHUTNEY

**Prep:** 15 minutes  **Grill:** 10 minutes

1 ripe mango, seeded, peeled, and sliced
¼ cup dried currants or raisins
¼ cup thinly sliced green onions
2 to 3 tablespoons cider vinegar
2 tablespoons brown sugar
½ teaspoon mustard seed, crushed
⅛ teaspoon salt
4 skinless, boneless chicken thighs (about 1 pound total)
1 teaspoon five-spice powder

**1** In a medium saucepan combine half of the mango slices, the currants, green onions, vinegar, brown sugar, mustard seed, and salt. Bring to boiling; reduce heat. Simmer, covered, for 5 minutes. Remove from heat.

**2** Meanwhile, chop the remaining mango slices; set aside. Rub both sides of chicken with five-spice powder.

**3** *For a charcoal grill,* grill chicken on the rack of an uncovered grill directly over medium coals for 10 to 12 minutes or until tender and no longer pink, turning once halfway through grilling. (*For a gas grill,* preheat grill. Reduce heat to medium. Place chicken on grill rack over heat. Cover and grill as above.)

**4** To serve, stir the chopped mango into the cooked mango mixture. Serve with chicken. Makes 4 servings.

Nutrition Facts per serving: 205 calories, 6 g total fat (2 g saturated fat), 54 mg cholesterol, 125 mg sodium, 22 g carbohydrate, 2 g fiber, 17 g protein. Daily Values: 22% vit. A, 26% vit. C, 3% calcium, 10% iron.

# Herb-Stuffed Chicken Breasts

**Prep:** 15 minutes    **Grill:** 35 minutes

*Leave the skin on the chicken, if you like. It will keep the chicken moist. You can remove it before eating, if you prefer.*

 1 3-ounce package cream cheese, softened
 2 tablespoons snipped fresh basil
 1 tablespoon snipped fresh chives
 1 clove garlic, minced
 3 whole small chicken breasts (about 2¼ pounds total), halved lengthwise
 2 tablespoons olive oil or cooking oil
 1 tablespoon lemon or lime juice
 1 tablespoon water

1 For stuffing, in a small bowl stir together cheese, basil, chives, and garlic. Set aside.

2 If desired, remove skin from chicken. Make a pocket in each chicken piece by cutting horizontally from 1 side almost to the opposite side. Spoon stuffing into pockets. If necessary, secure the openings with wooden toothpicks. In a small bowl combine oil, lemon juice, and water.

3 *For a charcoal grill,* grill chicken, bone side up, on the rack of an uncovered grill directly over medium coals for 35 to 45 minutes or until tender and no longer pink, turning once and brushing occasionally with oil mixture during the last half of grilling. (*For a gas grill,* preheat grill. Reduce heat to medium. Place chicken, bone side up, on grill rack over heat. Cover and grill as above.) Makes 6 servings.

Nutrition Facts per serving: 273 calories, 17 g total fat (6 g saturated fat), 94 mg cholesterol, 108 mg sodium, 1 g carbohydrate, 0 g fiber, 29 g protein. Daily Values: 8% vit. A, 2% vit. C, 2% calcium, 7% iron.

# NORTH INDIAN CHICKEN WITH YOGURT

**Prep:** 15 minutes    **Grill:** 35 minutes

 1 teaspoon grated fresh ginger
 ½ teaspoon ground allspice
 ½ teaspoon ground cinnamon
 ½ teaspoon crushed red pepper
 ¼ teaspoon curry powder
 2 cloves garlic, minced
 1 tablespoon lemon juice
 4 chicken drumsticks
 4 chicken thighs (about 3 pounds total)
   Plain yogurt or chutney

1 In a small mixing bowl stir together ginger, allspice, cinnamon, red pepper, curry powder, and garlic. Stir in lemon juice until a paste forms.

2 Loosen skin of chicken, but do not remove. Rub paste mixture under skin of chicken. Rub any remaining paste mixture over skin of the chicken.

3 *For a charcoal grill,* grill chicken on the rack of an uncovered grill directly over medium coals for 35 to 45 minutes or until tender and no longer pink, turning once halfway through grilling. (*For a gas grill,* preheat grill. Reduce heat to medium. Place chicken on grill rack over heat. Cover and grill as above.) Serve with yogurt or chutney. Makes 4 servings.

Nutrition Facts per serving: 235 calories, 12 g total fat (3 g saturated fat), 99 mg cholesterol, 97 mg sodium, 2 g carbohydrate, 0 g fiber, 28 g protein. Daily Values: 5% vit. A, 4% vit. C, 1% calcium, 10% iron.

# Honey-Glazed Drumsticks

**Prep:** 10 minutes   **Grill:** 35 minutes

    3 tablespoons honey
    3 tablespoons Dijon-style mustard
    1 teaspoon lemon juice
    1 teaspoon finely shredded orange
        peel
    8 chicken drumsticks (about
        1½ pounds total)

**1** For sauce, stir together honey, mustard, lemon juice, and orange peel. Set aside.

**2** *For a charcoal grill,* grill chicken on the rack of an uncovered grill directly over medium coals for 35 to 45 minutes or until chicken is tender and no longer pink, turning once halfway through grilling and brushing with sauce during the last 10 minutes of grilling. (*For a gas grill,* preheat grill. Reduce heat to medium. Place chicken on grill rack over heat. Cover and grill as above.) Makes 4 servings.

Nutrition Facts per serving: 215 calories, 6 g total fat (1 g saturated fat), 82 mg cholesterol, 368 mg sodium, 14 g carbohydrate, 0 g fiber, 26 g protein. Daily Values: 1% vit. A, 2% vit. C, 14% calcium, 8% iron.

# APRICOT-AND-MUSTARD-GLAZED CHICKEN

**Prep:** 15 minutes   **Grill:** 50 minutes

*Apricot spread is the foundation for this glaze, while rosemary and mustard add interesting flavor notes.*

    ½ cup apricot spreadable fruit
    1 tablespoon white vinegar
    1 tablespoon Dijon-style mustard
    1 tablespoon snipped fresh
        rosemary or 1 teaspoon dried
        rosemary, crushed
    2 cloves garlic, minced
    ¼ teaspoon pepper
    3 whole medium chicken breasts
        (about 3 pounds total), halved
        lengthwise

**1** For glaze, in a small saucepan combine spreadable fruit, vinegar, mustard, rosemary, garlic, and pepper. Cook and stir over low heat until heated through. Remove from heat.

**2** *For a charcoal grill,* arrange medium-hot coals around a drip pan. Test for medium heat above the pan. Place chicken, skin side down, on grill rack over drip pan. Cover and grill for 50 to 60 minutes or until tender and no longer pink, turning once and brushing occasionally with glaze during the last 10 minutes of grilling. [*For a gas grill,* preheat grill. Reduce heat to medium. Adjust for indirect cooking (see page 10). Grill as above.] Makes 6 servings.

Nutrition Facts per serving: 255 calories, 8 g total fat (2 g saturated fat), 83 mg cholesterol, 132 mg sodium, 17 g carbohydrate, 0 g fiber, 29 g protein. Daily Values: 2% vit. A, 1% calcium, 7% iron.

Jalapeño and Basil-Glazed Chicken

# Jalapeño and Basil-Glazed Chicken

**Prep:** 15 minutes **Grill:** 50 minutes

*Basil and jalapeño? Sure! They marry perfectly brushed on this red-pepper-rubbed chicken.*

2 whole medium chicken breasts
(about 2 pounds total), halved
lengthwise
1 tablespoon olive oil
1 clove garlic, minced
¼ teaspoon salt
¼ teaspoon ground red pepper
½ cup jalapeño pepper jelly
2 tablespoons snipped fresh basil
1 tablespoon lime juice

1 If desired, remove skin from chicken. For rub, in a small bowl combine oil, garlic, salt, and red pepper. Spoon rub evenly over chicken; rub in with your fingers. For sauce, in a small saucepan combine jalapeño jelly, basil, and lime juice. Cook and stir over low heat until jelly is melted. Remove from heat.

2 *For a charcoal grill,* arrange medium-hot coals around a drip pan. Test for medium heat above the pan. Place chicken, bone side up, on grill rack over drip pan. Cover and grill for 50 to 60 minutes or until tender and no longer pink, turning once and brushing with some of the sauce during the last 5 minutes of grilling. [*For a gas grill,* preheat grill. Reduce heat to medium. Adjust for indirect cooking (see page 10). Grill as above.] To serve, reheat and pass the remaining sauce with chicken. Makes 4 servings.

Nutrition Facts per serving: 377 calories,
13 g total fat (3 g saturated fat), 104 mg cholesterol,
226 mg sodium, 27 g carbohydrate, 0 g fiber,
37 g protein. Daily Values: 4% vit. A, 4% vit. C,
2% calcium, 12% iron.

# CRANBERRY-MAPLE CHICKEN

**Prep:** 15 minutes **Grill:** 1¼ hours

*Nothing beats a whole grilled chicken, especially one glazed in a distinctive New-England-style sauce (which goes great on turkey, too).*

½ cup whole cranberry sauce
¼ cup maple syrup
3 tablespoons catsup
2 tablespoons cider vinegar
½ teaspoon onion powder
1 3- to 3½-pound whole broiler-fryer
chicken, halved lengthwise

1 For sauce, in a small saucepan combine cranberry sauce, maple syrup, catsup, vinegar, and onion powder. Bring to boiling; reduce heat. Simmer, uncovered, for 5 minutes, stirring occasionally. Remove saucepan from heat.

2 *For a charcoal grill,* arrange medium-hot coals around a drip pan. Test for medium heat above the pan. Place chicken, bone side down, on grill rack over drip pan. Cover and grill for 1¼ to 1½ hours or until tender and no longer pink, brushing occasionally with some of the sauce during the last 10 minutes of grilling. [*For a gas grill,* preheat grill. Reduce heat to medium. Adjust for indirect cooking (see page 10). Grill as above.] To serve, cut each chicken half into 2 or 3 portions. Reheat and pass the remaining sauce with chicken. Makes 4 to 6 servings.

Nutrition Facts per serving: 385 calories,
15 g total fat (4 g saturated fat), 99 mg cholesterol,
255 mg sodium, 31 g carbohydrate, 1 g fiber,
31 g protein. Daily Values: 6% vit. A, 5% vit. C,
1% calcium, 12% iron.

# Garlic-Grilled Whole Chicken

**Prep:** 15 minutes  **Grill:** 1¼ hours
**Stand:** 10 minutes

*For the fullest effect on your taste buds, work the spices in well under the skin.*

- 1 3- to 3½-pound whole broiler-fryer chicken
- 3 cloves garlic
- ½ of a lemon, sliced
- ½ of a red sweet pepper, sliced
- 1 tablespoon snipped fresh basil or 1 teaspoon dried basil, crushed
- ⅛ teaspoon salt
- 1 tablespoon olive oil or cooking oil
- 1 tablespoon lemon juice

**1** Remove neck and giblets from chicken. Twist wing tips under the back. Cut 1 clove garlic in half lengthwise. Rub skin of chicken with cut edge of garlic. Place garlic halves, lemon slices, and sweet pepper slices in cavity of chicken. Mince remaining garlic. Combine garlic, basil, and salt; set aside.

**2** Starting at the neck on 1 side of the breast, slip your fingers between skin and meat, loosening the skin as you work toward the tail end. Once your entire hand is under the skin, free the skin around the thigh and leg area up to, but not around, the tip of the drumstick. Repeat on the other side of the breast. Rub garlic mixture under skin directly on meat. Securely fasten opening with wooden toothpicks. Combine oil and lemon juice; brush over chicken.

**3** *For a charcoal grill*, arrange medium-hot coals around a drip pan. Test for medium heat above the pan. Place chicken, breast side up, on grill rack over drip pan. Cover and grill for 1¼ to 1½ hours or until chicken is no longer pink and drumsticks move easily, brushing occasionally with oil mixture up to the last 15 minutes of grilling. [*For a gas grill*, preheat grill. Reduce heat to medium. Adjust for indirect cooking (see page 10). Grill as above, except place chicken on a rack in a roasting pan.]

**4** Remove chicken from grill. Cover with foil; let stand for 10 minutes before carving. Makes 5 servings.

Nutrition Facts per serving: 289 calories, 17 g total fat (4 g saturated fat), 95 mg cholesterol, 142 mg sodium, 3 g carbohydrate, 0 g fiber, 30 g protein. Daily Values: 10% vit. A, 37% vit. C, 2% calcium, 10% iron.

## FIVE-SPICE ROTISSERIE CHICKEN

**Prep:** 15 minutes  **Grill:** 1¼ hours
**Stand:** 10 minutes
**Special Equipment:** Spit rod

- 1 3- to 3½-pound whole broiler-fryer chicken
- 2 to 3 teaspoons five-spice powder
- 2 tablespoons soy sauce
- 1 tablespoon cooking oil
- 1 clove garlic, minced
  Cooked rice (optional)
- 2 tablespoons snipped fresh cilantro (optional)

**1** Remove neck and giblets from chicken. If desired, sprinkle salt lightly inside the body cavity of the chicken. Starting at the neck on 1 side of the breast, slip your fingers between skin and meat, loosening the skin as you work toward the tail end. Once your entire hand is under the skin, free the skin around the thigh and leg area up to, but not around, the tip of the drumstick. Repeat on the other side of the breast. Rub five-spice powder under the skin directly on meat. Securely fasten opening with wooden toothpicks. Skewer the neck skin to the back.

**2** In a small bowl combine soy sauce, cooking oil, and garlic. Lightly brush some of the mixture over chicken.

**3** To mount chicken on spit rod, place one holding fork on rod, tines toward point. Insert rod through chicken, neck end first, pressing tines of holding fork firmly into breast meat. To tie wings, slip a 30-inch piece of 100-percent-cotton string under back of chicken; bring ends of string to front, looping around each wing tip. Tie in center of breast, leaving equal string ends. To tie legs, slip a 24-inch piece of string under tail. Loop string around tail, then around crossed legs. Tie very tightly to hold bird securely on spit, again leaving string ends. Pull together the strings attached to wings and legs; tie tightly. Adjust second holding fork and tighten screws. Test the balance; make adjustments as necessary.

**4** *For a charcoal grill,* arrange medium-hot coals around a drip pan. Test for medium heat above the pan. Attach spit; turn on the motor and lower the grill hood. Let the chicken rotate over the drip pan for 1¼ to 1½ hours or until chicken is no longer pink and the drumsticks move easily in sockets, brushing occasionally with soy sauce mixture. [*For a gas grill,* preheat grill. Reduce heat to medium. Adjust for indirect cooking (see page 10). Grill as above.]

**5** To serve, remove chicken from spit. Cover with foil; let stand for 10 minutes before carving. If desired, serve with rice seasoned with snipped cilantro. Makes 4 servings.

Nutrition Facts per serving: 362 calories, 22 g total fat (6 g saturated fat), 118 mg cholesterol, 626 mg sodium, 2 g carbohydrate, 0 g fiber, 37 g protein. Daily Values: 6% vit. A, 3% calcium, 15% iron.

## Flaming Facts

**Free-range or field-grazed chickens are considered cream of the crop by many chefs and home cooks today. They believe chickens that have been allowed to roam outdoors are more flavorful than factory-raised chickens. For various reasons, however, there's no guarantee that the end result will be better than other chicken. Before paying for a higher-priced chicken, ask your butcher exactly how the chicken was raised, the benefits to the consumer; then decide if the additional cost is worth it to you.**

# Chicken Whirlibirds

**Prep:** 15 minutes **Grill:** 1¼ hours
**Stand:** 10 minutes
**Special Equipment:** Spit rod

¼ cup dry white wine
2 tablespoons cooking oil
2 tablespoons lemon juice
1 tablespoon snipped fresh parsley
1 tablespoon snipped fresh
 rosemary plus 2 sprigs fresh
 rosemary or 2 teaspoons dried
 rosemary, crushed
1 teaspoon prepared mustard
1 teaspoon Worcestershire sauce
½ teaspoon salt
¼ teaspoon celery seed
¼ teaspoon pepper
2 3- to 3½-pound whole broiler-fryer
 chickens
¼ cup apple jelly

**1** For sauce, in a small bowl combine wine, oil, lemon juice, parsley, the 1 tablespoon snipped fresh rosemary or 1 teaspoon of the dried rosemary, the mustard, Worcestershire sauce, salt, celery seed, and pepper. Set aside.

**2** Remove the necks and giblets from chickens. Rub additional salt and the remaining dried rosemary inside the body cavities (or place rosemary sprigs in birds). Skewer the neck skin to the backs.

**3** To mount one chicken on a spit rod, place one holding fork on rod, tines toward point. Insert rod through chicken cavity, pressing tines of holding fork firmly into breast meat. To tie wings, slip a 30-inch piece of 100-percent-cotton string under back of chicken; bring ends of string to front, looping around each wing tip. Tie in center of breast, leaving equal string ends. To tie legs, slip a 24-inch piece of string under tail. Loop string around tail, then around crossed legs. Tie tightly to hold bird securely on spit, again leaving string ends. Pull together the strings attached to wings and legs; tie tightly.

**4** Place the second chicken on spit rod so that the tails of both birds meet. Tie second chicken as for first. Place the second holding fork on rod, tines toward the chicken; press tines of holding fork firmly into breast meat. Adjust forks and tighten screws. Test the balance, making adjustments as necessary.

**5** For a charcoal grill, arrange medium-hot coals around a drip pan. Test for medium heat above the pan. Attach spit; turn on the motor and lower the grill hood. Let the chickens rotate over drip pan for 1¼ to 1½ hours or until chickens are no longer pink and drumsticks move easily, brushing every 15 minutes with sauce during the first 45 minutes of grilling.

**6** Add jelly to the remaining sauce; stir vigorously until smooth. Brush chickens occasionally with jelly sauce up to the last 15 minutes of grilling. [For a gas grill, preheat grill. Reduce heat to medium. Adjust for indirect cooking (see page 10). Grill as above.]

**7** To serve, remove chickens from spit. Cover with foil; let stand for 10 minutes before carving. Makes 8 to 10 servings.

Nutrition Facts per serving: 386 calories,
22 g total fat (6 g saturated fat),
118 mg cholesterol, 260 mg sodium,
7 g carbohydrate, 0 g fiber, 37 g protein. Daily
Values: 6% vit. A, 6% vit. C, 2% calcium, 13% iron.

## GREEN-TEA-AND-GINGER-SMOKED CHICKEN

**Prep:** 20 minutes **Marinate:** 4 to 24 hours
**Grill:** 1¼ hours **Stand:** 10 minutes

*Green tea leaves and ginger are smoked in a foil pan to give this chicken an exotic flavor.*

1 3- to 3½-pound whole broiler-fryer
 chicken
½ cup rice wine or dry sherry
2 tablespoons grated fresh ginger
2 tablespoons soy sauce
½ teaspoon pepper
3 tablespoons honey
1 teaspoon soy sauce
1 ½-inch slice peeled fresh ginger
½ cup green tea leaves
6 ¼-inch slices peeled fresh ginger

1 Remove the neck and giblets from chicken. Skewer the neck skin to the back. Twist wing tips under back. Tie legs to tail with 100-percent-cotton string. Place chicken in a plastic bag set in a deep bowl.

2 For marinade, in a small bowl combine rice wine, the grated ginger, the 2 tablespoons soy sauce, and the pepper. Pour over chicken; seal bag. Marinate in the refrigerator for 4 to 24 hours, turning bag occasionally.

3 For glaze, in a small saucepan combine honey, the 1 teaspoon soy sauce, and the 1 slice of ginger. Bring to boiling; reduce heat. Simmer, uncovered, for 1 minute. Remove from heat. Discard ginger.

4 Fold an 18×9-inch piece of heavy foil in half to make a 9-inch square. Fold up sides of foil, forming a pan. Place tea leaves and the 6 slices of ginger in foil pan. Drain chicken, discarding marinade.

5 *For a charcoal grill,* arrange medium-hot coals around a drip pan. Test for medium heat above pan. Place chicken, breast side up, on grill rack over drip pan. Place tea leaves and ginger in foil pan on grill rack directly over coals. Cover; grill for 1¼ to 1½ hours or until chicken is no longer pink and drumsticks move easily. [*For a gas grill,* preheat grill. Reduce heat to medium. Adjust for indirect cooking (see page 10). Grill as above, except place chicken on a rack in a roasting pan.]

6 Remove chicken from grill; discard tea leaves and ginger. Cover chicken with foil; let stand 10 minutes before carving. To serve, drizzle with glaze. Makes 4 servings.

Nutrition Facts per serving: 418 calories, 18 g total fat (5 g saturated fat), 118 mg cholesterol, 712 mg sodium, 17 g carbohydrate, 0 g fiber, 37 g protein. Daily Values: 6% vit. A, 2% calcium, 14% iron.

# Herbed Chicken

**Prep:** 15 minutes  **Grill:** 1¼ hours
**Stand:** 10 minutes

- 1 3- to 3½-pound whole broiler-fryer chicken
- 2 tablespoons margarine or butter, melted
- 3 tablespoons lemon juice
- 1 teaspoon dried thyme, savory, or sage, crushed
- 3 cloves garlic, minced
- ¼ teaspoon salt
- ¼ teaspoon pepper

1 Remove the neck and giblets from chicken. Skewer the neck skin to the back. Twist wing tips under back. Tie legs to tail with 100-percent-cotton string.

2 Stir together the melted margarine or butter, lemon juice, desired herb, garlic, salt, and pepper. Brush margarine mixture over chicken.

3 *For a charcoal grill,* arrange medium-hot coals around a drip pan. Test for medium heat above pan. Place chicken, breast side up, on grill rack over drip pan. Cover and grill for 1¼ to 1½ hours or until chicken is no longer pink and drumsticks move easily, brushing with margarine mixture the first 45 minutes of grilling. [*For a gas grill,* preheat grill. Reduce heat to medium. Adjust for indirect cooking (see page 10). Grill as above, except place chicken on a rack in a roasting pan.]

4 Remove chicken from grill. Cover chicken with foil; let stand 10 minutes before carving. Makes 4 servings.

Nutrition Facts per serving: 380 calories, 24 g total fat (6 g saturated fat), 118 mg cholesterol, 311 mg sodium, 2 g carbohydrate, 0 g fiber, 37 g protein. Daily Values: 13% vit. A, 10% vit. C, 2% calcium, 13% iron.

## HONEY-SOY GRILLED CHICKEN

**Prep:** 15 minutes  **Marinate:** 6 to 24 hours
**Grill:** 1¼ hours  **Stand:** 10 minutes

- 1 3- to 4-pound whole broiler-fryer chicken
- ¼ cup water
- ¼ cup soy sauce
- ¼ cup dry sherry
- 1 green onion, sliced
- 2 cloves garlic, minced
- ½ teaspoon five-spice powder
- 1 tablespoon cooking oil
- 1 tablespoon honey

**1** Remove the neck and giblets from chicken. Skewer the neck skin to the back. Twist wing tips under back. Tie legs to tail with 100-percent-cotton string. Place chicken in a plastic bag set in a deep bowl.

**2** For marinade, in a small bowl combine water, soy sauce, sherry, green onion, garlic, and five-spice powder. Pour over chicken; seal bag. Marinate in the refrigerator for 6 to 24 hours, turning bag occasionally. Drain chicken, discarding marinade. Brush chicken with oil.

**3** *For a charcoal grill*, arrange medium-hot coals around a drip pan. Test for medium heat above the pan. Place chicken, breast side up, on grill rack over drip pan. Cover and grill for 1¼ to 1¾ hours or until chicken is no longer pink and drumsticks move easily, brushing with the honey during the last 10 minutes of grilling. [*For a gas grill*, preheat grill. Reduce heat to medium. Adjust for indirect cooking (see page 10). Grill as above, except place chicken on a rack in a roasting pan.]

**4** Remove chicken from grill. Cover with foil; let stand for 10 minutes before carving. Makes 6 to 8 servings.

Nutrition Facts per serving: 251 calories, 14 g total fat (4 g saturated fat), 79 mg cholesterol, 245 mg sodium, 3 g carbohydrate, 0 g fiber, 25 g protein. Daily Values: 4% vit. A, 1% calcium, 8% iron.

## Herbed-Mustard Chicken

**Prep:** 20 minutes  **Grill:** 1¼ hours

- 2 tablespoons creamy Dijon-style mustard blend
- 1 tablespoon snipped fresh parsley
- 1 tablespoon snipped fresh oregano
- 1 tablespoon water
- ⅛ teaspoon ground red pepper
- 1 3- to 3½-pound whole broiler-fryer chicken
- 1 tablespoon cooking oil

**1** For sauce, in a small bowl combine mustard blend, parsley, oregano, water, and red pepper. Cover the sauce and refrigerate until ready to use.

**2** Remove the neck and giblets from chicken. Skewer the neck skin to the back. Twist wing tips under back. Tie legs to tail with 100-percent-cotton string. Brush cooking oil over chicken.

**3** *For a charcoal grill*, arrange medium-hot coals around a drip pan. Test for medium heat above the pan. Place chicken, breast side up, on grill rack over drip pan. Cover and grill for 1¼ to 1½ hours or until chicken is no longer pink and drumsticks move easily, brushing with the mustard sauce during the last 10 minutes of grilling. [*For a gas grill*, preheat grill. Reduce heat to medium. Adjust for indirect cooking (see page 10). Grill as above, except place chicken on a rack in a roasting pan.] Makes 4 servings.

Nutrition Facts per serving: 371 calories, 23 g total fat (6 g saturated fat), 118 mg cholesterol, 216 mg sodium, 2 g carbohydrate, 0 g fiber, 37 g protein. Daily Values: 7% vit. A, 2% vit. C, 1% calcium, 11% iron.

Honey-Soy Grilled Chicken

## MEDITERRANEAN GAME HENS WITH HERB SAUCE

**Prep:** 20 minutes  **Marinate:** 30 minutes
**Grill:** 40 minutes

- 2 1¼- to 1½-pound Cornish game hens, halved lengthwise
- ⅓ cup loosely packed fresh basil leaves
- ⅓ cup loosely packed fresh parsley
- ¼ cup olive oil
- 2 tablespoons lemon juice
- 1 tablespoon Dijon-style mustard
- 2 teaspoons snipped fresh rosemary
- 1 clove garlic, halved
- ¼ teaspoon salt
- ¼ teaspoon pepper
- ¼ cup dairy sour cream
  Fresh rosemary sprigs (optional)

**1** Place hens in a plastic bag set in a deep bowl. In a blender container or food processor bowl combine basil, parsley, oil, lemon juice, mustard, rosemary, garlic, salt, and pepper. Cover and blend or process until nearly smooth. Pour ¼ cup of herb mixture over hens; seal bag. Marinate at room temperature for 30 minutes or in the refrigerator for up to 6 hours, turning bag occasionally. Cover; chill remaining herb mixture for sauce. Drain Cornish hens, discarding the marinade.

**2** *For a charcoal grill,* arrange medium-hot coals around a drip pan. Test for medium heat above the pan. Place Cornish hens, skin sides up, on grill rack over drip pan. Cover and grill for 40 to 50 minutes or until tender and no longer pink. [*For a gas grill,* preheat grill. Reduce heat to medium. Adjust for indirect cooking (see page 10). Grill as above.]

**3** For sauce, in a small bowl stir together remaining herb mixture and sour cream. Serve with hens. If desired, garnish with additional rosemary. Makes 4 servings.

Nutrition Facts per serving: 489 calories,
38 g total fat (9 g saturated fat), 127 mg cholesterol,
300 mg sodium, 2 g carbohydrate, 0 g fiber,
37 g protein. Daily Values: 6% vit. A, 15% vit. C,
3% calcium, 2% iron.

## Cornish Game Hens Provençal

**Prep:** 15 minutes  **Marinate:** 24 hours
**Grill:** 40 minutes

- 2 1¼- to 1½-pound Cornish game hens, halved lengthwise
- ½ cup Merlot or other dry red wine
- 2 tablespoons olive oil
- 1 tablespoon snipped fresh rosemary
- 1 tablespoon snipped fresh thyme
- 4 cloves garlic, minced
- ½ teaspoon salt
- ½ teaspoon cracked pepper

**1** Place hen halves in a plastic bag set in a deep bowl. For marinade, in a small bowl combine the wine, olive oil, rosemary, thyme, garlic, salt, and pepper. Pour over hens; seal bag. Marinate in the refrigerator for 24 hours, turning bag occasionally.

**2** Drain hens, reserving marinade. *For a charcoal grill,* arrange medium-hot coals around a drip pan. Test for medium heat above the pan. Place Cornish hens, skin sides up, on grill rack over drip pan. Cover and grill for 40 to 50 minutes or until tender and no longer pink, brushing with reserved marinade during the first 30 minutes. [*For a gas grill,* preheat grill. Reduce heat to medium. Adjust for indirect cooking (see page 10). Grill as above.] Makes 4 servings.

Nutrition Facts per serving: 373 calories,
26 g total fat (5 g saturated fat), 100 mg cholesterol,
361 mg sodium, 2 g carbohydrate, 0 g fiber,
31 g protein. Daily Values: 2% vit. C., 1%calcium,
2% iron.

## TURKEY BURGERS WITH CURRY CATSUP

**Prep:** 20 minutes  **Grill:** 14 minutes

- 1 recipe Curry Catsup (recipe, page 275)
- 1 slightly beaten egg
- ¼ cup fine dry bread crumbs

2 tablespoons snipped fresh cilantro
2 teaspoons grated fresh ginger
1 clove garlic, minced
½ teaspoon salt
½ teaspoon curry powder
¼ teaspoon freshly ground pepper
1 pound uncooked ground turkey
2 large pita bread rounds, toasted
   (optional)

1 Prepare Curry Catsup. Set aside. Meanwhile, in a medium bowl combine egg, bread crumbs, cilantro, ginger, garlic, salt, curry powder, and pepper. Add ground turkey; mix well. Shape turkey mixture into four ¾-inch-thick patties. (If mixture is sticky, moisten hands with water.)

2 *For a charcoal grill,* grill burgers on the lightly greased rack of an uncovered grill directly over medium coals for 14 to 18 minutes or until no longer pink, turning once halfway through grilling. (*For a gas grill,* preheat grill. Reduce heat to medium. Place burgers on grill rack over heat. Cover and grill as above.)

3 To serve, spoon Curry Catsup over burgers. (Or, if using, cut pita bread in half; place burgers in pita halves; top with Curry Catsup.) Makes 4 servings.

Curry Catsup: Chop 4 medium plum tomatoes. In a medium saucepan combine tomatoes, ½ cup catsup, 3 tablespoons finely chopped onion, 2 tablespoons snipped fresh cilantro, and 2 teaspoons curry powder. Bring to boiling; reduce heat. Simmer, covered, for 5 minutes, stirring occasionally. Season to taste with salt and pepper.

Nutrition Facts per serving: 407 calories, 11 g total fat (3 g saturated fat), 95 mg cholesterol, 1,113 mg sodium, 52 g carbohydrate, 2 g fiber, 24 g protein. Daily Values: 10% vit. A, 33% vit. C, 8% calcium, 27% iron.

# Aloha Turkey Burgers

**Prep:** 15 minutes  **Grill:** 14 minutes

1 8-ounce can pineapple slices
1 tablespoon prepared mustard
2 teaspoons sugar
1 teaspoon cornstarch
1 tablespoon margarine or butter
1 beaten egg
½ cup soft bread crumbs
¼ cup finely chopped celery
¼ teaspoon salt
¼ teaspoon ground ginger
⅛ teaspoon pepper
1 pound uncooked ground turkey
4 cups shredded mixed salad greens

1 For sauce, drain pineapple, reserving juice. Set pineapple aside. In a saucepan combine mustard, sugar, and cornstarch. Stir in reserved pineapple juice. Cook and stir until thickened and bubbly. Cook and stir for 2 minutes more. Stir in margarine. Keep sauce warm.

2 In a medium bowl combine egg, bread crumbs, celery, salt, ginger, and pepper. Add ground turkey; mix well. Shape turkey mixture into four ¾-inch-thick patties.

3 *For a charcoal grill,* grill burgers on the lightly greased rack on an uncovered grill directly over medium coals for 14 to 18 minutes or until no longer pink, turning once halfway through grilling and brushing often with sauce. Place the pineapple slices on the grill rack the last 5 minutes of grilling or until heated through, turning once. (*For a gas grill,* preheat grill. Reduce heat to medium. Place burgers, then pineapple on grill rack over heat. Cover and grill as above.)

4 Divide mixed greens among 4 dinner plates. Top each with a grilled patty and a slice of grilled pineapple. Spoon any remaining sauce over all. Makes 4 servings.

Nutrition Facts per serving: 272 calories, 13 g total fat (3 g saturated fat), 95 mg cholesterol, 324 mg sodium, 20 g carbohydrate, 1 g fiber, 18 g protein. Daily Values: 8% vit. A, 18% vit. C, 4% calcium, 14% iron.

## TERIYAKI TURKEY PATTIES

**Prep:** 15 minutes  **Grill:** 14 minutes

1 beaten egg
½ cup soft bread crumbs
¼ cup chopped water chestnuts
2 tablespoons chopped onion
2 tablespoons teriyaki sauce
1 pound uncooked ground turkey
¼ cup orange marmalade
½ teaspoon sesame seed

**1** In a medium bowl combine egg, bread crumbs, water chestnuts, onion, and 1 tablespoon of the teriyaki sauce. Add ground turkey; mix well. Shape turkey mixture into four ¾-inch-thick patties (mixture will be soft).

**2** *For a charcoal grill,* grill patties on the lightly greased rack of an uncovered grill directly over medium coals for 14 to 18 minutes or until no longer pink, turning once halfway through grilling. (*For a gas grill,* preheat grill. Reduce heat to medium. Place patties on grill rack over heat. Cover and grill as above.)

**3** Meanwhile, in a small saucepan combine orange marmalade, the remaining 1 tablespoon teriyaki sauce, and sesame seed. Cook over low heat until marmalade melts, stirring occasionally. Spoon sauce over cooked patties. Makes 4 servings.

Nutrition Facts per serving: 241 calories, 10 g total fat (3 g saturated fat), 95 mg cholesterol, 444 mg sodium, 20 g carbohydrate, 1 g fiber, 18 g protein. Daily Values: 2% vit. A, 2% vit. C, 3% calcium, 23% iron.

## Turkey Steak and Portobello Sandwiches

**Prep:** 15 minutes  **Marinate:** 2 to 4 hours
**Grill:** 12 minutes

*Both the turkey breasts and mushrooms bathe in a balsamic vinegar marinade. How could something so good be made even better? Try it with Tomato Aioli!*

4 small fresh portobello mushrooms
    (2½ to 3 inches in diameter)
4 turkey breast tenderloin steaks,
    cut ½ inch thick (about 1 pound
    total)
⅓ cup balsamic vinegar
2 tablespoons brown sugar
2 tablespoons olive oil
1 teaspoon snipped fresh thyme or
    ½ teaspoon dried thyme, crushed
1 clove garlic, minced
½ teaspoon salt
½ teaspoon bottled hot pepper sauce
2 medium red sweet peppers,
    quartered lengthwise
1 recipe Tomato Aioli (recipe,
    page 44) (optional)
4 hamburger buns or kaiser
    rolls, split and toasted
8 lettuce leaves

**1** Cut off the mushroom stems even with the caps; discard stems. Rinse mushroom caps. Gently pat dry with paper towels. Place turkey and mushroom caps in a plastic bag set in a shallow dish.

**2** For marinade, in a small bowl combine vinegar, brown sugar, oil, thyme, garlic, salt, and hot pepper sauce. Pour over turkey and mushrooms; seal bag. Marinate in the refrigerator for 2 to 4 hours, turning bag occasionally. Drain turkey and mushrooms, discarding marinade. If desired, place mushrooms and the sweet peppers in a grill basket.

**3** *For a charcoal grill,* grill turkey, mushrooms, and sweet peppers on the rack of an uncovered grill directly over medium coals until turkey and vegetables are tender and turkey is no longer pink, turning once halfway through grilling. (Allow 12 to 15 minutes for turkey and 10 to 12 minutes for vegetables.) (*For a gas grill,* preheat grill. Reduce heat to medium. Place turkey, mushrooms, and sweet peppers on grill rack over heat. Cover and grill as above.) Remove turkey and vegetables from grill.

**4** If desired, spread some Tomato Aioli on toasted buns or kaiser rolls. Layer with lettuce, turkey, mushrooms, and sweet peppers. Makes 4 servings.

Nutrition Facts per serving: 294 calories, 7 g total fat (2 g saturated fat), 50 mg cholesterol, 427 mg sodium, 30 g carbohydrate, 1 g fiber, 27 g protein. Daily Values: 28% vit. A, 111% vit. C, 7% calcium, 24% iron.

## SPICY TURKEY SANDWICHES

**Prep:** 15 minutes  **Grill:** 16 minutes

*The American bird goes Deep South in these tongue-tingling, delightful sandwiches.*

- ½ cup bottled onion-hickory barbecue sauce
- 1 small fresh jalapeño pepper, seeded and finely chopped
- 1 tablespoon tahini (sesame seed paste)
- 4 fresh tomatillos, husked and halved lengthwise, or ½ cup salsa verde
- 2 turkey breast tenderloins (about 1 pound total)
- 4 French-style rolls, split and toasted
  Spinach leaves

**1** For sauce, in a small bowl combine barbecue sauce, jalapeño pepper, and tahini. Transfer half of the sauce to another bowl for basting. Reserve the remaining sauce until ready to serve. If using, thread tomatillos onto two 8- to 10-inch metal skewers. Set aside.

**2** Brush both sides of turkey with some of the basting sauce.

**3** *For a charcoal grill,* grill turkey and tomatillo kabobs on the rack of an uncovered grill directly over medium coals until turkey and tomatillos are tender and turkey is no longer pink, turning once and brushing turkey once with the remaining basting sauce halfway through grilling. (Allow 16 to 20 minutes for turkey and about 8 minutes for tomatillos.) (*For a gas grill,* preheat grill. Reduce heat to medium. Place turkey and tomatillo kabobs on grill rack over heat. Cover and grill as above.) Transfer turkey and tomatillos to a cutting board; cool slightly. Thinly slice turkey and chop tomatillos.

**4** Serve the turkey slices on toasted rolls with the reserved sauce, tomatillos or salsa verde, and spinach leaves. Makes 4 servings.

Nutrition Facts per serving: 378 calories, 8 g total fat (2 g saturated fat), 50 mg cholesterol, 776 mg sodium, 45 g carbohydrate, 1 g fiber, 30 g protein. Daily Values: 12% vit. A, 24% vit. C, 9% calcium, 25% iron.

# Turkey and Couscous Salad

**Prep:** 15 minutes    **Marinate:** 4 to 24 hours
**Grill:** 50 minutes

*Mint and kalamata olives in this summer salad take you away to the Mediterranean.*

    1 turkey thigh (about 1 pound)
    2 cups chicken broth
    3 tablespoons lemon juice
    2 tablespoons olive oil
    1 clove garlic, minced
    ¼ teaspoon salt
    ¼ teaspoon ground red pepper
    1 cup quick-cooking couscous
    1 stalk celery, chopped
    ½ cup whole pitted kalamata or ripe
       olives (sliced, if desired)
    2 tablespoons thinly sliced green
       onion
    2 tablespoons snipped fresh mint
       Shredded lettuce (optional)
    1 medium tomato, seeded and
       chopped

1 Place turkey in a plastic bag set in a deep bowl. In a screw-top jar combine ½ cup of the chicken broth, the lemon juice, oil, garlic, salt, and red pepper. Cover and shake well. Pour ¼ cup of the mixture over turkey; seal bag. Marinate in the refrigerator for 4 to 24 hours, turning bag occasionally. Cover and chill the remaining mixture for dressing.

2 Drain turkey, discarding marinade. *For a charcoal grill,* arrange medium-hot coals around a drip pan. Test for medium heat above the pan. Place turkey on grill rack over drip pan. Cover and grill for 50 to 60 minutes or until tender and no longer pink. [*For a gas grill,* preheat grill. Reduce heat to medium. Adjust for indirect cooking (see page 10). Grill as above.] Remove turkey from grill.

3 When turkey is cool enough to handle, remove skin and bone; shred meat or cut into cubes.

4 Meanwhile, in a medium saucepan bring remaining chicken broth to boiling; stir in couscous. Remove from heat. Cover; let stand about 5 minutes or until liquid is absorbed.

5 Transfer couscous to a large bowl. Add turkey, celery, olives, green onion, and mint; toss to combine. Drizzle with dressing; toss to coat. Serve warm or cover and chill for up to 24 hours. If desired, serve on shredded lettuce. Sprinkle with chopped tomato. Makes 4 servings.

Nutrition Facts per serving: 398 calories, 12 g total fat (3 g saturated fat), 68 mg cholesterol, 688 mg sodium, 40 g carbohydrate, 9 g fiber, 30 g protein. Daily Values: 3% vit. A, 21% vit. C, 4% calcium, 21% iron.

## TURKEY-PEACH SALAD

**Prep:** 20 minutes    **Grill:** 12 minutes

*Fruit and poultry take a peach of a turn. The cool but electric yogurt-and-onion dressing will bowl you over—big time.*

    4 turkey breast tenderloin steaks, cut
       ½ inch thick (about 1 pound
       total)
    1 teaspoon olive oil
       Salt and pepper
    2 peaches, pitted and cut up*
    2 plums, pitted and sliced
    2 tablespoons lemon juice
    ½ cup lemon low-fat yogurt
    2 tablespoons thinly sliced green
       onion
    ¼ teaspoon poppy seed
       Mixed salad greens

1 Rub both sides of turkey with oil. Sprinkle with salt and pepper. *For a charcoal grill,* grill turkey on the rack of an uncovered grill directly over medium coals for 12 to 15 minutes or until tender and no longer pink, turning once halfway through grilling. (*For a gas grill,* preheat grill. Reduce heat to medium. Place turkey on grill rack over heat. Cover and grill as above.) Transfer turkey to a cutting board; cool slightly. Cut turkey into bite-size strips.

**2** In a medium bowl combine the peaches and plums. Add lemon juice; toss gently to coat. For dressing, in a small bowl combine yogurt, green onion, and poppy seed. If necessary, stir in 1 to 2 teaspoons additional lemon juice to make of drizzling consistency.

**3** Divide greens among 4 dinner plates. (For peach bowls, see note below.) Arrange turkey and fruit on greens. Drizzle with dressing. Makes 4 servings.

Nutrition Facts per serving: 209 calories, 4 g total fat (1 g saturated fat), 51 mg cholesterol, 96 mg sodium, 20 g carbohydrate, 2 g fiber, 24 g protein. Daily Values: 6% vit. A, 22% vit. C, 5% calcium, 7% iron.

*Note:* To serve the salad in peach bowls, cut 2 large peaches in half crosswise; remove pits. Using a spoon, scoop out some of the pulp to create shallow "bowls." Place on salad greens and spoon turkey and plums into peach halves. Drizzle with dressing.

## Border Turkey Salad

**Prep:** 20 minutes  **Marinate:** 30 minutes
**Grill:** 12 minutes

**4 turkey breast tenderloin steaks, cut ½ inch thick (about 1 pound total)**
**¼ cup lime juice**
**1 teaspoon chili powder**
**1 teaspoon bottled minced garlic**
**¾ cup bottled dried tomato vinaigrette***
**1 medium fresh jalapeño pepper, seeded and finely chopped**
**4 cups purchased torn mixed salad greens**

**1 cup peeled, seeded, and chopped cucumber or peeled and chopped jicama**
**1 large tomato, coarsely chopped**
**8 baked tortilla chips, broken into bite-size pieces**

**1** Place turkey in a plastic bag set in a shallow dish. For marinade, combine lime juice, chili powder, and garlic. Pour over turkey; seal bag. Marinate in refrigerator at least 30 minutes or up to 3 hours, turning the bag occasionally.

**2** Drain turkey, reserving marinade. *For a charcoal grill,* grill turkey on the rack of an uncovered grill directly over medium coals for 12 to 15 minutes or until turkey is tender and no longer pink, turning once halfway through grilling and brushing occasionally with marinade up to the last 5 minutes of grilling. (*For a gas grill,* preheat grill. Reduce heat to medium. Place turkey on grill rack over heat. Cover and grill as above.) Transfer turkey to a cutting board; cool slightly. Cut turkey into bite-size strips.

**3** Meanwhile, for dressing, in a small bowl stir together vinaigrette and jalapeño pepper. Combine salad greens, cucumber, and tomato; toss to mix. Divide greens mixture among 4 dinner plates; arrange turkey on top of greens. Drizzle with dressing and sprinkle with tortilla chips. Makes 4 servings.

Nutrition Facts per serving: 363 calories, 19 g total fat (3 g saturated fat), 79 mg cholesterol, 402 mg sodium, 13 g carbohydrate, 2 g fiber, 36 g protein. Daily Values: 7% vit. A, 46% vit. C, 3% calcium, 14% iron.

*Note:* If you can't find bottled dried tomato vinaigrette, substitute ⅔ cup bottled red wine vinaigrette and 2 tablespoons snipped, drained, oil-packed dried tomatoes.

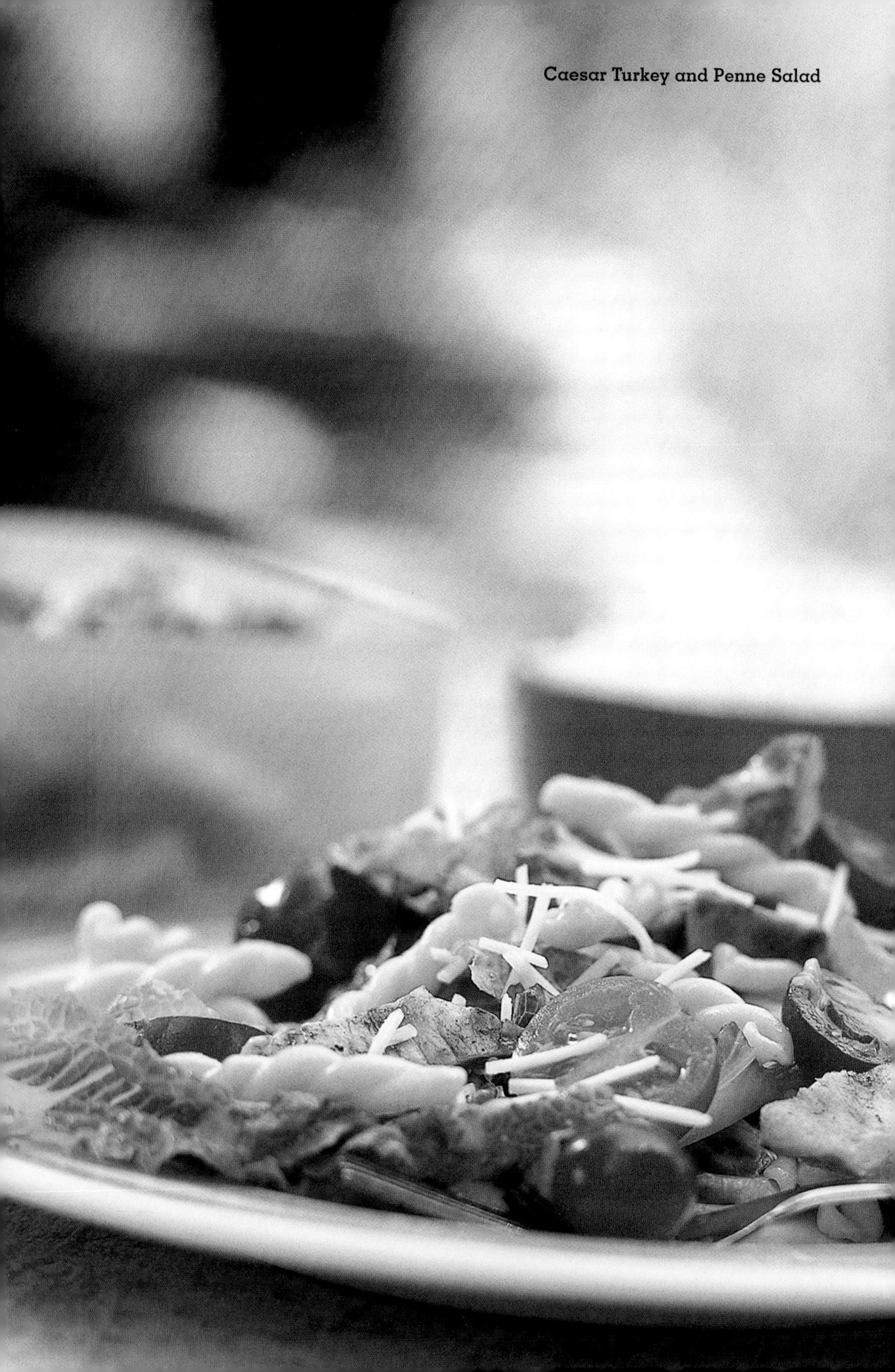

Caesar Turkey and Penne Salad

## CAESAR TURKEY AND PENNE SALAD

**Prep:** 20 minutes  **Grill:** 12 minutes

*Traditional Caesar salad gets a new spin with the addition of pasta.*

  6 ounces packaged dried gemelli or
     penne pasta
  4 turkey breast tenderloin steaks, cut
     ½ inch thick (about 1 pound
     total)
  ¾ cup bottled Caesar salad dressing
  6 cups torn romaine lettuce
  12 cherry tomatoes, halved
  ¼ cup finely shredded Parmesan
     cheese
     Cracked pepper (optional)

**1** Cook pasta according to package directions; drain.

**2** *For a charcoal grill,* grill turkey on the rack of an uncovered grill directly over medium coals for 12 to 15 minutes or until tender and no longer pink, turning and brushing once with ¼ cup of the salad dressing halfway through grilling. (*For a gas grill,* preheat grill. Reduce heat to medium. Place turkey on grill rack over heat. Cover; grill as above.) Transfer turkey to a cutting board; cool slightly.

**3** In a large salad bowl combine cooked pasta, romaine, and tomatoes. Add the remaining salad dressing; toss gently to coat. Slice turkey diagonally across the grain and arrange on greens mixture. Sprinkle with Parmesan cheese and, if desired, pepper. Makes 4 servings.

Nutrition Facts per serving: 538 calories,
26 g total fat (1 g saturated fat), 55 mg cholesterol,
138 mg sodium, 41 g carbohydrate, 4 g fiber,
32 g protein. Daily Values: 26% vit. A, 51% vit. C,
9% calcium, 25% iron.

## DON'T GET BURNED!

Poultry can "go bad" fairly quickly and should be purchased and stored carefully. Check the "sell by" date on the package label or the last day the product should be sold. (If properly refrigerated, poultry will retain its freshness a day or two after that date.) Store fresh poultry in the coldest part of your refrigerator as soon as you get it home. Poultry packaged in supermarket trays can be refrigerated in the original wrapping. Plan to use it within 1 to 2 days.

# Turkey Pasta Salad

**Prep:** 20 minutes  **Marinate:** 1 hour
**Soak:** 1 hour  **Grill:** 16 minutes

- 1 cup apple, cherry, or peach wood chips
- ½ cup olive oil
- 4 teaspoons finely shredded lemon peel
- 3 tablespoons lemon juice
- 2 tablespoons capers, drained (optional)
- 2 tablespoons snipped fresh parsley
- 2 teaspoons Dijon-style mustard
- ¼ teaspoon black pepper
- 2 turkey breast tenderloins (about 1 pound total)
- 2½ cups rotini
- 1 large green sweet pepper, quartered lengthwise
- 1 large red sweet pepper, quartered lengthwise
- 2 medium yellow summer squash, cut lengthwise into ½-inch slices
- 1 tablespoon olive oil

**1** At least 1 hour before grilling, soak wood chips in enough water to cover. For marinade, in a screw-top jar combine the ½ cup olive oil, lemon peel, lemon juice, capers (if using), parsley, mustard, and black pepper. Cover; shake well. Reserve ½ cup of the marinade to use later for salad dressing. Place turkey in a plastic bag set into a shallow dish. Pour remaining marinade over turkey; seal bag. Marinate in the refrigerator for 1 hour, turning bag occasionally.

**2** Meanwhile, cook rotini according to package directions. Drain and rinse in cold water. Drain; set aside.

**3** Drain turkey, discarding marinade. Drain wood chips. Brush green and red sweet peppers and yellow summer squash with the 1 tablespoon olive oil. *For a charcoal grill,* place medium coals in bottom of grill. Sprinkle wood chips over coals. Grill turkey, sweet pepper, and yellow summer squash on the rack of an uncovered grill directly over medium coals for 16 to 20 minutes or until turkey and vegetables are tender and turkey is no longer pink, turning once halfway through grilling. (*For a gas grill,* preheat grill. Reduce heat to medium. Place turkey, then vegetables on grill rack over heat. Cover and grill as above, except add soaked wood chips following manufacturer's directions.)

**4** Remove turkey and vegetables from grill. Remove and discard peel from peppers. Cut sweet peppers and squash into 1-inch squares. Cut turkey crosswise into ½-inch slices. In a large salad bowl toss together turkey, vegetables, cooked pasta, and the reserved dressing. Makes 4 servings.

Nutrition Facts per serving: 508 calories, 25 g total fat (4 g saturated fat), 50 mg cholesterol, 92 mg sodium, 43 g carbohydrate, 4 g fiber, 29 g protein. Daily Values: 19% vit. A, 153% vit. C, 4% calcium, 22% iron.

## TURKEY TENDERLOIN STEAKS WITH BANANA CHUTNEY

**Prep:** 15 minutes  **Grill:** 12 minutes

*You'll go bananas for this mild but radical fruit chutney. Serve it alongside these jalapeño-jelly-glazed turkey tenderloins.*

- 2 tablespoons dried cranberries, dried cherries, and/or raisins
- 2 tablespoons lime juice
- 1 small fresh jalapeño pepper, seeded and chopped
- 1 teaspoon sugar
- ½ teaspoon grated fresh ginger
- ¼ teaspoon ground allspice
- 2 firm, yet ripe, bananas, chopped
- ¼ cup jalapeño pepper jelly
- ⅛ teaspoon salt
- 4 turkey breast tenderloin steaks, cut ½ inch thick (about 1 pound total)
- 1 tablespoon cooking oil

1 For chutney, in a medium bowl stir together the dried fruit, 1 tablespoon of the lime juice, the jalapeño pepper, sugar, ginger, and allspice. Add bananas; toss gently to coat. Cover; chill until ready to serve.

2 Meanwhile, for glaze, in a small saucepan cook and stir the remaining lime juice, the jalapeño jelly, and salt over medium-low heat until jelly is melted. Remove from heat.

3 Lightly brush the turkey breast tenderloin steaks with oil.

4 *For a charcoal grill,* grill turkey on the rack of an uncovered grill directly over medium coals for 12 to 15 minutes or until tender and no longer pink, turning once and brushing occasionally with glaze during the last 5 minutes of grilling. (*For a gas grill,* preheat grill. Reduce heat to medium. Place turkey on grill rack over heat. Cover and grill as above.) Serve turkey with chutney. Makes 4 servings.

Nutrition Facts per serving: 265 calories, 6 g total fat (1 g saturated fat), 50 mg cholesterol, 117 mg sodium, 32 g carbohydrate, 1 g fiber, 22 g protein. Daily Values: 23% vit. C, 2% calcium, 9% iron.

## Turkey with Ginger Salsa

**Prep:** 20 minutes **Marinate:** 6 to 24 hours **Grill:** 12 minutes

*Try a new twist on basic salsa. A hint of ginger supplies the refreshing difference.*

- 4 turkey breast tenderloin steaks, cut ½ inch thick (about 1 pound total)
- ¼ cup vinegar
- 2 tablespoons dry sherry
- 2 tablespoons soy sauce
- 1 tablespoon grated fresh ginger
- 1 teaspoon crushed red pepper
- 1 clove garlic, minced
- 1 medium tomato, peeled, seeded, and chopped
- ¼ cup chopped green sweet pepper
- 1 green onion, thinly sliced
- 1 tablespoon snipped fresh cilantro
- 4 6-inch flour tortillas

1 Place turkey in a plastic bag set in a shallow dish. For marinade, in a small bowl combine vinegar, sherry, soy sauce, ginger, crushed red pepper, and garlic. Reserve 2 tablespoons of the marinade for salsa. Pour the remaining marinade over turkey; seal bag. Marinate in the refrigerator for 6 to 24 hours, turning bag occasionally.

2 Meanwhile, for salsa, in a small bowl combine the reserved 2 tablespoons marinade, the tomato, sweet pepper, green onion, and cilantro. Cover and chill until ready to serve. Drain turkey, reserving marinade. Stack the tortillas and wrap in a piece of foil.

3 *For a charcoal grill,* grill turkey and tortillas on the rack of an uncovered grill directly over medium coals until turkey is tender and no longer pink and tortillas are heated through, turning turkey and brushing once with marinade halfway through grilling. (Allow 12 to 15 minutes for turkey and about 5 minutes for tortillas.) (*For a gas grill,* preheat grill. Reduce heat to medium. Place turkey and tortillas on grill rack over heat. Cover and grill as above.) Serve turkey with tortillas and salsa. Makes 4 servings.

Nutrition Facts per serving: 196 calories, 4 g total fat (1 g saturated fat), 50 mg cholesterol, 399 mg sodium, 14 g carbohydrate, 1 g fiber, 24 g protein. Daily Values: 4% vit. A, 18% vit. C, 3% calcium, 13% iron.

## TURKEY STEAKS AND VEGETABLES

**Prep:** 10 minutes  **Grill:** 12 minutes

¼ cup vegetable juice
3 tablespoons mayonnaise or
   salad dressing
1 tablespoon snipped fresh chives or
   green onion tops
2 teaspoons snipped fresh thyme
   or ½ teaspoon dried
   thyme, crushed
1 clove garlic, minced
4 turkey breast tenderloin steaks,
   cut ½ inch thick (about 1 pound
   total)
   Salt and pepper
2 small zucchini, halved lengthwise
2 large plum tomatoes, halved
   lengthwise

1 For sauce, in a small bowl gradually stir vegetable juice into mayonnaise; stir in chives, thyme, and garlic. Set aside. Sprinkle turkey breasts with salt and pepper.

2 For a charcoal grill, grill turkey steaks on the rack of an uncovered grill directly over medium coals for 6 minutes. Turn turkey; brush with sauce.

3 Add zucchini and tomatoes, cut sides down, to grill. Grill for 6 to 9 minutes more or until turkey and zucchini are tender, turkey is no longer pink, and tomatoes are heated through, turning vegetables occasionally and brushing turkey and vegetables occasionally with sauce. (*For a gas grill,* preheat grill. Reduce heat to medium. Place turkey, then zucchini and tomatoes, cut sides down, on grill rack over heat. Cover and grill as above.) Serve with any remaining sauce. Serves 4.

Nutrition Facts per serving: 209 calories, 11 g total fat (2 g saturated fat), 56 mg cholesterol, 200 mg sodium, 6 g carbohydrate, 1 g fiber, 22 g protein. Daily Values: 7% vit. A, 29% vit. C, 2% calcium, 11% iron.

# Stuffed Turkey Tenderloins

**Prep:** 15 minutes  **Grill:** 16 minutes

*There's no nonsense in this stuffing. For a smoother and mellower flavor, use the chèvre; for a bolder, edgier taste, go with the feta.*

2 cups chopped fresh spinach leaves
¾ cup crumbled semisoft goat cheese
   (chèvre) or feta cheese (3 ounces)
½ teaspoon black pepper
2 turkey breast tenderloins (about
   1 pound total)
1 tablespoon olive oil
1 teaspoon paprika
½ teaspoon salt
⅛ to ¼ teaspoon ground red pepper

1 For stuffing, in a medium bowl combine spinach, cheese, and black pepper. Make a pocket in each tenderloin by cutting lengthwise from 1 side almost to the opposite side. Spoon stuffing into pockets. Tie 100-percent-cotton string around each tenderloin in 3 or 4 places.

2 In a small bowl combine oil, paprika, salt, and ground red pepper; brush mixture evenly over turkey.

3 For a charcoal grill, grill turkey on the rack of an uncovered grill directly over medium coals for 16 to 20 minutes or until tender and no longer pink, turning once halfway through grilling. (*For a gas grill,* preheat grill. Reduce heat to medium. Place turkey on grill rack over heat. Cover and grill as above.) To serve, remove and discard strings; slice turkey crosswise. Makes 4 servings.

Nutrition Facts per serving: 220 calories, 12 g total fat (4 g saturated fat), 68 mg cholesterol, 458 mg sodium, 1 g carbohydrate, 1 g fiber, 26 g protein. Daily Values: 24% vit. A, 14% vit. C, 5% calcium, 13% iron.

## TURKEY TENDERS WITH SWEET-PEPPER SALSA

**Prep:** 15 minutes **Marinate:** 2 to 4 hours
**Grill:** 12 minutes

6 turkey breast tenderloin steaks, cut
   ½ inch thick (about 1½ pounds)
⅓ cup olive oil
¼ cup lemon juice
1 teaspoon finely shredded orange
   peel
¼ cup orange juice
4 cloves garlic, minced
¼ teaspoon salt
¼ teaspoon pepper
1 recipe Sweet Pepper-Citrus Salsa

1 Place turkey in a plastic bag set in a shallow bowl. For marinade, in a small bowl combine oil, lemon juice, orange peel, orange juice, garlic, salt, and pepper. Pour over turkey. Seal bag. Marinate in the refrigerator for 2 to 4 hours, turning occasionally.

2 Drain turkey, reserving marinade. *For a charcoal grill,* grill turkey on the rack of an uncovered grill directly over medium coals for 12 to 15 minutes or until turkey is tender and no longer pink, turning once halfway through grilling and brushing with marinade during the first 6 minutes of grilling. (*For a gas grill,* preheat grill. Reduce heat to medium. Place turkey on grill rack over heat. Cover and grill as above.) Serve with Sweet Pepper-Citrus Salsa. Makes 6 servings.

**Sweet Pepper-Citrus Salsa:** In a small bowl combine one 7-ounce jar roasted red sweet peppers, drained and chopped; 1 orange, peeled, seeded, and cut up; 2 green onions, sliced; 2 tablespoons balsamic vinegar; and 1 tablespoon snipped fresh basil or 1 teaspoon dried basil, crushed. Cover and refrigerate the salsa until serving time. Makes 1½ cups salsa.

Nutrition Facts per serving: 206 calories, 10 g total fat (2 g saturated fat), 50 mg cholesterol, 107 mg sodium, 6 g carbohydrate, 1 g fiber, 22 g protein. Daily Values: 11% vit. A, 122% vit. C, 2% calcium, 10% iron.

## Spicy Turkey Tenderloins

**Prep:** 15 minutes **Marinate:** 20 minutes
**Grill:** 12 minutes

4 turkey breast tenderloin steaks, cut
   ½ inch thick (about 1 pound)
1 teaspoon finely shredded orange
   peel
¼ cup orange juice
2 tablespoons olive oil or cooking oil
1 teaspoon ground cumin
1 teaspoon dried thyme, crushed
½ teaspoon salt
¼ teaspoon black pepper
¼ teaspoon crushed red pepper

1 Place turkey in a shallow nonmetal dish. For marinade, in a small bowl combine orange peel, orange juice, olive oil or cooking oil, cumin, thyme, salt, black pepper, and crushed red pepper. Pour marinade over turkey. Cover and let stand 20 minutes.

2 Drain turkey, reserving marinade. *For a charcoal grill,* grill turkey on the rack of an uncovered grill directly over medium coals for 12 to 15 minutes or until turkey is tender and no longer pink, turning once halfway through grilling and brushing with marinade during the first 6 minutes of grilling. (*For a gas grill,* preheat grill. Reduce heat to medium. Place turkey on grill rack over heat. Cover and grill as above.) Makes 4 servings.

Nutrition Facts per serving: 182 calories, 9 g total fat (2 g saturated fat), 50 mg cholesterol, 315 mg sodium, 2 g carbohydrate, 0 g fiber, 22 g protein. Daily Values: 10% vit. C, 11% iron.

## PINEAPPLE-RUM TURKEY KABOBS

**Prep:** 15 minutes  **Marinate:** 4 to 24 hours
**Grill:** 12 minutes

*When you eat this rum-and-lemongrass kabob,*
*you won't know whether you're in the Caribbean*
*or the South Seas, but you'll like it just the same.*

12 **ounces turkey breast tenderloin**
    **steaks, cut ½ inch thick, or**
    **boneless turkey breast**
⅓ **cup unsweetened pineapple juice**
3 **tablespoons rum or unsweetened**
    **pineapple juice**
1 **tablespoon brown sugar**
1 **tablespoon finely chopped**
    **lemongrass or 2 teaspoons finely**
    **shredded lemon peel**
1 **tablespoon olive oil**
1 **medium red onion, cut into**
    **thin wedges**
3 **plums or 2 nectarines, pitted and**
    **cut into thick slices**
2 **cups fresh or canned pineapple**
    **chunks**
    **Hot cooked rice (optional)**
    **Thinly sliced sugar snap peas**
    **(optional)**

**1** Cut turkey into 1-inch cubes. Place turkey
in a plastic bag set in a shallow dish. For
marinade, in a small bowl combine the ⅓ cup
pineapple juice, the rum or 3 tablespoons
pineapple juice, brown sugar, lemongrass,
and oil. Pour over turkey; close bag. Marinate
in the refrigerator for 4 to 24 hours, turning
the bag occasionally.

**2** Drain turkey, reserving marinade. In a
small saucepan bring marinade to boiling.
Boil gently, uncovered, for 1 minute. Remove
from heat. On four 12-inch metal skewers,
alternately thread turkey and onion, leaving
about a ¼-inch space between each piece.
Alternately thread plums and pineapple onto
4 more skewers.

**3** *For a charcoal grill,* grill turkey and fruit
kabobs on the rack of an uncovered grill
directly over medium coals until turkey and
onion are tender, turkey is no longer pink, and
fruit is heated through, turning once and
brushing occasionally with marinade during
the last half of grilling. (Allow 12 to
14 minutes for turkey and onion and about
5 minutes for fruit.) (*For a gas grill,* preheat
grill. Reduce heat to medium. Place turkey
and fruit kabobs on grill rack over heat. Cover
and grill as above.)

**4** To serve, if desired, toss hot cooked rice
with snap peas; serve turkey, onion, and
fruit with rice. Makes 4 servings.

Nutrition Facts per serving: 235 calories,
6 g total fat (1 g saturated fat), 37 mg cholesterol,
37 mg sodium, 24 g carbohydrate, 2 g fiber,
17 g protein. Daily Values: 1% vit. A, 34% vit. C,
2% calcium, 8% iron.

## WISE ADVICE

**Don't think of turkey as just
for Thanksgiving. If you
haven't tried turkey on the
grill, then you're missing out.
Turkey white meat is
naturally low in fat. It has a
slightly heartier taste than
chicken and is versatile
enough to be used as a
substitute in place of higher
fat meat. Like all meats,
turkey is a good source of
iron, zinc, and vitamin B-12.**

Pineapple-Rum Turkey Kabobs

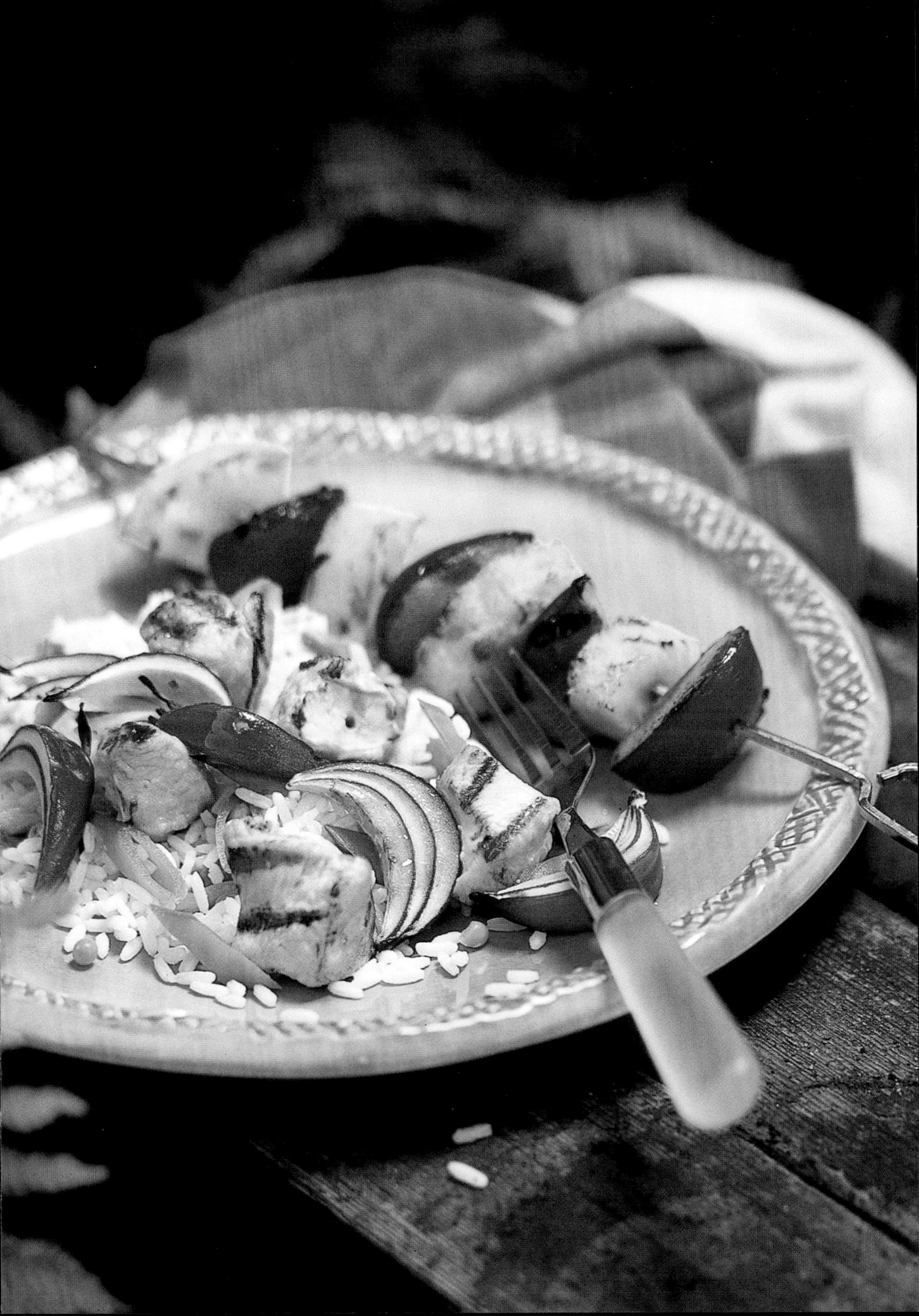

# Mayan Turkey with Peanut Mole

**Prep:** 40 minutes   **Grill:** 1½ hours
**Stand:** 10 minutes

*You won't sacrifice a thing when you dine on these dark and fiery turkey breasts. The peanut mole sauce seals in the juiciness as a glaze and adds a wonderful kick as the serving sauce.*

  1  **cup chopped onion**
  2  **tablespoons olive oil**
  1  **cup chopped seeded tomato**
  2  **tablespoons chili powder**
  4  **cloves garlic, minced**
  ½  **teaspoon ground cinnamon**
  1  **14½-ounce can chicken broth**
  2  **6-inch corn tortillas, torn into small pieces**
  1 to 3 **canned chipotle peppers in adobo sauce plus 1 tablespoon of the sauce**
  ½  **cup creamy peanut butter**
  3  **tablespoons honey or brown sugar**
  1  **3- to 4-pound boneless whole turkey breast**
  2  **tablespoons olive oil**
  2  **cloves garlic, minced**
  1½ **teaspoons chili powder**
  1  **teaspoon ground cumin**
  ½  **teaspoon salt**

1 For mole, in a large skillet cook the onion in 2 tablespoons hot oil over medium-high heat for 2 minutes. Stir in tomato, the 2 tablespoons chili powder, the 4 cloves garlic, and the cinnamon. Cook and stir for 4 minutes more. Add ½ cup of the chicken broth, the tortillas, and the chipotle peppers and adobo sauce. Bring to boiling; reduce heat. Simmer, uncovered, for 4 minutes. Cool mole slightly.

2 Transfer mixture to a blender container or food processor bowl. Cover and blend or process until smooth. Return mixture to skillet; stir in the remaining broth, the peanut butter, and 1 tablespoon of the honey. Simmer, uncovered, about 10 minutes more or until desired consistency. (Mole may be made up to 2 days ahead; store, covered, in the refrigerator.) For basting sauce, transfer ½ cup of the mole to a small bowl; stir in the remaining 2 tablespoons honey. Place remaining sauce in a small bowl and reserve to pass with turkey. Cover and refrigerate both sauces.

3 Spread open turkey. For rub, in a small bowl combine 2 tablespoons oil, the 2 cloves garlic, the 1½ teaspoons chili powder, the cumin, and salt. Spoon rub evenly over turkey; rub in with your fingers. Insert a meat thermometer into center of turkey.

4 For a charcoal grill, arrange medium-hot coals around a drip pan. Test for medium heat above the pan. Place turkey, skin side up, on grill rack over drip pan. Cover and grill for 1½ to 2 hours or until meat thermometer registers 170°, brushing with the ½ cup mole basting sauce during the last 10 minutes of grilling. Discard sauce. [*For a gas grill,* preheat grill. Reduce heat to medium. Adjust for indirect cooking (see page 10). Grill as above, except place turkey on a rack in a roasting pan.] Remove turkey from grill. Cover with foil; let stand for 10 minutes. To serve, slice turkey. Reheat and pass reserved mole with the turkey. Makes 12 servings.

Nutrition Facts per serving: 264 calories,
13 g total fat (2 g saturated fat), 50 mg cholesterol,
333 mg sodium, 12 g carbohydrate, 2 g fiber,
26 g protein. Daily Values: 8% vit. A, 9% vit. C,
3% calcium, 13% iron.

# TURKEY WITH PEAR-CHIPOTLE SALSA

**Prep:** 20 minutes  **Soak:** 1 hour
**Grill:** 1½ hours  **Stand:** 10 minutes

*The zingy pear-chipotle salsa provides a flavor burst and will leave you begging for more.*

    4 cups fruit wood or hickory chips
    1 2- to 2½-pound turkey breast half
        with bone
    2 teaspoons finely shredded
        lemon peel
    2 cloves garlic, minced
    1 or 2 dried chipotle peppers
    2 medium pears, cored and finely
        chopped
    2 tablespoons lemon juice or lime
        juice
    ¼ cup snipped dried apricots or dried
        cranberries
    2 tablespoons snipped fresh cilantro
    1 tablespoon honey

**1** At least 1 hour before grilling, soak wood chips in enough water to cover.

**2** Slip your fingers between skin and meat to loosen turkey skin, leaving skin attached at 1 side. For rub, in a small bowl combine lemon peel and garlic. Lift turkey skin and spoon rub evenly over turkey meat; rub in with your fingers. Fold skin back over meat, covering as much as possible. Insert a meat thermometer into the thickest part of the turkey breast without the thermometer touching bone.

**3** Drain wood chips. *For a charcoal grill,* arrange medium-hot coals around a drip pan. Test for medium heat above the pan. Sprinkle half of the wood chips over the coals. Place turkey on grill rack over drip pan. Cover and grill for 1½ to 2 hours or until meat thermometer registers 170°. Add the remaining wood chips halfway through grilling. [*For a gas grill,* preheat grill. Reduce heat to medium. Adjust for indirect cooking (see page 10). Grill as above, except place turkey on a rack in a roasting pan and add soaked wood chips following manufacturer's directions.] Remove turkey from grill. Cover with foil; let stand for 10 minutes.

**4** Meanwhile, remove stems from chipotle peppers. In a small bowl combine peppers and enough hot water to cover. Let peppers stand for 30 minutes to soften; drain. Finely chop peppers.

**5** For salsa, in a medium bowl stir together pears and lemon juice. Stir in chipotle peppers, dried fruit, cilantro, and honey. Cover and let stand at room temperature about 30 minutes to blend flavors.

**6** To serve, remove skin from turkey. Slice turkey; serve with salsa. Makes 8 servings.

Nutrition Facts per serving: 181 calories, 5 g total fat (2 g saturated fat), 61 mg cholesterol, 77 mg sodium, 12 g carbohydrate, 2 g fiber, 21 g protein. Daily Values: 5% vit. A, 7% vit. C, 2% calcium, 13% iron.

# Cider-Glazed Turkey Thighs with Sweet Potatoes

**Prep:** 15 minutes  **Grill:** 50 minutes

½ cup apple cider or juice
2 tablespoons apple jelly
1½ teaspoons cornstarch
½ teaspoon apple pie spice
2 medium sweet potatoes (about 12 ounces total), peeled, halved lengthwise, and cut into ½-inch slices
2 medium cooking apples (such as Braeburn or Golden Delicious), cored and cut into wedges
2 turkey thighs (about 2 pounds)

1 For sauce, in a small saucepan stir together apple cider, apple jelly, cornstarch, and apple pie spice. Cook and stir over medium heat until thickened and bubbly. Cook and stir for 1 minute more. Remove from heat.

2 In a large bowl toss together sweet potatoes and apples. Fold a 36×18-inch piece of heavy foil in half to make an 18-inch square. Place sweet potato mixture in center of foil. Drizzle with half of the sauce. Bring up opposite edges of foil and seal with a double fold. Fold remaining edges together to completely enclose mixture, leaving space for steam to build. Chill until ready to grill.

3 If desired, remove skin from turkey. *For a charcoal grill,* arrange medium-hot coals around a drip pan. Test for medium heat above the pan. Place turkey, bone side down, and sweet potato mixture on grill rack over drip pan. Cover and grill until turkey is tender and no longer pink and sweet potatoes and apples are just tender, turning packet once and brushing turkey frequently with the remaining sauce during the last 20 minutes of grilling. (Allow 50 to 60 minutes for turkey and 30 to 40 minutes for sweet potato mixture.) [*For a gas grill,* preheat grill. Reduce heat to medium. Adjust for indirect cooking (see page 10). Grill as above.]

4 To serve, cut turkey meat from bones. Serve with sweet potatoes and apples. Makes 4 servings.

Nutrition Facts per serving: 265 calories, 6 g total fat (2 g saturated fat), 47 mg cholesterol, 50 mg sodium, 37 g carbohydrate, 4 g fiber, 16 g protein. Daily Values: 144% vit. A, 33% vit. C, 4% calcium, 13% iron.

# CRANBERRY MARGARITA TURKEY LEGS

**Prep:** 20 minutes  **Marinate:** 2 hours
**Grill:** 45 minutes

6 turkey drumsticks (about 3 pounds total)
¼ cup cranberry juice
¼ cup tequila
1 tablespoon finely shredded lime peel
¼ cup lime juice
2 cloves garlic, minced
1 teaspoon salt
¼ teaspoon ground red pepper (optional)
1 16-ounce can whole cranberry sauce
2 or 3 canned chipotle peppers in adobo sauce, mashed

1 Place turkey in a plastic bag set in a shallow dish. For marinade, in a small bowl stir together cranberry juice, 2 tablespoons of the tequila, 1½ teaspoons of the lime peel, 2 tablespoons of the lime juice, the garlic, salt, and, if desired, red pepper. Pour over turkey; seal bag, Marinate in the refrigerator for 2 to 24 hours, turning bag occasionally. Drain turkey, discarding marinade.

2 For sauce, in a small saucepan combine remaining tequila, remaining lime peel, remaining lime juice, the cranberry sauce, and chipotle peppers. Bring to boiling; reduce heat. Simmer, uncovered, for 5 minutes. Reserve 1¼ cups of the sauce.

3 *For a charcoal grill,* arrange medium-hot coals around a drip pan. Test for medium heat above the pan. Place turkey on grill rack

over drip pan. Cover; grill for 45 to 60 minutes or until tender and no longer pink, turning and brushing occasionally with the remaining sauce during the last 10 minutes of grilling. [*For a gas grill*, preheat grill. Reduce heat to medium. Adjust for indirect cooking (see page 10). Grill as above.] To serve, reheat and pass the reserved sauce with turkey. Makes 6 servings.

Nutrition Facts per serving: 372 calories, 9 g total fat (3 g saturated fat), 105 mg cholesterol, 290 mg sodium, 32 g carbohydrate, 1 g fiber, 36 g protein. Daily Values: 6% vit. A, 12% vit. C, 4% calcium, 21% iron.

# Rosemary-and-Orange Turkey

**Prep:** 20 minutes  **Soak (optional):** 1 hour
**Grill:** 2½ hours  **Stand:** 15 minutes

> 4 cups hickory wood chips (optional)
> 2 tablespoons margarine or butter, softened
> 2 tablespoons snipped fresh rosemary
> 2 tablespoons finely shredded orange peel
> 1 8- to 10-pound turkey
> 2 tablespoons cooking oil

**1** If using wood chips, at least 1 hour before grilling, soak wood chips in enough water to cover. In a small bowl combine softened margarine or butter, rosemary, and orange peel; set aside.

**2** Remove the neck and giblets from turkey. Slip your fingers between skin and meat to loosen turkey skin over breast area. Lift turkey skin and carefully spread margarine mixture directly over turkey meat. Skewer the neck skin to the back. Twist wing tips under back. Tuck drumsticks under the band of skin across the tail or tie legs to tail with 100-percent-cotton string. Place turkey, breast side up, on a rack in a roasting pan. Insert a meat thermometer into the center of an inside thigh muscle without the thermometer touching bone. Brush turkey with oil.

**3** Drain wood chips. *For a charcoal grill*, arrange medium-hot coals around edge of grill. Test for medium heat above center of grill. Sprinkle one-fourth of the wood chips over the coals. Place turkey in pan on grill rack over center of grill. Cover; grill for 2½ to 3 hours or until thermometer registers 180° to 185°. Add more wood chips every 30 minutes. [*For a gas grill*, preheat grill. Reduce heat to medium. Adjust for indirect cooking (see page 10). Grill as above, except add soaked wood chips, if using, following manufacturer's directions.] Remove turkey from grill. Cover with foil; let stand for 15 minutes before carving. Makes 10 to 12 servings.

Nutrition Facts per serving: 307 calories, 17 g total fat (4 g saturated fat), 122 mg cholesterol, 113 mg sodium, 0 g carbohydrate, 0 g fiber, 36 g protein. Daily Values: 11% vit. A, 2% vit. C, 3% calcium, 17% iron.

**Grilling Know-How**

When grilling whole turkey, follow these wise guidelines:
*Only grill unstuffed birds because they cook more evenly than if stuffed. Stuffed birds are also more prone to food-borne pathogens since it takes longer to heat the interior of the bird to a safe temperature.
*For best results, the turkey should weigh less than 16 pounds; bigger birds are too large for some grills and may be difficult to remove from the grill.
*Check the doneness of the turkey with a meat thermometer inserted into the deepest section of the inside thigh. The temperature should register 180° to 185° for a whole turkey.

If desired, remove the skin from the poultry. Test for desired coal temperature (see How Hot is It? page 11). Place poultry on the grill rack, bone side up, directly over the preheated coals (for direct grilling) or directly over drip pan (for indirect grilling). Grill (uncovered for direct grilling or covered for indirect grilling) for the time given below or until tender and no longer pink. (Note: White meat will cook slightly faster.) Turn poultry over halfway through the grilling time.

# Grilling Chart

| Type of Bird | Weight | Coal Temperature | Doneness | Direct Grilling* Time | Indirect Grilling* Time |
|---|---|---|---|---|---|
| **Chicken broiler, fryer, half** | 1¼ to 1½ pounds | Medium | Tender, no longer pink | 40 to 50 min. | 1 to 1¼ hrs. |
| **Chicken breast half, skinned and boned** | 4 to 5 ounces each | Medium | Tender, no longer pink | 12 to 15 min. | 15 to 18 min. |
| **Chicken quarters** | 2½ to 3 pounds each | Medium | Tender, no longer pink | 40 to 50 min. | 50 to 60 min. |
| **Meaty chicken pieces** | 2½ to 3 pounds total | Medium | Tender, no longer pink | 35 to 45 min. | 50 to 60 min. |
| **Turkey breast tenderloin steak** | 4 to 6 ounces each | Medium | Tender, no longer pink | 12 to 15 min. | 15 to 18 min. |

*Note: For differences in direct and indirect grilling methods, see page 10.*

# FISH

## AND
## SHELLFISH

7

# Fish and Shellfish

# Orange and Dill Sea Bass

**Prep:** 15 minutes  **Grill:** 6 minutes

*When it's time to give the fish-and-lemon combo
a vacation, explore other citrus possibilities.
Here, sea bass is perfumed orange by "baking"
it on your grill on a bed of orange slices.*

> 4  5- to 6-ounce fresh or frozen sea
>    bass or orange roughy fillets,
>    ¾ inch thick
> 2  tablespoons snipped fresh dill
> 2  tablespoons olive oil
> ¼  teaspoon salt
> ¼  teaspoon white pepper
> 4  large oranges, cut into ¼-inch
>    slices
> 1  orange, cut into wedges
>    Fresh dill sprig (optional)

**1** Thaw fish, if frozen. Rinse fish; pat dry
with paper towels. In a small bowl stir
together the dill, oil, salt, and pepper. Brush
both sides of fish with dill mixture.

**2** *For a charcoal grill*, place medium coals in
bottom of grill. Arrange a bed of orange
slices on the greased grill rack directly over
coals. Arrange fish on orange slices. Cover;
grill for 6 to 9 minutes or until fish flakes
easily when tested with a fork (do not turn
fish). (*For a gas grill*, preheat grill. Reduce
heat to medium. As above, arrange orange
slices and fish on greased grill rack over heat.
Grill as above.)

**3** To serve, use a spatula to transfer fish and
grilled orange slices to a serving platter or
serving plates. Squeeze the juice from orange
wedges over fish. If desired, garnish with dill
sprig. Makes 4 servings.

Nutrition Facts per serving: 207 calories,
10 g total fat (2 g saturated fat), 59 mg cholesterol,
230 mg sodium, 2 g carbohydrate, 0 g fiber,
26 g protein. Daily Values: 7% vit. A, 22% vit. C,
1% calcium, 3% iron.

# SEA BASS WITH BLACK BEAN AND AVOCADO

**Prep:** 15 minutes
**Grill:** 4 to 6 minutes per ½-inch thickness

*Sea bass is perfect for grilling. It is meaty
enough to take the rigors of an outdoor grill.*

> 4  4- to 5-ounce fresh or frozen sea
>    bass or haddock fillets, ¾ to
>    1 inch thick
> 2  tablespoons snipped fresh cilantro
> 2  tablespoons snipped fresh oregano
> ½  teaspoon finely shredded lime peel
> 2  tablespoons lime juice
> 1  tablespoon olive oil
> 1  clove garlic, minced
> ¼ to ½ teaspoon bottled hot pepper
>    sauce
> 1  15-ounce can black beans, rinsed
>    and drained
> 1  avocado, seeded, peeled, and
>    chopped

**1** Thaw fish, if frozen. Rinse fish; pat dry
with paper towels. Place fish in a shallow
dish. In a small bowl stir together cilantro,
oregano, lime peel, lime juice, oil, garlic, and
hot pepper sauce. For relish, place
2 tablespoons of the cilantro mixture in a
bowl. Add beans and avocado; toss lightly to
coat. Cover and chill.

**2** Brush remaining cilantro mixture over fish.
Place fish in a greased grill basket, tucking
under any thin edges.

**3** *For a charcoal grill*, grill fish on the rack of
an uncovered grill directly over medium
coals until fish flakes easily when tested with a
fork (allow 4 to 6 minutes per ½-inch
thickness of fish), turning basket once halfway
through grilling. (*For a gas grill*, preheat grill.
Reduce heat to medium. Place fish on grill
rack over heat. Cover and grill as above.)
Serve relish with fish. Makes 4 servings.

Nutrition Facts per serving: 303 calories,
15 g total fat (2 g saturated fat), 47 mg cholesterol,
348 mg sodium, 20 g carbohydrate, 6 g fiber,
29 g protein. Daily Values: 9% vit. A, 16% vit. C,
4% calcium, 13% iron.

# Miso-Sesame Grilled Sea Bass

**Prep:** 15 minutes **Marinate:** 30 minutes
**Grill:** 6 minutes

    4 4- to 5-ounce fresh or frozen sea
        bass or halibut steaks, cut
        ¾ inch thick
    ⅓ cup Japanese yellow miso
        (soybean paste) (see tip below)
    2 tablespoons sesame seed
    2 tablespoons water
    2 tablespoons reduced-sodium soy
        sauce
    1 tablespoon cooking oil
    1 orange, cut into wedges
        Fresh dill sprig (optional)

**1** Thaw fish, if frozen. Rinse fish and pat dry. Place fish in a shallow dish. For marinade, in a small bowl stir together miso, sesame seed, water, soy sauce, and oil. Pour over fish; turn fish to coat. Cover and marinate at room temperature for 30 minutes, turning fish once. Drain fish, discarding marinade.

**2** Lightly grease grill rack or lightly coat with nonstick spray. *For a charcoal grill,* grill fish on the greased rack of an uncovered grill directly over medium coals for 6 to 9 minutes or until fish flakes easily when tested with a fork, gently turning once halfway through grilling. (*For a gas grill,* preheat grill. Reduce heat to medium. Place fish on greased grill rack over heat. Cover; grill as above.)

**3** To serve, squeeze the juice from orange wedges over fish. If desired, garnish with fresh dill. Makes 4 servings.

Nutrition Facts per serving: 193 calories, 8 g total fat (1 g saturated fat), 47 mg cholesterol, 1,076 mg sodium, 8 g carbohydrate, 1 g fiber, 24 g protein. Daily Values: 6% vit. A, 21% vit. C, 2% calcium, 12% iron.

## Did You Know?

Miso, or bean paste, has the consistency of peanut butter and comes in a variety of flavors and colors. Made from fermented soybean paste, miso has three basic categories—barley, rice, and soybean. All three are used as basic flavorings in much of Japanese cooking. The lighter versions are used more in delicate soups and sauces, and the darker versions in heavier dishes. It is easily digested and is very nutritious, containing high amounts of B vitamins and protein. Miso can be found in Japanese markets and health-food stores. To keep it fresh, store in an air-tight container in the refrigerator.

# FRAGRANT SWORDFISH BROCHETTES

**Prep:** 25 minutes **Marinate:** 1 to 2 hours
**Grill:** 8 minutes

*Loaded with herbs and spices, these brochettes are sure to make your neighbors jealous as the breeze wafts exotic aromas into their yards.*

    1½ pounds fresh or frozen swordfish or
        salmon steaks, cut 1½ inches
        thick
    ⅓ cup lightly packed fresh parsley
        leaves
    ⅓ cup lightly packed fresh mint
        leaves
    ⅓ cup lightly packed fresh cilantro
        leaves
    3 tablespoons lemon juice
    3 tablespoons olive oil
    6 cloves garlic
    2 teaspoons paprika
    ½ teaspoon ground coriander
    ½ teaspoon ground cumin
    8 bay leaves*
        Hot cooked couscous or rice pilaf
        (optional)

1 Thaw fish, if frozen. Rinse fish; pat dry. Cut fish into 1½-inch cubes. Place fish in a shallow dish. For marinade, in a blender container or food processor bowl combine parsley, mint, cilantro, lemon juice, oil, garlic, paprika, coriander, and cumin. Cover and blend or process until combined, scraping down sides of blender or food processor as necessary. Pour over fish; turn fish to coat. Cover and marinate in the refrigerator for 1 to 2 hours, turning fish once.

2 Drain fish, discarding marinade. On 4 long metal skewers, alternately thread fish and bay leaves.

3 *For a charcoal grill,* grill kabobs on the greased rack of an uncovered grill directly over medium coals for 8 to 12 minutes or until fish flakes easily when tested with a fork, gently turning once halfway through grilling. (*For a gas grill,* preheat grill. Reduce heat to medium. Place kabobs on greased grill rack over heat. Cover and grill as above.)

4 If desired, serve kabobs over couscous. Makes 4 servings.

*Note:* Bay leaves flavor the fish during grilling, but are not to be eaten.

Nutrition Facts per serving: 319 calories, 17 g total fat (3 g saturated fat), 67 mg cholesterol, 159 mg sodium, 5 g carbohydrate, 0 g fiber, 35 g protein. Daily Values: 17% vit. A, 34% vit. C, 4% calcium, 28% iron.

## Swordfish with Spicy Tomato Sauce

**Prep:** 15 minutes   **Grill:** 8 minutes

*Firm, steaklike fish, such as swordfish, can stand up to a spicy tomato sauce such as this one.*

- 4 5- to 6-ounce fresh or frozen swordfish or salmon steaks, cut 1 inch thick
- 4 teaspoons cooking oil
- ½ teaspoon salt
- ¼ teaspoon black pepper

- ¼ cup chopped onion
- 1 small fresh serrano pepper, seeded and finely chopped
- 1 clove garlic, minced
- ½ teaspoon ground turmeric
- ¼ teaspoon ground coriander
- 1½ cups chopped plum tomatoes
- 1 tablespoon snipped fresh cilantro
  Hot cooked couscous (optional)

1 Thaw fish, if frozen. Rinse fish; pat dry with paper towels. Drizzle fish with 2 teaspoons of the oil. Sprinkle with ¼ teaspoon of the salt and the black pepper. Cover and chill fish until ready to grill.

2 For sauce, in a medium skillet cook onion, serrano pepper, garlic, turmeric, and coriander in the remaining hot oil until onion is tender, stirring often. Add remaining salt and the tomatoes. Cook until tomatoes are just tender, stirring often. Remove from heat; stir in cilantro. Set aside.

3 *For a charcoal grill,* grill fish on the greased rack of an uncovered grill directly over medium coals for 8 to 12 minutes or until fish flakes easily when tested with a fork, gently turning once halfway through grilling. (*For a gas grill,* preheat grill. Reduce heat to medium. Place fish on greased grill rack over heat. Cover and grill as above.)

4 Serve sauce over fish. If desired, serve with couscous. Makes 4 servings.

Nutrition Facts per serving: 237 calories, 11 g total fat (2 g saturated fat), 56 mg cholesterol, 402 mg sodium, 5 g carbohydrate, 1 g fiber, 29 g protein. Daily Values: 9% vit. A, 39% vit. C, 1% calcium, 11% iron.

Garden-Stuffed Fish Steaks

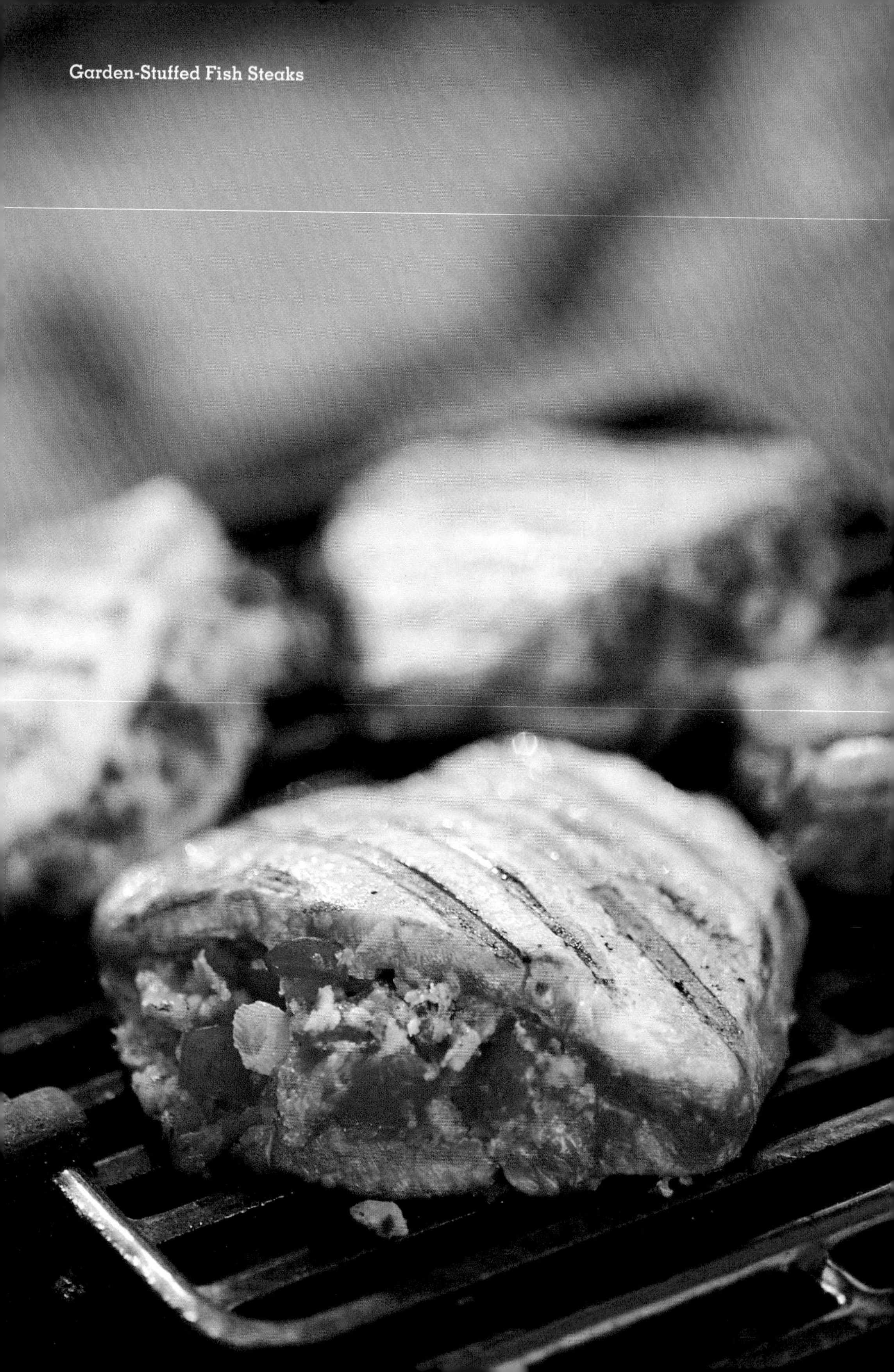

## GARDEN-STUFFED FISH STEAKS

**Prep:** 25 minutes  **Grill:** 14 minutes

*These swordfish steaks, an elegant entrée for guests, are stuffed with vegetables, bread crumbs, and cheese, then grilled to perfection.*

4 5- to 6-ounce fresh or frozen
    swordfish or tuna steaks, cut
    1 inch thick
½ cup coarsely shredded carrot
¼ cup sliced green onions
1 clove garlic, minced
2 tablespoons margarine or butter
1 small tomato, seeded and chopped
2 tablespoons fine dry seasoned
    bread crumbs
2 tablespoons grated Parmesan
    cheese

**1** Thaw fish, if frozen. Rinse fish; pat dry with paper towels. If necessary, remove bones and skin. Make a pocket in each steak by cutting horizontally from one side almost through to the other side. Cover; chill until ready to grill.

**2** For stuffing, in a small saucepan cook carrot, green onions, and garlic in hot margarine or butter until vegetables are tender. Remove from heat. Add tomato, bread crumbs, and cheese; toss lightly to mix. Spoon about ¼ cup stuffing into each pocket. Secure the openings with wooden toothpicks.

**3** *For a charcoal grill,* grill fish on the greased rack of an uncovered grill directly over medium-hot coals for 14 to 18 minutes or until fish flakes easily when tested with a fork, gently turning once halfway through grilling. (*For a gas grill,* preheat grill. Reduce heat to medium-hot. Place fish on greased grill rack over heat. Cover and grill as above.) Makes 4 servings.

Nutrition Facts per serving: 293 calories, 16 g total fat (4 g saturated fat), 58 mg cholesterol, 352 mg sodium, 5 g carbohydrate, 1 g fiber, 30 g protein. Daily Values: 53% vit. A, 12% vit. C, 5% calcium, 9% iron.

## Swordfish with Citrus Salsa

**Prep:** 20 minutes  **Marinate:** 30 minutes
**Grill:** 8 minutes

1 pound fresh or frozen swordfish
    steaks, cut 1 inch thick
¼ cup orange juice
2 tablespoons lemon juice
2 tablespoons lime juice
1 tablespoon cooking oil
½ teaspoon ground ginger
1 clove garlic, minced
1 orange, peeled and chopped
⅓ cup finely chopped fresh or canned
    pineapple
2 tablespoons finely chopped onion
2 tablespoons finely chopped red
    sweet pepper
2 tablespoons snipped fresh parsley
2 tablespoons lime juice
1 fresh jalapeño pepper, seeded and
    finely chopped

**1** Thaw fish, if frozen. Rinse fish; pat dry. Place fish in a shallow dish. For marinade, combine orange juice and next 5 ingredients. Pour over fish; turn fish to coat. Cover; marinate at room temperature for 30 minutes or in the refrigerator for 1 hour, turning once.

**2** For salsa, stir together orange, pineapple, onion, sweet pepper, parsley, 2 tablespoons lime juice, and jalapeño pepper. Cover; chill.

**3** Drain fish, discarding marinade. Place fish in a greased grill basket. *For a charcoal grill,* grill fish on the rack of an uncovered grill directly over medium coals for 8 to 12 minutes or until fish flakes easily when tested with a fork, turning basket once halfway through grilling. (*For a gas grill,* preheat grill. Reduce heat to medium. Place fish on grill rack over heat. Cover and grill as above.) To serve, cut fish into 4 pieces. Serve with salsa. Makes 4 servings.

Nutrition Facts per serving: 208 calories, 8 g total fat (2 g saturated fat), 45 mg cholesterol, 104 mg sodium, 10 g carbohydrate, 1 g dietary fiber, 23 g protein. Daily Values: 8% vit. A, 82% vit. C, 2% calcium, 8% iron.

## BLACKENED SWORDFISH

**Prep:** 15 minutes
**Grill:** 4 to 6 minutes per ½-inch thickness

*Blackened fish is delicious, but able to set off smoke alarms within seconds. Thank goodness for grills, perfect for cooking blackened foods.*

  2 8- to 10-ounce fresh or frozen
       swordfish or tuna steaks, cut
       ¾ to 1 inch thick
  ¾ teaspoon white pepper
  ¾ teaspoon black pepper
  ½ teaspoon onion powder
  ½ teaspoon garlic powder
  ½ teaspoon ground red pepper
  ½ teaspoon dried thyme, crushed
  ¼ teaspoon salt
  3 tablespoons margarine or butter,
       melted

**1** Thaw fish, if frozen. Cut each steak in half. Rinse fish; pat dry with paper towels.

**2** For rub, in a shallow bowl stir together white pepper, black pepper, onion powder, garlic powder, red pepper, thyme, and salt. Brush fish with some of the melted margarine or butter. Sprinkle rub evenly over fish; rub in with your fingers.

**3** *For a charcoal grill,* place hot coals in bottom of an uncovered grill. Place a 12-inch cast-iron skillet directly on coals. Preheat about 5 minutes or until a drop of water sizzles when added to skillet. Place fish in hot skillet. Drizzle with the remaining margarine. Grill until fish flakes easily when tested with a fork (allow 4 to 6 minutes per ½-inch thickness of fish), gently turning once halfway through grilling. (*For a gas grill,* place skillet on grill rack; preheat grill and skillet. Reduce heat to medium. Place fish in hot skillet. Drizzle with remaining margarine. Cover and grill as above.) Makes 4 servings.

Nutrition Facts per serving: 219 calories,
13 g total fat (3 g saturated fat), 45 mg cholesterol,
336 mg sodium, 1 g carbohydrate, 0 g fiber,
23 g protein. Daily Values: 15% vit. A, 2% vit. C,
1% calcium, 8% iron.

## Shark with Nectarine Salsa

**Prep:** 30 minutes   **Grill:** 8 minutes

  1 ripe nectarine, cut into ½-inch
       pieces
  1 small cucumber, seeded and cut
       into ½-inch pieces
  1 ripe kiwi fruit, peeled and cut into
       ½-inch pieces
  ¼ cup thinly sliced green onions
  3 tablespoons orange juice
  1 tablespoon white wine vinegar
  1 1-pound fresh or frozen shark or
       orange roughy fillet, 1 inch thick
  1 teaspoon olive oil
  ½ teaspoon freshly ground pepper

**1** For salsa, in a bowl combine nectarine, cucumber, kiwi fruit, green onions, orange juice, and vinegar. Cover and refrigerate until ready to serve.

**2** Thaw fish, if frozen. Rinse fish; pat dry with paper towels. Brush oil over both sides of fish; sprinkle with pepper. Place fish in a greased grill basket. *For a charcoal grill,* grill fish on the rack of an uncovered grill directly over medium coals for 8 to 12 minutes or until fish flakes easily when tested with a fork, turning basket once halfway through grilling. (*For a gas grill,* preheat grill. Reduce heat to medium. Place fish on grill rack over heat. Cover and grill as above.)

**3** To serve, cut fish into 4 serving-size pieces. Top with salsa. Makes 4 servings.

Nutrition Facts per serving: 158 calories,
3 g total fat (1 g saturated fat), 60 mg cholesterol,
94 mg sodium, 10 g carbohydrate, 1 g fiber,
22 g protein. Daily Values: 6% vit. A, 55% vit. C,
3% calcium, 5% iron.

**Prep:** 20 minutes  **Marinate:** 30 minutes
**Grill:** 8 minutes

*Plums bring a touch of freshness to these Asian-inspired kabobs.*

  1 pound fresh or frozen tuna,
    swordfish, or shark steaks, cut
    1 inch thick
  3 tablespoons soy sauce
  2 tablespoons cooking oil
  2 tablespoons dry sherry
  1 tablespoon black sesame seed or
    sesame seed, toasted
  1 teaspoon brown sugar
  1 clove garlic, minced
  4 plums, pitted and quartered
 32 snow peas

**1** Thaw fish, if frozen. Rinse fish; pat dry with paper towels. Cut fish into 1-inch cubes. Place fish in a shallow dish. For marinade, in a small bowl combine soy sauce, oil, sherry, 2 teaspoons of the sesame seed, brown sugar, and garlic. Pour over fish; turn fish to coat. Cover and marinate at room temperature for 30 minutes or in refrigerator for 2 hours, turning fish occasionally.

**2** Drain fish, reserving marinade. On 8 long metal skewers, alternately thread fish, plums, and snow peas, leaving a ¼-inch space between pieces. Brush with marinade.

**3** *For a charcoal grill,* grill kabobs on the greased rack of an uncovered grill directly over medium coals for 8 to 12 minutes or until fish flakes easily when tested with a fork, gently turning once halfway through grilling. (*For a gas grill,* preheat grill. Reduce heat to medium. Place kabobs on greased grill rack over heat. Cover and grill as above.)

**4** To serve, sprinkle remaining sesame seed over kabobs. Makes 4 servings.

Nutrition Facts per serving: 323 calories,
14 g total fat (3 g saturated fat), 47 mg cholesterol,
823 mg sodium, 14 g carbohydrate, 3 g fiber,
32 g protein. Daily Values: 75% vit. A, 47% vit. C,
2% calcium, 17% iron.

# Tuna Steaks with Hot Chile Pepper Sauce

**Prep:** 15 minutes  **Grill:** 8 minutes

  ⅓ cup mayonnaise or salad dressing
  1 fresh jalapeño pepper, finely
    chopped*
  1 tablespoon Dijon-style mustard
  1 teaspoon lemon juice
  4 6-ounce fresh or frozen tuna or
    halibut steaks, cut 1 inch thick
  4 teaspoons olive oil or cooking oil
    Dash ground red pepper

**1** For sauce, in a small bowl combine mayonnaise, jalapeño pepper, mustard, and lemon juice. Cover; chill until serving time.

**2** Thaw fish, if frozen. Rinse fish; pat dry with paper towels. Combine oil and red pepper; brush half of the oil mixture over both sides of fish.

**3** *For a charcoal grill,* grill fish on the greased rack of an uncovered grill directly over medium coals for 8 to 12 minutes or until fish flakes easily when tested with a fork, gently turning and brushing once with remaining oil mixture halfway through grilling. (*For a gas grill,* preheat grill. Reduce heat to medium. Place fish on greased grill rack over heat. Cover and grill as above.) Serve fish with sauce. Makes 4 servings.

Nutrition Facts per serving: 443 calories,
28 g total fat (5 g saturated fat), 81 mg cholesterol,
271 mg sodium, 1 g carbohydrate, 0 g fiber,
44 g protein. Daily Values: 111% vit. A, 10% vit. C,
1% calcium, 13% iron.

*Note:* When seeding and chopping a fresh chile pepper, protect your hands with plastic gloves. The oils in the pepper can irritate your skin. Also, avoid direct contact with your eyes. When finished with the chile pepper, wash hands thoroughly.

## TUNA FAJITAS

**Prep:** 25 minutes    **Marinate:** 30 minutes
**Grill:** 8 minutes

*Generally thought of as a dish that contains beef, fajitas (fah-HEE-tuhs) can be converted to a fish lover's dish with ease.*

    2  5- to 6-ounce fresh or frozen tuna or
        halibut steaks, cut 1 inch thick
    ¼ cup lemon juice
    2  tablespoons snipped fresh cilantro
        or parsley
    2  teaspoons olive oil
    2  cloves garlic, minced
    ¼ teaspoon coarsely ground black
        pepper
    ⅛ teaspoon ground red pepper
    1  recipe Tomatillo Salsa
    8  8-inch fat-free flour tortillas
    2  medium red sweet peppers,
        quartered lengthwise

**1** Thaw fish, if frozen. Rinse fish; pat dry. Place fish in a shallow dish. For marinade, in a small bowl stir together lemon juice, cilantro, oil, garlic, black pepper, and red pepper. Pour over fish; turn fish to coat. Cover and marinate at room temperature for 30 minutes or in the refrigerator for 1 hour, turning fish occasionally.

**2** Meanwhile, prepare Tomatillo Salsa. Cover and chill salsa until ready to serve. Stack tortillas and wrap in a piece of foil. Drain fish, reserving marinade.

**3** *For a charcoal grill,* grill fish, sweet peppers, and tortillas on the greased rack of an uncovered grill directly over medium coals until fish flakes easily when tested with a fork, peppers are tender, and tortillas are heated through, gently turning fish and peppers and brushing once with marinade halfway through grilling. (Allow 8 to 12 minutes for fish, 8 to 10 minutes for peppers, and about 5 minutes for tortillas.) (*For a gas grill,* preheat grill. Reduce heat to medium. Place fish, sweet peppers, and tortillas on greased grill rack over heat. Cover; grill as above.)

**4** Flake fish into large chunks with a fork. Cut sweet peppers into ½-inch-wide strips. Immediately fill warm tortillas with fish and sweet pepper strips. Serve with Tomatillo Salsa. Makes 4 servings.

Tomatillo Salsa: Halve 2 fresh serrano peppers lengthwise; remove stems, seeds, and membranes. Finely chop peppers. Remove husks from 3 fresh tomatillos. Finely chop tomatillos (you should have about 1½ cups).

In a medium bowl stir together serrano peppers; tomatillos; 3 green onions, thinly sliced; 2 tablespoons finely chopped onion; 1 tablespoon snipped fresh cilantro or parsley; 1 tablespoon lemon juice; 1 clove garlic, minced; and ¼ teaspoon salt. Makes about 1⅔ cups salsa.

Nutrition Facts per serving: 361 calories, 6 g total fat (1 g saturated fat), 30 mg cholesterol, 711 mg sodium, 52 g carbohydrate, 3 g fiber, 23 g protein. Daily Values: 73% vit. A, 113% vit. C, 1% calcium, 18% iron.

# Panzanella with Tuna

**Prep:** 20 minutes
**Grill:** 4 to 6 minutes per ½-inch thickness
**Stand:** 5 minutes

*This panzanella is easy to assemble.*

    4  4- to 5-ounce fresh or frozen tuna or
        halibut steaks, cut ¾ to 1 inch
        thick
    ½ cup bottled balsamic vinaigrette or
        red wine vinegar salad dressing
    ½ teaspoon finely snipped fresh
        rosemary
    2  cups torn mixed salad greens
    1½ cups broccoli florets
    2  small tomatoes, seeded and
        chopped
    ¼ cup thinly sliced green onions
    4  cups 1-inch cubes day-old Italian
        bread
        Finely shredded Parmesan cheese
        (optional)

Thaw fish, if frozen. Rinse fish; pat dry with paper towels. For brushing sauce, in a small bowl combine balsamic vinaigrette and rosemary; reserve 2 tablespoons for dressing. In a large salad bowl combine greens, broccoli, tomatoes, and green onions; toss gently to combine. Cover and chill greens mixture until ready to serve.

*For a charcoal grill*, grill fish on the greased rack of an uncovered grill directly over medium coals until fish flakes easily when tested with a fork (allow 4 to 6 minutes per ½-inch thickness of fish), gently turning and brushing once with the remaining sauce halfway through grilling. (*For a gas grill*, preheat grill. Reduce heat to medium. Place fish on greased grill rack over heat. Cover and grill as above.)

Flake fish into large chunks with a fork. Add fish to greens mixture. Drizzle with reserved dressing; toss gently to coat. Add bread cubes; toss gently to combine. Let stand for 5 minutes before serving. If desired, sprinkle with cheese. Makes 4 servings.

Nutrition Facts per serving: 80 calories, 17 g total fat (3 g saturated fat), 47 mg cholesterol, 608 mg sodium, 24 g carbohydrate, 2 g fiber, 33 g protein. Daily Values: 82% vit. A, 69% vit. C, 5% calcium, 19% iron.

## TUNA WITH WILTED SPINACH

**Prep:** 15 minutes   **Marinate:** 5 minutes
**Grill:** 6 minutes

*Grilling does not have to be matter of running from the kitchen to your patio. Wilt the spinach and watch the tuna without leaving your post.*

> 1 4- to 5-ounce fresh or frozen tuna or salmon fillets, ¾ inch thick
>   Salt and black pepper
> 3 tablespoons balsamic vinegar
> 1 tablespoon olive oil
> ¼ teaspoon salt
> ¼ teaspoon garlic pepper
> 1 medium red onion, cut into ¼-inch slices

> 6 cups torn fresh spinach or torn mixed salad greens
> 2 cups grape tomatoes or cherry tomatoes, halved
> 2 tablespoons water

Thaw fish, if frozen. Rinse fish; pat dry with paper towels. Place fish in a shallow dish. Lightly sprinkle fish with salt and black pepper. Set aside.

In a small bowl stir together the vinegar, oil, the ¼ teaspoon salt, and the garlic pepper. Pour 2 tablespoons of the vinegar mixture over fish; turn fish to coat. Cover and marinate at room temperature for 5 minutes. Cover and chill the remaining vinegar mixture until ready to serve. Drain fish, reserving marinade.

*For a charcoal grill*, grill fish and onion slices on the greased rack of an uncovered grill directly over medium coals for 6 to 9 minutes or until fish flakes easily when tested with a fork and onion is tender, gently turning and brushing once with reserved marinade the first half of grilling. (*For a gas grill*, preheat grill. Reduce heat to medium. Place fish and onion slices on grill rack over heat. Cover and grill as above.) Remove fish and onion slices from grill. Discard any remaining marinade.

While the fish is cooking, in a large heavy skillet* combine the spinach, tomatoes, and water. Place skillet on grill rack over heat. Grill for 3 to 4 minutes or until spinach begins to wilt, stirring occasionally. To serve, transfer the spinach mixture to a serving platter. Top spinach with fish and onion slices. Drizzle with the remaining vinegar mixture. Makes 4 servings.

Nutrition Facts per serving: 299 calories, 11 g total fat (2 g saturated fat), 59 mg cholesterol, 315 mg sodium, 10 g carbohydrate, 3 g fiber, 39 g protein. Daily Values: 134% vit. A, 58% vit. C, 6% calcium, 26% iron.

*Note:* The heat from the grill will blacken the outside of the skillet, so use a cast-iron or an old skillet.

# Fish Kabobs with Cucumber Sauce

**Prep:** 25 minutes **Grill:** 8 minutes

*Taste this and you'll know why it's a favorite. It's big on flavor and low on calories. If you like, tuck the fish inside pita bread for sandwiches.*

- 1 10-ounce fresh or frozen salmon steak, cut 1 inch thick
- 1 10-ounce fresh or frozen halibut steak, cut 1 inch thick
- 1 8-ounce fresh or frozen tuna steak, cut 1 inch thick
- ¼ cup bottled Italian salad dressing
- 1 tablespoon snipped fresh cilantro
- 1 teaspoon chili powder
- ½ cup plain low-fat yogurt
- ¼ cup finely chopped, seeded tomato
- ¼ cup finely chopped, seeded cucumber

**1** Thaw fish, if frozen. Rinse fish; pat dry with paper towels. If necessary, remove bones and skin. Cut fish into 1-inch cubes. On 6 long metal skewers, alternately thread the different types of fish, leaving about ¼-inch space between pieces.

**2** In a small bowl combine Italian salad dressing, cilantro, and chili powder. Brush fish with dressing mixture. Set aside.

**3** For cucumber sauce, in a small bowl combine yogurt, tomato, and cucumber. Cover and chill until ready to serve.

**4** *For a charcoal grill*, grill kabobs on the greased rack of an uncovered grill directly over medium coals for 8 to 12 minutes or until fish flakes easily when tested with a fork, gently turning once halfway through grilling. (*For a gas grill*, preheat grill. Reduce heat to medium. Place kabobs on greased grill rack over heat. Cover and grill as above.)

**5** Serve fish kabobs with cucumber sauce. Makes 6 servings.

Ⓥ Nutrition Facts per serving: 215 calories, 10 g total fat (2 g saturated fat), 41 mg cholesterol, 166 mg sodium, 3 g carbohydrate, 0 g fiber, 27 g protein. Daily Values: 30% vit. A, 4% vit. C, 5% calcium, 8% iron.

## SALMON WITH CUCUMBER-HORSERADISH SAUCE

**Prep:** 10 minutes **Grill:** 8 minutes

- ⅓ cup finely chopped, seeded cucumber
- 2 tablespoons mayonnaise or salad dressing
- 2 tablespoons plain yogurt
- 1 teaspoon prepared horseradish
- 4 6-ounce fresh or frozen salmon steaks, cut 1 inch thick
- 1 tablespoon margarine or butter, melted
- 1 teaspoon snipped fresh dill or ¼ teaspoon dried dillweed

**1** For sauce, in a small bowl combine cucumber, mayonnaise, yogurt, and horseradish. Cover and refrigerate until ready to serve.

**2** Thaw fish, if frozen. Rinse fish; pat dry with paper towels. Combine melted margarine and dill; set aside. *For a charcoal grill*, grill fish on the greased rack of an uncovered grill directly over medium coals for 8 to 12 minutes or just until fish flakes easily when tested with a fork, gently turning once halfway through grilling and brushing occasionally with dill mixture. (*For a gas grill*, preheat grill. Reduce heat to medium. Place fish on greased grill rack over heat. Cover and grill as above.) Serve salmon with sauce. Makes 4 servings.

Nutrition Facts per serving: 237 calories, 14 g total fat (3 g saturated fat), 35 mg cholesterol, 193 mg sodium, 1 g carbohydrate, 0 g fiber, 25 g protein. Daily Values: 7% vit. A, 1% vit. C, 2% calcium, 8% iron.

# Minty Halibut with Yellow Squash

**Prep:** 15 minutes    **Grill:** 8 minutes

*Healthy, quick, and easy, this is both a gardener's and a busy cook's delight. But even if you don't have the herbs growing in your own garden, they're usually easy to find at the supermarket.*

>     4 5- to 6-ounce fresh or frozen halibut
>        or salmon steaks, cut
>        1 inch thick
>     ¼ cup lemon juice
>     2 tablespoons olive oil
>     3 cloves garlic, minced
>     2 tablespoons snipped fresh basil
>     1 tablespoon snipped fresh mint
>     2 medium yellow summer squash or
>        zucchini, halved lengthwise
>        Salt and pepper

**1** Thaw fish, if frozen. Rinse fish; pat dry with paper towels. In a small bowl stir together lemon juice, oil, and garlic. Transfer 3 tablespoons of the lemon juice mixture to a small bowl; stir in basil and mint. Set aside. Brush remaining lemon juice mixture on fish and the cut sides of squash. Lightly sprinkle fish and squash with salt and pepper.

**2** *For a charcoal grill,* grill fish and squash on the greased rack of an uncovered grill directly over medium coals for 8 to 12 minutes or until fish flakes easily when tested with a fork and squash is tender, gently turning once halfway through grilling. (*For a gas grill,* preheat grill. Reduce heat to medium. Place fish and squash on greased grill rack over heat. Cover and grill as above.)

**3** Transfer squash to a cutting board; cool slightly. Cut squash into ⅛-inch slices; arrange on a serving platter. Drizzle with some of the reserved lemon-basil mixture. Top with fish; drizzle with remaining lemon-basil mixture. Makes 4 servings.

Nutrition Facts per serving: 233 calories, 10 g total fat (1 g saturated fat), 46 mg cholesterol, 112 mg sodium, 5 g carbohydrate, 1 g fiber, 30 g protein. Daily Values: 8% vit. A, 19% vit. C, 7% calcium, 11% iron.

# MUSTARD-GLAZED HALIBUT STEAKS

**Prep:** 10 minutes    **Grill:** 8 minutes

*Although basil is the herb suggested for this easy fish entrée, other herbs, such as oregano or tarragon, are also good choices.*

>     4 6-ounce fresh or frozen halibut
>        steaks, cut 1 inch thick
>     2 tablespoons margarine or butter
>     2 tablespoons lemon juice
>     1 tablespoon Dijon-style mustard
>     2 teaspoons snipped fresh basil or
>        ½ teaspoon dried basil, crushed

**1** Thaw fish, if frozen. Rinse fish; pat dry with paper towels. In a small saucepan heat margarine, lemon juice, mustard, and basil over low heat until melted. Brush both sides of steaks with mustard mixture.

**2** *For a charcoal grill,* grill fish on the greased rack of an uncovered grill directly over medium coals for 8 to 12 minutes or until fish flakes easily when tested with a fork, gently turning once halfway through grilling and brushing occasionally with mustard mixture. (*For a gas grill,* preheat grill. Reduce heat to medium. Place fish on greased grill rack over heat. Cover and grill as above.) Makes 4 servings.

Nutrition Facts per serving: 243 calories, 10 g total fat (2 g saturated fat), 55 mg cholesterol, 254 mg sodium, 1 g carbohydrate, 0 g fiber, 36 g protein. Daily Values: 14% vit. A, 5% vit. C, 6% calcium, 9% iron.

Caramelized Salmon with Citrus Salsa

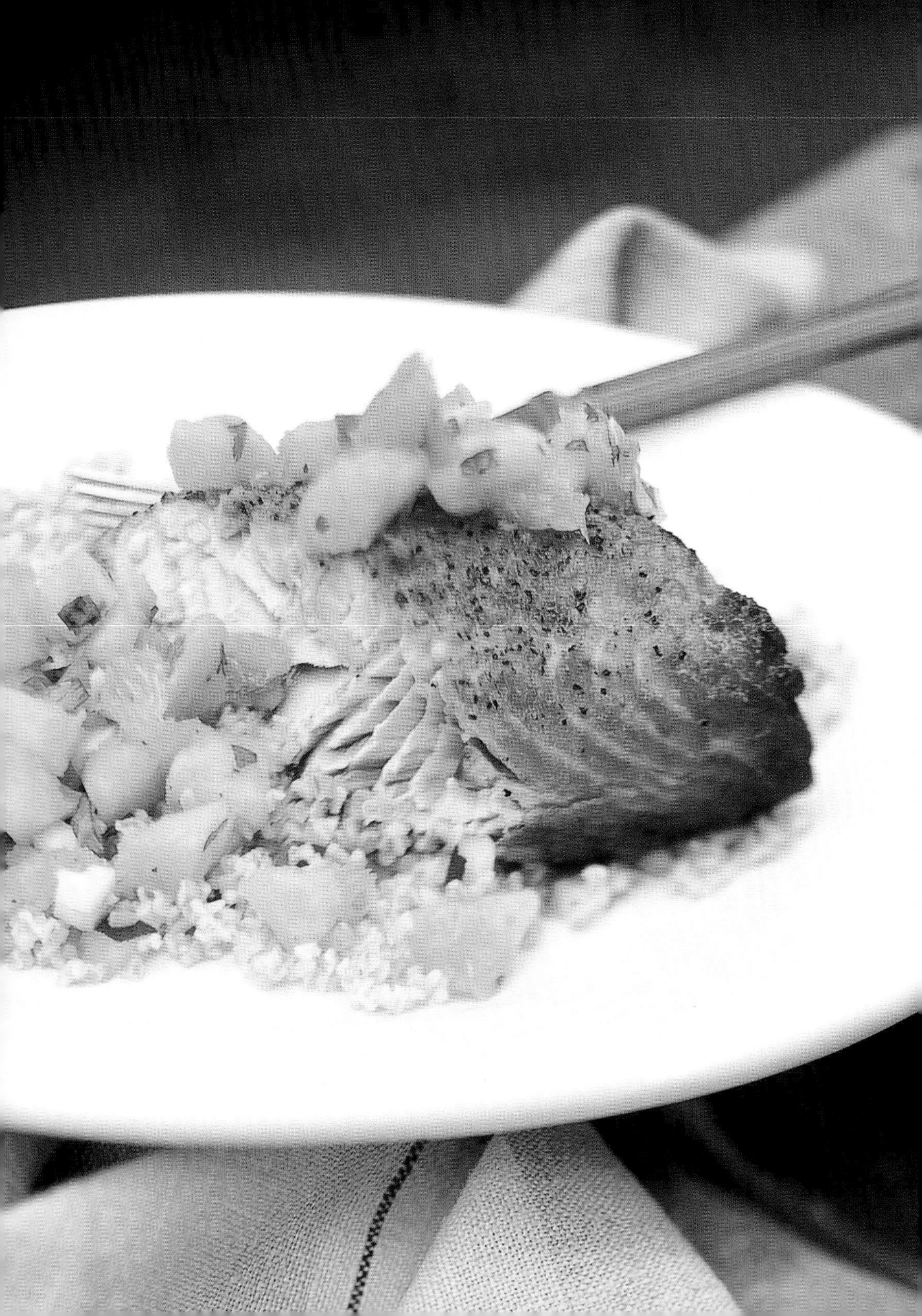

# Caramelized Salmon with Citrus Salsa

**Prep:** 20 minutes   **Marinate:** 8 to 24 hours
**Grill:** 15 minutes

*Fragrant and delicious, this do-ahead recipe is especially impressive because the orange-scented sugar rub turns a rich golden brown during grilling. Because jalapeños vary in their level of heat, you might want to taste the salsa before adding all of the jalapeño.*

> 1   1½-pound fresh or frozen salmon or halibut fillet (with skin), 1 inch thick
> 2   tablespoons sugar
> 1½  teaspoons finely shredded orange peel
> 1   teaspoon salt
> ¼   teaspoon freshly ground black pepper
> 1   teaspoon finely shredded orange peel
> 2   oranges, peeled, sectioned, and coarsely chopped
> 1   cup chopped fresh pineapple or canned crushed pineapple, drained
> 2   tablespoons snipped fresh cilantro
> 1   tablespoon finely chopped shallot
> 1   fresh jalapeño pepper, seeded and finely chopped

**1** Thaw fish, if frozen. Rinse fish; pat dry with paper towels. Place fish, skin side down, in a shallow dish. For rub, in a small bowl stir together sugar, the 1½ teaspoons orange peel, the salt, and black pepper. Sprinkle rub evenly over fish (not on skin side); rub in with your fingers. Cover and marinate in the refrigerator for 8 to 24 hours.

**2** Meanwhile, for salsa, in a small bowl stir together the 1 teaspoon orange peel, the oranges, pineapple, cilantro, shallot, and jalapeño pepper. Cover and chill until ready to serve or for up to 24 hours. Drain fish, discarding liquid.

**3** *For a charcoal grill,* arrange medium-hot coals around a drip pan. Test for medium heat above the pan. Place fish, skin side down, on greased grill rack over drip pan. Cover and grill about 12 minutes or until fish flakes easily when tested with a fork. [*For a gas grill,* preheat grill. Reduce heat to medium. Adjust for indirect cooking (see page 10). Grill as above.]

**4** To serve, cut fish into 4 serving-size pieces, cutting to but not through the skin. Carefully slip a metal spatula between fish and skin, lifting fish up and away from skin. Serve fish with salsa. Makes 4 servings.

Nutrition Facts per serving: 145 calories, 4 g total fat (1 g saturated fat), 20 mg cholesterol, 424 mg sodium, 10 g carbohydrate, 1 g fiber, 17 g protein. Daily Values: 5% vit. A, 31% vit. C, 2% calcium, 6% iron.

## DON'T GET BURNED!

**Fish is a great candidate for the grill, if you're willing to take a little extra care to prevent it from falling apart. It helps to place fish on a double layer of heavy-duty foil and to use a wide spatula if you must turn it, or to place it in a grill basket. Also, cut slits in the foil before placing fish on foil. This will allow the juices to drain so the fish doesn't poach in the juices. Be sure to lightly grease or brush the foil or grill basket with cooking oil or lightly coat it with nonstick cooking spray before adding the fish. Firmer-textured fish steaks can be grilled directly on top of a greased grill rack.**

## SALMON AND SCALLOP KABOBS

**Prep:** 15 minutes    **Marinate:** 1 to 2 hours
**Grill:** 8 minutes

*Pineapple and tarragon combine for a marinade and brush-on that will wow your dinner guests.*

8 ounces fresh or frozen salmon or
    tuna fillets, 1 inch thick
8 ounces fresh or frozen sea scallops
¼ cup pineapple juice
2 tablespoons lemon juice
1 tablespoon snipped fresh tarragon
    or 1 teaspoon dried tarragon,
    crushed
¼ teaspoon salt
¼ teaspoon dry mustard
2 medium zucchini, sliced ½ inch
    thick
1 medium red or green sweet
    pepper, cut into 1-inch squares
½ of a fresh pineapple, cut into
    chunks, or one 16-ounce can
    pineapple chunks, drained

1 Thaw fish and scallops, if frozen. Rinse fish and scallops; pat dry with paper towels. Cut fish into 1-inch cubes. Place fish and scallops in a plastic bag set into a shallow dish. For marinade, in a small bowl combine pineapple juice, lemon juice, tarragon, salt, and mustard. Pour over fish and scallops; seal bag. Marinate in refrigerator for 1 to 2 hours, turning bag occasionally.

2 Meanwhile, in a covered medium saucepan cook zucchini in a small amount of boiling water for 3 to 4 minutes or until nearly tender. Drain and cool.

3 Drain fish and scallops, reserving marinade. On 8 long metal skewers, alternately thread fish, scallops, zucchini, sweet pepper, and pineapple, leaving a ¼-inch space between pieces. Brush with marinade.

4 *For a charcoal grill*, grill kabobs on the greased rack of an uncovered grill directly over medium coals for 8 to 12 minutes or until fish flakes easily when tested with a fork and scallops are opaque, turning once halfway through grilling. (*For a gas grill*, preheat grill. Reduce heat to medium. Place kabobs on greased grill rack over heat. Cover and grill as above.) Makes 4 servings.

Nutrition Facts per serving: 150 calories, 3 g total fat (0 g saturated fat), 27 mg cholesterol, 255 mg sodium, 16 g carbohydrate, 2 g fiber, 17 g protein. Daily Values: 24% vit. A, 95% vit. C, 5% calcium, 13% iron.

# Gingered Salmon Fillet

**Prep:** 15 minutes    **Grill:** 6 minutes

*Need something classy in a hurry? Think fish, think grill, then turn to the reliable trio of soy sauce, ginger, and garlic. You can't go wrong.*

1 1½-pound fresh or frozen salmon or
    orange roughy fillet, ¾ inch
    thick
3 tablespoons lemon juice
1 tablespoon cooking oil
1 tablespoon soy sauce
2 teaspoons grated fresh ginger or
    ½ teaspoon ground ginger
1 teaspoon Worcestershire sauce
2 cloves garlic, minced
¼ teaspoon pepper
    Nonstick cooking spray

1 Thaw fish, if frozen. Rinse fish and pat dry with paper towels. For sauce, in a small bowl stir together lemon juice, oil, soy sauce, ginger, Worcestershire sauce, garlic, and pepper. Brush both sides of fish with some of the sauce.

2 Cut several slits in a piece of heavy foil. Lightly coat foil with nonstick cooking spray; place fish on foil, tucking under any thin edges.

3 *For a charcoal grill*, arrange medium-hot coals around a drip pan. Test for medium heat above the pan. Place foil with fish on

grill rack over drip pan. Cover and grill for 6 to 9 minutes or until fish flakes easily when tested with a fork, brushing twice with sauce during the last half of grilling. [*For a gas grill*, preheat grill. Reduce heat to medium. Adjust for indirect cooking (see page 10). Grill as above.] Makes 6 servings.

Nutrition Facts per serving: 129 calories, 6 g total fat (1 g saturated fat), 20 mg cholesterol, 248 mg sodium, 1 g carbohydrate, 0 g fiber, 16 g protein. Daily Values: 2% vit. A, 8% vit. C, 1% calcium, 6% iron.

## Did You Know?

**Pacific salmon are in season from spring through fall. Among the best Pacific salmon is the Chinook or king salmon. Its high-fat, soft-textured flesh ranges from off-white to bright red. Other high-fat salmon include the coho or silver salmon, with firm-textured, pink to red-orange flesh, and the sockeye or red salmon (often used for canning), with firm, deep red flesh. Not as fatty are the pink or humpback salmon and the chum or dog salmon, which has the lightest color of all. Atlantic salmon has diminished greatly over the years due to industrial pollution; Canada currently supplies most of the Atlantic salmon. Depending on the variety, salmon is sold whole or in fillets or steaks.**

## DILLY SALMON FILLETS

**Prep:** 15 minutes   **Marinate:** 10 minutes
**Grill:** 5 minutes

*Sauces don't need to be rich, nor do they need to be complicated. Here's a dazzling salmon recipe that's as easy as tossing fish on the grill.*

4   5- to 6-ounce fresh or frozen salmon or halibut fillets, ½ to ¾ inch thick
3   tablespoons lemon juice
2   tablespoons snipped fresh dill
2   tablespoons mayonnaise or salad dressing
2   teaspoons Dijon-style mustard
   Dash pepper

1 Thaw fish, if frozen. Rinse fish; pat dry with paper towels. Place in a shallow dish. For marinade, in a small bowl combine the lemon juice and 1 tablespoon of the dill. Pour over fish; turn fish to coat. Cover and marinate at room temperature for 10 minutes.

2 Meanwhile, in a small bowl stir together the remaining dill, the mayonnaise, mustard, and pepper. Set aside.

3 *For a charcoal grill*, arrange medium-hot coals around a drip pan. Test for medium heat above the pan. Drain fish, discarding the marinade. Place fish on greased grill rack over drip pan. Cover and grill for 3 minutes. Turn fish; spread with the mayonnaise mixture. Cover and grill for 2 to 6 minutes more or until fish flakes easily when tested with a fork. [*For a gas grill*, preheat grill. Reduce heat to medium. Adjust for indirect cooking (see page 10). Grill as above.] Makes 4 servings.

Nutrition Facts per serving: 211 calcium, 11 g total fat (2 g saturated fat), 35 mg cholesterol, 204 mg sodium, 1 g carbohydrate, 0 g fiber, 25 g protein. Daily Values: 4% vit. A, 8% vit. C, 1% calcium, 7% iron.

# Fish Sandwiches

**Prep:** 10 minutes
**Grill:** 4 to 6 minutes per ½-inch thickness

*These fresh-off-the-grill fish sandwiches put any drive-through fast-food fish sandwich to shame. Pick your seasoning—lemon pepper, Jamaican jerk, or Cajun—then top with a mayonnaise spread. You'll never go back for the drive-through kind again.*

4 4- to 5-ounce fresh or frozen fish
    fillets, ½ to ¾ inch thick
1 tablespoon lemon or lime juice
1 teaspoon lemon-pepper seasoning,
    Jamaican jerk seasoning, or
    Cajun seasoning
½ cup mayonnaise or salad dressing
4 teaspoons Dijon-style mustard
1 teaspoon honey
4 hamburger buns or kaiser rolls,
    split and toasted
    Watercress or lettuce leaves
    (optional)
    Roasted red sweet pepper strips or
    fresh tomato slices (optional)

## Smokin' Hot Tip

**Testing fish for doneness can be a tricky job for even expert grillers. A few tips will help: If grilling fish with the skin on, let the skin brown and begin to pull away from the grill before trying to turn the fish. Grill fish just until it is opaque through the thickest part. Don't cook until it's dry, though! It will turn tough. The best test of all is to take a quick peek at the thickest part of the fish using a fork. When done, the fish will flake easily.**

**1** Thaw fish, if frozen. Rinse fish; pat dry with paper towels. Brush fish with lemon juice. Sprinkle desired seasoning evenly over all sides of fish. For sandwich spread, in a small bowl stir together mayonnaise, mustard, and honey. Cover and chill until ready to serve.

**2** Place fish in a greased grill basket, tucking under any thin edges. *For a charcoal grill,* grill fish on the rack of an uncovered grill directly over medium coals until fish flakes easily when tested with a fork (allow 4 to 6 minutes per ½-inch thickness of fish), turning basket once halfway through grilling. (*For a gas grill*, preheat grill. Reduce heat to medium. Place fish on grill rack over heat. Cover and grill as above.)

**3** Remove fish from grill. To serve, spread bottom half of buns with mayonnaise mixture. Top with watercress (if desired), fish, additional mayonnaise mixture, red pepper strips (if desired), and top halves of buns. Makes 4 servings.

Nutrition Facts per serving with bun:
311 calories, 14 g total fat (2 g saturated fat),
51 mg cholesterol, 676 mg sodium,
24 g carbohydrate, 1 g fiber, 22 g protein. Daily
Values: 2% vit. A, 4% vit. C, 3% calcium, 10% iron.

## GROUPER WITH RED PEPPER SAUCE

**Prep:** 25 minutes
**Grill:** 4 to 6 minutes per ½-inch thickness

1 large red sweet pepper, chopped
1 tablespoon margarine or butter
2 medium tomatoes, peeled, seeded,
    and chopped
1 tablespoon sugar
1 teaspoon red wine vinegar
¼ teaspoon salt
⅛ teaspoon garlic powder
    Dash ground red pepper
4 4-ounce fresh or frozen grouper
    fillets, ½ to 1 inch thick
2 tablespoons lemon juice
1 tablespoon olive oil
¼ teaspoon dried rosemary, crushed

**1** For sauce, in a medium saucepan cook sweet pepper in hot margarine over medium heat until tender. Stir in tomatoes, sugar, vinegar, salt, garlic powder, and ground red pepper. Cook for 5 minutes, stirring occasionally. Transfer mixture to a blender container or food processor bowl. Cover and blend or process until smooth. Return to saucepan; cover and keep warm.*

**2** Thaw fish, if frozen. Rinse fish; pat dry with paper towels. In a small bowl combine lemon juice, oil, and rosemary. Brush both sides of fish with lemon mixture. Place fish in a greased grill basket, turning under any thin edges. *For a charcoal grill*, grill fish on the rack of an uncovered grill directly over medium coals until fish flakes easily when tested with a fork (allow 4 to 6 minutes per ½-inch thickness of fish), turning basket once halfway through grilling. (*For a gas grill*, preheat grill. Reduce heat to medium. Place fish on grill rack over heat. Cover and grill as above.) Serve the fish with the sauce. Makes 4 servings.

Nutrition Facts per serving: 194 calories, 8 g total fat (1 g saturated fat), 60 mg cholesterol, 266 mg sodium, 9 g carbohydrate, 1 g fiber, 22 g protein. Daily Values: 27% vit. A, 97% vit. C, 2% calcium, 5% iron.

*Note:* If desired, you may prepare the sauce ahead of time. Cover and refrigerate until ready to grill. Before serving, reheat the sauce in a saucepan.

## Wasabi-Glazed Whitefish with Vegetable Slaw

**Prep:** 20 minutes
**Grill:** 4 to 6 minutes per ½-inch thickness

4 4-ounce fresh or frozen white-fleshed fish fillets, ½ to ¾ inch thick
2 tablespoons reduced-sodium soy sauce
1 teaspoon toasted sesame oil
½ teaspoon sugar

¼ teaspoon wasabi powder or 1 tablespoon prepared horseradish
1 medium zucchini, coarsely shredded (about 1⅓ cups)
1 cup sliced radishes
1 cup fresh pea pods, strings removed
3 tablespoons snipped fresh chives
3 tablespoons rice vinegar

**1** Thaw fish, if frozen. Rinse fish; pat dry with paper towels. In a small bowl combine soy sauce, ½ teaspoon of the sesame oil, ¼ teaspoon of the sugar, and the wasabi powder. Brush soy mixture over both sides of fish. Place fish in a greased grill basket, tucking under any thin edges.

**2** *For a charcoal grill*, grill fish on the rack of an uncovered grill directly over medium coals until fish flakes easily when tested with a fork (allow 4 to 6 minutes per ½-inch thickness of fish), turning basket once halfway through grilling. (*For a gas grill*, preheat grill. Reduce heat to medium. Place fish on greased grill rack over heat. Cover and grill as above.)

**3** Meanwhile, for vegetable slaw, in a medium bowl combine the zucchini, radishes, pea pods, and 2 tablespoons of the chives. Stir together the remaining sesame oil, remaining sugar, and vinegar; drizzle over the zucchini mixture, tossing to coat. To serve, sprinkle remaining chives over fish. Serve with vegetable slaw. Makes 4 servings.

Nutrition Facts per serving: 141 calories, 3 g total fat (1 g saturated fat), 60 mg cholesterol, 363 mg sodium, 6 g carbohydrate, 1 g fiber, 24 g protein. Daily Values: 3% vit. A, 46% vit. C, 3% calcium, 10% iron.

## MAHI MAHI WITH VEGETABLE SLAW

**Prep:** 15 minutes    **Marinate:** 30 minutes
**Grill:** 4 to 6 minutes per ½-inch thickness

- 4 5- to 6-ounce fresh or frozen mahi mahi or pike fillets, ½ to ¾ inch thick
- 1 teaspoon finely shredded lime peel (set aside)
- ¼ cup lime juice
- ¼ cup snipped fresh cilantro
- 3 tablespoons olive oil
- 1 tablespoon honey
- 1 fresh jalapeño pepper, seeded and finely chopped
- 3 cloves garlic, minced
- ⅛ teaspoon salt
- 1½ cups packaged shredded cabbage with carrot (coleslaw mix)
- 1 cup shredded jicama

**1** Thaw fish, if frozen. Rinse fish; pat dry. Place fish in a shallow dish. For dressing, in a small bowl combine lime juice, cilantro, oil, honey, jalapeño pepper, garlic, and salt; divide in half. Stir lime peel into one portion of dressing. Pour dressing with lime peel over fish; turn fish to coat. Cover; marinate at room temperature for 30 minutes.

**2** For slaw, in a medium bowl combine cabbage mixture and jicama. Pour remaining dressing over slaw; toss to coat. Cover and chill until ready to serve.

**3** Drain fish, discarding marinade. Place fish in a greased grill basket, tucking under any thin edges. *For a charcoal grill*, grill fish on the rack of an uncovered grill directly over medium coals until fish flakes easily when tested with a fork (allow 4 to 6 minutes per ½-inch thickness of fish), turning basket once halfway through grilling. (*For a gas grill*, preheat grill. Reduce heat to medium. Place fish on grill rack over heat. Cover and grill as above.) Serve fish with slaw. Serves 4.

Ⓝutrition Facts per serving: 276 calories, 10 g total fat (1 g saturated fat), 67 mg cholesterol, 130 mg sodium, 12 g carbohydrate, 1 g fiber, 34 g protein. Daily Values: 23% vit. A, 60% vit. C, 9% calcium, 10% iron.

## Parsley Sole Fillets

**Prep:** 20 minutes    **Grill:** 14 minutes

- 4 3- to 4-ounce fresh or frozen sole or flounder fillets, ¼ inch thick
- 2 tablespoons mayonnaise or salad dressing
- 1 tablespoon Dijon-style mustard
- 1 tablespoon honey
- ¼ cup finely chopped pecans
- ¼ cup snipped fresh parsley
- ¼ cup shredded carrot
  Nonstick spray coating
- 1 tablespoon snipped fresh parsley

**1** Thaw fish, if frozen. Rinse fish; pat dry with paper towels. Stir together mayonnaise, mustard, and honey. Brush one side of each fillet with about 1½ teaspoons of the mustard mixture. Sprinkle fillets with pecans, the ¼ cup parsley, and carrot. Roll fish up, starting from one of the short sides. Secure with wooden toothpicks that have been soaked in water. Fold a 24×18-inch piece of heavy foil in half crosswise. Trim to make a 12-inch square. Cut several slits in foil. Lightly coat foil with nonstick cooking spray. Place fish rolls on foil.

**2** *For a charcoal grill*, arrange medium-hot coals around drip pan. Test for medium heat above pan. Place foil with fish rolls on grill rack over drip pan. Cover; grill for 14 to 16 minutes or until fish flakes easily when tested with fork. [*For a gas grill*, preheat grill. Reduce heat to medium. Adjust for indirect cooking (see page 10). Grill as above.]

**3** To serve, brush remaining mustard mixture on fish rolls; sprinkle with the 1 tablespoon parsley. Makes 4 servings.

Ⓝutrition Facts per serving: 189 calories, 11 g total fat (1 g saturated fat), 44 mg cholesterol, 201 mg sodium, 7 g carbohydrate, 1 g fiber, 15 g protein. Daily Values: 23% vit. A, 11% vit. C, 1% calcium, 4% iron.

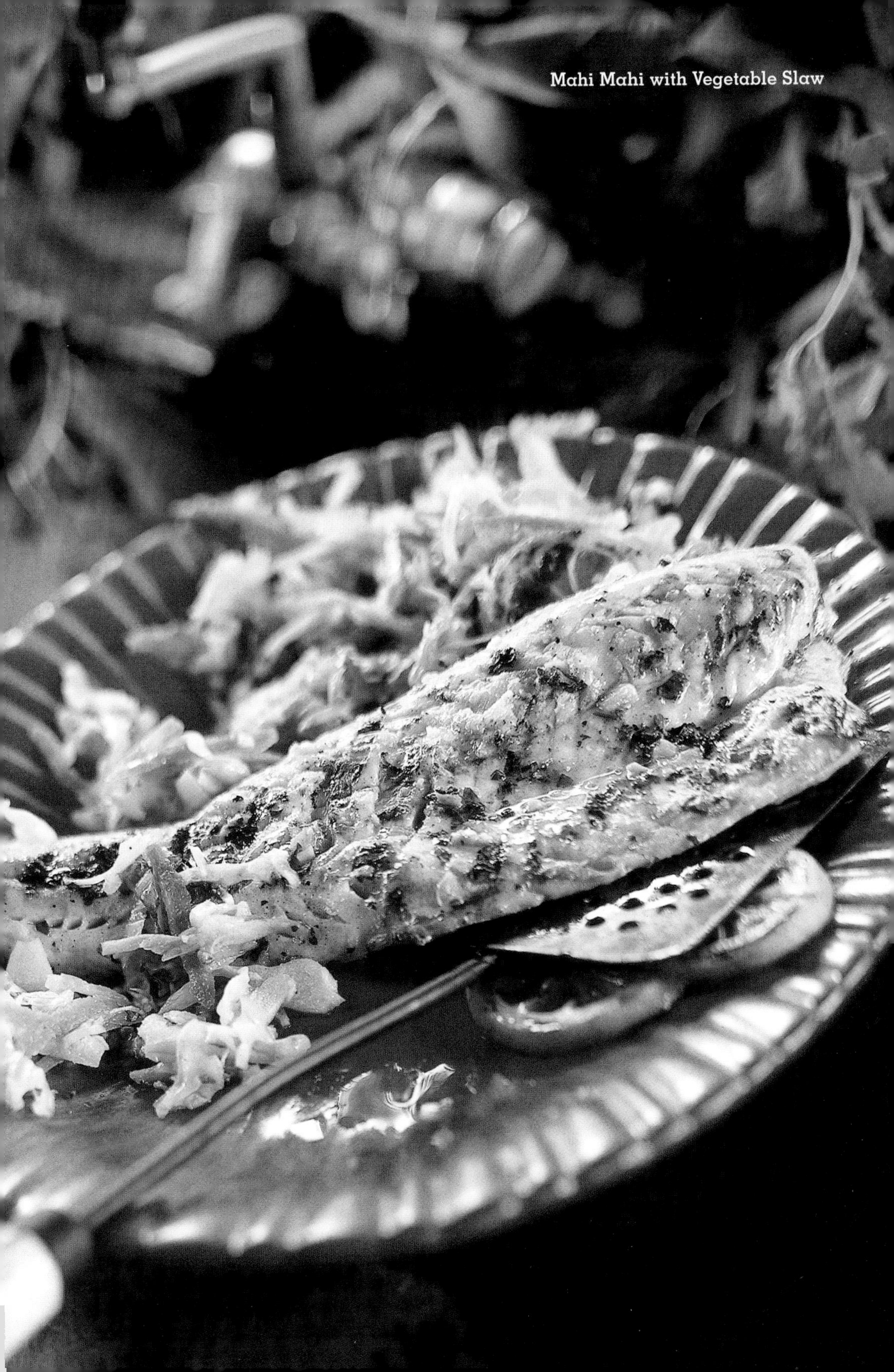
Mahi Mahi with Vegetable Slaw

## RED SNAPPER WITH HERB-PECAN CRUST

**Prep:** 15 minutes
**Grill:** 4 to 6 minutes per ½-inch thickness

*Thanks to its nutty crust, this grilled fish stays juicy. For a lovely combination, serve this with grilled summer squash brushed with lemon butter and a simple toss of steamed rice and snipped fresh tarragon.*

- 4 5- or 6-ounce fresh or frozen red snapper or salmon fillets (with skin), ½ to ¾ inch thick
- ⅓ cup finely chopped pecans
- 2 tablespoons fine dry bread crumbs
- 2 tablespoons margarine or butter, softened
- 1 tablespoon snipped fresh Italian flat-leaf parsley
- 1 teaspoon finely shredded lemon peel
- 2 cloves garlic, minced
- ¼ teaspoon salt
- ⅛ teaspoon black pepper
  Dash ground red pepper
  Snipped fresh Italian flat-leaf parsley (optional)
  Lemon wedges (optional)

**1** Thaw fish, if frozen. Rinse fish; pat dry with paper towels. In a small bowl combine pecans, bread crumbs, margarine or butter, parsley, lemon peel, garlic, salt, black pepper, and red pepper.

**2** *For a charcoal grill,* place fish, skin sides down, on the greased rack of an uncovered grill directly over medium coals. Spoon the pecan mixture on top of the fish; spread slightly. Grill until fish flakes easily when tested with a fork (allow 4 to 6 minutes per ½-inch thickness of fish). (*For a gas grill,* preheat grill. Reduce heat to medium. Place fish on greased grill rack over heat. Cover and grill as above.)

**3** Transfer to a serving platter with a wide spatula. If desired, sprinkle fish with additional snipped parsley and serve with lemon wedges. Makes 4 servings.

Nutrition Facts per serving: 268 calories, 14 g total fat (2 g saturated fat), 52 mg cholesterol, 287 mg sodium, 7 g carbohydrate, 8 g fiber, 30 g protein. Daily Values: 7% vit. A, 4% vit. C, 4% calcium, 4% iron.

## Snapper with Cilantro Pesto

**Prep:** 15 minutes
**Grill:** 4 to 6 minutes per ½-inch thickness

*Cilantro, used in a pesto, has a freshness that goes beautifully with fish. Don't use the pesto with just this recipe. Try stirring it into angel hair pasta to create a side dish for grilled fish.*

- 4 4- to 5-ounce fresh or frozen red snapper or halibut fillets, ½ to ¾ inch thick
- 1 cup loosely packed fresh parsley leaves
- ½ cup loosely packed fresh cilantro leaves
- 3 tablespoons grated Parmesan cheese
- 2 tablespoons pine nuts or slivered almonds
- 3 cloves garlic, minced
- 2 teaspoons lemon juice
- ⅛ teaspoon salt
- 2 tablespoons olive oil
- 1 tablespoon lemon juice
- 2 teaspoons olive oil
  Salt and pepper
- 1 plum tomato, seeded and chopped

**1** Thaw fish, if frozen. Rinse fish; pat dry with paper towels. For pesto, in a blender container or food processor bowl combine the parsley, cilantro, Parmesan cheese, pine nuts, garlic, the 2 teaspoons lemon juice, and the salt. Cover and blend or process with several on-off turns until nearly smooth, stopping the machine and scraping down sides as necessary. With the machine running slowly, gradually add the 2 tablespoons oil; blend or process until the consistency of softened butter, scraping sides as necessary. Transfer to a small bowl. Set aside.

**2** In a small bowl stir together the 1 tablespoon lemon juice and the 2 teaspoons oil. Brush fish with lemon mixture. Sprinkle fish with salt and pepper.

**3** Place fish in a greased grill basket, tucking under any thin edges. *For a charcoal grill*, grill fish on the rack of an uncovered grill directly over medium coals until fish flakes easily when tested with a fork (allow 4 to 6 minutes per $\frac{1}{2}$-inch thickness of fish), turning basket once halfway through grilling. (*For a gas grill*, preheat grill. Reduce heat to medium. Place fish on grill rack over heat. Cover and grill as above.)

**4** To serve, spoon pesto over fish and top with tomato. Makes 4 servings.

Nutrition Facts per serving: 254 calories, 15 g total fat (3 g saturated fat), 45 mg cholesterol, 281 mg sodium, 4 g carbohydrate, 0 g fiber, 27 g protein. Daily Values: 10% vit. A, 44% vit. C, 10% calcium, 12% iron.

## TROUT WITH FENNEL STUFFING

**Prep:** 25 minutes    **Grill:** 15 minutes

    4  8- to 10-ounce fresh or frozen dressed trout or other dressed fish
    2  medium fennel bulbs
    1  clove garlic, minced
    $\frac{1}{4}$  teaspoon salt
    $\frac{1}{8}$  teaspoon pepper
    2  tablespoons margarine or butter
    1  tablespoon snipped fresh parsley
    3  tablespoons margarine or butter
    1  tablespoon lemon juice
    $\frac{1}{2}$  teaspoon dried rosemary, crushed
       Dash pepper
       Nonstick spray coating
       Lemon wedges (optional)
       Fresh parsley sprigs (optional)

**1** Thaw fish, if frozen. Rinse fish; pat dry with paper towels. For stuffing, cut off and discard upper stalks of fennel. Remove any wilted outer layers; wash fennel. Chop fennel (you should have about $2\frac{1}{2}$ cups). In a medium saucepan cook and stir fennel, garlic, salt, and the $\frac{1}{8}$ teaspoon pepper in 2 tablespoons margarine for 10 minutes or until fennel is tender but not brown. Stir in parsley; set aside.

**2** For sauce, in a small saucepan cook and stir the 3 tablespoons margarine, lemon juice, rosemary, and dash pepper until the margarine is melted. Spoon one-fourth of the stuffing into each fish cavity. Tie the fish with 100-percent-cotton string in 2 or 3 places to close the cavity. Brush fish with sauce. Cut several slits in a piece of heavy foil large enough to hold fish. Lightly coat foil with nonstick cooking spray; place fish on foil.

**3** *For a charcoal grill*, arrange medium-hot coals around a drip pan. Test for medium heat above the pan. Place foil with fish on grill rack over drip pan. Cover and grill for 15 to 20 minutes or until fish begins to flake easily when tested with a fork, brushing often with any remaining sauce. [*For a gas grill*, preheat grill. Reduce heat to medium. Adjust for indirect cooking (see page 10). Grill as above.]

**4** To serve, remove string. Garnish with lemon wedges and parsley, if desired. Makes 4 servings.

Nutrition Facts per serving: 414 calories, 22 g total fat (4 g saturated fat), 130 mg cholesterol, 385 mg sodium, 4 g carbohydrate, 11 g fiber, 48 g protein. Daily Values: 22% vit. A, 25% vit. C, 15% calcium, 29% iron.

# Rosemary Trout with Lemon Butter

**Prep:** 15 minutes  **Grill:** 6 minutes

*This lemon-shallot butter is a true friend of grilled food. Make extra and brush over grilled zucchini, or simply melt a spoonful of this butter over a good steak.*

2  8- to 10-ounce fresh or frozen dressed, boned rainbow trout or other dressed fish
1  tablespoon snipped fresh rosemary
1  tablespoon finely chopped shallot or onion
   Salt and pepper
1  teaspoon finely shredded lemon peel (set aside)
1  tablespoon lemon juice
2  teaspoons olive oil
4  teaspoons butter, softened
2  medium tomatoes, halved crosswise
1  tablespoon snipped fresh parsley

1 Thaw fish, if frozen. Rinse fish; pat dry with paper towels. Spread each fish open, skin side down. Rub the rosemary and half of the shallot over fish; sprinkle with salt and pepper and drizzle with lemon juice and oil. Set aside.

2 For lemon butter, in a small bowl stir together the remaining shallot, the lemon peel, and butter. Sprinkle with salt and pepper. Dot each tomato half with ¼ teaspoon of the butter mixture.

3 *For a charcoal grill,* grill fish, skin sides down, and tomatoes on the greased rack of an uncovered grill directly over medium coals until fish flakes easily when tested with a fork and tomatoes are heated through. (Allow 6 to 8 minutes for fish and about 5 minutes for tomatoes.) (*For a gas grill,* preheat grill. Reduce heat to medium. Place fish, skin sides down, and tomatoes on greased grill rack over heat. Cover and grill as above.)

4 To serve, in a small saucepan melt remaining butter mixture. Cut each fish in half lengthwise. Sprinkle fish with parsley. Drizzle butter mixture over fish and tomatoes. Makes 4 servings.

Ⓥ Nutrition Facts per serving: 206 calories, 10 g total fat (3 g saturated fat), 75 mg cholesterol, 109 mg sodium, 4 g carbohydrate, 1 g fiber, 24 g protein. Daily Values: 13% vit. A, 31% vit. C, 7% calcium, 17% iron.

## SHRIMP AND TROPICAL FRUIT

**Prep:** 25 minutes  **Grill:** 10 minutes

*A riot of tropical fruit turns barbecued shrimp into a festival of flavor and color. Simply baste shrimp with a tangy, gingery barbecue sauce and serve over a tropical fruit.*

1¼  pounds fresh or frozen jumbo shrimp in shells
1  cup bottled barbecue sauce
⅔  cup unsweetened pineapple juice
2  tablespoons cooking oil
4  teaspoons grated fresh ginger or 1½ teaspoons ground ginger
¼  of a fresh pineapple, sliced crosswise
1  medium papaya, peeled, seeded, and cut up
3  medium kiwi fruit, peeled and cut up

1 Thaw shrimp, if frozen. Peel and devein shrimp, leaving tails intact. Rinse shrimp; pat dry. Thread shrimp onto six 10- to 12-inch metal skewers, leaving a ¼-inch space between pieces. Set aside.

2 For sauce, in a medium bowl stir together barbecue sauce, pineapple juice, oil, and ginger. Brush shrimp with sauce.

3 *For a charcoal grill,* grill kabobs and pineapple on the greased rack of an uncovered grill directly over medium coals until shrimp are opaque and pineapple is heated through, turning once and brushing occasionally with some of the sauce up to the

last 5 minutes of grilling. (Allow 10 to 12 minutes for shrimp and about 5 minutes for pineapple.) (*For a gas grill*, preheat grill. Reduce heat to medium. Place kabobs and pineapple on greased grill rack over heat. Cover and grill as above.)

**4** In a small saucepan bring the remaining sauce to boiling. Boil gently, uncovered, for 1 minute. Cool slightly. Pass for dipping. Serve shrimp and pineapple with papaya and kiwi fruit. Makes 6 servings.

Nutrition Facts per serving: 199 calories, 6 g total fat (1 g saturated fat), 116 mg cholesterol, 474 mg sodium, 21 g carbohydrate, 1 g fiber, 14 g protein. Daily Values: 13% vit. A, 115% vit. C, 5% calcium, 17% iron.

## Asparagus and Shrimp with Dill Butter

**Prep:** 20 minutes   **Grill:** 15 minutes

1 pound fresh or frozen medium
 shrimp in shells
1 pound asparagus spears
¼ cup butter, softened
1 tablespoon snipped fresh dill or
 1 teaspoon dried dillweed
1 tablespoon dry white wine
½ teaspoon finely shredded lemon
 peel
⅛ teaspoon salt
⅛ teaspoon pepper
1 medium leek, thinly sliced
3 cups hot cooked rice or pasta

**1** Thaw shrimp, if frozen. Peel and devein shrimp, removing tails, if desired. Rinse shrimp; pat dry with paper towels. Set aside.

**2** Snap off and discard woody bases from asparagus. Cut asparagus diagonally into 2-inch pieces. In a bowl stir together the butter, dill, wine, lemon peel, salt, and pepper. Set aside.

**3** Fold a 36×18-inch piece of heavy foil in half to make an 18-inch square. Place shrimp, asparagus, and leek in center of foil. Top with dill mixture. Bring up opposite edges of foil and seal with a double fold. Fold remaining edges together to completely enclose shrimp mixture, leaving space for steam to build.

**4** *For a charcoal grill*, grill shrimp mixture on the rack of an uncovered grill directly over medium coals about 15 minutes or until shrimp are opaque, turning packet once halfway through grilling. (*For a gas grill*, preheat grill. Reduce heat to medium. Place shrimp mixture on grill rack over heat. Cover and grill as above.)

**5** Serve shrimp and vegetables over rice or pasta. Drizzle with juices from foil packet. Makes 4 servings.

Nutrition Facts per serving: 350 calories, 13 g total fat (2 g saturated fat), 131 mg cholesterol, 357 mg sodium, 39 g carbohydrate, 2 g fiber, 19 g protein. Daily Values: 25% vit. A, 35% vit. C, 5% calcium, 28% iron.

**Did You Know?**

The price of shrimp, generally sold by the pound, is determined by the size—the bigger the shrimp, the higher the price, and the fewer per pound. Shrimp vary in size from small to jumbo. Here's a general guideline for determining approximately how many shrimp are in a pound: 50 to 60 small, 30 to 40 medium, 15 to 25 large, and 10 to 15 jumbo shrimp.

Garlic and Shrimp Pasta Toss

## GARLIC AND SHRIMP PASTA TOSS

**Prep:** 25 minutes   **Grill:** 38 minutes

*As any Italian cook knows, garlic, butter, shrimp, and pasta were made for each other. But using roasted garlic can make the best even better.*

- 1 **pound fresh or frozen large shrimp in shells**
- 1 **large garlic bulb**
- 1 **tablespoon olive oil**
- 2 **tablespoons lemon juice**
- 1 **red or yellow sweet pepper, quartered lengthwise**
- 1 **onion, cut into ½-inch slices**
- 3 **cups packaged dried cavatelli (curled shells) or bow tie pasta (farfalle) (about 8 ounces)**
- 2 **tablespoons butter, softened**
- ½ **teaspoon salt**
- ½ **teaspoon freshly ground black pepper**
- ⅓ **cup shredded Asiago or Parmesan cheese**

1 Thaw shrimp, if frozen. Peel and devein shrimp, leaving tails intact. Rinse shrimp; pat dry with paper towels. Cover and refrigerate until ready to grill.

2 With a sharp knife, cut off the top ½ inch from garlic bulb to expose the ends of the individual cloves. Leaving garlic bulb whole, remove any loose, papery outer layers.

3 Fold an 18×9-inch piece of heavy foil in half to make a 9-inch square. Place garlic bulb, cut side up, in center of foil. Drizzle bulb with 1½ teaspoons of the oil. Bring up opposite edges of foil and seal with a double fold. Fold remaining edges together to completely enclose garlic, leaving room for steam to build.

4 *For a charcoal grill,* arrange medium-hot coals around a drip pan. Test for medium heat above the pan. Place garlic on greased grill rack over drip pan. Cover and grill for 30 minutes. [*For a gas grill,* preheat grill. Reduce heat to medium. Adjust for indirect cooking (see page 10). Grill as above.]

5 Meanwhile, thread shrimp onto long metal skewers, leaving a ¼-inch space between pieces. In a small bowl combine the remaining oil and 1 tablespoon of the lemon juice; brush over shrimp and vegetables.

6 Add skewers to grill over drip pan; add vegetables to grill directly over coals. Cover and grill for 8 to 10 minutes more or until garlic is soft, shrimp are opaque, and vegetables are tender, turning shrimp and vegetables once halfway through grilling. Remove from grill. Cool garlic and vegetables slightly. Coarsely chop vegetables.

7 While shrimp and vegetables are grilling, cook pasta according to package directions; drain. Return pasta to hot pan.

8 Squeeze garlic pulp into a small bowl. Thoroughly mash garlic pulp. Add butter, salt, and black pepper; mix well. In a large bowl combine pasta and garlic mixture; toss to coat. Add shrimp, vegetables, remaining lemon juice, and cheese; toss gently to mix. Serve immediately. Makes 4 servings.

Nutrition Facts per serving: 404 calories, 16 g total fat (7 g saturated fat), 174 mg cholesterol, 567 mg sodium, 44 g carbohydrate, 3 g fiber, 21 g protein. Daily Values: 25% vit. A, 66% vit. C, 12% calcium, 28% iron.

## WISE ADVICE

**How do you tell if the seafood you're buying is fresh? Give it a sniff. If it smells fishy, move on. Whole fish should have red or pink gills and clear, slightly bulging eyes. Fillets, steaks, and shrimp should have shiny surfaces; clams and oysters should have tightly closed shells. Farm-raised fish are often freshest because they can be brought to market more quickly than fish caught in the wild.**

# Shrimp and Papaya Salad

**Prep:** 20 minutes  **Grill:** 10 minutes

1¼ pounds fresh or frozen jumbo
  shrimp in shells
½ cup plain yogurt
¼ cup mayonnaise or salad dressing
1 tablespoon honey
¾ teaspoon curry powder
⅛ teaspoon salt
  Leaf lettuce
1 cup coarsely shredded cucumber
  or zucchini
1 cup coarsely shredded carrot
2 papayas, seeded, peeled, and
  thinly sliced
8 red or green sweet pepper rings
¼ cup sliced almonds, toasted
  (optional)

1 Thaw shrimp, if frozen. Peel and devein shrimp, leaving tails intact. Rinse shrimp; pat dry with paper towels. Thread shrimp onto four 10-inch metal skewers, leaving a ¼-inch space between pieces. For dressing, in a small bowl stir together yogurt, mayonnaise, honey, curry powder, and salt. Cover and chill until ready to serve.

2 *For a charcoal grill,* grill kabobs on the greased rack of an uncovered grill directly over medium coals for 10 to 12 minutes or until shrimp are opaque, turning once halfway through grilling. *(For a gas grill,* preheat grill. Reduce heat to medium. Place kabobs on greased grill rack over heat. Cover and grill as above.)

3 Remove shrimp from skewers. Brush shrimp lightly with some of the dressing. Arrange lettuce each plate. Sprinkle cucumber and carrot over lettuce. Arrange shrimp, papaya, and sweet pepper on each salad. If desired, top with almonds. Serve salad with remaining dressing. Serves 4.

Nutrition Facts per serving: 260 calories, 13 g total fat (2 g saturated fat), 162 mg cholesterol, 354 mg sodium, 18 g carbohydrate, 2 g fiber, 19 g protein. Daily Values: 114% vit. A, 123% vit. C, 9% calcium, 20% iron.

# GINGERED SHRIMP WITH COUSCOUS

**Prep:** 20 minutes  **Marinate:** 1 to 2 hours
**Grill:** 6 minutes

1 pound fresh or frozen medium to
  large shrimp in shells
1 medium mango, peeled, seeded,
  and chopped
3 teaspoons grated fresh ginger
½ teaspoon finely shredded lime
  peel
2 tablespoons lime juice
2 tablespoons cooking oil
¼ teaspoon salt
¼ teaspoon crushed red pepper
½ cup finely chopped red onion
½ cup orange juice
½ cup water
¾ cup quick-cooking couscous
1 tablespoon snipped fresh cilantro

1 Thaw shrimp, if frozen. Peel and devein shrimp, leaving tails intact. Rinse shrimp; pat dry with paper towels. Place shrimp in a medium bowl.

2 For marinade, place ½ cup of the chopped mango in a blender container; cover and blend until smooth. (Or, mash with a potato masher or fork.) In a small bowl stir together the blended mango, 2 teaspoons of the ginger, the lime peel, lime juice, 1 tablespoon of the cooking oil, the salt, and crushed red pepper. Pour marinade over shrimp in bowl; toss to coat. Cover and marinate in the refrigerator for 1 to 2 hours, stirring occasionally. Drain shrimp, discarding marinade. Thread shrimp onto 4 long metal skewers, leaving a ¼-inch space between each piece.

3 *For a charcoal grill,* grill kabobs on the greased rack of an uncovered grill directly over medium coals for 6 to 10 minutes or until shrimp are opaque, turning once halfway through grilling. *(For a gas grill,* preheat grill. Reduce heat to medium. Place kabobs on greased grill rack over heat. Cover and grill as above.)

4 Meanwhile, in a medium saucepan cook the remaining 1 teaspoon ginger and the onion in the remaining 1 tablespoon oil until tender. Stir in orange juice and water. Bring to boiling. Stir in couscous. Cover and remove from heat. Let stand for 5 minutes. Stir in remaining mango and the cilantro.

5 To serve, remove shrimp from skewers. Serve with couscous. Makes 4 servings.

⊛Nutrition Facts per serving: 315 calories, 8 g total fat (1 g saturated fat), 131 mg cholesterol, 290 mg sodium, 41 g carbohydrate, 7 g fiber, 19 g protein. Daily Values: 28% vit. A, 59% vit. C, 4% calcium, 17% iron.

# Shrimp and Sausage over Creamy Garlic Pasta

**Prep:** 25 minutes    **Grill:** 6 minutes

*Shrimp can stand up to sausage, even smoked versions. Here it's served on a bed of angel hair pasta bathed in a luscious cream sauce.*

  8 ounces fresh or frozen medium
     shrimp in shells
  8 ounces packaged dried capellini
     (angel hair)
  3 cloves garlic, minced
  2 tablespoons butter or margarine
  ¾ cup whipping cream
  ½ cup chicken broth
  ⅓ cup grated Romano cheese
  1 tablespoon olive oil
  1 clove garlic, minced
  8 ounces cooked smoked sausage,
     cut into ½-inch slices
  2 tablespoons snipped fresh Italian
     flat-leaf parsley

1 Thaw shrimp, if frozen. Peel and devein shrimp. Rinse shrimp; pat dry with paper towels. Cover and chill until ready to grill. Cook pasta according to package directions; drain. Return pasta to hot pan.

2 Meanwhile, in a large skillet cook the 3 cloves garlic in hot butter or margarine over medium heat for 1 minute, stirring constantly. Stir in whipping cream and broth.

Bring to boiling; reduce heat. Boil gently about 8 minutes or until slightly thickened (you should have about ¾ cup sauce). Stir in cheese. Pour sauce over pasta; toss gently to coat. Keep warm.

3 In a small bowl combine oil and the 1 clove garlic. On 4 long metal skewers, alternately thread shrimp and sausage, leaving a ¼-inch space between pieces. Brush shrimp and sausage with oil mixture.

4 *For a charcoal grill*, grill kabobs on the greased rack of an uncovered grill directly over medium coals for 6 to 8 minutes or until shrimp are opaque and sausage is heated through, turning once halfway through grilling. (*For a gas grill*, preheat grill. Reduce heat to medium. Place kabobs on greased grill rack over heat. Cover and grill as above.)

5 To serve, transfer pasta to serving platter. If desired, remove shrimp and sausage from skewers. Place shrimp and sausage on pasta. Sprinkle with parsley. Makes 4 servings.

Nutrition Facts per serving: 733 calories, 48 g total fat (23 g saturated fat), 191 mg cholesterol, 896 mg sodium, 49 g carbohydrate, 2 g fiber, 28 g protein. Daily Values: 30% vit. A, 9% vit. C, 16% calcium, 28% iron.

## WISE ADVICE

**When selecting shrimp, look for those that are moist and firm, have translucent flesh, and smell fresh. Avoid those that have an ammonia smell and blackened edges or spots on the shells. Since most of the shrimp available today has been previously frozen, always check to see if thawed shrimp is firm and shiny. If purchased frozen, make sure it is frozen solidly and has no signs of freezer burn. Thaw frozen shrimp overnight in the refrigerator, or place under cold running water.**

## Soft-Shell Crabs and Spinach

**Prep:** 25 minutes    **Grill:** 5 minutes

*Here's the epitome of regionally inspired cooking. In spring soft-shell crabs appear briefly. The butternut, also referred to as a white walnut, is a walnut variety found in New England.*

    4 large or 8 small soft-shell crabs
      (about 12 ounces total)
      Cooking oil
  ¼ cup butter (no substitutes)
    1 teaspoon finely shredded lemon
      peel
    1 tablespoon lemon juice
  ¼ cup coarsely chopped butternuts
      or walnuts
    1 10-ounce package fresh spinach,
      washed and trimmed

**1** To clean each soft-shell crab, hold the crab between the back legs. Using kitchen scissors, remove the head by cutting horizontally across the body about ½ inch behind the eyes, removing the face. Lift the pointed, soft top shell to expose the "devil's fingers" (the spongy projectiles) on one side. Using your fingers, push up on the devil's fingers and pull off. Replace the soft top shell over the body. Repeat on the other side. Turn crab over. Pull off the apron-shape piece and discard. Handle each crab carefully while thoroughly rinsing under cold running water to remove the mustard-colored substance; pat dry. Brush crabs with cooking oil. Cover and chill until ready to grill.

**2** *For a charcoal grill*, grill crabs, back sides down, on the greased rack of an uncovered grill directly over medium coals for 5 to 7 minutes or until golden brown, turning once halfway through grilling. (*For a gas grill*, preheat grill. Reduce heat to medium. Place crabs, back sides down, on greased grill rack over heat. Cover and grill as above.)

**3** Meanwhile, for lemon butter, in a small saucepan melt 2 tablespoons of the butter. Stir in lemon peel and juice. Set aside. In a large skillet melt the remaining butter. Stir in nuts; cook for 4 to 5 minutes or until toasted, stirring constantly. Remove walnuts from skillet; set aside. Add spinach to skillet; cook for 2 to 3 minutes or until just wilted, stirring often.

**4** To serve, divide spinach among 4 serving plates. Arrange crabs on spinach. Sprinkle with nuts and drizzle with lemon butter. Makes 4 servings.

Nutrition Facts per serving: 209 calories, 18 g total fat (8 g saturated fat), 55 mg cholesterol, 251 mg sodium, 4 g carbohydrate, 1 g fiber, 9 g protein. Daily Values: 17% vit. A, 12% vit. C, 4% calcium, 6% iron.

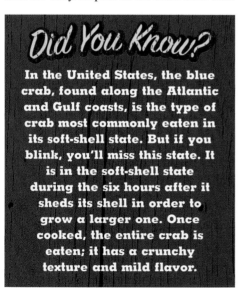

## Did You Know?

**In the United States, the blue crab, found along the Atlantic and Gulf coasts, is the type of crab most commonly eaten in its soft-shell state. But if you blink, you'll miss this state. It is in the soft-shell state during the six hours after it sheds its shell in order to grow a larger one. Once cooked, the entire crab is eaten; it has a crunchy texture and mild flavor.**

# Lobster Tails with Basil-Walnut Butter

**Prep:** 15 minutes   **Grill:** 12 minutes

*As with many things so easy, this is sinfully delicious. Combine melted butter, garlic, walnuts, and fresh basil and serve it over sweet lobster meat. A combination this delectable deserves a good bottle of chilled champagne.*

   4  8-ounce frozen lobster tails
   2  teaspoons olive oil
   ⅓  cup butter
   2  tablespoons snipped fresh basil
   2  tablespoons finely chopped
       walnuts, toasted
   1  clove garlic, minced

**1** Thaw lobster. Rinse lobster; pat dry with paper towels. Place lobster, shell sides down, on a cutting board. To butterfly, with kitchen scissors, cut each lobster in half lengthwise, cutting to but not through the back shell. Bend backward to crack back shell and expose the meat. Brush lobster meat with oil.

**2** *For a charcoal grill*, grill lobster, shell sides down, on the greased rack of an uncovered grill directly over medium coals for 12 to 15 minutes or until lobster meat is opaque and shells are bright red, turning once halfway through grilling. (*For a gas grill*, preheat grill. Reduce heat to medium. Place lobster, shell sides down, on greased grill rack over heat. Cover and grill as above.)

**3** While lobster is cooking, in a small saucepan melt butter over low heat without stirring; cool slightly. Pour off clear top layer; discard milky bottom layer. In a small bowl combine butter, basil, walnuts, and garlic. To serve, spoon butter mixture over lobster meat. Makes 4 servings.

Nutrition Facts per serving: 321 calories, 21 g total fat (10 g saturated fat), 145 mg cholesterol, 706 mg sodium, 3 g carbohydrate, 0 g fiber, 30 g protein. Daily Values: 17% vit. A, 8% calcium, 4% iron.

# SCALLOP BROCHETTES

**Prep:** 15 minutes   **Marinate:** 30 minutes
**Grill:** 5 minutes

*It's hard to imagine a dish this good that involves no slicing, dicing, or mincing. The simple honey-mustard marinade does beautiful things with sweet scallops. Shrimp can be added to the skewers, too.*

   1  pound fresh or frozen sea scallops
       and/or peeled and deveined
       shrimp
   2  tablespoons cooking oil
   2  tablespoons dry sherry
   2  tablespoons stone-ground mustard
   1  tablespoon honey
   1½  teaspoons soy sauce

**1** Thaw scallops, if frozen. Rinse scallops; pat dry with paper towels. Halve any of the large scallops (you should have about 20 pieces). Place scallops in a shallow dish. For marinade, in a small bowl combine oil, sherry, mustard, honey, and soy sauce. Pour over scallops; turn scallops to coat. Cover and marinate in the refrigerator for 30 minutes.

**2** Drain scallops, discarding marinade. Thread scallops onto long metal skewers, leaving a ¼-inch space between pieces. (If using scallops and shrimp, thread a scallop in the "curl" of each shrimp.)

**3** *For a charcoal grill*, grill kabobs on the greased rack of an uncovered grill directly over medium coals for 5 to 8 minutes or until scallops are opaque, gently turning once halfway through grilling. (*For a gas grill*, preheat grill. Reduce heat to medium. Place kabobs on greased grill rack over heat. Cover and grill as above.) Makes 4 servings.

Nutrition Facts per serving: 119 calories, 5 g total fat (1 g saturated fat), 34 mg cholesterol, 284 mg sodium, 4 g carbohydrate, 0 g fiber, 15 g protein. Daily Values: 6% calcium, 13% iron.

# Thai-Spice Scallops

**Prep:** 20 minutes   **Grill:** 15 minutes

*Start a pan of fragrant jasmine rice to serve with the scallops; then decide if you want to steer dinner toward China with five-spice powder or Thailand with thai seasoning. Either way, it's a quick trip. The whole meal can be ready in 30 minutes.*

　　1 **pound fresh or frozen sea scallops**
　　⅔ **cup bottled sweet-and-sour sauce**
　　2 **tablespoons snipped fresh basil**
　　1 **teaspoon Thai seasoning or**
　　　　**five-spice powder**
　　1 **clove garlic, minced**
　　2 **medium yellow summer squash**
　　　　**and/or zucchini, quartered**
　　　　**lengthwise and sliced ½ inch**
　　　　**thick**
　1½ **cups packaged peeled baby**
　　　　**carrots**
　　　　**Salt and pepper**

**1** Thaw scallops, if frozen. Rinse scallops; pat dry with paper towels. Halve any large scallops. Thread scallops onto 4 long metal skewers, leaving a ¼-inch space between pieces. Cover and chill until ready to grill.

**2** For sauce, in a small bowl combine sweet-and sour sauce, basil, Thai seasoning, and garlic. Transfer ¼ cup of the sauce to a small bowl for basting. Reserve remaining sauce until ready to serve.

**3** Fold a 36×18-inch piece of heavy foil in half to make an 18-inch square. Place squash and carrots in center of foil. Sprinkle with salt and pepper. Bring up opposite edges of foil; seal with a double fold. Fold remaining edges together to completely enclose vegetables, leaving space for steam to build.

**4** *For a charcoal grill,* grill vegetables on the greased rack of an uncovered grill directly over medium coals for 10 minutes, turning once or twice. Add kabobs to grill. Grill for

5 to 8 minutes more or until scallops are opaque and vegetables are crisp-tender, turning and brushing skewers once with sauce halfway through grilling. (*For a gas grill,* preheat grill. Reduce heat to medium. Place vegetables, then kabobs on greased grill rack over heat. Cover; grill as above.) Serve scallops and vegetables with remaining sauce. Makes 4 servings.

Ⓥ Nutrition Facts per serving: 168 calories, 1 g total fat (0 g saturated fat), 34 mg cholesterol, 370 mg sodium, 25 g carbohydrate, 3 g fiber, 16 g protein. Daily Values: 122% vit. A, 17% vit. C, 9% calcium, 18% iron.

## Did You Know?

There are two basic types of scallops: sea and bay. Bays are smaller and can be tastier, except they're more likely to become overcooked. Sea scallops are larger and easier to grill. When purchasing scallops, avoid those that smell fishy or sour; these are signs that they aren't fresh. Scallops are sold according to size, and the smaller the number count per pound, the larger and more expensive the scallops. Be aware that a stark bleached-white color or excessive milky liquid in the display tray can be a sign the scallops have been treated heavily with sodium tripolyphosphate (STP). While STP is useful to help bind natural moisture in seafood during the freezing and thawing process, it can be overused and cause scallops to soak up additional water.

Thaw fish or shellfish, if frozen. Test for desired temperature. For fish fillets, place in a well-greased grill basket. For fish steaks and whole fish, grease the grill rack. Place the fish on the rack directly over the preheated coals (for direct grilling) or over a drip pan (for indirect grilling). Grill (uncovered for direct grilling or covered for indirect grilling) for the time given below or until the fish just begins to flake easily when tested with a fork; scallops and shrimp should look opaque. Turn the fish over halfway through the grilling time. If desired, brush fish with melted margarine or butter.

## Grilling Chart

| Form of Fish | Weight, Size, or Thickness | Coal Temperature | Doneness | Direct Grilling* Time | Indirect Grilling* Time |
|---|---|---|---|---|---|
| **Dressed Fish** | ½ to 1½ pounds | Medium | Flakes | 7 to 9 min. per ½ pound | 20 to 25 min. per ½ pound |
| **Fillets, steaks, cubes** (for kabobs) | ½ to 1 inch thick | Medium | Flakes | 4 to 6 min. per ½-inch thickness | 15 to 18 min. per ½-inch thickness |
| **Lobster tail, butterflied** (rock lobster) | 5 ounces | Medium | Opaque | 12 to 14 min. | 13 to 15 min. |
| | 8 ounces | Medium | Opaque | 16 to 18 min. | 18 to 20 min. |
| **Sea scallops** (for kabobs) | 12 to 15 per | Medium | Opaque | 5 to 8 min. | 5 to 7 min. |
| **Shrimp** (for kabobs) | Medium (20 per pound) | Medium | Opaque | 6 to 8 min. | 6 to 8 min. |
| | Jumbo (12 to 15 per pound) | Medium | Opaque | 10 to 12 min. | 10 to 12 min. |

*Note: For differences in direct and indirect grilling methods, see page 10.*

# Game and Fowl

# Bison Cheeseburgers

**Prep:** 10 minutes **Grill:** 18 minutes

*When you don't feel at home on the kitchen range, move the action outside with buffalo burgers. Buffalo is leaner than most ground beef and has a flavor that stands up to the Garlic-Mustard Mayonnaise and smoked Swiss cheese.*

1 recipe Garlic-Mustard Mayonnaise
1 large sweet onion,* cut into ½-inch slices
2 teaspoons olive oil
1 pound ground bison
4 1-ounce slices smoked Swiss cheese
4 kaiser rolls or whole wheat buns, split and toasted
4 lettuce leaves

**1** Prepare Garlic-Mustard Mayonnaise; cover and chill until ready to serve. Lightly brush onion slices with oil; set aside. Shape ground bison into four ¾-inch-thick patties.

**2** *For a charcoal grill,* grill onion slices on the rack of an uncovered grill directly over medium coals for 5 minutes, turning once halfway through grilling. Add burgers to grill. Grill for 12 to 16 minutes more or until onion is tender and meat is no longer pink, turning once halfway through grilling. (*For a gas grill,* preheat grill. Reduce heat to medium. Place onion slices, then burgers on grill rack over heat. Cover and grill as above.)

**3** Top burgers with cheese. Grill for 1 to 2 minutes more or until cheese is melted. Remove burgers from grill. Serve the burgers on toasted rolls with Garlic-Mustard Mayonnaise, lettuce, and grilled onion slices. Makes 4 servings.

**Garlic-Mustard Mayonnaise:** In a small bowl combine ⅓ cup mayonnaise or salad dressing, 1 tablespoon country-style Dijon mustard, and 2 cloves garlic, minced. Makes about ⅓ cup.

*\*Note:* Different varieties of sweet onion include Georgia Vidalia, Texas Supersweet, Washington Walla Walla, or Hawaiian Maui Sweet.

Nutrition Facts per serving: 570 calories, 29 g total fat (9 g saturated fat), 107 mg cholesterol, 642 mg sodium, 36 g carbohydrate, 1 g fiber, 39 g protein. Daily Values: 9% vit. A, 4% vit. C, 29% calcium, 34% iron.

## Flaming Facts

**Ground bison is a great substitute for beef in most of your everyday recipes. Because bison contains very little fat, it is a healthful alternative. As with ground beef, bison should be cooked thoroughly to an internal temperature of 160°. Because bison will cook a bit faster than ground beef, it's important to take extra care in avoiding overcooking it, as it will become dried out.**

## COFFEE AND PEPPERCORN CRUSTED BISON STEAKS

**Prep:** 15 minutes **Grill:** 8 minutes

*Coffee beans isn't a misprint. In fact, they are the secret ingredient of the crust that coats a tender buffalo steak. Find out what cowboys have known all along—coffee isn't just for breakfast.*

1 recipe Garlic Butter
2 tablespoons coffee beans
2 tablespoons black peppercorns
1 tablespoon coarse salt
½ teaspoon ground cumin
4 6-ounce boneless bison top loin
  steaks, cut 1 inch thick

1 Prepare Garlic Butter; cover and set aside. For rub, in a coffee grinder container or mini food processor bowl combine coffee beans and peppercorns. Cover; grind or process with several on-off turns until mixture is coarsely ground. Transfer to a small bowl; stir in salt and cumin.

2 Sprinkle rub on both sides of the steaks; gently press into surface of steaks.

3 *For a charcoal grill*, grill steaks on the rack of an uncovered grill directly over medium coals until desired doneness, turning once halfway through grilling. (Allow 8 to 12 minutes for medium doneness.) (*For a gas grill*, preheat grill. Reduce heat to medium. Place steaks on grill rack over heat. Cover and grill as above.) Serve Garlic Butter with steaks. Makes 4 servings.

Garlic Butter: In a small bowl stir together ¼ cup softened butter, 1 tablespoon snipped fresh parsley, and 1 small clove garlic, minced. Makes about ¼ cup.

Nutrition Facts per tablespoon: 331 calories,
15 g total fat (8 g saturated fat), 148 mg cholesterol,
1,802 mg sodium, 5 g carbohydrate, 1 g fiber,
42 g protein. Daily Values: 10% vit. A, 8% vit. C,
4% calcium, 42% iron.

## Catalina-Style Buffalo Burgers

**Prep:** 10 minutes **Grill:** 12 minutes

1 pound ground bison
2 tablespoons finely chopped onion
¼ teaspoon salt
¼ teaspoon pepper
4 onion buns or kaiser rolls, split
  and toasted
1 medium avocado, seeded, peeled,
  and thinly sliced
1 4½-ounce can whole green chile
  peppers, drained

1 In a medium bowl combine the ground bison, onion, salt, and pepper; mix well. Shape mixture into four ¾-inch-thick patties.

2 *For a charcoal grill*, grill burgers on the rack of an uncovered grill directly over medium coals for 12 to 16 minutes or until meat is no longer pink, turning once halfway through grilling. (*For a gas grill*, preheat grill. Reduce heat to medium. Place burgers on grill rack over medium heat. Cover and grill as above.)

3 Remove burgers from grill. Serve burgers on toasted buns or kaiser rolls with avocado slices and chile peppers. Makes 4 servings.

ⓋNutrition Facts per serving: 375 calories,
12 g total fat (2 g saturated fat), 70 mg cholesterol,
588 mg sodium, 34 g carbohydrate, 2 g fiber,
32 g protein. Daily Values: 2% vit. A, 21% vit. C,
8% calcium, 36% iron.

## OLD ENGLISH VENISON STEAKS

**Prep:** 10 minutes  **Marinate:** 4 to 24 hours
**Grill:** 8 minutes

*You'll love the simplicity of this recipe. Port and sage contribute all the flavor needed to allow the flavor of the meat to shine through.*

4  4- to 5-ounce boneless venison or bison top loin steaks, cut 1 inch thick
½ cup port or dry red wine
1 teaspoon dried sage, crushed
¼ teaspoon salt
¼ teaspoon pepper

**1** Place steaks in a plastic bag set in a shallow dish. Pour port over steaks; seal bag. Marinate in the refrigerator for 4 to 24 hours, turning bag occasionally. Drain steaks, discarding marinade. In a small bowl combine sage, salt, and pepper. Sprinkle sage mixture on both sides of the steaks; gently press into surface of steaks.

**2** *For a charcoal grill,* grill steaks on the rack of an uncovered grill directly over medium coals until desired doneness, turning once halfway through grilling. (Allow 8 to 12 minutes for medium-rare doneness.) (*For a gas grill,* preheat grill. Reduce heat to medium. Place steaks on grill rack over heat. Cover and grill as above.) Makes 4 servings.

Nutrition Facts per serving: 146 calories, 2 g total fat (1 g saturated fat), 93 mg cholesterol, 193 mg sodium, 2 g carbohydrate, 0 g fiber, 25 g protein. Daily Values: 1% calcium, 21% iron.

# Elk Burgers

**Prep:** 15 minutes  **Grill:** 14 minutes

*Go ahead—be adventurous! Try these elk burgers next time you want something more exotic than ordinary burgers.*

1 beaten egg
3 tablespoons catsup
1 teaspoon Worcestershire sauce
¼ cup soft bread crumbs
¼ cup finely chopped onion
1 teaspoon prepared horseradish
½ teaspoon salt
1½ pounds ground elk or bison
6 hamburger buns, split and toasted
Assorted condiments

**1** In a medium bowl combine the egg, catsup, and Worcestershire sauce. Stir in bread crumbs, onion, horseradish, and salt. Add the elk; mix well. Shape elk mixture into six ¾-inch-thick patties.

**2** *For a charcoal grill,* grill burgers on the rack of an uncovered grill directly over medium coals for 14 to 18 minutes or until meat is no longer pink, turning once halfway through grilling. (*For a gas grill,* preheat grill. Reduce heat to medium. Place burgers on grill rack over medium heat. Cover and grill as above.)

**3** Remove burgers from grill. Serve burgers on toasted buns with condiments. Makes 6 servings.

Nutrition Facts per serving: 273 calories, 5 g total fat (1 g saturated fat), 98 mg cholesterol, 393 mg sodium, 25 g carbohydrate, 1 g fiber, 30 g protein. Daily Values: 29% iron.

Marinated Bison London Broil

## MARINATED BISON LONDON BROIL

**Prep:** 20 minutes  **Marinate:** 2 to 8 hours
**Grill:** 8 minutes

*The aroma of dried porcini mushrooms evokes the wild outdoors like nothing else. While this mushroom-garlic butter is great over game, you'll also love it over beef and chicken.*

½ **ounce dried porcini mushrooms**
1 **cup boiling water**
½ **cup butter, softened**
2 **cloves garlic, minced**
1 **teaspoon finely snipped fresh parsley**
⅛ **teaspoon salt**
1 **2-pound bison flank steak**
¾ **cup dry red wine**
¼ **cup water**
2 **tablespoons finely chopped shallots**
2 **tablespoons olive oil**
1 **tablespoon snipped fresh oregano, thyme, or basil or ¼ teaspoon dried oregano, thyme, or basil, crushed**
¼ **teaspoon salt**
⅛ **teaspoon pepper**
   **Italian bread, bias-sliced and toasted (optional)**

**1** For mushroom-garlic butter, in a small bowl cover porcini mushrooms with 1 cup boiling water. Let stand for 15 minutes. Drain mushrooms; finely chop. In a small bowl thoroughly combine chopped mushrooms, butter, garlic, parsley, and the ⅛ teaspoon salt. Cover and chill until ready to serve.

**2** Score steak on both sides in a diamond pattern by making shallow diagonal cuts at 1-inch intervals. Place in a shallow dish. For marinade, in a small bowl stir together the wine, the ¼ cup water, the shallots, oil, herb, the ¼ teaspoon salt, and the pepper. Pour wine mixture over steak; turn to coat. Cover and marinate in the refrigerator for 2 to 8 hours, turning steak occasionally. Drain steak, discarding marinade.

**3** *For a charcoal grill*, grill steak on the rack of an uncovered grill directly over medium coals until steak is desired doneness, turning once halfway through grilling. (Allow 8 to 12 minutes for medium-rare and 12 to 14 minutes for medium doneness.) (*For a gas grill*, preheat grill. Reduce heat to medium. Place steak on grill rack over heat. Cover and grill as above.)

**4** Thinly slice steak diagonally across the grain. In a small saucepan melt the mushroom-garlic butter. Spoon over meat slices. If desired, serve as open-face sandwiches on toasted Italian bread slices. Makes 8 servings.

Nutrition Facts per serving: 262 calories, 15 g total fat (8 g saturated fat), 101 mg cholesterol, 238 mg sodium, 6 g carbohydrate, 1 g fiber, 25 g protein. Daily Values: 12% vit. A, 3% vit. C, 1% calcium, 21% iron.

## Did You Know?

**There's no need to feel guilty every time you order a juicy steak. Simply order farm-raised game, the naturally lean red meat. It is generally less tough and gamy tasting than meat from animals hunted in the wild. With fewer fat grams and more iron per serving than skinless chicken breasts, game meats such as venison, bison, and ostrich allow meat-lovers to savor the guilt-free pleasure of thick, succulent steak or fillet again.**

# Game by Mail

THE FOLLOWING COMPANIES WILL SHIP
INDIVIDUAL CUTS OF GAME MEAT.

### BROKEN ARROW RANCH, INC.
P.O. Box 530 • Ingram, TX 78025 • 800-962-4263
Carries a full range of game, including antelope,
deer, and wild boar.

### D'ARTAGNAN, INC.
280 Wilson Ave. • Newark, NJ 07105
800-327-8246 • Carries a wide range of domestic animals and game,
including game sausages.

### POKANOKET OSTRICH FARM OF NEW ENGLAND
107 Gulf Rd. • South Dartmouth, MA 02748 • 508-992-6188

### LOBELS, INC.
1096 Madison Ave. • New York, NY 10028
212-737-1372 • Carries quality beef, poultry, and game.

### HILLS FOODS LTD.
109-3650 Bonneville Place
Burnaby, British Columbia • Canada V3N 4T7
604-421-3100 • Supplier of organic meats and game,
specialty poultry, and reptile meat.

### ATLANTIC GAME MEATS
P. O. Box 84 • Hampden, ME 04444 • 207-862-4217
Provides farm-raised venison and venison products.

# Soy-Ginger Marinated Venison Chops

**Prep:** 12 minutes   **Marinate:** 2 hours
**Grill:** 17 minutes

*Soy sauce and ginger can dominate or collaborate. With venison it's a collaboration of the first order. Serve these chops with grilled tri-color peppers and rice.*

4 8-ounce venison rib chops, cut
  1 inch thick
2 green onions, finely chopped
2 tablespoons brown sugar
2 tablespoons lime juice
2 tablespoons soy sauce
1 tablespoon grated fresh ginger
1 fresh jalapeño pepper, seeded and
  finely chopped
2 cloves garlic, minced

**1** Place chops in a plastic bag set in a shallow dish. For marinade, in a small bowl combine green onions, brown sugar, lime juice, soy sauce, ginger, jalapeño pepper, and garlic. Pour marinade over chops; seal bag. Marinate in the refrigerator for 2 to 4 hours, turning bag occasionally. Drain chops, discarding marinade.

**2** *For a charcoal grill*, grill chops on the rack of an uncovered grill directly over medium coals until desired doneness, turning once halfway through grilling. (Allow 17 to 20 minutes for medium doneness.) (*For a gas grill*, preheat grill. Reduce heat to medium. Place chops on grill rack over heat. Cover and grill as above.) Makes 4 servings.

Nutrition Facts per serving: 157 calories, 2 g total fat (1 g saturated fat), 70 mg cholesterol, 577 mg sodium, 8 g carbohydrate, 0 g fiber, 26 g protein. Daily Values: 1% vit. A, 16% vit. C, 2% calcium, 22% iron.

# VENISON TENDERLOINS WRAPPED IN BACON

**Prep:** 15 minutes   **Marinate:** 4 to 24 hours
**Grill:** 25 minutes

2 8- to 10-ounce venison tenderloins
¾ cup dry red wine
1 tablespoon olive oil
6 cloves garlic, minced
2 bay leaves
10 juniper berries, slightly crushed
½ teaspoon dried thyme, crushed
6 to 8 slices bacon, partially cooked
  and drained

**1** Place meat in a plastic bag set in a shallow dish. For marinade, combine wine, olive oil, garlic, bay leaves, juniper berries, and thyme. Pour over meat; seal bag. Marinate in the refrigerator for 4 to 24 hours, turning bag occasionally. Drain meat, reserving the marinade. Wrap 3 or 4 slices of partially cooked bacon around each tenderloin; secure with wooden toothpicks. Insert a meat thermometer into center of meat.

**2** *For a charcoal grill*, arrange medium-hot coals around a drip pan. Test for medium heat above pan. Place meat on grill rack over drip pan. Cover; grill until meat thermometer registers 145° to 155° for medium (25 to 35 minutes), brushing with reserved marinade during the first 15 minutes of grilling. [*For a gas grill*, preheat grill. Reduce heat to medium. Adjust for indirect cooking (see page 10). Grill as above except place meat on a rack in a roasting pan.] Makes 4 servings.

Nutrition Facts per serving: 246 calories, 10 g total fat (3 g saturated fat), 101 mg cholesterol, 240 mg sodium, 3 g carbohydrate, 0 g fiber, 28 g protein. Daily Values: 7% vit. C, 2% calcium, 24% iron.

# Venison Tenderloin and Onions

**Prep:** 25 minutes  **Marinate:** 2 to 3 hours
**Grill:** 25 minutes

> 2 8- to 10-ounce venison tenderloins
> 3 tablespoons olive oil
> 2 tablespoons balsamic vinegar
> 2 teaspoons coarsely cracked mixed
>     peppercorns
> 1 teaspoon Dijon-style mustard
> 1 large onion, sliced
> 4 green onions, cut into 1-inch pieces
> 4 shallots, sliced
> 2 leeks (whites only), cut in half
>     lengthwise and sliced
> 3 cloves garlic, sliced
> 2 tablespoons balsamic vinegar
> 1 teaspoon brown sugar

**1** Place meat in plastic bag set in shallow dish. For marinade, in bowl combine oil, the 2 tablespoons balsamic vinegar, the peppercorns, and mustard. Pour over meat; seal bag. Marinate in the refrigerator for 2 to 3 hours, turning bag occasionally. Drain meat, discarding marinade. Insert a meat thermometer into the center of meat.

**2** Fold a 36×18-inch piece of heavy foil in half to make an 18-inch square. Place onion slices, green onions, shallots, leeks, and garlic in the center of foil. Stir together 2 tablespoons balsamic vinegar and the brown sugar. Drizzle over vegetables. Bring up opposite edges of foil and seal with a double fold. Fold remaining edges together to completely enclose vegetables, leaving space for steam to build.

**3** *For a charcoal grill,* arrange medium-hot coals around a drip pan. Test for medium heat above the drip pan. Place the meat on the grill rack over the drip pan. Place vegetables on grill rack directly over the coals. Cover and grill until the meat thermometer registers 145° to 155° for medium doneness (25 to 35 minutes), turning the vegetable packet once halfway through grilling. [*For a gas grill,* preheat the grill. Reduce heat to medium. Adjust for indirect cooking (see page 10). Grill as above, except place the meat on a rack in a roasting pan.]

**4** To serve, cut meat crosswise into 4 serving-size slices. Transfer vegetables to a large serving platter. Arrange meat slices on top. Makes 4 servings.

Nutrition Facts per serving: 211 calories, 5 g total fat (1 g saturated fat), 93 mg cholesterol, 80 mg sodium, 14 g carbohydrate, 3 g fiber, 26 g protein. Daily Values: 15% vit. A, 16% vit. C, 4% calcium, 29% iron.

## BROCHETTE OF GAME WITH PEAR-BALSAMIC SALSA

**Prep:** 30 minutes  **Marinate:** 8 to 24 hours
**Grill:** 12 minutes

> 1 large onion, cut into 8 wedges
> 1 medium red or yellow sweet
>     pepper, cut into 1-inch pieces
> 1 medium green sweet pepper, cut
>     into 1-inch pieces
> 12 ounces boneless elk or venison
>     loin
> ½ cup dry red wine
> 2 tablespoons olive oil
> 1 tablespoon dried Italian
>     seasoning, crushed
> 1 tablespoon ground cumin
> 1 recipe Pear-Balsamic Salsa
> 8 cherry tomatoes
>     Hot cooked couscous (optional)

**1** In a saucepan cook onion in a small amount of boiling water for 3 minutes. Add sweet peppers. Cook for 2 minutes more; drain and rinse immediately in cold running water.

**2** Cut meat into 1-inch pieces. Place meat, onion, and sweet peppers in a plastic bag set in a shallow dish. For marinade, in a small bowl combine wine, oil, Italian seasoning, and cumin. Pour over meat and vegetables; seal bag. Marinate in the refrigerator for 8 to 24 hours, turning bag occasionally.

**3** Meanwhile, prepare Pear-Balsamic Salsa; cover and chill until ready to serve (let stand at room temperature for 30 minutes before serving).

**4** Drain meat and vegetables, discarding marinade. On eight 8-inch metal skewers, alternately thread meat, onion, and sweet peppers, leaving a ¼-inch space between each piece.

**5** *For a charcoal grill*, grill kabobs on the rack of an uncovered grill directly over medium coals for 12 to 14 minutes or until meat is slightly pink in center, turning once halfway through grilling. Add a cherry tomato to the end of each kabob during the last 2 minutes of grilling. (*For a gas grill*, preheat grill. Reduce heat to medium. Place kabobs on grill rack over heat. Cover and grill as above.) Serve kabobs with Pear-Balsamic Salsa. If desired, serve with couscous. Makes 4 servings.

**Pear-Balsamic Salsa:** In a medium saucepan bring ¼ cup white balsamic vinegar to boiling. Add 1½ cups peeled, chopped pears (about 2 small pears); reduce heat to medium. Cook for 5 minutes, stirring occasionally. Remove salsa from heat; cool. Just before serving, stir in ½ cup finely chopped red sweet pepper; ⅓ cup finely chopped red onion; 2 tablespoons snipped fresh cilantro; and 1 to 2 fresh jalapeño peppers, seeded and finely chopped. Makes about 1½ cups.

Nutrition Facts per serving: 220 calories, 4 g total fat (1 g saturated fat), 47 mg cholesterol, 65 mg sodium, 25 g carbohydrate, 4 g fiber, 21 g protein. Daily Values: 27% vit. A, 145% vit. C, 3% calcium, 29% iron.

# Duck Salad with Orange-Hazelnut Dressing

**Prep:** 20 minutes   **Marinate:** 4 to 24 hours
**Grill:** 10 minutes

3 skinless, boneless wild duck
    breasts (about 12 ounces total)
¼ cup water
¼ cup olive oil
3 tablespoons frozen orange juice
    concentrate, thawed
2 tablespoons finely chopped
    shallots

2 tablespoons balsamic vinegar
3 cloves garlic, minced
¼ teaspoon salt
¼ teaspoon pepper
8 cups mesclun or torn mixed salad
    greens
2 oranges, peeled and sectioned
⅓ cup chopped hazelnuts or
    almonds, toasted

**1** Rinse duck breasts; pat dry. Place duck breasts in a plastic bag set in a shallow dish. For marinade, in a small bowl combine water, oil, orange juice concentrate, shallots, vinegar, garlic, salt, and pepper. Transfer ⅓ cup of the mixture to a small bowl for salad dressing; cover and chill until ready to serve (let stand at room temperature for 30 minutes before serving). Pour remaining marinade over duck; seal bag. Marinate in refrigerator for 4 to 24 hours, turning bag occasionally. Drain duck, discarding marinade.

**2** *For a charcoal grill*, grill duck on the rack of an uncovered grill directly over medium coals for 10 to 12 minutes or until tender and no longer pink, turning once halfway through grilling. (*For a gas grill*, preheat grill. Reduce heat to medium. Place duck on grill rack over heat. Cover and grill as above.)

**3** Meanwhile, for salad, in a large bowl combine mesclun, oranges, and hazelnuts; toss gently to mix. Shake dressing. Pour dressing over salad; toss gently to coat. To serve, divide among serving plates. Thinly slice duck breasts. Arrange slices on top of salad. Makes 4 servings.

Nutrition Facts per serving: 246 calories, 19 g total fat (3 g saturated fat), 19 mg cholesterol, 126 mg sodium, 13 g carbohydrate, 2 g fiber, 7 g protein. Daily Values: 7% vit. A, 59% vit. C, 4% calcium, 9% iron.

Duck Breast with Lime Sauce

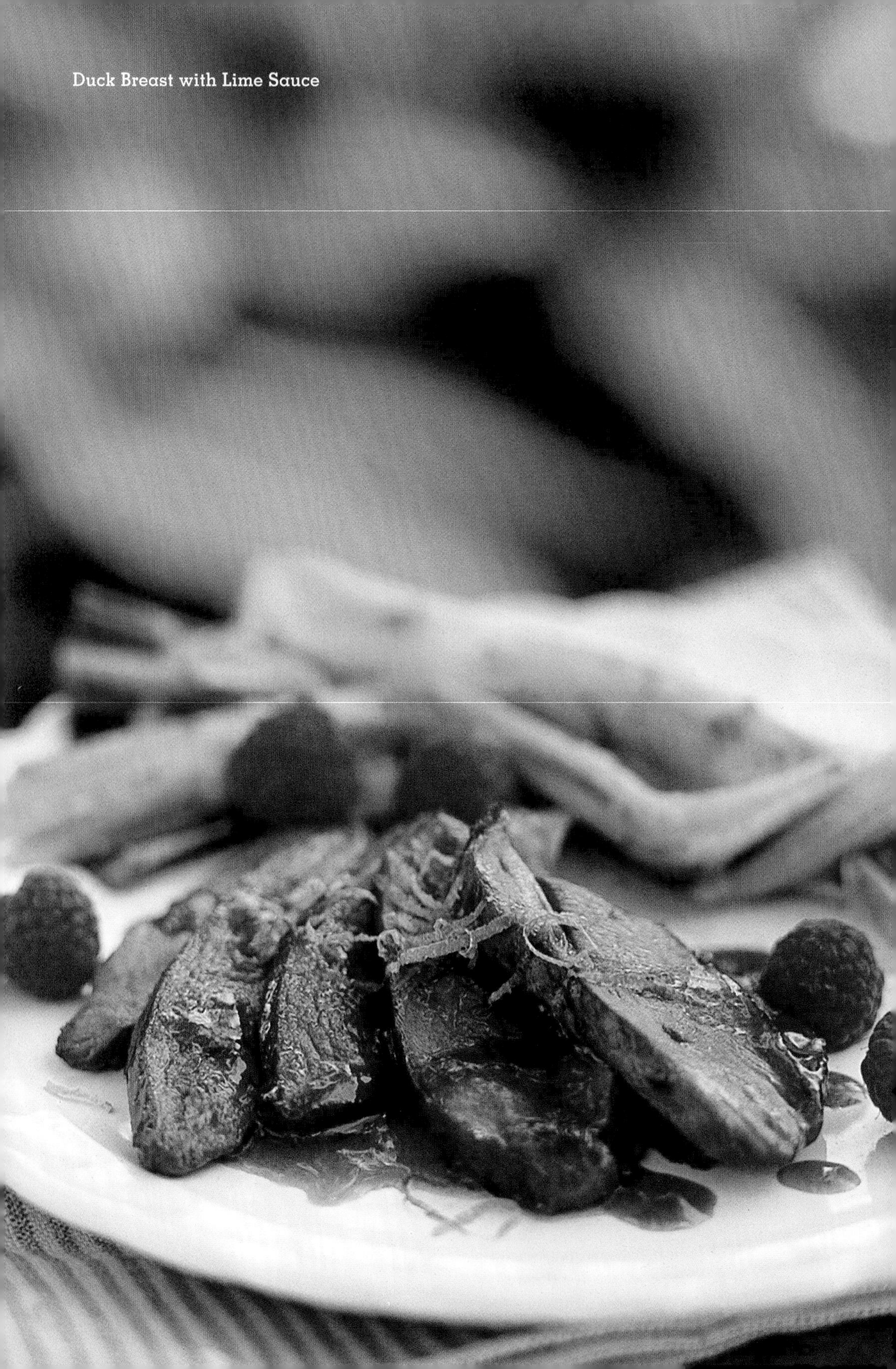

## DUCK BREAST WITH LIME SAUCE

**Prep:** 20 minutes **Grill:** 10 minutes

*Commercially raised ducks have sweet, tender meat. Serve with wild rice and grilled asparagus.*

½ cup currant jelly
¼ cup sweet or semi-dry white wine, such as Riesling or sauterne
1 tablespoon raspberry vinegar
1 teaspoon finely shredded lime peel
1 tablespoon lime juice
¼ teaspoon grated fresh ginger
⅛ teaspoon salt
Dash pepper
1 tablespoon margarine or butter
4 skinless, boneless wild duck breasts (about 1 pound)
2 teaspoons olive oil
Fresh red raspberries (optional)

**1** For sauce, in a small saucepan combine jelly, wine, vinegar, lime peel, lime juice, ginger, salt, and pepper. Bring just to boiling; reduce heat. Simmer, uncovered, about 12 minutes or until sauce is slightly thickened and reduced to ½ cup. Remove from heat; stir in margarine or butter. Transfer ¼ cup of the sauce to a small bowl for basting. Reserve remaining sauce until ready to serve.

**2** Rinse duck; pat dry. Brush oil over both sides of duck breasts.

**3** *For a charcoal grill*, grill duck on the rack of an uncovered grill directly over medium coals for 10 to 12 minutes or until tender and no longer pink, turning once and brushing occasionally with the ¼ cup sauce during the last 5 minutes of grilling. (*For a gas grill*, preheat grill. Reduce heat to medium. Place duck on grill rack over heat. Cover and grill as above.)

**4** Serve duck with reserved sauce. If desired, garnish with raspberries. Makes 4 servings.

Nutrition Facts per serving: 222 calories, 8 g total fat (2 g saturated fat), 22 mg cholesterol, 124 mg sodium, 29 g carbohydrate, 6 g protein. Daily Values: 4% vit. A, 5% vit. C, 1% calcium, 8% iron.

## Duck with Cranberry-Orange Glaze

**Prep:** 5 minutes **Grill:** 10 minutes

½ cup cranberry-orange sauce
⅓ cup orange marmalade
1 tablespoon vinegar
1 teaspoon grated fresh ginger
4 skinless, boneless wild duck breast halves (about 1 pound)
2 teaspoons cooking oil

**1** For glaze, in a small bowl combine cranberry-orange sauce, orange marmalade, vinegar, and ginger. Set aside.

**2** Rinse duck; pat dry. Brush oil over both sides of duck breast halves.

**3** *For a charcoal grill*, grill duck on the rack of an uncovered grill directly over medium coals for 10 to 12 minutes or until tender and no longer pink, turning once and brushing frequently with glaze during the last 5 minutes of grilling. (*For a gas grill*, preheat grill. Reduce heat to medium. Place duck on grill rack over heat. Cover and grill as above.) Makes 4 servings.

Nutrition Facts per serving: 253 calories, 5 g total fat (1 g saturated fat), 142 mg cholesterol, 111 mg sodium, 25 g carbohydrate, 1 g fiber, 28 g protein. Daily Values: 7% vit. C, 1% calcium, 30% iron.

**Flaming Facts**

**Both wild and domestic ducks are known for their distinctive flavor and moist dark meat. The flavor of duck is affected by the diet of the bird, as well as its age and weight. Generally, older and heavier birds are stronger flavored and less tender. Domestic ducks have a layer of fat under their skins that is not present in wild ducks.**

## OSTRICH BURGERS WITH CRANBERRIES

**Prep:** 20 minutes   **Grill:** 14 minutes

*Ostrich is coming on strong as a meat option because it combines the virtues of poultry (lean) with the virtues of beef (flavor). Add to that a sauce of red wine and dried cranberries and you have a burger combo everyone will ask for.*

   ¼ **cup dry red wine**
   2 **tablespoons red wine vinegar**
   1 **tablespoon finely chopped shallot**
   ½ **teaspoon coarsely ground pepper**
   ½ **cup butter (no substitutes), cut into 8 pieces**
   ¼ **cup dried cranberries**
   2 **pounds ground ostrich meat**
      **Salt**
   6 **hamburger buns, split and toasted**

1 For sauce, in a small saucepan combine wine, vinegar, shallot, and pepper. Bring to boiling; reduce heat to medium-high. Boil gently about 5 minutes or until liquid is reduced to about 1 tablespoon. Reduce heat to low. Add butter, one piece at a time, stirring until completely melted before adding next piece. Stir in cranberries. Remove from heat; keep warm.

2 Shape ground ostrich into six ¾-inch-thick patties. Sprinkle lightly with salt.

3 *For a charcoal grill*, grill burgers on the rack of an uncovered grill directly over medium coals for 14 to 18 minutes or until no longer pink, turning once halfway through grilling. (*For a gas grill*, preheat grill. Reduce heat to medium. Place burgers on grill rack over heat. Cover and grill as above.)

4 Remove burgers from grill. Serve burgers on buns with sauce. Makes 6 servings.

Nutrition Facts per serving: 453 calories, 21 g total fat (10 g saturated fat), 41 mg cholesterol, 477 mg sodium, 26 g carbohydrate, 1 g fiber, 37 g protein. Daily Values: 16% vit. A, 3% calcium, 52% iron.

## Peppered Ostrich Steak

**Prep:** 10 minutes   **Grill:** 14 minutes

   2 **teaspoons cracked mixed peppercorns**
   1 **large clove garlic, minced**
   ⅛ **teaspoon salt**
   4 **4-ounce ostrich thigh fan or venison steaks, cut 1 inch thick**
   1 **tablespoon balsamic vinegar**

1 In a small bowl combine peppercorns, garlic, and salt. Sprinkle evenly over both sides of meat; rub in with your fingers.

2 *For a charcoal grill*, grill steaks on the greased rack of an uncovered grill directly over medium coals until desired doneness, turning once halfway through grilling. (Allow 14 to 18 minutes for medium-rare doneness.) (*For a gas grill*, preheat grill. Reduce heat to medium. Place steaks on grill rack over heat. Cover and grill as above.)

### DON'T GET BURNED!

**What's the number one rule for grilling wild game? Don't overcook it. Farm-raised game doesn't have fat running through it, so it's not naturally moist and juicy. Aside from paying careful attention to timing and doneness tests, you can retain moisture by marinating it first, which also will add flavor. It's also a good idea to lightly brush the cold grill rack with oil so the meat won't stick.**

**3** Transfer steaks to a serving platter. Drizzle with vinegar. Cover and let stand for 5 minutes before serving. Makes 4 servings.

Nutrition Facts per serving: 141 calories, 5 g total fat (0 g saturated fat), 65 mg cholesterol, 121 mg sodium, 2 g carbohydrate, 1 g fiber, 22 g protein. Daily Values: 19% iron.

## JERK OSTRICH WITH MANGO SALSA

**Prep:** 15 minutes **Grill:** 1¼ hours
**Stand Time:** 15 minutes

*Heat it up with island spices; then cool it down with tropical fruit. That's the way it's done on the islands. Ostrich meat is rubbed with tongue-tingling flavors, and Mango Salsa cools it down.*

    1 recipe Mango Salsa
    3 tablespoons chopped green onions
    2 teaspoons lime juice
    2 teaspoons grated fresh ginger
    2 cloves garlic, minced
    ½ to 1 fresh Scotch bonnet or serrano
        pepper, finely chopped
    1 teaspoon brown sugar
    ½ teaspoon salt
    ½ teaspoon ground allspice
    1 3-pound ostrich thigh fan roast

**1** Prepare Mango Salsa; cover and chill until ready to serve. In a bowl combine green onions, lime juice, ginger, garlic, Scotch bonnet pepper, brown sugar, salt, and allspice.

**2** Sprinkle onion mixture on both sides of roast; gently press into surface. Insert a meat thermometer into center of roast.

**3** *For a charcoal grill*, arrange medium-hot coals around a drip pan. Test for medium heat above the pan. Place roast on the grill rack over drip pan. Cover and grill 1¼ to 1½ hours or until meat thermometer registers 145°. [*For a gas grill*, preheat grill. Reduce heat to medium. Adjust for indirect cooking (see page 10). Grill as above.] Remove from grill. Cover with foil; let stand for 15 minutes before carving.

**4** To serve, slice roast. Serve with Mango Salsa. Makes 8 servings.

**Mango Salsa:** In a small bowl stir together 2 cups chopped mango, 1 cup chopped red sweet pepper, ¼ cup snipped fresh cilantro, 2 tablespoons lime juice, and ⅛ teaspoon ground red pepper. Makes about 2½ cups.

Nutrition Facts per serving: 465 calories, 8 g total fat (0 g saturated fat), 218 mg cholesterol, 446 mg sodium, 22 g carbohydrate, 3 g fiber, 73 g protein. Daily Values: 70% vit. A, 143% vit. C, 1% calcium, 56% iron.

## Flaming Facts

Because ostrich is not considered a domesticated bird, such as chicken and turkey, it does not fall under the Poultry Product Inspection Act. Legislation has been drafted to redefine "poultry" to include ostrich, but currently federal and state inspection of these birds is voluntary. According to the American Ostrich Association, the vast majority of ostrich farmers comply with voluntary inspection by the United States Department of Agriculture (USDA). The USDA seal on packaged ostrich products ensures the meat is safe and wholesome.

# Classic French-Style Quail

**Prep:** 15 minutes    **Marinate:** 4 to 6 hours
**Grill:** 7 minutes

*For a semi-boneless quail, check a good butcher shop. They can provide you with a whole quail prepared for cooking in the "European style." This means the bird is split open, rib cages removed, with the wing and leg bones left intact.*

    8 semi-boneless quail
    ¾ cup dry white wine
    2 tablespoons fresh rosemary leaves
    1 tablespoon olive oil
    4 cloves garlic, sliced
        Salt and pepper
    2 lemons, cut into wedges

**1** Rinse quail; pat dry. Using kitchen shears, cut down center of back of each quail and press open on firm surface to lay flat. Twist wing tips under back. Tie legs together with 100-percent-cotton string. Place quail in a plastic bag set in a shallow dish.

**2** For marinade, in a small bowl combine wine, rosemary, oil, and garlic. Pour over quail; seal bag. Marinate in the refrigerator for 4 to 6 hours, turning bag occasionally. Drain quail, discarding marinade. Sprinkle lightly with salt and pepper.

**3** *For a charcoal grill*, grill quail on the rack of an uncovered grill directly over medium coals for 7 to 10 minutes or until tender and no longer pink, turning once halfway through grilling. (*For a gas grill*, preheat grill. Reduce heat to medium. Place quail on grill rack over heat. Cover and grill as above.)

**4** To serve, place quail on serving platter and garnish with lemon. Squeeze lemon over quail before eating. Makes 4 servings.

Nutrition Facts per serving: 438 calories,
27 g total fat (7 g saturated fat), 0 mg cholesterol,
183 mg sodium, 1 g carbohydrate, 0 g fiber,
43 g protein. Daily Values: 16% vit. A, 28% vit. C,
2% calcium, 58% iron.

## WINE-MARINATED PHEASANT

**Prep:** 15 minutes    **Marinate:** 6 to 24 hours
**Grill:** 50 minutes

    1 2- to 2½-pound domestic pheasant
    ¾ cup dry sherry
    ¼ cup lime juice or lemon juice
    3 tablespoons snipped fresh parsley
    2 tablespoons cooking oil
    2 cloves garlic, crushed
    ½ teaspoon salt
    ½ teaspoon dried savory, crushed
    ½ teaspoon bottled hot pepper sauce

**1** Rinse pheasant; pat dry. Using poultry shears, cut closely along one side of backbone the entire length of bird. Repeat on other side. Discard backbone. Cut pheasant into quarters. Place pheasant quarters in a plastic bag set in a shallow dish. For marinade, in a small bowl combine sherry, lime juice, parsley, oil, garlic, salt, savory, and hot pepper sauce. Pour over pheasant; seal bag. Marinate in the refrigerator for 6 to 24 hours, turning bag occasionally. Drain pheasant, reserving marinade. Remove garlic cloves; discard.

**2** *For a charcoal grill*, arrange medium-hot coals around a drip pan. Test for medium heat above the pan. Place pheasant quarters on grill rack over drip pan. Cover and grill for 50 to 60 minutes or until tender and no longer pink, turning once halfway through grilling and brushing occasionally with marinade during the first 15 minutes of grilling. [*For a gas grill*, preheat grill. Reduce heat to medium. Adjust for indirect cooking (see page 10). Grill as above.] Makes 4 servings.

Nutrition Facts per serving: 446 calories,
23 g total fat (6 g saturated fat), 0 mg cholesterol,
261 mg sodium, 4 g carbohydrate, 0 g fiber,
46 g protein. Daily Values: 11% vit. A, 27% vit. C,
2% calcium, 17% iron.

# Smoke Cooking

# Texans' Beef Brisket

**Prep:** 15 minutes  **Soak:** 1 hour
**Smoke:** 5 hours

*Texans get mighty cantankerous about their
barbecue. This brisket—with a mopping sauce,
dry rub, and passing sauce—covers all the bases.*

15 to 20 **mesquite, hickory, or pecan
   wood chunks**
1 **recipe Vinegar Mop Sauce**
1 **3- to 3½-pound fresh beef brisket**
2 **teaspoons seasoned salt**
1 **teaspoon paprika**
1 **teaspoon chili powder**
1 **teaspoon garlic pepper**
½ **teaspoon ground cumin**
1 **recipe Spicy Beer Sauce**

**1** At least 1 hour before smoke-cooking, soak
wood chunks in enough water to cover.
Prepare Vinegar Mop Sauce; set aside. Trim
fat from meat. For rub, in a small bowl
combine seasoned salt, paprika, chili powder,
garlic pepper, and cumin. Sprinkle mixture
evenly over meat; rub in with your fingers.

**2** Drain wood chunks. In a smoker arrange
preheated coals, about one-fourth of the
drained wood chunks, and the water pan
according to the manufacturer's directions.
Pour water into pan. Place meat on grill rack
over water pan. Cover and smoke for 5 to
6 hours or until meat is tender, brushing
occasionally with Vinegar Mop during the
last hour of smoking. Add more coals, wood
chunks, and water as needed.

**3** Shortly before serving, prepare Spicy Beer
Sauce. To serve, thinly slice meat across
the grain. Serve meat with Spicy Beer Sauce.
Makes 12 servings.

**Vinegar Mop Sauce:** In a small bowl stir
together ¼ cup of beer, 4 teaspoons
Worcestershire sauce, 1 tablespoon cooking
oil, 1 tablespoon vinegar, ½ teaspoon
jalapeño mustard or other hot-style mustard,
and a few dashes hot pepper sauce.

**Spicy Beer Sauce:** In a medium saucepan
melt 2 tablespoons margarine or butter. Add
1 large peeled, seeded, and chopped tomato
(¾ cup); 1 medium chopped onion; and ½ cup
chopped green sweet pepper. Cook about
5 minutes or until onion is tender, stirring
occasionally. Stir in 1 cup bottled chili sauce,
½ cup beer, ½ cup cider vinegar,
2 tablespoons brown sugar, 1 to 2 tablespoons
chopped chipotle peppers in adobo sauce,
1¼ teaspoons black pepper, and ½ teaspoon
salt. Bring to boiling; reduce heat. Boil
gently, uncovered, about 10 minutes or until
reduced to about 2¼ cups.

Nutrition Facts per serving: 277 calories,
14 g total fat (4 g saturated fat), 78 mg cholesterol,
689 mg sodium, 11 g carbohydrate, 1 g fiber,
26 g protein. Daily Values: 10% vit. A, 20% vit. C,
2% calcium, 20% iron.

## DON'T GET BURNED!

**Smoking is popular in the fall
and winter, which are good
seasons to enjoy hearty
briskets, pulled pork, and
smoked game. But be aware
that the greater temperature
variations during cold or
windy weather can make
smoking more difficult. If
possible, place your smoker
where it has a shelter from
the wind. However, don't be
tempted to use your smoker in
your garage. The smoke will
most likely make its way into
your home.**

## PEPPER-CRUSTED BEEF RIB EYE ROAST

**Prep:** 15 minutes  **Soak:** 1 hour
**Cook:** 45 minutes  **Smoke:** 3 hours
**Stand:** 15 minutes

*Here's a beef lover's nirvana. A glorious rib eye roast, a pepper crust, a good long smoke, and tomato chutney make for a great entrée.*

  10 to 12 oak wood chunks
   1 4- to 5-pound beef rib eye roast
   1 to 2 tablespoons cracked pepper
   2 large cloves garlic, minced
   4 ripe tomatoes, chopped (about
       3 cups)
   1 to 1¼ cups packed brown sugar
   1 large onion, chopped
   1 cup raisins
   ½ cup balsamic vinegar or red wine
       vinegar
   2 to 3 tablespoons chopped
       crystallized ginger
   1 to 2 fresh jalapeño peppers, finely
       chopped
   ½ to 1 teaspoon dry mustard
       Salt and pepper (optional)

**1** At least 1 hour before smoke-cooking, soak wood chunks in enough water to cover.

**2** Trim fat from meat. For rub, in a small bowl combine pepper and garlic. Sprinkle rub evenly over meat; rub in with your fingers. Insert a meat thermometer into the thickest part of the meat.

**3** Drain wood chunks. In a smoker arrange preheated coals, drained wood chunks, and water pan according to the manufacturer's directions. Pour water into pan. Place meat, fat side up, on grill rack over water pan. Cover and smoke for 3 to 4 hours or until meat thermometer registers 140° for medium-rare doneness. Add more coals, wood chunks, and water as needed. Remove meat from smoker. Cover with foil; let stand for 15 minutes before carving. (The meat's temperature will rise 5° during standing.)

**4** Meanwhile, for chutney, in a small saucepan combine tomatoes, brown sugar, onion, raisins, vinegar, ginger, jalapeño peppers, and mustard. Bring to boiling; reduce heat. Simmer, uncovered, about 45 minutes or until desired consistency. If desired, cover and chill until ready to serve.

**5** If desired, season meat with salt and pepper. Serve meat with warm or chilled chutney. Makes 10 to 12 servings.

Nutrition Facts per serving: 458 calories, 19 g total fat (8 g saturated fat), 107 mg cholesterol, 113 mg sodium, 36 g carbohydrate, 2 g fiber, 37 g protein. Daily Values: 4% vit. A, 30% vit. C, 4% calcium, 35% iron.

## Hickory-Smoked Pork Loin

**Prep:** 10 minutes  **Soak:** 1 hour
**Marinate:** 30 minutes  **Smoke:** 1¾ hours
**Stand:** 10 minutes

*The barbecue kings of the Deep South wouldn't think of using any wood but hickory. It's fine for beef, but it really shines on all kinds of pork.*

  10 to 12 hickory wood chunks
   1 2- to 2½-pound boneless pork top
       loin roast (single loin)
   2 tablespoons light brown sugar
   1 tablespoon finely shredded orange
       peel
   1 teaspoon ground coriander
   1 teaspoon paprika
   ½ teaspoon ground ginger
   ½ teaspoon salt
   ¼ teaspoon pepper

**1** At least 1 hour before smoke-cooking, soak wood chunks in enough water to cover.

**2** Meanwhile, trim fat from meat. Place meat in a shallow dish. For rub, in a small bowl stir together brown sugar, orange peel, coriander, paprika, ginger, salt, and pepper. Sprinkle rub evenly over meat; rub in with your fingers. Cover and marinate at room temperature for 30 minutes or in the refrigerator for 2 hours. Insert a meat thermometer into the center of meat.

**3** Drain wood chunks. In a smoker arrange preheated coals, half of the drained wood chunks, and the water pan according to the manufacturer's directions. Pour water into pan. Place meat on grill rack over water pan. Cover and smoke for 1¾ to 2 hours or until meat thermometer registers 155°. Add more coals, wood chunks, and water as needed. Remove meat from smoker.

**4** Cover meat with foil; let stand for 10 minutes before carving. (The meat's temperature will rise 5° during standing.) Makes 6 to 8 servings.

Nutrition Facts per serving: 199 calories, 10 g total fat (3 g saturated fat), 68 mg cholesterol, 231 mg sodium, 5 g carbohydrate, 0 g fiber, 22 g protein. Daily Values: 2% vit. A, 3% vit. C, 1% calcium, 7% iron.

## COASTAL CAROLINA PULLED PORK BBQ

**Prep:** 15 minutes  **Soak:** 1 hour
**Smoke:** 4 hours  **Stand:** 15 minutes

*The Carolinas may well offer more variations on barbecue than anywhere else in the country. These shredded pork sandwiches get dressed up with slaw and a simple vinegar sauce.*

　10 to 12 oak or hickory wood chunks
　　1 4½- to 5-pound boneless pork
　　　　shoulder roast
　1½ teaspoons salt
　1½ teaspoons black pepper
　　2 cups cider vinegar
　　3 tablespoons brown sugar
　　　　(optional)
　　1 tablespoon salt
　　1 tablespoon crushed red pepper
　12 hamburger buns, split and toasted
　　　　Coleslaw (optional)
　　　　Bottled hot pepper sauce (optional)

**1** At least 1 hour before smoke-cooking, soak wood chunks in enough water to cover.

**2** Trim fat from meat. For rub, in a small bowl combine the 1½ teaspoons salt and the black pepper. Sprinkle rub evenly over meat; rub in with your fingers. For sauce, in a medium bowl combine vinegar, brown sugar (if desired), the 1 tablespoon salt, and the red pepper. Set aside.

**3** Drain wood chunks. In a smoker arrange preheated coals, drained wood chunks, and the water pan according to the manufacturer's directions. Pour water into pan. Place meat on grill rack over water pan. Cover and smoke for 4 to 5 hours or until meat is very tender. Add more wood chunks, coals, and water as needed. Remove meat from smoker.

**4** Cover with foil; let stand for 15 minutes. Using 2 forks, gently shred the meat into long, thin strands. Add enough of the sauce to the meat to moisten.

**5** Place shredded meat on toasted buns. If desired, top meat with coleslaw. Pass remaining sauce and, if desired, hot pepper sauce. Makes 12 servings.

Nutrition Facts per serving: 314 calories, 11 g total fat (3 g saturated fat), 64 mg cholesterol, 1,096 mg sodium, 24 g carbohydrate, 1 g fiber, 31 g protein. Daily Values: 3% vit. A, 1% vit. C, 4% calcium, 17% iron.

### Did You Know?

Supermarkets that stock charcoal usually will carry wood chips and chunks as well. But there are companies that will ship what you want to your front door. Check out these companies for your favorite woods: Woodbridge Vintage Barrel Chips (407-382-3256) are made from oak wine barrels; Blanton Mesquite Wood (877-891-3597) carries pecan and mesquite woods; and the Barbecue Store (888-789-0650) offers mesquite, alder apple, or hickory woods, and Cabernet and Chardonnay wine-soaked oak woods.

# Memphis-Style Smoked Pork with Bourbon Sauce

**Prep:** 25 minutes  **Marinate:** 24 hours
**Soak:** 1 hour  **Smoke:** 4 hours
**Stand:** 15 minutes

*Tennessee is famed for its bourbon and its
barbecue, so isn't it time to put the two together?
The bourbon flavor is stout enough to withstand
a long smoke and still come through in the
finished dish.*

1 8-ounce can tomato sauce
1 cup chopped onion
1 cup cider vinegar
½ cup bourbon or beef broth
¼ cup Worcestershire sauce
2 tablespoons brown sugar
¼ teaspoon black pepper
  Dash bottled hot pepper sauce
1 4½- to 5-pound boneless pork
  shoulder roast
8 to 10 hickory wood chunks

**1** For sauce, in a medium saucepan combine
tomato sauce, onion, ½ cup of the vinegar,
the bourbon, Worcestershire sauce, brown
sugar, black pepper, and hot pepper sauce.
Bring to boiling; reduce heat. Simmer,
covered, for 15 minutes; cool. Reserve 1 cup
of sauce. Cover reserved sauce and chill until
ready to serve.

**2** Meanwhile, trim fat from meat. Place meat
in a plastic bag set in a shallow dish. For
marinade, combine the remaining sauce and
the remaining vinegar. Pour over meat; seal
bag. Marinate in the refrigerator for 24 hours,
turning bag occasionally. Drain meat,
reserving marinade.

**3** At least 1 hour before smoke-cooking, soak
wood chunks in enough water to cover.

**4** Drain wood chunks. In a smoker arrange
preheated coals, half of the drained wood
chunks, and the water pan according to the
manufacturer's directions. Pour water into
pan. Place meat on grill rack over water pan.
Cover and smoke for 4 to 5 hours or until
meat is tender, basting occasionally with
marinade during the first 3 hours of smoking.
Add more coals, wood chunks, and water as
needed. Remove meat from smoker.

**5** Cover with foil; let stand for 15 minutes
before carving. Meanwhile, in a small
saucepan cook the reserved 1 cup sauce over
medium heat until heated through. Slice
meat. Serve meat with sauce. Serves 12.

Nutrition Facts per serving: 324 calories,
17 g total fat (6 g saturated fat), 112 mg cholesterol,
253 mg sodium, 6 g carbohydrate, 0 g fiber,
30 g protein. Daily Values: 2% vit. A, 18% vit. C,
1% calcium, 16% iron.

**Smokin' Hot Tip**

**Have a little patience when
cooking on a smoker.
Smoking, unlike grilling,
takes a matter of hours, not
minutes. Resist opening the
smoker lid during smoking
because the temperature
inside the smoker will be
greatly reduced. It may take
as long as 15 minutes to
return to the correct
temperature. Also, be sure to
use wood chunks rather than
chips when cooking for more
than a few hours, and
add more chunks every 2 to
4 hours to keep the
temperature constant.**

Memphis-Style Smoked Pork
with Bourbon Sauce

## PECAN-SMOKED PORK CHOPS

**Prep:** 25 minutes   **Soak:** 1 hour
**Smoke:** 1¾ hours

*Though milder than other woods, pecan wood punches up these thick chops with plenty of flavor. Rubbed-on allspice comes alive when it meets the cherry relish.*

**6 to 8 pecan wood chunks**
**4 pork loin chops, cut 1½ inches thick**
**1 tablespoon brown sugar**
**½ teaspoon salt**
**½ teaspoon paprika**
**¼ teaspoon ground allspice**
**¼ teaspoon pepper**
**1 tablespoon cider vinegar**
**1 recipe Apple-Cherry Relish**

**1** At least 1 hour before smoke-cooking, soak wood chunks in enough water to cover.

**2** Trim fat from chops. For rub, in a small bowl stir together brown sugar, salt, paprika, allspice, and pepper. Brush the chops with vinegar. Sprinkle rub evenly over chops; rub in with your fingers.

**3** Drain wood chunks. In a smoker arrange preheated coals, drained wood chunks, and water pan according to the manufacturer's directions. Pour water into pan. Place chops on grill rack over water pan. Cover and smoke for 1¾ to 2¼ hours or until chops are slightly pink in center and juices run clear, adding more coals as needed. Serve chops with Apple-Cherry Relish. Makes 4 servings.

**Apple-Cherry Relish:** In a small saucepan combine 1 cup chopped, peeled apple; ½ cup dried tart cherries; and 3 tablespoons water. Bring to boiling; reduce heat. Simmer, covered, about 5 minutes or until apple is tender. In a small bowl combine

2 tablespoons brown sugar, 2 tablespoons vinegar, 1 teaspoon cornstarch, and ¼ teaspoon ground allspice. Stir into apple mixture. Cook and stir until thickened and bubbly. Cook and stir for 2 minutes more. Just before serving, stir in ¼ cup chopped pecans, toasted. Makes about 1 cup.

Nutrition Facts per serving: 417 calories, 19 g total fat (5 g saturated fat), 102 mg cholesterol, 348 mg sodium, 27 g carbohydrate, 2 g fiber, 33 g protein. Daily Values: 11% vit. A, 4% vit. C, 1% calcium, 12% iron.

# Memphis-Style Ribs

**Prep:** 5 minutes   **Soak:** 1 hour
**Marinate:** 30 minutes   **Smoke:** 3 hours

**8 to 10 hickory wood chunks**
**4 pounds pork loin back ribs or meaty spareribs**
**3 tablespoons brown sugar**
**3 tablespoons paprika**
**2 tablespoons chili powder**
**1 tablespoon ground cumin**
**1 tablespoon garlic pepper**
**1 teaspoon seasoned salt**
**½ to 1 teaspoon ground red pepper**

**1** At least 1 hour before smoke-cooking, soak wood chunks in enough water to cover.

**2** Meanwhile, trim fat from ribs. Place ribs in a shallow dish. For rub, in a small bowl combine the brown sugar, paprika, chili powder, cumin, garlic pepper, seasoned salt, and red pepper. If desired, reserve 2 tablespoons of the rub to sprinkle on ribs near the end of smoking. Sprinkle the remaining rub evenly over ribs; rub in with your fingers. Cover and marinate at room temperature for 30 minutes or in the refrigerator for 4 to 24 hours.

**3** Drain wood chunks. In a smoker arrange preheated coals, drained wood chunks, and the water pan according to the manufacturer's directions. Pour water into pan. Place ribs on grill rack over water pan. (Or, place ribs in a rib rack; place on grill rack.) Cover and smoke for 3 to 4 hours or until ribs are tender. Add more coals, wood chunks, and water as needed. If desired, sprinkle ribs with the reserved rub during the last 15 minutes of smoking. Makes 4 servings.

Nutrition Facts per serving: 509 calories, 27 g total fat (9 g saturated fat), 118 mg cholesterol, 163 mg sodium, 15 g carbohydrate, 1 g fiber, 51 g protein. Daily Values: 43% vit. A, 11% vit. C, 6% calcium, 36% iron.

## TEXAS BEER-SMOKED RIBS

**Prep:** 10 minutes  **Marinate:** 24 hours
**Soak:** 1 hour  **Smoke:** 3 hours

*Some Texans wouldn't think of starting a marinade with anything but Shiner Bock, but any good flavorful beer will do. The ancho pepper gives these Lone Star ribs a little border flair.*

    6 pounds meaty pork spareribs or
        loin back ribs
    1 12-ounce bottle beer
    2 tablespoons chili powder
    2 tablespoons lime juice
    1 teaspoon ground cumin
    3 cloves garlic, minced
    ¾ teaspoon salt
    4 to 6 mesquite or hickory wood
        chunks
    3 dried ancho or other dried large
        chile peppers (optional)

**1** Trim fat from ribs. Cut ribs into 8-rib portions. Place ribs in a large plastic bag set in a large shallow dish. For marinade, in a medium bowl combine beer, chili powder, lime juice, cumin, garlic, and salt. Pour over ribs; seal bag. Marinate in the refrigerator for 24 hours, turning bag occasionally. Drain ribs, reserving marinade.

**2** At least 1 hour before smoke-cooking, soak wood chunks in enough water to cover.

**3** Drain wood chunks. In the smoker arrange preheated coals, drained wood chunks, and the lined water pan according to the manufacturer's directions. Pour the marinade into pan; add the dried peppers (if desired). Place ribs on grill rack over pan. Cover and smoke for 3 to 4 hours or until ribs are tender. Add more coals, wood chunks, and water as needed. Makes 6 servings.

Nutrition Facts per serving: 580 calories, 43 g total fat (17 g saturated fat), 133 mg cholesterol, 232 mg sodium, 1 g carbohydrate, 0 g fiber, 43 g protein. Daily Values: 2% vit. A, 1% vit. C, 7% calcium, 22% iron.

## WISE ADVICE

When using a smoker, there are a few preliminary steps that will make clean-up much easier when you're finished. Line the water pan of the smoker with heavy foil. This keeps any stray drips from the meat from burning onto the pan, which can be difficult to clean later. Also, lightly coat the insides of the smoker and the lid with nonstick cooking spray. This will also make washing off any grease easier.

# Sugar-Smoked Pork Ribs

**Prep:** 15 minutes  **Soak:** 1 hour
**Marinate:** 1 hour  **Smoke:** 3 hours

*The taste sensations of tart, sweet, and salt come together in these riotous ribs. Using apple wood rather than hickory will give them fruity appeal.*

    10 to 12 apple or hickory wood chunks
     4 pounds meaty pork spareribs
     1 lemon, cut in half
     1 to 2 tablespoons soy sauce
    ¼ cup packed brown sugar

1 At least 1 hour before smoke-cooking, soak wood chunks in enough water to cover.

2 Meanwhile, trim fat from ribs. Place ribs in a shallow dish. Squeeze and rub the cut surfaces of the lemon halves over ribs. Brush ribs with the soy sauce. Cover and marinate in the refrigerator for 1 hour.

3 Drain wood chunks. In a smoker arrange preheated coals, drained wood chunks, and the water pan according to the manufacturer's directions. Pour water into pan. Place ribs on grill rack over water pan. (Or, place ribs in a rib rack; place on grill rack.) Cover and smoke for 3 to 4 hours or until tender. Add more coals, wood chunks, and water as needed.

4 Sprinkle the ribs with brown sugar. Cover and smoke for 5 minutes more. Makes 4 to 6 servings.

Nutrition Facts per serving: 530 calories, 37 g total fat (14 g saturated fat), 148 mg cholesterol, 375 mg sodium, 12 g carbohydrate, 0 g fiber, 36 g protein. Daily Values: 8% vit. C, 5% calcium, 17% iron.

# SWEET AND SALTY SMOKED HALIBUT

**Prep:** 10 minutes  **Soak:** 1 hour
**Smoke:** 1 hour

*You also can grill these steaks indirectly on a gas or charcoal grill. Use timings recommended in the fish grilling chart on page 326 and use wood chips as directed by the manufacturer.*

     4 apple or other fruit wood chunks
     4 6-ounce fresh or frozen halibut
       steaks, 1 inch thick
    ½ cup packed brown sugar
     1 to 2 tablespoons balsamic vinegar
     2 teaspoons kosher salt
     1 tablespoon olive oil

1 At least 1 hour before smoke-cooking, soak wood chunks in enough water to cover.

2 Thaw fish, if frozen. Rinse fish; pat dry with paper towels. In a small bowl combine brown sugar, vinegar, and kosher salt. Brush both sides of halibut with olive oil. Use your fingers to rub sugar and salt mixture into tops of fish steaks.

3 Drain wood chunks. In a smoker arrange preheated coals, drained wood chunks, and the water pan according to manufacturer's directions. Pour water into pan. Place fish on grill rack over water pan. Cover and smoke for about 1 hour or until fish flakes easily when tested with a fork. Makes 4 servings.

Nutrition Facts per serving: 323 calories, 7 g total fat (1 g saturated fat), 55 mg cholesterol, 1,169 mg sodium, 28 g carbohydrate, 0 g fiber, 35 g protein. Daily Values: 7% vit. A, 9% calcium, 13% iron.

# Honeyed Smoked Trout

**Prep:** 10 minutes  **Marinate:** 2 hours
**Soak:** 1 hour  **Smoke:** 1½ hours

*Trout welcomes a sweet kiss in many a dish—
honey in this case. Smoking adds another
dimension, and the cream sauce makes the
finished fish magnificent.*

> 4 8- to 10-ounce fresh or frozen
>   dressed, boned rainbow trout
> ¼ teaspoon salt
> ¼ teaspoon ground white pepper
> 3 tablespoons honey
> 2 tablespoons orange juice
> 4 hickory or apple wood chunks
> ⅓ cup whipping cream
> 2 tablespoons lemon juice
> 1 tablespoon prepared horseradish
>   Salt and white pepper
>   Fresh dill sprigs

**1** Thaw fish, if frozen. Rinse fish; pat dry. In
a large shallow dish spread the fish open,
skin side down and overlapping as necessary.
Sprinkle with salt and white pepper. In a
small bowl stir together the honey and orange
juice; spoon evenly over the fish. Cover and
marinate in the refrigerator for 2 hours.

**2** At least 1 hour before smoke-cooking, soak
wood chunks in enough water to cover.

**3** Meanwhile, for sauce, in a medium bowl
beat the whipping cream just until it starts
to thicken. Stir in the lemon juice and
horseradish. Season to taste with additional
salt and white pepper. Cover and chill until
ready to serve.

**4** Drain wood chunks. In a smoker arrange
preheated coals, drained wood chunks, and
water pan according to the manufacturer's
directions. Pour water into pan. Fold the fish
closed and place on grill rack over water pan.

Cover and smoke for 1½ to 2 hours or until
fish flakes easily when tested with a
fork. Add more coals, wood chunks, and
water as needed.

**5** Serve fish with the sauce. Garnish with dill
sprigs. Makes 4 servings.

Nutrition Facts per serving: 395 calories,
15 g total fat (6 g saturated fat), 157 mg cholesterol,
277 mg sodium, 15 g carbohydrate, 0 g fiber,
47 g protein. Daily Values: 12% vit. A, 241% vit. C,
14% calcium, 29% iron.

**Did You Know?**

**Trout is gaining in popularity,
as evidenced by its frequent
inclusion on restaurant menus
and in food magazines. While
trout is relatively lean and
makes a delicious addition to
modern diets, the overriding
reason is availability. Trout
has become more plentiful.
Overfishing and pollution had
caused the trout population to
diminish, but trout hatcheries
and other regenerative
measures have forestalled the
extinction of the fish. Today
trout is plentiful. Probably the
best known of the freshwater
species is the rainbow trout,
which can weigh up to 50
pounds, but averages around
8 ounces. Brook or speckled
trout, considered by many as
the best trout for eating, are
small, only about 6 to 8 inches
long. Trout is available
whole—fresh and frozen—
and in fillets.**

Double-Smoked Salmon with
Horseradish Cream

## DOUBLE-SMOKED SALMON WITH HORSERADISH CREAM

**Prep:** 15 minutes **Soak:** 1 hour
**Smoke:** 30 minutes

*What makes this doubly smoked—and doubly good—is the fresh salmon is stuffed with smoked salmon and then is smoked in your smoker.*

    4  hickory or apple wood chunks
    4  6-ounce fresh or frozen salmon
         fillets (with skin), about 1 inch
         thick
    4  slices smoked salmon (about
         3 ounces)
    2  tablespoons snipped fresh dill
    1  tablespoon lemon juice
         Salt and pepper
    ½ cup dairy sour cream
    4  teaspoons prepared horseradish
    1  green onion, thinly sliced

**1** At least 1 hour before smoke-cooking, soak wood chunks in enough water to cover.

**2** Thaw fish, if frozen. Rinse fish; pat dry. Make a pocket in each fish fillet by cutting horizontally from one side almost through to the other side. Fill with slices of smoked salmon and 2 teaspoons of the dill, folding salmon slices as necessary to fit. Brush fish with lemon juice and top with 2 teaspoons of the dill. Sprinkle with salt and pepper.

**3** Drain wood chunks. In a smoker arrange preheated coals, drained wood chunks, and water pan according to the manufacturer's directions. Pour water into pan. Place fish, skin side down, on grill rack over water pan. Cover and smoke about 30 minutes or until fish flakes easily when tested with a fork.

**4** Meanwhile, for sauce, in a small bowl combine the remaining dill, the sour cream, horseradish, and green onion. Serve fish with the sauce. Makes 4 servings.

Nutrition Facts per serving: 245 calories,
13 g total fat (5 g saturated fat), 48 mg cholesterol,
337 mg sodium, 2 g carbohydrate, 0 g fiber,
29 g protein. Daily Values: 11% vit. A, 6% vit. C,
4% calcium, 9% iron.

## Smoked Salmon with Lemon Dill Aïoli

**Prep:** 20 minutes **Soak:** 1 hour
**Smoke:** 2½ hours

*Classic flavors for fish adorn this salmon entrée. Dill, lemon, and mayonnaise combine for a dish that is simply the best.*

    10 to 12 alder or apple wood chunks
    ¾ cup mayonnaise or salad dressing
    2  tablespoons snipped fresh dill
    1½ teaspoons finely shredded lemon
         peel
    1  tablespoon lemon juice
    ¼ teaspoon lemon-pepper seasoning
    1  3½- to 4-pound dressed salmon
    8  sprigs fresh dill

**1** At least 1 hour before smoke-cooking, soak wood chunks in enough water to cover.

**2** Meanwhile, for sauce, in a small bowl combine mayonnaise, snipped dill, lemon peel, lemon juice, and lemon-pepper seasoning. Cover and chill until serving.

**3** Rinse salmon; pat dry with paper towels. Fill cavity of fish with fresh dill sprigs. Place salmon on an 18×12-inch piece of greased heavy foil.

**4** Drain wood chunks. In a smoker arrange preheated coals, drained wood chunks, and water pan according to manufacturer's directions. Pour water into pan. Place fish and foil on grill rack over water pan. Cover and smoke for 2½ to 3 hours or until fish flakes easily when tested with a fork. Add more coals, wood chunks, and water as needed.

**5** To serve, remove skin from one side of salmon and serve fish with sauce. Makes 4 to 6 servings.

Nutrition Facts per serving: 661 calories,
46 g total fat (8 g saturated fat), 95 mg cholesterol,
541 mg sodium, 2 g carbohydrate, 0 g fiber,
57 g protein. Daily Values: 11% vit. A, 4% vit. C,
3% calcium, 19% iron.

## SMOKED CHICKEN-CABBAGE SALAD

**Prep:** 25 minutes  **Soak:** 1 hour
**Smoke:** 2½ hours

*This is not your basic chicken salad. This one gets a flavor punch from smoke, fresh oranges, and a dressing of oil, vinegar, and hot Thai chili sauce.*

  6 to 8 apple or other fruit wood
      chunks
  1 tablespoon olive oil or cooking oil
  2 cloves garlic, minced
  ½ teaspoon salt
  ¼ teaspoon pepper
  1 3- to 3½-pound whole broiler-fryer
      chicken
  3 tablespoons olive oil
  3 tablespoons balsamic vinegar
  2 tablespoons bottled Thai chili
      sauce or chili sauce plus several
      dashes bottled hot pepper sauce
  4 cups shredded cabbage
  1 cup orange sections (about
      3 oranges)
  1 large tomato, chopped
  2 green onions, chopped

1 At least 1 hour before smoke-cooking, soak wood chunks in enough water to cover.

2 In a small bowl stir together the 1 tablespoon oil, the garlic, salt, and pepper. Remove the neck and giblets from chicken. Twist wing tips under back. Starting at the neck on 1 side of the breast, slip your fingers between skin and meat, loosening the skin as you work toward the tail end. Repeat on the other side of the breast. Lift chicken skin and carefully rub the garlic mixture under skin directly on meat. Skewer the neck skin to the back. Tie legs to tail with 100-percent-cotton string.

3 Drain wood chunks. In a smoker arrange preheated coals, drained wood chunks, and water pan according to the manufacturer's directions. Pour water into pan. Place chicken, breast side up, on grill rack over water pan. Cover and smoke for 2½ to 3 hours or until chicken is no longer pink and drumsticks move easily. Add more coals, wood chunks, and water as needed.

4 Transfer chicken to a cutting board. Cool slightly. Remove skin from chicken; remove meat from bones. Discard skin and bones. Cut meat into bite-size pieces.

5 Meanwhile, for dressing, in a screw-top jar combine the 3 tablespoons oil, the balsamic vinegar, and chili sauce. Cover and shake well. In a large salad bowl combine cabbage, orange sections, tomato, and green onions. Add chicken; toss gently to combine. Pour dressing over chicken mixture; toss gently to coat. Makes 4 to 6 servings.

Nutrition Facts per serving: 379 calories, 24 g total fat (5 g saturated fat), 66 mg cholesterol, 450 mg sodium, 19 g carbohydrate, 3 g fiber, 23 g protein. Daily Values: 10% vit. A, 145% vit. C, 7% calcium, 15% iron.

# Smoked Gremolata Chicken

**Prep:** 20 minutes  **Soak:** 1 hour
**Smoke:** 3¼ hours  **Stand:** 15 minutes

*Gremolata—the garnish of garlic, lemon, and parsley that's traditionally sprinkled over osso buco—gives this smoked bird great flavor.*

  10 to 12 apple or cherry wood chunks
  1 6- to 7-pound whole roasting
      chicken
  2 to 3 tablespoons snipped fresh
      Italian flat-leaf parsley
  2 teaspoons finely shredded
      lemon peel
  ¼ teaspoon coarsely ground pepper
  1 garlic bulb
  1 small lemon, cut into wedges

1 At least 1 hour before smoke-cooking, soak wood chunks in enough water to cover.

2 Remove the neck and giblets from chicken. In a small bowl combine parsley, lemon peel, and pepper. Sprinkle rub evenly over

chicken; rub in with your fingers. With a sharp knife, cut off the top ½ inch from garlic bulb to expose the ends of the individual cloves. Leaving garlic bulb whole, remove any loose, papery outer layers. Place the garlic bulb and lemon wedges in cavity of chicken. Skewer the neck skin to the back. Twist wing tips under back. Tie legs to tail with 100-percent-cotton string. Insert a meat thermometer into the center of an inside thigh muscle without touching bone.

**3** Drain wood chunks. In a smoker arrange preheated coals, drained wood chunks, and water pan according to the manufacturer's directions. Pour water into pan. Place chicken, breast side up, on grill rack over water pan. Cover and smoke for 3¼ to 4 hours or until meat thermometer registers 180° to 185°. Add more coals, wood chunks, and water as needed. Remove chicken from smoker. Cover with foil; let stand for 15 minutes before carving the chicken.

**4** Remove garlic and lemon wedges from chicken cavity. If desired, season chicken with salt. Makes 6 to 8 servings.

Nutrition Facts per serving: 363 calories, 20 g total fat (6 g saturated fat), 162 mg cholesterol, 120 mg sodium, 2 g carbohydrate, 0 g fiber, 41 g protein. Daily Values: 29% vit. A, 8% vit. C, 2% calcium, 17% iron.

## HICKORY-SMOKED TURKEY

**Prep:** 15 minutes **Soak:** 1 hour
**Smoke:** 5 hours **Stand:** 15 minutes

> 10 to 12 hickory wood chunks
> 1 10- to 12-pound turkey
> 2 tablespoons olive oil
> 1 teaspoon dried thyme, crushed
> 1 teaspoon dried sage, crushed
> ½ teaspoon salt
> ¼ teaspoon pepper

**1** At least 1 hour before smoke-cooking, soak wood chunks in enough water to cover.

**2** Remove the neck and giblets from turkey. Rub skin of turkey with oil. Sprinkle inside

and out with thyme, sage, salt, and pepper. Skewer the neck skin to the back. Twist wing tips under back. Tuck drumsticks under the band of skin across the tail or tie the legs to tail with 100-percent-cotton string. Insert a meat thermometer into the center of an inside thigh muscle without it touching bone.

**3** Drain wood chunks. In a smoker arrange preheated coals, drained wood chunks, and the water pan according to the manufacturer's directions. Pour water into pan. Place turkey, breast side up, on grill rack over water pan. Cover and smoke about 5 hours or until meat thermometer registers 180° to 185°. Add more coals, wood chunks, and water as needed. Cut band of skin or string between drumsticks two-thirds of the way through cooking. Remove turkey from smoker. Cover with foil; let stand for 15 minutes before carving. Makes 12 to 14 servings.

Nutrition Facts per serving: 277 calories, 14 g total fat (4 g saturated fat), 120 mg cholesterol, 173 mg sodium, 0 g carbohydrate, 0 g fiber, 35 g protein. Daily Values: 8% vit. A, 2% calcium, 17% iron.

## Smokin' Hot Tip

**To moisten meats and add flavor during smoking, try spraying meats with fruit juices before smoking. This puts moisture back into the meat as it dries during cooking. Or, for a water smoker, try varying the liquid in the water pan. Fruit juices—orange, apple, white grape, or cranberry—are great with poultry. For pork, try cider or red wine vinegar. Beer mixed with half water is a good companion for beef ribs or roasts.**

# Five-Spice Smoked Turkey

**Prep:** 20 minutes **Soak:** 1 hour
**Smoke:** 2 hours **Stand:** 15 minutes

      4 cups apple wood chips
      1 teaspoon ground cinnamon
      1 teaspoon aniseed, crushed
      ½ teaspoon salt
      ¼ teaspoon fennel seed, crushed
      ¼ teaspoon coarsely ground pepper
         or Szechwan pepper
      ⅛ teaspoon ground cloves
      1 2- to 3-pound turkey breast half
         with bone
      1 tablespoon cooking oil

**1** At least 1 hour before smoke-cooking, soak wood chips in enough water to cover.

**2** Stir together cinnamon, aniseed, salt, fennel seed, pepper, and cloves. If desired, remove skin from turkey breast and discard.

Brush turkey breast with cooking oil. Use your fingers to rub the seasoning mixture onto the turkey breast. Insert a meat thermometer into turkey breast.

**3** Drain wood chips. In a smoker arrange preheated coals, wood chips, and the water pan according to manufacturer's directions. Pour water into pan. Place the turkey breast on grill rack over water pan. Cover; smoke for 2 to 2½ hours or until thermometer registers 170°. (The seasoning mixture will cause the outside of the turkey breast to appear dark.) Remove turkey from smoker. Cover with foil; let stand for 15 minutes before carving. Makes 4 to 6 servings.

Nutrition Facts per serving: 335 calories,
15 g total fat (4 g saturated fat), 118 mg cholesterol,
367 mg sodium, 1 g carbohydrate, 0 g fiber,
46 g protein. Daily Values: 4% calcium, 18% iron.

# Grilling Chart

| CUT | Weight, Thickness | Doneness | Smoke Time |
|---|---|---|---|
| Beef, fresh brisket | 3 to 3½ lbs. | Tender | 5 to 6 hrs. |
| Beef, rib eye roast | 4 to 5 lbs. | 140° (medium rare) | 3 to 4 hrs. |
| Pork, boneless top loin | 2 to 2½ lbs. | 155° | 1¾ to 2 hrs. |
| Pork, boneless shoulder | 4½ to 5 lbs. | tender | 4 to 5 hrs. |
| Pork, loin chops | 1½ inches thick | juices run clear | 1¾ to 2¼ hrs. |
| Pork, ribs | | tender | 3 to 4 hrs. |
| Halibut, steaks | 1 inch thick | flakes easily | 1 hr. |
| Salmon, fillets | 1 inch thick | flakes easily | 30 min. |
| Salmon, dressed | 3½ to 4 lbs. | flakes easily | 2½ to 3 hrs. |
| Trout, dressed | 8 to 10 ounces | flakes easily | 1½ to 2 hrs. |
| Chicken, whole broiler fryer | 3 to 3½ lbs. | 180° to 185° | 2½ to 3 hrs. |
| Chicken, whole roasting | 6 to 7 lbs. | 180° to 185° | 3¼ to 4 hrs. |
| Turkey | 10 to 12 lbs. | 180° to 185° | 5 hrs. |
| Turkey, breast half with bone | 2 to 3 lbs. | 170° | 2 to 2½ hrs. |

## D-E

## METRIC COOKING HINTS

By making a few conversions, cooks in Australia, Canada, and the United Kingdom can use the recipes in this book with confidence. The charts on this page provide a guide for converting measurements from the U.S. customary system, which is used throughout this book, to the imperial and metric systems. There also is a conversion table for oven temperatures to accommodate the differences in oven calibrations.

**Product Differences:** Most of the ingredients called for in the recipes in this book are available in English-speaking countries. However, some are known by different names. Here are some common American ingredients and their possible counterparts:
■ Sugar is granulated or castor sugar.
■ Powdered sugar is icing sugar.
■ All-purpose flour is plain household flour or white flour. When self-rising flour is used in place of all-purpose flour in a recipe that calls for leavening, omit the leavening agent (baking soda or baking powder) and salt.
■ Light-colored corn syrup is golden syrup.
■ Cornstarch is cornflour.
■ Baking soda is bicarbonate of soda.
■ Vanilla is vanilla essence.
■ Green, red, or yellow sweet peppers are capsicums.
■ Golden raisins are sultanas.

**Volume and Weight:** Americans traditionally use cup measures for liquid and solid ingredients. The chart, below, shows the approximate imperial and metric equivalents. If you are accustomed to weighing solid ingredients, the following approximate equivalents will be helpful.
■ 1 cup butter, castor sugar, or rice = 8 ounces = about 250 grams
■ 1 cup flour = 4 ounces = about 125 grams
■ 1 cup icing sugar = 5 ounces = about 150 grams
  Spoon measures are used for smaller amounts of ingredients. Although the size of the tablespoon varies slightly in different countries, for practical purposes and for recipes in this book, a straight substitution is all that's necessary.
  Measurements made using cups or spoons always should be level unless stated otherwise.

### EQUIVALENTS: U.S. = AUSTRALIA/U.K.

⅛ teaspoon = 0.5 ml
¼ teaspoon = 1 ml
½ teaspoon = 2 ml
1 teaspoon = 5 ml
1 tablespoon = 1 tablespoon
¼ cup = 2 tablespoons = 2 fluid ounces = 60 ml
⅓ cup = ¼ cup = 3 fluid ounces = 90 ml
½ cup = ⅓ cup = 4 fluid ounces = 120 ml
⅔ cup = ½ cup = 5 fluid ounces = 150 ml
¾ cup = ⅔ cup = 6 fluid ounces = 180 ml
1 cup = ¾ cup = 8 fluid ounces = 240 ml
1¼ cups = 1 cup
2 cups = 1 pint
1 quart = 1 liter
½ inch = 1.27 cm
1 inch = 2.54 cm

### BAKING PAN SIZES

| American | Metric |
|---|---|
| 8×1½-inch round baking pan | 20×4-cm cake tin |
| 9×1½-inch round baking pan | 23×3.5-cm cake tin |
| 11×7×1½-inch baking pan | 28×18×4-cm baking tin |
| 13×9×2-inch baking pan | 30×20×3-cm baking tin |
| 2-quart rectangular baking dish | 30×20×3-cm baking tin |
| 15×10×1-inch baking pan | 30×25×2-cm baking tin (Swiss roll tin) |
| 9-inch pie plate | 22×4- or 23×4-cm pie plate |
| 7- or 8-inch springform pan | 18- or 20-cm springform or loose-bottom cake tin |
| 9×5×3-inch loaf pan | 23×13×7-cm or 2-pound narrow loaf tin or pâté tin |
| 1½-quart casserole | 1.5-liter casserole |
| 2-quart casserole | 2-liter casserole |

### OVEN TEMPERATURE EQUIVALENTS

| Fahrenheit Setting | Celsius Setting* | Gas Setting |
|---|---|---|
| 300°F | 150°C | Gas Mark 2 (slow) |
| 325°F | 160°C | Gas Mark 3 (moderately slow) |
| 350°F | 180°C | Gas Mark 4 (moderate) |
| 375°F | 190°C | Gas Mark 5 (moderately hot) |
| 400°F | 200°C | Gas Mark 6 (hot) |
| 425°F | 220°C | Gas Mark 7 |
| 450°F | 230°C | Gas Mark 8 (very hot) |
| Broil | | Grill |

*Electric and gas ovens may be calibrated using Celsius. However, for an electric oven, increase the Celsius setting 10 to 20 degrees when cooking above 160°C. For convection or forced-air ovens (gas or electric), lower the temperature setting 10°C when cooking at all heat levels.

## FOOD SAFETY AT THE GRILL

*Cooking and keeping foods safe is easy if you follow a few guidelines.*

- Use a thermometer when cooking large cuts of meats or poultry. Be sure to place the thermometer deep into the center of the meat. Smaller cuts, such as hamburgers, boneless chicken breasts, or pork chops, don't lend themselves to the use of a thermometer. Carefully check your timings and doneness descriptions for smaller cuts.
- Cook roasts and steaks to a temperature of at least 145°. Whole chicken or turkey should reach 180° to 185°. The center of the stuffing should reach 165°.
- Cook ground beef to at least 160° because bacteria can spread during processing. The Centers for Disease Control and Prevention believes there is a connection between eating undercooked, pink ground beef and a higher risk of illness. To keep from becoming ill, it's best to avoid eating ground beef that is still pink.
- Fish that is cooked properly should be opaque and flake easily when tested with a fork.
- After marinating, if using the marinade to serve with the meat, heat the marinade to a full rolling boil, stirring often during heating. Leftover sauces should also be heated to a full rolling boil. The temperature should reach at least 165°.

## RECOMMENDED DEGREE OF DONENESS

|  | Medium-Rare | Medium | Well Done |
|---|---|---|---|
| Beef | 145° | 160° | 170° |
| Veal | * | 160° | 170° |
| Lamb | 145° | 160° | 170° |
| Pork | * | 160° | 170° |
| Ground Meats | * | 160° | 170° |

*Not recommended for less than medium degree of doneness.
Source: The Guide to Identifying Meat Cuts, © 1998 National Cattlemen's Beef Association and National Pork Producers Council.

## IN A PINCH: HOW HOT IS HOT?

Unless you have a thermometer built into your grill, you'll need a good way to measure the approximate temperature of the coals. This simple test will help: Hold your hand at the level the food will cook for as long as it's comfortable. The number of seconds you can hold it there will give you an estimate for the heat of the fire.

| Temperature | Number of Seconds |
|---|---|
| High | 2 |
| Medium-high | 3 |
| Medium | 4 |
| Medium-low | 5 |
| Low | 6 |

*For More Information*

If you would like to know more or have questions about meat or poultry, contact the USDA Meat and Poultry Hotline (800-535-4555), The National Cattlemen's Beef Association (312-467-5520), or National Pork Producers Council (515-223-2600). For grilling tips and recipes, visit the Better Homes Kitchen® at bhglive.com/food/index.